ALLEN COUNTY PUBLIC LIBRARY

D1602179

Automotive Engine Design

William H. Crouse

McGraw-Hill Book Company

New York St. Louis San Francisco
Düsseldorf London Mexico
Panama Sydney Toronto

5-6-74

McGraw-Hill Automotive Technology Series

BOOKS BY WILLIAM H. CROUSE

Automotive Chassis and Body
Automotive Electrical Equipment
Automotive Engines
Automotive Fuel, Lubricating, and Cooling Systems
Automotive Transmissions and Power Trains
Workbook for Automotive Chassis
Workbook for Automotive Electricity
Workbook for Automotive Engines
Workbook for Automotive Service and Troubleshooting
Workbook for Automotive Tools
(Other books in process)

OTHER BOOKS BY WILLIAM H. CROUSE

Automotive Mechanics
General Power Mechanics
Science Marvels of Tomorrow
Understanding Science

AUTOMOTIVE ENGINE DESIGN

Library of Congress Catalog Card Number 70-129110
ISBN 07-014671-3

3 4 5 6 7 8 9 10 VHVH 7 9 8 7 6 5 4 3

This book was set in Helvetica by Typographic Sales, Incorporated, and printed on permanent paper and bound by Von Hoffmann Press, Inc. The designer was Audry Sinclare; the cover was designed by Edward A. Butler. The editors were D. Eugene Gilmore and Julia Ziercher. Al Lambiase supervised production.

Preface

The proliferation of automotive vehicles and other machines powered by internal-combustion engines has brought with it vast social and economic changes in our society. Our world turns, in effect, to the sound of running engines. They are everywhere. They power our automobiles, trucks, buses, airplanes, and motor boats; they saw our wood, cut our lawns, trim our hedges, operate our road-building and construction equipment, plow our fields, pick our corn, reap our wheat—even thrust our astronauts in their space vehicles out toward the moon, or Mars. The list is almost endless.

With all of these developments, there has come a greatly increased interest in automotive engines: how they became what they are; why they developed to their present designs; what caused engineers to select the materials for automotive engines—chromium or molybdenum coatings for piston rings, or forged steel for crankshafts, for example; why the gasoline engine, rather than the diesel, the turbine, or the steam engine, is used in most automobiles. —Again, the list is almost endless.

This book is designed to answer many of those questions—to explain how automotive engines came to be what they are today and how today's automotive engines are designed and manufactured. The book is devoted almost exclusively to the modern, four-stroke-cycle, multiple-cylinder, liquid-cooled, overhead-valve, internal-combustion engine for vehicular use. This is the engine which has received the most intensive engineering attention and presently is the focus of much of today's engine-design activities. However, most of the other internal-combustion engines in use today, including diesel, two-stroke-cycle, Wankel, turbine, and so on, are also discussed in the book. The engineering background of these various engines, however, is not covered in any detail.

A selective bibliography has been compiled and appears at the end of the book. The entries have been arranged according to chapter to aid the user in finding the best source for additional reference.

Mathematical treatment has been held to a minimum in the text, but engineering considerations that have led to modern engine designs are discussed in detail. Practical aspects of design, rather than theory, are stressed because this is the way automotive engineers often work. Much of present-day automotive-engineering knowledge was arrived at empirically: that is, by experiment—by trial and error. And although the automotive engineer must be well versed in theory, he often arrives at his new design by a process of trying a variety of configurations in his journey to the best compromise. He may, for example, try a dozen—or a hundred—intake-manifold cross sections before he arrives at one that provides the best performance. This book, therefore, which stresses the engineering methods in actual use, should meet the needs of the student and young engineer who desire an insight into the practical, day-to-day aspects of automotive engineering.

WILLIAM H. CROUSE

Contents

1. Interchangeability, Mass Production, and Automation 1

1. Mass production and interchangeability
2. Automation of machine tools
3. Modern automatic machine tools
4. Automated cylinder-block processing
5. Automation of assembling
6. Factors to be considered in automation
7. Designing for automation
8. Mass distribution
9. The automobile and our modern world
10. Opportunities in the automotive industry

2. Designing an Automobile 10

11. Under the skin
12. The idea
13. The decision
14. Mechanical design
15. The stylists
16. The stylist's job
17. From clay to steel
18. Designing the Camaro—a case history
19. Mechanical design vs. styling
20. Cutting the lead time
21. Designing for safety
22. The design job
23. The role of the SAE

3. Internal-Combustion-Engine Operation 27

24. Engine cylinders
25. Piston rings
26. Reciprocating to rotary motion
27. Engine valves
28. Actions in engine cylinder
29. Multiple-cylinder engines
30. Flywheel

4. Internal-Combustion-Engine Types 34

31. Cylinder arrangements
32. Two-cylinder engine
33. Three-cylinder engines
34. Four-cylinder engines
35. Five-cylinder engines
36. Six-cylinder engines
37. Eight-cylinder engines
38. Twelve- and sixteen-cylinder engines
39. Valve arrangments
40. Overhead-camshaft engines
41. Two-stroke-cycle engines
42. Diesel engine
43. Diesel engine applications
44. Gas turbine
45. Free-piston engine
46. Wankel engine
47. Sterling engine
48. Other rotary engines

5. Physical Principles of Engine Operation 59

49. Atoms
50. Size of atoms
51. The elements
52. Molecules
53. Combustion
54. Heat
55. The gas laws
56. Heat flow and specific heat
57. Idealized cycles
58. The constant-volume cycle
59. Thermal efficiency
60. *PV* curve of a four-stroke-cycle engine
61. Volumetric efficiency

6. Engine Measurements 68

62. Bore and stroke
63. Piston displacement
64. Compression ratio
65. Horsepower
66. Indicated horsepower
67. Brake horsepower
68. Dynamometer
69. Dynamometer tests
70. Friction
71. Static and kinetic friction
72. Coefficient of kinetic friction
73. Three classes of kinetic friction
74. Friction horsepower

75. Relating ihp, bhp, and fhp
76. SAE horsepower
77. Torque
78. Torque compared with bhp
79. Mechanical efficiency
80. Engine heat losses

7. Engine Construction 79

81. Engine cylinder block
82. Cylinder heads
83. Gaskets
84. Oil pan
85. Exhaust manifold
86. Intake manifold
87. Crankshaft
88. Flywheel
89. Torsional-vibration damper
90. Engine bearings
91. Engine-bearing lubrication
92. Connecting rod
93. Pistons and piston rings
94. Piston rings
95. Cams and camshafts
96. Valves
97. Valve seat
98. L-head valve train
99. I-head valve train
100. F-head valve train
101. Hydraulic valve lifter
102. Valve timing

8. Engine Accessory Systems 100

103. Fuel system
104. Lubricating system
105. Electric system
106. Operation of ignition system
107. Operation of ignition-advance mechanisms
108. Cooling system

9. Engine Design 111

109. What design means
110. The life of a design
111. Engine design considerations
112. Thermal efficiency
113. Volumetric efficiency
114. Mechanical efficiency

10. Engine Fuel 116

115. Automotive-engine fuels
116. Volatility of gasoline
117. Antiknock value
118. Compression ratio and bore size
119. Heat of compression
120. Causes of knocking
121. Study of knocking
122. Control of knocking
123. Measuring antiknock values of fuels
124. Knock, preignition, and rumble
125. Chemical control of knocking
126. Environmental factors affecting knocking
127. Octane requirements
128. Gasoline additives
129. Chemistry of combustion

11. Combustion-Chamber Design 132

130. Combustion-chamber requirements
131. Designing a combustion chamber
132. Factors in combustion-chamber design
133. Turbulence
134. Volumetric efficiency
135. Hemispheric vs. wedge combustion chambers
136. Hemispheric chamber with squish-quench
137. Valve cooling, size, and placement
138. Spark-plug placement
139. The s/v ratio

12. Pistons and Rings 143

140. Piston and piston-ring requirements
141. Piston design
142. Piston-design considerations
143. Piston material
144. Piston scuffing and its prevention
145. Piston-head design
146. Heat control in piston
147. Expansion control in piston
148. Piston skirts
149. Piston weight
150. Piston-pin attachment and lubrication
151. Piston-pin offset
152. Ring-groove stresses
153. Ring-groove fortification
154. Piston tests
155. The Chevrolet 427 piston—a case history
156. Piston-failure analysis

13. Piston Rings 164

157. Purpose of piston rings
158. Compression rings
159. Why two compression rings?
160. Compression-ring wear and materials
161. Ring dimensions
162. Trends in compression-ring design
163. Laboratory tests of compression rings

164. Life expectancy of compression rings
165. Oil-control rings
166. Types of oil-control rings
167. Why only one ring?
168. What is good oil control?
169. Speed and oil control
170. Piston-ring-failure analysis

14. Connecting Rods, Crankshafts, and Bearings 178

171. Connecting rod
172. Engine bearings
173. Main-thrust bearing
174. Engine-bearing lubrication
175. Engine-bearing types
176. Bearing requirements
177. Bearing materials
178. Bearing loading
179. The effective bearing load
180. The bearing-load graph
181. Bearing design
182. Bearing failures
183. Crankshaft
184. Crankshaft design
185. Crankshaft-balance analysis
186. Crankshaft-crankpin throw
187. Crankshaft-journal size
188. Crankshaft-journal geometry and finishes
189. Crankshaft tests
190. Torsional-vibration dampers
191. Engine-vibration mountings

15. Valve Trains 207

192. L-head vs. I-head
193. Valve and valve-train requirements
194. Valve and valve-train design
195. Valve lift
196. Intake valve and gas flow
197. Exhaust valve and gas flow
198. Valve size
199. Valve-face angle
200. Interference angle
201. Valve-head proportions
202. Valve-stem size
203. Valve-head shape
204. Valve materials
205. Sodium valves
206. Valve facings
207. Valve stem and tips
208. Valve-port design
209. Valve guide
210. Valve-seat design
211. Valve temperature and cooling
212. Valve lubrication
213. Valve rotation
214. Rocker arms
215. Cams
216. Valve spring
217. Valve-train dynamics[7]
218. The Chevrolet Turbo-Jet engine valves—a case history
219. Cams for hydraulic lifters
220. High-performance cams
221. Overhead camshaft
222. Valve-failure analysis

16. Cylinder Block and Head 247

223. Basic considerations
224. Foundry practice
225. Casting a cylinder block
226. Designing Ford's 240 engine cylinder block—a case history
227. Finishing a cylinder block
228. Designing a cylinder head
229. Engine assembly
230. Aluminum cylinder blocks

17. Automotive Fuel Systems 265

231. Fuel-system requirements
232. Carburetor requirements
233. Fuel gauge
234. Carburetor fundamentals
235. Carburetor circuits
236. Air cleaner
237. Float circuit
238. Idling and low-speed circuit
239. Off-idle or low-speed circuit
240. High-speed, part-load circuit
241. High-speed, full-power circuit
242. Accelerator-pump circuit
243. Choke
244. Manifold heat control
245. Other carburetor devices
246. Typical carburetors
247. One-barrel carburetors
248. Two-barrel, or dual, carburetors
249. Four-barrel, or quadrijet, carburetors
250. Carburetor design
251. Intake manifold
252. Tuned intake manifold
253. The Ford Mark II-427 GT intake manifold
254. The Chevrolet Turbo-Jet engine intake manifold
255. Supercharging

256. Exhaust manifold
257. Smog control
258. Fuel injection
259. Volkswagen electronic fuel injection
260. Binder fluidic carburetor—an experimental unit

18. Engine Cooling Systems 309

261. Purpose of cooling system
262. Water jackets
263. Water pumps
264. Engine fan
265. Radiator
266. Thermostat
267. Radiator pressure cap
268. Antifreeze solutions and temperature indicators
269. Cooling-system design
270. The Chevrolet Turbo-Jet engine cooling system

19. Engine Lubricating Systems 324

271. Purpose of engine lubricating systems
272. Source and properties of oil
273. Service ratings of oil
274. Testing engine oil
275. Automotive lubricants
276. Types of lubricating systems
277. Oil pumps
278. Relief valve
279. Oil filters
280. Oil-pressure indicators
281. Oil changes
282. Oil consumption
283. Water-sludge formation
284. Blow-by diversion
285. Lubricating-system design

20. Ignition System 348

286. Function of ignition system
287. Ignition distributor
288. Construction of the ignition coil
289. Mutual and self-induction in ignition coil
290. Action in primary winding during build-up
291. Action in the secondary winding during build-up
292. Self-induction in primary winding after current stops
293. Condenser
294. Action in the secondary winding during magnetic collapse
295. Spark plugs
296. Secondary wiring
297. Ignition-spark advance
298. Determination of spark-advance curve
299. Centrifugal spark advance
300. Intake-manifold vacuum advance
301. Combining centrifugal and vacuum advances
302. Piezoelectric ignition
303. Special ignition devices
304. Low-frequency vs. high-frequency ignition systems

BIBLIOGRAPHY 369

INDEX 372

Acknowledgments

Many individuals and organizations have contributed to *Automotive Engine Design*. During the many long months the book was in preparation, the author was in touch with scores of automotive engineers, through personal contact or by means of technical reports and papers. Thus, the book cannot be said to be the work of a single person, but rather is the result of the combined effort of many individuals who have a professional interest in automotive engine design.

Space is too brief to permit the naming of all who contributed to the book, but special thanks are due to the following individuals: Harry Clary, TRW Inc.; William C. Grindrod, Cincinnati Milling Machine Co.; W. S. Giles, TRW Inc.; J. Dudley Binford, Dana Corporation; William L. Weertman, Chrysler Corporation; Frederick C. Tew, Chrysler Corporation; D. P. Hammial, Pontiac Motor Division, General Motors Corporation; J. F. Aldrighetti, Cadillac Motor Car Division, General Motors Corporation; Marshall Huntzinger, Delco-Remy Division, General Motors Corporation; D. I. Connor, Bohn Aluminum and Brass Company; Donald Patterson, General Motors Engineering Staff; Clifford G. Studaker, Buick Motor Division, General Motors Corporation; George E. Trainor, Ford Division, Ford Motor Company; K. A. Stonex, General Motors Engineering Staff; and Donald Stoltman, General Motors Corporation.

Special thanks are also due to the following organizations for information and illustrations they supplied: AC Spark Plug Division, Buick Motor Division, Cadillac Motor Car Division, Chevrolet Motor Division, Delco-Remy Division, Detroit Diesel Engine Division, Oldsmobile Division, Pontiac Motor Division, and Rochester Products Division of General Motors Corporation; American Motors Corporation; American Petroleum Institute; Carter Carburetor Company; Caterpillar Tractor Company; Dodge Division and Chrysler-Plymouth Division of Chrysler Motors Corporation; Cincinnati Milling Machine Company; Cross Company; Eaton Manufacturing Company; Esso Research and Engineering Company; Federal-Mogul-Bower Bearings, Inc.; Ford Motor Company; Ford Division and Lincoln-Mercury Division of Ford Motor Company; Hercules Motors Corporation; Houdaille Industries, Inc.; International Harvester Company; Johnson Bronze Company; Lord Manufacturing Company; Muskegon Piston Ring Company; Outboard Marine Corporation; Perfect Circle Company; The Pure Oil Company; The Rover Company Ltd.; Sealed Power Corporation; Shell Oil Company; Standard Oil Company; Standard-Triumph Motor Company, Inc.; Studebaker Corporation; Thompson, Ramo, Wooldridge, Inc.; and Waukesha Motor Company.

The author appreciates the advice and counsel of the following men who took time from busy schedules to read the manuscript and who offered many helpful suggestions: Dennis Chapman, Oklahoma State Tech, Okmulgee, Olkahoma; George R. Kinsler, Wisconsin Board of Vocational, Technical and Adult Education; H. C. MacDonald, Ford Motor Company; Joseph W. Menconi, John A. O'Connell School, San Francisco, California; Arthur J. Oettmeier, Delta College, University Center, Michigan; Donald F. Reynolds, Los Angeles City Unified School District; and Mr. H. C. Rotrock, Oregon Technical Institute, Klamath Falls, Oregon.

To all these people and the organizations they represent, the author offers his sincere thanks!

WILLIAM H. CROUSE

CHAPTER 1

Interchangeability, Mass Production, and Automation

The automotive engine designer must have a thorough understanding of manufacturing methods and automation. Not only must his new engine be better than earlier engines in specified ways, it must also be acceptable to his management from the manufacturing standpoint. Thus, we begin this book with a brief discussion of mass production and automation. The bibliography at the end of the chapter will lead the reader to more extensive treatments of these subjects.

§1. Mass production and interchangeability Modern manufacturing methods demand that the component parts of any device being manufactured must be made as uniform as possible. For example, such engine parts as pistons, piston rings, and crankshafts that are going into a particular model of an engine must have as nearly identical weights, dimensions, strength, heat conductivity, and so on, as manufacturing methods can make. These parts thus become interchangeable, within manufacturing limits, as will be discussed in more detail later.

Although numerous small automobile manufacturers started businesses in the first years of the twentieth century, it was not until the concepts of interchangeability and mass production took hold that the automotive industry really came of age.

Interchangeability was a relatively new idea to most people in 1900, even though it was first demonstrated publicly in 1798 in Washington, D.C. In that year, Eli Whitney, the inventor of the cotton gin, stood before a group of high dignitaries, including President Adams and Thomas Jefferson. On a table before him were 10 disassembled muskets. He picked up pieces at random, and assembled the muskets, proving that the parts could be made so nearly alike that they would fit together without special work.

Before that time, each part was made by hand, and no two parts were exactly alike. Thus, each part had to be fitted as it was assembled into the musket. Therefore assembly work was very slow and required expert craftsmen. However, Whitney had devised a new method of making the parts. He used machine tools and jigs which enabled unskilled men to turn out nearly identical musket parts by the hundreds. During the next few years, Whitney's factory produced tens of thousands of muskets for the government.

Another early episode in the development of interchangeability occurred in a small town in Connecticut where, in about 1807, Eli Terry set up a factory to make clocks. Little is known about this venture except that in three years Terry made 4,000 clocks. The first year was spent in tooling up; in the second year he made 1,000 clocks; and in the third year he made 3,000. These early clocks had works made of wood parts, and they were satisfactory in places where the humidity did not vary too much. Then, in about 1840, Chauncey Jerome, another early inventor, developed tooling for a clock that had metal works. His factory in Waterbury, Connecticut, was soon producing clocks that retailed for $1.50, only a fraction of the cost of handmade clocks at that time. All parts were made so accurately with machine tools that they fitted together in the completed assembly without any special work. Soon Jerome was manufacturing clocks by the tens of thousands per year.

There were many other men who further developed the concept of interchangeability. By the turn of the century, this concept was commonplace in American industrial plants. At the same time, the interrelated idea of mass production was developing. The basic concept was simple: If all parts were interchangeable, it was not necessary to stop to fit each part. All that was required was to break down the total assembly procedure into small segments, with men specializing in a single segment. In an engine-building factory, for example, one group of men would attach pistons to connecting rods, a second group would install the piston rings, a third group would install the rod and piston assemblies in the engine block, and so on.

Later came the idea of having the assemblers stand in one place, while the items that were being assembled moved along in front of them on an endless belt. Within a few years, automotive factories were using many conveyer belts, and mass production was in full swing.

Fig. 1-1. Modern turret lathe, or screw machine. Although an operator is shown running the lathe, lathes of this type can be operated automatically. (*Warner and Swasey Company*)

Fig. 1-2. Automatic turret lathe, operated by a computer. A tape on which the sequence of operations is programmed passes through the computer; the computer signals the controls on the lathe so that the programmed sequence of operations is performed. The operator is shown inspecting a workpiece that the lathe has just completed. (*Warner and Swasey Company*)

§2. Automation of machine tools Automation of parts manufacturing was a natural development, flowing out of the concepts of interchangeability and mass production. When large numbers of an identical part or mechanism are produced, it becomes feasible to spend large amounts of money on production machinery. For example, if you were going to make 1,000 clocks, you could not afford to spend very much for tooling. If you spent $10,000, then amortizing the costs over the total production run would amount to $10 a clock. However, it is a different story if you plan to make 10,000,000 clocks. You could then afford to spend 10 million dollars installing automatic equipment to make the clock parts. In this case, amortization of tooling costs would come to only $1 a clock.

Thus, as the automobile industry grew, it turned more and more to automatic processes to reduce manufacturing costs and assure more uniform products. An early example of automation is the automatic turret lathe, also called an *automatic screw machine*. Typical examples of this lathe are shown in Figs. 1-1 and 1-2. In this lathe, the workpiece is revolved, and a succession of tools is brought to bear on the workpiece. For example, let us examine the setup required to produce automatically the shaft shown in Fig. 1-3.

The shaft is produced from bar stock which is fed into the lathe through the revolving spindle

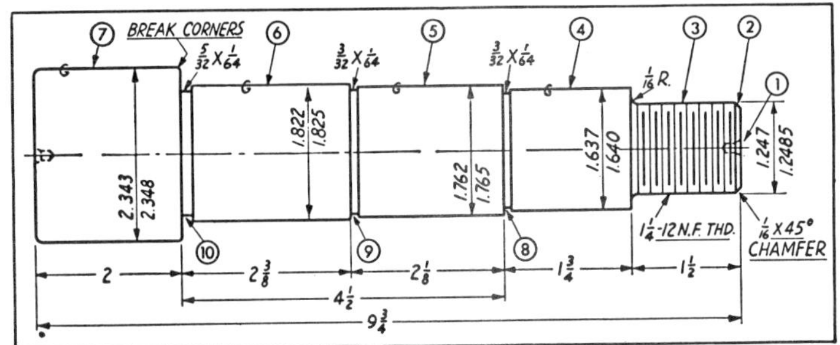

Fig. 1-3. Typical job for an automatic turret lathe: a shaft. (*Warner and Swasey Company*)

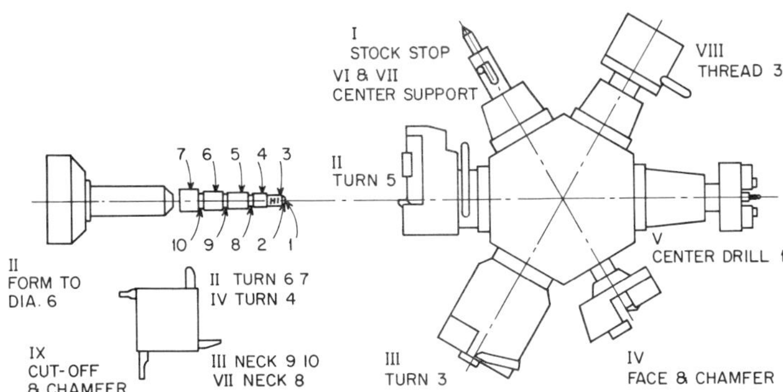

Fig. 1-4. Tooling setup for the shaft shown in *Fig. 1-3*. (*Warner and Swasey Company*)

(see Fig. 1-1). The tooling setup required to finish the shaft from the bar stock is shown in the top view of Fig. 1-4. Visualize first that the two turrets—the square turret to the lower left and the hexagonal turret to the right—can move toward and away from the workpiece. The square turret moves in from the side. The hexagonal turret moves in from the end. Also, both turrets can turn on their centers so that different tools can be brought to bear on the workpiece.

Figure 1-5 shows the sequence of events. This illustration is correlated with Figs. 1-3 and 1-4. A study of these illustrations will disclose the sequence of operations. Remember that after each machining operation, the turret is withdrawn from the workpiece, rotated to position the next tool, and moved into the workpiece again.

As a piece is finished, it is cut off and drops down into a chute that directs it into a tub or bin below the lathe. Meantime, the bar stock is automatically

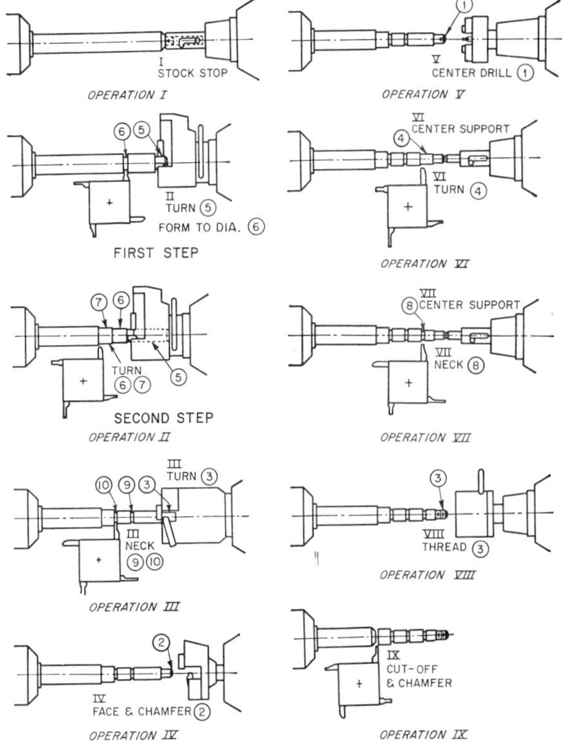

Fig. 1-5. Sequence of operations for machining the shaft shown in *Fig. 1-3*. (*Warner and Swasey Company*)

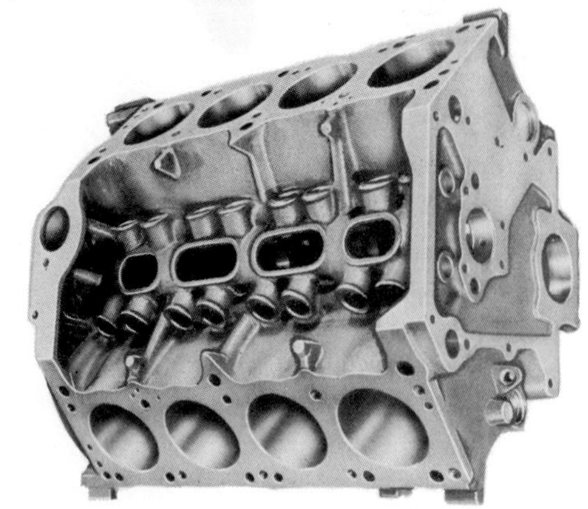

Fig. 1-6. Top and bottom views of the engine block for a V-8 engine, showing holes, cylinder bores, surfaces, and oil and water passages that require machining. (*Chrysler Motors Corporation*)

advanced to the stop (operation 1 in Fig. 1-5), and the whole sequence is repeated automatically.

Over the years that followed, a variety of such machine tools were developed to fabricate machine parts such as screws, nuts, collars, shafts, and similar items. Automatic punch presses made their appearance; some of these, fed from coiled sheet metal, can operate for hours with no attention, turning out stampings by the thousands per hour. As plastics of various types came into use, automatic presses were developed to produce plastic parts. Automatic metal-casting machines appeared. These machines have molds that operate automatically, plus semiautomatic or fully automatic molten-metal dispensers. By the mid-1920's, there were automated foundries that were automatically casting, from gray iron, small automotive parts such as distributor housings, generator- and cranking-motor end frames, and so on.

§3. Modern automatic machine tools Many of the basic castings or other parts that become components of products such as automotive engines must be machined in a variety of ways. For instance, an engine block, after it has been cast, must be cleaned, machined on various surfaces, drilled, and tapped; cylinders must be bored, oil galleries must be drilled, and so on. Modern automatic machines have been set up to perform all of these operations on the engine block, with a minimum of attention from human operators. A typical finished engine block is shown in Fig. 1-6. Study this illustration to see how many machine operations are necessary.

§4. Automated cylinder-block processing In modern automotive engine manufacturing plants, unfinished cylinder blocks from the foundry are put on one end of an extensive block-processing line. This line includes a series of machines that perform all the machining operations required on the block. Referring to Fig. 1-6 again, it will be noted that the block has drilled holes and passages for water and oil circulation and tapped holes for attaching the cylinder heads, front cover, manifolds, bearings, and other parts. In addition, the cylinder bores are bored and honed. Also, the surfaces on which parts are mounted are finished. All of the machining operations must be done to precise dimensions and at precise locations so that all parts will fit onto or into the block and have the proper relations to each other. The block is automatically turned into various positions as it moves down the line so that the machine tools can perform their prescribed operations. (More information about this is given in Chap. 16, "Cylinder Block and Head," which describes the designing and processing of cylinder blocks and heads.)

§5. Automation of assembling After all component parts of the engines are finished, the next step in production is to put them together, that is, to assemble the engine. The various parts, as they are finished, are brought to the main assembly line, where men and machines put them together. In the modern engine manufacturing plant, as many as possible of the assembling operations are automated, that is, performed automatically by machines.

While modern automated factories look quite complicated, the principles used are really simple. An assembling operation that engineers want to automate is carefully studied to see what sort of machine could be designed to replace the human hand. A simple example might be the placement of bolts in tapped holes. This could be done manually by having an operator pick up the bolts from a pan before him and then put them, one by one, into the tapped holes of the workpiece moving down the line before him. Then, the next person on the assembly line would use a hand wrench to tighten the bolts. This process can be automated by a device into which the bolts are fed from a hopper. The bolts are all facing in the proper direction, threaded end down. As the workpiece moves into position, the automated device brings the bolts down to the tapped holes, and a power wrench automatically turns them down and tightens them to the proper tension. This is a simple example. Six, a dozen, or more bolts can be installed on the workpiece in this manner simultaneously, or one after another.

Much more complex assembling operations can be automated. In fact, engineers say that nearly any operation that is repetitive can be turned over to a machine. The cost, however, may be prohibitive for many assembling operations. There are many factors to be considered.

§6. Factors to be considered in automation Some of the basic factors to be considered by management investigating the automation possibilities of any particular manual manufacturing operation, or set of operations, include:

1. Labor costs and savings
2. Material costs and savings
3. Automation costs and amortization
4. Possible improvement of product
5. Union problems

There are other factors, of course, but the above are some of the more important ones. As an example of item 1, labor costs and savings, let us take a case where labor costs average $2 per hour and it takes 10 hours to complete a sequential series of manufacturing operations to produce a device. Suppose, further, that 1 million of these devices are produced per year. Direct labor costs are, therefore, 20 million dollars. Now suppose labor costs increase to an average of $5 per hour. Direct labor costs per year, therefore, increase to 50 million dollars, all other factors remaining unchanged. Now suppose management had been considering a partial automation job that would cut labor costs in half. At $2 per hour, the savings amount to 10 million dollars per year. At $5 per hour, the savings amount to 25 million dollars. The costs of designing and installing the necessary automating equipment might be too great to make it feasible with the $2 per hour labor costs. But it could be another story if labor costs were $5 per hour.

This oversimplified example hardly begins to tell the story of labor-cost considerations. Chances are, if labor costs increase, so will the costs of automation. Then there is the problem as to what resistance to automation will be made by the labor unions. Also, amortization of the automation costs must be considered. For instance, if automation is going to save 20 million dollars per year in labor costs, and the automation equipment is to be written off in five years, then—without considering any other factors—it could be said that the break-even point on automation costs would be 100 million dollars. That is, management could afford to spend that amount on automation.

However, we must also think of possible material costs and customer satisfaction. Will automation reduce scrap and customer complaints; that is, will automation make a better product? Also, can the design of the manufactured device be altered so that it is easier to manufacture with automated methods?

There are, of course, many other questions to be answered.

§7. Designing for automation With wages going up, it becomes increasingly important for the designers to work toward designs that are easier to manufacture with automatic machinery. This applies to designers of bathroom scales, electric fans, food packages, television sets, and cash registers, as well as to designers of automotive engines. Today, in the design of any mass-produced object, automation possibilities must be carefully analyzed.

Often, a preliminary design is altered extensively to make it easier to manufacture. Also, when the designer comes to the point of considering alternate configurations of a design, he usually selects the one that lends itself most readily to automatic manufacturing processes. A design engineer cannot design a mechanism "in the clouds" as it were. He must ask himself whether or not the mechanism can be built on the production line. He must find out whether special tools, dies, and jigs are required. He must estimate the cost of special tooling, and provide data on the man-hours required to produce *x* numbers of the mechanism.

If all factors are not favorable, the designer may have to redesign the complete mechanism, perhaps to use available manufacturing facilities, or to fit into a newly proposed automatic manufacturing setup. Further, he must also be aware of servicing problems on the mechanism. Sometimes, the design must be altered substantially so as to make the servicing of the mechanism easier after it is out in the field. (All of these factors are discussed in more detail later.)

§8. Mass distribution Mass production requires mass distribution. It would be of no value to produce large quantities of automobiles or other goods if there were not adequate means of distributing and marketing them. Each industry has its own special problems of distribution. Electrical appliances are distributed in one way, milk in another; furniture, food, and automobiles have still other distribution and marketing methods. Let us take a look at how the automotive industry does it.

Each automobile company has its own network of dealers, each dealer being located in a defined marketing area. Smaller communities have one Ford dealer, for example, while large metropolitan areas may have several. Each dealer has a building, or buildings, which include a showroom where new cars are exhibited, a service department, a parts department, business offices, and a used-car lot.

Before the start of a new-model year, for example, when cars are introduced, each dealer orders a quantity of the new cars in various models. His order and its mix are based on his past experience and how he thinks the new models will "go." These cars are delivered to the dealer, and he prepares them for exhibit and sale. Meantime, some customers may already have ordered new cars, and the dealer includes these in his order.

On introduction day, his salesmen are ready with the facts and figures about the new cars and armed with various brochures describing their merits. Advertising in local newspapers, in magazines, and on radio and television encourages people to come in and see the new models. Some years, considerable excitement attends the introduction of new models, particularly when interesting innovations, such as front-wheel drive, are introduced.

Many things must happen, however, before the introduction of a new car. It must be designed (Chap. 2) and put into production. Repair and service parts must be made and sent to regional warehouses and dealers. Servicing tools and printed instructions for automotive mechanics must be prepared and sent to dealer-service departments. Often, the automobile manufacturer also prepares films and holds service schools so that automotive mechanics will know how to service the new cars. This is especially important when new designs or devices are introduced on the new cars.

The advertising and sales-promotion departments of the manufacturer must work out advertising campaigns, establish their budgets, and map out how much they are going to spend (and in what media) to promote the new cars. The company advertising men work with their advertising agency to develop several series of ads for the printed media—magazines and newspapers. The agency negotiates with radio and TV networks for time in which they can tell the listener or viewer about the merits of their cars. Advertising and factual pamphlets and brochures are developed which describe features of the new cars.

Meantime, well before the new cars are introduced, dealers and their representatives assemble in regional or national conventions to hear about the new models. A little later, local meetings are held for dealer salesmen so that they can learn about the new cars.

All this prepares the dealer and his staff for the new cars. The salesmen get ready to sell them, and the service and parts departments get ready to service and repair them.

§9. The automobile and our modern world Before the coming of the automobile, travel was difficult, and most people stayed close to home. As a rule, they found work within walking distance, and every community was pretty much on its own, producing almost everything the inhabitants needed. A journey to the "city" 10 miles away was a day's trip, and if the "city" was 20 miles away, that could mean an overnight stay.

Then, with the coming of the automobile and the development of good roads, people were able to spread out and no longer had to cluster about the factories and shops where they worked. They could drive to work from miles away. This made it possible to build huge factory complexes which were more efficient than anything that had gone before. With mass production, however, it was essential to have large work forces, and the automobile made this possible. The automobile and truck also made it easier to distribute the products of a factory over many states so that many more people could enjoy the fruits of mass production—that is, more products for less money.

The automobile has thus changed, in a few decades, from a novelty and a toy for the wealthy to a basic necessity of modern living. It is difficult to imagine a world without automobiles, but if our country were somehow deprived of all motor vehicles tomorrow, our civilization, as we know it, would collapse in a few days.

§10. Opportunities in the automotive industry More than 12 million people in the United States are employed in the manufacture, distribution, maintenance, and commercial operation of motor vehicles. This means that almost one in every six persons who work owes his employment to the automotive industry. Within this vast employment area there are hundreds of thousands of good job opportunities, particularly for the trained technician or engineer. In fact, many of the top executives are men who have moved up from the engineering department.

This book is written especially for the technician and engineer, and thus it is relevant to examine some of the job opportunities open to technical- or engineering-school graduates. Not only are engineers and technicians employed in the engineering department, where improvements and new developments are worked out; they also are the key personnel in tool design, plant engineering, parts design and distribution, testing laboratories, testing grounds, sales engineering, production engineering, and so on. Engineers and technicians are essential in nearly every aspect of the industrial scene. It would take a book to describe all of the ways that these trained men and women contribute their brainpower and skills to the American economy.

Let us take a brief look at one facet of engineering and technician activity in the automotive industry—their work in the engineering department. We might do this by observing an entirely hypothetical case—for example, a design engineer at work as he plays around with possible new designs for an electric clock for automobiles. Perhaps certain problems have arisen with previous designs. They have failed to keep good time. Variations in battery charge and weather (temperature and humidity) throw the clock off.

The design engineer "dreams up" a new design. This may take him days or weeks, during which his main activity seems to be sitting at his desk, studying books and various reports, and sending one of his assistants—a junior engineer or technician—on various errands. Such errands might involve looking up technical data in the company library, phoning or writing a metal-processing company for information on, or samples of, certain bimetal springs, taking samples into the testing laboratory to run temperature-action curves, or laying out a tentative cam contour. As soon as a possible design for the new clock crystalizes in the engineer's mind, he begins to doodle with his pencil. Soon, he has some rough sketches. He, and perhaps one of his assistants, will take these sketches to a draftsman who has been assigned by the head of the drafting department to work with the engineer.

Over a period of days or weeks, the engineer, his assistants, and the draftsman will prepare a series of drawings based on the engineer's ideas. These drawings will show in full detail every separate part required to make the new design, as well as how these parts go together. Finally, when everyone is satisfied with the drawings, blueprints are made of them, and the engineer or one of his assistants carries or sends the prints to the model shop.

Incidentally, the drawings are all marked "EX" (experimental), with a set of consecutive numbers (as a rule) from a special block of numbers that identify the general area in which the work falls. For example, there may be one block of numbers for engines, another for accessories (subdivided perhaps into subblocks for lighting, clocks, and gauges), still another for transmissions, and so on. Thus, the category of the part can be instantly determined by the number. Of course, the drawings also carry the name of the part, the assembly into which it is to go, and the names of the draftsman and the engineer. As a rule, the engineer will sign the drawing, or at least he will sign the work order that accompanies the blueprints to the model shop.

Once in the model shop, the prints are assigned to one or more technicians or model makers who fashion, out of metal stock, the separate parts that are required. This calls for considerable ingenuity on the part of the model makers. Sometimes, if a part is difficult to make, the model department may report back informally to the engineer, suggesting an alternative which will be easier to produce. Also, there are times when a design—say, of a carburetor or an intake manifold—requires a casting. In such cases, a pattern maker steps in to make the required patterns, and these are then used to make the casting. In some cases, it is possible to take production parts and alter them enough to make the experimental parts.

Finally, after all parts have been handmade and assembled, the assembly is subjected to a series of tests. To start this activity, the engineer writes a work order and sends it, with the assembled model, to the experimental laboratory. There, a technician or engineer puts the model through the tests called for in the work order. He may operate the model at varying temperatures, air pressures, humidities, and voltages, recording performances under all of these variables. The results of the tests are then embodied in a report which goes back to the design engineer. The tests may point up deficiencies that require modifications in the design. In such case, new drawings and parts are made, and the model is rebuilt and retested. This might be repeated several times as the design engineer refines his design and tries to eliminate all the "bugs." The design engineer reports periodically to his superior—the chief engineer or section head—on his activities. The design engineer may have several projects in the works at one time.

After perhaps half a dozen models have been built and tested, a decision is made by the engineer and the staff as to the feasibility of the tentative design. The decision might be to continue work on it (refining it further), to drop the project as being impractical, or to put the new design into production. In the latter case, the project usually is turned over to production engineers who examine the design from the standpoint of manufacture and who may alter the design to make it easier or less expensive to manufacture. Service engineers may suggest changes that will make servicing of the new product easier in the field. Production engineers will also consult with plant and production engineering to determine where the new design will be manufactured and what special tooling and equipment will be required. The purchasing department will then procure any special equipment and material needed to manufacture the new device.

Next the scheduling department sets a schedule — so many assemblies a day starting on such and such a date. This schedule is based on many factors, such as when the special manufacturing equipment can be delivered and the assembly line set up in the factory, or when necessary metal, screws, nuts, and other material can be purchased by the purchasing department or made by other manufacturing departments of the factory. Also, and perhaps most important, the schedule must take into account the date on which the new design will be adopted for use in the completed automobile.

Inspection engineers must design and set up their testing equipment to test the subassemblies and finished assemblies as they come off the end of the assembly line. Packaging and shipping engineers must design the necessary packaging and decide on methods of shipping the assemblies in quantity to the point of use. This could be in a plant a few blocks away, or in another city halfway across the country.

Meantime, service engineers decide what special servicing tools and instructions might be required, design the tools, and prepare printed instructions as necessary.

This is only a thumbnail sketch of the contributions that the engineers and technicians make to the design, development, and manufacture of a new or improved device. Only a hint is given of the engineer's and technicians's activities and responsibilities. They sample production by taking samples off the assembly line and running them through special tests. They continue to consider alternate and possibly better designs. If something goes wrong with the device in the field, defective units are shipped back to the factory for detailed analysis, and engineers may be sent out to the users to find out what went wrong and why. This information is then used to improve the design.

All of these activities require many engineers and technicians. It is to this great reservoir of talent that management often turns for the management personnel they need. A good engineer not only must know his way around in every department of his company, but he also must know how to get along with others and secure their cooperation in whatever his work requires.

Percentages are hard to come by, but it is estimated that the large majority of mid- and top-management people in the automotive industry came up through the engineering department. This seems only fair, because everything really starts with the engineer and his technicians. Nothing happens until they put pencil to paper, which starts a whole avalanche of activities, as we have seen, with hundreds, thousands, and possibly millions of people ultimately involved.

In this modern world, it is not only interesting to be an engineer or a technician, it is also essential to a healthy economy that the number of these trained people be greatly increased.

Designing an Automobile

CHAPTER **2**

As we noted in the previous chapter, the automotive engine designer must have manufacturing methods very much in mind as he designs his new engine. It is equally important for him to fit his new design into the style and model of automobile for which the engine is intended. To a great extent, the configuration and performance specifications of the new car model or models will dictate the engine-design specifications. It is thus necessary for the engine designer to thoroughly understand how a new car model is born.

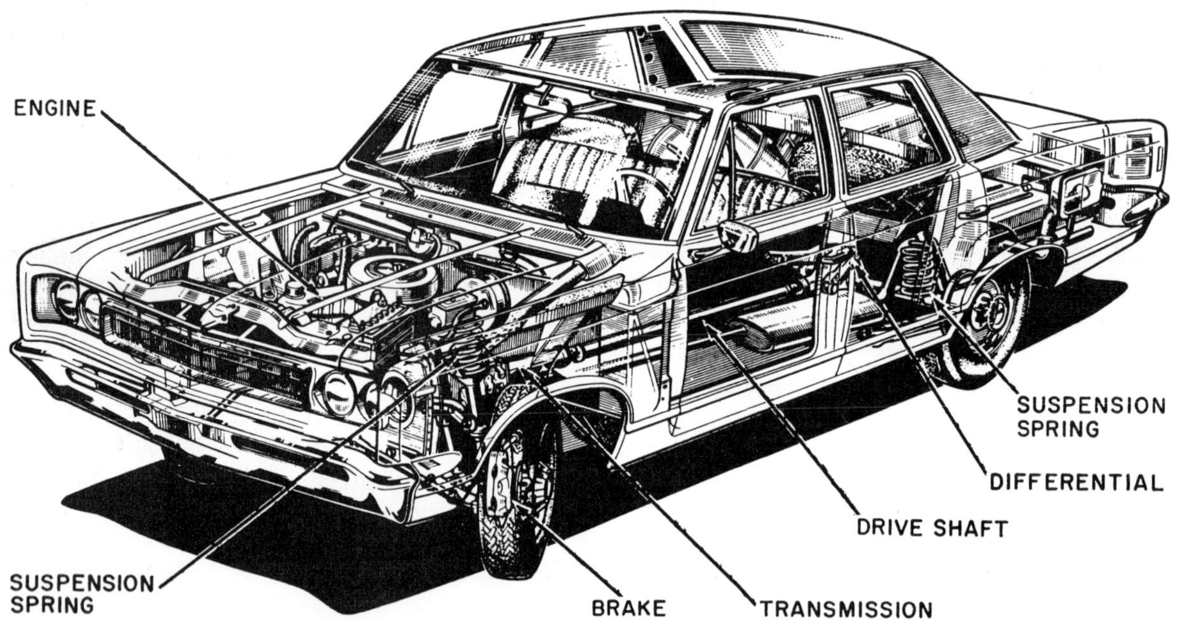

Fig. 2-1. Phantom view of a passenger car with the major components named. (*American Motors Corporation*)

§11. Under the skin Figures 2-1 and 2-2 are phantom views of late-model passenger cars which show the locations of various components that the driver seldom sees. These include the engine, transmission, drive shaft, differential, suspension, steering, and brakes. The vast majority of cars made in the United States have the engine up front, with the rear wheels being driven, as shown in Figs. 2-1 and 2-2. This arrangement requires a long drive shaft, stretching from the transmission at the front to the differential at the rear-wheel axles. This is by no means the only arrangement used. Some cars have the engine mounted in the rear and driving the rear wheels. Others have the engine

Fig. 2-2. Phantom view of a passenger car, the Camaro. (*Chevrolet Motor Division of General Motors Corporation*)

up front and driving the front wheels. Some vehicles have four-wheel drive; that is, all four wheels can be driven by the engine. The engine may be mounted fore and aft, or longitudinally, with the crankshaft parallel to the direction of car motion. Other engines are mounted sideways, or transversally, with the crankshaft perpendicular to the direction of car motion. (These various arrangements are described in detail and illustrated later.)

§12. The idea Everyone is aware, of course, that automobile companies bring out new car models each year, if not more often. It is also well known that, in the past, it has taken as long as three or four years to carry a new model from idea to production. What is perhaps less well known is that this long interval of time is being drastically shortened by modern design methods, which include the use of computers. (This is discussed more fully in §20.)

Engineering departments of automobile companies are constantly at work improving their cars. Laboratory and testing grounds have thousands of tests going on at all times—testing new devices, materials, and processes. As these new developments are proved out, they are either adopted for current car production or held in readiness for the new car models.

Meantime, other new developments, aimed specifically at the new car model, are coming along. First, of course, top management must decide that the new model is needed, and that the many millions of dollars required to develop it will be a worthwhile expenditure.

§13. The decision A decision to go ahead with a new car model is based on economic as well as technical considerations. Will the new model sell well enough for the company to recoup the costs of development? Are the technical and manufacturing facilities of the company adequate for the job? How much new plant and tooling wiil be required to produce the number of cars that the company thinks it will sell? What is the capital investment required, and how will the new plant and tooling be financed?

There are also many other factors that are not directly related to economic or financial aspects. What will be the general specifications of the new car—type, size, retail price? What will be the impact of the new model on the competition? That is, what competitive advantage can the new model give the company? What will be the lead time between crystalizing the design and getting cars into the dealer showrooms?

These and many other factors are considered by management. Car companies have market research and economic departments, as well as design engineers, plant engineers, tool engineers, and stylists, that help management reach their decision. Only after exhaustive analysis of all factors is a decision made.

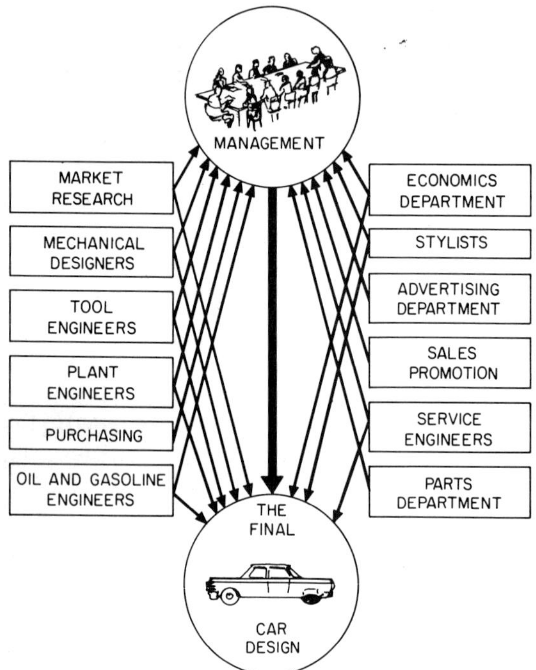

Fig. 2-3. Graphic representation of the interplay of various departments in an automotive company as they work out the final design of a new car model.

If management decides to go ahead, the various departments of the company become involved in a complex, but orderly, manner (Fig. 2-3). At an early stage, the two principle groups, engineering (or mechanical design) and styling, are brought in to begin their preliminary work. Later, the tooling and manufacturing departments study the preliminary design work and decide what new tools and manufacturing facilities will be needed. The safety engineers study the design from the standpoint of driver and passenger protection, as well as ease and safeness of operation. The purchasing department is advised, at some later date, what types and quantities of material will be needed for the new model. The advertising and promotion departments are brought in at the appropriate time so they can lay out an advertising campaign to promote the new model. The sales department begins to plan its regional and local meetings to introduce the new model to the dealers. Extensive sales literature is developed for mailing and for direct distribution to p,ospective buyers entering the dealerships. The service department starts its engineers working on the design of new tools to service the new model; it also begins to develop the necessary service manuals and other material required to train the automotive mechanics in the dealerships in the proper methods to service the new model. The parts department determines what and how many spare parts must be stocked in regional warehouses and dealerships to service the new models. Meantime, automobile-company engineers are working with the oil companies to make sure that the proper gasoline, oil, and other lubricants will be available when the new model comes out.

There is still another consideration in the development of new products—patent infringement. A good engineer is usually pretty well aware of new developments and patent activities in his field. He must always be careful to avoid designing anything that resembles too closely something already patented. On the other hand, if he arrives at something new, he will usually refer it to the company's patent attorney for patent investigation. If feasible, patent application is filed, and then, normally, the patent is assigned to the company. Sometimes, engineers may find that the developments or improvements they seek are already covered by patents owned by another company or individual. In such a case, any of three different courses may be taken. The project may be abandoned; it may be turned in another direction that will not be likely to result in patent infringement; or the company may try to work out an agreement with the owner of the patent. This last course would require the payment of a royalty to the patent owner on every mechanism manufactured using the patented mechanism or process.

As you can see, this is an enormously complicated business that requires the utmost in close cooperation among all the departments of the company. If even one department fails, the new model might well become a complete failure. For example, even though the new model is mechanically excellent, if the buying public does not like the grillwork on the front end, then the new model might not sell as well as expected and the company could lose many millions of dollars. Another example might be that the service department fails to provide the proper tools to service some new device—say, a new automatic transmission. If transmission troubles then develop and automotive mechanics do not have the proper tools to correct them, there could be many serious complaints from owners, and the new model, as well as the company, could be severely condemned.

§14. Mechanical design Let us look more closely at two major design activities that enter into the total car design: *mechanical design* and *styling*. The mechanical design work is focused on the engine, the transmission and drive line, steering, suspension, brakes, frame, and other such items. At an early stage certain tentative decisions are reached in conferences with top management, the styling department, market research, and other interested departments as to the size of the car, its seating capacity, type and horsepower of the engine, type of transmission and suspension, and so on. Almost all car models today have many options, from which the buyer can select the size of engine he wants, the type of brakes, transmission, steering wheel, rear-axle ratio, as well as body-paint colors and interiors, the type of seats, and so on. All these options are examined carefully during the development of the new model so that every option that can be selected will fit and be suitable for the car.

Meantime, new developments from the laboratories that have been proved out are considered. Many of these, such as better materials, improved placement of suspension parts, better valving of the engine, and so on, are automatically included in the new model. Other developments may not be considered suitable from the standpoint of adaptability, cost, possible patent infringement, or other factors. For example, a newly developed lightweight automatic transmission might be considered satisfactory for a small car with a small engine; however, if the new car model is to have a high horsepower engine, then the lightweight automatic transmission might not be suitable. On the other hand, engineers might analyze the possibilities of making a heavier transmission for the new model. They might make cost analyses and run tests with handmade transmissions. Ultimately, a tentative decision might be made that a modified design of the transmission would be satisfactory. However, much further analysis would have to be made, including cost studies, availability of manufacturing facilities, and so on, to determine whether or not the modified design of the new transmission actually would be selected for the new car model.

The new car model might also have mechanical innovations that must be developed almost from the idea stage. For example, suppose top management has made the decision that the new model is to be a front-drive car, with the engine driving the front wheels. Even before this decision is made, much research must be done in order to confirm the feasibility of the proposed design. This research may develop ultimately into the building of actual vehicles that embody the new design so it can be tested on the road. In any event, the engineers must be able to come up with a firm "Can do!" before the decision is made to go ahead.

In this section we have barely scratched the surface of the mechanical design of an automobile. Almost every conceivable aspect of automotive design, manufacture, operation, and service must be considered. Even such factors as car theft are analyzed; that is, engineers try to make their cars as theftproof as possible, along with such less important touches as arranging the ash trays for maximum convenience and safety. Very little is overlooked. Thousands of engineers, technicians, laboratory and field workers, plant engineers, tool engineers, and management men, including sales and service engineers, play a part in the design decision. Sometimes, a man working on the assembly line comes up with a suggestion that results in a change of design. Also, once in a while, an automotive mechanic working in a dealer's service shop suggests an idea that is incorporated into the design.

So you see, the ultimate configuration of the new car model is arrived at through the cooperative efforts of thousands of men and women. A transmission engineer, for example, embarking on the design of a new transmission, may find his work modified greatly as his original design is studied by other members of the team. For example, the engine or chassis engineer might suggest different mounting arrangements or different operating characteristics to better match the torque curve of the new engine. The plant and tool engineers, who are responsible for providing the tools and manufacturing equipment to make the new transmission, might suggest design modifications that would make the tooling or manufacturing of the transmission easier, less expensive, higher in quality, or more adaptable to existing tooling and plant layouts. Meantime, the metallurgists might have their say as to the specifications of the metals that the transmission designer selected for the parts in the assembly. Also, the service engineers look at the design from the standpoint of ease of servicing, need for new service tools, automotive-mechanics training requirements, and possible difficulties in servicing procedures. They may make suggestions for design changes that will facilitate servicing of the transmission in the field or that will utilize servicing tools that are already available in the dealer-service shops. Other members of the team have a say in the ultimate design, too. The director of sales, or advertising, for example, might suggest that a different shifting speed in the transmission could be a strong talking point in advertising or sales literature.

Ultimately, all of these diverse opinions and suggestions are considered and either rejected or incorporated in one way or another into the final transmission design. Now, the modified design has to clear another obstacle, that of management approval. Not only must management look at the design itself, how it will fit into the manufacturing plant, and what the tooling costs and servicing requirements will be, but also they must consider the possible competitive advantage the proposed new transmission will give the company. Ultimately, they must make the decision, shall we go ahead with the new design, or shall we stick with what we have?

Many knowledgeable outsiders, viewing the complex process of decision making in modern industry, wonder how any decision is ever made. Yet the decision-making machinery is well designed and functions effectively, we know. For new models and new processes are constantly being released.

§15. The stylists The stylists play a very important part in the overall design of the new car model. In many ways, their work is far more difficult and much less predictable. Design work is relatively straightforward for the engine designer, for example, as he arrives at a new intake-manifold design. He is dealing with factors that can be weighed and measured in the laboratory. When the extrapolation of existing laws or formulas and prior engineering experience do not provide him with the answers he seeks, he can alter the design, have experimental manifolds made, and find out exactly in what way this altered design affects engine performance.

The stylist has no such set of rules or formulas to fall back on. He must follow precedent and not wander too far from what the public has accepted. To help him, the market research people make studies of public taste by means of questionnaires and personal interviews. But the results of these studies may turn out to be of little actual value. Public tastes in car styles change, sometimes in unpredictable ways. The tail-fin fad is an example. Relatively few stylists would have given the tail fin a vote of confidence at first. Cadillac used tail fins in 1948, but the idea did not catch on in the lower-priced cars. Then, the Chrysler Corporation decided to put tail fins on its Plymouth in 1957, and the public liked it. Plymouth's sales zoomed.

The stylist, however, does have precedents to follow—many rules of design, his own good taste, the results of market research, and preliminary commentary on his ideas from others, as he feels his way along toward his new design.

§16. The stylist's job After the preliminary decisions are reached by management as to the general characteristics of the new car model, the stylists begin their detailed development work.[1-3] They must reach decisions on the general appearance of the new model, body shape and style, placement of glass, roof, pillars, trim, and so on. Further, their work involves the type and placement of seats, interior trim, dash design, color schemes, and many other items.

Fig. 2-4. Preliminary artist's sketches of possible designs for a new car. (*Chevrolet Motor Division of General Motors Corporation*)

Fig. 2-5. Preliminary design study by stylists to show their ideas of how a new car model might look.

Stylists enter into the preliminary management decisions in several ways. They supply renderings, that is, artwork, showing what the various details and the overall design might look like. Numerous rough sketches and renderings are made as different ideas are tried out on interested personnel in styling and management (Figs. 2-4 and 2-5).

A relatively new design tool is now being used to some extent by car stylists in their early body-design work. It is a computer device which includes a modified cathode-ray tube, on the display face of which drawings can be made. The device has various names. It is called SKETCHPAD by MIT (Massachusetts Institute of Technology) personnel who helped to develop it. A modification of the device used by General Motors Research is called DAC (Design Augmented by Computer).

One way that the device is used by car stylists is as follows: During their preliminary planning of the new car model, stylists want to know how possible design contours would look from different angles. To achieve this quick look, the designer picks up a special electronic pencil and makes a sketch of the proposed design on the tube face by moving the pencil tip across the tube face (Fig. 2-6). Actually, the drawing is an electronic pattern produced by the moving electronic pencil tip. After a drawing has been made, the computer can be asked to analyze the proposed design in a number of ways, according to the manner in which the computer has been programmed. For example, a stylist might sketch out the side view of a prototype car design. Then, DAC could be asked to show how this design would look from other

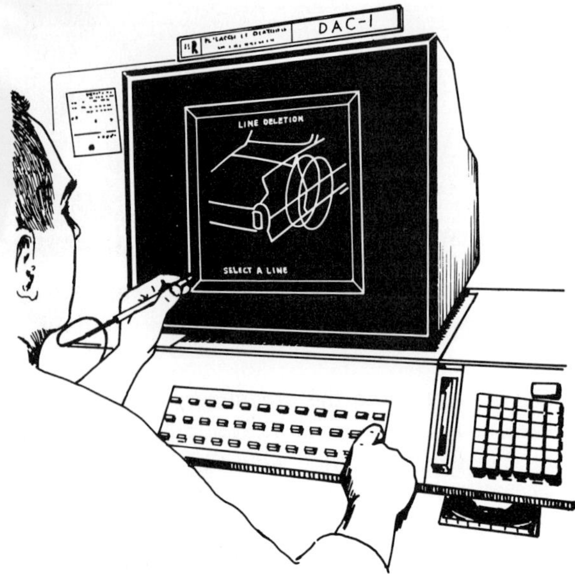

Fig. 2-6. DAC (Design Augmented by Computer) in use to assess configuration of a preliminary car-body styling idea. (*General Motors Corporation*)

angles (front, top, three-quarter, and so on), and it would display on the tube face these other views of the prototype car design as they are requested. Furthermore, if properly programmed, the computer could analyze the prototype design as to structural strength, aerodynamic properties, and so on. (You will appreciate how valuable this device can be to the stylist in his preliminary design work.)

After much study and consultation with all interested parties, stylists begin to crystalize the semifinal design of the car body, inside and out. They may then prepare, on vertical blackboards or drawing boards, full-scale silhouette outlines of the car. These are studied by the stylists, top management, and manufacturing specialists, and the design may be further altered to suit stylistic preferences and in recognition of possible effects on future tooling and production problems. An extra long hood, for example, might mean the installation of new larger stamping presses. Shortening the hood slightly, however, might make it possible to stamp out hoods on the smaller presses which the company already has.

After many modifications, the general appearance of the new model is established. At this point, scale models of the new model are prepared. These scale models may be from one-quarter to full size. They are made of clay on a wood framework, carefully shaped and contoured, with the trim, grillwork, and other touches as accurately simulated as possible. The models are covered with plastic film to imitate paint, and metal foil is used to imitate chrome so that the models look as nearly like actual cars as possible. These models are studied from all angles for appearance, comfort, convenience, aerodynamic properties, safety, and relationship to the mechanical features of the proposed vehicle. For example, there must be room enough under the hood for the engine, power brakes, power steering, air-induction system, air-conditioning, and so on. Likewise, the design must permit adequate bracing and interior padding to protect the driver and passengers in case of accident.

Several scale models may be prepared in succession (Fig. 2-7), each embodying the changes suggested by the various interested members of the design team—engine and chassis engineers, safety engineers, production people, purchasing agents, sales and advertising personnel, service engineers, top management, and so on. Finally, a design configuration is arrived at that is approved by everyone.

§17. From clay to steel After the general design has crystalized, a full-scale model is made out of modeling clay. After further looks by everyone concerned (and possibly further modifications), skilled template makers begin their work. The templates are made from sheets of cardboard that are cut and recut until they match the contours of the clay model. These templates are made to match the body contours at about 5-inch intervals—less in rapid transitional areas or sharp curves. This is extremely painstaking work. The clay is soft and must be approached carefully with the cardboard templates to avoid changing the contours.

After the templates are completed, loftsmen take over. Loft lines are a series of curves, correspond-

Fig. 2-7. Stages in the evolution of a luxury sports car, the Cougar, as reflected in clay models. Note how the general configuration changed from 1 through 4, which was the final design of the Cougar. (*Ford Motor Company*)

ing to the contours, which were picked up by the template makers on their templates. The loftsmen usually modify the body design slightly because the clay model is not perfectly contoured and the cardboard templates probably do not follow the contours exactly. The loftsmen transfer the contour lines from the templates to drawing paper or sheets of aluminum.

The contour lines, or loft lines, are used to make metal templates. These templates are then used by master woodworkers who carve, from laminated mahogany blocks that are fitted together, a full-scale *mockup* of the car. This mockup is then painted and decorated with chrome for additional analysis by all interested departments.

After perhaps still further modification, the mahogany blocks become the master models from which the body-stamping dies are made. From this point on, the design of the new car model is fixed. The body-stamping dies are made from blocks of special die steel on a special milling machine. This machine uses a cutting tool that can move in three directions. The operator has duplicates of the mahogany blocks that show the contours of one part of the body, say, the car roof. He places this in a holding fixture and then moves a stylus over the contours of the model. As he does this, the cutting tool moves in synchronism over the work-piece, or block of steel, from which the roof-stamping die is being cut so that ultimately the steel block has been cut to contours matching the model. This is a long process called *die-sinking.* Hundreds of hours may be required to produce a single die.

As a final step, the stamping surfaces of the die must be "barbered," a process during which small irregularities are cleaned up, male and female dies are properly mated, and so on.

Other activities are proceeding at the same time. Segmental plaster casts are made to guide the toolmakers who will prepare the tools needed to manufacture the small parts such as bumpers, door handles and other hardware, head and tail lights, and so on. In addition, interior stylists prepare interior "bucks," or dimensioned forms, in which they can arrange the steerling wheel, seats, instrument panels, and so on, and also try out different color schemes and interior arrangements.

Meantime, several handmade models are built so that the new design can be tested by driving the cars under various road and weather conditions. These test drives may also embody testing of some of the new mechanical components which have been adopted for the new car model. The handmade bodies are produced by first preparing cast-iron or hardwood prototypes of the final dies. The sheet metal is then hand hammered to shape over these preliminary dies.

At every stage of the procedure, the appearance, roadability, safety, comfort, and serviceability of the new design are evaluated by the several groups already mentioned. During early stages, it is possible to make rather major changes, but, as the final design begins to emerge, changes become fewer and smaller. For example, it would be possible in the early stages to change bumper or roof-pillar shapes and locations. Later, trim locations could be adjusted. But, finally, the complete design is crystalized, and the manufacturing dies and tools are completed.

§18. Designing the Camaro—a case history[1] Let us finish our discussion of the stylist's job by looking at a specific project, the design of the 1967 Chevrolet Camaro.[1] A phantom view of this car is shown in Fig. 2-2. A basic specification of the new car was that it would be a four-passenger vehicle. This predetermined, in a general way, the size and shape of the passenger envelope.

As a first step, the artists in the styling section began making preliminary sketches (Fig. 2-4). These sketches showed possible new design details and how the new car might look from every angle. After much consultation with everyone concerned with the new design and many further sketches, a general configuration began to take shape. This shape was then translated from two-dimensional drawings to a three-dimensional full-scale model, or "buck." The model (Fig. 2-8) was made with a wood frame, which gave the stylists a better feel for the developing new style, the comfort and convenience that the interior offered the passengers and driver, the ease of entry and exit, driver visibility, and so on.

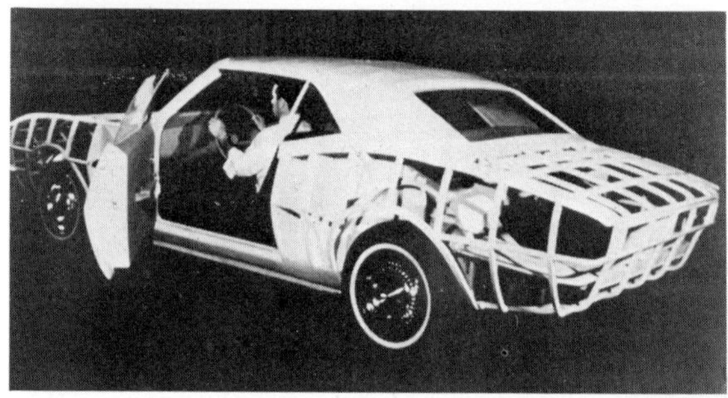

Fig. 2-8. Preliminary wood-frame buck of a new car model. (*Chevrolet Motor Division of General Motors Corporation*)

Then, a full-scale clay model was developed. This clay model was, in effect, a piece of sculpture that could be altered in order to try different lines, curves, headlight mountings, grillwork, windshield and window shapes (or "greenhouse areas" as the glass is called), and so on. Out of all this work and study ultimately emerged a clay model that represented the consensus of the styling section, sales, mechanical design, production, research, and top management (Fig. 2-9).

As the next step, an accurate quarter-scale clay model was constructed and tested in a wind tunnel for an analysis of the aerodynamic properties of the new design (Fig. 2-10). A total of 76 data runs were made in the 78 hours that the new design was tested in the wind tunnel. These tests proved the basic aerodynamic stability of the new design. Some modifications of the shape were made (for

Fig. 2-9. Full-scale clay model. (*Chevrolet Motor Division of General Motors Corporation*)

Fig. 2-10. Testing a one-quarter scale model of a new car in a wind tunnel. (*Chevrolet Motor Division of General Motors Corporation*)

instance, on the leading surfaces of the front fenders) to further improve the aerodynamic properties.

Next, the results of the wind-tunnel tests were incorporated into the basic design, and a final configuration was agreed upon (Fig. 2-9). From this point on, the final design was translated from clay to tools and dies, and finally to steel, as already described (§17).

§19. Mechanical design vs. styling You are aware by now that the designers of the mechanical components and the stylists (the designers of the "look") have two greatly different chores. The stylists, in effect, treat the vehicle as a whole; where a major style change is called for, their job is to produce a substantially new body look. On the other hand, the mechanical designers are working on individual components—the engine, transmission, suspension, steering, brakes, and so on. This fragmentation permits the engineers in the engine section, for example, to develop a new engine without special consultation or close cooperation with the steering or brake engineers. In addition, the mechanical designers maintain a more or less steady flow of new designs or mechanical improvements which are ready for application on new models. In effect, this provides a reservoir of new or improved models of mechanical components upon which management can draw.

§20. Cutting the lead time The basic bottleneck in the introduction of new models, as already indicated, is the lead time between the conception of the new design and the delivery of the new models to the car dealers. The traditional procedure, outlined above in some detail, requires three years or more. Thus, the style that you see in the dealer's showroom today was conceived three years ago or more. This long gestation period has been due to the necessarily slow work of making the full-scale silhouette outlines, converting these into small-scale models, then into full-scale models, then into actual running, handmade models, and finally preparing the tools and dies needed to put the new model on the assembly line.

Traditionally, this meant that an automotive manufacturer had two, three, or four years of car models in some stage of development. As an example, some years ago, when a company introduced its 1955 model in the fall of 1954, its 1956 model was already pretty well crystalized, and the tools and dies for it might already be in preparation. Meantime, its 1957 model might be in the clay-model stage, its 1958 model in the silhouette-outline stage, and its 1959 model in the first-sketch, or "dreaming," stage.

The dangers of this long lead time are obvious. Suppose a competitor were to come out with a radical departure in design, say, in the fall of 1956. Suppose this caught the public fancy so that the company's projected designs for 1957, 1958, and so on, apparently lost their appeal. The company could suffer a major loss of business under such circumstances. A case in point was the decision of the Plymouth manufacturers to add tail fins to their 1957 car models. Their sales leaped upward as this innovation caught the public fancy, and this increase in sales was at the expense, at least in part, of the other automotive manufacturers.

On the other hand, designers can introduce an innovation that has a negative impact on sales. For example, in 1959, Chevrolet had horizontal, wing-like fins at the rear, so the design was called "the Martian Ground Chariot" by certain competitors. Then, in 1960, Ford's sales suffered, it was reported, when they brought out a slope-nosed model that the Ford competition called "the Ant-eater."

All of these factors have forced designers to shorten their lead time as much as possible. The use of computers has been a great help in this regard. We have already mentioned SKETCHPAD and DAC (§16), which enable the designer to see how the new design looks from various angles at a very early stage in the design work.

Another recent innovation is the use of computer-controlled milling machines that pick up the die-contour data directly from the loft lines. They work in the following manner. The loft drawings are laid out in sequence, one after another, on a large table fitted with a special electronic viewer—somewhat like a television camera. This viewer moves methodically back and forth across each drawing that is placed on the table, recording on computer tape the contour lines on the drawings.

After all the loft drawings related to a single body stamping are scanned in this manner and the contours programmed on computer tape, the tape is placed in a special computer-control device. This device is connected to the motors that move the cutting tool of the milling machine (Fig. 2-11). From this point on, making the die is automatic. As the tape feeds through the machine, the cutting tool is automatically moved along the contours, cutting away steel to reveal, at last, the final die shape that is required to stamp out the body part.

As you can see, this innovation greatly shortens the lead time because it is no longer necessary to prepare metal templates and a mahogany-block full-scale mockup of the car.

Fig. 2-11. Computer-controlled milling machine in operation, machining a car-body die. (*Cincinnati Milling Machine Company*)

But it is still necessary to prepare cardboard templates and loft drawings. It has been suggested, however, that these steps could be eliminated if a means could be found to go directly from the clay model to the computer-controlled milling machine. One way to do this is to immerse the clay model in water and then pull it out in increments of 2 or 3 inches, taking photographs of the water line around the clay model at each step. These photographs could then be examined by a special electronic viewer so it could prepare the computer tape on which the contour data is recorded. This tape could then be used to guide the computer-controlled milling machine. No doubt other methods are possible.

§21. Designing for safety In recent years, increased attention has been focused by designers on making automobiles more crashworthy, that is, designing cars so that they provide greater protection for the driver and passengers in case of an accident. However, this has been a matter of special interest to automotive designers for many years. Witness, for example, the introduction of all-steel bodies, safety glass, four-wheel brakes, padded instrument panels, seat belts, and so on.

Research into the matter of automotive safety is a continuing activity, and special sections of

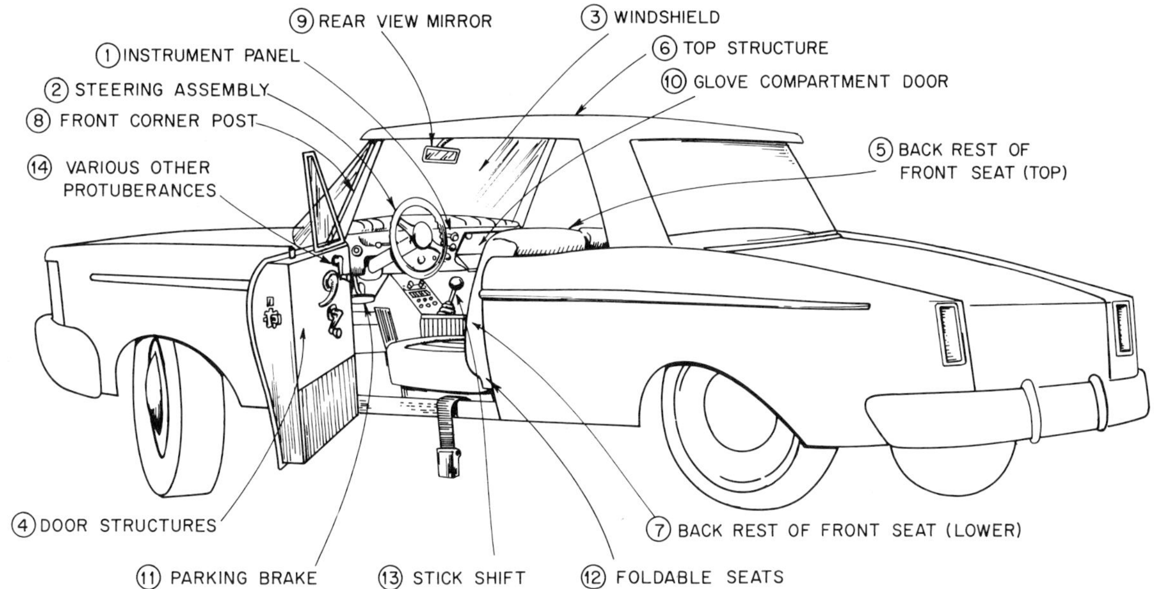

Fig. 2-12. Fouteen areas, or parts, of the automobile that are most commonly involved in injuring or killing passengers and drivers, numbered according to the frequency with which they are responsible for injuries in accidents.

engineering departments devote their full time to it. Recent studies show that the most dangerous sectors of the automobile, insofar as passengers and driver are concerned, are as shown in Fig. 2-12. Two separate actions occur, in sequence, when a crash takes place: There is the *first collision,* during which the car encounters another object that brings it to a very rapid halt. This collision takes place somewhere on the perimeter of the car, and an inward and crushing movement on the car takes place, starting from the impact point. The rapid halt of the car itself then causes the passengers to be thrown forward. More accurately, the inertia of the passengers causes them to continue to move forward after the car has halted until they are restrained by their seat belts, or until they meet some stationary part of the car.

This secondary action is called the *second collision,* and it is often the cause of serious injury or death to passengers or driver. A variety of methods are used to study the effects of the second collision. One method uses impact sleds (Fig. 2-13); a second method uses actual cars, operated by remote control (Fig. 2-14). In both methods, dummies equipped with sensing devices record their motions and decelerations during the second

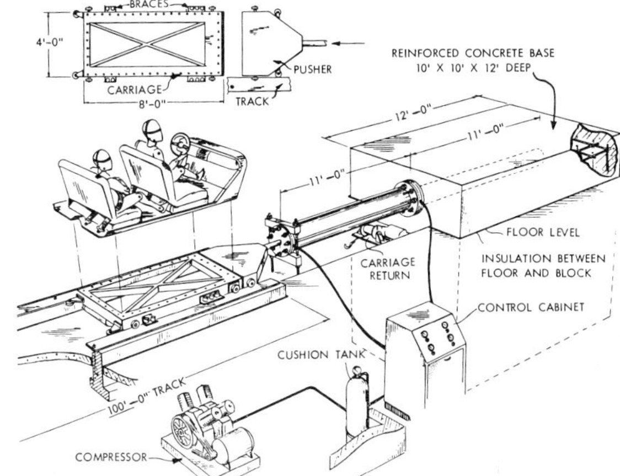

Fig. 2-13. Impact sled used to simulate sudden deceleration of passengers during an automobile accident. Dummies in the sled have sensors that report decelerations. In addition, high-speed photographs are taken during the action. (*General Motors Corporation*)

Fig. 2-14. Cars operated by remote control are crashed in a variety of ways to study effects on occupants and on the car structure. (*General Motors Corporation*)

collision. Cars are also lifted by crane and dropped from various heights on their front ends to test the strength and collapsibility of the frame and other parts.

Partial protection of passengers and driver can be achieved by the use of seat belts. A seat belt helps to hold a person in his seat so he is not thrown forward and into the part of the car just ahead of him. Fig. 2-15 shows the motions of a dummy in the front passenger seat, with and without a seat belt, at various decelerations. Note that, while the seat belt protects the passenger from going through the windshield, his body will jackknife and his head will be thrown into the instrument panel at the higher decelerations. The use of a shoulder belt (Fig. 2-16) generally will prevent this jackknifing.

Even though the driver or passengers are held in their seats by seat and shoulder belts, the collision may drive some part of the car toward them, causing injury or death. Protection of the driver

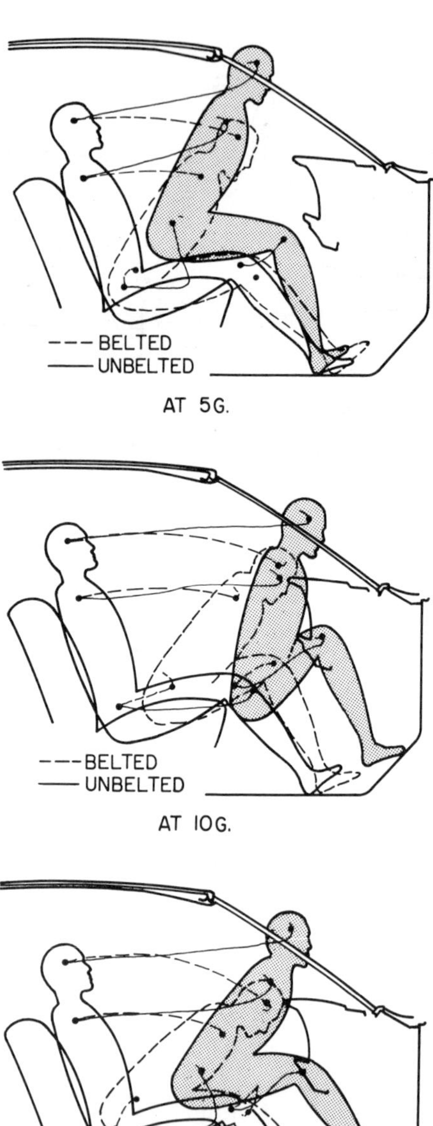

Fig. 2-15. Motions of a dummy passenger in the front seat of a car, with and without a seat belt, at impacts that impose decelerations of 5, 10, and 15 g on the dummy passenger. The dots indicate the starting and ending points of the head, shoulder, and other parts of the dummy. The lines connecting the points are their paths of travel. (*General Motors Corporation*)

Fig. 2-16. Use of a shoulder strap, as well as a seat belt, restrains the car occupants so they will not jackknife.(*Dodge Division of Chrysler Motors Corporation*)

and front-seat passenger has been increased by making the steering shaft partly collapsible so that it shortens under impact (Fig. 2-17), and by using a strong fire wall in back of the engine. This will force the engine down, under the front passenger compartment, in case of a front collision, instead of into the compartment.

In addition, frames and bodies are being designed to selectively collapse during a front-end collision so that the energy of the moving car is more gradually absorbed. This reduces the deceleration of the passengers and driver so that the second collision will be less severe.

These are a few of the steps being taken to make automobiles safer and more crashworthy. Automotive engineers, whether their field is engines, frames, bodies, or transmissions, and so on, think about and work toward safer automobiles.

§22. The design job The past few pages have given you an idea of some of the things the automotive engineer-designer must consider as he works out his ideas, first in his head, then on paper, then in three-dimensional models, then in the laboratory, and finally on the assembly line and in the field. He must consider many factors: reliability, relative simplicity of design, ease of manufacturing and servicing, safety, applicability

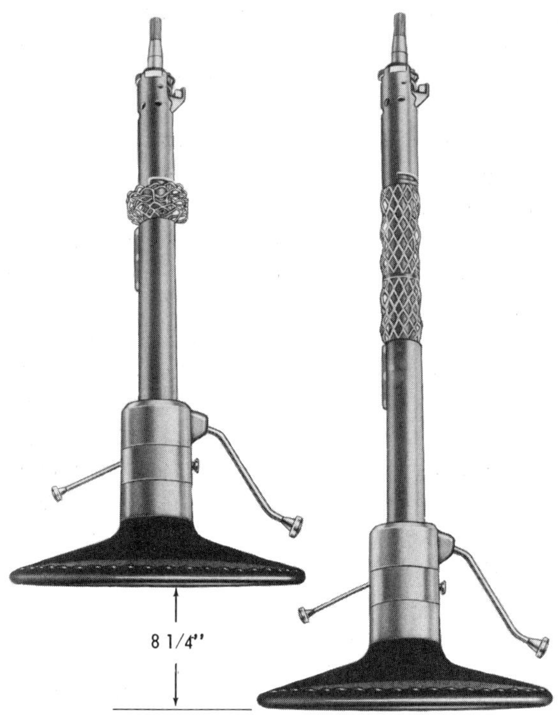

Fig. 2-17. Collapsible steering shaft. The mesh section will collapse under impact, as shown at left, thus shortening the shaft length to protect the driver. (*Cadillac Motor Car Division of General Motors Corporation*)

of available manufacturing facilities, cost factors, availability of materials and parts, competitive advantage, promotional features that will appeal to the public, how top management will react to the design, and so on.

Each of these factors and many others enter into the final decisions on the proposed design. It might seem difficult, if not impossible, for a new design to see the light of day, having to clear so many hurdles. However, automotive manufacturers, and other manufacturers as well, have long since set up the necessary decision-making machinery so that American industry continues to bring out new designs of their products and to improve these designs after they go into production. This teamwork among the many different departments of a company is a basic factor in the economic strength of any manufacturing concern.

§23. The role of the SAE The SAE (Society of Automotive Engineers) has as members most engineers and management personnel in the automotive and aircraft industry, including parts and materials suppliers. Also, there are many members from the fields of education and publishing.

The SAE, with its numerous activities and publications, serves several extremely important functions. First, the society provides channels of communication through which engineers can exchange ideas and compare notes, as it were. The society publishes a magazine which is filled with technical articles on automotive and aircraft design, manufacture, and operation *(The SAE Journal).* Each year it holds a number of local and national meetings which are attended by thousands of SAE members. In these meetings, technical papers (on new developments) are presented and discussed. These papers are also published for distribution to members, libraries, and schools.*

The SAE maintains about 415 committees and subcommittees (as of 1968), made up of members of the society, that study various aspects of automotive engineering, manufacture, and maintenance. Based on these studies, the committees set standards and recommended practices. For example, there are committees on ball and roller bearings, ball joints (front suspension), brakes, screw threads, suspension springs, bumpers, and so on. Committees meet as necessary to discuss standards and recommended practices in their special fields. Whenever changes are required, they revise their papers or reports on standards and recommended practices and reissue them. Each year, all of these data are gathered together into a published book. This is the *SAE Handbook*, which consists of more than a thousand pages and contains thousands of tables, illustrations, standards, and recommended practices.

The *Handbook* is an invaluable tool to the engineer. If he is designing a machine that will have a spline shaft, he does not have to worry about designing the splines. This has already been done by the splines committee, and their standards paper contains numerous tables giving spline dimensions for shafts of various sizes with varying numbers of splines. Also, recommended materials, manufacturing methods, and inspection procedures are given. The same holds true for screw threads, hydraulic tube fittings, generator mountings, cranking-motor-pinion and flywheel-ring gears, shaft seals, piston rings, cigar lighters, electrical wiring, including color codes, seat-belt anchorage, and thousands of other items in the automobile.

Think, for a moment, how extremely difficult it would be for engineers to design an automobile if they did not have these thousands of standards and recommended practices to utilize. Fortunately, however, the design of screw threads, spark-plug mounting, splines, lock washers, sealing rings, springs, bearings, and so on, have already been worked out. The whole industrial complex of the United States agrees on these standards, so that a 1/4 = 20 UNC = 2A thread will be the same regardless of whether it is manufactured in California or New York. Millions of decisions have already been made by qualified engineers regarding all these items, and thus the designer of a new mechanism does not have to reconsider any of them.

The SAE also has another function. It places SAE members on committees of other technical organizations. For instance, it has members on the Committee for Standardization and Unification of Screw Threads, which is a committee of the American Standards Association. These composite committees assure general acceptance of all standards and recommended practices by all technical societies and thus by the entire manufacturing industry in the United States.

There is another interesting aspect of all this committee work: with standards being set for screws, nuts, pipe fittings, splines, and so on, the tooling and equipment to manufacture and utilize all of these parts can also be standardized. It is easy to see that without such standardization, life would be much more difficult for anyone designing, manufacturing, or repairing machines such as automobiles. For example, what would happen if

*The references at the ends of chapters in this book list many SAE papers.

Chrysler used one type of screw thread, Ford a second, and General Motors a third, with none of them being interchangeable? Special tooling would have to be developed for each, and, furthermore, each repair shop, garage, or service station would have to carry complete stocks of all these different screws, nuts, and bolts. And even if they did this, the parts would constantly be getting mixed up. Fortunately, however, a $1/4 = 20$ UNC $= 2$A thread is the same anywhere in the country and will fit an automobile, airplane, submarine, electric toaster, or any other device where specifications call for it.

In addition to the many activities of the SAE mentioned above, the society is also active in the field of education. For example, committees are formed and special sessions are held in the interest of aiding in the training of automotive mechanics or engineers. Young men and women still in college are encouraged to become junior members of the society. The society also encourages the exchange of information between manufacturers and educators in technical institutes and colleges.

Because the SAE provides so much technical information and assistance to its members, every eligible engineer or technician in the automotive field should belong to the society. Management, well aware of the value of membership in the SAE to the engineer or technician, encourages their qualified employees to join. Further, management sees to it that qualified people get to the appropriate regional and national SAE conventions, generally paying their expenses to assure this attendance. However, one does not have to be in the employ of an automotive or accessory manufacturer to join the SAE. Engineering students can also join. Students usually find that such association is of great value in furthering their careers.

SUMMARY

Designing an automobile is an exceedingly complex matter, involving thousands of individuals who must make tens of thousands of decisions. The decision of an automotive company to produce a new model is based on economic and technical considerations. Once a decision to go ahead is made, all departments of a company begin to make their plans; the car must be designed, and also the manufacturing, distribution, and servicing departments must get ready for the new model.

The design of the new car can be divided into two interrelated parts: styling and mechanical, or, you might say, the looks and the performance. Mechanical design can be segmented to a considerable degree, with various groups working on different components such as engine, transmission, steering, brakes, and so on. But styling requires an integrated approach—the "look" cannot be broken down into separate components, at least to begin with. However, after the general style has been crystalized, specialist groups can refine such details as seat placement and configurations, arrangement of interiors, bumper and trim, and so on.

Stylists must work two or three years ahead, and various electronic aids have come into use to shorten this lead time. Computer-controlled milling machines can now work directly (via tapes) from the loft lines to make the body-stamping dies. It has been suggested that even more time could be saved by a device that could operate the milling machine directly from photographs of the clay model immersed at various depths in water.

Car companies continue their research on safety, with greater emphasis than ever, and many protective devices for the driver and passengers have been developed. These include seat belts, collapsible steering shafts, padded instrument panels and rear-view mirrors, more collapsible car bodies to absorb impact, stronger framing around the passenger compartment, improved brakes, and so on. For many years, we have already had such safety features as all-steel bodies, four-wheel brakes, and safety glass.

REFERENCES

1. McPherson, D. H., C. M. Rubly, and V. D. Valade, The Chevrolet Camaro, SAE (Society of Automotive Engineers) 670016, 1967 (paper).

2. Lunn, R. C., The Ford GT Sports Car, SAE (Society of Automotive Engineers) 670065, 1967 (paper).

3. Andren, B. T., and T. J. Feaheny, The Mercury Cougar—Why and How, SAE (Society of Automotive Engineers) 670017, 1967 (paper).

QUESTIONS

1. Make an organization chart of an automobile company, using the information given in the chapter and showing the function of each department in the design and manufacture of a new model.

2. Write a short paper contrasting the work of the styling and mechanical departments in designing a new model car.

3. Explain why patent research is so important to a design engineer.

4. Describe briefly the steps that stylists take as they start a new design and bring it to completion.

5. Write a short paper on die-sinking, referring to books in the bibliography as necessary.

6. Describe recent research and its results in the field of car safety.

7. Write a report outlining the steps that engineers take in designing and putting into production a new "gizmo."

CHAPTER 3

Internal-combustion-engine Operation

This chapter provides a brief review of the operation of the most widely used automotive engine—the piston-type, internal-combustion, four-stroke-cycle, overhead-valve, liquid-cooled engine. Chapter 4 describes different types of the piston-type, internal-combustion engine, as well as internal-combustion engines which do not use pistons.

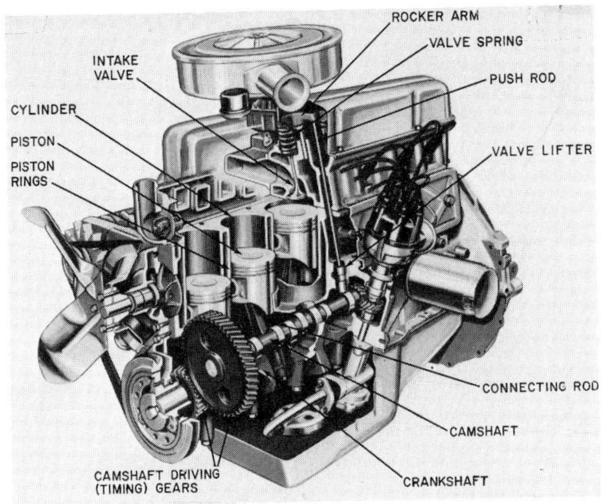

Fig. 3-1. Cutaway view of a six-cylinder, overhead-valve, in-line engine. (*Chevrolet Motor Division of General Motors Corporation*)

§24. Engine cylinders Most piston-type automotive engines have four, six, or eight cylinders. Inasmuch as the actions are similar in all cylinders, we can concentrate on one cylinder in order to study the actions that take place in the engine. Figure 3-1 shows an engine in a phantom view so that the features of one cylinder can be seen. Essentially, the engine cylinder is a cylindrical air pocket which is closed at one end. The piston—a snug-fitting metal plug—is inserted through the open end of the cylinder. The piston can slide up and down in the cylinder.

When the piston is moved up into the cylinder, it traps air ahead of it, thus compressing the air (Fig. 3-2). If gasoline vapor were mixed with the air and the compressed mixture were ignited by a spark, the resulting explosion would blow the piston out of the cylinder (Fig. 3-2*c*). This is similar to what happens in the engine cylinder, except, of course, that the piston is not blown clear out. Actually, the piston moves up and down, moving up to compress the air-fuel mixture and down when the air-fuel mixture is ignited and burns.

§25. Piston rings The piston must have a fairly loose fit in the cylinder. If it were a tight fit when cold, it might expand so much as it heated up that it would actually stick tight in the cylinder. However, it must not have too loose a fit because this would allow excessive leakage of air-fuel mixture and combustion pressures past it. This loss would seriously reduce engine performance.

Piston rings are used to make a good sealing fit between the piston and cylinder wall. The piston has three or more grooves cut in its side, and metal rings are fitted into these grooves (Fig. 3-3). The rings are split at one point so they can be expanded and slid over the piston head into the grooves. Then they are compressed when the piston is installed in the cylinder. This brings the split ends of the rings almost together. The rings fit tightly against the cylinder wall and against the sides of the grooves in the piston. This provides a good seal

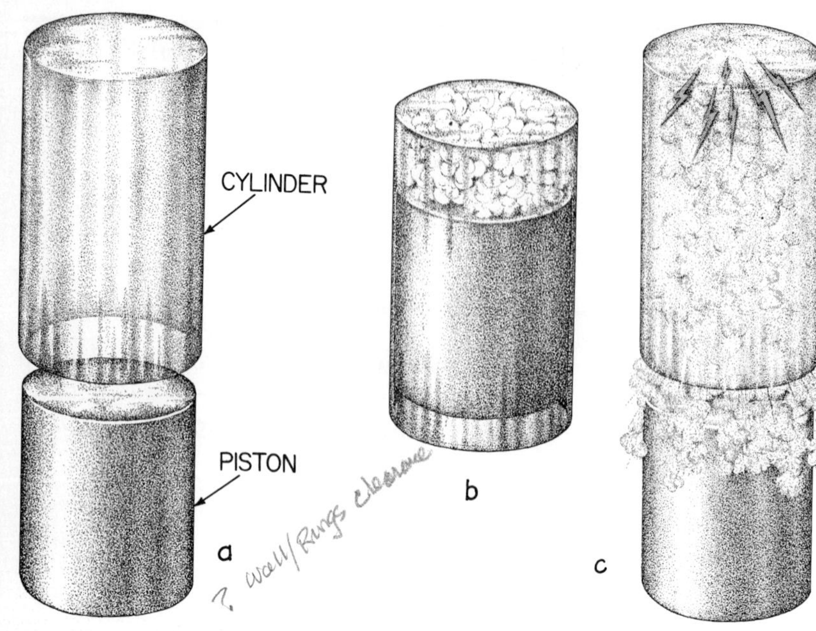

Fig. 3-2. Three views showing the actions in an engine cylinder: (*a*) The piston is a metal plug that fits snugly into the engine cylinder. (*b*) When the piston is pushed up into the cylinder, air is trapped and compressed. The cylinder is drawn as though it were transparent, so that the piston can be seen. (*c*) The increase of pressure as the gasoline-vapor and air mixture is ignited pushes the piston out of the cylinder.

between the piston and cylinder wall, while still permitting the piston and ring assembly to slide up and down in the cylinder.

Two types of piston rings are used: compression rings and oil-control rings. Compression rings hold the pressure, or compression, in the cylinder by forming a seal between the piston and cylinder wall, as already noted. Oil-control rings wipe excessive oil off the cylinder walls, thus preventing it from passing up into the combustion chamber where it would be burned. (Piston rings are discussed in detail in Chaps. 7 and 12.)

§26. Reciprocating to rotary motion The reciprocating motion of the pistons in the cylinders must be changed to rotary motion to produce rotary motion of the vehicle wheels. To achieve this change, the piston is connected by a linkage to a crank on a crankshaft. The connecting link is called a *connecting rod* (Figs. 3-3 to 3-5). The crank is an offset section of the crankshaft that swings around in a circle as the crankshaft rotates.

The piston end of the connecting rod is attached to the piston by a *piston pin*, sometimes called a *wrist pin*. The crank end of the connecting rod is attached to the crank by a cap, called the *rod-bearing cap* (Figs. 3-4 and 3-5). That part of the crank to which the rod is connected is called the *crankpin*. A bearing in the piston end of the connecting rod permits the rod to swing back and forth on the piston pin. (On some engines, there are two bearings in the piston.) The crank end of the connecting rod has a bearing that permits the crankpin to rotate in the connecting rod.

Note: In shop parlance, the crank end of the connecting rod is sometimes called the rod "big end" and the piston end is called the rod "small end."

Figure 3-6 shows how the reciprocating motion of the piston is changed to rotary motion by the connecting rod and crank on the crankshaft. As the piston moves down, the connecting rod tilts to one side so that the crank end can follow the circular path of the crankpin. Follow the sequence from 1 to 8 in Fig. 3-6 to see the different positions that the connecting rod and crank take as the piston moves up and down. The rod tilts, or swings back and forth, as the crankpin moves in a circle.

§27. Engine valves There must be a means of removing the products of combustion from the cylinder and replacing them with fresh charges of air-fuel mixture. In the typical four-stroke-cycle engine, the means is provided by a pair of valves.

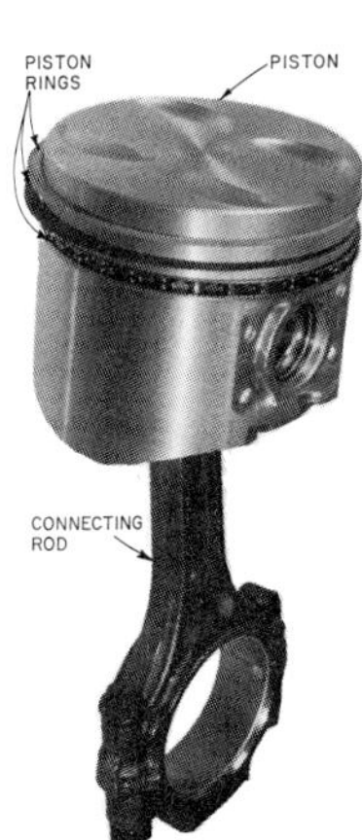

Fig. 3-3. Typical piston with the piston rings in place and the connecting rod attached. When the piston is installed in the cylinder, the rings are compressed into the grooves in the piston. (*Chrysler Motors Corporation*)

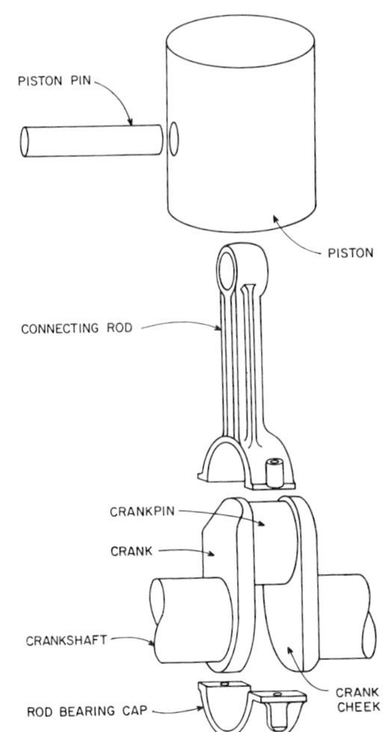

Fig. 3-4. Piston, connecting rod, piston pin, and crankpin on an engine crankshaft in disassembled view. The piston rings are not shown.

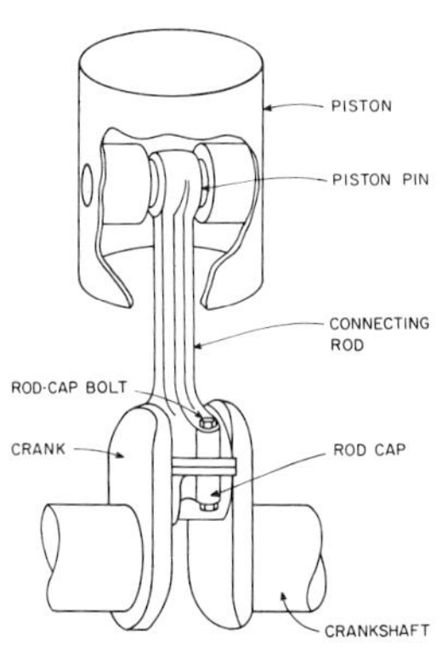

Fig. 3-5. Piston and connecting-rod assembly attached to the crankpin on a crankshaft. The piston rings are not shown. The piston is partly cut away to show how it is attached to the connecting rod.

These valves are located at the top of the cylinder in openings, or valve ports (see Fig. 3-1). One port permits the air-fuel mixture to enter the cylinder. The other port permits the burned gases, after combustion, to exhaust, or escape, from the cylinder.

The valves move up and down in these two ports during the various stages of engine operation. The valves close off one or the other of the ports, or both ports, during the piston movements in the cylinder.

Each valve is an accurately machined plug on the end of a long stem (Fig. 3-7). The head of the valve has a beveled face, shaped like a section of a cone, and this beveled face fits against a matching face called the *valve seat*, in the top, or head end, of the cylinder (Fig. 3-8). When the valve is closed, the matching faces fit tightly against each other so that the valve port is sealed closed. No air-fuel mixture or combustion pressures can pass through the port.

The valves must be opened, that is, pushed down off their seats, periodically to permit the entrance of air-fuel mixture or the exit of burned gases. This valve motion is produced by the valve train, which consists, in a typical engine, of a small sprocket on the crankshaft, a drive chain, a large sprocket, a camshaft, valve lifters, push rods, rocker arms, and springs (Fig. 3-9). The camshaft is rotated by the chain and sprocket arrangement from the crankshaft. (Alternatively, a pair of gears is used to drive the camshaft, as shown in Fig. 3-1.) There is a separate cam on the camshaft for each valve (Fig. 3-10). Each cam has a single lobe, or high spot. As the cam rotates, the lobe moves up under the valve lifter and forces the lifter to move upward. This upward motion is carried by the push rod to the rocker arm, causing the rocker arm to rock on its ball pivot (Fig. 3-11). As the push-rod end of the rocker arm is pushed up, the valve end is pushed down. This downward push on the valve stem forces the valve to move downward. Normally,

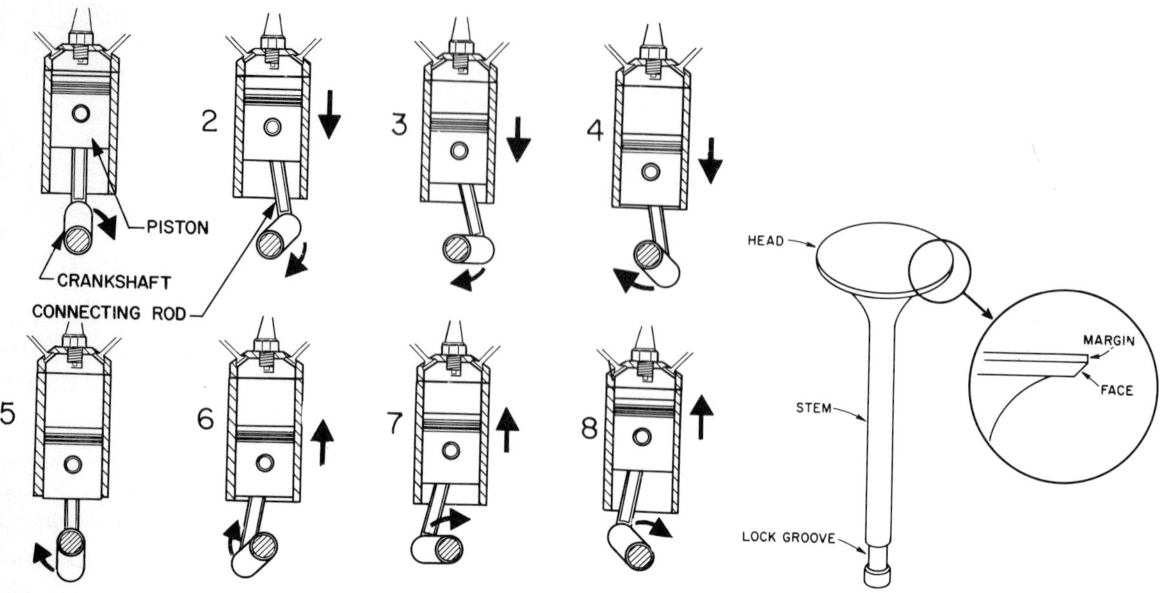

Fig. 3-6. Sequence of actions as the crankshaft completes one revolution and the piston moves from top to bottom to top again.

Fig. 3-7. Typical engine valve.

the valve is held closed by the pressure of a coil spring (Fig. 3-12), but the movement of the rocker arm causes the valve to move to the opened position, further compressing the spring. As soon as the cam lobe passes from under the valve lifter, the spring pressure forces the valve to move up into its closed position; this motion moves the rocker arm back and forces the push rod and valve lifter down.

Note: The above is a description of an I-head engine. The L-head engine has a different arrangement (see §39).

§28. Actions in engine cylinder Now that we have sketched the basic components entering into the actions in the engine cylinder, let us put everything together and see how the piston, rod, crankshaft, and valve train cooperate.

The actions that take place in the cylinder of a four-stroke-cycle engine can be divided into four stages, or strokes. The word "stroke" refers to piston movement; a stroke occurs when the piston moves from one limiting position to the other. The upper limit of piston movement (position 1 in Fig. 3-6) is called TDC (top dead center). The lower limit of piston movement (position 5 in Fig. 3-6) is called BDC (bottom dead center). A stroke is piston movement from TDC to BDC or from BDC to TDC. The piston changes its direction of motion each time it completes a stroke.

The four piston strokes that make up the complete cycle of actions in the four-stroke-cycle engine are intake, compression, power, and exhaust.

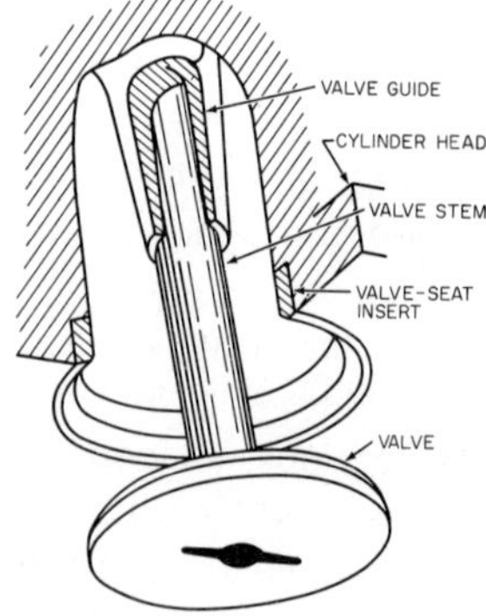

Fig. 3-8. Valve and valve seat in a cylinder head. The cylinder head, valve-seat insert, and valve guide have been partly cut away so that the valve stem can be seen.

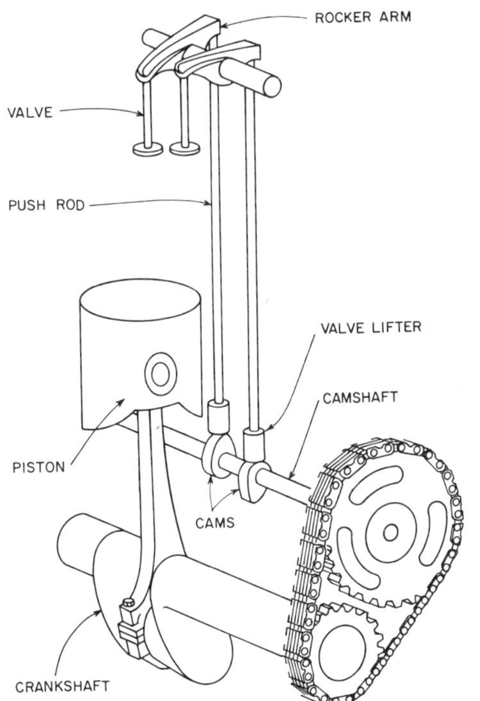

Fig. 3-9. Valve-operating mechanism for an I-head, or overhead-valve, engine. Only the essential moving parts for one cylinder are shown.

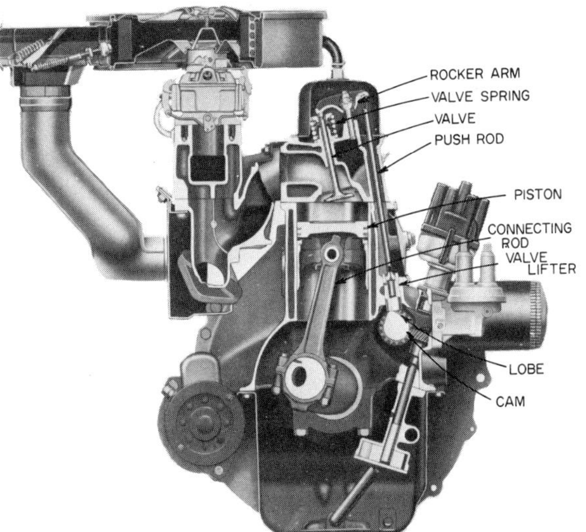

Fig. 3-10. Valve mechanism used in an I-head, or overhead-valve, engine. The valve lifter is raised each time the lobe on the cam passes under it.

This cycle requires two crankshaft revolutions. (In two-stroke-cycle engines, the entire cycle of events is completed in two strokes, or one crankshaft revolution.)

The four-stroke cycle described here is known as the *Otto cycle*, after N. A. Otto (1832 to 1891), who built a successful engine using the four-stroke-cycle principle in 1862.

Note: In the following discussion, the valves are considered to open and close at TDC and BDC for the sake of simplicity. However, as we will learn in a later chapter, the valves actually do not open and close at these points.

1. *Intake (Fig. 3-13).* On the intake stroke, the intake valve is opened. The piston moves down, and a mixture of air and fuel flows through the intake-valve port into the cylinder. The air-fuel mixture is delivered to the cylinder by the carburetor.

2. *Compression (Fig. 3-14).* At the end of the intake stroke, as the piston reaches BDC, the intake valve closes. The exhaust valve is also closed so that the upper end of the cylinder is sealed. Now, as the piston moves up on the compression stroke, the air-fuel mixture is compressed. By the time the piston has reached TDC, the mixture has been compressed to one-eighth or less of its original volume.

3. *Power (Fig. 3-15).* As the piston reaches TDC on the compression stroke, the ignition system delivers a high-voltage surge to the spark plug in the top of the cylinder. This causes an electric spark to take place that ignites the compressed air-fuel mixture. The mixture now begins to burn very rapidly, and the pressure in the cylinder rises to a peak that may exceed 600 psi (pounds per square inch). Thus, on a piston that is 3 inches in diameter (head area of about 7 square inches), there will be a total pressure, or push, of more than 2 tons. This pressure forces the piston to move downward; the downward thrust of the pressure is carried through the connecting rod to the crank on the crankshaft. The crankshaft is therefore forced to rotate.

4. *Exhaust (Fig. 3-16).* As the piston reaches BDC on the power stroke, the exhaust valve opens.

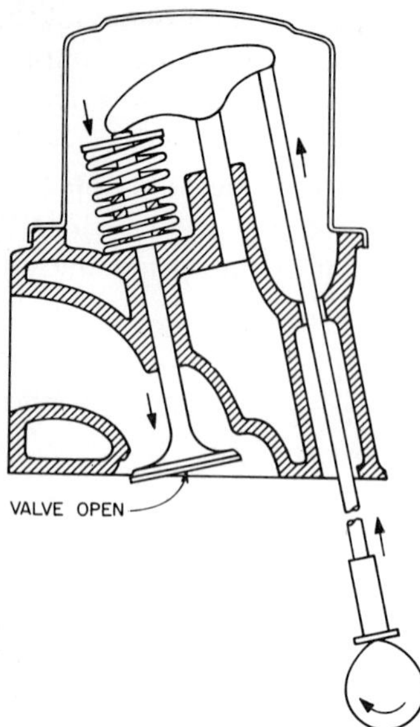

Fig. 3-11. When the cam lobe passes under the valve lifter, the lifter moves upward, raising the push rod, causing the rocker arm to rock and the valve to move down to the opened position.

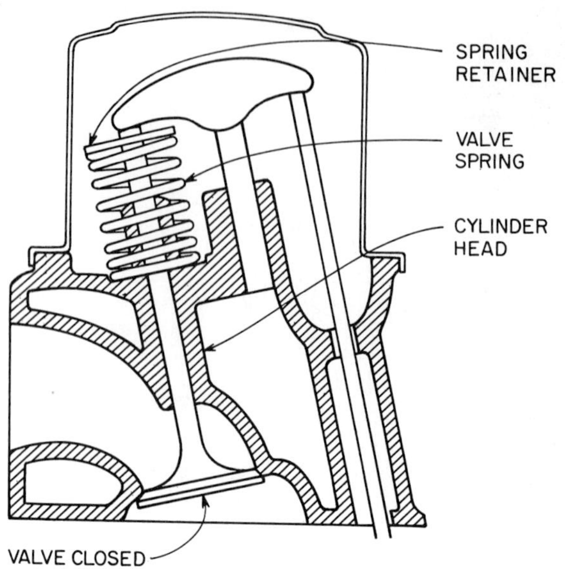

Fig. 3-12. Valve spring which, positioned between cylinder head and spring retainer on the end of the valve stem, normally keeps the valve closed when cam lobe is not under valve lifter.

Now, as the piston moves back up on the exhaust stroke, it pushes the burned gases out through the exhaust port. Then, as soon as the piston reaches TDC on the exhaust stroke, the exhaust valve closes, the intake valve opens, and the entire sequence of events (the four piston strokes) is repeated. The four strokes are continuously repeated as long as the engine is running.

§29. Multiple-cylinder engines A single-cylinder, four-stroke-cycle engine provides only one power stroke for every two crankshaft revolutions and is delivering power only one-fourth of the time. To provide for a more continuous flow of power, most automotive engines use four, six, or eight cylinders. The power strokes are so arranged that they follow one another, or overlap, in a continuous pattern. This permits a more even flow of power from the engine. This is illustrated in Fig. 3-17.

§30. Flywheel In a multicylinder engine, even though the power strokes follow one another, or overlap, continuously, there is still some unevenness in power flow from the engine. The reason for this is that the pistons on the power strokes do not supply an even pressure to the cranks on the crankshafts. At the start of the power stroke, the combustion pressures are high, and the thrust on the crank through the connecting rod is strong. But as the piston moves down, the combustion pressures are reduced, and the thrust on the crank is also reduced. Combustion pressures, in a typical situation, may fall from over 600 psi at the start of the power stroke to less than 200 psi at the midway point in the power stroke.

To compensate for this variance, the engine crankshaft has a flywheel (Fig. 3-18). The flywheel is a steel wheel which is attached to the end of the crankshaft and which rotates with it. The inertia of the flywheel as it rotates tends to combat the tendency of the engine to slow down or speed up in synchronization with the variations of pressure during the individual power strokes. For example, on a single-cylinder, four-stroke-cycle engine, the engine is delivering power only one-fourth of the time—during the power stroke. This power impulse is not uniform because, as we have seen,

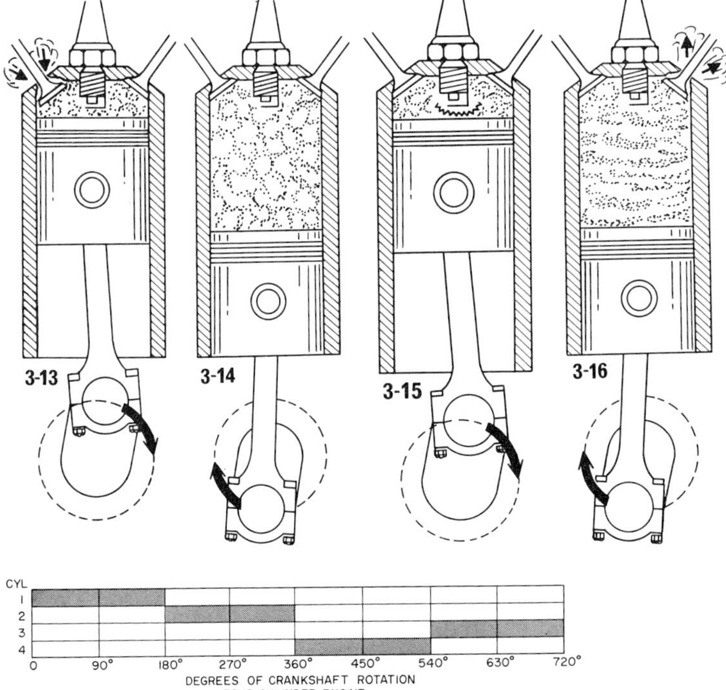

Fig. 3-13. Intake stroke. The intake valve (at left) has opened, and the piston is moving downward, drawing air and gasoline vapor into the cylinder.

Fig. 3-14. Compression stroke. The intake valve has closed, and the piston is moving upward, compressing the mixture.

Fig. 3-15. Power stroke. The ignition system produces a spark that ignites the mixture. As it burns, high pressure is created, pushing the piston downward.

Fig. 3-16. Exhaust stroke. The exhaust valve (right) has opened, and the piston is moving upward, forcing the burned gases from the cylinder.

CYL
1
2
3
4
0 90° 180° 270° 360° 450° 540° 630° 720°
DEGREES OF CRANKSHAFT ROTATION
FOUR CYLINDER ENGINE

1
2
3
4
5
6
120° 240° 360° 480° 600° 720°
DEGREES OF CRANKSHAFT ROTATION
SIX CYLINDER ENGINE

1
2
3
4
5
6
7
8
90° 180° 270° 360° 450° 540° 630° 720°
DEGREES OF CRANKSHAFT ROTATION
EIGHT CYLINDER ENGINE

Fig. 3-17. Power impulses (shown in dark gray) in four-, six-, and eight-cylinder engines. Note the power overlap in the six- and eight-cylinder engines.

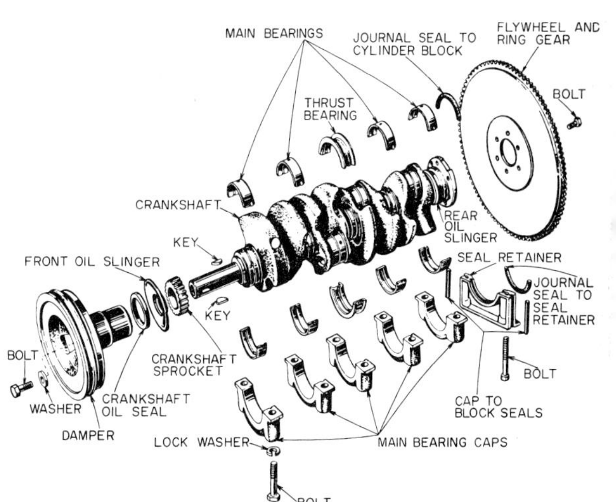

Fig. 3-18. Crankshaft and related parts used in an eight-cylinder V-type engine. (*Lincoln-Mercury Division of Ford Motor Company*)

the pressure is much higher at the beginning than at the end of the power stroke. During the other three piston strokes, the engine is absorbing power to move the piston up on the compression stroke. Thus, during the power stroke, the engine tends to speed up, while during the other three strokes, the engine tends to slow down. However, the inertia of the flywheel minimizes this tendency. In effect, the flywheel absorbs power during the power stroke and feeds power back out to the engine during the other three strokes.

This analogy also holds true for multicylinder engines. In these, the flywheel keeps the engine turning over more smoothly, with less of a pulsating motion than it would have without a flywheel.

Internal-combustion-engine Types

CHAPTER **4**

The internal-combustion piston engine has been made in many configurations with from 1 to 16 cylinders. Multiple-cylinder engines have had the cylinders arranged in a single row, in two or four rows, and radially, with a variety of valve arrangements. In addition, numerous rotary and nonpiston internal-combustion-engine designs have been tried, but most of these have not been commercially successful. This chapter describes various piston, as well as nonpiston, internal-combustion engines. The engine designer should have at least a nodding acquaintance with engine designs that have failed as well as those that have succeeded. One never knows when some new design might come along that will succeed. A good example is the Wankel or rotating-combustion engine (§46). Few automotive engineers gave it much chance for success when it was first introduced, but it is now in use in several automobiles.

§31. Cylinder arrangements The cylinders in multicylinder engines can be arranged in a variety of ways. Figure 4-1 shows four arrangements: in-line, V-type, flat, and radial. In-line engines can have two, three, four, six, or eight cylinders. For reasons explained in §37, the eight-cylinder in-line engine is no longer being produced. Instead, eight-cylinder engines have the V-8 arrangement. V-type engines are available as V-4, V-6, V-8, and V-12. Flat engines, with the cylinders opposed in two rows, are available as two-, four-, and six-cylinder engines. The following sections describe these various engines.

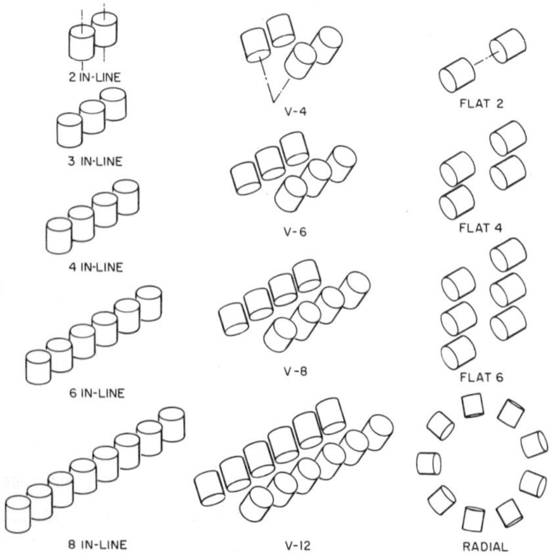

2 IN-LINE
3 IN-LINE
4 IN-LINE
6 IN-LINE
8 IN-LINE
V-4
V-6
V-8
V-12
FLAT 2
FLAT 4
FLAT 6
RADIAL

Fig. 4-1. Several cylinder arrangments.

Fig. 4-2. Cutaway view of a two-cylinder engine with cylinders opposing each other. (*DAF of Holland*)

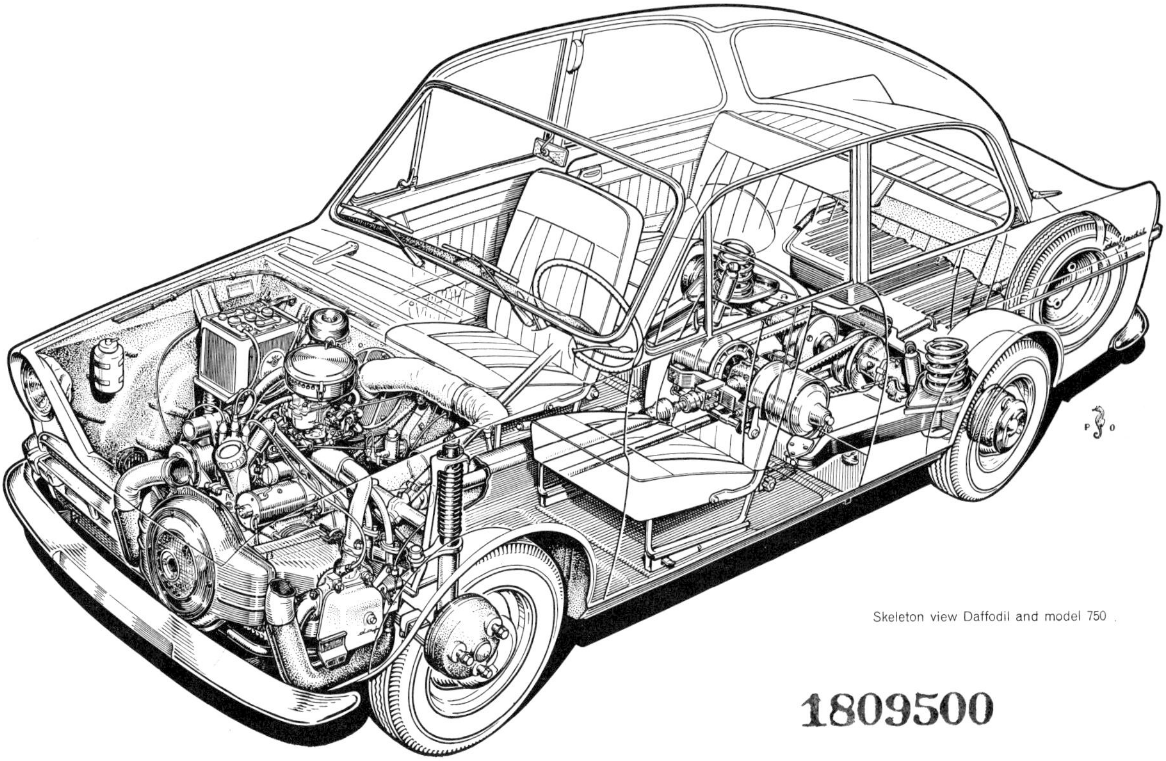

Skeleton view Daffodil and model 750 .

1809500

Fig. 4-3. Cutaway view of a Daffodil car which uses the two-opposed-cylinder engine shown in *Fig. 4-2.* (*DAF of Holland*)

§32. Two-cylinder engines Two two-cylinder engines have been produced: a flat opposed-cylinder engine and an in-line engine. A cutaway view of a flat two-cylinder engine used in the DAF of Holland car is shown in Fig. 4-2. This engine is air-cooled (see Chap. 18), and the two cylinders oppose each other. The crankshaft and camshaft are located between the two cylinders. The valves are in the cylinder heads (I-head arrangement, as explained in §39). Figure 4-3 shows the engine mounted in the automobile. Note that the engine actually hangs out in front of, or ahead of, the front axles.

§33. Three-cylinder engines Three-cylinder engines are in-line engines. Figures 4-5 and 4-6 are cutaway and sectional views of two similar three-cylinder, in-line engines. These are two-stroke-cycle engines (not four-stroke-cycle); the two-stroke-cycle principle is explained in §41. Briefly,

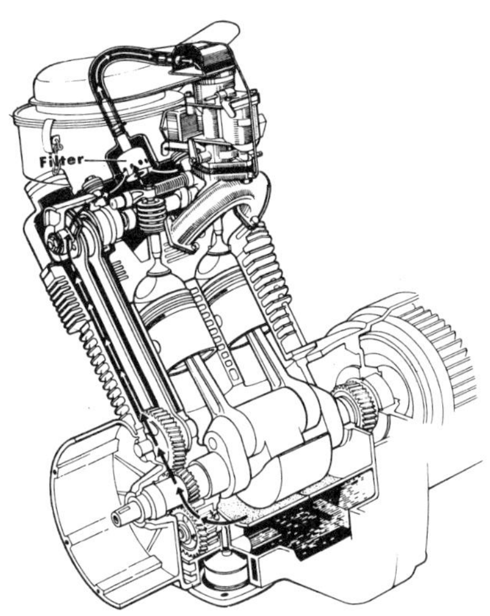

Fig. 4-4. Cutaway view of the two-cylinder, in-line, air-cooled NSU Prinz engine. The arrows show the action of the crankcase ventilating system. (*NSU of Germany*)

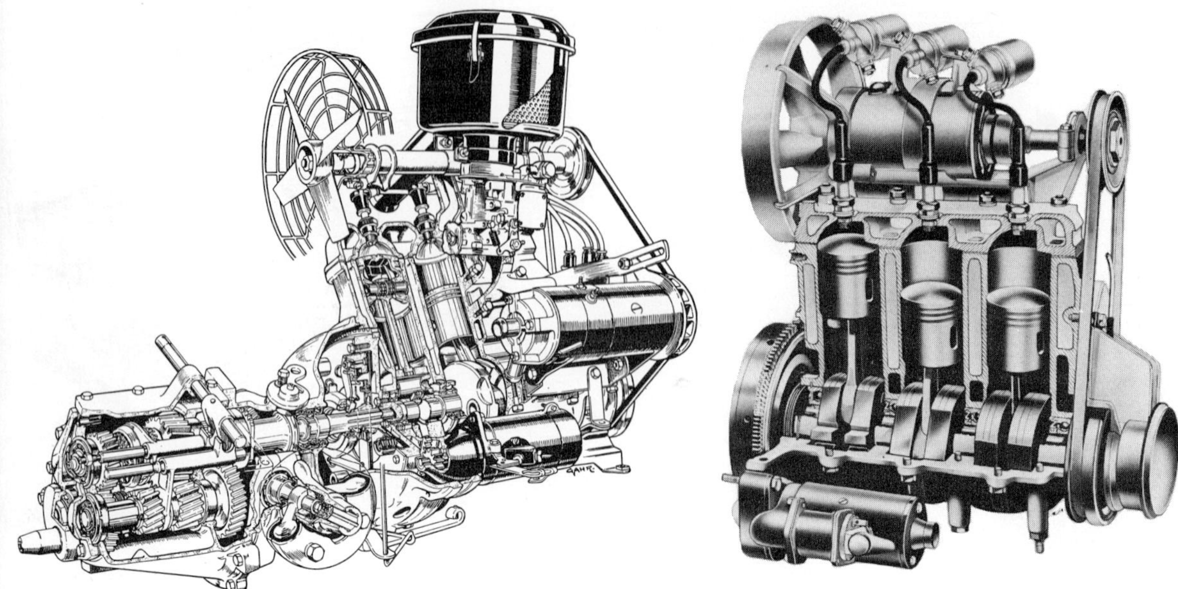

Fig. 4-5. Cutaway view of a three-cylinder, two-stroke-cycle, in-line engine. (*SAAB of Sweden*)

Fig. 4-6. Sectional view of a three-cylinder, two-stroke-cycle, in-line engine. (*Daimler-Benz*)

the crankcase in these engines serves as an intake and precompression chamber. Each cylinder must have its own sealed-off section of the crankcase. Thus, the main bearings that support the crankshaft are of the sealed type, so that the crankcase, in effect, is divided into three separate compartments, one for each cylinder.

Figure 4-5 also shows the details of the transmission. This engine is used on a front-drive automobile, and the differential is located between the engine and the transmission. A similar arrangement is shown in Fig. 4-7. The engine is mounted between the front wheels, with each wheel being driven by a half shaft. The disk brakes are located on the inboard ends of the half shafts.

The engines shown in Figs. 4-5 to 4-7 are lubricated by oil mixed with the gasoline. In those shown in Figs. 4-6 and 4-7, oil is kept in a tank separate from the gasoline tank. An injector pump meters the oil and injects it into the ingoing gasoline, according to engine load and speed.

§34. Four-cylinder engines The cylinders of a four-cylinder engine can be arranged in any of three ways: in-line, V, or opposed. In the V-type engine, the cylinders are in two banks, or rows, of two cylinders each; the two rows are set at an angle to each other. In the opposed-type engine, the

Fig. 4-7. Mounting arrangement of a three-cylinder, two-stroke-cycle, in-line engine. Note that the automobile is front drive and that inboard disk brakes are used. (*Mercedes-Benz*)

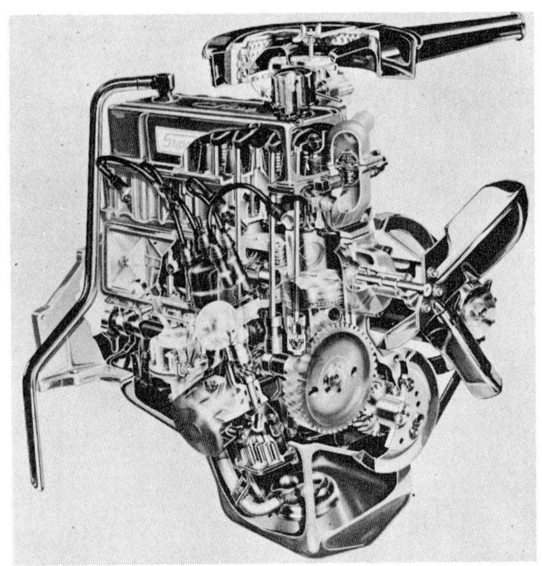

Fig. 4-8. Partial cutaway view of a four-cylinder, in-line, overhead-valve engine. (*Chevrolet Motor Division of General Motors Corporation*)

Fig. 4-9. Sectional view (from the end) of a four-cylinder, in-line, overhead-valve engine. The cylinders are slanted to one side to permit a lower hood line. (*Pontiac Motor Division of General Motors Corporation*)

cylinders are in two banks, or rows, of two cylinders each, set opposite each other. This makes a flat engine, so it is sometimes referred to as a "pancake engine."

1. In-line engines. Figure 4-8 is a cutaway view of a four-cylinder, in-line engine. The cylinders are arranged in one row, or line. A very similar engine is shown in Fig. 4-9. In this engine, the cylinders are slanted to one side to permit a lower hood line.

The engine shown in Fig. 4-10 is a four-cylinder, in-line unit, with an integrated clutch and transmission. The transmission, in effect, is folded under the engine. The engine is mounted at the rear of the automobile in a transverse position, with two half shafts connecting to the two rear wheels.

Another rear-mounted engine, with transmission and differential, is shown in Fig. 4-11. The engine cylinders are slanted to one side to provide space above the engine for a luggage compartment. The engine block is die-cast from aluminum with cast-in iron cylinder liners. (Chapter 16 discusses aluminum blocks and iron cylinder liners in detail.) Another interesting feature of this engine

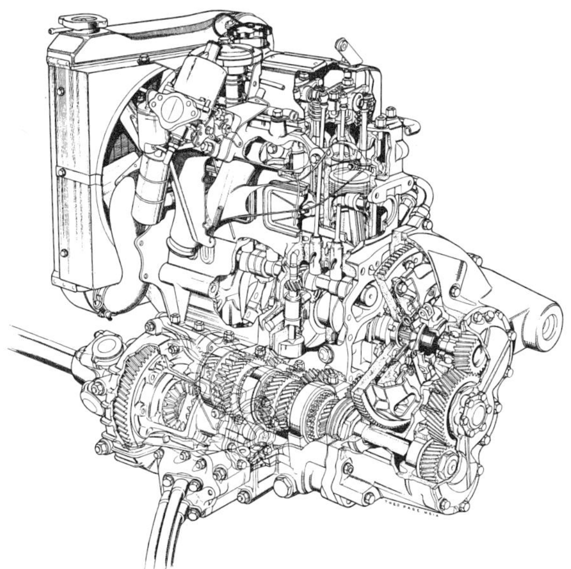

Fig. 4-10. Cutaway view of a four-cylinder, in-line engine with integrated clutch and transmission. (*English Austin*)

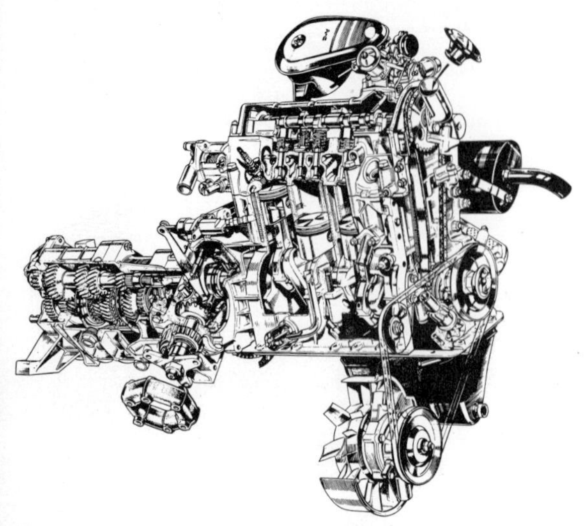

Fig. 4-11. Four-cylinder, in-line engine with overhead camshaft (OHC). The engine, with transmission and differential, mounts at the rear of the vehicle. (*Hillman Imp*)

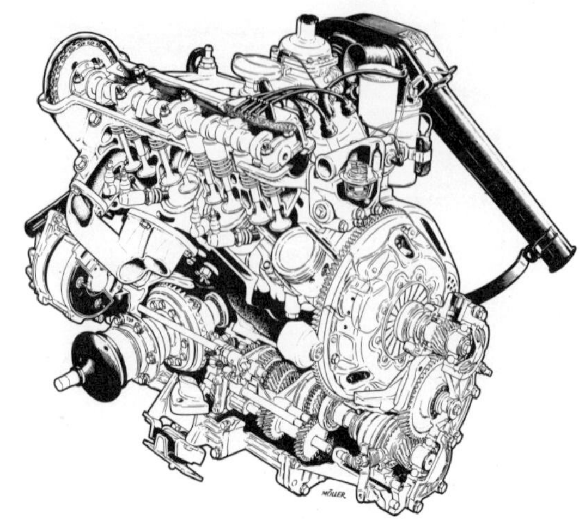

Fig. 4-12. Slant four-cylinder OHC engine with integrated clutch and transmission (*SAAB of Sweden*)

is that it has an overhead camshaft. Many of the engines previously described have the camshaft in the lower part of the engine, with the valves operated by lifters, push rods, and rocker arms (§27). However, when the camshaft is located in the cylinder head, as shown in Fig. 4-11, there is no need for push rods, or, in some engines, rocker arms, or lifters. This has certain advantages, as explained in §40.

Another slant-four engine, with overhead camshaft and integrated clutch, transmission, and differential, is shown in Fig. 4-12. The camshaft is driven by a chain and sprockets from the crankshaft.

2. V-4 engines.[1] The V-4 engine has two rows of two cylinders each, set at an angle, or a V, to each other. The crankshaft has only two cranks, with connecting rods from opposing cylinders in the two banks attached to the same crankpin. Each crankpin has two connecting rods attached to it. Relatively few companies have produced this engine because there is an inherent lack of balance in the engine that tends to make it rock in its mounting. This is difficult to correct with counterweights on the crankshaft. The engines described and illustrated herein achieved balance by use of a balance shaft that turns in the opposite direction to the crankshaft. Figure 4-13 is a phantom view of this engine, emphasizing the internal mov-

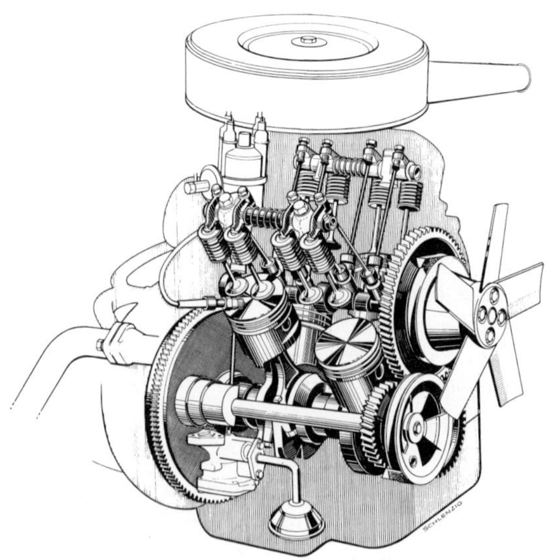

Fig. 4-13. Phantom view of V-4 engine, showing major moving parts. (*Ford Motor Company of Germany*)

ing parts of the engine. The engine was brought out for use in the German Taunus 12-M automobile. Later, Ford of Britain used a larger version in their Corsair. Original developmental work was done on this engine by Ford Motor Company of the United States for a proposed compact car that was to be called the "Cardinal." The Cardinal was never brought into production, but German and British firms utilized the engine design.

The details of the balance shaft and its driving arrangement are shown in Fig. 4-14. Specifications of the two versions of the V-4 mentioned above are interesting. Both are 60-degree engines; that is, the two banks of cylinders are set at a 60-degree angle from each other. The Taunus 12-M engine had a displacement* of 72.2 cubic inches and produced 50 hp (horsepower*) at 5,000 rpm (revolutions per minute). Ford of Britain brought out two larger versions. One had a displacement of 101.5 cubic inches (3.69-inch bore* and 2.37-inch stroke*) and developed 81.5 hp at 4,750 rpm. The larger Ford of Britain version had a displacement of 121.8 cubic inches (3.69-inch bore and 2.85-inch stroke) and developed 93 hp at 4,750 rpm.

Figure 4-15 shows the front end of the Taunus 12-M car, with the engine arranged for front drive.

* All of these terms are defined in Chap. 6.

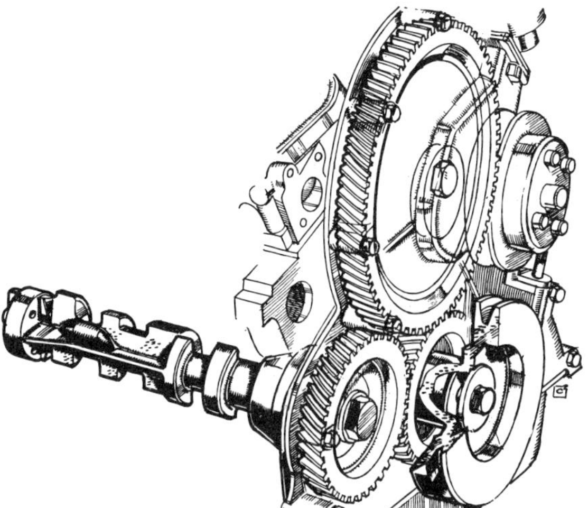

Fig. 4-14. Balance shaft used in V-4 engine to counteract rocking tendency in engine. (*Ford of Britain*)

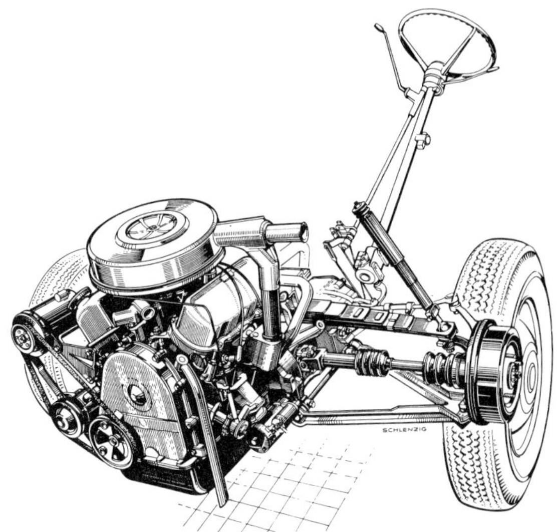

Fig. 4-15. V-4 engine and power-train arrangement for front-drive car. (*Ford Motor Company of Germany*)

Fig. 4-16. Flat four-cylinder engine, with two banks of two cylinders opposing one another. (*Volkswagen*)

The engine, transmission, differential, and clutch are compactly located between the front wheels, with the front wheels connected to the differential by half shafts.

3. Flat four-cylinder engines. Figure 4-16 shows the flat four-cylinder engine used by Volkswagen. The two banks, or rows, of cylinders oppose each other, and the engine is air-cooled. Figure 4-17 shows the manner in which the engine is mounted at the rear of the car. It requires very little headroom because the cylinders are opposed, which makes for a very compact engine compartment.

Fig. 4-17. Mounting arrangement of the flat four-cylinder engine at the rear of the automobile. (*Volkswagen*)

Fig. 4-18. Five-cylinder radial engine for light aircraft. (Designed by McCulloch Corporation)

§35. Five-cylinder engines There are not many five-cylinder engines in existence. It is hard to conceive of a five-in-line or a V-5 engine. However, arranging the five cylinders like the spokes of a wheel gives us a radial engine. This engine is inherently well-balanced and lightweight. Radial engines have been used for many years on aircraft, in various versions up to nine cylinders. Moreover, one manufacturer put two nines together, one back of the other, to produce the most powerful radial engine ever made. One version of this aircraft engine was rated at about 1,600 hp.

The radial engine shown in Fig. 4-18 is new. Five pistons and connecting rods work to a single crank on the crankshaft. The fuel system is the injection type, and the engine uses the two-stroke-cycle principle (described in detail in §41).

Fig. 4-19. Six-cylinder, in-line engine with overhead valves, partly cut away to show internal construction. (*Ford Division of Ford Motor Company*)

§36. Six-cylinder engines Most six-cylinder engines are in-line engines, although there are V-6 and flat-six engines. This compares with four-cylinder engines (§34), which also can be either in-line, V-type, or flat.

1. *In-line engines.* Figure 4-19 shows a six-cylinder, in-line engine, partly cut away so the internal

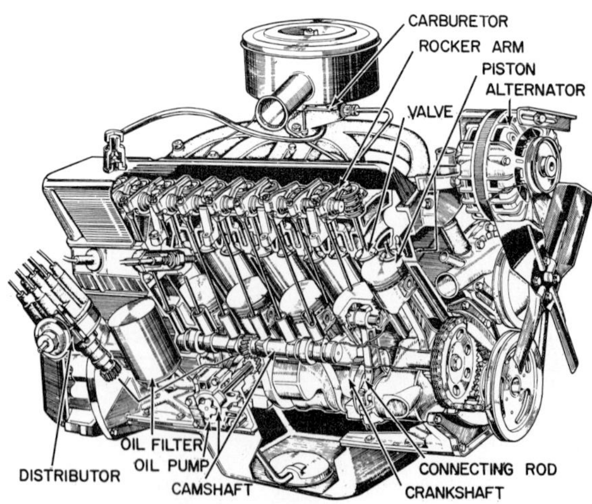

Fig. 4-20. Slant-six, in-line, overhead-valve engine, cut away to show internal parts. Cylinders are slanted to permit a lower hood line. (*Dodge Division of Chrysler Motors Corporation*)

construction can be seen. The valves are overhead; this is an I-head engine (see §39). Figure 4-20 shows a slant-six engine. This engine is similar to other in-line engines, except that the cylinders are slanted to one side (similar to the four-cylinder engine shown in Fig. 4-9) so that the hood line may be lowered.

2. V-6 engines.[1] Several varieties of the V-6 engine have been built. In this engine, two three-cylinder banks are set at an angle, or V, to each other. The crankshaft has only three cranks, with connecting rods from opposing cylinders in the two banks attached to the same crankpin. Each crankpin has two connecting rods attached to it. Figure 4-21 shows one version of this engine. One model of this version has a displacement of 121.9 cubic inches and is rated at 106 or 113 hp at 5,300 rpm, according to compression ratio (defined in Chap. 6). Another model, with a displacement of 139.8 cubic inches, has a rating of 126 hp at 5,800 rpm.

Buick Motor Division and Truck and Coach Division, both of General Motors Corporation, have brought out their own versions of V-6 engines; generally speaking, these have a somewhat higher power output. Figure 16-6 shows a V-6 engine block with one bank partly cut away so the internal construction of the block can be seen.

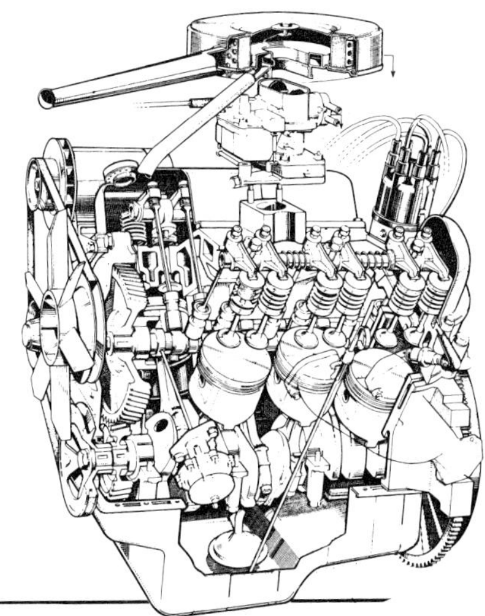

Fig. 4-21. Cutaway view of a V-6, overhead-valve engine. (*Ford Motor Company of Germany*)

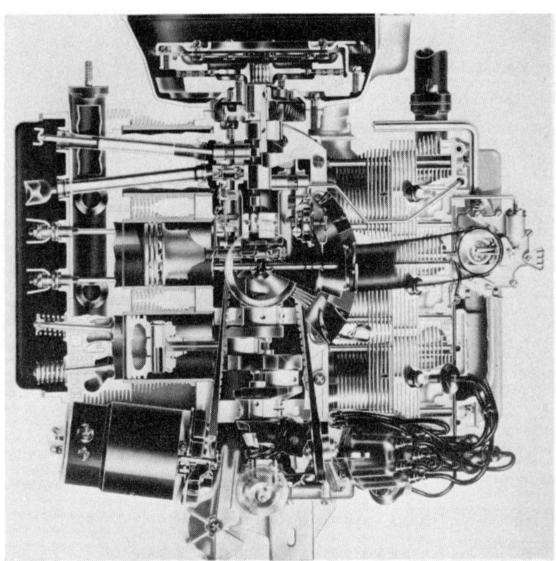

Fig. 4-22. Sectional view from top of a six-cylinder, overhead-valve, air-cooled engine. This type of engine is sometimes referred to as a *pancake engine.* (*Chevrolet Motor Division of General Motors Corporation*)

3. Flat-six engines. Figure 4-22 shows the flat-six (sometimes called a "pancake-six") engine which was used in the Chevrolet Corvair. This engine is air-cooled (Chap. 18).

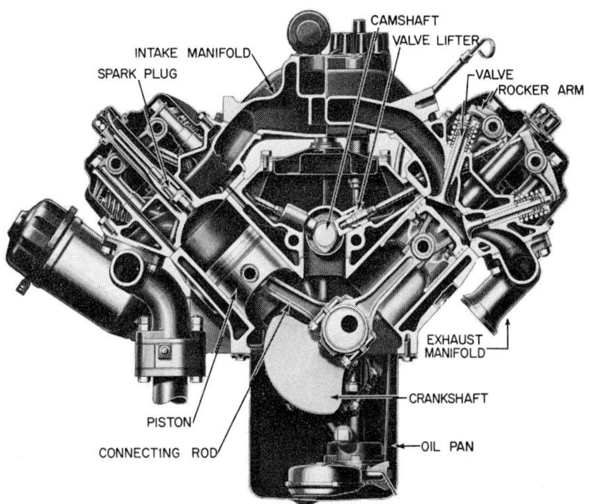

Fig. 4-23. Sectional view from the end of a V-8 engine with overhead valves. (*Dodge Division of Chrysler Motors Corporation*)

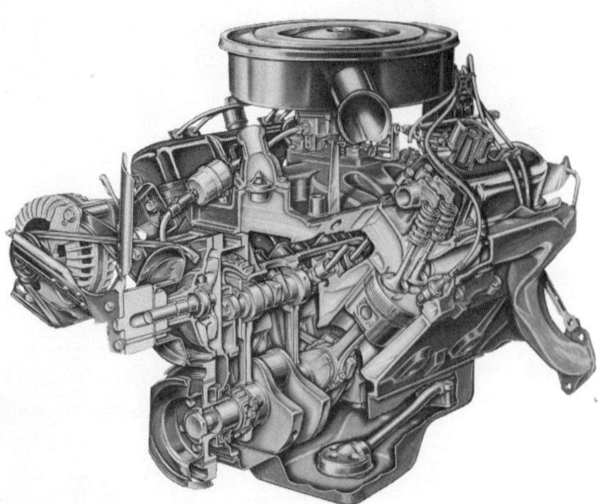

Fig. 4-24a. Cutaway view of a V-8, 273-cubic-inch displacement engine. (*Chrysler Motors Corporation*)

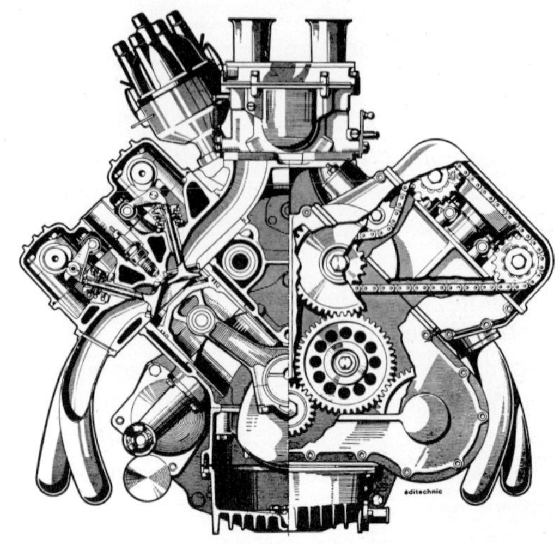

Fig. 4-25a. Sectional view from the end of a V-8 engine with four overhead camshafts. Right bank has been cut away to show camshaft drive arrangement. Left bank has been cut away to show internal construction and locations of valves and other components. (*Renault*)

§37. Eight-cylinder engines At one time, most eight-cylinder engines were the in-line type, with all eight cylinders lined up in a single row. There are disadvantages to this arrangement, however, and this type of engine is no longer manufactured for automotive use. Instead, the V-8 engine has been widely adopted. There are several reasons for this. First, the V-8 is a more compact assembly that takes less room under the hood. More importantly, from the engineering standpoint, the V-type engine is much more rigid structurally, and the cylinder block can be made much lighter and still have adequate strength. Also, the arrangement of the cylinders permits a more even distribution of air-fuel mixture from the carburetor to the cylinders. This is in contrast with the in-line engine,

Fig. 4-24b. Cutaway view of a 460 cubic inch, 365-hp, V-8 engine for Continental Mark III. (*Lincoln-Mercury Division of Ford Motor Company*)

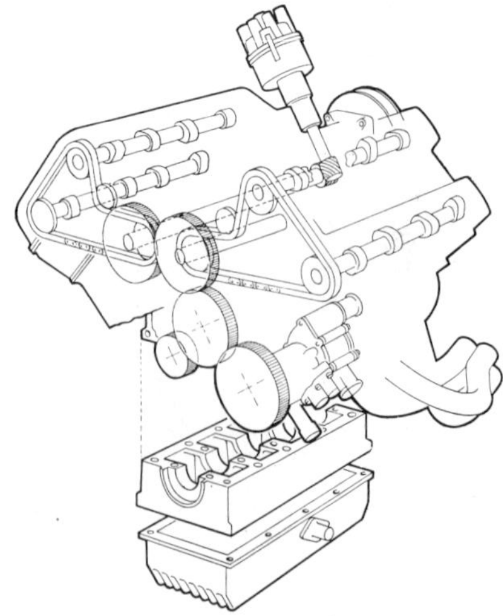

Fig. 4-25b. Phantom view of a V-8 engine with four overhead camshafts, showing layout of timing gears and chains to drive the camshaft. (*Renault*)

Fig. 4-26. V-8 racing engine, partly cut away to show internal construction. (*Ford of Britain*)

where cylinders 1 and 8 were so distant from the carburetor, comparatively, that they were apt to be "starved" and thus did not contribute their fair share to the engine operation.

In the V-8 engines [Figs. 4-23 and 4-24*a* and *b*], the cylinders are arranged in two banks of four cylinders each, set at an angle, or a V, to each other. In effect, this engine is like two four-cylinder engines, set at an angle to each other, and working to a common crankshaft. In V-8 engines, the crankshaft has only four cranks, with connecting rods from opposing cylinders in the two banks being attached to the same crankpin.

The V-8 engines shown in Figs. 4-23 and 4-24*a* and *b* have overhead valves operated by valve lifters, push rods, and rocker arms from a single camshaft located between the two cylinder banks. Some high-performance V-8 engines have overhead camshafts, with the camshafts located in the cylinder heads. One version of this engine has a single overhead camshaft in each cylinder head. Another version has two overhead camshafts in each cylinder head—one for the intake valves, the other for the exhaust valves. Engines of this latter type are shown in Figs. 4-25 and 4-26. As previously mentioned, the overhead-camshaft engine requires no push rods or, in some designs, rocker arms. The overhead-camshaft engine has other advantages (§40). The engine shown in Fig. 4-25*a* and *b* is a high-performance engine designed for rear mounting in the Alpine Le Mans sports car. It has a displacement of 182 cubic inches with a 3.42-inch bore and 2.48-inch stroke. It will develop up to 325 hp at 8,000 rpm.

A still more powerful V-8 engine, developed for racing, is shown in Fig. 4-26. This engine is credited with 410 hp at 9,000 rpm, with a displacement of 182.6 cubic inches. The bore is 3.375 inches, the stroke is 2.55 inches, and the compression ratio is 11:1. It weighs less than 370 pounds, or only about 0.9 pound per hp, achieving this favorable ratio by using aluminum for all major castings. The engine has four overhead camshafts, four valves per cylinder, and fuel injection. The fuel is injected into the eight inlet ports.

Many other V-8 racing engines have been built, some using overhead camshafts and other using push rods. The Ford Mark II 427 engine[2] (427 cubic inches displacement), which performed so well at Le Mans and elsewhere, has a bore of 4.2346 inches, a stroke of 3.784 inches, and a rating of 485 hp at 6,200 to 6,400 rpm. This engine was unusual in that it used as many Ford-engine production parts as possible. On the other hand, most racing engines are "special" more or less all the way through, with most of the major components especially designed for the job.

§38. Twelve- and sixteen-cylinder engines Twelve- and sixteen-cylinder engines have been used in passenger cars, buses, trucks, ships, and industrial installations. Few automobiles today, however, are fitted with anything more than eight-cylinder engines. An exception is the Italian Ferrari, among others, which has a V-12 engine.

For certain heavy-duty installations, twelve- and sixteen-cylinder engines are used. In these, the cylinders are usually arranged in either two banks (V-12 or V-16), three banks (W type), or four banks (X type).

§39. Valve arrangements The intake and exhaust valves can be arranged in various positions in the cylinder head, or block. There are four basic

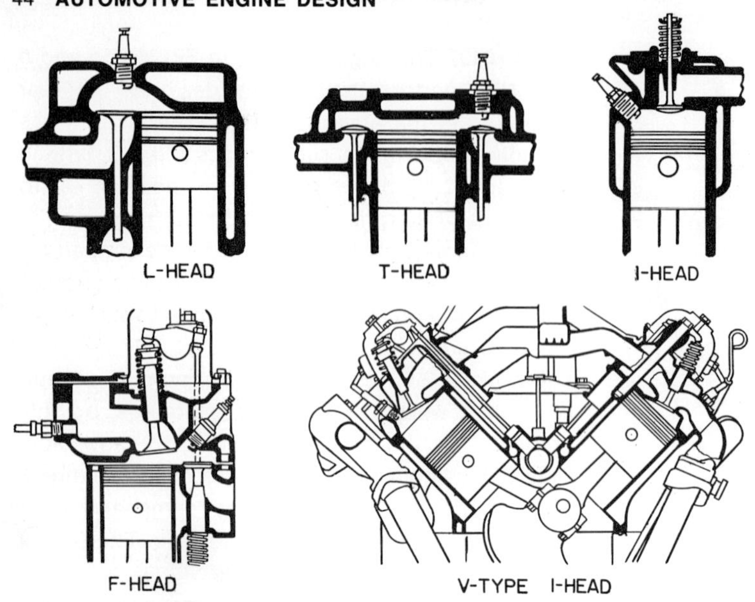

Fig. 4-27. Valve arrangements. (Compare these line drawings with the sectional views of various engines shown elsewhere in the book.)

arrangements: "L," "I," "F," and "T." Remember the word "LIFT," and it will be easy to recall the four valve arrangements. Of all arrangements, the I-head design is by far the most common.

1. L-head engine. In the L-head-engine arrangement (Figs. 4-27 and 4-28), the valves are located in the cylinder block. The combustion chamber and cylinder form an inverted L. The intake and exhaust valves are located side by side in the cylinder block, with all valves for an in-line engine arranged in one line (Fig. 4-29). In a V-8 engine, the valves would be arranged in two lines, one line in each bank of cylinders. The valve train in an L-head engine is relatively simple, with only a valve lifter interposed between a cam on the camshaft and a valve. Service operations are relatively simple, also. Removal of the cylinder head and valve covers from the block exposes the valves (see Fig. 4-29). On the other hand, the L-head-engine configuration does not lend itself to the higher compressions required by modern high-performance engines. The I-head, or overhead-valve, engine can be designed to attain very high compressions. (A detailed discussion of this matter will be found in §192.)

2. I-head engine. In the I-head, or overhead-valve, engine, the valves are carried in the cylinder head (Figs. 3-9 and 4-27). The valves may have various placements because there are many designs of combustion chambers and valve arrangements. In some in-line engines, the valves are placed in a single row (Fig. 4-20). Another arrangement is to place the valves in two rows, one row being the intake valves and a second row the ex-

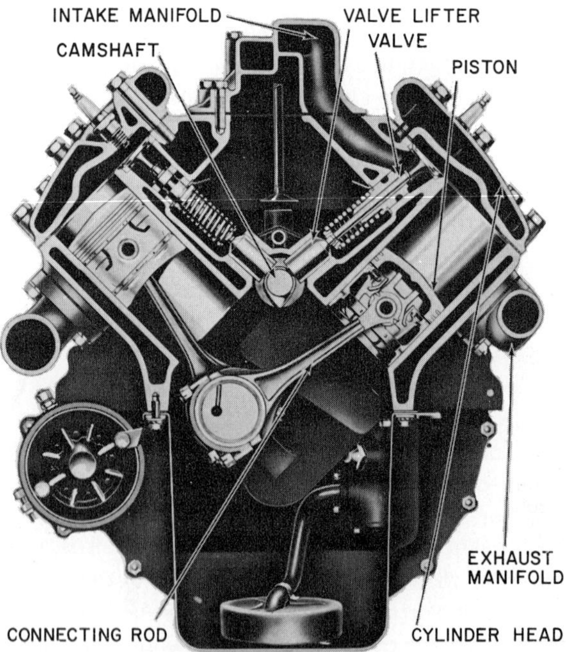

Fig. 4-28. Sectional view from the end of a V-8 engine with L heads. (*Ford Motor Company*)

haust valves (Fig. 4-23). Most I-head engines, both the in-line and the V-type, use a single camshaft, with the push rods and rocker arms arranged as required to accommodate the single- or two-row valve placements. (Numerous illustrations of I-head engines are given throughout the book.)

3. *F-head engine.* The F-head engine combines the L-head and I-head arrangements (Figs. 4-27 and 4-30). The intake valves are in the head, convenient to the carburetor. The exhaust valves are in the block. Both sets of valves are operated from the same camshaft.

4. *T-head engine.* With this arrangement, the intake valves are in the block on one side of the cylinder, and the exhaust valves are in the block on the other side of the cylinder (Fig. 4-27). However, this arrangement is no longer used.

§40. Overhead-camshaft engines The I-head-engine design, in its most common version, uses push rods and rocker arms to operate the valves (Figs. 3-9, 4-19, and so on) and is often called a *push-rod engine.* These elements impose inertia that must be overcome as the valves open and close. At high speeds, the inertia is felt more than at low speeds. As a consequence, the valve action lags more at high speed. This tends to limit maximum engine speed. However, with the overhead-camshaft engine, the cams work directly on the rocker arms or valve lifters. This results in greater valve fidelity at high engine speed. Higher engine speeds and outputs are thus possible.* The V-8 engine with four overhead camshafts, shown in Fig. 4-26, will peak out at 9,000 rpm, producing 410 hp at this speed. The single-overhead-camshaft engine (one overhead camshaft in each cylinder head) is known as an *SOHC* engine. The double overhead-camshaft engine is a *DOHC* engine.

Fig. 4-29. Six-cylinder, L-head, in-line engine with head and the intake and exhaust valves of two cylinders removed.

Fig. 4-30. Cutaway view of an F-head engine. (*Rolls-Royce Limited*)

The push-rod I-head engine is satisfactory for passenger cars, trucks, and other vehicles, under the demands of normal operation. However, where the engine designer is required to take more power from an engine of a given size, one way to do it is to increase engine speed with the help of one or more overhead camshafts. The overhead camshaft also makes the engine more agile. That is, with a more direct connection from camshaft to valves and with fewer moving parts (and thus less inertia), the engine responds more quickly to the opening of the throttle. This is very important for a racing engine, for example. Very fast acceleration when coming out of turns onto straightaways is essential for a winning racing car. One model of the Ford V-8 engine that has been so successful at the Indianapolis 500 and elsewhere has four camshafts —two in each cylinder head.

*A more technically advanced discussion of the advantages of the overhead camshaft will be found in §221.

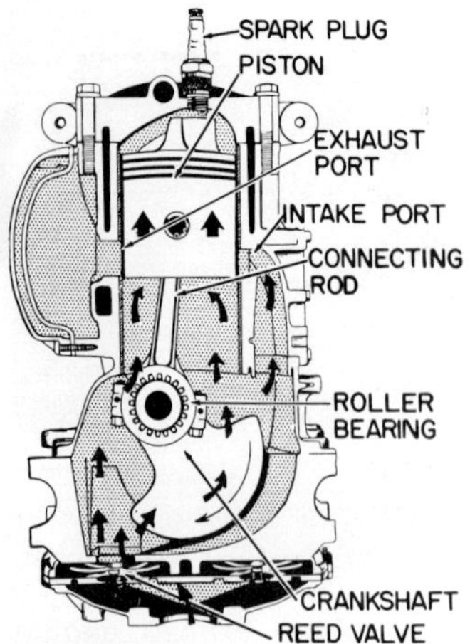

Fig. 4-31. Sectional view of a two-cycle engine with the piston nearing TDC. Ignition of the compressed air-fuel mixture occurs approximately at this point. (*Johnson Motors*)

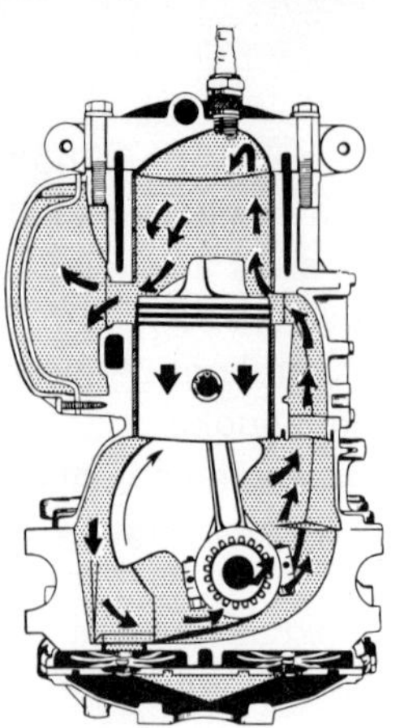

Fig. 4-32. As the piston approaches BDC, it uncovers the intake and exhaust ports. Burned gases stream out through the exhaust port, and a fresh charge of air-fuel mixture enters the cylinder, as shown by the arrows. (*Johnson Motors*)

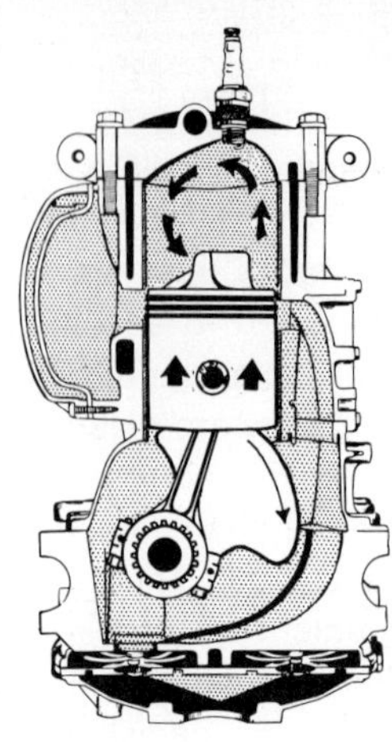

Fig. 4-33. After the piston passes BDC and moves up again, it covers the intake and exhaust ports. Further upward movement of the piston traps and compresses the air-fuel mixture. (*Johnson Motors*)

§41. Two-stroke-cycle engines In the four-stroke-cycle engine (previously discussed), the complete cycle of events requires four piston strokes (intake, compression, power, and exhaust) and two crankshaft revolutions. In the two-stroke-cycle engine, the intake and compression strokes and the power and exhaust strokes are, in a sense, combined. Thus, the complete cycle of events requires only two piston strokes and one crankshaft revolution.

In the two-stroke-cycle engine, the piston acts as a valve, clearing valve ports in the cylinder wall as it nears BDC (bottom dead center). A fresh air-fuel charge enters through the intake port, and the burned gases exit through the exhaust port. The complete cycle of operation is as follows: As the piston nears TDC (top dead center), ignition takes place (Fig. 4-31). The high combustion pressures drive the piston down, and the thrust through the connecting rod turns the crankshaft. As the piston nears BDC, it passes the intake and exhaust ports in the cylinder wall (Fig. 4-32). Burned gases, still under some pressure, begin to stream out through the exhaust port. At the same time, the intake port, now cleared by the piston, begins to deliver air-fuel mixture, under pressure, to the cylinder. The top of the piston is shaped to give the incoming mixture an upward movement. This helps to sweep the burned gases ahead and out through the exhaust port. After the piston has passed through BDC and starts up again, it passes both ports, thus sealing them off (Fig. 4-33). Now the fresh air-fuel charge above the piston is compressed and ignited. The same series of events takes place again and continues as long as the engine runs.

It was mentioned that the air-fuel mixture is delivered to the cylinder under pressure. In many engines, this pressure is put on the mixture in the crankcase. The crankcase is sealed, except for a leaf, or reed, valve at the bottom. The reed valve is a flexible, flat metal plate that rests snugly against the floor of the crankcase. There are holes under the reed valve that connect to the engine carburetor. When the piston is moving up, a partial vacuum is produced in the sealed crankcase. Atmospheric pressure lifts the reed valve off the holes, and air-fuel mixture enters the crankcase (Fig. 4-31). After the piston passes TDC and starts down again, pressure begins to build up in the crankcase. This pressure closes the reed valve so that further downward movement of the piston compresses the trapped air-fuel mixture in the crankcase. The pressure which is built up on the air-fuel mixture then causes it to flow up through the intake port into the engine cylinder when the piston moves down enough to clear the intake port (Fig. 4-33).

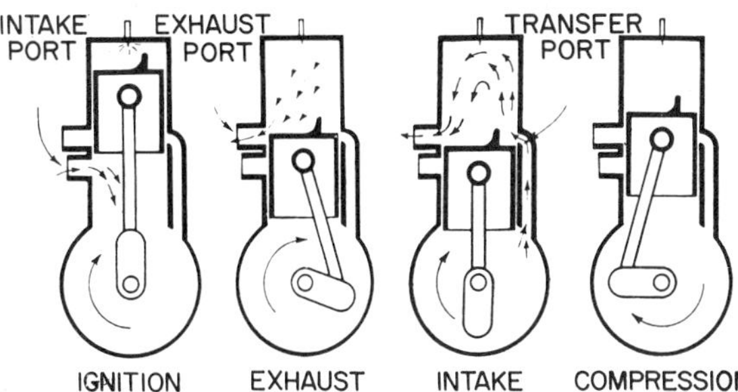

Fig. 4-34. Intake and exhaust port action in a three-port, two-cycle engine.

Fig. 4-35. Transfer-port action in a three-port, two-cycle engine.

Instead of using a reed valve in the crankcase, some engines have a third, or transfer, port in the cylinder (Figs. 4-34 and 4-35). In this type of engine, the intake port is cleared by the piston as it approaches TDC. When this happens, the air-fuel mixture pours into the crankcase, filling the partial vacuum left by the upward movement of the piston. Then, as the piston moves down, the intake port is cut off by the piston. The air-fuel mixture in the crankcase is compressed, and the other actions then take place as already described.

An engine with transfer ports is shown in Fig. 4-6. This is a three-cylinder, two-cycle engine of a somewhat different construction. The crankshaft is supported on four sealed ball bearings, and roller bearings are used at both ends of the connecting rod (at the crankpin and the piston pin). The crankpins are 120 degrees apart. The crankcase is separated into three compartments, one for each cylinder, so as to utilize the crankcase pressure as the piston moves down to transfer the air-fuel mixture from the crankcase to the cylinder.

The five-cylinder radial engine shown in Fig. 4-18 operates on the two-stroke-cycle principle. However, it uses a different system for supplying air and fuel to the cylinders. A turbo-supercharger, driven by the pressure of the exhaust gas, supplies air at relatively high pressure to a chamber that surrounds the cylinders. When a piston moves down into the cylinder far enough to clear the intake port, air from this chamber passes into the cylinder. At the same time, the exhaust port is cleared by the piston so the exhaust gases are driven out as the clean air from the turbo-supercharger enters the cylinder.

Fuel is supplied by an injection system. At the right instant on the compression stroke of the piston, as it nears TDC, the injection pump delivers a metered quantity of gasoline to the cylinder. This sprays into the cylinder and mixes with the compressed air to form a combustible mixture. Then the spark occurs at the spark plug, the mixture is ignited, and the piston is forced downward. As it again clears the intake and exhaust ports, fresh air enters, the burned gases exhaust, and the complete cycle is repeated.

Another type of two-stroke-cycle engine uses a valve in the cylinder head to exhaust the burned gases (Fig. 4-36). As the piston moves down past the intake ports (notice there is a ring of them around the cylinder), the exhaust valve opens. Now, the incoming air, under pressure from the blower, can efficiently clear the cylinder of exhaust gases. The engine shown in Fig. 4-36 is a diesel engine, and only air enters through the intake ports. (§42 discusses diesel engines.)

Note that the two-stroke-cycle engine produces a power stroke every crankshaft revolution. The four-stroke-cycle engine requires two crankshaft revolutions for each power stroke per cylinder. You might conclude from this that a two-stroke-cycle engine could produce twice as much horsepower as a four-stroke-cycle engine of the same size, running at the same speed. However, this is not true. In the two-stroke-cycle engine, when the intake and exhaust ports have been cleared by the piston, there is always some mixing of the fresh charge and the burned gases. Not all of the burned gases escape, and this prevents a fuller fresh charge from entering. Therefore, the power stroke that follows is not as powerful as it could be if all the burned gases were exhausted and a full charge of air-fuel mixture entered. In the four-stroke-cycle engine, nearly all the burned gases are forced from the combustion chamber by the upward-moving piston. Also, a comparatively full charge of air-fuel mixture can enter because a complete piston stroke is devoted to the intake of the mixture (con-

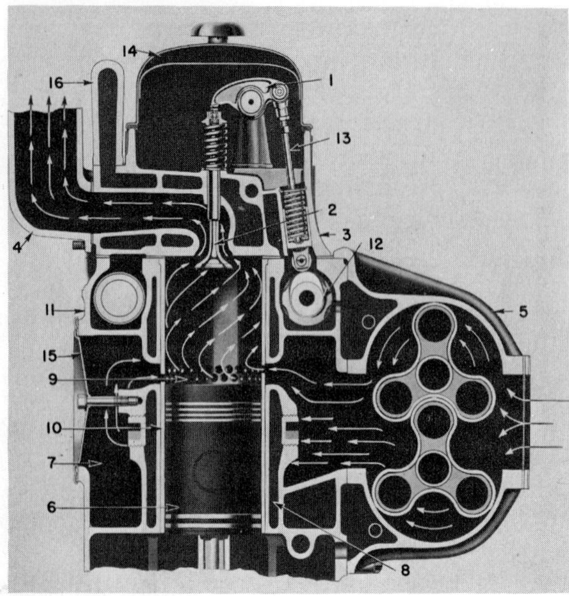

Fig. 4-36. Two-stroke-cycle diesel engine with exhaust valve in top of cylinder. Arrows show flow of air from the blower, through the cylinder, and out the exhaust manifold. (*Detroit Diesel Engine Division of General Motors Corporation*)

1. Exhaust-valve rocker
2. Exhaust valve
3. Cylinder head
4. Exhaust manifold
5. Blower
6. Piston
7. Air box
8. Cooling-water passage
9. Port admitting air to cylinder
10. Cylinder liner
11. Cylinder block
12. Camshaft
13. Push rod
14. Rocker cover
15. Hand-hole cover
16. Water manifold

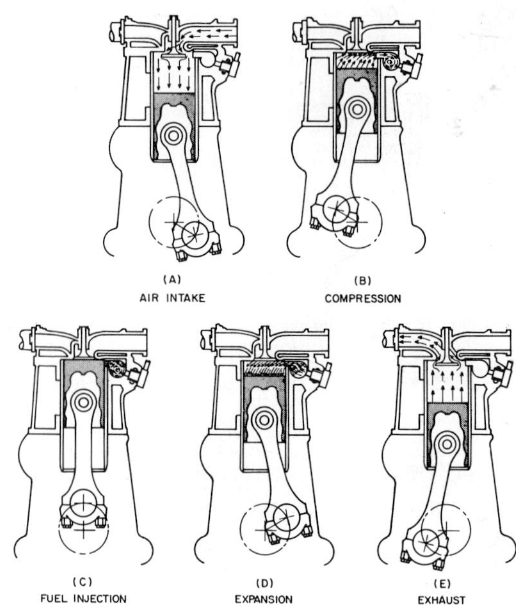

Fig. 4-37. Sequence of events in four-stroke-cycle diesel engine. Intake and exhaust valves are side by side or, as shown, the exhaust valve is behind the intake valve. The intake valve is shown in *A* to *D*, and the exhaust valve is shown in *E*. (*Hercules Motor Corporation*)

trasted with only part of a stroke in the two-stroke-cycle engine). Therefore, in the four-stroke-cycle engine the power stroke produces more power.

§42. Diesel engine The diesel engine operates on a somewhat different principle from the Otto-cycle engine. In the Otto-cycle engine, a combustible mixture of fuel vapor and air is drawn into the cylinder and compressed. In the diesel engine, however, the fuel is not mixed with the air entering the cylinder during the intake stroke. Instead, air alone is compressed during the compression stroke, and the fuel (a light oil) is injected or sprayed into the cylinder at the end of the compression stroke. In diesel engines the compression ratios (§64) used are as high as 21:1 and provide pressures of above 500 psi (pounds per square inch) at the end of the compression stroke. When air is rapidly compressed to this pressure, it is heated to a temperature of approximately 1000°F. This temperature is high enough to ignite spontaneously the fuel oil injected or sprayed into the cylinder at this instant. The combustion of the oil can be controlled by the speed with which the oil is introduced into the cylinder. Thus, in the diesel engine, the combustion is not a rapid burning of fuel that is already present in the cylinder, as in the gasoline engine; rather, it is a slower burning that produces an even increase of pressure. This allows a more complete utilization of the energy in the fuel.

The four-stroke-cycle diesel engine requires four piston strokes for each power stroke, as in the gasoline engine: intake, compression, power, and exhaust (Fig. 4-37). On the intake stroke the piston

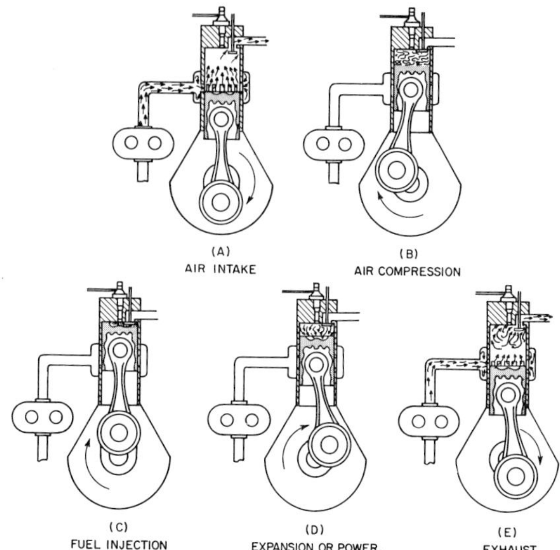

Fig. 4-38. Sequence of events in the two-stroke-cycle diesel engine. (*Detroit Diesel Engine Division of General Motors Corporation*)

moves downward and pulls air into the cylinder past the intake valve. The intake valve closes as the compression stroke starts, and the air is compressed. At the end of the compression stroke the fuel is sprayed or injected into the combustion chamber, where it burns and creates high pressures. The piston is pushed down during the power stroke, at the end of which the exhaust valve opens to allow the burned gases to escape during the exhaust stroke.

In the two-stroke-cycle diesel engine, a blower, or rotary-type pump, is used to create an initial pressure on the incoming air (Fig. 4-38). The piston serves as a valve or valves, clearing, on its downward stroke, the ports through which the air enters and exhaust gases escape. The type of diesel engine shown in Fig. 4-38 has an exhaust valve in the top of the cylinder, through which the burned gases are forced when the valve opens and the piston clears the intake ports (Fig. 4-36). As the piston moves upward, it passes the intake ports, and the exhaust valve closes. The air thus trapped in the cylinder is highly compressed, the fuel is sprayed into the cylinder, and the power stroke takes place.

The fuel oil used in diesel engines does not burn rapidly unless it is finely atomized and thoroughly mixed with the compressed air. To assure adequate mixing, particularly in the smaller engines, various shapes of combustion chambers are used. These special shapes produce turbulence, or whirling, of the compressed air, which improves the mixing of the fuel with the air during the combustion process.

Figure 4-39 illustrates the turbulence chamber used in Hercules diesel engines. Toward the end of the compression stroke, the air is forced into the turbulence chamber at a high velocity, so it is whirling rapidly. The fuel is injected into the turbulent air, and this produces a thorough mixing of the fuel and air, so that better combustion is attained.

§43. Diesel engine applications Diesel engines have been made in a great variety of sizes and outputs, ranging from a few to 5,000 hp (horsepower). They are used in passenger cars, trucks, buses, farm and construction machinery, ships, electric power plants (up to about 5,000 kilowatts), and other mobile and stationary applications.

Diesel engines are not used in the passenger cars manufactured in the United States, although they are common in trucks, buses, and other commercial equipment. However, in Europe, passenger

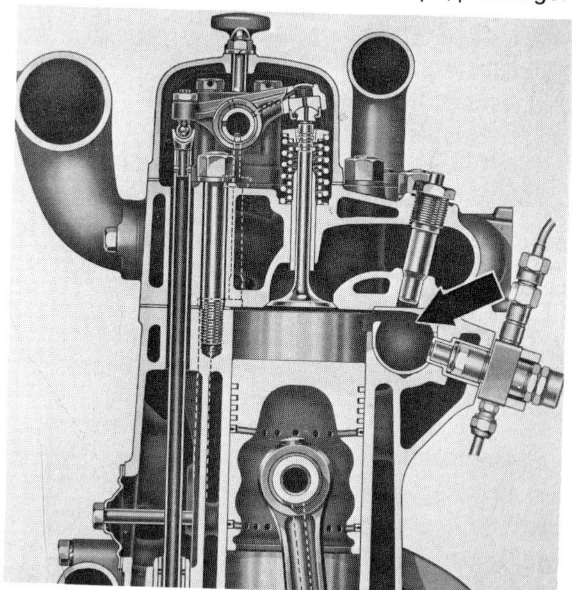

Fig. 4-39. Turbulence chamber (indicated by arrow) and fuel injector in the Hercules diesel engine. (*Hercules Motor Corporation*)

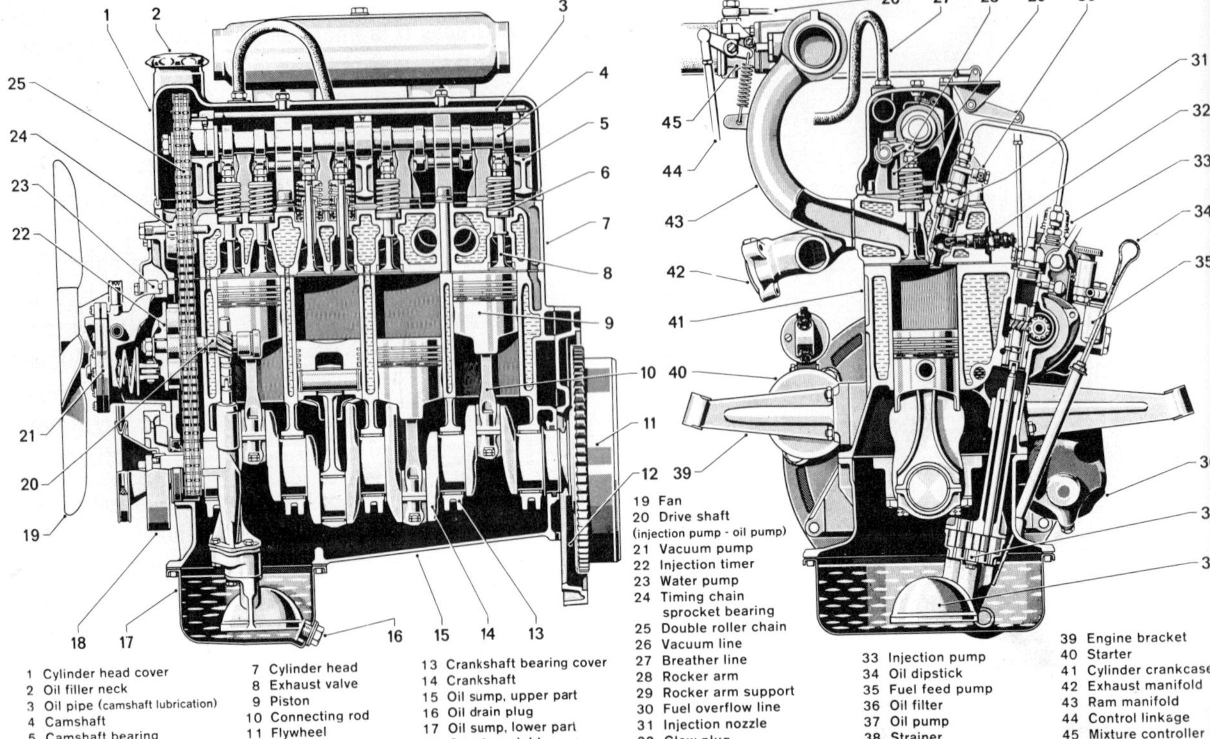

Fig. 4-40. Sectional views of a four-cylinder diesel engine for passenger cars. (*Mercedes-Benz*)

cars equipped with diesel engines are rather common. For example, Mercedes-Benz has produced about half a million diesel-powered automobiles since 1950. Figure 4-40 shows sectional views of a four-cylinder, in-line, diesel engine for passenger cars. This engine has a 121-cubic-inch displacement, with a 3.43-inch bore and a 3.29-inch stroke. The compression ratio is 21:1 (see §64). It peaks at 60 hp at 4,200 rpm, and the engine weighs around 400 pounds. This works out to 6.67 pounds per hp.

Contrast 6.67 pounds per hp with the Ford 427-cubic-inch GT engine that was so successful in the 1966 Le Mans races and at other races. This engine has a dry weight of 580 pounds and peaks at 485 hp at 6,400 rpm. The pound per hp here is only 1.19. Also, the V-8 engine shown in Fig. 4-26, with displacement of only 182.6 cubic inches and weight of 370 pounds, puts out 410 hp (at 9,000 rpm), so it checks out at only 0.9 pound per hp. Of course, it is unfair to compare the two engines in this way, but the comparison was made to point out an essential difference between the diesel and the Otto-cycle engines: The diesel engine, generally speaking, is heavier, slower, and less agile. On the other hand, the Otto-cycle engine of fifty years ago was also relatively heavy for its output and was slow and not very agile. However, very intensive engineering work on the Otto-cycle engine has brought it to its present state of performance. Some engineers might argue that a somewhat similar improvement might have been made on the diesel engine, had it been given the same amount of developmental work. Yet the fact remains that the diesel engine is inherently a slow-speed engine. As originally conceived by R. Diesel, the rpm was about 300, with the fuel injection controlled and prolonged to give a constant pressure during the combustion stroke. The high-speed diesel engine departs from this constant-pressure specification because the time for fuel injection is so short. This tends to produce very high momentary peak pressures which, in turn, require comparatively heavy construction.

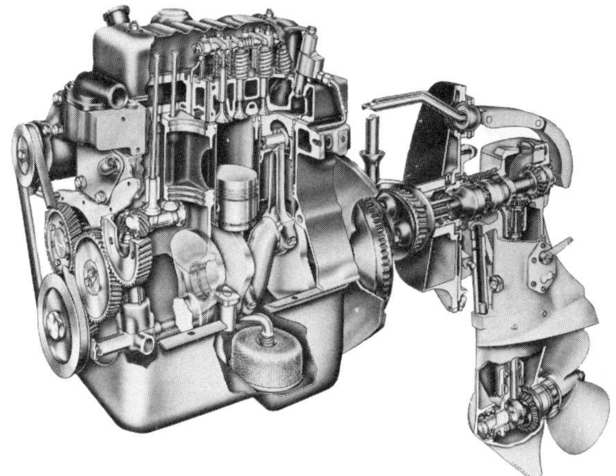

Fig. 4-41. Three-cylinder diesel engine for inboard-outboard motor boat. The propeller drive is to the right. (*Perkins Engines, Limited*)

The sequential actions in the diesel engine tend to limit top speed. The air must first be compressed sufficiently for it to reach combustive temperatures. Then, the fuel must be injected, ignited by the heated air, and burned. This all requires time, even if it is measured only in microseconds. In contrast, the Otto-cycle engine, compressing an already combustible air-fuel mixture, requires only the spark at the spark plug to start the combustion process. In fact, one problem in the Otto-cycle engine is to slow down the combustion process, that is, to prevent excessively rapid combustion of the compressed air-fuel mixture. (This problem is discussed in detail in later chapters.)

The diesel engine is favored by many bus and truck operators (and, in Europe, by many passenger-car owners) because it is sturdy, reliable, and economical to operate. Diesel fuel is considerably cheaper than gasoline (especially in Europe), and the efficiency of the diesel engine in utilizing the fuel is higher (especially at part throttle).

Figure 4-41 is a partially cutaway view of a three-cylinder, four-cycle diesel engine for marine use. The diesel engine is well suited to this type of application for a number of reasons. Rapid acceleration is not required, but, rather, steady, one-speed operation for hours at a time. Furthermore, diesel fuel does not evaporate and form an explosive mixture with air as does the gasoline used in Otto-cycle engines. This greatly reduces the risk of

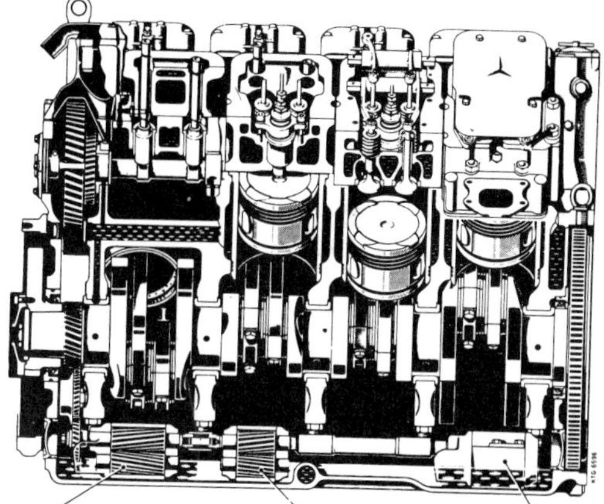

Fig. 4-42. Sectional view of a V-8 diesel engine. (*Daimler-Benz A. G.*)

explosion and fire, especially in boats or ships in which the engine is located in a closed engine compartment or room.

Figure 4-42 is a partial sectional view of a V-8 diesel engine for heavy-duty stationary or mobile applications.[3] The bore is 6.5 inches and the stroke is 6.9 inches, with a displacement of 1,806 cubic inches. The engine produces 800 hp in its turbocharged version at 2,200 rpm. Figure 4-43 illustrates the valve train of this engine, and Fig. 4-44 shows the reciprocating parts. Note that this engine uses four valves per cylinder: two intake valves and two exhaust valves. This improves engine breathing; that is, air can enter and exhaust gases can exit more freely. The piston uses five

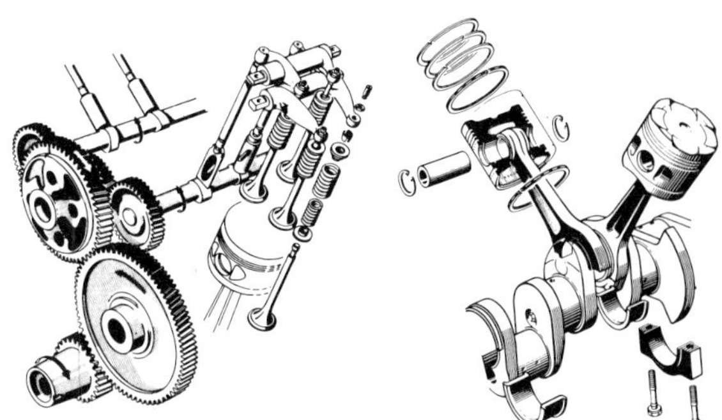

Fig. 4-43. Valve train of a V-8 diesel engine; four valves per cylinder. (*Daimler-Benz A. G.*)

Fig. 4-44. Pistons and other reciprocating parts of a V-8 diesel engine. (*Daimler-Benz A. G.*)

piston rings, as you will note. Two of these are oil-control rings, and three are compression rings. (Chapters 7 and 12 discuss piston rings in detail.)

Figure 4-45 is a partially cutaway view of a V-8 diesel engine that is similar in many ways to the one shown in Fig. 4-42. This engine also has four valves per cylinder. However, in this engine, the

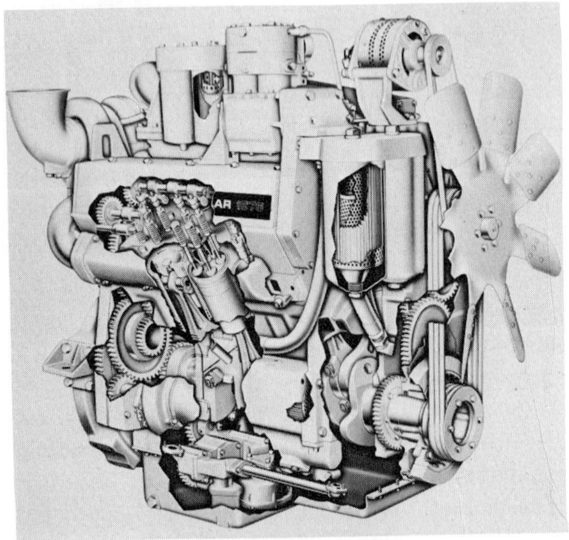

Fig. 4-45. Partial cutaway view of a V-8, four-cycle diesel engine. (*Caterpillar Tractor Company*)

valves are operated from overhead camshafts. This engine also has wet cylinder liners, which are replaceable sleeves that form the cylinder walls and are also in contact with the cooling water in the cooling system.

§44. Gas turbine The gas turbine, now under development as a possible automotive power plant, consists essentially of two sections: a gasifier section and a power section. Figure 4-46 is a simplified sectional view of a turbine, and Fig. 4-47 is a cutaway view of an actual unit. The compressor in the gasifier has a rotor with a series of blades around its outer edge. As it rotates, air between the blades is carried around and thrown out by centrifugal force. This action supplies the burner with air at relatively high pressure. Fuel is sprayed into the compressed air. The fuel used can be gasoline, kerosene, or oil. As the fuel burns, a further increase in pressure results. The high-pressure,

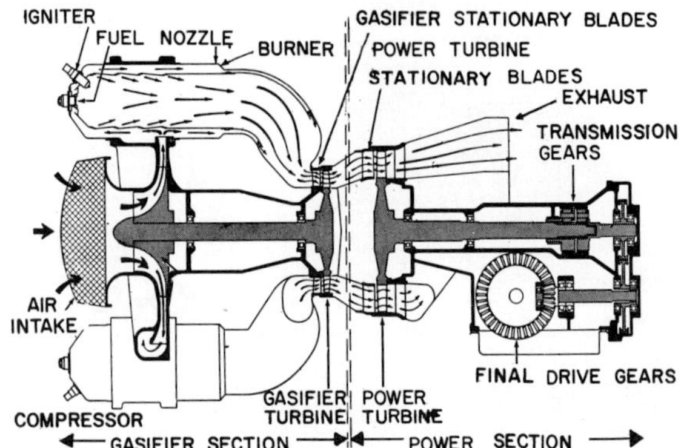

Fig. 4-46. Experimental gas turbine for automotive vehicles. The gasifier section burns fuel in a burner and delivers the resulting gas to the power section, where it spins the power turbine. The power turbine then turns the vehicle wheels through a series of gears. (*General Motors Corporation*)

high-temperature gas then passes through the gasifier nozzle diaphragm. A series of stationary blades directs this high-pressure gas against a series of curved blades on the outer edge of the gasifier turbine rotor. The resulting high pressure against the curved blades causes the gasifier turbine rotor to spin at high speed. Since the gasifier turbine rotor and the compressor rotor are mounted on the same shaft, the compressor rotor is also spun at high speed. This action continues to supply the burner with an ample amount of compressed air. The action continues as long as fuel is supplied to the burner.

After the high-pressure, high-temperature gas leaves the gasifier section, it enters the power turbine. Here it strikes another series of stationary curved blades and is directed against a series of curved blades on the outer edge of the power turbine rotor. The resulting high pressure against these rotor blades spins the rotor at high speed. In some models, the turbine may turn up to 50,000 rpm. This high rpm is reduced by a series of transmission gears before power is applied to the vehicle wheels.

§45. Free-piston engine This is not really a complete engine in the sense that it provides power. It is no more than a device to supply high-pressure gas to drive a power turbine. In this sense, it would simply substitute for the gasifier section of the turbine engine described above. The free-piston

Fig. 4-47. Cutaway view of a gas turbine. (*Caterpillar Tractor Co.*)

engine (Figs. 4-48 to 4-51) contains a pair of piston assemblies that oppose each other in a cylinder. Each piston assembly consists of a relatively small power piston attached to a relatively large bounce piston. The principle of operation is this: The piston assemblies are driven in (or bounced in) to compress air between the power pistons. As the pistons complete their inward travel, fuel is injected into the combustion space between the pistons. At this instant, the engine functions like a diesel engine (see §42); that is, the heat of compression ignites the fuel, and combustion takes place. The resulting high pressure drives the pistons apart. They clear the exhaust and intake ports, and fresh air enters the power cylinder. At the same time, the air back of the bounce pistons becomes compressed (in the bounce cylinders), and this pressure drives the piston assemblies toward each other again. The gas, as it exhausts from the power cylinder, still has sufficient pressure to drive a turbine (Fig. 4-46). This action continues as long as fuel is supplied to the engine.

The valves in the compression cylinders are spring-loaded to open against pressure. Thus, when the bounce pistons are moving inward, air is compressed ahead of them, and this forces the intake valves to open and admit this air to the air box. When the bounce pistons are moving outward, the pressure in the compression cylinders drops below atmospheric, and atmospheric pressure forces the intake valves open to admit air into the compression cylinders.

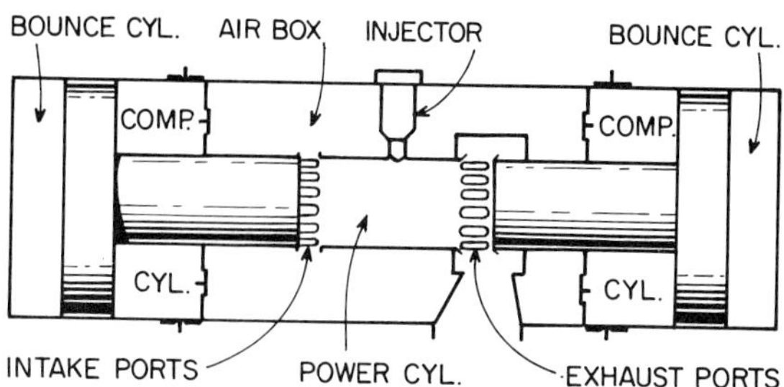

Fig. 4-48. Schematic drawing of a free-piston engine.

Fig. 4-49. Action as the compression cycle starts. The bounce pistons are moving inward, compressing air between the two power pistons.

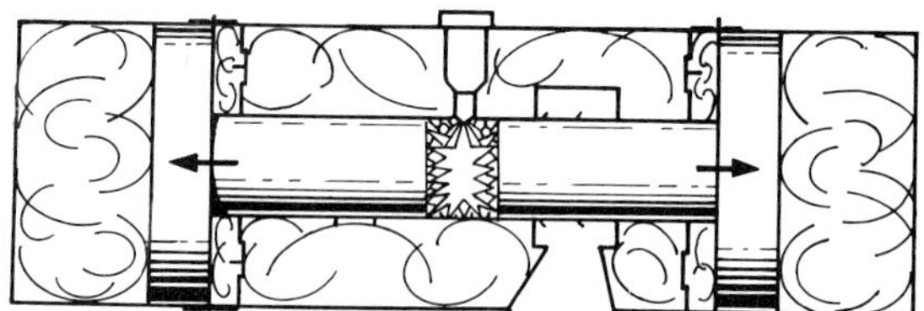

Fig. 4-50. Combustion starts when fuel is injected into the compressed and hot air between the power pistons.

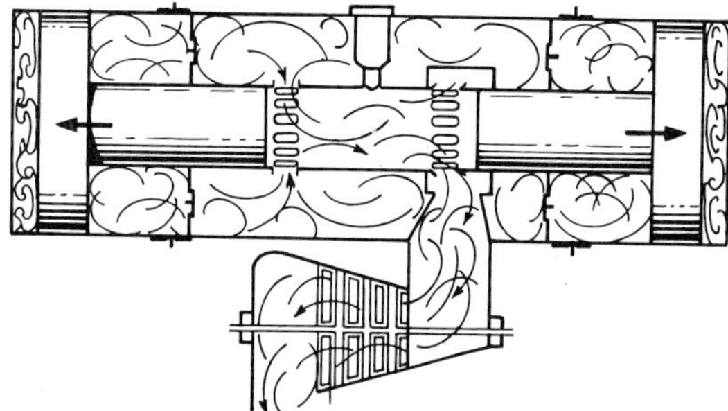

Fig. 4-51. The combustion pressures drive the power pistons outward. As the right-hand piston clears the exhaust ports, the high-pressure gases escape from the power cylinder and drive the turbine. As the left-hand piston clears the intake ports, air from the air box enters the power cylinder and scavenges it.

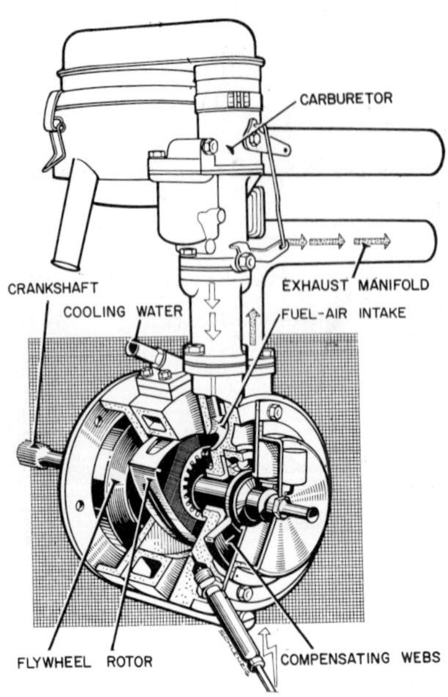

Fig. 4-52. Cutaway view of the Wankel engine.

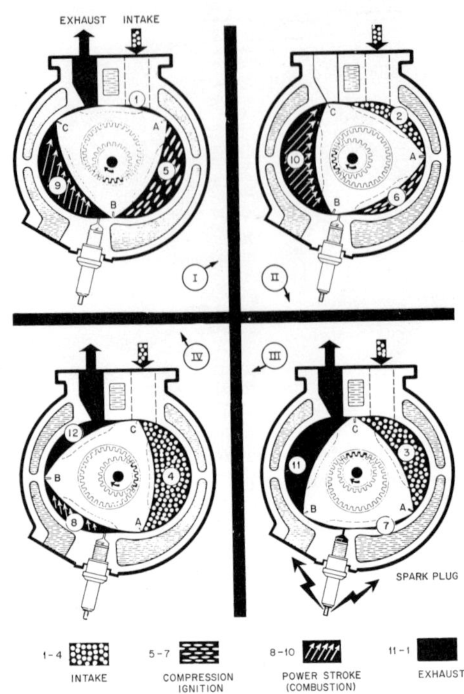

Fig. 4-53. Actions in the Wankel engine during one complete rotation of the rotor.

§46. Wankel engine This engine makes use of a three-lobe rotor that rotates eccentrically in an oval chamber (Fig. 4-52). The rotor is mounted on the crankshaft through external and internal gears. The four cycles—intake, compression, power, and exhaust—are going on simultaneously around the rotor when the engine is running. Figure 4-53 will give you an idea of how the engine works. The rotor lobes (A, B, and C) seal tightly against the side of the oval chamber. The rotor has oval depressions on its three faces between the lobes (shown by dashed lines in Fig. 4-53). Let us follow the rotor around as it goes through the four cycles. At I (upper left), lobe A has passed the intake port, and the air-fuel mixture (I) is ready to enter. At II (upper right), lobe A has moved on around so that the space between lobes A and C and the chamber wall (2) is increasing and the air-fuel mixture is entering. At III (lower right), the intake is continuing as the combustion space (3) continues to increase. It has reached its maximum at IV(4).

To see what happens to the air-fuel mixture, let us go back to I (upper left) again. Here, an air-fuel charge has been trapped between lobes A and B (5) as lobe A passes the intake port. Further rotation of the rotor reduces the combustion space (6), as shown at II. Then, at III, the combustion space (7) is at a minimum, so that the mixture reaches maximum compression. At this instant, the spark plug fires and ignites the mixture. Now the power cycle begins. At IV, the expanding gases (8) force the rotor around, and this action is shown continuing in I (9) and II (10). With further rotation of the rotor, the leading lobe clears the exhaust port, and the burned gases are forced out as shown at III (11) and IV (12).

As will be seen, there are three power cycles for each rotor revolution, and the engine delivers power almost continuously. Early experimental models of this engine had some difficulty with the sealing between the rotor lobes, the rotor sides, and the walls of the oval chamber, according to some engineers. The sealing system now used (Fig. 4-54) is designed to provide effective sealing at all points.

A later version of the Wankel engine uses two rotors and, with a displacement of 60.7 cubic inches, produces 136 hp at 5,500 rpm. This engine is shown in a cutaway view in Fig. 4-55. The engine, as used in the German NSU sedan (known as the

RO-80), has a torque converter and a friction clutch that is electrically operated. Figure 4-56 shows how the engine is mounted in the automobile. Note that the car is front drive, with the engine mounted between the front wheels. There are disk brakes on the inboard ends of the half shafts that drive the front wheels.

Besides the NSU, other companies have been licensed to manufacture the engine and install it in their automobiles. These include Daimler-Benz, Perkins in England, Citroen in France, and Kogya and Mazda in Japan. Curtiss-Wright in the United States has been working on the engine for a number of years and apparently has solved all the major problems that would deter an American automobile manufacturer from adopting it for one or more of his models. However, no United States automobile maker has publicly expressed interest in doing this.

Fig. 4-55. Cutaway view of a two-rotor Wankel engine with attached torque converter and transmission. (*NSU of Germany*)

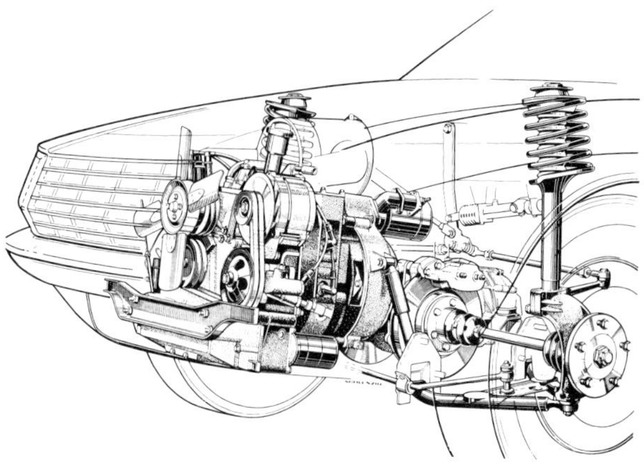

Fig. 4-56. Method of mounting two-rotor Wankel engine in RO-80 sedan. (*NSU of Germany*)

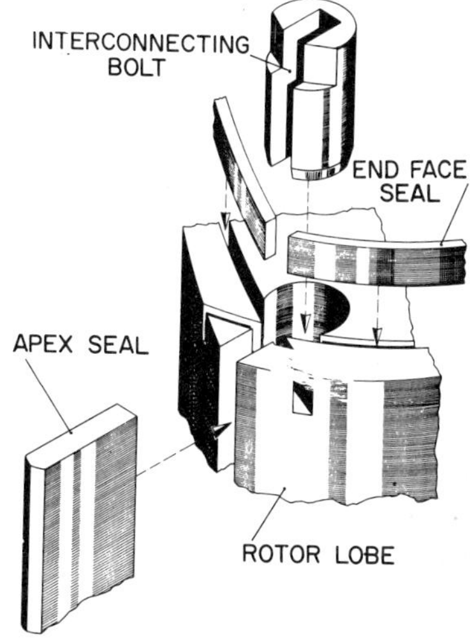

Fig. 4-54. Details of rotor sealing in the Wankel engine.

§47. Sterling engine This engine makes use of the fact that the pressure in a container of gas goes up when the gas is heated and goes down when the gas is cooled. A specific amount of gas is sealed into the engine and alternately heated and cooled. When it is heated, its increasing pressure pushes a power piston down. When it is cooled, its lowered pressure in effect pulls the power piston up.

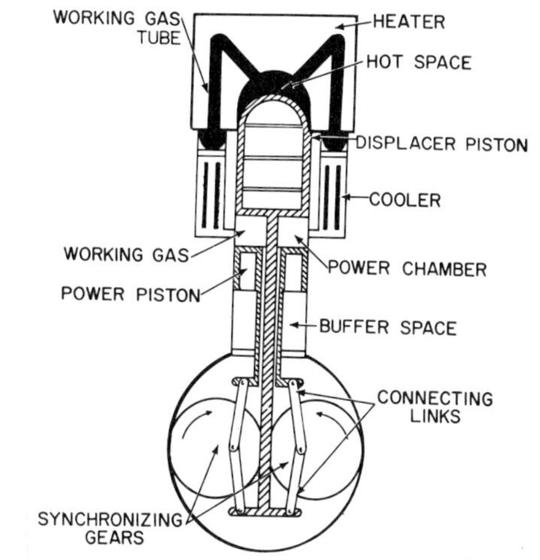

Fig. 4-57. Schematic drawing of a Sterling engine.

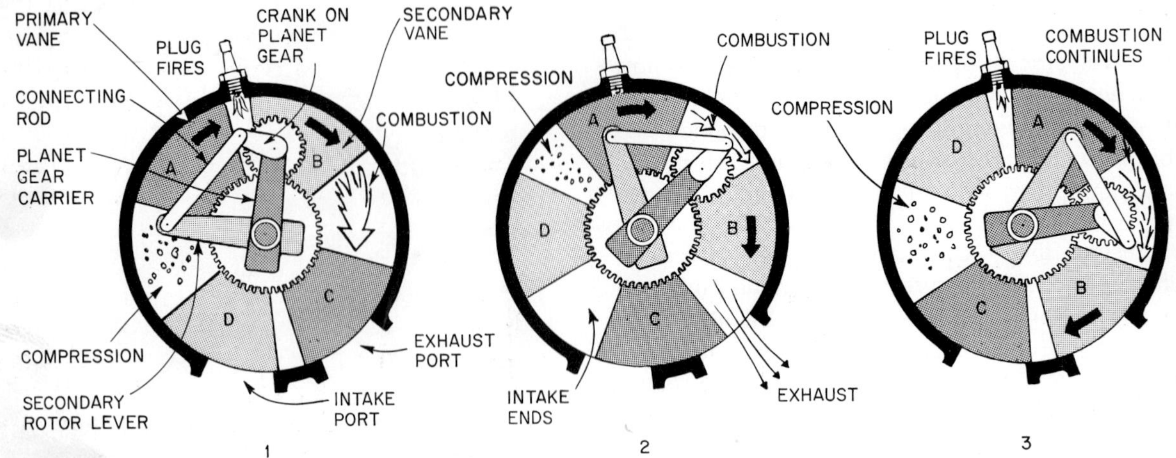

Fig. 4-58. Operation of Kauertz rotary engine.

Figure 4-57 shows the Sterling engine. The upper, or displacer, piston does not produce power, but simply causes the air to move between the heated and cooled sections of the engine. The power piston moves up and down between the power chamber and the buffer space. The two pistons are linked by a rhombic drive to a pair of synchronizing gears which, in turn, drive the output shaft. The name "rhombic" comes from the fact that the four links form a rhombus, which is a geometric figure of four sides, the opposing sides of which are parallel.

Let us follow the engine through a complete cycle of events and see how it operates. We will start with the pistons in the position shown in Fig. 4-57. The working gas has been heated, and therefore its pressure has increased. This increase of pressure, applied to the head of the power piston, forces the piston to move down. Note that the working gas expands during this action.

The power piston, in moving down, pushes downward through its two connecting links against the two gears. The gears therefore rotate and turn the engine-output shaft. Meanwhile, the rotation of the gears causes the two links to the displacer piston to pull the displacer piston down. This increases the hot space above the displacer piston so that some of the working gas can flow from the power chamber toward this space. As it moves through the cooler on the way to this upper space, the gas is cooled, and its pressure drops.

Notice that there is a buffer space below the power piston. This buffer space contains a specific amount of gas. When the power piston moves down, this gas is compressed, and its pressure goes up. Now, after the power piston has reached BDC, the pressure of this buffer gas becomes higher than the pressure of the working gas. Remember that the working gas has been cooled, so that its pressure has dropped. Now, with the buffer gas at a higher pressure than the working gas, the power piston is pushed up. This motion is transmitted through the two links to the gears, rotating them on around to the position shown in Fig. 4-57.

Meanwhile, the working gas that has flowed into the hot space becomes heated. The heating effect results from the continuous combustion of a fuel such as kerosene or oil. The heating of the working gas causes its pressure to increase, and once again the power piston is forced down by the increasing pressure.

The action, therefore, results from the repeated heating and cooling of the working gas. When the working gas is heated, it drives the power piston down. When it cools, the buffer-gas pressure forces the piston up. You might think that this heating and cooling would take considerable time and result in an awkward, slow, and inefficient engine. However, recent experimental engines, using helium as the working gas at an average pressure of 1,500 pounds per square inch, have operated at 3,000 rpm with an efficiency of 30 percent, which is as good as, or better than, most automotive engines.

Some engineers have proposed the Sterling engine for such small-engine applications as lawnmowers. They are very easy to start, silent in operation, and simple in basic design. Other engineers believe that they will appear first for large stationary applications, such as remote electric power plants or pumping stations. One possibility is that they will be used to power space satellites and space stations. In space, no source of heat other than the sun would be needed. With a large reflector to gather heat from the sun and a large radiator to radiate the heat away, a Sterling engine would operate without any fuel at all.

§48. Other rotary engines The idea of a rotary internal-combustion engine has fascinated inventors for many years. Wankel, of course, has enjoyed some success, as noted previously. Several other designs are discussed in this section. Some of these use pistons of odd shapes; others use vanes that are linked together in one way or another. In some, the engine block itself rotates.

1. Kauertz. This engine (Fig. 4-58) has two rotors, each with a pair of opposing vanes. The two rotors, with their vanes, are linked together with levers, connecting rods, and a pair of gears. In Fig. 4-58, primary vanes A and C are attached to the primary rotor, and secondary vanes B and D are attached to the secondary rotor. In operation, the spaces between the vanes increase and decrease (due to the gear and linkage action) to produce the four cycles, intake, compression, power, and exhaust. For example, note that in 1 of Fig. 4-58 the air-fuel mixture, compressed between vanes A and B, is ignited as the spark plug fires. The resulting pressure drives vane B ahead of vane A so that the space between the two vanes increases, as shown at 2 and 3. At the same time, the opposing vanes on the two rotors act to produce intake and compression. As vane B moves ahead of A, so also does vane D move ahead of C. This produces intake between C and D and compression between D and A. The oscillation of the secondary rotor with vanes B and D (combined with the actual rotation of the rotor) could be likened to a sort of "catch-up and fall-behind" action. The primary rotor turns at a steady speed; however, the secondary rotor, while turning, also oscillates so that it moves ahead and then falls behind the primary rotor. This action is produced by the stationary sun gear and the rotating planet gear and their linkages. The planet-gear carrier is attached to the primary rotor and the output shaft. When combustion pressure pushes a secondary vane ahead of the primary vane just behind it, the secondary-rotor lever pushes the connecting rod forward; this turns the crank on the planet gear. The planet gear therefore turns on the stationary sun gear, causing the planet-gear carrier and primary rotor to rotate. The output shaft therefore turns.

2. Virmel. The Virmel engine is very similar to the Kauertz engine. It has two sets of vanes, the primary and secondary. They are linked by a more complex set of levers and gears than in the Kauertz engine. This linkage causes one set of vanes to be brougnt to a complete stop twice each revolution. The action thereby produces the four cycles between the vanes: intake, compression, power, and exhaust.

3. Mercer. The Mercer engine contains two pistons in a single cylinder, which are held in place by long piston pins that have rollers on their ends. The rollers run on a track made up of two intersecting circles (almost like a modified figure 8). The engine operates on the two-stroke-cycle principle. Combustion takes place between the two pistons, driving them outward. This outward pressure is carried through the piston pins to the rollers, which roll along the track formed by the two intersecting circles. This forces the entire inner part of the engine, with the cylinder, to rotate. As the pistons complete their power strokes, they clear the inlet and exhaust ports. Fresh charges of air-fuel mixture which have been compressed at the outer ends of the pistons now pass through the transfer passages, as shown, into the combustion chamber while, at the same time, the burned gases are escaping through the exhaust ports. Further rotation of the cylinder, with pistons, forces the pistons inward on the compression stroke. Ignition then takes place, and the entire cycle is repeated.

4. Jernaes. The Jernaes engine has a three-lobe rotor, like the Wankel, and is similar in operation to the Wankel. There are differences, however, in the manner in which the rotor is supported. It has no internal gearing as does the Wankel. Instead, it is mounted on three eccentric planet gears meshed with a stationary concentric reaction gear. This produces the eccentric rotor motion that is essential to the action of the engine.

SUMMARY

Internal-combustion engines come in many sizes, shapes, and types, including the four-stroke-cycle, two-stroke-cycle, diesel, turbine, Wankel, and Sterling engines. The four-stroke-cycle engine is by far the most widely used in automobiles and is the subject of the engine chapters in this book. Most automotive engines have four, six, or eight cylinders, and sixes may be in-line or V type. Eight-cylinder engines are all V-8.

The piston, with rings, moves up and down in the cylinder in the four strokes of the cycle: intake, compression, power, and exhaust. This reciprocating motion is translated into rotary motion by the connecting rod and crankshaft. There are four general valve arrangements: L, I, F, and T. The I arrangement is almost universal in the field.

In two-stroke-cycle engines, the piston acts as the valve, clearing the intake and exhaust ports as it moves down to BDC. The complete cycle of events takes place in two piston strokes and one crankshaft revolution.

The diesel engine compresses air alone on the compression stroke, and the fuel is injected or sprayed into the cylinder at the end of the compression stroke. Heat of compression produces ignition of the fuel.

The gas-turbine, free-piston, Wankel, and Sterling engines are all internal-combustion devices and may someday play a more important role in automobiles. For the present, however, the four-stroke-cycle engine is far in the lead.

REFERENCES

1. Aitken, A., Ford of Britain's Vee Engine Range, SAE (Society of Automotive Engineers) 670004, 1967 (paper).

2. Bowers, J., and J. F. Macura, Mark II-427 GT Engine, SAE (Society of Automotive Engineers) 670066, 1967 (paper).

3. Herschmann, O., Daimler-Benz High Output Engines—A Study in Compact Design, SAE (Society of Automotive Engineers) 670519, 1967 (paper).

QUESTIONS

1. Describe the major moving parts in the engine and explain their functions.

2. Describe the actions taking place during the four strokes in the four-stroke-cycle engine.

3. Explain the purpose of the flywheel.

4. Describe three of the most common cylinder arrangements used in automobiles.

5. Describe and illustrate with simple sketches the four valve arrangements used in four-stroke-cycle engines.

6. Describe the operation of the two-stroke-cycle engine that uses a reed valve. A transfer port. An exhaust valve in the head.

7. Explain the operation of the diesel engine and contrast it with the Otto-cycle engine.

8. Describe the gas turbine and its operation.

9. What is the purpose of the free-piston engine? Describe its construction and operation.

10. Describe the construction and operation of the Wankel engine.

11. Describe the construction and operation of the Sterling engine.

Physical Principles of Engine Operation

CHAPTER **5**

This chapter considers the physical principles involved in the operation of an internal-combustion engine. Much of the material covered may be familiar to the reader, but it is included in order to provide a review of fundamentals leading up to the discussions of air-fuel cycles and pressure-volume curves of four-stroke-cycle engines.

§49. Atoms The world is made up of a tremendous variety of substances; water, blood, steel, bone, wood, copper, coal, glass, paper—the list is endless. Yet all of these substances are made up of about a hundred types of basic "building blocks" called *atoms.* Each type of atom, in quantity, is called an *element.* Moreover, each atom, regardless of how complex it is, is composed of three basic particles: electrons, protons, and neutrons.*

The number of protons that an atom contains determines whether the atom is hydrogen, carbon, iron, uranium, or some other substance. Thus, an atom of hydrogen is made up of 1 proton at its center, or nucleus, and an electron circling, or orbiting, around the proton (Fig. 5-1). The proton has a positive electric charge (indicated by a + sign), the electron has a negative electric charge (indicated by a − sign). The attraction between the opposing electric charges (positive and negative) holds the electron to its orbit around the proton.

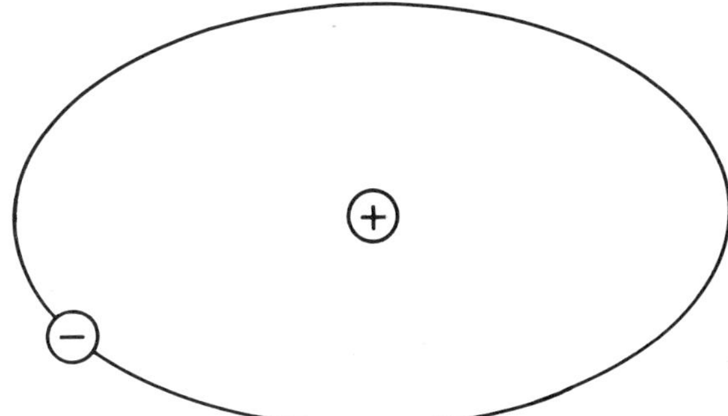

Fig. 5-1. An atom of hydrogen.

An atom of helium has 2 protons in its nucleus and 2 electrons circling the nucleus (Fig. 5-2). In addition, the helium nucleus contains 2 neutrons. The neutron has no electric charge, but it does play a part in holding the 2 protons in the nucleus. If it were not for the neutrons, the 2 protons would fly apart. For just as two opposing electric charges attract each other, so do two like electric charges repel each other. The presence of the neutrons in the nucleus permits the 2 protons to remain in close proximity within the nucleus.

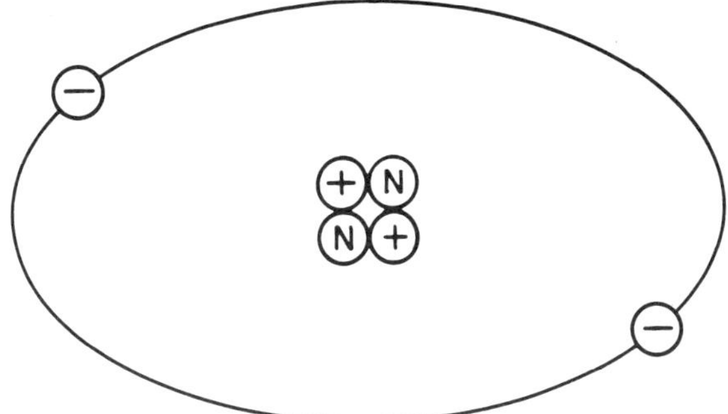

Fig. 5-2. An atom of helium.

Next in the order of atomic complexity is lithium (Fig. 5-3), with 3 protons and 4 neutrons in its

*In this discussion, we consider only the two "basic" particles in the nucleus, the proton and neutron, ignoring for the sake of simplicity the numerous other particles that have been detected in the nuclear jungle.

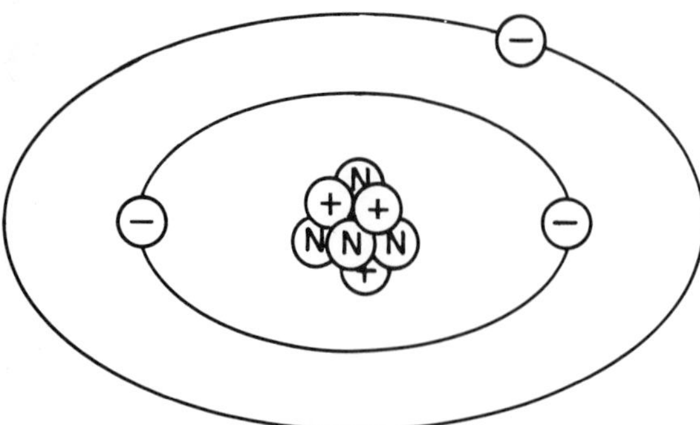

Fig. 5-3. An atom of lithium.

nucleus and 3 electrons circling the nucleus. Then there is beryllium, with 4 protons, 5 neutrons, and 4 electrons in an atom; boron, with 5 protons, 5 neutrons, and 5 electrons; carbon, with 6, 6, and 6; nitrogen, with 7, 7, and 7; oxygen, with 8, 8, and 8; and so on. Note that each atom normally has the same number of electrons as protons; this makes the atom electrically neutral because the positive and negative charges are equal in number.

§50. Size of atoms Individual atoms are far too small for us to observe directly, even with the most powerful microscopes. Yet we do know a great deal about them—for instance, their size. Start with a cubic inch of hydrogen gas at 32°F and atmospheric pressure. This cube contains about 88×10^{19} (880 billion billion) atoms (Fig. 5-4). Suppose we were able to expand this cube until it was large enough to contain the earth. This means that each edge would measure 8,000 miles. Now, on this tremendously expanded scale, if all atoms were enlarged in the same proportion, each atom would measure about 10 inches in diameter.

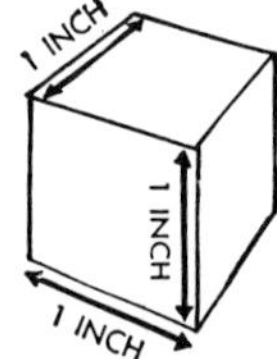

Fig. 5-4. A cubic inch of hydrogen gas at atmospheric pressure and at 32° F, which contains about 880 billion billion atoms.

§51. The elements The Table of Elements gives a partial listing of the elements, with names, chemical symbols, atomic numbers and weights, and electron arrangements. The atomic number is the number of protons in the nucleus of an atom of the element. The atomic weight is the weight of the atom as compared to hydrogen; it takes into consideration the presence of neutrons in the nucleus. The odd numbers (for example, copper, with an atomic weight of approximately 63.6) are due to the fact that some atoms of the element have more neutrons in their nuclei than others. These variants are called *isotopes.*

§52. Molecules It is rare to find elements in their pure forms. Usually, they are combined with other elements. When elements do combine, their atoms enter into close association to form larger particles called *molecules.* The water molecule is a simple example. It is made up of two hydrogen atoms and one oxygen atom and has the chemical formula H_2O. Figure 5-5 is a greatly enlarged and simplified diagram which shows the formation of a molecule of water.

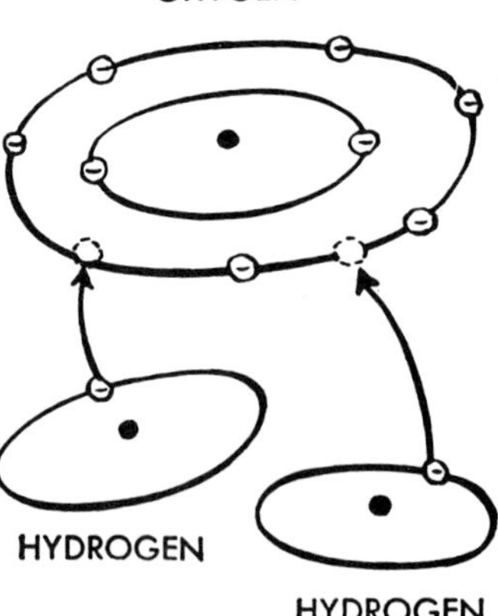

Fig. 5-5. An atom of oxygen uniting with two atoms of hydrogen to form a molecule of water, or H_2O.

The formation of molecules from atoms or from other molecules is called a *chemical reaction.* During a chemical reaction, there is a sharing, or interchange, of electrons between the atoms involved. The nuclei of the atoms remain unchanged.

TABLE OF ELEMENTS

Name	*Symbol*	*Atomic number*	*Approximate atomic weight*	*Electron arrangement*
Aluminum	Al	13	27	2)8)3
Calcium	Ca	20	40	2)8)8)2
Carbon	C	6	12	2)4
Chlorine	Cl	17	35.5	2)8)7
Copper	Cu	29	63.6	2)8)18)1
Hydrogen	H	1	1	1
Iron	Fe	26	56	2)8)14)2
Magnesium	Mg	12	24	2)8)2
Mercury	Hg	80	200	2)8)18)32)18)2
Nitrogen	N	7	14	2)5
Oxygen	O	8	16	2)6
Phosphorus	P	15	31	2)8)5
Potassium	K	19	39	2)8)8)1
Silver	Ag	47	108	2)8)18)18)1
Sodium	Na	11	23	2)8)1
Sulfur	S	16	32	2)8)6
Zinc	Zn	30	65	2)8)18)2

Some elements are highly reactive; others are chemically inert. The difference lies in the number and arrangement of the electrons (see the Table of Elements). Electrons are arranged in orbits, or "shells," of varying sizes around the atomic nuclei. These orbits, or shells, hold maximum specific numbers of electrons. The inside shell, for example, will hold only 2 electrons; the second shell, 8 electrons; the third shell, 18; and the fourth shell, 32. There are additional shells in the more complex atoms.

A reactive element is hydrogen, the atom of which has only 1 electron in the inner shell (which can hold two electrons). Another highly reactive element is oxygen, the atom of which has 2 electrons in the inner shell and 6 electrons in the next outer shell (which can hold 8 electrons). A nonreactive element is helium, which has 2 electrons in its inner shell (all the shell can hold). Another nonreactive element is neon, which has 2 electrons in its inner shell and 8 in the next outer shell (all this shell can hold). Note that reactive elements have unfilled outer shells, and that inert, or nonreactive, elements have filled outer shells.*

*This is a highly simplified explanation.

§53. Combustion Combustion is a common chemical reaction in which the element oxygen combines with other elements, such as hydrogen or carbon. The combustion process in the automobile engine is an example. Here, the fuel (gasoline), which is a hydrocarbon, combines with oxygen from the air to form hydrogen oxide (Fig. 5-5), that is, water, and carbon dioxide (Fig. 5-6).

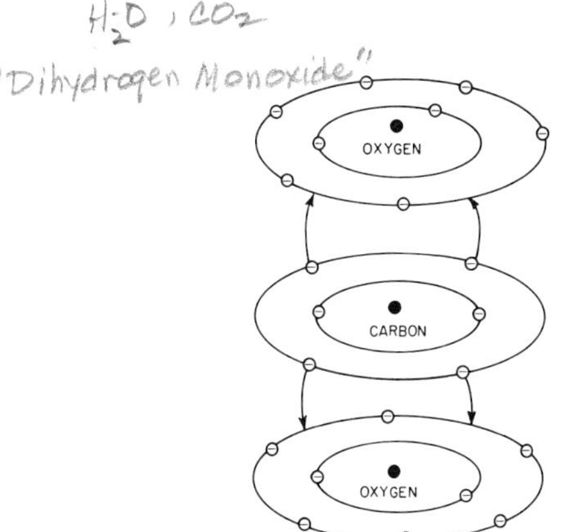

Fig. 5-6. One atom of carbon uniting with two atoms of oxygen to form a molecule of carbon dioxide, or CO_2.

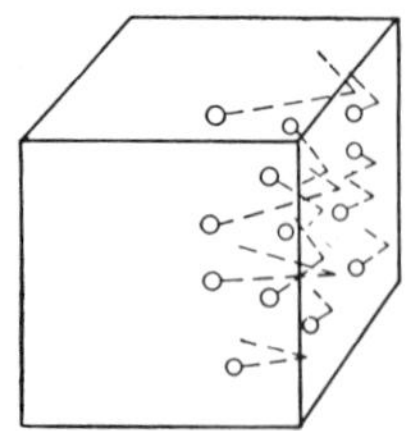

Fig. 5-7. Gas pressure in a container is the result of the ceaseless bombardment of the inner sides of the container by the fast-moving molecules of gas. For simplicity, this "bombardment" is shown on only one side of the container. It actually takes place against all the inner sides. The molecules are shown tremendously enlarged. Also, of course, there are billions of molecules entering into the action, not just a few as shown.

§54. Heat Combustion produces heat. Heat causes the pressure on the gases confined in the combustion chamber of the engine cylinder to increase. This high pressure forces the piston down so that the engine produces power.

From the molecular point of view, an explanation of how heat increases gas pressure might be stated thus: The molecules of gas are in rapid motion, and the hotter the gas, the more rapid this motion is. The pressure of gas in a container results from the ceaseless bombardment of the gas molecules on the insides of the container (Fig. 5-7). Of course, a few molecules bumping the walls of the container would not bê significant. However, in a cubic inch of gas at atmospheric pressure there are billions of molecules. At high temperatures, these molecules are moving very rapidly, and the consequent bombardment does become significant. We know, for example, that in a typical automotive engine, the bombardment of molecules on the head of the piston, during the power stroke, may add up to more than two tons of pressure.

§55. The gas laws Gas pressure, temperature, and volume are related in specific ways, as set forth in the gas laws. One of these is Boyle's law, which states that, as long as the temperature of the gas remains unchanged, the volume (V) of a specific mass (m) of gas is inversely proportional to the pressure (P). Thus, for a given mass of gas at constant temperature,

$$V \propto \frac{1}{P}$$

To express it another way, for a gas at a specific pressure and temperature,

$$V \propto m$$

Also

$$V \propto \frac{m}{P}$$

If the constant of proportionality is designated as k, then

$$V = \frac{mk}{P}$$

or

$$PV = mk$$

The constant k differs for different gases.

A second important law is Charles' law, which states that, at constant pressure, the volume (V) of a given mass of gas increases a specific amount for each degree, Centigrade, of temperature (T) rise. This specific amount is 1/273.16 of its volume at 0°C. Thus

$$V = k_1 T$$

The two laws may be combined, as follows:

$$\frac{P_1 V_1}{T_1} = \frac{P_2 V_2}{T_2}$$

The above laws are for "ideal" gases, that is, gases that obey the laws strictly. Actual gases vary from the ideal, with the deviations increasing as pressure increases and temperature decreases. However, the laws are cited because they indicate, in a general way, how gases perform under varying pressures and temperatures.

§56. Heat flow and specific heat It is a basic law of nature that heat flows from areas of high concentration (hot areas) to areas of low concentration (cold areas). In other words, heat passes from hotter substances to cooler substances. To look at this matter from the molecular point of view, consider once again the proposition that heat is a measure of molecular activity: the higher the temperature, the faster the molecules are moving. Thus, when we place a hot object next to a cool object, the molecules composing the hot object are moving faster then those of the cool object. In this case, the fast-moving molecules gradually lose velocity to the slow-moving molecules until finally all are moving at the same average speed; that is, both objects are at the same temperature.

For example, drop an ice cube into a glass of water. The molecules in the ice cube are moving at relatively slow speeds, compared with the molecules in the liquid water. Gradually, however, the water molecules lose velocity, while the ice molecules gain velocity. That is, the ice melts, and the resultant water from the ice increases in temperature while the original liquid water decreases in temperature. Thus, the result is a cool drink.

It takes different amounts of heat to raise the temperature of different substances a specific number of degrees; that is, these substances have different heat or thermal capacities. The starting point for the definition of the amount of heat required is a characteristic of water. When water at 15°C is increased in temperature 1°C, it requires 1 calorie per gram of water; or, it requires 1 Btu (British thermal unit) to raise one pound of water 1°F, starting at 60°F. Actually, these are the definitions of calorie and Btu. That is, a calorie is the amount of heat required to raise the temperature of 1 gram of water from 15 to 16°C; or, a Btu is the amount of heat required to raise the temperature of 1 pound of water 1°F, starting at 60°F.

These definitions set out the specific heat of water which has the value of unity, or 1. Few substances have a greater specific heat, or thermal capacity, than water. Most other substances have a lower thermal capacity, or specific heat. Thus, steel has a specific heat of 0.12. That is, it would take only 0.12 calorie to raise a gram of steel from 15 to 16° (or 0.12 Btu to raise a pound of steel 1°F, starting at 60°F). Gasoline has a specific heat of 0.53; oak wood, 0.57; ordinary air, 0.24.

Gases have two specific heats—one when their temperature is increased at constant volume, and the other when their temperature is increased at constant pressure. These are, for air (a mixture of gases) at room temperature,

Specific heat at constant volume, or $C_v = 0.171$
Specific heat at constant pressure, or $C_p = 0.240$

Note that it requires less heat to raise the temperature of air if the volume is kept constant, that is, if the size of the container remains the same. More heat is required if the air is kept at constant pressure, that is, if the size of the container is increased so the pressure remains constant. The reason for this is that if the volume remains constant, the pressure goes up with temperature, and, as we have seen (§54), this increased pressure also adds heat. On the other hand, if the pressure remains constant, then only the heat added from the external source raises the air temperature, and more heat is required.

§57. Idealized cycles To arrive at an understanding of the thermodynamic processes involved in the operation of internal-combustion engines, reference is made to idealized cycles. These cycles can be graphed to illustrate, in modification, the conditions which take place inside the engine cylinder, for example, during the four strokes in a four-stroke-cycle engine.

§58. The constant-volume cycle There are three basic thermodynamic cycles, and the one that is directly applicable to the four-stroke-cycle spark-ignition engine is the constant-volume cycle. A typical idealized constant-volume cycle is graphed in Fig. 5-8; the working medium in the cylinder is air. To start with, the cylinder is filled with air at atmospheric pressure (point 1). This air is then compressed adiabatically (without heat being added or subtracted) to point 2. At this point, heat is added at a constant volume to cause a pressure increase to point 3. This is followed by an adiabatic expansion to point 4, after which the charge is allowed to exhaust to atmospheric pressure at a constant volume. The constant-volume name is applied because the heat is supplied and lost at

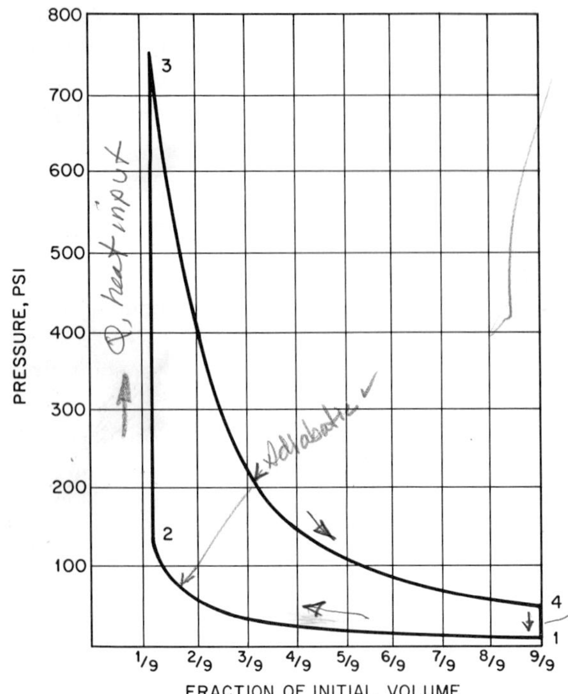

Fig. 5-8. Pressure-volume diagram for a constant-volume four-stroke cycle, using an idealized working medium having the properties of air at room temperature.

constant volume (or from points 2 to 3 and points 4 to 1).

Now we know, of course, that these are not the actual conditions in the engine cylinder. They would be, however, if it were possible to achieve the ideal cycle. The actual work that would come out of such an ideal cycle is measured by the area enclosed by the graph lines (1 to 2 to 3 to 4 to 1). The work that goes in is measured by the pressure increase from point 1 to point 2. It takes a certain amount of work to compress the air, as shown. This is the reason that the total area under the curve from point 3 to point 4 cannot be taken as the work produced by the cycle. The area below the curve from point 1 to point 2 must be subtracted.

All this can be described mathematically, and we will do this before we pass on to a comparison of the graph of the ideal cycle with the *PV* (pressure-volume) graph of the activities in an engine cylinder. The symbols for the various quantities involved are as follows:

P = pressure, lb-ft^2
V = volume, ft^3
c = specific heat of working medium
T = temperature
W = weight, lb
Q = quantity of heat added, Btu
N_{th} = thermal efficiency

Subscripts denote points on the graph (Fig. 5-8). Work input to the working medium by the piston is

$$\text{Work input} = Wc(T_2 - T_1)$$

The work output from the working medium to the piston is

$$\text{Work output} = Wc(T_3 - T_4)$$

The net work is output minus input or

$$\text{Net work} = Wc(T_3 - T_4 - T_2 + T_1)$$

The heat energy put into the cycle is

$$Q = Wc(T_3 - T_2)$$

§59. Thermal efficiency Efficiency is the ratio between the results obtained and the efforts exerted. Thermal efficiency is a measure of how efficiently the heat Q is used. It is the ratio between the net work obtained and the heat energy put into the cycle (Fig. 5-8), or

$$N_{th} = \frac{\text{net work}}{Q} = \frac{Wc(T_3 - T_4 - T_2 + T_1)}{Wc(T_3 - T_2)}$$

$$= \frac{T_3 - T_2}{T_3 - T_2} - \frac{T_4 - T_1}{T_3 - T_2}$$

$$= 1 - \frac{T_4 - T_1}{T_3 - T_2}$$

Now, to analyze this last equation, we can see that the thermal efficiency is unity (100 percent) minus the heat lost by the discharge of the working medium into the atmosphere $(T_4 - T_1)$, divided by the net temperature rise as the heat energy Q is added $(T_3 - T_2)$.

§60. *PV* curve of a four-stroke-cycle engine The more nearly the idealized cycle can be achieved in the engine, the more efficient the engine will be. However, it is obvious that the *PV* curve of an actual running engine will fall short of the ideal. In the first place, compression of the air-fuel charge and expansion of the hot burned gases are not adiabatic. In compression, heat is added to the working medium from the surrounding cylinder wall, head, and piston, all of which are at high temperatures. On the other hand, during expansion, the working medium, or combusted gases, are much hotter than the surrounding metal engine parts; the medium gives off some of its heat to these parts. But much more heat is lost in this manner than is gained by the air-fuel mixture during compression. This heat loss lowers the thermal efficiency because the lost heat is not available to produce work on the piston.

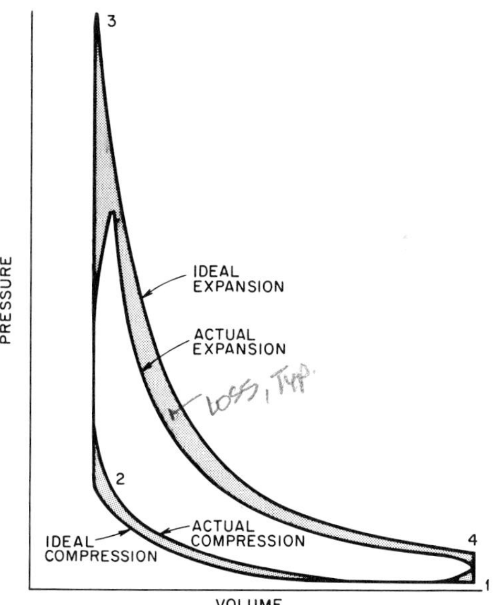

Fig. 5-9. Comparison of idealized pressure-volume diagram with pressure-volume diagram of four-stroke-cycle engine.

Other differences will become obvious when you compare the real cycle as superimposed over the ideal cycle (Fig. 5-9). The shaded areas represent losses. Note that ideal compression (points 1 to 2) is not achieved because as the air-fuel mixture is compressed in the cylinder it absorbs heat from the engine parts. This increases gas pressure above the ideal. Also, in the actual engine, the addition of heat (ignition of air-fuel mixture) starts before the compression stroke is completed.

Then, as ignition of the compressed air-fuel mixture takes place, the combustion is not instantaneous. This means that heat is not injected instantaneously, as in the ideal cycle (points 2 to 3). Furthermore, during expansion, some of the heat from the charge is lost to the surrounding engine parts, and the actual expansion (points 3 to 4) is at lower pressures. Finally, there is a heat loss at points 4 to 1 because heat is lost in the hot exhaust gases.

§61. Volumetric efficiency One of the practical reasons why the four-stroke-cycle engine does not achieve an ideal cycle is that volumetric efficiency is always less than 100 percent. Volumetric efficiency is the ratio between the amount of air-fuel mixture actually entering the cylinder and the amount that could enter under ideal conditions. If the mixture were drawn into the cylinder very slowly and adiabatically (no heat added to it), then it would be possible to get a full charge into the cylinder. However, the intake stroke lasts a very short time—it is about 1/10 second with the engine idling, and less than 1/100 second at high speeds. Therefore, pressure in the cylinder is always less than atmospheric at the end of the intake stroke (Fig. 5-10). Also, as the air-fuel mixture enters the cylinder, it receives heat from the hotter engine parts and expands nonadiabatically.

Thus, the operating engine never receives a "full" charge of air-fuel mixture. Engineers refer to this condition as difficulty in "breathing." The faster the engine is running, the more difficult it is for the engine to "breathe" and draw in the charges of air-fuel mixture. That is to say, volumetric efficiency falls off with increasing engine speed.

As a simple example, let us suppose that the volume of the cylinder with the piston at BDC (bottom dead center) is 47 cubic inches. This cylinder can hold, at atmospheric pressure, about 0.034 ounce

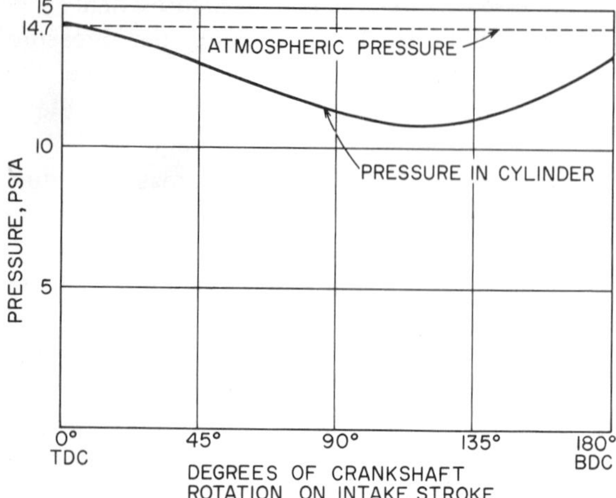

Fig. 5-10. As the intake stroke proceeds, the pressure in the engine cylinder drops below atmospheric and does not regain atmospheric pressure throughout the stroke. Curve is for one particular engine and one set of operating conditions. Curve will vary greatly according to engine rpm and other operating conditions.

of air. However, with the engine running at a given speed somewhat above idle, then only about 0.027 ounce can enter. This means that the volumetric efficiency (N_v) of the engine at the speed it is operating is

$$N_v = \frac{0.027}{0.034} = 80 \text{ percent}$$

The higher the engine speed, the shorter the time available for the air-fuel mixture to flow into the cylinder and therefore the lower the volumetric efficiency. This is one reason why an engine cannot continue to increase in speed indefinitely. It finally reaches a speed at which the volumetric efficiency is so low that the engine can produce only enough power to overcome the internal losses in the engine. This is its top speed.

Several things can be done to improve engine breathing, or volumetric efficiency, and these are discussed in detail in the chapters on engine design. First, the intake valve can be timed to open well before the piston reaches TDC (top dead center), and it can stay open well after the piston has passed BDC at the end of the intake stroke. This gives additional time for the inflow of the air-fuel mixture. Also, intake valves and intake manifolds can be made larger so there is less restriction on the inflowing air-fuel mixture. The carburetor can be made with more than one barrel to provide additional air-fuel passages through it. Some carburetors—the four-barrel units—are made with two barrels that come into action only at high engine speeds to open up additional flow areas for the ingoing air-fuel mixture. In addition, some intake manifolds are designed to employ a modified "ram-jet" action and thereby increase the amount of air-fuel mixture entering the cylinder. These are called "tuned" intake manifolds. Also, some engines employ supercharging. These engines have a compressor or "blower" that applies several pounds pressure on the ingoing air-fuel mixture so that more air-fuel mixture is delivered. The compressor is commonly called a *blower* in the automotive field, and the engine is therefore a *blown* engine.

SUMMARY

Atoms are the smallest bits of specific elements. They are composed of protons and neutrons in their nuclei, with electrons circling in orbits around the nuclei. The number of protons in the nucleus determines which element the atom is. Atoms combine to form molecules, and this is called a *chemical reaction*. The chemical reaction that is combustion, or fire, occurs when atoms of oxygen combine with atoms of hydrogen or carbon.

Boyle's law states that the volume of a specific mass of gas is inversely proportional to the pressure as long as the gas temperature remains unchanged.

Charles' law states that, at constant pressure, the volume of a given mass of gas increases a specific amount for each degree Centigrade of temperature rise.

Heat flows from areas of higher temperature to areas of lower temperature. Thermal capacities of different substances vary, and these capacities are indicated by their specific heat.

Idealized cycles are of value in the study of internal-combustion engines, and the one that is directly applicable is the constant-volume cycle. The *PV* curve is also of value in understanding engine theory. This understanding leads to appreciation of the losses that prevent higher efficiencies.

QUESTIONS

1. *Explain the basic difference between various elements from the atomic viewpoint.*
2. *Describe combustion.*
3. *State and explain Boyle's law.*
4. *State and explain Charles' law.*
5. *Explain the term "specific heat."*
6. *Explain why gases have two specific heats.*
7. *Describe the constant-volume cycle.*
8. *What is thermal efficiency?*
9. *Why does the* PV *curve of an operating engine fall short of the ideal?*
10. *Explain why the engine cannot achieve 100 percent volumetric efficiency.*

Engine Measurements

CHAPTER **6**

This chapter describes the various measurements that are applied to internal-combustion engines, as to both physical dimensions (bore, stroke, piston displacement, compression ratio, and so on) and operating characteristics (volumetric efficiency, brake horsepower, torque, indicated horsepower, efficiency, and so on).

§62. Bore and stroke The size of an engine cylinder is referred to in terms of the bore, or diameter, and stroke, or distance, the piston travels from BDC (bottom dead center) to TDC (top dead center) (Fig. 6-1). Note that the bore is always mentioned first as a 4.0 × 3.5 inch cylinder. This means that the diameter, or bore, is 4.0 inches and the stroke is 3.5 inches. The bore and stroke measurements are used to figure piston displacement (§63).

In the engine of many years ago, the stroke was always greater than the bore. The ideal of the early engine designer was a small-bore cylinder and a long piston stroke. Today, however, most engines are designed to have a short piston stroke and a large-bore cylinder. When the bore measurement is larger than the piston stroke, as, for instance, a 4.0 × 3.5 inch cylinder, then the engine is said to be *oversquare.* A "square" engine would, of course, be one in which both measurements were the same.

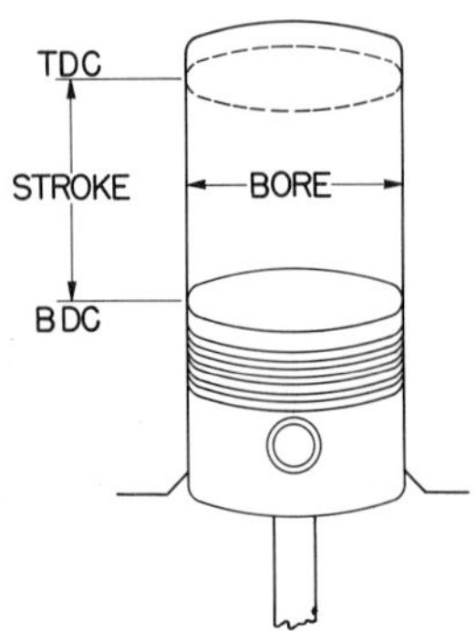

Fig. 6-1. Bore and stroke of an engine cylinder.

Fig. 6-2 is a graph of the average bore and stroke of automobile engines in recent years. Note that the measurements crossed over in 1955, and that the bore has increased and the stroke has decreased since that time. One reason for this is that with the shorter piston stroke, there is less loss from friction (§74). In addition, the shorter stroke reduces inertia and centrifugal loads on the bearings (§178). It also permits a reduction of engine height and thus a lower hood line.

§63. Piston displacement Piston displacement is the volume that the piston displaces as it moves from BDC to TDC. You can visualize this as a cylinder with the diameter of the engine cylinder, the top and bottom being the piston head at TDC and BDC. Thus, piston displacement of a 4.0 × 3.5 inch cylinder would be,

$$\frac{\pi \times D^2 \times L}{4} = \frac{3.1416 \times 4^2 \times 3.5}{4} = 43.98 \text{ cu in.}$$

If the engine has eight cylinders, then the total displacement of the engine would be 351.84 cubic inches (8 × 43.98). This measurement is an important one, especially in the field of racing, because, for any particular race, maximum allowable displacement is usually specified. Thus, at the Indianapolis 500, the 1966 maximum displacement was specified as follows:

American stock production block design, single non-

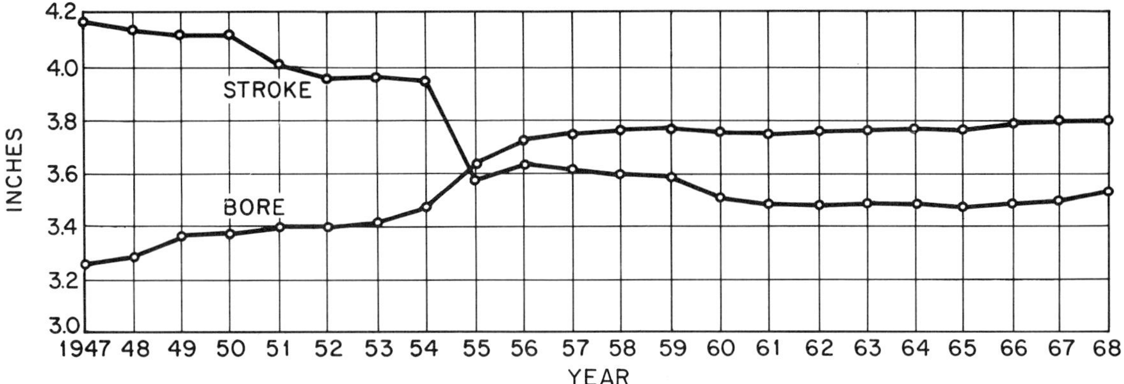

Fig. 6-2. Average bore and stroke of automotive engines in recent years.

overhead camshaft, removable head engines, not more than 203.4 cu in. if supercharged and not more than 305.1 cu in. if non-supercharged, are eligible to compete against the special racing engines which are limited to 171 cu in. supercharged and 256 cu in. non-supercharged.

§64. Compression ratio The compression ratio of an engine is a measure of how much the air-fuel mixture is compressed. It is the volume in a cylinder with the piston at BDC divided by its volume with the piston at TDC (Fig. 6-3). The volume above the piston with the piston at TDC is called the *clearance volume* since it is the clearance that remains above the piston at TDC.

Suppose that an engine has a cylinder volume of 48.0 cubic inches at BDC (*A* in Fig. 6-3) and a clearance volume of 5.0 cubic inches (B in Fig. 6-3). Thus, the compression ratio would be 48 divided by 5, or 9.6/1. That is, during the compression stroke, the air-fuel mixture would be compressed from 48 cubic inches to 5 cubic inches or to 1/9.6 of its original volume.

The compression ratio of an engine is an important factor in engine performance. In a limited sense, increasing the compression ratio increases engine power output, other factors being equal.

Figure 6-4 illustrates the trend in automobile-engine compression ratios during recent years. Note that they have gone up from about 7.5:1 to about 9.5:1 in the past 10 years. Some recent engines have compression ratios of above 10:1. For example, some of the V-8 engines used by Buick, Chrysler, and Oldsmobile in 1968 had compression ratios of 10.25:1. Also, one optional V-8 Ford engine had a compression ratio of 11.1:1.

These higher compression ratios cannot be achieved in L-head engines, but they are possible in I-head engines (§39). One reason for this is that, in the L-head engine, the valves require space into which they can move, and this space is in addition to the space above the piston. In the I-head engine, on the other hand, the valves work into the space above the piston, and thus the total space, or clearance volume, can be made smaller. Study the various illustrations of L-head and I-head engines in this book to clarify this point in your mind. Because increasing the compression ratios has certain inherent advantages, most automotive engines today are I-head engines.

One important advantage of higher compression ratios is that the air-fuel mixture is more highly compressed at the start of the power stroke. There-

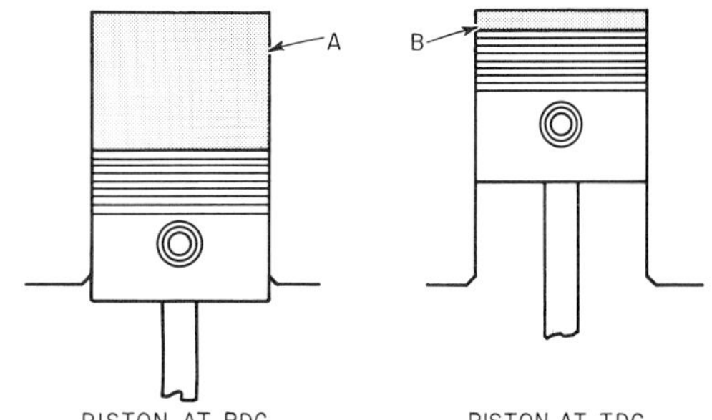

Fig. 6-3. The compression ratio is the volume in a cylinder with the piston at BDC divided by its volume with the piston at TDC, or A divided by B.

fore, higher combustion pressures will be attained as the power stroke begins. Further, the combusting mixture will expand more as the power stroke proceeds. Thus, there is more push on the piston for a larger part of the power stroke, and more power is obtained from each power stroke.

As we have already seen (§59), thermal efficiency is

$$N_{th} = 1 - \frac{T_4 - T_1}{T_3 - T_2}$$

This means that thermal efficiency increases as $T_4 - T_1$ decreases, that is, as the difference in temperature between points 4 and 1 in Fig. 5-8 decreases. Thermal efficiency also increases as Q, the quantity of heat added between points 2 and 3, increases.

Increasing the compression ratio has both of these effects: it decreases the net heat loss as the burned gases are exhausted; and, also, as the air-fuel mixture is more highly compressed, more heat is added during the power stroke. Increasing the compression ratio also tends to reduce exhaust-valve temperature because the exhaust gases are at a lower temperature [due to the higher thermal efficiency (see §211)].

§65. Horsepower Power is the rate at which work is done. The rate at which an engine can do work is measured in horsepower (hp). One horsepower is 33,000 foot-pounds per minute or

$$\text{hp} = \frac{\text{ft-lb per minute}}{33{,}000} = \frac{L \times W}{33{,}000 \times t}$$

where

hp = horsepower
L = length, in feet, through which W is forced
W = push, in pounds, that is exerted through L
t = time, in minutes, required to force W through L

§66. Indicated horsepower The amount of power that an engine can deliver at the output shaft is always less than the power that is actually developed inside the engine by the pressure of the expanding combusted gases on the piston heads. The power that is actually developed inside the engine is called *indicated horsepower* (ihp). A special indicating device is required to determine ihp. This device includes a sensor in the combustion chamber which reports almost instantaneous pressures reached in the engine cylinder during the four piston strokes (intake, compression, power, and exhaust). Figure 6-5 shows the pressure curve of an engine cylinder as related to crankshaft rotation. The four small drawings show the piston strokes during the four-stroke cycle. Note that the pressure is about atmospheric at the beginning of the intake stroke. It then falls a little below atmospheric as air-fuel delivery lags slightly behind piston movement (that is, volumetric efficiency is less than 100 percent).

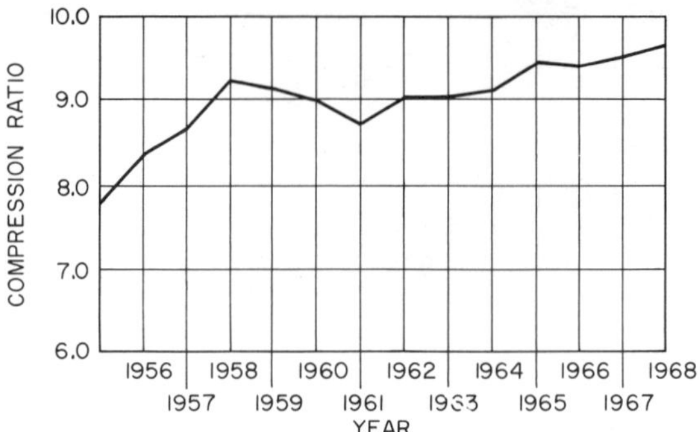

Fig. 6-4. Average compression ratio of automotive engines in recent years.

When the compression stroke begins, the pressure starts to increase. At a few degrees before TDC on the compression stroke, ignition takes place. The ignition system (Chap. 20) includes advance mechanisms that advance the spark so it takes place earlier in the compression stroke at higher speeds. This gives the compressed charge more time to ignite and burn.

As the compressed charge burns (Fig. 6-5), the pressure increases very rapidly, reaching a peak of about 680 psi (pounds per square inch) at about 25° past TDC on the power stroke. (This data is for one specific engine operating at one specific speed.) Pressure falls off rapidly as the power stroke continues, but there is still a pressure of about 50 psi at the end of the power stroke. When the exhaust stroke begins, the pressure drops further as the piston moves up, forcing the burned gases from the cylinder. At the end of the exhaust stroke, the pressure has fallen to nearly atmospheric.

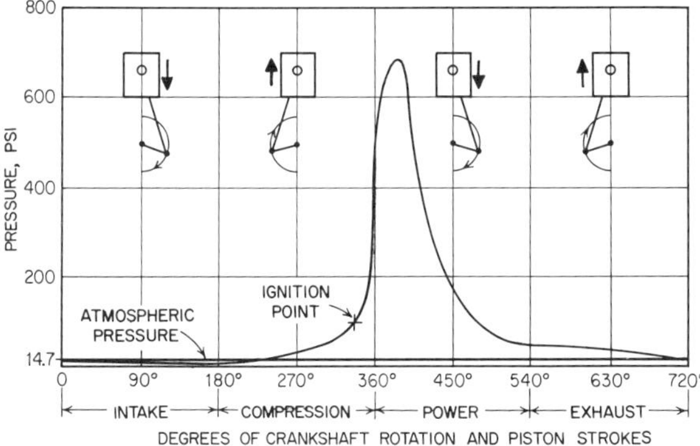

Fig. 6-5. Pressures in an engine cylinder during the four piston strokes. The four strokes require two crankshaft revolutions (360 degrees each), a total of 720 degrees of rotation. This curve is for a particular engine operating at one definite speed and throttle opening. Changing the speed and throttle opening would change the curve (particularly the power curve).

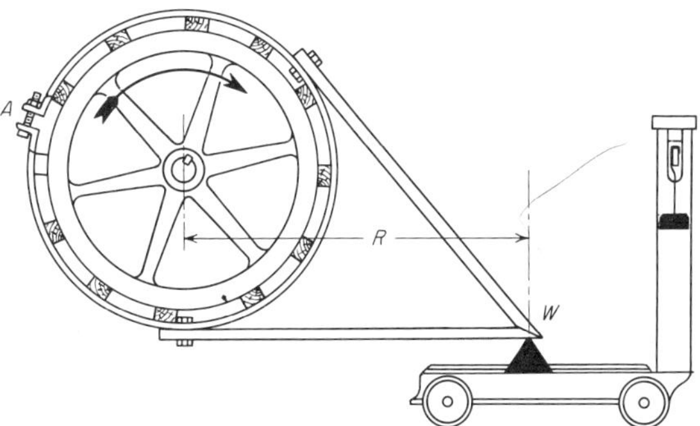

Fig. 6-6. Prony brake for determining the power of an engine. *A* is the adjustment for tightening the brake on the brake drum, *R* is the length of the arm (from the center of the shaft to the end supported on scales), and *W* is the weight, or force, exerted on the scales.

From a graph such as shown in Fig. 6-5, the mep (mean effective pressure) can be determined. The mep is the average pressure during the power stroke, minus the average pressures during the other three strokes. In effect, the mep is the pressure that actually forces the piston down during the power stroke. From the mep and other engine data, the following formula can be used to calculate ihp.

$$\text{ihp} = \frac{PLANK}{33{,}000}$$

where

P = mean effective pressure, in psi
L = length of stroke, in feet
A = area of cylinder section, in square inches
N = number of power strokes per minute (rpm/2)
K = number of cylinders

In operation, some of the power developed in the engine is used up in overcoming friction of engine parts. Thus, ihp is always greater than the horsepower delivered [measured in bhp (brake horsepower)].

§67. Brake horsepower The term "brake horsepower" is related to the fact that a braking device was originally used to determine the power that a running engine was delivering. This device is a *Prony brake* (Fig. 6-6). It includes a large brake drum, around which a brake is clamped. A brake arm is attached to the brake at one end, and it rests on a scale at the other. The brake has a device that can be tightened to exert a greater braking effect on the rotating drum. During the test, the engine drives the brake drum. The engine is operated at a steady speed, and the brake is gradually tightened to exert an increased load on the engine. At the same time, the throttle is opened so as to maintain a steady engine speed.

Increasing the load on the engine in this way also increases the load, or weight, on the scales. To find the maximum power that the engine can develop at any one speed, the load is increased gradually, while at the same time the throttle is opened wider and wider until it is wide open. Further loading would then cause the engine speed and power output to drop off.

The maximum load on the scales and engine rpm (revolutions per minute) are then used to determine the horsepower that the engine developed:

$$\text{bhp} = \frac{2\pi RNW}{33{,}000} = \frac{RNW}{5{,}252}$$

where

R = length of arm (from center of drum) in feet
N = engine speed, in rpm
W = load on scales, in pounds

§68. Dynamometer In the modern shop or laboratory, a dynamometer, rather than the Prony brake, is used to measure engine horsepower.[1] The dynamometer includes a generator that is driven by the engine. The number of watts of electric energy produced by the generator during the test is a direct measure of the amount of power that the engine is producing. The wattage output of the generator can be measured very accurately, and thus the dynamometer will very accurately report the horsepower output of the engine.

Another type of engine tester uses a water brake. The water brake contains a rotating device with numerous blades. When water is put into the device, the rotating member has a restriction placed on it because the blades must pass through the water. The more water added, the greater the restriction and the greater the load placed on the engine that is driving the rotor. As can be seen, this device can place varying loads on the engine as water is added or removed.

§69. Dynamometer tests Dynamometer tests of engines, even under controlled laboratory conditions, usually will not show test results that agree with the advertised horsepower ratings of the engines. For example, an engine advertised as being a "300-hp engine," might show only about 260 or 270 hp maximum on the dynamometer. One reason for this is that the advertised ratings are arrived at without such accessories as a generator, air cleaner, and exhaust system.

In addition, the advertised rating has been corrected for both temperature and atmospheric pressure. Other factors being equal, power output of an engine will increase with increased pressure and decrease with increased temperature. Increased pressure delivers more air-fuel mixture to the engine. Increased temperature causes a reduction in the amount of air-fuel mixture delivered, because it causes the air to expand and weigh less per unit volume.

To take into account these variables, a test code[1] has been adopted that does the following: After an engine is tested on the dynamometer, the actual test results are changed so as to take into account the actual pressure and temperature during the test. The engine test code requires adjustment of the test results to a standard pressure and temperature, which correspond to dry air at 60°F and 15 psi (sea-level atmospheric pressure).

§70. Friction Friction losses occur in the engine as a result of the relative motion between engine parts. Friction is the resistance to relative motion between two parts in contact. It varies with the pressure applied between the moving surfaces, the roughness of the surfaces, and the material of which the surfaces are made.

For example, suppose you were to pull an object weighing 100 pounds across a surface and found that it required a pull of 50 pounds to keep it moving (Fig. 6-7). Then you could be sure that if you were to pull a smaller object of the same material, weighing only 10 pounds, across the same surface, it would take only 5 pounds of pull: *Friction varies with the load.* Also, if you smoothed the two surfaces in contact, you would find it took less pull to move the objects: *Friction varies with the roughness of the surfaces.*

Friction also varies with the type of material. For example, to move a block of rubber along a concrete surface might require a pull of 120 pounds

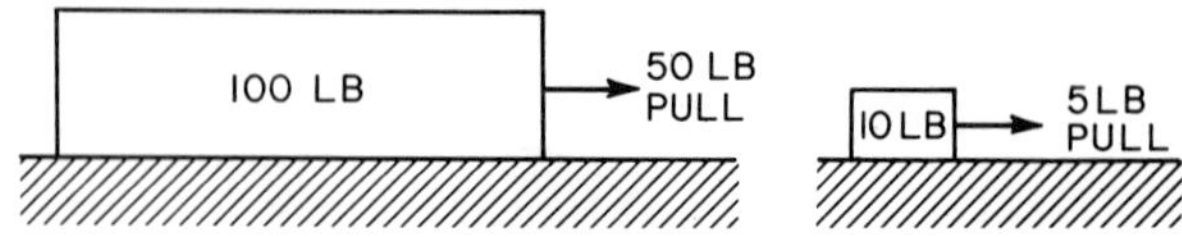

Fig. 6-7. Friction varies with the load.

or more (Fig. 6-8). On the other hand, a block of ice weighing 100 pounds might require a pull of only 2 pounds to keep it moving on the concrete surface. This, of course, explains why rubber is used for automobile tires. It has great resistance to slipping on concrete and thus resists skidding better than most any other material.

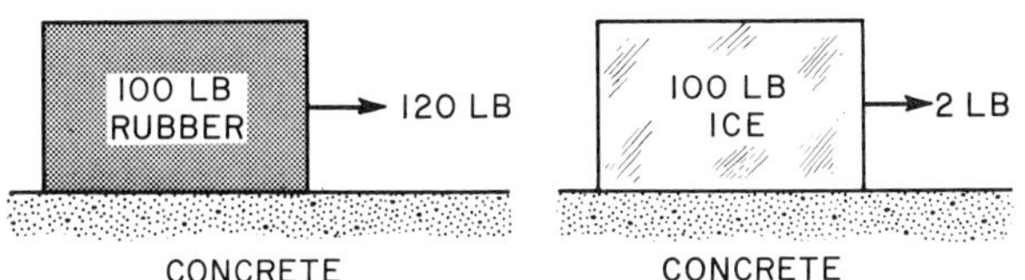

Fig. 6-8. Friction varies with the materials in contact.

§71. Static and kinetic friction There are two types of friction: *static* and *kinetic*. Static friction is the resistance to motion between two objects in contact, both of which are stationary. Kinetic friction is the resistance to motion between two objects that are in relative motion. Static friction is greater than kinetic friction.

§72. Coefficient of kinetic friction The amount of friction there will be between two surfaces that are in relative motion, or sliding contact, is indicated by the coefficient of friction:

$$\mu = \frac{F}{W}$$

where

W = the force holding the two surfaces together
F = the force required to keep W moving (Fig. 6-9)

§73. Three classes of kinetic friction There are three classes of kinetic friction: dry, greasy, and viscous. Dry friction is the resistance to relative motion of two dry objects. Greasy friction occurs when the two surfaces are separated by layers of fluid of microscopic thickness. Viscous friction occurs between layers of fluid. Viscosity, from which the term "viscous" is derived, relates to the tendency of liquids, such as oil, to resist flowing. A fluid of low viscosity, such as water, flows easily.

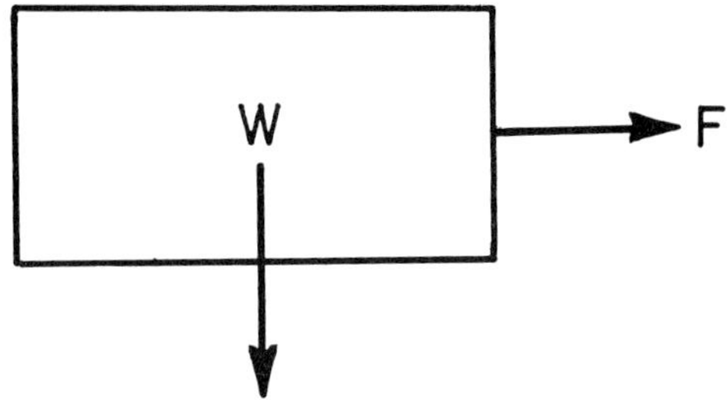

Fig. 6-9. The value of the coefficient of friction is *F* divided by *W*.

But heavy oil flows slowly; it has a high viscosity.

With viscous friction, the two objects in relative motion are separated by a layer of fluid. Actually, for purposes of discussion, let us say that there are several layers of fluid, as shown in Fig. 6-10. An object of weight *W* moves over a stationary surface, as shown, and the two surfaces are separated by the fluid. Layer *A* adheres to the moving object *W*, and layer *E* adheres to the stationary surface. Thus, there must be relative motion between the layers of oil, and the resistance to this interflow is called *viscous friction*.

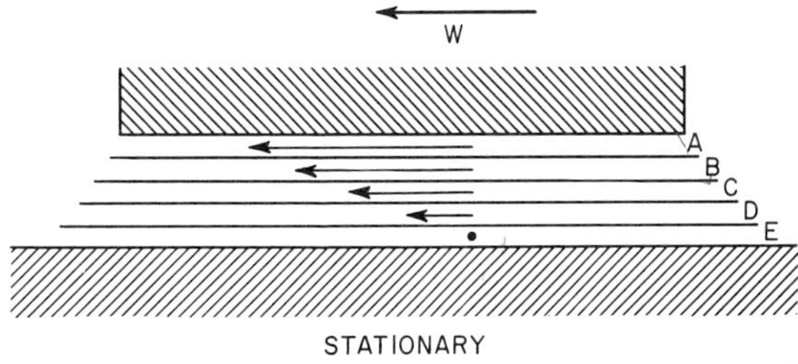

Fig. 6-10. Viscous friction is the friction between layers of fluid moving at different speeds or, as shown, between layers A, B, C, D, and E. W represents a moving object.

§74. Friction horsepower Numerous parts in the engine move in relation to each other: Pistons and rings slide up and down in the cylinders, the camshaft and crankshaft turn in bearings, the crank journal turns within the connecting-rod bearing, the valve-train parts move back and forth, and so on. In the running engine, there is viscous friction at all these points. Power is required to overcome this friction, and this friction loss is called *friction horsepower* (fhp).

The fhp of an engine can be determined by driving the engine with an electric motor. To make the test, the engine is first operated for a while to bring it up to operating temperature. Then, with no fuel in the carburetor and the throttle wide open, the motor drives the engine at various speeds. The electric power required to drive the engine in this manner is a direct measure of the viscous friction in the engine.

The amount of power required to overcome engine friction is somewhat proportional to engine speed. At higher speeds, the power required increases, because the moving parts are moving greater distances per unit of time.

Figure 6-11 shows the relationship between fhp and engine rpm. Note that at 1,000 rpm the fhp is only about 4 hp. But at 2,000 rpm the fhp is 10 hp, and at 4,000 the fhp is about 40 hp.

One of the major causes of fhp in the engine is piston-ring friction. Under some conditions, the friction of the rings on the cylinder walls accounts for 75 percent of all friction losses in the engine.

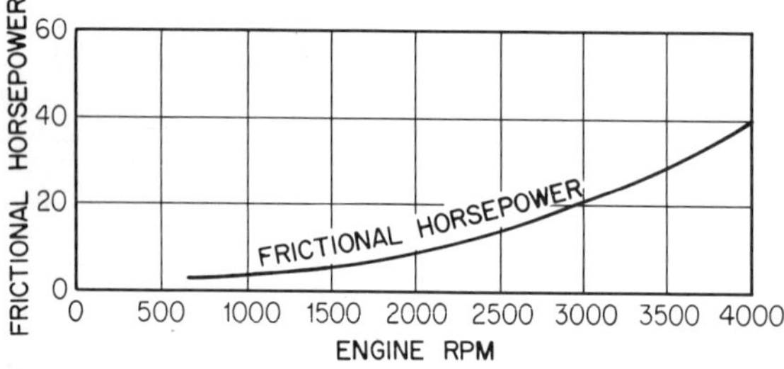

Fig. 6-11. A friction-horsepower (fhp) curve, showing the relationship between fhp and engine speed.

§75. Relating ihp, bhp, and fhp Bhp is the power delivered by the engine; ihp is the power developed against the moving pistons; and fhp is the horsepower used up in overcoming engine friction. The relationship between these three is

$$\text{bhp} = \text{ihp} - \text{fhp}$$

In other words, the horsepower delivered by the engine (bhp) is equal to the horsepower developed in the engine minus the horsepower losses resulting from engine friction.

§76. SAE horsepower The SAE (Society of Automotive Engineers) horsepower rating is used to compare engines on a uniform basis (for tax purposes usually). The formula is

$$\text{SAE hp} = \frac{D^2N}{2.5}$$

where D = diameter of cylinder, or bore
N = number of cylinders

Note that this formula does not consider such factors as mep, stroke, rpm, and so on.

§77. Torque Torque is another very important measure of engine performance. Torque is turning effort. When the piston is moving down on the power stroke, it applies torque to the crankshaft through the connecting rod and crank (Fig. 6-12). The harder the push on the piston, the greater the torque.

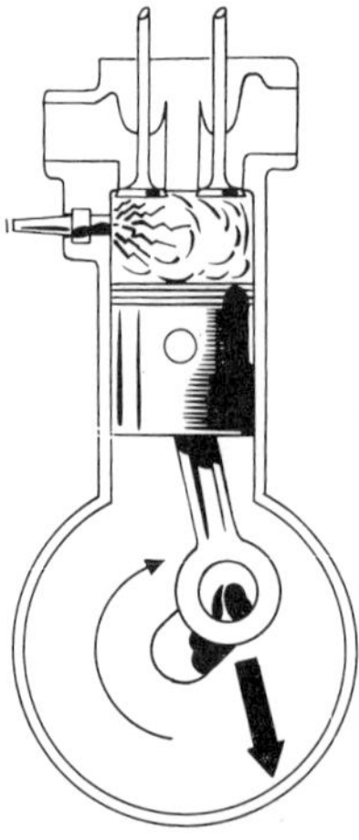

Fig. 6-12. As it moves down on the power stroke, the piston applies torque to the crankshaft.

Torque should not be confused with power. Torque is the twisting effort that the engine supplies through the crankshaft. Power is the rate at which the engine works. Power requires motion. Torque does not. Torque is the force applied times the distance the force is acting from the center of the shaft, or pound-feet. (Remember that work is indicated in foot-pounds.)

§78. Torque compared with bhp The torque that

an engine can develop changes with engine speed. An engine develops more torque at intermediate speeds (with wide-open throttle) than at high speeds. This is because, at the lower speeds, the volumetric efficiency is higher. Thus, there is a greater amount of air-fuel mixture to burn during the power stroke; higher combustion pressures result, and greater torque is applied to the crankshaft.

At higher speeds, volumetric efficiency is lower; combustion pressures are also lower, and thus torque is lower. Also, at high speeds, the piston is moving so much faster that it tends to "keep step" with the increasing pressure as combustion starts; less thrust is exerted on the piston.*

Figure 6-13 shows a typical torque curve of an engine. Note that torque is highest at intermediate speeds, and that it falls off rapidly at higher speeds.

Horsepower also increases with engine speed (Fig. 6-14). This is obviously so because horsepower depends on rpm as well as on torque. Look at the brake-horsepower formula in §67. The *W* and *R* in the formula are pounds of force and distance in feet from the shaft center (or pound-feet torque), while *N* is rpm. Thus, as long as torque and rpm increase, the horsepower output will also increase. Figure 6-14 illustrates this; it gives the horsepower curve of the same engine for which the torque curve is given in Fig. 6-13. Note that at low speeds (400 rpm) the bhp is small (only about 14 bhp). However, the bhp goes up steadily with increasing speed until a maximum of about 110 bhp is reached at around 3,500 rpm. Then, the bhp falls off rapidly. This tapering-off results from the rapid decrease of engine torque in the higher-speed ranges, as well as from the rapid increase of fhp (friction horsepower) at the higher speeds. The relationships can be readily seen in Fig. 6-15, which shows all three curves. Note that the bhp continues to increase for some time even after the torque starts to drop. This is the effect of increasing engine speed. Soon, however, fhp uses up

* The advance mechanism on the ignition distributor is designed to reduce this undesirable effect. It starts the combustion process earlier in the cycle at higher speeds (§107).

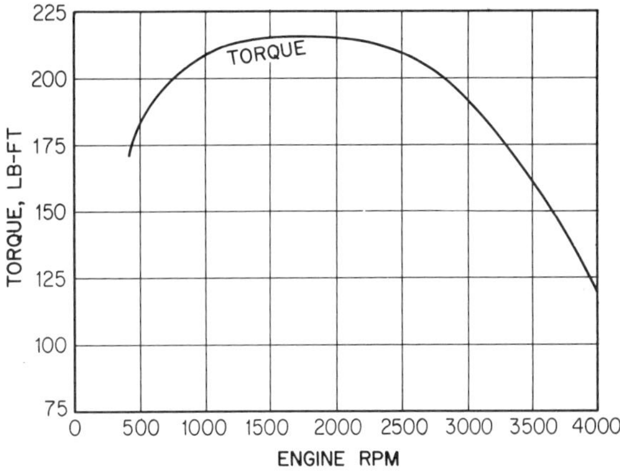

Fig. 6-13. The torque curve of an engine, showing the relationship between torque and speed.

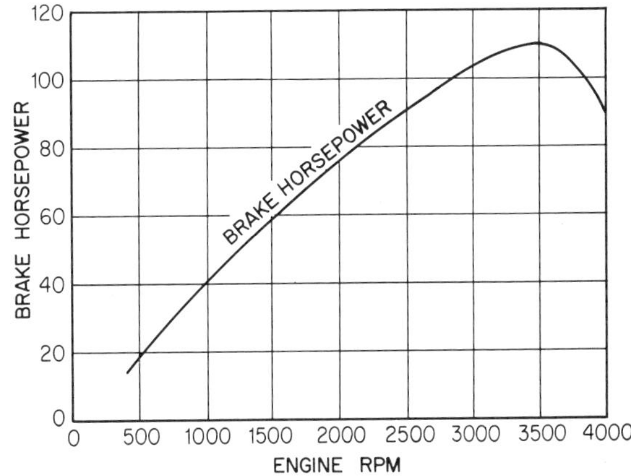

Fig. 6-14. Curve showing relationship between bhp and engine speed.

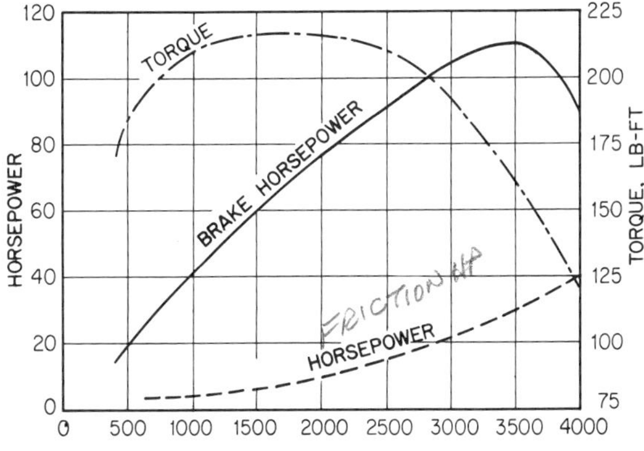

Fig. 6-15. Torque-bhp-fhp curves of an engine.

so much horsepower that the bhp starts falling off. Contributing to this bhp-curve drop is the torque-curve drop.

Note: The curves shown in Figs. 6-13 to 6-15 are for one particular engine only. Different engines have different torque, fhp, and bhp curves. Peaks may occur at higher or lower speeds, and the torque-bhp-fhp-speed relationships may not be as indicated.

In recent years, engineers have come to rely more and more on torque as a measure of engine performance rather than horsepower. For example, it is the torque produced by the engine and delivered to the car wheels that gives the car "zip" during passing and gets it around the other car. The torque curves for late-model, oversquare engines are flatter than for engines of older design. Torque is higher at low speeds and does not fall off so much at high speeds. This is because the bore and valves are larger, giving better volumetric efficiency. At the same time, the shorter stroke reduces engine power losses from piston and ring friction.

There is another advantage to be found in the larger-bore, higher-displacement engines: improved torque at low speeds. That is, these engines produce greater horsepower at lower speeds (because horsepower depends on torque as well as on speed). With greater horsepower at intermediate speeds, it is possible to use a higher gear ratio in the power train so that a lower engine speed will produce the same car speed. In the 1930s, for example, a typical engine had to turn 50 rpm for each mile per hour (mph) of car speed. This meant that to drive a car at 40 mph the engine would have to turn 2,000 rpm. The newer engines, on the other hand, turn only about 35 rpm for each mph of car speed; at 40 mph they would turn only 1,400 rpm. You can see how this materially reduces both frictional horsepower (friction losses) and engine wear.

§79. Mechanical efficiency The mechanical efficiency (N_m) of an engine is the relation between the power delivered (bhp) and the power developed in the engine cylinders (ihp) or

$$N_m = \frac{\text{bhp}}{\text{ihp}}$$

We have already seen (§75) that

$$\text{bhp} = \text{ihp} - \text{fhp}$$

Thus we can write

$$N_m = \frac{\text{ihp} - \text{fhp}}{\text{ihp}}$$

§80. Engine heat losses If it were possible for the engine to operate on an idealized cycle, as described in §58 and Fig. 5-8, there would be no heat gain or loss during the compression stroke and power stroke. Thermal efficiency would therefore be much higher than it actually is, and considerably more energy would be realized from the fuel burned during the power stroke. In actuality, two-thirds or more of the heat energy in the fuel is lost. A rough indication of the energy loss measured during a typical engine test is shown in Fig. 6-16. Note that about 35 percent of the energy is lost as heat to the cooling water and lubricating oil. Another 35 percent is lost in the hot exhaust gases, which still contain much heat energy as they exit from the engine. A 10 percent loss due to engine friction is shown, leaving 20 percent of the total energy in the fuel to actually produce the power output from the engine.

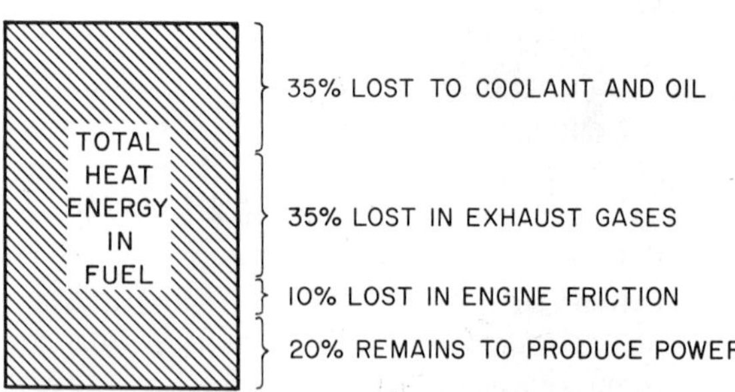

Fig. 6-16. Energy from fuel lost due to various causes in operating engine.

Engineers, recognizing these factors, do have some tricks in engine design that can increase thermal efficiency. For example, larger cylinder bores reduce heat losses somewhat because the heat has a greater distance to travel from the center of the combustion area to the cooler cylinder walls. Also, operating the engine at higher cylinder-wall, piston-head, and cylinder-head temperatures reduces heat losses because the temperature differential between the combustion gases and surrounding engine surfaces is reduced. This creates other problems, however. The lubricating oil must be able to withstand these higher temperatures without breaking down (see Chap. 19). Critical parts such as pistons and valves must be designed and made of materials that can hold up under the higher temperatures. Other factors are also involved, as will be discussed in following chapters on engine design.

SUMMARY

Bore is the diameter of the cylinder, and stroke is the distance that the piston travels in the cylinder. The bore has been increased, and the stroke has been reduced in engines over the years, until now engines are oversquare (the bore is greater than the stroke). A shorter stroke reduces friction losses, inertia and centrifugal loads on bearings, and engine height. A larger bore improves volumetric efficiency, torque characteristics, and intermediate-speed-horsepower output.

Piston displacement is the volume that the piston displaces as it moves from BDC to TDC. The volume remaining above the piston at TDC is called *clearance volume*. Compression ratio is the total volume of the cylinder with the piston at BDC (or piston displacement plus clearance volume) divided by clearance volume. Increasing the compression ratio increases thermal efficiency and power output.

Horsepower (hp) is the rate at which work is done; 1 hp is 33,000 foot-pounds per minute. Indicated horsepower (ihp) is the power that is actually developed inside the engine cylinders, and brake horsepower (bhp) is the power the engine can deliver. Friction horsepower (fhp) is the power used up in overcoming friction in the engine. Thus,

$$\text{bhp} = \text{ihp} - \text{fhp}$$

There are two types of friction: static and kinetic. There are three classes of kinetic friction: dry, greasy, and viscous.

Mechanical efficiency is the relationship between *bhp* and *ihp* or

$$N_m = \frac{\text{bhp}}{\text{ihp}}$$

Up to two-thirds of the energy in the fuel is lost in heat losses to the cooling water and lubricating oil and in the hot exhaust gases. There is also a loss due to friction. Thus, thermal efficiency may be as low as 20 percent. Engineers work to improve thermal efficiency because this means better utilization of the fuel. However, there are limitations imposed by the temperatures at which lubricating oil, valves, pistons, and rings can be worked. Also, heat loss in the exhaust gases is inevitable.

REFERENCE

1. *Engine Test Code, SAE Standard J816a, 1963, in "SAE Handbook" (latest annual edition).*

QUESTIONS

1. Determine the average bore, stroke, piston displacement, clearance volume, and compression ratio of the latest models of passenger cars. Pick half a dozen models of different makes for your averages.

2. *What are some of the advantages of a shorter stroke? A larger bore?*

3. *What is the piston displacement of a 4.2 × 3.5 cylinder?*

4. *If the clearance volume of a 4.2 × 3.5 cylinder is 5.0 cubic inches, what is the compression ratio?*

5. *Write a short paper on the advantages of increasing compression ratios.*

6. *An engine has a compression ratio of 9:1 and a clearance volume of 5.0 cubic inches. Accumulations of carbon in the combustion chamber, after months of adverse service, amount to 1.0 cubic inch per cylinder. What is the effective compression ratio?*

7. *An engine raises 66,000 pounds 50 feet in 20 seconds. Ignoring friction losses, what horsepower is the engine delivering?*

8. *In a Prony-brake test of an engine, the brake arm is 4 feet long, and the load on the scales is 300 pounds at 1,500 rpm. What horsepower is the engine delivering?*

9. *What is the ihp of an eight-cylinder 3 × 4 inch engine which, when running at 2,000 rpm, shows a mep of 360 psi?*

10. *It requires a pull of 30 pounds to keep a 75-pound object moving on a flat surface. What is the coefficient of friction?*

11. *Explain the three classes of kinetic friction. Which is most common in a running engine?*

12. *An engine under test rates 30 fhp at 3,000 rpm while developing 200 bhp at the same speed. What is its ihp under these conditions? What is its mechanical efficiency?*

13. *What is thermal efficiency? Explain the heat losses that keep it low.*

Engine Construction

CHAPTER **7**

This chapter describes in some detail the construction and function of the various engine components. Later chapters analyze the engine components and assembly from the standpoint of design.

§81. Engine cylinder block The cylinder block, on liquid-cooled engines (Fig. 7-1), forms the basic framework of the engine. (In air-cooled engines, the cylinders are often separate parts, as in Fig. 7-6.) Other parts are attached to the cylinder block or assembled in it (Fig. 7-2). The block is cast in one piece from gray iron or iron alloyed with other metals, such as nickel or chromium. Some blocks are cast from aluminum. The engine shown in Fig. 4-20, for example, has been supplied with either a die-cast aluminum or a cast-iron block. The block contains not only the cylinders, but also the water jackets that surround them. In aluminum blocks, cast-iron cylinder sleeves (also called *cylinder liners*) are used. These metals have better wearing qualities than aluminum, so they can better withstand the wearing effects of the pistons and rings moving up and down in the cylinders. In the engine shown in Fig. 4-20, the aluminum block has iron cylinder liners cast into the die-cast block. In some small engines, the cylinder walls are plated with chromium, a very hard metal, to reduce wall wear and lengthen service life.

The casting for the engine block is normally rather intricate, since it contains not only the engine cylinders, but the water jackets that surround them. In addition, passageways are provided to accommodate the valve mechanisms and, on L-head engines (Figs. 4-29 and 7-3), the openings for the intake and exhaust ports. In L-head engines the intake-valve seats are part of the cylinder block, but in many engines the exhaust-valve seats are made of special metal rings (Fig. 7-30) inserted into recesses in the block. Such exhaust-valve-seat inserts are used because they can better withstand the high temperatures of the burned gases passing through the exhaust ports. The lower part of the cylinder block contains the supporting bearings for the engine crankshaft (called the *main bearings*) so that the crankshaft, in effect, is suspended from the bottom of the block (Figs. 7-1 and 7-4).

The upper halves of the crankshaft, or main, bearings are assembled directly into half-round sections in the cylinder block; the lower halves of the main bearings are held in place by bearing caps that are attached to the cylinder block by bolts (Fig. 7-4).

On most engines, the camshaft is supported in the cylinder block by bushings that fit into machined holes in the block (Fig. 4-20). On some engines, the camshaft is located on the cylinder head, as shown in Fig. 4-25 (see also §221).

The intake and exhaust manifolds are attached to the side of the cylinder block on L-head, in-line engines (Fig. 7-5). On L-head, V-8 engines, the intake manifold is located between the two banks of cylinders. In this engine, there are two exhaust manifolds, one on the outside of each bank. On I-head engines, the manifolds are attached to the cylinder head (Figs. 3-1 and 7-2).

Other parts attached to the block include the water pump (attached at the front as shown in Fig. 7-2), the timing-gear or timing-chain cover (at

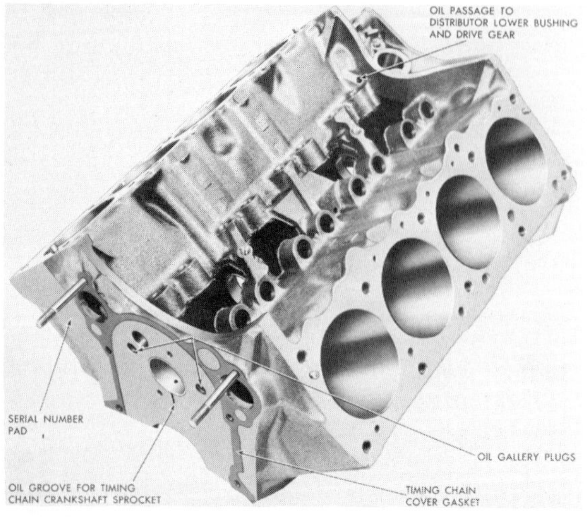

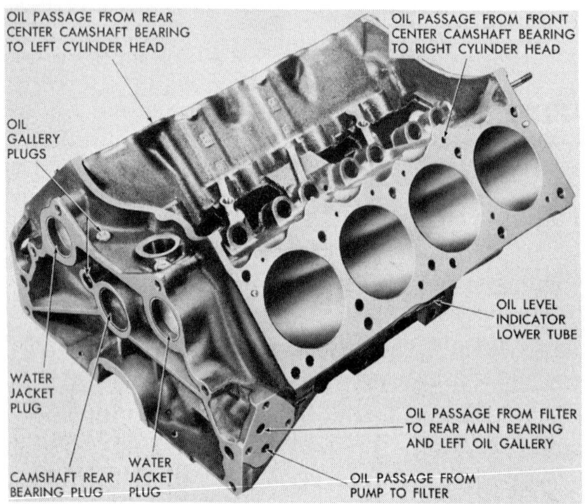

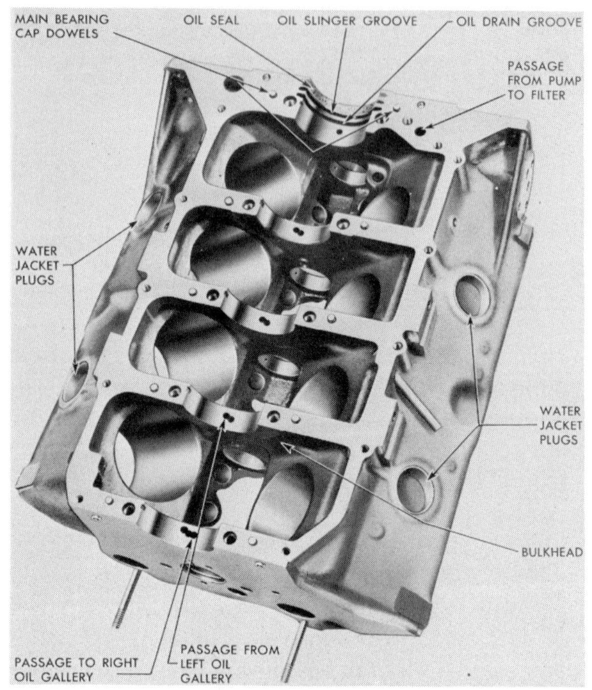

Fig. 7-1. Three views of a cylinder block from a V-8, overhead-valve, liquid-cooled engine, showing the locations of water and oil passages and plugs. (*Pontiac Motor Division of General Motors Corporation*)

the front), the flywheel and clutch housing (at the rear), the ignition distributor, and the fuel pump. The cylinder head mounts on top of the block.

The various parts are attached to the cylinder block with sealing gaskets. Each gasket (§83) is placed between the part and the block. Then, tightening the attaching bolts or nuts flattens the gasket to provide a good seal, which prevents leakage (of water, oil, or gas).

Some parts are attached with bolts; others, with nuts and studs. Studs are threaded at both ends; one end is tightened into a threaded hole in the block, the part to be attached is put into place, and a nut is tightened on the other end of the stud to hold the part in position. In some places, retaining or lock washers are put under the nuts or bolt-heads.

A cylinder from the air-cooled Chevrolet Corvair engine is shown in Fig. 7-6, along with the piston and related parts. The cylinders are installed on the crankcase, and the cylinder head is installed on top of the cylinders. Figure 7-9 shows the cylinder head.

§82. Cylinder heads. The cylinder heads are usually cast in one piece in a manner similar to the way the cylinder block is cast. Iron alloyed with various other metals is often used; the alloys add such desirable characteristics as strength, toughness, and heat conductivity. Aluminum alloy is also used, since this material combines lightness with a high degree of heat conductivity. The latter characteristic is especially desirable because it assures that

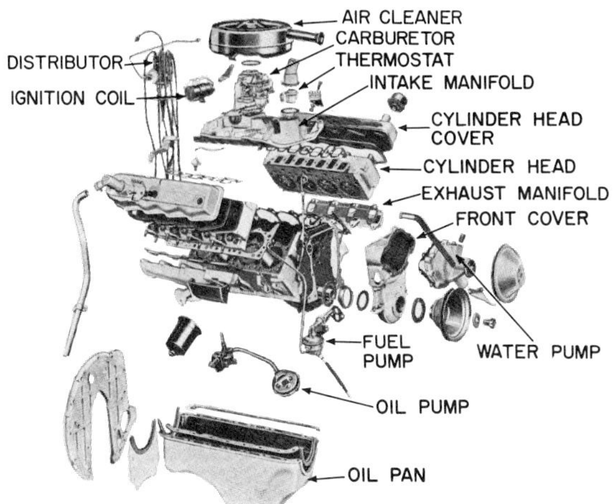

Fig. 7-2. External parts which are attached to an engine block when the engine is assembled. (*Chrysler-Plymouth Division of Chrysler Motors Corporation*)

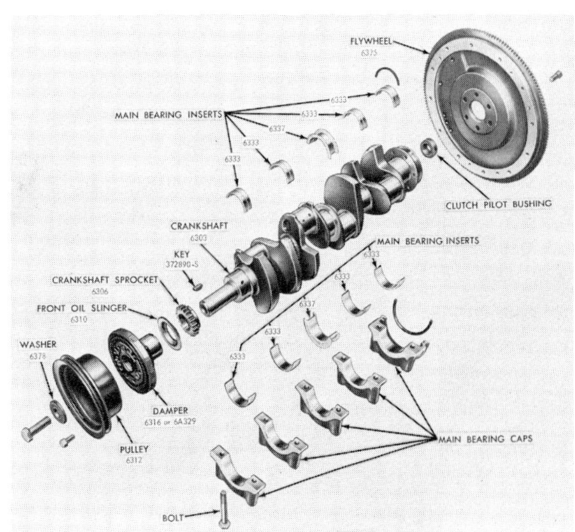

Fig. 7-4. Crankshaft and related parts for a V-8 engine. (*Ford Division of Ford Motor Company*)

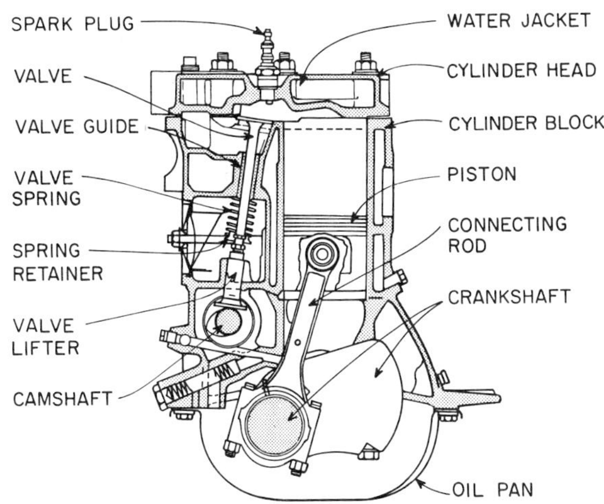

Fig. 7-3. Sectional view of an L-head, in-line engine. (*American Motors Corporation*)

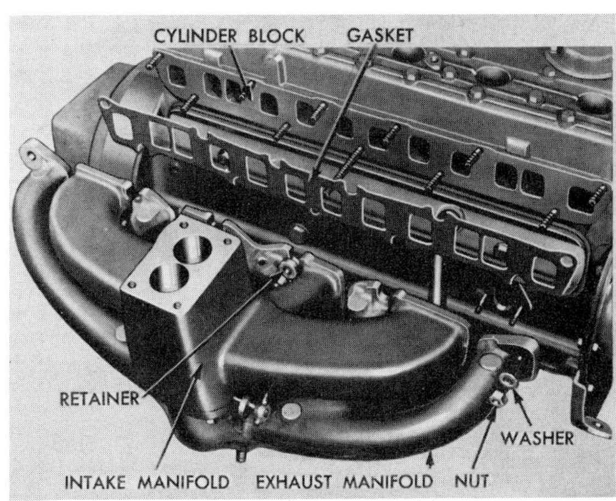

Fig. 7-5. Installation of intake and exhaust manifolds on the cylinder block of a typical L-head engine.

the heat of combustion will be rapidly carried away, preventing the formation of "hot spots," which would cause preignition, or premature ignition, of the air-fuel mixture in the cylinder. Two types of cylinder heads are in general use: the L-head type (Fig. 7-3) and the I-head, or overhead-valve, type (Figs. 7-2 and 7-7).

1. L head. The L-head type of cylinder head, also known as a *flat head*, is a comparatively simple casting. It contains water jackets for cooling, which, in the assembled engine, are connected through openings to the water jackets in the cylinder block. Spark-plug openings are provided, along with pockets into which the valves operate (Fig. 7-3). Each pocket also serves as the top of the combustion chamber; the air-fuel mixture is compressed into the pocket as the piston reaches the end of the compression stroke. It will be noted that the pockets have a rather complex curved surface. This shape has been carefully designed so that the air-fuel mixture, when compressed into the pocket, will be subjected to violent whirling, or turbulence. Turbulence assures a more uniform mixing of the fuel and air, which improves the combustion process and helps prevent local high-pressure, high-temperature areas that would cause detonation, or knocking.

2. *I head.* The I-head, or overhead-valve, type of cylinder head not only contains water jackets for cooling, spark-plug openings, and valve and combustion-chamber pockets, but also contains and supports the valves and valve-operating mechanisms (Figs. 7-2 and 7-7). In addition, on overhead-camshaft engines, the cylinder head also has bearings to support the camshaft and the rocker-arm shafts (Fig. 7-8). It is obvious that the I head is more complex than the L head. However, most automotive engines are of the I-head type. A major reason is that this engine offers a greater opportunity for increasing compression ratios. The I head, since it does carry the intake and exhaust valves, must have additional means of cooling. If you will examine the various engine illustrations in this book, you will note that the water jackets in the I heads are larger than those in the L heads.

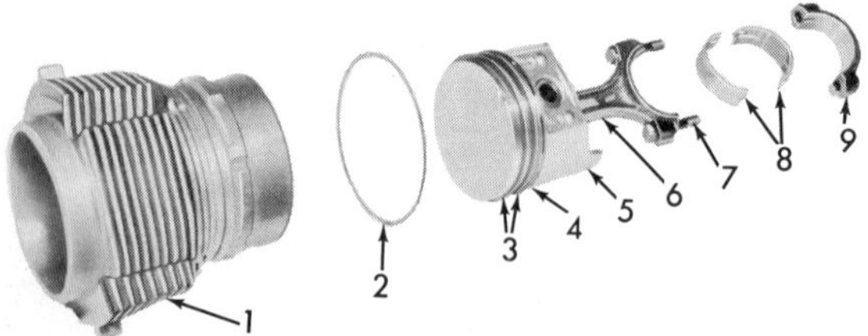

Fig. 7-6. Piston, connecting rod, cylinder, and related parts from a six-cylinder, air-cooled, pancake engine: (1) cylinder, (2) cylinder gasket, (3) compression rings, (4) oil ring, (5) piston, (6) connecting rod, (7) connecting-rod bolt, (8) connecting-rod bearing, (9) connecting-rod cap. (*Chevrolet Motor Division of General Motors Corporation*)

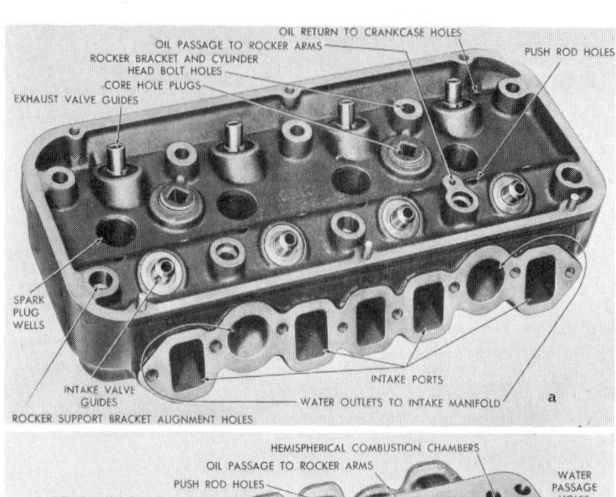

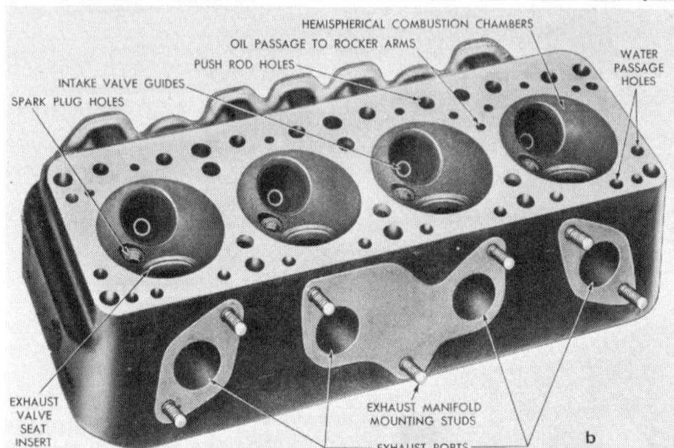

Fig. 7-7. (*a*) Top view of cylinder head from a V-8, overhead-valve engine; (*b*) bottom view. (*Dodge Division of Chrysler Motors Corporation*)

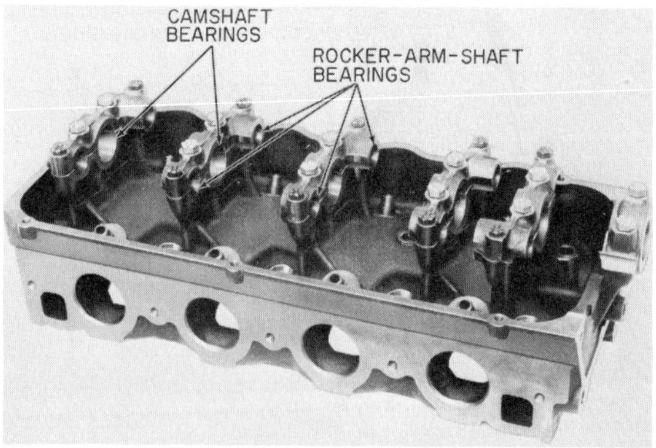

Fig. 7-8. Cylinder head for an overhead camshaft engine, showing bearings to support the camshaft and the rocker-arm-shaft bearings. (*Ford Division of Ford Motor Company*)

3. *Heads for air-cooled engines.* Figure 7-9 shows the cylinder head for the Chevrolet Corvair air-cooled engine. The head mounts on top of three cylinders; thus, the engine uses two cylinder heads. The head carries the valves and rocker arms, just as in other I heads.

§83. Gaskets The joint between the cylinder block and the cylinder head must be tight and able to withstand the pressure and heat developed in the cylinders. For production cars, it is not practical to machine the cylinder-block and cylinder-head surfaces flat and smooth enough to produce such a tight joint. Consequently, gaskets (Fig. 7-10) are used. Head gaskets are made of sheets that are cut out to conform with all water, cylinder, valve, and head-bolt openings in the block and the head. When they are placed in position between the block and the head, tightening of the head bolts squeezes the soft metal between the head and the cylinder block so that the joint is effectively sealed. Head gaskets are made of several materials. They may be made of plain copper, two thin copper sheets with asbestos between, steel and copper sheets with asbestos between, or crimped steel. In the last type, the crimping is flattened out as the head bolts are tightened, which produces the sealing effect. As a rule, gaskets can be used only once. If they are removed and reinstalled, they cannot be further compressed to provide an effective seal. Gaskets are also used to seal joints between other engine parts, for example, between the oil pan and cylinder block and between the cylinder head or block and manifolds.

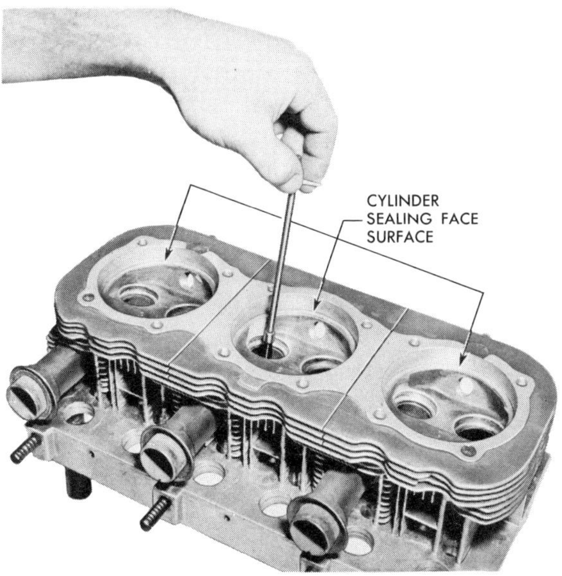

Fig. 7-9. One of the two cylinder heads used on a six-cylinder, air-cooled, pancake engine. The tool is being used to clean the valve-guide bores. (*Chevrolet Motor Division of General Motors Corporation*)

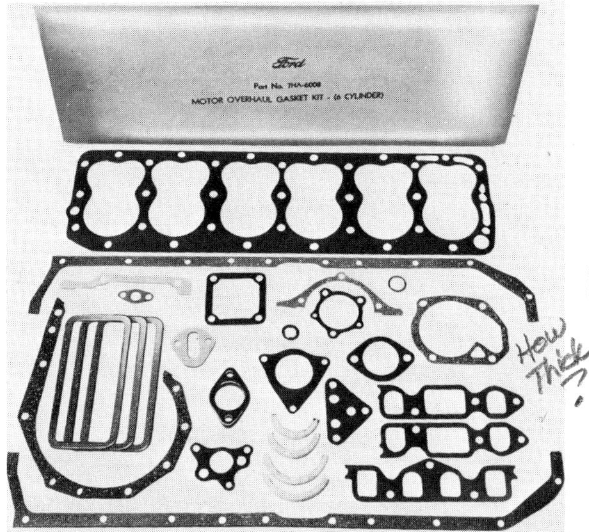

Fig. 7-10. Motor-overhaul-gasket kit for a six-cylinder engine, showing the various gaskets used in the engine. (*Ford Division of Ford Motor Company*)

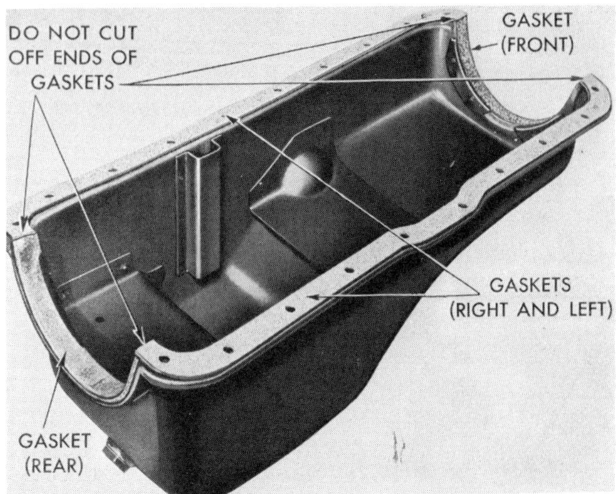

Fig. 7-11. Oil pan with gaskets in place, ready for pan replacement. (*Chrysler-Plymouth Division of Chrysler Motors Corporation*)

§84. Oil pan The oil pan, usually formed of pressed steel (Fig. 7-11), provides a sump, or

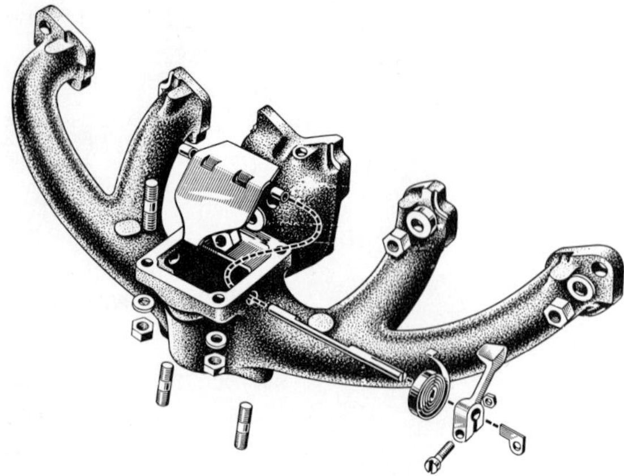

Fig. 7-12. Exhaust manifold for a six-cylinder, L-head, in-line engine with the heat-control valve and its parts in disassembled view.

reservoir, for the engine lubricating oil. The oil pan holds from 4 to 9 quarts of oil, depending on the engine. Most passenger car engines take about 4 quarts; the high-performance and heavy-duty engines require larger reservoirs of engine oil and thus oil pans or separate oil reservoirs of larger capacity. The oil pump in the lubricating system pumps oil from the pan to all working parts. The oil drains off and runs down into the pan, where the oil pump draws it up and sends it back through the lubricating system. The oil pan is attached to the underside of the cylinder block, with gaskets placed between the pan and the block to produce a tight seal. On many engines an oil strainer or filter is placed in the oil pan, and the oil must pass through it before entering the oil pump. The lubricating system, which includes the pump, filter, and oil lines, is considered in detail in Chaps. 8 and 19.

§85. Exhaust manifold The exhaust manifold is essentially a tube for carrying the burned gases away from the engine cylinders. On L-head, in-line engines the exhaust manifold is bolted to the side of the cylinder block (Fig. 7-12). On I-head, in-line engines the exhaust manifold is bolted to the side of the cylinder head. On V-8 engines there are two exhaust manifolds, one for each bank of cylinders. The exhaust manifolds are bolted to the outsides of the two banks (to the block in L-head engines, and to the cylinder heads in I-head engines). On some cars, they are interconnected by a crossover pipe, and they exhaust through a common muffler and tail pipe. On other cars, each manifold is connected to a separate exhaust pipe, muffler, and tail pipe (Fig. 7-13). The exhaust manifold normally is tied in closely with the intake manifold in order to provide a certain amount of heat transfer from the exhaust manifold to the intake manifold during engine warm-up. This improves vaporization of the fuel and provides better initial engine performance just after the engine is started.

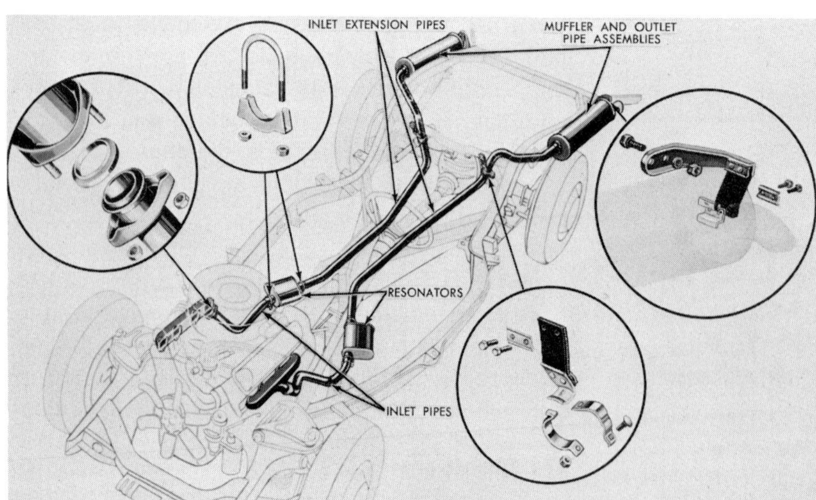

Fig. 7-13. Dual-exhaust system for a V-8 engine. Each bank of cylinders has its own exhaust system. The circles show details of assembly and attachment. (*Lincoln-Mercury Division of Ford Motor Company*)

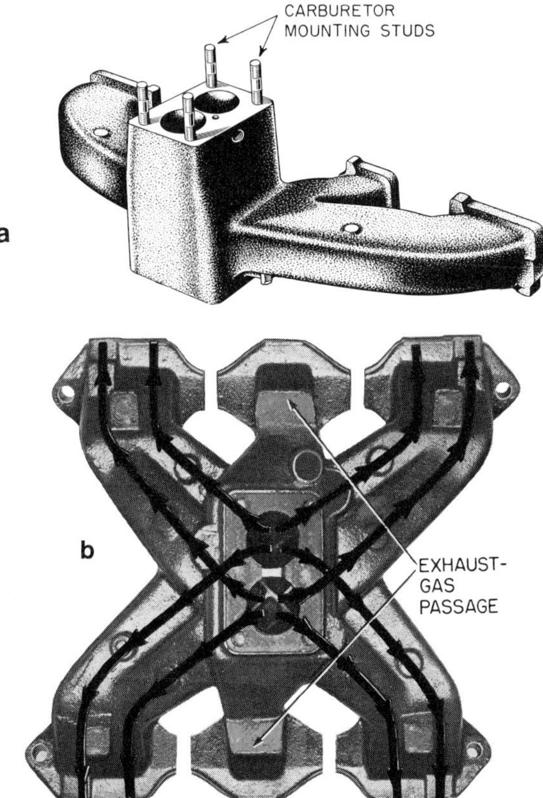

Fig. 7-14. (*a*) Intake manifold for an L-head, in line, six-cylinder engine; (*b*) intake manifold for an I-head, V-8 engine. The white arrows in (*b*) show the air-fuel-mixture flow between the two barrels of the carburetor and the eight cylinders in the engine. The central passage connects between the two exhaust manifolds; exhaust gas flows through this passage during engine warm-up. (*Studebaker Corporation*)

Dual-exhaust system. The dual-exhaust system used on one V-8 engine is shown in Fig. 7-13. Each exhaust manifold exhausts into a separate exhaust pipe which, in turn, exhausts into its own muffler, resonator, and tail pipe. The resonators further reduce exhaust noises; they are, in effect, secondary mufflers. The use of two separate exhaust systems, one for each bank of cylinders, improves the "breathing" ability of the engine, allowing it to exhaust more freely. This tends to reduce the amount of exhaust gas remaining in the cylinder at the end of the exhaust stroke, and thus engine performance is improved.

§86. Intake manifold Essentially, the intake manifold (Fig. 7-14) is a tube for carrying the air-fuel mixture from the carburetor to the engine intake-valve ports. The carburetor is normally mounted in a central position on the intake manifold. The intake manifold is attached to the side of the cylinder block on L-head, in-line engines, and to the side of the cylinder head on I-head, in-line engines. On L-head, V-8 engines the intake manifold is situated between the two banks of cylinders and is attached to each bank of cylinders in the block. On I-head, V-8 engines, the intake manifold is also situated between the two banks of cylinders, but it is attached to the insides of the two cylinder heads. Figure 7-7 shows the intake ports on an I-head from a V-8 engine, over which the intake

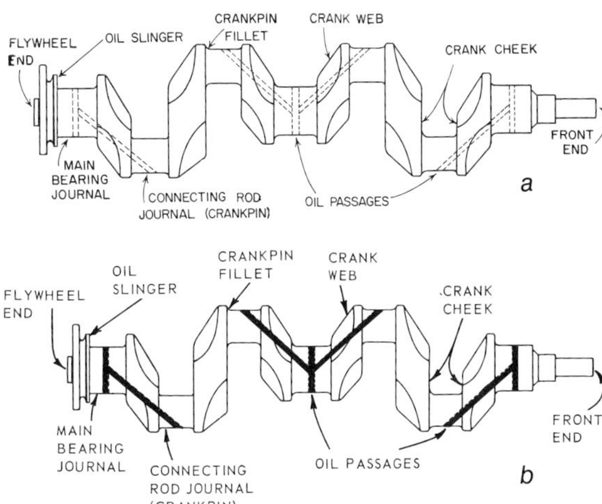

Fig. 7-15. (*a*) Line drawing of a typical crankshaft, showing the names of the parts; (*b*) cutaway view of a crankshaft for a V-8 engine. Note the oil passages drilled to the crankpins for lubricating rod bearings. (*Johnson Bronze Company and Ford Division of Ford Motor Company*)

manifold is attached. A gasket is used between the intake manifold and the mating surface of the block, or head. Figure 7-14*b* shows an intake manifold from an I-head, V-8 engine. A two-barrel carburetor mounts on the intake manifold, each barrel supplying four of the eight cylinders with air-fuel mixture.

A two-barrel carburetor is, in effect, two separate carburetors assembled together. Each barrel has its own venturi, throttle valve, and fuel nozzles. (See Chap. 17 for more information on carburetors.) The arrows in Fig. 7-14*b* indicate the pattern of air-fuel distribution from the two carburetor barrels to the eight cylinders of the engine. Note that each carburetor barrel supplies four cylinders. This arrangement permits a very even distribution of air-fuel mixture; each cylinder receives its "share," and no cylinder is starved.

Many V-8 engines use four-barrel carburetors, often called "quad" (for the number four) carburetors. In these carburetors, two of the barrels make up the primary side, and the other pair form the secondary side. For most operating conditions, the primary side takes care of the engine requirements. However, for acceleration and high-power operation, the secondary side supplies additional air-fuel mixture. (Chapter 17 describes carburetors in detail.)

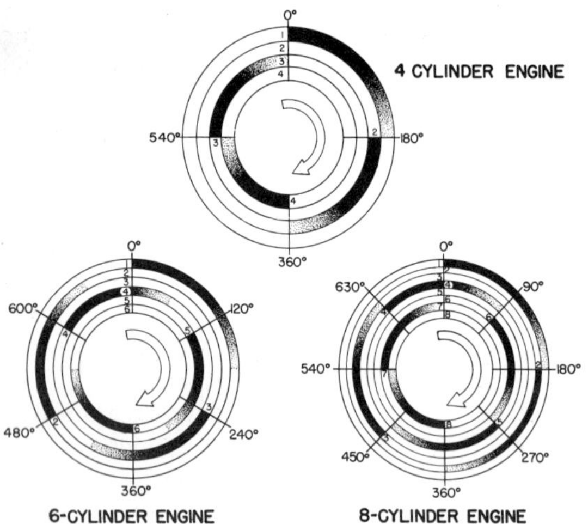

Fig. 7-16. Power impulses in four-, six-, and eight-cylinder engines during two crankshaft revolutions. The complete circle represents two crankshaft revolutions, or 720 degrees. Less power is delivered toward the end of the power stroke, as indicated by lightening of the shaded areas that show power impulses. Note the power overlap on six- and eight-cylinder engines.

§87. Crankshaft The crankshaft is a one-piece casting or forging of heat-treated alloy steel which is of considerable mechanical strength (Figs. 7-4 and 7-15). The crankshaft, it will be remembered, takes the downward thrust of the piston during the power stroke. Pressure exerted by the pistons through the connecting rods against the crankpins on the crankshaft causes the shaft to rotate. This rotary motion is transmitted through the power train to the car wheels. Crankshafts generally have drilled oil passages (Fig. 7-15) through which oil can flow from the main bearings to the connecting-rod bearings (see §91 on bearing lubrication).

In the assembled engine, the front end of the crankshaft carries three devices. One of these is a gear, or sprocket, that drives the camshaft (Fig. 7-26); the camshaft is driven at one-half the speed of the crankshaft. A second device is the vibration damper (see §89), which combats torsional vibration in the crankshaft. As a part of the vibration damper, there is a pulley with one or more grooves. V belts fit these grooves and drive the engine fan and water pump as well as the alternator. On cars equipped with power steering, there is an additional groove in the pulley; this additional groove is fitted with a V belt that drives the power-steering hydraulic pump. In cars equipped with air-conditioning, there may also be another groove for belt-driving the compressor.

§88. Flywheel The flow of power from the engine is not smooth. Although the power strokes from the various cylinders may overlap to some extent in engines with six or more cylinders, there are periods when more power is being delivered to the crankshaft than at other times (Fig. 7-16). When more power is being delivered, the crankshaft tends to speed up; with less power, it tends to slow down. This would produce a roughly running engine if it were not for the flywheel. The flywheel, a comparatively heavy wheel bolted to the rear end of the crankshaft (Fig. 7-4), tends to resist any change of speed because of its *inertia*. Inertia is the property that causes a body to resist any attempt to change its speed or direction of motion.

Fig. 7-17. Arrangement of one of the center main, or crankshaft, bearings. The engine is lying on its side; the bearing cap has been removed. Connecting rods have also been removed. (*Chrysler-Plymouth Division of Chrysler Motors Corporation*)

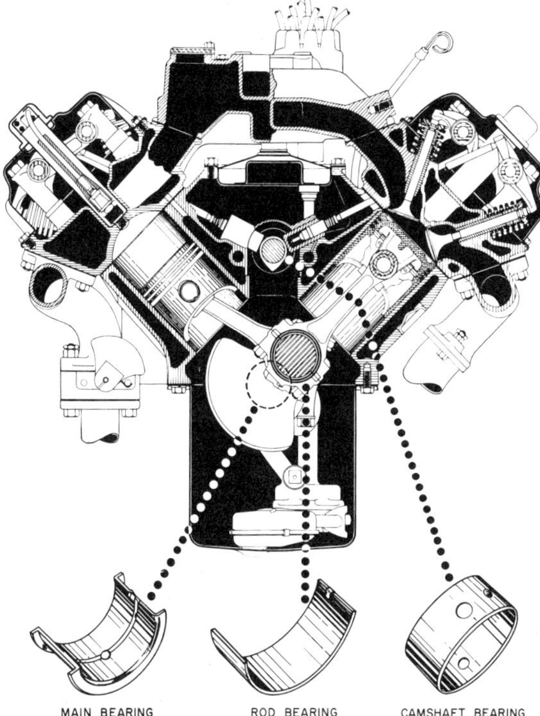

Fig. 7-18. Main, connecting-rod, and camshaft-bearing locations in a V-8 engine. (*Federal-Mogul-Bower Bearings, Inc.*)

The flywheel absorbs power during the intervals that the engine attempts to speed up. During the intervals when less power is produced by the engine, the flywheel resists the engine's attempts to slow down by giving up part of its energy of rotation. In addition to this function, the flywheel has gear teeth around its outer rim that mesh with the cranking-motor drive pinion when the cranking motor is operated to crank the engine for starting. On installations that use a clutch, the rear face of the flywheel also serves as the driving member of the engine clutch.

§89. Torsional-vibration damper The transmission of the power impulses to the crankshaft tends to set up torsional vibration in the crankshaft. When a piston moves down on the power stroke, it imparts considerable force to the crankpin, to which it is connected by the connecting rod. This force tends to twist the crankshaft (the shaft is actually twisted slightly). When the end of the power stroke is reached, the push against the crank is relieved, so the shaft, having been twisted, attempts to return to its original shape. It acts as a spring, however, and overrides this position, going beyond the original shape and twisting slightly in the opposite direction. It then returns, overriding in the other direction. This sets up an oscillating motion within the crankshaft, which is repeated with every power stroke. If this torsional vibration were not controlled, succeeding power impulses would continue to add to the original oscillations of the shaft until, at certain speeds, the shaft might be broken by excessive twisting. To control this torsional vibration, devices variously called *torsional-vibration dampers, torsional*

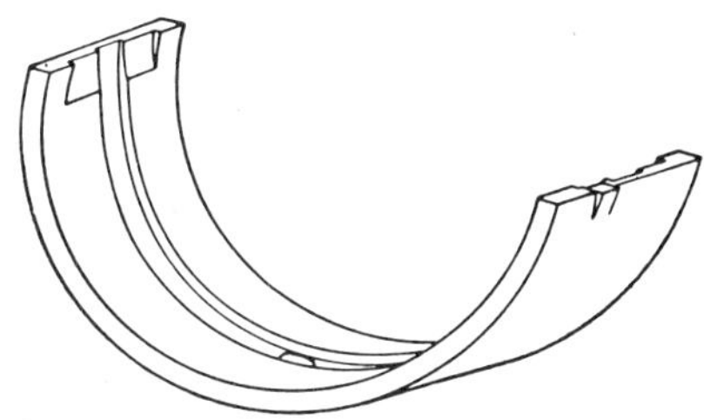

Fig. 7-19. Typical sleeve-type bearing half. (*Federal-Mogul-Bower Bearings, Inc.*)

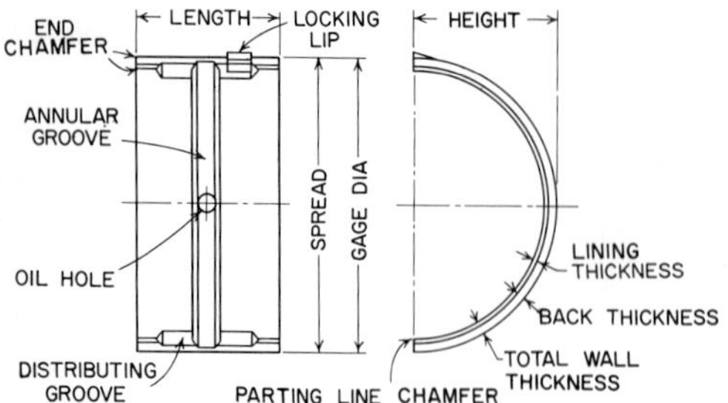

Fig. 7-20. Typical sleeve-type bearing half with its parts named. Many bearings do not have annular and distributing grooves. (*Federal-Mogul-Bower Bearings, Inc.*)

balancers, or *crankshaft-torque impulse neutralizers* are used. They are usually mounted to the front end of the crankshaft (Fig. 7-4) and include the fan-belt pulley.

One type of torsional-vibration damper consists of two parts, a small damper flywheel and the pulley, bonded to each other by a rubber insert about 1/4 inch thick. The pulley is mounted on the front end of the crankshaft. As the crankshaft tends to speed up or slow down, the damper flywheel imposes a dragging effect (because of its inertia). This effect, which slightly flexes the rubber insert, tends to hold the pulley and crankshaft to a constant speed. The action tends to check the twist-untwist, or torsional vibration, of the crankshaft. (This is discussed further in §190.)

§90. Engine bearings In the engine, there must be relative motion between the piston and the connecting rod, between the connecting rod and the crankpin on the crankshaft, and between the crankshaft and the supporting bearings in the cylinder block. At all these points (as well as at other places in the engine) bearings must be installed (Figs. 7-17 and 7-18). These bearings are called *sleeve bearings* because they are in the shape of a sleeve that fits around the rotating journal. Connecting-rod and crankshaft, or "main," bearings are of the split, or half, type; that is, the bearing is split into two halves. Figure 7-19 illustrates a typical sleeve-type bearing half. With main bearings, the upper half is assembled into the counterbore in the cylinder block, and the lower half is held in place in the bearing cap. Figure 7-17 shows the lower bearing half and bearing cap. Figure 7-21 shows the bearings (Nos. 4 and 7) used in a connecting rod (in disassembled and assembled views). The big-end bearing is the split type, but the piston-pin bearing is not; it is the full-round or bushing type.

§91. Engine-bearing lubrication The engine bearings are flooded with oil by the lubricating system. For example, the bearing shown in Fig. 7-20 has an oil hole that aligns with an oil hole in the engine block. Oil feeds through this hole constantly, keeping the annular groove and the distributing grooves in the bearing filled with oil. Oil constantly feeds from these grooves onto the

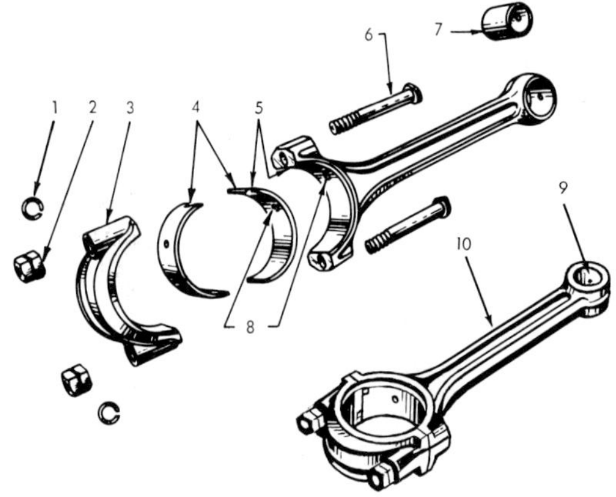

Fig. 7-21. Connecting rod with bearing and a bearing cap in disassembled view (top) and assembled view (bottom). (*Chrysler-Plymouth Division of Chrysler Motors Corporation*)

1. Cap-bolt-nut lock washer
2. Cap-bolt nut
3. Cap
4. Rod bearings
5. Tongue and groove
6. Cap bolt
7. Piston-pin bearing
8. Oil holes
9. Oil hole
10. Assembled rod

bearing surfaces. The oil works its way outward to the edges of the bearing. As it reaches the outer edges, it is thrown off and falls back into the oil pan. Thus oil is constantly circulating across the faces of the bearings in the engine. Not all bearings have or need annular and distributing grooves.

One function of the oil, of course, is to provide lubrication; that is, the bearing and rotating jour-

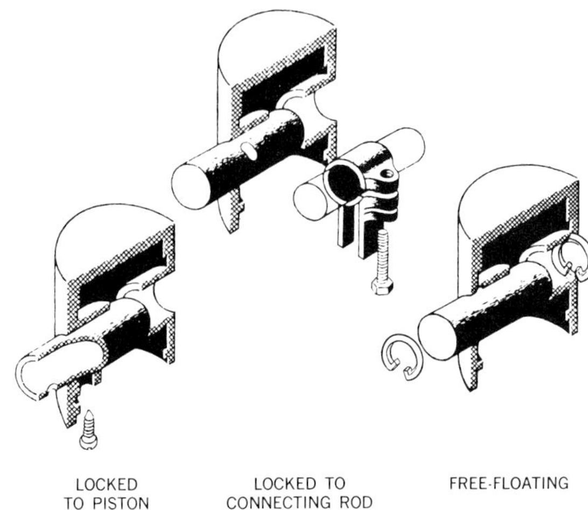

Fig. 7-22. Three piston-pin arrangements.

nal are separated by a film of oil so that there is no actual metal-to-metal contact. In addition, the oil helps to cool the bearing. The oil is relatively cool as it comes from the oil pan; as it spreads across the bearing and passes off the bearing edges, it warms up, thus removing heat from the bearing. This keeps the bearings at lower operating temperatures. A third function of the oil is to act as a flushing medium. It tends to flush out particles of dirt or grit that may have worked into the bearing (and other engine parts). These particles are then carried back to the oil pan by the circulating oil and are removed from the oil by the oil filter, or screen.

In addition to these functions, the "throwoff" of oil from the engine bearings helps to lubricate other engine parts. For example, the cylinder walls, pistons, and rings are lubricated by the oil that is thrown onto the walls by the rotating crankshaft and connecting rods.

§92. Connecting rod The connecting rod (Fig. 7-21) is attached at one end to a crankpin on the crankshaft, and at the other end to a piston (through a piston pin or wrist pin). The connecting rod must combine great strength and rigidity with light weight. It must be strong enough to maintain rigidity when carrying the thrust of the piston during the power stroke. At the same time, it must be as light as possible so that the centrifugal and inertia loads on the bearings will be no greater than necessary.

The crankpin end of the connecting rod (rod big end) is provided with a split-type sleeve bearing, as shown in Fig. 7-21. It is attached to the crankpin by means of the bearing cap, rod bolts, and nuts.

The piston end of the connecting rod (rod small end) is attached to the piston by means of a *piston pin* (also called a *wrist pin*). Bosses are provided in the piston (Fig. 7-22), with holes into which the piston pin is assembled. The pin also goes through the bearing provided for it in the connecting rod.

Three methods are used to attach the piston and the connecting rod with the piston pin (Fig. 7-22). One method locks the piston pin in the piston by a lock bolt. On this type of installation, the connecting rod has a sleeve bearing that provides a bearing surface between the rod and the pin, so that the rod can rock back and forth on the pin.

A second design provides a press fit of the piston pin in the connecting rod. The press fit is tight enough to prevent the piston pin from moving out of position. (This is a commonly used design in American car engines.) There are sleeve bearings in the two piston bosses in which the pin can turn back and forth.

A third design has sleeve bearings in both the piston bosses and the connecting rod, the pin not being locked to either. In this latter design, the pin is prevented from moving out and scoring the cylinder walls by means of *lock rings* (also called *snap rings*) in the piston bosses (Fig. 7-23).

To provide lubrication of the piston pin, an oil-passage hole is often drilled the entire length of the connecting rod from the crankpin-journal bearing to the piston-pin bearing. A hole in the rod bearing (not the cap bearing) feeds oil to the connecting-rod oil passage from oil lines drilled in the crankshaft. Oil circulates through the connecting-rod oil passage to the piston-pin bearing. On some applications, a second hole is drilled on one side of the connecting rod. This hole is called the *oil-spit* hole because, as the crankshaft rotates within the bearing, an oil-passage hole in the crankshaft indexes with this hole. Oil feeds through

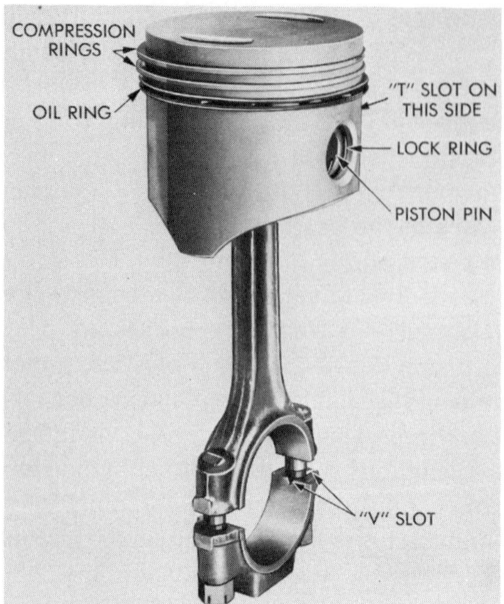

Fig. 7-23. Piston and connecting-rod assembly of the type that uses lock rings to hold the piston pin in position in the piston and connecting rod. (*Dodge Division of Chrysler Motors Corporation*)

so that for a moment oil spits, or streams, from the hole in the connecting rod. This oil is thrown against the cylinder wall to provide additional cylinder-wall lubrication. The holes are arranged to index just as the piston approaches TDC (top dead center); thus, a large area of the cylinder wall is covered with oil.

On many V-8 engines, cylinder walls and piston pins are lubricated by oil jets from opposing connecting rods. That is, each rod has a groove, or hole, that indexes with an oil-passage hole in the crank journal at every crankshaft revolution. When this happens, a jet of oil spurts into the opposing cylinder in the other cylinder bank.

To maintain good engine balance, connecting rods and caps are carefully matched in sets for engines. All rods in an engine must have the same weight; if they do not, noticeable vibration may result. In original assembly, rods and caps are individually matched to each other and usually carry identifying numbers so that they will not be mixed if the engine is disassembled for service. They must not be mixed during any service job, since this could result in poor bearing fit and bearing failure.

§93. Pistons and piston rings Essentially, the piston is a long cylinder that is open at the bottom and closed at the top, and that is attached to the connecting rod at an intermediate point (Figs. 7-22 and 7-23). The piston moves up and down in the engine cylinder, compressing the air-fuel mixture, transmitting the combustion pressure to the crankpin through the connecting rod, forcing out the burned gases on the exhaust stroke, and producing a vacuum in the cylinder that "draws in" the air-fuel mixture on the intake stroke. The piston may seem to be a fairly simple part, but actually it has been the subject of possibly more study and design than any other engine part. It must be light so as to keep inertia loads to a minimum, but it must also be rigid and strong enough to take the punishing heat and pressure developed in the combustion chambers. (Piston design is described in Chap. 12.)

§94. Piston rings A good seal must be maintained between the piston and the cylinder walls so that "blow-by" is prevented. "Blow-by" is a word used to describe the escape of burned gases from the combustion chamber, past the piston,

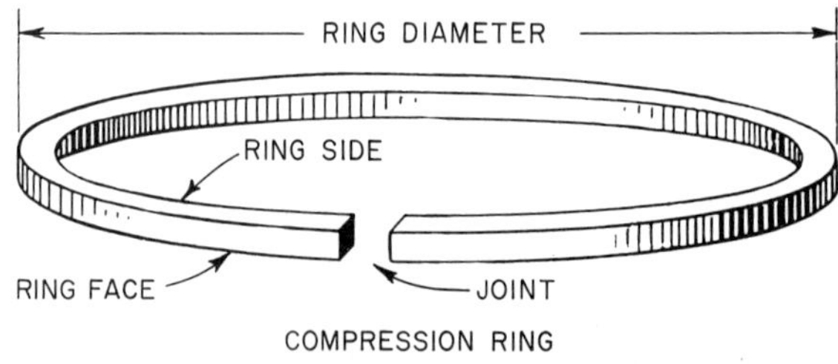

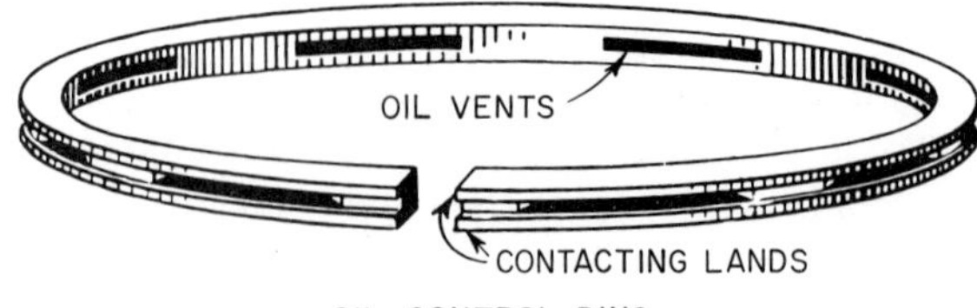

Fig. 7-24. A compression ring (top) and an oil-control ring (bottom), with the various parts named. (*Sealed Power Corporation*)

into the crankcase. In other words, these gases "blow by" the piston. They represent a loss of energy because they do not contribute to engine operation. Instead, they tend to damage the lubricating oil in the oil pan by adulteration. It would be difficult to machine a piston to fit the cylinder accurately enough to prevent excessive blow-by. Even if this were possible, the differences in expansion between the cylinder and the piston during engine operation, caused by variations in temperature, would change the fit so that it would be either too loose or too tight.

Piston rings, assembled into grooves in the piston as shown in Fig. 7-23, are used to provide a good seal so that blow-by is kept at a minimum. Also, they seal in the compressed air-fuel mixture, thus maintaining good compression. Piston rings also perform a second function: they scrape oil off the cylinder walls on the piston downstrokes (power and intake). This prevents excessive amounts of oil from working up past the piston and getting into the combustion chamber. Oil in the combustion chamber burns, leaving a residue of carbon that fouls spark plugs, valves, and piston rings. Finally, piston rings perform a third function: they help cool the piston by transmitting a considerable amount of heat from the piston to the cylinder walls. The cylinder walls are cooled by the water circulating in the water jackets, and this cooling effect is thus carried through the rings to the piston. This helps guard against excessive and possibly damaging piston temperatures.

Piston rings on modern engines are of two types, according to their purpose: compression rings and oil-control rings. There are usually three or more rings on a piston. The upper rings are of the compression type and have the job of sealing in compression and preventing blow-by. The lower rings are of the oil-control type and have the job of controlling the oil on the cylinder walls. That is, these rings scrape off the excess oil and return it to the crankcase, leaving only enough oil on the cylinder walls to provide piston and ring lubrication.

Figure 7-24 shows a compression ring (top) and an oil-control ring (bottom), naming the various parts. Note that the rings have a joint (they are split) so that they can be expanded and slipped over the piston head into the recessed grooves that are cut in the piston.

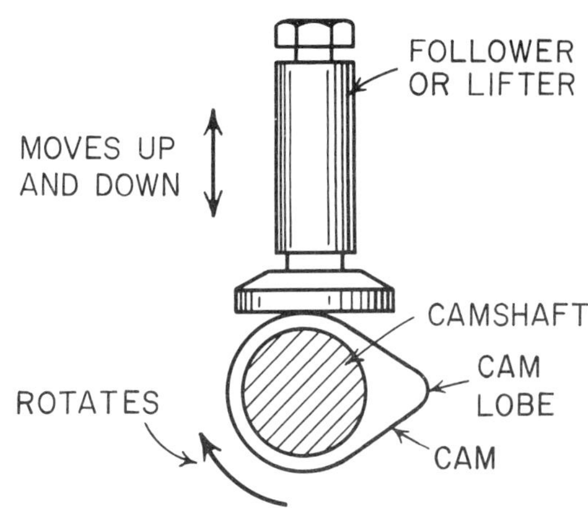

Fig. 7-25. A simple cam and follower, or lifter. As the cam revolves, the follower follows the cam surface by moving up and down.

Two compression rings are used on a piston (instead of only one) because more than one ring is required to do the job. For example, the top compression ring may seal in most of the combustion pressure, but the second ring is required to complete the job. Even with two rings, some slight

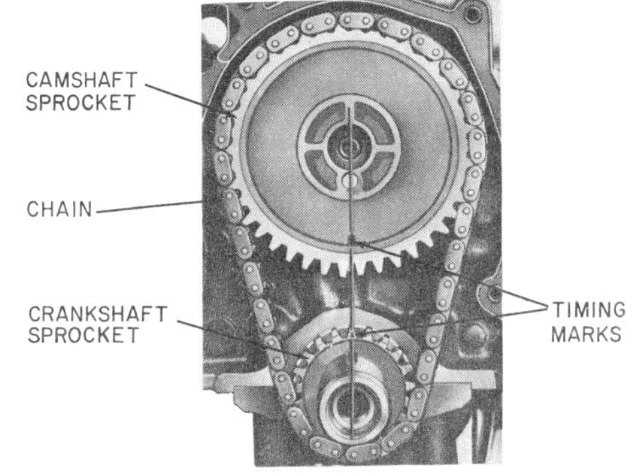

Fig. 7-26. Crankshaft and camshaft sprockets, using a chain drive and showing the timing marks on the sprockets. Note that the larger of the two sprockets is on the camshaft, making it turn at one-half crankshaft speed. (*Ford Motor Company*)

Fig. 7-27. Camshaft and crankshaft gears to drive the camshaft. The mechanic is checking the clearance, or backlash, between the gear teeth. (*General Motors Corporation*)

amount of blow-by may be experienced. However, two rings keep it down to an unimportant minimum (when rings, cylinder wall, and other engine parts are in good condition). Most automobile engines have two compression rings, but some heavy-duty engines have more.

Two oil-control rings are used on some engines (most use only one) to provide adequate oil control. The lower ring removes most of the oil from the cylinder wall, and then the upper oil-control ring removes the remainder of the excess oil. Actually, a thin film of oil is left on the cylinder wall. If *all* the oil were removed, actual metal-to-metal contact between the rings and the wall would result, causing very rapid ring and wall failure.

Initially, the rings are of a somewhat larger diameter than they are in the cylinder. When they are placed in the cylinder, the rings are compressed so that the joints are nearly closed. Compressing the rings into the cylinder in this way places an initial tension on them, and they press tightly against the cylinder wall.

§95. Cams and camshafts A cam is a device that can change rotary motion into linear, or straight-line, motion. The cam has one or more high spots, or lobes; a follower riding on the cam will move

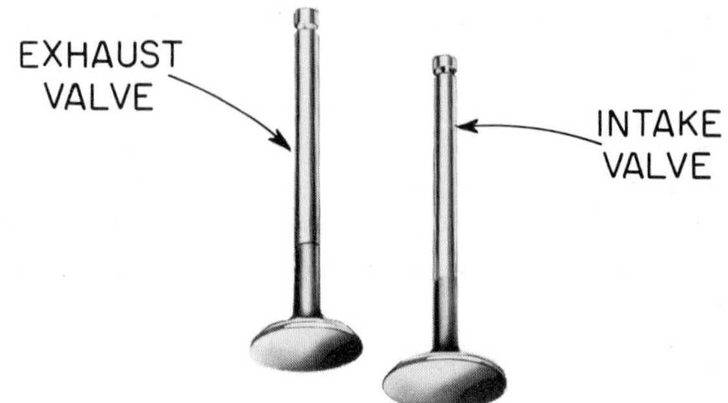

Fig. 7-28. Typical poppet valves. (*Ford Motor Company*)

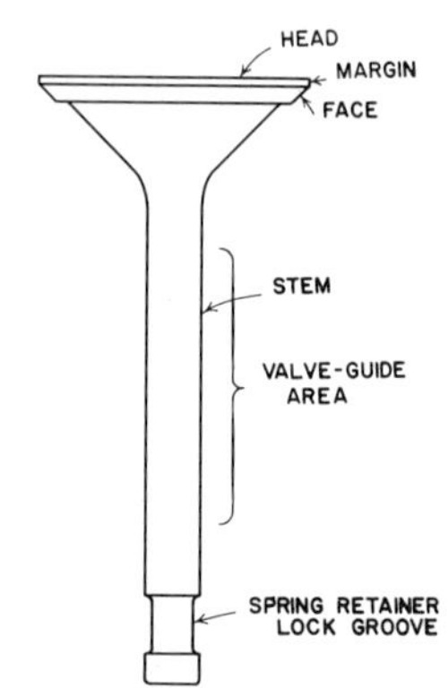

Fig. 7-29. Valve with the parts named.

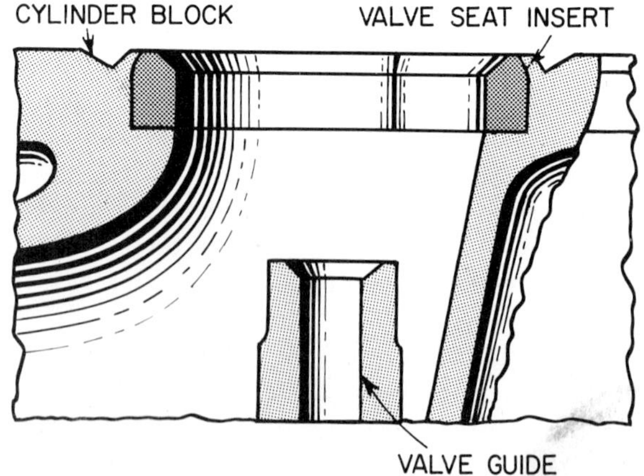

Fig. 7-30. Cutaway view of a valve-seat insert in cylinder block. The insert is indicated by an arrow. In I-head engines, the insert is in the cylinder head. (*Chrysler-Plymouth Division of Chrysler Motors Corporation*)

away from or toward the camshaft as the cam rotates (Fig. 7-25).

In the engine, cams are used to control the opening and closing of the intake and exhaust valves. Figures 3-10 and 4-28 show the valve mechanisms (also called *valve trains*) on L-head and I-head engines. The cams are formed as integral sections of the camshaft; each cam has one lobe, or high spot. There are two cams for each engine cylinder, one each for the intake valve and the exhaust valve. In addition, the camshaft has another cam (or eccentric) to operate the fuel pump, as well as a gear to drive the ignition distributor and the oil pump. The camshaft is driven from the crankshaft by sprockets and a chain (Fig. 7-26), or by two gears (Fig. 7-27). The camshaft sprocket or gear is twice as large as the crankshaft sprocket, or gear. This gives a 1:2 gear ratio: the camshaft turns at half the speed of the crankshaft (four-stroke-cycle engine). Thus, every two crankshaft revolutions gives one camshaft revolution and one cycle of valve action; that is, the intake valve and the exhaust valve open and close once every two crankshaft revolutions. In in-line engines the camshaft is mounted in bearings in the lower part of the cylinder block. In V-type engines the camshaft is located directly above the crankshaft between the two banks of cylinders (Fig. 4-23). In some engines the camshaft is located overhead or on top of the cylinder head (Fig. 4-25). (See also, §221.)

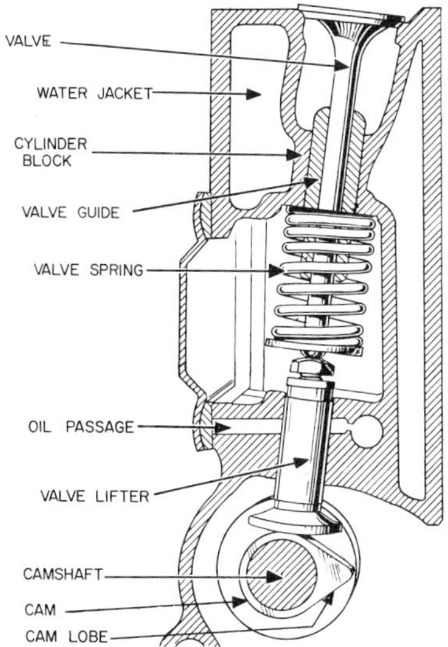

Fig. 7-31. Valve mechanism used in an L-head engine. The valve is raised off its seat with every camshaft rotation.

§96. Valves In most engines there are two valves for each cylinder: an intake valve and an exhaust valve. (Two-cycle engines may have one or none, and certain heavy-duty engines may have more, as shown in Figs. 4-42 and 4-43.) The intake valve opens during the intake stroke to admit the air-fuel mixture into the cylinder. The exhaust valve opens during the exhaust stroke to permit the burned gases to be exhausted from the cylinder. The cam lobes on the camshaft are related to the crankshaft crankpins (through the gears or sprockets and chain) so as to cause the valves to open and close with the proper relationship to the piston strokes (see §102).

In the past, various types of valves have been used for internal-combustion engines, among them sliding-sleeve and rotary valves. However, now almost all internal-combustion engines use the mushroom, or "poppet," valve (Figs. 7-28 and 7-29).

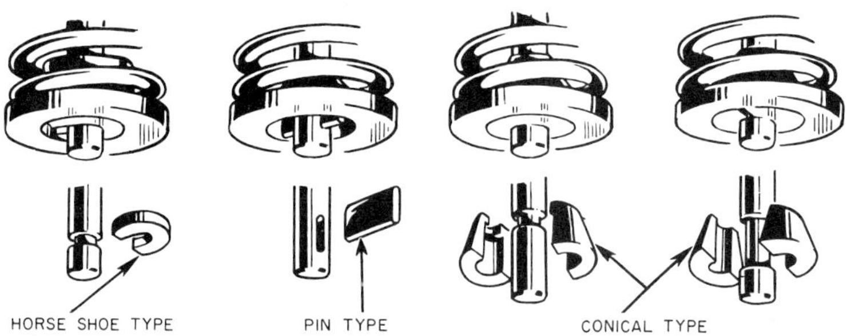

Fig. 7-32. Types of valve-spring-retainer locks (also called *keepers*).

The valve is normally held closed and firmly seated by one or more heavy springs and by the pressures in the combustion chamber. (The manner in which the spring is fastened to the valve stem is described in §98.) As the camshaft rotates, the cam lobe raises the valve lifter, causing the spring to compress and the valve to be lifted off its seat. When closed, the valve face makes uniform contact with the valve seat around the entire circumference of the valve. The seat and valve face are ground at the same angle, and both are circular, so a good seal is formed.

Fig. 7-33. Rocker arm used in an overhead-valve engine. (*Chevrolet Motor Division of General Motors Corporation*)

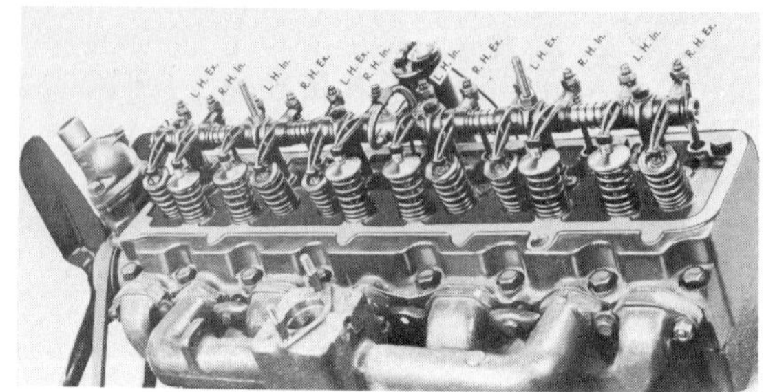

Fig. 7-34. Rocker-arm assembly for a six-cylinder, overhead-valve engine. (*Chevrolet Motor Division of General Motors Corporation*)

§97. Valve seat The exhaust-valve seat, as well as the exhaust valve, are subjected to the high temperatures of the burned gases passing from the engine cylinder through the exhaust port. For this reason, the exhaust-valve seat is often made of a special heat-resistant, steel-alloy insert in the form of a ring. This ring is set into a counterbore in the cylinder block, or head (Fig. 7-30). The ring, which is made of a very hard, heat-resistant metal, is better able to withstand the high exhaust-gas temperatures than the block or head materials. Consequently, it holds up better and gives longer service life. After it has become worn or rough, it can be serviced by a valve-seat grinding machine. A seat reamer, or cutter, cannot be used on this type of valve seat. If the seat has become badly worn or damaged, the seat insert can be removed and a new one installed.

§98. L-head valve train The L-head engine uses a relatively simple valve train, or valve mechanism: the valves are located near, and in a straight line with, the camshaft. Figure 7-31 shows this valve mechanism, with the various parts named. The valve spring is compressed between the cylinder block at one end and a spring retainer at the other. The spring retainer is attached to the end of the valve stem with a retainer lock (Fig. 7-32). The most commonly used lock is the conical type. It consists of two halves that fit into a conical recess in the retainer and into an undercut, or groove, in the valve stem. To remove the lock, the valve spring must be compressed by moving the retainer up out of the way. The lock is then free and can be removed. With the lock out, the valve can be pulled (from the top of the block) and the spring and retainer removed.

The valve rides in a valve guide assembled into the cylinder block (Fig. 7-31). Essentially, the valve guide consists of nothing more than a hollow steel tube, carefully dimensioned to be a tight fit in a drilled hole in the block, and having a close clearance fit with the valve stem. Although the valve could be installed directly in a hole drilled in the block, this method of installation would make it difficult to correct for wear. With the guide, however, excessive wear can be corrected by installation of a new guide.

The valve lifter (or *tappet*, as it is sometimes called) rides on the cam and moves up and down as the cam lobe passes under it. This motion is carried to the valve, causing it to open. Valve-spring pressure then recloses the valve as the cam lobe moves out from under the valve lifter. There are two types of lifters: the so-called "solid," or "mechanical," lifter and the hydraulic lifter (§101).

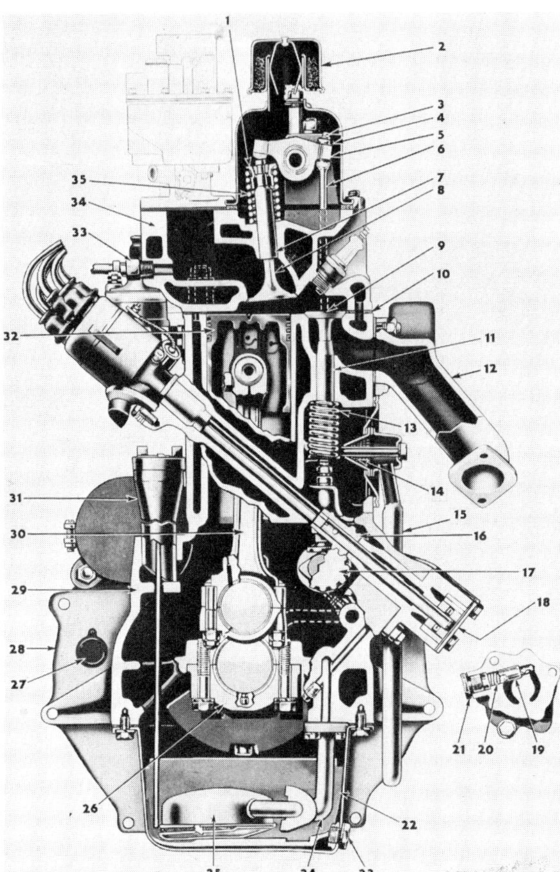

Fig. 7-35. End sectional view of an F-head engine with its intake valves in the head and its exhaust valves in the block.

1. Intake-valve-spring retainer
2. Breather cap
3. Adjusting screw
4. Adjusting-screw nut
5. Rocker arm
6. Push rod
7. Intake-valve guide
8. Intake valve
9. Exhaust valve
10. Cylinder-head gasket
11. Exhaust-valve guide
12. Exhaust manifold
13. Exhaust-valve spring
14. Ventilator baffle
15. Crankcase ventilator
16. Oil-pump-driven gear
17. Camshaft
18. Oil pump
19. Relief plunger
20. Relief-plunger spring
21. Relief-spring retainer
22. Oil pan
23. Oil-pan drain plug

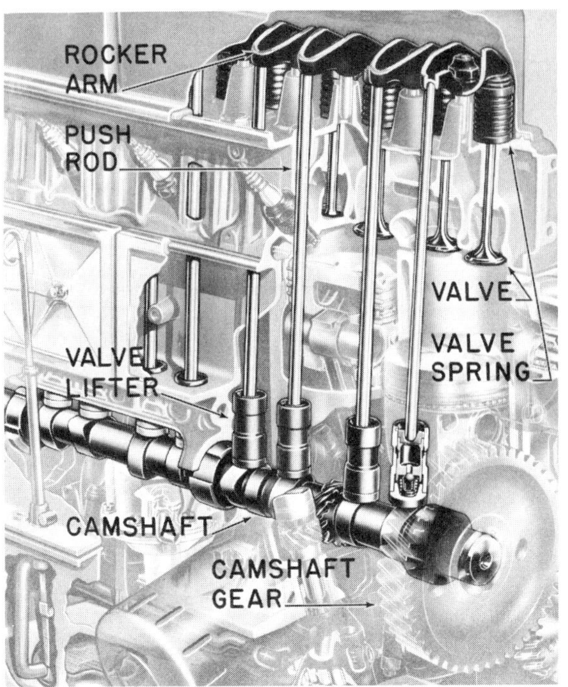

Fig. 7-36. Cutaway view of an I-head engine, showing the location of the hydraulic valve lifter in the valve train. (*Pontiac Motor Division of General Motors Corporation*)

The mechanical lifter is essentially nothing more than a cylinder with a flat face on the lower end, which rides on the cam. On the other end there is an adjustment screw which can be turned into or out of the lifter to adjust the clearance in the valve train. It is this adjustment screw that makes contact with the end of the valve stem. Some clearance must be maintained in the system to allow for dimensional changes resulting from temperature variations. If the screw were adjusted to give zero clearance with the engine cold, then, as the engine warmed up, the valve stem would lengthen so that the valve would not seat. This would cause

24. Oil-float support
25. Oil float
26. Crankshaft
27. Timing-hole cover
28. Rear-engine plate
29. Cylinder block
30. Connecting rod
31. Oil-filler tube
32. Piston
33. Vacuum-tube connection
34. Cylinder head
35. Intake-valve spring

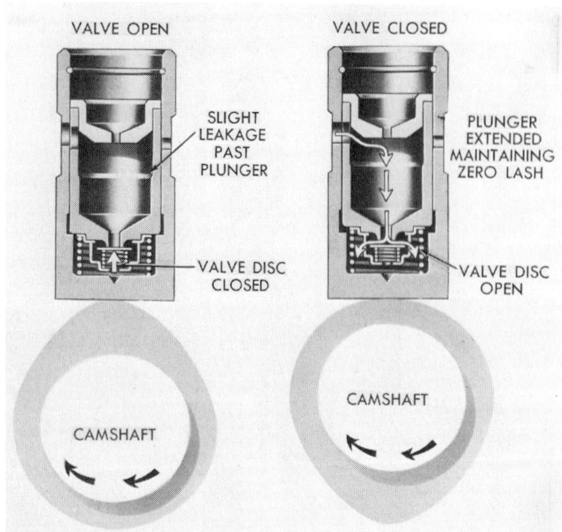

Fig. 7-37. Two positions of the hydraulic valve lifter: valve open and valve closed. (*Ford Motor Company*)

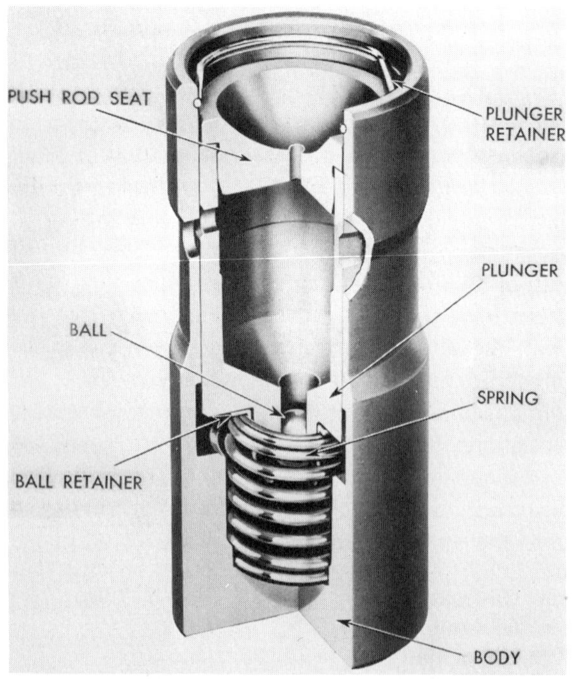

Fig. 7-38. Cutaway view of a hydraulic valve lifter. (*Chevrolet Motor Division of General Motors Corporation*)

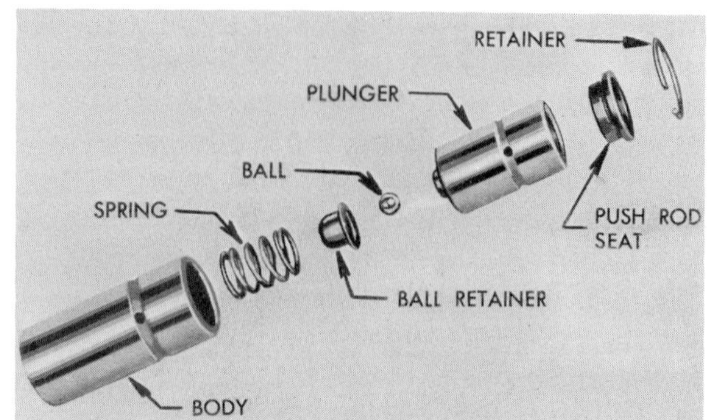

Fig. 7-39. Disassembled view of the hydraulic valve lifter shown in *Fig. 7-38.* (*Buick Motor Division of General Motors Corporation*)

valve leakage and such troubles as burned exhaust valves. Either the adjustment screw is self-locking, or there is a lock nut which is tightened after adjustment is made to keep the screw from turning and thereby changing the adjustment.

The valve lifter is free in its mounting and normally revolves as the cam rotates against its face. This distributes the wear over a larger area of the lifter face.

§99. I-head valve train In the I-head, or overhead, valve design (Figs. 3-10 and 4-20), two parts are installed in the valve train in addition to those required by the L-head train. These parts are the push rod and the rocker arm (Fig. 7-33). The push rods extend through openings in the cylinder head and block to the valve lifters above the cams on the camshaft. As the push rod is moved upward by the lifter, it causes the rocker arm to pivot, or rock, on its mounting shaft. The valve end of the rocker arm then bears down on the valve stem, pushing it down, so that the valve opens. Figure 7-34 shows how rocker arms, of the design shown in Fig. 7-33, are assembled to a shaft mounted on the cylinder head. In this design, proper clearance between the valve stem and the rocker arm is maintained by an adjustment screw and a lock nut assembled into the rocker arm. The lower end of the adjustment screw is ball-shaped, and it rests in a socket in the upper end of the push rod. Measurement of the clearance is made between the valve stem and the rocker arm, but adjustment is made in the push-rod side of the rocker arm.

§100. F-head valve train The F-head design combines both the L-head and the I-head design in one engine (Figs. 4-27, 4-30, and 7-35). In the engines shown, the intake valves are in the head, and the exhaust valves are in the block. The intake valves are operated from the camshaft through lifters, push rods, and rocker arms, exactly as in a conventional I-head engine. The exhaust valves are operated through valve lifters as in an L-head engine. Both sets of valves are operated from the same camshaft. The F-head arrangement permits the use of large intake valves and short, direct air-fuel mixture passages between the carburetor and intake ports (thus improving volumetric efficiency). At the same time, the exhaust valves, being located in the block, incorporate the simplicity of the L-head design.

§101. Hydraulic valve lifter Many engines use a hydraulic valve lifter. This type of lifter, which provides zero valve clearance, is very quiet in operation. There is no "click" (or *tappet noise*, as it is

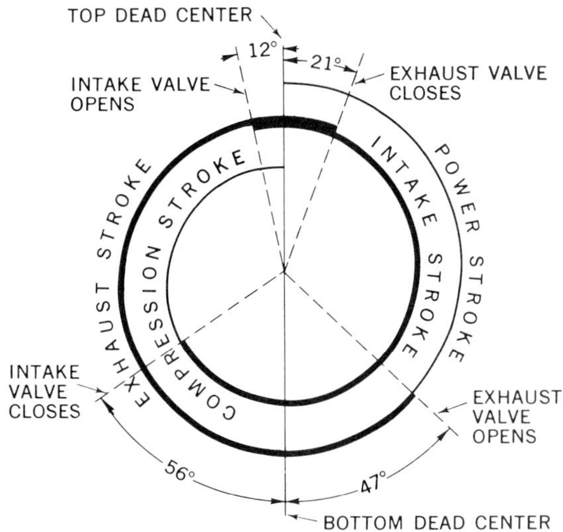

Fig. 7-40. Intake- and exhaust-valve timing. The complete cycle of events is shown as 720-degree spiral, which represents two complete crankshaft revolutions. The timing of valves differs among various engines.

called) as the adjustment screw on the valve lifter meets the valve stem (or push rod), as there may be with other lifters, particularly when clearances are high. On the hydraulic valve lifter, there is no adjustment screw and there is no clearance. As a rule, this type of valve lifter requires no adjustment in normal service. Variations due to wear of parts or temperature changes are taken care of automatically within the valve lifter.

Figure 7-36 shows a hydraulic valve lifter installed on an overhead-valve engine. Figure 7-37 shows the operation of this type of valve lifter, and Figs. 7-38 and 7-39 show details of the construction of the lifter. In operation, oil is fed into the valve lifter under engine-oil-pump pressure from an oil gallery that runs the length of the engine (a V-8 would have two oil galleries, one for each bank).

When the valve is closed, oil (from the engine oil-pump) is forced into the hydraulic valve lifter through the oil holes in the lifter body and plunger (see Fig. 7-37 for an illustration of the following action story). As the oil enters the plunger, it acts on the ball-check valve in the bottom of the plunger, forcing it open. Oil now passes the ball-check valve and enters the space under the plunger. The plunger is therefore forced upward until it comes into contact with the valve push rod (or valve stem on an L-head engine). This takes up any clearance in the system.

Now, when the cam lobe moves around under the lifter body, the lifter is raised. Since there is no clearance, there is no tappet noise. As the lifter is raised, the sudden increase in oil pressure in the body chamber under the lifter causes the ball-check valve to close. The oil is therefore trapped in the chamber, and the lifter acts as a simple one-piece lifter. It moves up as an assembly and causes the valve to open. Then, when the lobe moves out from under the lifter, the valve spring forces the valve to close and the lifter to move down. The pressure on the oil in the chamber under the plunger is reduced, and the ball-check valve opens. Oil from the engine oiling system is again forced past the ball-check valve to replace whatever oil may have leaked from the chamber. Slight amounts of oil may leak past the ball-check valve and between the plunger and the lifter body. As this oil is replaced, the plunger moves up as necessary to bring the push-rod seat into contact with the push rod. This eliminates any clearance in the valve train.

§102. Valve timing In previous discussions of engine and valve action, it was assumed that the intake and exhaust valves opened and closed at TDC and BDC. Actually, as can be seen from Fig. 7-40, the valves are not timed to open or close at these points in the engine cycle of operation. For example, in the valve-timing diagram illustrated, the exhaust valve starts to open at 47 degrees before BDC on the power stroke. It remains open through the remainder of the power stroke and through the entire exhaust stroke. It does not close until 21 degrees after TDC on the intake stroke. This additional exhaust-valve opening gives more time for the exhaust gases to leave the cylinder. When the exhaust valve starts to open (47 degrees before BDC), the combustion pressures have dropped considerably; most of the available power of the burning charge has already been transmitted to the downward-moving piston. Opening the exhaust valve this early gives the exhaust gases additional time to exhaust from the cylinder.

Note: For an idea of how much the combustion pressure has dropped at 47 degrees before BDC on the power stroke, refer to Fig. 6-5, which shows the pressures in an engine cylinder during the four piston strokes. In the curve shown, the pressure has dropped from a peak combustion pressure of almost 700 psi (pounds per square inch) to about 100 psi at 47 degrees before BDC on the power stroke.

The intake valve starts to open at 12 degrees before TDC on the exhaust stroke, thus giving a 33-degree overlap during which both valves are at least partly open. The intake valve then stays open until 56 degrees past BDC on the compression stroke. This gives the air-fuel mixture additional time to enter the cylinder. As you will recall from our discussion of volumetric efficiency (§61), delivery of adequate amounts of air-fuel mixture to the cylinders is a critical item in engine operation. Actually, the cylinder is never quite "filled up" when the intake valve closes. Thus, there is no loss of compression resulting from the intake valve staying open well past BDC on the compression stroke. At BDC, as the compression stroke starts, pressure in the cylinder is below atmospheric (see Fig. 6-5). Pressure does not reach atmospheric until the piston is well past BDC.

The illustration of valve timing (Fig. 7-40) is for one engine. Different engines have different degrees of valve timing. In some engines, valves open and close earlier or later than shown in Fig. 7-40, remaining open for different degrees of cam rotation.

SUMMARY

The engine block forms the basic framework of the engine. Assembled on and in it are the other engine components such as the piston and rod assemblies, crankshaft, bearings, camshaft, valve-train components, cylinder head, and so on. Blocks are made of intricate castings of iron or, in some engines, aluminum. Heads are also cast of iron or aluminum, and they are of two types—L heads or I heads.

Gaskets must be used between the head and block to assure a good seal. They are also used at many other places where seals are required between mating surfaces.

The exhaust manifold carries the burned gases from the exhaust-valve ports to the exhaust pipe and muffler. The intake manifold has the carburetor mounted on it and is connected to the intake-valve ports.

The crankshaft, with the vibrating damper and the flywheel, is hung from the bottom of the cylinder block by the main-bearing caps. The connecting rods connect the cranks on the crankshaft and the pistons. The bearings are lubricated by oil that is pumped to them from the reservoir in the oil pan.

The piston rings are necessary to maintain a

good sliding seal between the moving pistons and stationary cylinder walls. They are of two types: compression rings, for holding compression and combustion pressures; and oil-control rings, for wiping excess oil from the cylinder walls and preventing it from getting up into the combustion chambers where it would burn to leave carbon that could foul spark plugs, valves, and piston rings.

The valve train consists of the valves, valve springs, spring retainers, valve lifters, camshaft, and, on I-head engines, push rods and rocker arms. Some exhaust-valve seats are formed from seat inserts—rings of special heat-resistant steel alloy.

Many engines use hydraulic valve lifters. They automatically take up any clearance in the valve train during the time that the valves are closed, so that there is no tappet noise. The hydraulic valve lifter has a plunger that is raised by engine oil pressure to take up clearance in the valve train. When the cam raises the lifter to initiate valve opening, a ball-check valve traps the oil under the plunger so that the lifter acts like a simple, one-piece lifter.

Valves are timed by the shape of the cam contours to open and close at the proper times for best engine performance. The exhaust valve starts to open well before the piston reaches BDC on the power stroke; it remains open until the piston has reached TDC and has started down on the intake stroke. The intake valve starts to open before the piston reaches TDC on the exhaust stroke; it remains open until well after the piston has passed BDC and has moved up on the compression stroke. All this improves volumetric efficiency. Timing varies for different engines and for different performance requirements.

QUESTIONS

1. List the major components that are assembled on or in a cylinder block.

2. Describe the essential differences between an L-head engine and an I-head engine.

3. Explain the purpose of the vibration damper. The flywheel.

4. Explain briefly how the main bearings are lubricated.

5. Describe the three methods of attaching the connecting rod to the piston.

6. Explain the purposes of the two types of piston rings.

7. List and explain the purpose of each part in the L-head valve train. In the I-head valve train.

8. Describe the construction and operation of a hydraulic valve lifter.

9. Draw a valve-timing diagram which shows the intake valve opening at 15 degrees before TDC and closing at 40 degrees past BDC, and which shows the exhaust valve opening at 35 degrees before BDC and closing at 15 degrees after TDC.

Engine Accessory Systems

CHAPTER **8**

This chapter describes briefly the four accessory systems required by the engine for operation: the fuel system, lubricating system, ignition system, and cooling system. Each of these is an integral part of the engine and, in engine design work, must be treated as such. Following chapters discuss the design requirements of these four systems.

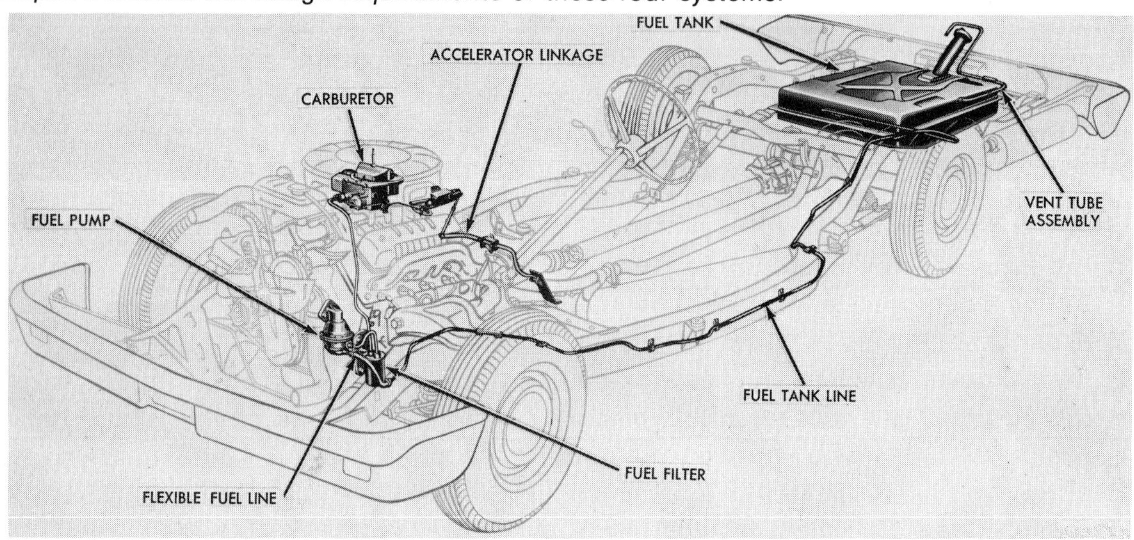

Fig. 8-1. Fuel system for a car with a V-8 engine. (*Ford Division of Ford Motor Company*)

§103. Fuel system The fuel system supplies the engine with a combustible mixture of fuel and air (Fig. 8-1). It consists of the fuel tank, fuel pump, fuel filter and screens, carburetor, engine intake manifold, and connecting fuel lines. The fuel pump draws liquid fuel from the fuel tank and delivers it to the carburetor. The carburetor mixes the fuel with air and delivers the mixture to the intake manifold. From there, it passes the intake-valve ports (when valves are open) and enters the engine cylinders. The carburetor varies the proportion of fuel and air to suit different operating conditions. For example, a rich mixture of about 9 pounds of air for every pound of gasoline is delivered for starting, initial warm-up, and accelerating. A relatively *lean* mixture of about 15 pounds of air for every pound of gasoline is delivered for normal over-the-road operation.

1. Fuel tank. The fuel tank is essentially a sheet-metal tank, with a filler tube for filling it and an outlet near the bottom to which the fuel line is attached.

2. Fuel pump. The fuel pump (Fig. 8-2) pumps gasoline from the fuel tank and delivers it to the carburetor. It contains, as the essential working parts, a rocker arm, a flexible diaphragm, and two valves. The pump is mounted on the side of the cylinder block. The rocker arm enters an opening

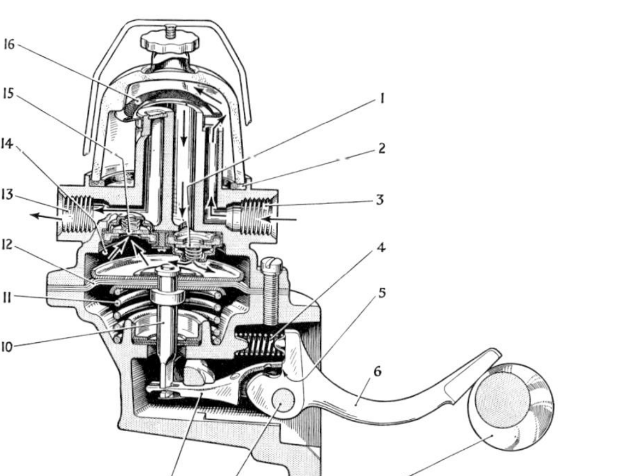

Fig. 8-2. Sectional view of a fuel pump. (*Hillman Motor Car Company, Limited*)

1. Inlet valve
2. Joint under cover bowl
3. Fuel inlet
4. Operating-arm return spring
5. Abutment on operating arm
6. Rocker arm
7. Eccentric on camshaft
8. Pivot
9. Connecting link
10. Pull rod
11. Diaphragm return spring
12. Diaphragm
13. Fuel outlet
14. Pump chamber
15. Outlet valve
16. Gauze filter

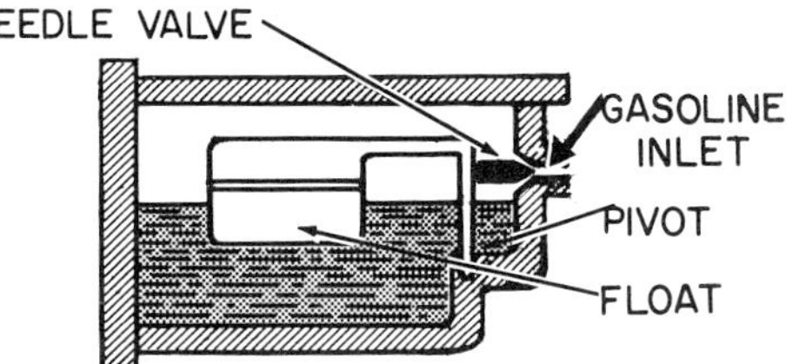

Fig. 8-3. Simplified drawing of a carburetor-float system.

in the block and rests on an eccentric on the camshaft (Fig. 19-10). The eccentric is an offset ring on the camshaft. As the camshaft rotates, the eccentric causes the rocker arm to rock, or move back and forth. This movement causes the diaphragm in the pump to fluctuate down and up, alternately creating vacuum and pressure. When vacuum is created, the inlet valve is lifted off its seat, allowing gasoline to be drawn from the fuel tank, through the fuel line, into the pump chamber. On the return stroke, the diaphragm is released, and the diaphragm spring forces it upward. This

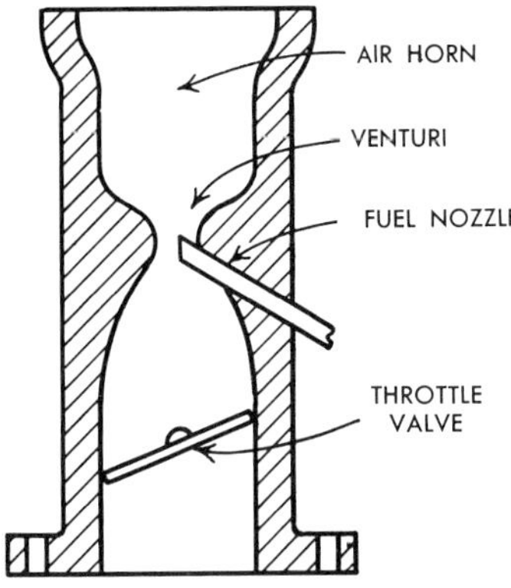

Fig. 8-4. Simple carburetor consisting of an air horn, a fuel nozzle, and a throttle valve.

creates pressure in the pump chamber. The inlet valve is closed by the pressure, the outlet valve is opened. Gasoline is forced from the pump through a fuel line to the carburetor. The rocker arm spring keeps the rocker arm in contact with the eccentric on the camshaft. The diaphragm spring maintains pressure on the diaphragm and the fuel in the pump chamber during the return stroke.

3. *Carburetor.* The gasoline is delivered through an inlet to a bowl on the side of the carburetor (Figs. 8-3 and 8-7). The bowl serves as a sort of constant-level gasoline reservoir. It contains a float that operates a needle valve. When the proper level of gasoline in the bowl is reached, the float has risen enough to force the needle valve into the opening, thus sealing it off. Now no further gasoline can be delivered. However, when the gasoline level falls in the bowl, the float drops down enough to allow the needle valve to open, and gasoline can enter the float bowl. In actual operation, the float positions the needle valve so that entering gasoline just balances the gasoline being withdrawn by the carburetor.

Aside from the float bowl, the carburetor contains three essentials: an air horn with a venturi (or constriction), a fuel nozzle, and a throttle valve (Fig. 8-4). The air horn is a passageway for air as it moves from outside the engine toward the engine cylinders. An air cleaner mounted on the air horn filters dirt and dust particles from the entering air. This action prevents such particles from getting into the engine, where they could damage engine bearings, cylinder walls, and piston rings. After the air passes through the air horn (where it picks up a charge of fuel), it enters the intake manifold on which the carburetor is mounted. The intake manifold (Fig. 7-14) is essentially nothing more than a series of passages leading from the carburetor to the engine cylinders. Generally, these passages are made to be as short and as straight as possible (minimum of bends) so that the air-fuel

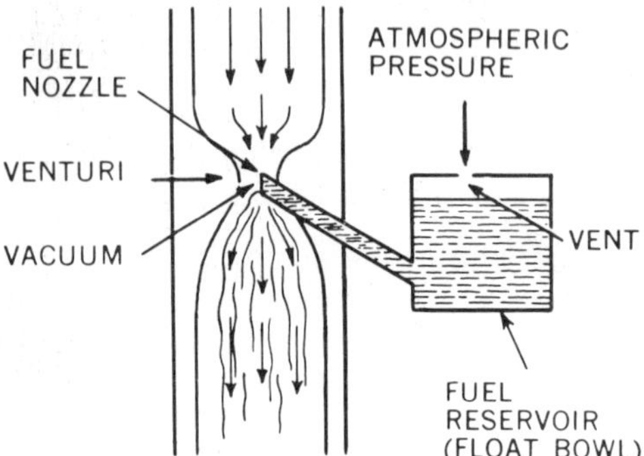

Fig. 8-5. The venturi, or constriction, causes a vacuum in the air stream just below the restriction. Atmospheric pressure then pushes fuel from the float bowl out through the fuel nozzle.

mixture will not be excessively restricted, or held back, on its way to the cylinders. There is an exception to this. In some engines, the manifolds are "tuned" to improve engine breathing at high speeds. This increases the lengths of the manifold passages considerably over the minimum possible distances. (Manifold tuning is described in §252.)

When the engine is running, air is moving constantly through the carburetor air horn and intake manifold to the engine cylinders. Each time a piston moves down on an intake stroke, a partial vacuum is produced in that cylinder. Atmospheric pressure (or pressure of the air) then pushes air through the air horn and intake manifold and through the opened intake-valve port into the cylinder.

As the air moves through the air horn, it picks up a "charge" of gasoline vapor, as already mentioned. The fuel nozzle, which extends upward from the float bowl into the center of the air horn

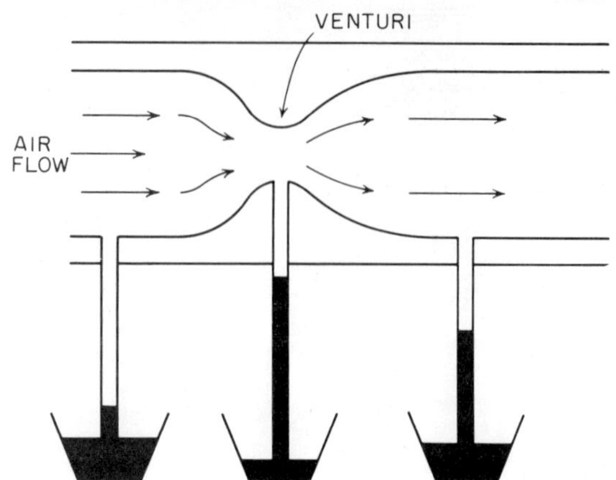

Fig. 8-6. Three dishes of mercury and three tubes connected to an air horn show differences in vacuum by the amount that the mercury rises in the tubes. The venturi has the highest vacuum.

(Fig. 8-5), delivers gasoline to the passing air. Its upper end is centered in a venturi, or constriction, in the air horn. When air is passing through a venturi, a partial vacuum is produced in it. This effect is shown in Fig. 8-6, which illustrates three dishes of mercury (a very heavy liquid) connected by tubes to an air horn with a venturi. The greater the vacuum, the greater the rise of the mercury in the tube. Note that the center tube, which opens into the venturi, shows the greatest mercury rise (greatest vacuum effect).

Thus, when the engine is running and air is passing through the air horn, the vacuum at the venturi (or at the fuel nozzle) causes gasoline to be delivered from the float bowl into the passing air. Atmospheric pressure, acting through a vent, or opening, in the float bowl (Fig. 8-5), pushes the gasoline up through the fuel nozzle. It leaves the fuel nozzle in the form of a fine spray which rapidly turns into vapor as the droplets of gasoline evaporate. The more air that moves through, the faster it moves and the greater the amount of gasoline delivered.

The throttle valve (Fig. 8-4) controls the amount of air-fuel mixture moving through and being delivered to the engine cylinders. The throttle valve is a round disk mounted on a shaft. When the shaft is turned, the valve tilts more or less to open or close the air passage. When the valve is tilted only slightly from the horizontal, the throttle

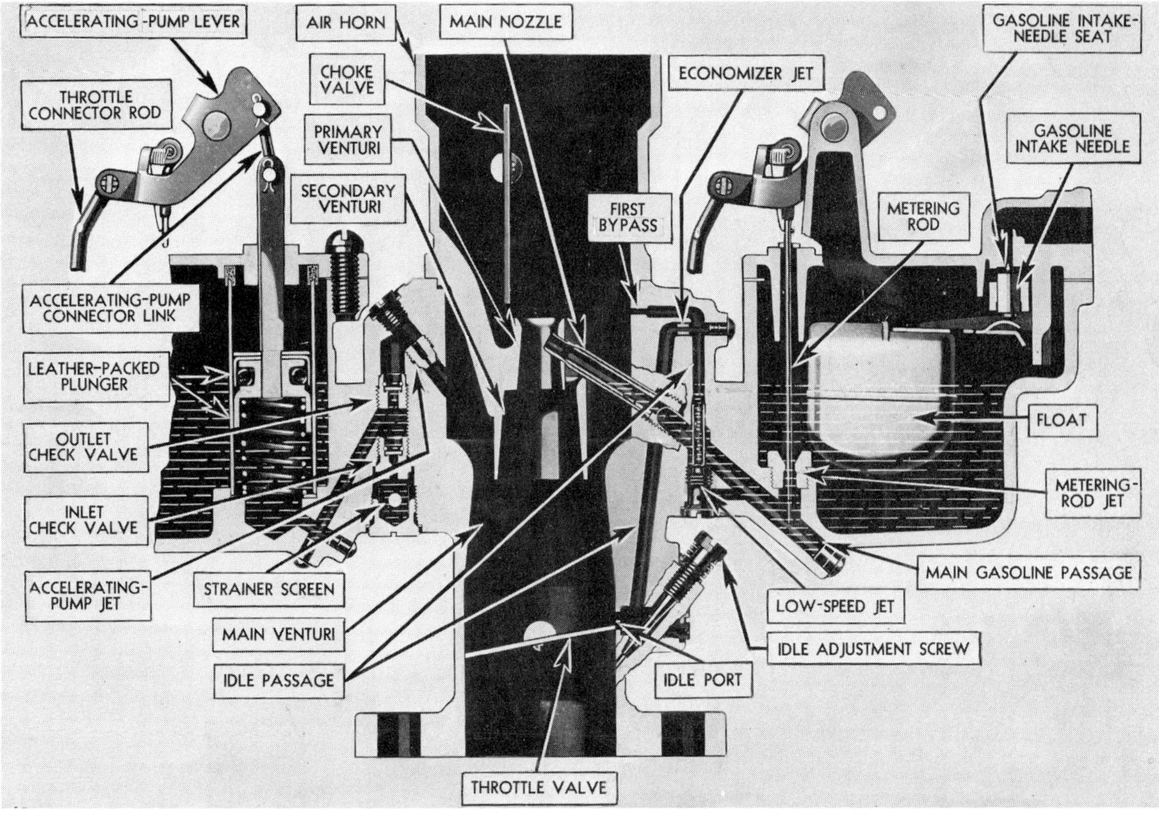

Fig. 8-7. Sectional view of a carburetor. The accelerator-pump system (left) is actually part of the float-bowl system (right), but it is shown on the left in order that its construction can be seen more clearly. (*Chevrolet Motor Division of General Motors Corporation*)

is said to be closed. Only a small amount of air can get through. Only small amounts of air-fuel mixture are delivered to the engine cylinders, and the engine runs slowly. It is "throttled down," or idling. When the throttle valve is opened, more air-fuel mixture gets through to the engine cylinders, and engine speed increases.

Figure 8-7 shows a carburetor in a schematic view. Note that the venturi arrangement is more complicated than that shown in the previous illustrations; it consists of three related venturis. This assures better fuel delivery and mixing. The actual carburetor has several circuits, or fuel passages, that provide balanced performance for different operating conditions. For instance, while the car is accelerating, the accelerator is pushed down. A linkage to the accelerator pump (at left in Fig. 8-7) causes the pump piston to move down and to force a stream of gasoline into the carburetor air horn. This greatly enriches the air-fuel mixture so that the engine responds quickly. The idle circuit includes an idle port under the throttle valve, which feeds gasoline when the throttle is closed. This assures satisfactory mixture richness for smooth idling.

Some fuel systems use superchargers. These devices deliver more air-fuel mixture to the engine to improve engine performance, particularly at higher speeds. Another system does not use a carburetor; instead, it has pumps which inject the fuel into the intake manifold. (Fuel systems are discussed in detail in Chap. 17.)

§104. Lubricating system The lubricating system used in the automotive engine is designed to supply oil to all moving parts. In a sense, these

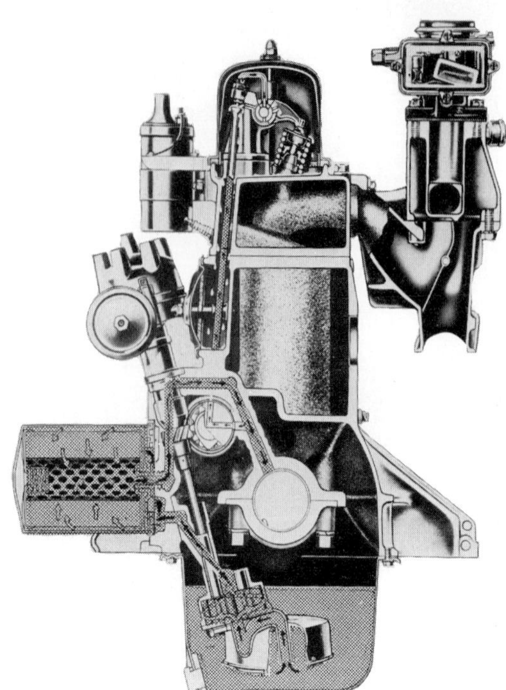

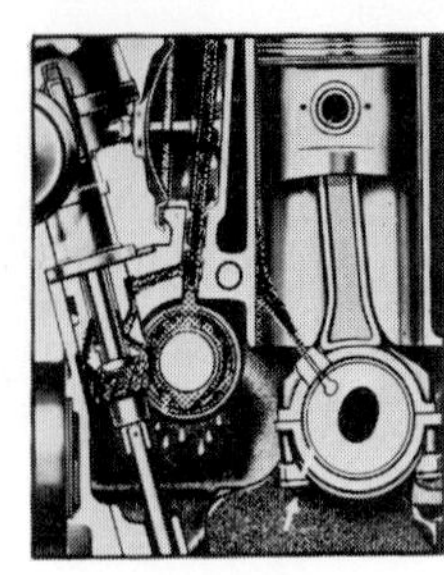

Fig. 8-8. Engine lubrication system of a six-cylinder, overhead-valve engine. Arrows show the direction of oil flow to the moving parts of the engine. (*Ford Division of Ford Motor Company*)

parts "float" in a film of oil which prevents actual metal-to-metal contact. In the engine, oil is supplied to crankshaft and camshaft journals, rotating in their supporting bearings. Oil is supplied to the cylinder walls so that the pistons and rings will slide easily and smoothly without undue piston, ring, or wall wear. In a like manner, other moving engine parts are supplied with oil.

Automotive-engine lubricating systems are of several types that splash or force (or both splash and force) oil onto the sliding and rolling metal surfaces in the engine. Figure 8-8 illustrates the full-pressure system. In this system, holes are drilled through the cylinder block and crankshaft, and oil is forced through these holes by an oil pump. The oil is fed onto the bearing and journal surfaces and is then thrown off in a fine spray. This spray effectively covers the cylinder walls. In addition, oil is forced through drilled leads to the camshaft bearings and valve mechanisms. The oil drains off the various engine parts and returns to the oil pan in the bottom of the engine. Then, it is picked up by the oil pump and recirculated.

In addition to providing lubrication, the oil also carries away some of the heat from the moving engine parts. The oil picks up heat, becomes hotter, and then, when it returns to the oil pan, gives up heat and cools off. The oil pan gives up heat to the passing air which circulates around and under it. (Further details of engine-lubricating systems are given in Chap. 19.)

§105. Electric system The electric system (Fig. 8-9) includes the storage battery, cranking motor, generator, regulator, ignition distributor, coil, and spark plugs, as well as the wires and switches for connecting their various units. The lights, radio, heater, indicating gauges, and other electrically operated devices, while part of the electric system, are usually considered accessory items since they are not essential to operation of the car.

1. Storage battery. The storage battery is an *electrochemical* device, which means that its operation depends upon both chemical and electrical actions. The battery is a source of electric current when the engine is being cranked with the cranking motor. It also supplies current when the generator is not able to carry the electric load. When current is withdrawn from the battery, chemical actions take place to produce the flow of current. In a sense, the chemicals in the battery are used up by this action. Thus, after a certain

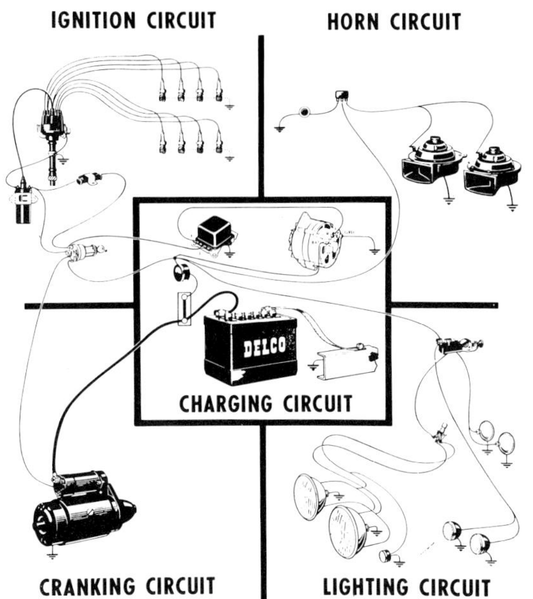

Fig. 8-9. Typical automotive electric system. Return circuits between electric units are formed by the engine block and the car frame. The symbol ⏚ means ground, or the return circuit. (*Delco-Remy Division of General Motors Corporation*)

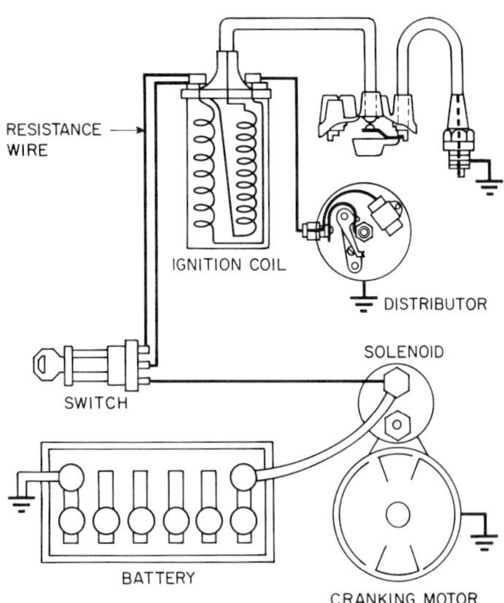

Fig. 8-10. Schematic wiring diagram of an ignition system with distributor, using contact points. (*Delco-Remy Division of General Motors Corporation*)

amount of current has been withdrawn for a certain length of time, the battery becomes "discharged." To "recharge" the battery, current from some external source, such as a generator or battery charger, must be forced through it in the reverse, or charging, direction.

2. *Cranking motor.* The cranking motor is a special direct-current electric motor that starts the engine by rotating the crankshaft when the cranking-motor switch is closed. Closing the switch connects the motor to the battery. There is a special gearing arrangement between the cranking-motor drive pinion and the engine flywheel that causes the flywheel and crankshaft to turn when the cranking motor operates.

3. *Alternator.* The alternator, or generator, is a device that converts mechanical energy (from the automobile engine) into a flow of electric current. This current restores the battery to a charged condition when it has become run down, or discharged. It also operates electrical devices, such as the ignition system, lights, radio, and so forth. The alternator is usually mounted on one side of the engine and is driven by the engine fan belt.

4. *Regulator.* If the alternator produces too much current, the various connected electrical devices are damaged. To prevent such damage, an alternator-output regulator is used. The regulator controls the amount of current produced by the alternator, allowing it to produce a high current when the battery is in a discharged condition and electrical devices are turned on. When the battery becomes charged and electric units are turned off, the regulator cuts down the current being produced to the amount needed to meet the operating requirements of the system.

5. *Lights, heater, radio, indicating devices.* The lights and heater add to the flexibility, comfort, and convenience of the car; the indicating devices keep the driver informed as to the engine temperature, oil pressure, amount of fuel in the tank, and the battery-charging rate.

6. *Wiring and switches.* The wiring (Fig. 8-9) connects the various electric units and switches and serves as a path through which the electric current can flow from one to another unit. Switches placed in these circuits are forms of valves that can close or open the circuits to permit or prevent the flow

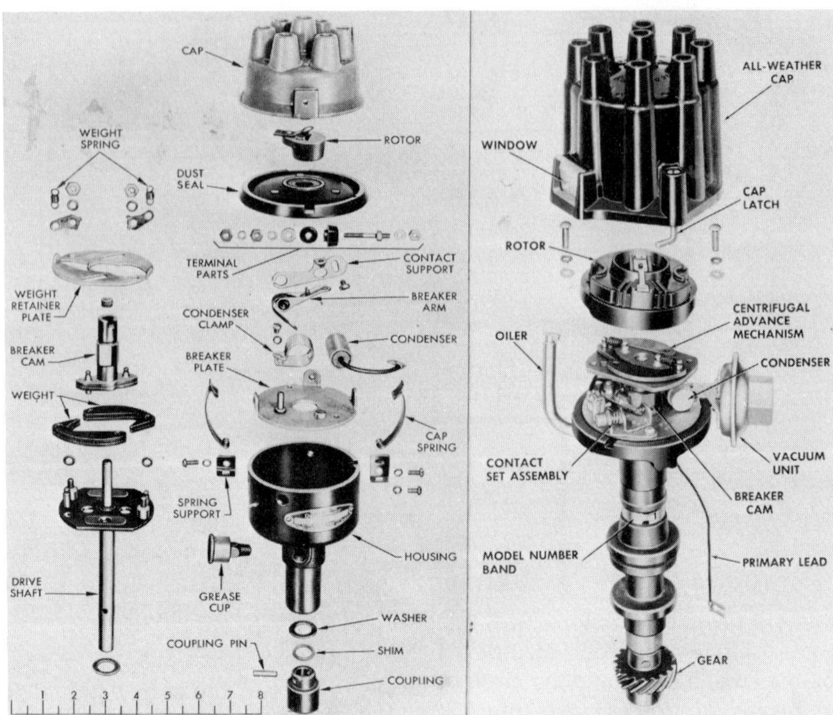

Fig. 8-11. Partly disassembled distributors. (*Delco-Remy Division of General Motors Corporation*)

of current. The wires are made up of conducting materials, such as copper, that freely conduct current between the electric units. Some materials, such as rubber and glass, are nonconductors, or insulators; they will not allow current to flow through them. Such substances are used to cover and insulate the wires so that the current will be kept within the proper circuits and paths (and will not *short-circuit*). Note that the automotive wiring system shown in Fig. 8-9 is a one-wire system; that is, the electric units are normally connected to each other by one wire. The return circuit is through the car frame and the engine block. This return circuit is also called the *ground;* all the electric units are connected to it.

7. *Ignition system.* The ignition system (Fig. 8-10) provides the high-voltage surges, or electric sparks, that ignite the compressed air-fuel mixture in the engine cylinders. After the fuel system has delivered the air and gasoline-vapor mixture to the engine cylinder and the mixture has been compressed by the piston compression stroke, it must be ignited. The ignition system does this job by producing sparks at the spark-plug gap in the engine cylinders. The sparks set the compressed mixture on fire so that it burns and creates the high pressure that drives the piston down on the power stroke. The following articles describe the operation of the ignition system in detail. Chapter 20 discusses various types of ignition systems in detail.

§106. Operation of ignition system The ignition system consists of the source of electric energy (battery or generator), ignition switch, ignition coil, ignition distributor, spark plugs, and wiring (Fig. 8-10). The ignition system might be said to have two jobs. First, it must take the low voltage (6 or 12 volts) from the battery and step it up to the several thousand volts needed to produce the igniting sparks at the spark plugs in the engine cylinders. Second, it must deliver the "sparks" to the proper cylinders at the proper time. That is, the ignition system must deliver a high-voltage surge (or spark) to cylinder 1 just as piston 1 nears TDC (top dead center) on the compression stroke. Then, a moment later, it must deliver another spark to cylinder 5 (or whichever cylinder is next in the

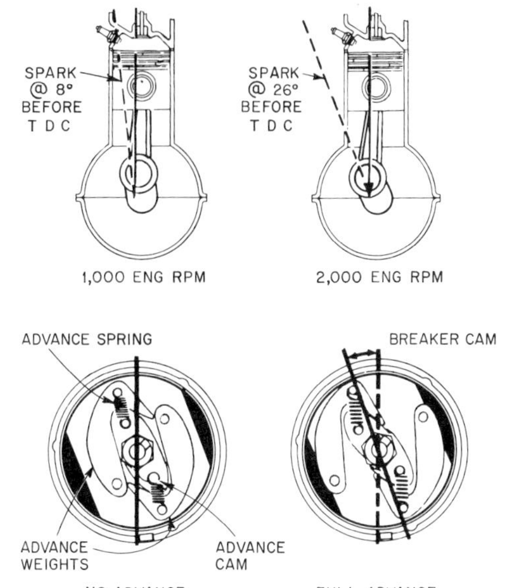

Fig. 8-12. Centrifugal-advance mechanism in the no-advance and full-advance positions. In the typical example shown, the ignition is timed at 8 degrees before TDC on idle. There is no centrifugal advance at 1,000 engine rpm, but there is 26 degrees' total advance (18 degrees centrifugal plus 8 degrees due to original timing) at 2,000 engine rpm. (*Delco-Remy Division of General Motors Corporation*)

order of firing) when it is ready to fire, and so on.

The voltage step-up job is done by the ignition coil, the distributor contacts, and the breaker cam. The breaker cam is mounted on the distributor shaft (which is driven from the engine camshaft at camshaft speed) and rotates with it. As the cam turns, lobes on the cam open and close the contacts. When the contacts are closed, they connect the ignition coil to the battery. Current then flows through the coil and the coil, in effect, becomes "loaded" with electric energy. Then, a moment later, as the cam turns further, a lobe on the cam opens the contacts, and the coil then unloads its energy in the form of a high-voltage surge.

Note: An ignition condenser (or capacitor) is connected across the contacts in order to prevent a high-voltage surge from jumping across the contacts as they separate. If this should happen, the energy in the coil would be wasted, and the contacts would be burned by the arc between the contacts. There would be insufficient electric energy to produce sparks in the cylinders, where they are needed to ignite the compressed air-fuel mixture.

The high-voltage surge that the coil produces as the contacts separate must be delivered to the proper cylinder. The distributor cap and rotor and the ignition wiring do this job. The high-voltage surge is led from the coil to the center terminal of the distributor cap by a high-tension lead. From there it passes to the distributor rotor. The rotor is mounted on the distributor cam and turns with it. It connects between the center terminal of the cap and the several outer cap terminals, in turn, as it rotates. Each outer terminal is connected by high-tension wires to a spark plug in one of the cylinders. Thus the rotor, as it turns, connects the ignition coil to the several cylinder spark plugs, one after the other. As each high-voltage surge is "manufactured" (by the closing and opening of the contacts), it is delivered through the cap and rotor to the cylinder that needs it; that is, it is delivered to the cylinder that is ready to fire (the piston nearing the end of its compression stroke).

Some ignition systems use transitors to reduce the load on the distributor contact points. A transistor is an electronic device, much like a vacuum tube, which can be used as an electric switch. In the transistorized system, the contact points merely operate the transistor, requiring only a very small current to do so (§287). The transistor then closes and opens the circuit between the battery and the ignition coil; it interrupts a much greater current. Because the contact points interrupt only a small current, they last longer.

Another type of ignition system does not use contact points. Instead, it has a magnetic pick-up device on the distributor. As the distributor shaft rotates, the magnetic pick-up sends electrical impulses to a transistor-control unit. The transistor-control unit then opens and closes the circuit between the battery and the ignition coil. (See §287 for a detailed discussion.)

§107. Operation of ignition-advance mechanisms When the engine is idling, the sparks are timed to appear in the engine cylinders just before the pis-

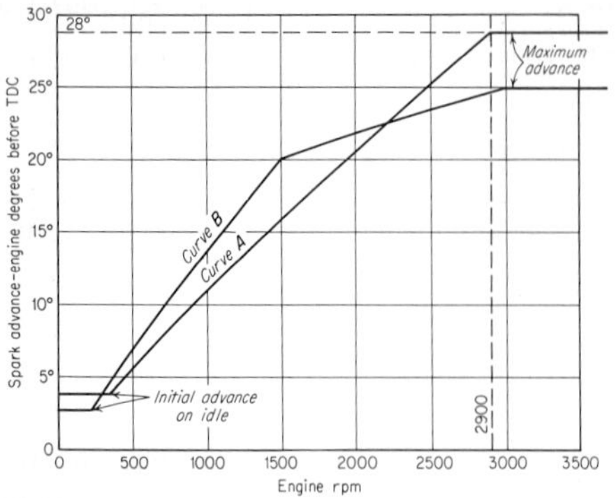

Fig. 8-13. Typical centrifugal-advance curves.

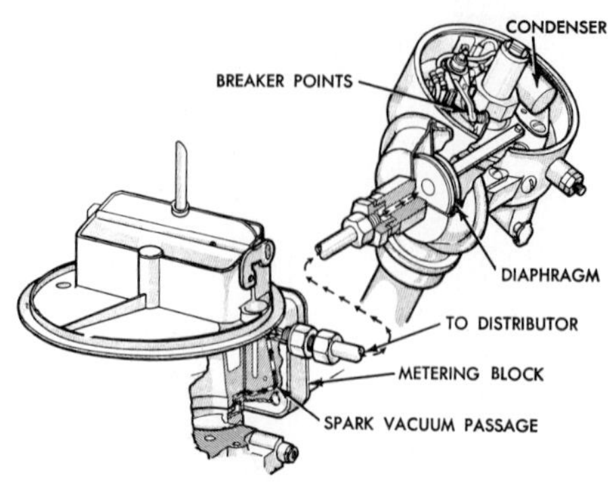

Fig. 8-14. Connection of the vacuum line between the carburetor and the vacuum-advance mechanism on the distributor. (*Ford Division of Ford Motor Company*)

tons reach TDC on their compression strokes. But at higher speeds, the air-fuel mixture has less time to ignite and burn. If ignition still took place just before TDC on the compression stroke, the piston would be up over the top and moving down before the mixture were well ignited. This means that the piston would be moving away from the pressure rise, and much of the energy in the burning fuel would be wasted. However, if the mixture were ignited earlier in the compression stroke (at high engine speeds), the mixture would be well ignited by the time the piston reached TDC. Pressure would increase, and more of the fuel energy would be used.

1. *Advance based on speed.* To ignite the mixture earlier at high engine speeds, a spark-advance mechanism is used. This mechanism is incorporated in the ignition distributor. One type consists of a centrifugal device that pushes the breaker cam ahead of the distributor shaft as engine speed increases. Figure 8-11 shows the parts of this mechanism. The breaker cam is attached to an oval-shaped advance cam, and this assembly sets down on a plate attached to the drive shaft. Two crescent-shaped advance weights are also assembled on the plate, as shown in Fig. 8-12. Figure 8-12 also shows how the mechanism operates to move the breaker cam ahead as engine speed increases. With increasing engine speed, the advance weights move out against the weight-spring tension. This movement pushes the breaker cam ahead so that the cam lobes close and open the contacts earlier. The sparks thus occur earlier; the spark is advanced so that ignition occurs earlier in the compression stroke.

Different engines require different amounts of spark advance at various speeds. Typical advance curves are shown in Fig. 8-13. In curve *A*, the spark is timed to occur just a few degrees of crankshaft rotation before TDC during idle. Then, as engine speed is increased, the spark moves ahead, or advances, until it reaches a maximum of 28 degrees at 2,900 rpm (revolutions per minute). Curve *B* is a little more complicated. It "dog-legs," or changes slope, at 1,500 rpm. A curve is worked out for each engine so that at any particular speed the advance will provide best performance. The mechanism is then built to provide this advance.

Excessive spark advance must be avoided because this will result in a knocking condition, often called *spark knock*. This occurs when the combustion is started too early in the cycle so that excessive pressures occur (§120).

2. *Advance based on intake-manifold vacuum.* With a partly closed throttle valve, there is a partial vacuum in the intake manifold. Less air-fuel mixture gets into the engine cylinders, and it is therefore less highly compressed. This means that the mixture burns more slowly. An additional spark advance, under these conditions, will allow the mixture ample time to burn and give up its energy to the piston. Spark advance, based on intake-manifold vacuum, is achieved by an airtight diaphragm linked to a movable breaker plate. This

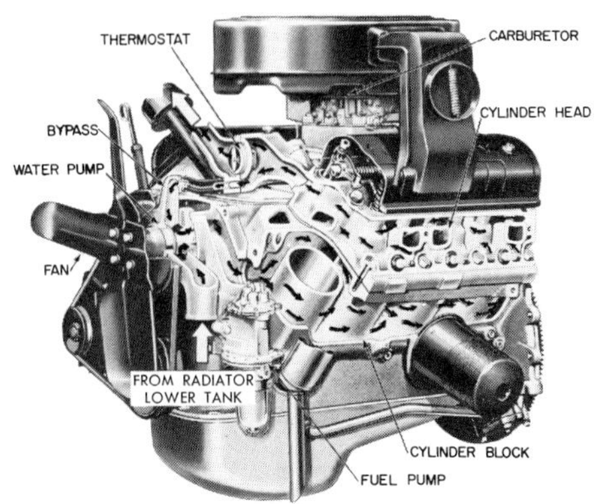

Fig. 8-15. Cooling system for a V-8 engine. The engine is partly cut away to show (by arrows) the circulation of coolant. The radiator is not shown. (*Lincoln-Mercury Division of Ford Motor Company*)

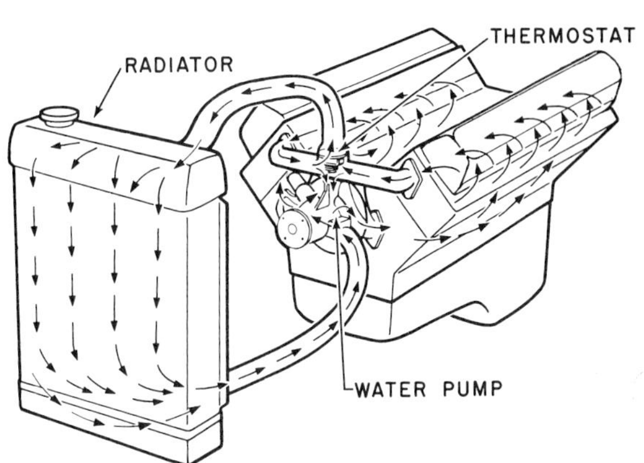

Fig. 8-16. Cooling system for a V-8 engine. Arrows show coolant flow through the system. (*Cadillac Motor Car Division of General Motors Corporation*)

type of arrangement is shown in Fig. 8-14. A vacuum connection is made to an opening just above the edge of the throttle plate in the carburetor. Whenever the throttle is opened, its edge moves past the opening, thus introducing intake-manifold vacuum into the tube. This vacuum then causes diaphragm and breaker-plate movement. The spark is advanced. Note that in this arrangement advance is based on manifold vacuum, which is part-throttle vacuum. When the throttle is opened wide, there is no appreciable manifold vacuum, and thus there will be no vacuum advance from this effect.

§108. Cooling system The burning of the air-fuel mixture in the engine cylinders produces a great deal of heat. Temperatures of several thousand degrees Fahrenheit are generated in the cylinders as the mixture burns. Some of this heat is carried out of the engine by the lubricating oil, some of it escapes in the hot exhaust gases, and some of it is absorbed by the evaporating fuel entering the the cylinders in the air-fuel mixture.* The cooling

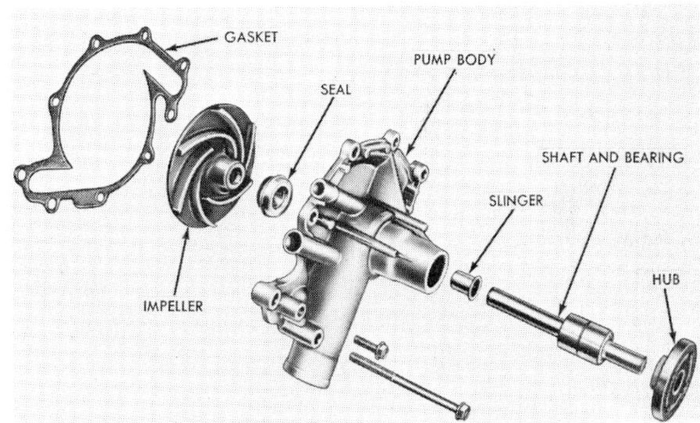

Fig. 8-17. Disassembled view of a water pump. (*Lincoln-Mercury Division of Ford Motor Company*)

system (Figs. 8-15 and 8-16) carries away most of the remaining excess heat. This prevents the engine from becoming too hot. Excessive engine temperature would damage or ruin the engine. At excessive temperatures, the lubricating oil would lose its effectiveness, and wear would increase very rapidly. High temperatures would also damage various engine parts.

Circulating water is used as the conducting medium in the cooling system. The combustion chambers of the engine are surrounded by pockets, or water jackets (Fig. 8-15), through which the water can flow. A water pump (Fig. 8-17) causes the water to be pumped from the bottom of the radiator through the water jackets and back to the radiator again. As the water passes through the

* When a liquid evaporates (undergoes a change of state), it absorbs heat. This action utilizes some of the heat developed in the engine and provides a certain amount of cooling as the fuel evaporates. In aircraft piston engines this effect is of great importance, and under certain circumstances requiring maximum power, the pilot may enrich the mixture in order to keep engine temperature down.

water jackets, it absorbs heat and becomes hot. Then, as it enters the top of the radiator, it starts to cool off. The radiator has numerous water passages through which the water flows. Around these small water passages are numerous air passages. The engine fan pulls air through these air passages, thus removing heat from the radiator. Thus, as the water passes down through the radiator, it is cooled. The cooler water is then pumped back through the water jackets in the engine. The pump keeps the water in continual circulation so that it continues to transfer heat from the engine to the air passing through the radiator. (See Chap. 19 for details of cooling-system requirements.)

SUMMARY

Four accessory systems are required by the internal-combustion engine: a fuel system to supply the fuel that is burned in the engine; a lubricating system to lubricate the moving engine parts; an ignition system to provide high-voltage surges, or sparks, which ignite the compressed mixtures in the combustion chambers and thus start the combustion processes; and a cooling system to carry away heat so that excessive temperatures do not occur in engine parts.

The fuel system consists of a tank, fuel lines, fuel pump, and carburetor. The carburetor is essentially a mixing device which mixes fuel and air in the proper proportions to meet various engine requirements. Basic control is achieved by the throttle valve.

The lubricating system includes a pump that pumps oil, under pressure, through oil lines or holes drilled in the engine parts to the surfaces that have relative motion.

The ignition system is part of the electric system, which also includes the battery, cranking motor, generator (or alternator), regulator, lights, wiring, switches, and so on. The ignition system steps up the low voltage of the battery or generator to the thousands of volts needed to jump the gaps at the spark plugs in the combustion chambers. This produces the sparks that initiate combustion. The sparks are timed to occur at the optimum time in the engine cycles by advance mechanisms. As engine speed increases, these mechanisms advance the spark to give the compressed charges ample time to burn. They also advance the spark at part throttle because the less highly compressed charges under this condition need more time to burn.

The cooling system has a water pump which circulates water, the cooling medium, between the water jackets in the engine and the radiator. This transfers heat from the engine to the radiator and then to the air passing through the radiator, so that engine parts are kept within acceptable temperature limits.

QUESTIONS

1. *Name the major components in the fuel system, and explain briefly how each works.*
2. *In the carburetor, what is the purpose of the venturi? Of the float bowl and float?*
3. *Explain the purpose of the throttle valve.*
4. *In the lubricating system, explain briefly how the oil is circulated.*
5. *List the major components of the electric system, and state the purpose of each.*
6. *Explain briefly how the contact points and ignition coil produce high-voltage surges.*
7. *What are the two types of spark-advance mechanisms? Explain how each works.*
8. *Explain briefly how the engine cooling system works.*

Engine Design

CHAPTER **9**

This is the first of several chapters which deal with the fundamentals of engine design. In the design of any intricate mechanism, such as an internal-combustion engine, there are many interrelated factors to consider. No one item can be considered with absolute independence because its design will have an effect on other engine components. Valve size and configurations, for example, have an intimate relationship with the design of the combustion chamber, piston, and intake manifold. Thus, even though there are separate sections and chapters on individual engine components, it must be remembered that their design cannot be considered independently of the other components or of the engine itself.

§109. What design means We can define design in many ways. In automotive engineering, we generally understand it to mean taking existing mechanisms or ideas and altering or adapting them to meet new needs. For example, the fundamental configuration of the four-stroke-cycle, internal-combustion engine was set a hundred years ago. But millions of man-hours have been spent in improving the design, so that the engine of today bears only faint resemblance to its distant ancestor.[1,2]

It is somewhat different with devices that have no direct ancestor, such as the space modules that are designed to carry men to the moon and Mars. Yet, even here, the designers have a fund of knowledge and experience to fall back on—the results of experiments, flybys, unmanned vehicle landings, and so on.

In its broadest sense, design consists of the following steps:

1. Determining the purpose. In an automobile engine, you might select as the purpose improving fuel economy, increasing torque, increasing horsepower output, increasing top speed, or improving the life of bearings, valves, or piston rings. You can see that some of these purposes are nearly mutually exclusive. Thus, if you improve the torque or horsepower output, bearings and other parts will be worked harder and will have a shorter service life. On the other hand, redesigning of these parts will prolong their life, even under the harsher demands of higher output or speed.

In any event, the first determination is that of the basic purpose of embarking on the development of a new design. You must know in which direction you are going.

2. Setting up an ideal. After determining your purpose, you must set up an ideal toward which you can strive in your design work. For instance, suppose you determine to improve valve life. You must then say how much you want to improve it. In other words, what is the ideal? A life of 50,000 miles under the most severe service? 100,000 miles? Or eliminate poppet valves altogether, with a radical valving design?

3. Gathering information. Next comes the job of gathering all related information on the matter. This means referring to the handbooks, the engineering archives of the company, and the latest scientific and engineering papers presented at the society meetings, and talking to other engineers who are working along the same lines. In other words, you must find out what has been done in the past, what is going on now, and what other men may be planning in the future that relates to the design problem facing you.

4. Selecting the most logical alternatives. A study of the previous designs and their performance, as well as what is going on at the present, may point the way to the most logical approaches. At this time, or perhaps earlier, you would be thinking about other factors besides the fundamental one of the ideal solution. You would consider such factors as costs of developing, testing, and proving out the design; the economic practicality of the design; possible hazards to manufacturing personnel, the vehicle driver, and the general public; its possible interest to top management; possible costs of tooling the factory to make the new design; economic advantages to the company; its possible acceptance in the market place; and so on. Out of your consideration of all of these sometimes contradictory factors might come one logical approach, or perhaps a few alternatives. There are several ways of improving piston or valve life, for example, but some would require very expensive materials, extensive design changes in the engine, or sacrifice of engine performance, and so on. Ultimately, however, you would be faced with perhaps two or three alternatives that would seem more or less equally attractive.

5. Picking the best alternative. Perhaps until this time, you have done practically no sketching of design configurations, let alone building and testing of prototypes. This may be the time that you now settle down to serious paper work, perhaps drafting actual design drawings, possibly programming the alternatives and running them through the company computer.[3] As the next step, you may have handmade models built to test out the alternatives. This is not always the proper approach, but it is sometimes desirable. Now, armed with the data accumulated from these activities, you are ready to firm up your design. Even this is only the beginning, however, because further laboratory and field testing may be required. Also, the design must clear the hurdles of process and plant engineering, service engineering, the economics and sales departments, as well as top management.

After that, if the new design goes into production, it may require modification if manufacturing "bugs" show up. Then, when it reaches the hands of the consumer, it will receive its ultimate testing, which may reveal certain weaknesses or lacks that would require still further modification.

You can see, therefore, that design is a continuing process, and, especially as applied to automotive engines, a continuous altering and modifying of the basic design are required.

§110. The life of a design Of basic importance to all mechanical design work is a consideration of design life; that is, how long will a particular design last and find favorable reception in the market place? How much and how many times can a design be improved to hold its place against competition? How costly will it be to carry a new design from the idea stage through to the completed product? How costly will it be to change the design for improved performance?

It has been said, by some automotive engineers, that the cost of designing a new engine, proving it, setting up the production machinery to make 8,000 engines a day, and getting the parts, tools, and knowledge out to the service men, runs well over $100,000,000. Whether or not this figure is high or low, it becomes obvious that the designer of any mechanical device must concern himself with the long-term future of his design. For example, take the automotive engine. We have already noted that the trend is to increase compression ratios, torque, and horsepower (Chap. 6). The engine designer must keep this trend in mind whenever he alters a design or begins a new design. The design must have plenty of "reserve," as it were, so it can grow and change in accordance with the trend. It is just too costly to produce a "dead-end" design that cannot be altered in future years to improve performance.

§111. Engine design considerations The design of the piston type of automotive engine, which is the subject of this and several succeeding chapters, is already fairly well fixed insofar as basics are concerned. A piston moves back and forth in a cylinder. During the power stroke, the piston transmits power through the connecting rod to the crankshaft. During the other three strokes, the crankshaft moves the piston. The valves open and close to admit fresh charges of air-fuel mixture and to permit burned gases to exhaust.

Thus, the engine design engineer is not faced with the problem of starting out to design a completely new mechanism. Instead, his problem is to provide improvements of an existing structure. These improvements focus on such aspects of the engine as valve and cylinder arrangement, combustion-chamber shapes, manifolding, cooling-system efficiency, lubrication methods, compression ratio, and so on.[2] All of these factors have an effect on the thermal, volumetric, and mechanical efficiency of the engine.

These factors, of course, determine the overall efficiency of the engine as well as its performance. Actually, the car owner usually thinks of engine performance in terms of economy, power, reliability, and smoothness. He wants an engine that will give him high power and torque at low fuel cost, with maximum smoothness. He wants all this for as long as he owns the car. And he does not want any repair bills.

Of course, these desires present the engine designer with a challenge to produce a reliable engine of high output and high efficiency that will operate smoothly at all speeds and loads. It is not easy to do this because, as already noted, high power and low fuel costs are opposing characteristics, as are high power and low wear rates of engine parts, or maximum performance and smooth engine operation.

Smoothness, for example, results from a combination of factors: absence of combustion roughness and knock, good engine balance, freedom from engine vibration, and lively acceleration without flat spots.

In following articles, we will consider factors affecting the three efficiencies referred to above: thermal, volumetric, mechanical. Later chapters discuss the design problems of specific components such as pistons, rings, valves, and so on.

§112. Thermal efficiency Thermal efficiency is defined in §59. It is a measure of how effectively the engine can use the thermal energy in the fuel. Naturally, high thermal efficiency means low fuel costs and is therefore desirable from that standpoint. However, compromises must be made because many factors that improve thermal efficiency reduce engine smoothness and increase wear rates. The major factors that improve thermal efficiency include:

1. Reducing heat losses to exhaust and cooling water.
2. Achieving ideal air-fuel ratio for operating condition.
3. Increasing compression ratio.
4. Achieving ideal burn rate of charge.

If you will refer to §60, which compares the *PV* (pressure-volume) curve of an actual engine with the ideal, you will see how reducing the heat loss improves the thermal efficiency. However, in certain engines, it is necessary to *increase* heat loss to prevent knock and engine roughness. Engines with a wedge-shaped combustion chamber require a quench area (Fig. 9-1). This area is the farthest point from the spark plug and always holds the last part of the charge to be burned. The quench area provides metal surfaces to which heat in the tail end of the burning charge can radiate. This pre-

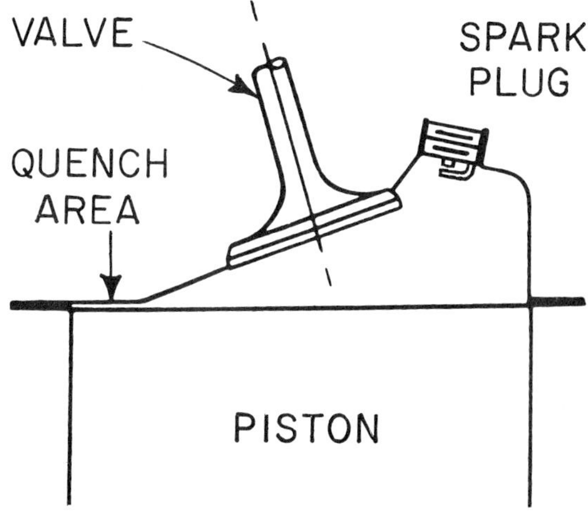

Fig. 9-1. Location of quench area in combustion chamber.

vents excessive heat rise and subsequent detonation of the last part of the charge. (The following chapter discusses this in greater detail.)

Another way to reduce heat loss is to increase the size of the cylinder bore. This increases the length of the heat path to the cylinder walls, either directly or through the piston. More heat energy is thus available during the power stroke. However, the piston will run hotter and, if an engine is redesigned to have a larger bore, then the piston probably would require redesigning too. Possibly it would require the use of another material which can accept higher temperatures without damage. In addition, a larger bore is more likely to knock and requires higher octane fuel (§120).

A similar problem occurs with increased compression ratios and burn rates of the compressed charges. Increasing the compression ratio raises point 2 on the *PV* curve and also provides a greater differential pressure between points 3 and 4 (see Fig. 5-9), all of which permits greater utilization of the heat energy in the fuel. But increasing the compression ratio increases the burn rate and the tendency for detonation and knocking to occur. This must be compensated for by changes of the combustion-chamber shape, as well as by changes in the chemical structure of the fuel and the use of additives in the fuel. (All of this is discussed in the following chapter.)

§113. Volumetric efficiency Getting more air-fuel mixture into the engine cylinders during the intake strokes improves the volumetric efficiency and engine performance, especially at high speeds (see §61). Volumetric efficiency can be improved by decreasing any restriction to the flow of air or air-fuel mixture through the induction system—air cleaner, carburetor, and intake manifold. It can also be increased by reducing the amount of heat that is injected into the air-fuel mixture as it moves toward the cylinders. Increasing the size and lift of the intake valves also increases volumetric efficiency. In addition, reducing the restrictions in the exhaust system to permit freer exhausting of the burned gases from the engine cylinders improves volumetric efficiency.

However, every one of these activities has limitations, and with some there are adverse effects on engine performance or design characteristics. For example, reducing the amount of heat injected into the ingoing air-fuel mixture may retard evaporation of the fuel droplets so that complete evaporation will not take place. If liquid gasoline enters the cylinders, it will wash the lubricant off the cylinder walls and increase cylinder-wall and piston-ring wear. Further, it may seep down into the crankcase and dilute the lubricating oil, thus hastening the wear of other engine parts. Also, of course, the unburned gasoline represents a loss of thermal efficiency because its heat energy is never realized.

In a like manner, there are limits to the reduction of restrictions in the induction system. For example, good turbulence of the air-fuel charge before ignition reduces knock tendencies. But good turbulence requires restrictions in the intake-port area which promote high entering velocities. In addition, the venturi, or venturis, in the carburetor must impose a restriction in order to function and cause fuel to feed from the fuel nozzles. In many engines, four-barrel carburetors are used, with two barrels coming into action only at high speed, to improve volumetric efficiency. Also, some engines have tuned intake manifolds that provide a ramjet action which improves volumetric efficiency at certain speeds. In addition, some engines use superchargers which apply pressure on the ingoing air-fuel mixture so as to induct a greater weight of the mixture on the intake strokes. All of these, however, bring additional problems (as will be explained in later chapters).

§114. Mechanical efficiency Mechanical efficiency (§79) is the ratio of power delivered to power developed in the engine cylinders. It can be increased by reducing frictional losses in the engine caused by relative motion between pistons, rings, and cylinder walls, as well as between bearings, crankshaft, and camshaft.

We have already mentioned the oversquare engine (§62), in which the stroke is shorter than the bore diameter, thus decreasing the frictional path of the piston and piston rings on the cylinder walls. This reduces the frictional losses and increases mechanical efficiency.

Another power loss in the engine, called *pumping loss*, results from the power used up on the intake and exhaust strokes. Reducing restrictions in the induction and exhaust systems reduces this loss (see §113).

In addition, power is used up by parasitic mechanisms such as the engine fan, water pump, generator, and power-steering pump. These losses must be accepted, as a rule. However, there are devices that will reduce fan losses. These include the flex-fan, which has blades that flex at higher speeds to reduce power requirements and noise, and the variable-speed fan, which holds down fan speed at higher engine rpms. Such fans may save more than 15 hp (horsepower) at higher engine speeds.

SUMMARY

In the automotive field, *design* usually refers to improving present designs to meet new needs. These steps are generally followed in design work: determining the purpose, setting up an ideal, gathering information, selecting the most logical alternatives, and picking the best alternative.

The life of a design is very important. A design should be capable of being modified for further improvement. For example, a new engine design should be such that it can be modified in subsequent years to increase compression ratios. If it is not, then when the demand for higher compression ratios is made, a new design must be brought out, and this is costly.

The three efficiencies with which the engine designer must contend include thermal efficiency, volumetric efficiency, and mechanical efficiency.

REFERENCES

1. Lucas, A. G., Spark Ignition Engine Progress, SAE (Society of Automotive Engineers) 670199, 1967 (paper).

2. Aiken, A., Ford of Britain's Vee Engine Range, SAE (Society of Automotive Engineers) 670004, 1967 (paper).

3. Borman, G. L., Computer Aided Engine Design, SAE (Society of Automotive Engineers) 670523, 1967 (paper).

QUESTIONS

1. What are the five steps that have been listed as comprising the design process? Explain each.

2. Explain what design life means and why it is so important.

3. What are some of the basic engine design considerations?

4. What is thermal efficiency? What factors tend to improve engine thermal efficiency?

5. What is volumetric efficiency? What are some of the factors involved in improving volumetric efficiency of the engine?

6. What is meant by the term "parasitic" as applied to such mechanisms as the engine fan, water pump, and so on?

Engine Fuel

CHAPTER **10**

This chapter discusses the hydrocarbon fuel, gasoline, that is used in automotive engines; the following chapter examines the closely related matter of combustion-chamber design. For good thermal efficiency, a smoothly running engine, absence of knock, low wear rate, and high horsepower and torque, the gasoline must have a rather specific chemical structure and must be burned in a combustion chamber that will conform mechanically to the chemical action of combustion.

§115. Automotive-engine fuels Most automobiles use the hydrocarbon, gasoline, as fuel. Gasoline appears to be a simple substance, but analysis shows it to be a complex mixture of several compounds plus a number of additives that do not contribute directly to engine operation. These additives (described in §128) serve various purposes, such as preventing gum formation, rust, engine knocking, dirt accumulation in the carburetor, icing in the carburetor, and so on.

Gasoline is produced from crude oil or petroleum. Petroleum is composed largely of a mixture of thousands of different compounds of hydrogen and carbon. Some of the lighter fractions, or compounds, of the petroleum can be separated by distillation to become gasoline. Others must be converted to gasoline by various conversion processes, one of which is called *thermal cracking*. By applying heat and pressure to the petroleum, some of the heavier hydrocarbon compounds are *cracked*, or broken down, into lighter hydrocarbons such as gasoline. Another process, *catalytic cracking*, or *cat cracking*, uses a catalytic agent to assist the conversion process. A variation of this process is called *fluid cat cracking*. The catalyst is in powdered form and flows through the petroleum. Another process is called *reforming*; this process reshapes the molecular structure of the hydrocarbons.

The purpose of all these processes is to produce a liquid hydrocarbon that can serve satisfactorily as fuel for the internal-combustion engine. A satisfactory gasoline must have the proper volatility, antiknock (or octane) rating; it must also have various additives (as mentioned above) to combat ice formation, rust, gum, and so on. The following articles discuss each of these attributes in detail.

§116. Volatility of gasoline Volatility refers to the ease with which a liquid evaporates. Alcohol has a high volatility; it evaporates at a relatively low temperature. Heavy oil has a low volatility; one type, for example, will not evaporate until it is heated to above 600°F.

Gasoline is blended from different hydrocarbon compounds having different volatilities.[1] Some of these evaporate at low temperatures more readily than others. The following combination is necessary for satisfactory engine operation under varying conditions.

1. Easy starting. For easy starting with a cold engine, gasoline must be highly volatile so that it vaporizes readily as it passes through the carburetor, even when air and fuel temperatures are low. Thus, a certain percentage of the gasoline must be volatile enough to permit easy starting. In winter the percentage of high-volatility gasoline is increased for good cold-weather starting. Also, the percentage of high-volatility gasoline varies in different parts of the country; the percentage is higher in the colder northern states.

2. *Freedom from vapor lock.* If gasoline is too volatile, heat from the engine will cause it to vaporize in the fuel lines and fuel pump. This action results in gas pockets, or *vapor locks*, that prevent normal fuel-pump action. When gas pockets exist, the increasing and decreasing pressures in the fuel line (due to fuel-pump action) simply cause the pockets to contract and expand. Thus, little or no fuel is pumped from the fuel tank into the carburetor. The engine then loses power or completely stalls from fuel starvation. To prevent vapor locks, the percentage of highly volatile gasoline must be kept relatively low. Thus, it can be seen that the requirements for easy starting and requirements for freedom from vapor lock are in opposition. That is, there must be enough high-volatility gasoline for easy starting, but not so much as to cause vapor lock.

3. *Quick warm-up.* The speed with which the engine will warm up depends in part on the percentage of gasoline that will vaporize immediately after the engine is started (and thus contribute to engine operation). Volatility for this purpose does not have to be quite as high as for easy starting. This is because, immediately after starting, the air speed through the carburetor is greater, and turbulence in the manifold and cylinder during intake and compression helps to vaporize the gasoline.

4. *Smooth acceleration.* When the throttle is opened for acceleration, there is a sudden increase of air rushing through the carburetor into the engine cylinders. At the same time, the accelerator pump delivers an extra amount of gasoline. If the gasoline does not vaporize quickly during this interval, a large mass of air will reach the cylinders without carrying its proper proportion of gasoline vapor. The mixture entering the cylinders will be too lean for good combustion, and the engine will hesitate or stutter. Immediately afterward, as the gasoline metered out by the accelerator pump begins to vaporize, the mixture reaching the cylinders will become too rich. This again produces poor combustion and a logy engine. The result is uneven and inferior acceleration. A sufficient percentage of the gasoline must be volatile enough to prevent this condition. On the other hand, if too large a percentage of the gasoline is highly volatile, there will be an overrich mixture on acceleration. This would cause the engine to "roll" or "load up," resulting in poor acceleration.

5. *Good economy.* For good fuel economy, or maximum miles per gallon, the fuel must have a high heat, or energy, content and relatively low volatility. High overall volatility tends to reduce economy, since the mixture may become overrich under many conditions of operation. On the other hand, the lower-volatility fuels tend to burn more efficiently, providing better fuel economy. However, the lower-volatility gasolines increase starting difficulty, reduce speed of warm-up, and do not give good acceleration. Thus, only a limited percentage of the gasoline can be of low volatility.

6. *Freedom from crankcase dilution.* When gasoline is not sufficiently volatile, some of it will enter the cylinder in liquid form as tiny unevaporated droplets. These droplets spray on the cylinder walls, washing off the film of lubricating oil. Removing the lubricating-oil film in this manner increases the rate at which the cylinder wall, piston rings, and piston will wear. Furthermore, the liquid gasoline passes the piston rings and enters the oil pan or crankcase. The lubricating oil is thus diluted by the gasoline, and it loses some of its lubricating ability. This means that all moving engine parts will wear more rapidly. After the engine has operated for a while and has thoroughly warmed up, this liquid gasoline in the crankcase begins to vaporize and is removed by the crankcase ventilating system (described in §257). To avoid damage to the engine before it warms up, the gasoline must be sufficiently volatile to avoid crankcase dilution.

7. *The volatility blend.* It is obvious from the above discussion that no one volatility would satisfy all engine operating requirements. On the one hand, the fuel must have high volatility for easy starting and acceleration. But it must also be of low volatility to give good fuel economy and com-

bat vapor lock. Thus, gasoline must be blended from various amounts of fuels that have different volatilities. Such a gasoline will then satisfy the various operating requirements.

§117. Antiknock value During normal combustion in the engine cylinder, an even increase of pressure occurs. However, if the fuel burns too rapidly, or "explodes," there is a sudden and sharp pressure increase. This sudden pressure increase produces a rapping or knocking noise that sounds almost as though the piston head had been struck a hard hammer blow. Actually, the sudden pressure increase does impose a sudden heavy load on the piston that is almost like a hammer blow. This can be very damaging to the engine, wearing moving parts rapidly and perhaps even causing parts to break. Furthermore, the energy in the gasoline is wasted since the sudden pressure increase does not contribute much to the production of power.

It has been found that some types of gasoline burn very rapidly in engine cylinders and thus knock very badly. Other types of fuel burn more slowly and therefore do not knock. Also, certain chemicals have been found which, when added to the gasoline, slow down the rate of burning so that knocking is eliminated. Gasoline is rated according to how easily it will knock, that is, by its antiknock value. The actual rating is by ONR (*octane number rating*). This term, and the theory of knocking are discussed in following articles.

§118. Compression ratio and bore size Before we discuss further the antiknock value of gasoline, let us talk once again about compression ratio and cylinder-bore size because both of these have a direct influence on knocking tendencies in an engine. As previously noted (in §64), increasing the compression ratio increases thermal efficiency and engine output. Also, increasing the cylinder bore improves volumetric efficiency and engine torque (§78). All of these improvements are desirable.

However, increasing the compression ratio and bore size increases knocking tendencies. It has therefore been necessary for engineers to develop fuels with greater knock resistance and also to do much research on combustion-chamber shapes. The shape of a combustion chamber has a profound effect on knock tendencies, and thus a great deal of work has been done in this area, as is detailed in Chap. 11.

§119. Heat of compression To understand why knocking occurs, let us first see what happens to any gas when it is compressed. As an example, consider what happens to the temperature of air at atmospheric pressure when it is compressed adiabatically to one-fifteenth of its original volume (in an engine with a compression ratio of 15:1). When this happens, the temperature of the air rises more than 1,000°F. When the air is compressed, work is done on it; this work is converted into heat energy, thus raising the temperature of the air. This temperature rise is called the *heat of compression.*

To consider the matter from the molecular point of view, compressing the air moves the air molecules closer together so they collide with much greater frequency, thus causing the molecules to move at a greater rate of speed (see §54).

§120. Causes of knocking During normal burning of fuel in the combustion chamber, the spark at the spark plug starts the burning process. A wall of flame spreads out in all directions from the spark, almost like a rubber balloon being blown up. The wall of flame travels rapidly outward through the compressed mixture in the combustion chamber until all the charge is burned. The speed with which the flame spreads is called the *rate of flame propagation*. The movement of the flame wall through the combustion chamber during normal combustion is shown in the row of pictures at the left in Fig. 10-1. During combustion, the pressure in the combustion chamber increases to several hundred pounds per square inch (psi). It may exceed 1,000 psi in the modern high-compression engine.

Under certain conditions, the last part of the compressed air-fuel mixture, or end gas, will ex-

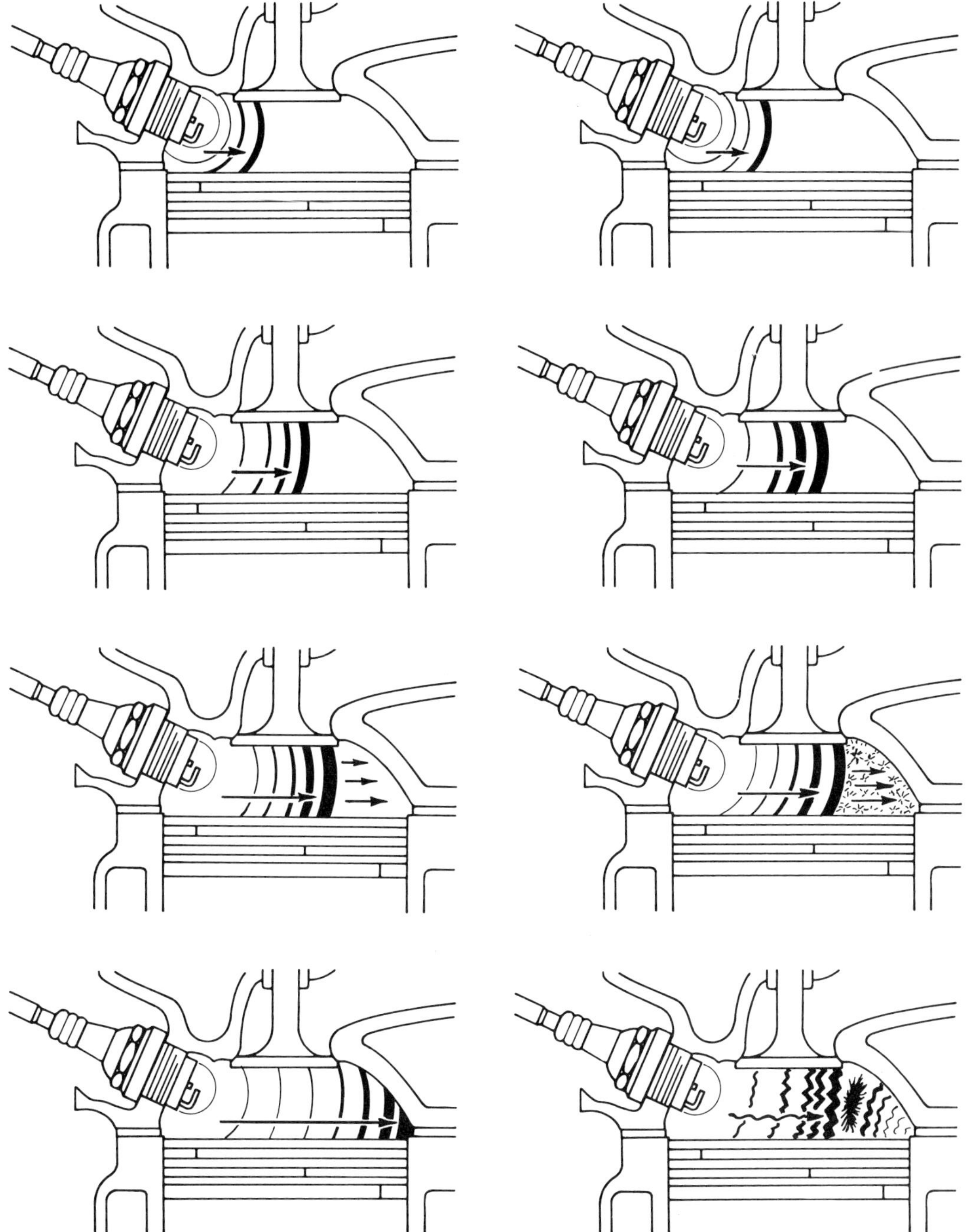

Fig. 10-1. Normal combustion without knocking is shown in the vertical row on the left. The fuel charge burns smoothly from beginning to end, providing an even, powerful thrust to the piston. Knocking is shown in the vertical row on the right. The last part of the fuel explodes, or burns almost instantaneously, to produce detonation, or knocking. (*General Motors Corporation*)

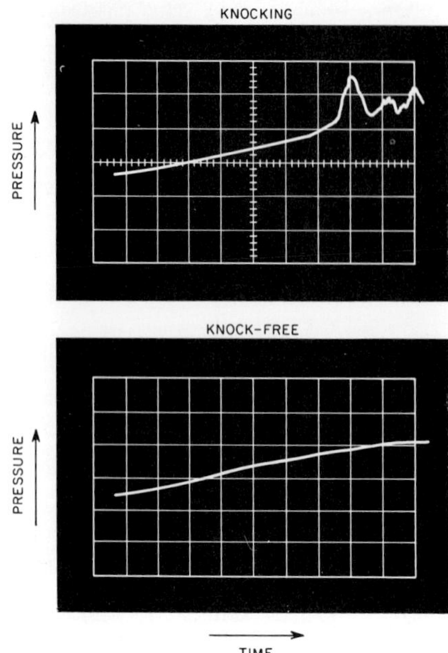

Fig. 10-2. Single-cycle oscilloscope pressure traces (sweep rate, 100 microseconds per centimeter), showing knocking and knock-free combustion conditions. (*Shell Oil Company*)

plode before the flame front reaches it (right, Fig. 10-1). It must be remembered that the end gas is subjected to increasing pressure as the flame progresses through the air-fuel mixture. This increases the end-gas temperature (due to heat of compression and also radiated heat from the combustion). If this temperature increases beyond the critical point or is maintained for a sufficient time, the end gas will detonate, as previously noted, before the flame front arrives.

It requires an appreciable time, even though it may be measured in microseconds (0.000001 second), for any chemical reaction to start. Increasing the temperature reduces this time. Thus, if the temperature goes high enough or is maintained long enough, the end gas will explode. This may be prevented by one of three methods: increasing the rate of flame propagation so that the flame arrives at the end gas in time; subtracting some heat from the end gas; or using a chemically more stable fuel that will take the higher temperatures without detonation. (These three methods are discussed in great detail later.)

NOTE: The first two methods are related to combustion-chamber design. Different designs have greatly varying knock characteristics (Chap. 11). This is one reason that the I-head engine has supplanted the L-head engine. The L-head engine has a longer flame-travel path and thus greater knock tendencies, which must be combatted by the inclusion of a large quench area (§132).

When the last part of the compressed air-fuel mixture, or end gas, explodes before the flame front reaches it, there will be a sudden and sharp pressure increase, followed by a very rapid oscillation of pressure in the combustion chamber.[2] This is illustrated in Fig. 10-2. The lower curve shows the steady pressure rise during a few microseconds of knock-free combustion. The upper curve shows what happens to the pressure when the last part of the charge detonates, or explodes. The pressure rises sharply and almost instantaneously. Shock waves from this explosion progress rapidly through the burned gases in the combustion chamber and strike the exposed surfaces of the piston, cylinder head, and cylinder walls. These shock waves, or pressure pulses, bounce off the metal surfaces and pass back and forth at sonic speeds through the gases, creating a series of pressure pulses in the gases. These pressure pulses, repeatedly striking the metal surfaces of the combustion chamber, cause the characteristic noise of knocking. The repeated blows of the shock waves on the metal surfaces can impose severe stresses on engine parts. Shock loads are applied to the piston, connecting rod, crankshaft, and bearings. Bearings, in particular, are susceptible to rapid failure under severe knocking conditions, although pistons, rods, and crankshafts have also failed from this condition.

§121. Study of knocking Many studies of knocking have been made.[1] One method uses a standard engine, running it on various fuels to determine the fuel sensitivity to knock (see §123). This method uses ignition spark advance as a control factor. As will be recalled (§107), the ignition-advance mechanism in the ignition distributor provides an advance based on engine speed. This initiates the combustion process earlier in the cycle at higher engine speeds. The air-fuel charge thus is given more time to burn and give up its energy to the piston. Excessive spark advance, however, will cause knocking. If the combustion process starts too early for any specific piston speed, it will near completion before, or by the time that, the piston reaches TDC (top dead center). With this condition, pressures will go so high that the last part of the charge will explode before the flame front reaches it. In other words, knocking will result. Some fuels are more knock resistant than others and can take more spark advance before they knock. Thus, one method of comparing knock resistance of various fuels is to determine how much spark advance they can stand without knocking (§123).

A second method of studying knocking uses a special engine, with a means of varying the compression ratio and with special sensing devices to measure the effects of such variations. This is the method we wish to discuss now to provide an insight into how automotive engineers study design problems.[2] The experimental work reported in the reference paper was designed to throw light on the actual mechanism of knock, its causes and effects. A special one-cylinder CFR (Cooperative Fuel Research) engine was used, similar to the one illustrated in Fig. 10-3. The engine was equipped with a special spacer plate between the cylinder block and head. This spacer plate can be replaced with thicker or thinner plates to decrease or increase the compression ratio. Also, the engine had several probe holes, or passages, into which various sensing devices could be placed to measure pressure, detect the flame front, and sense light radiations (Fig. 10-4).

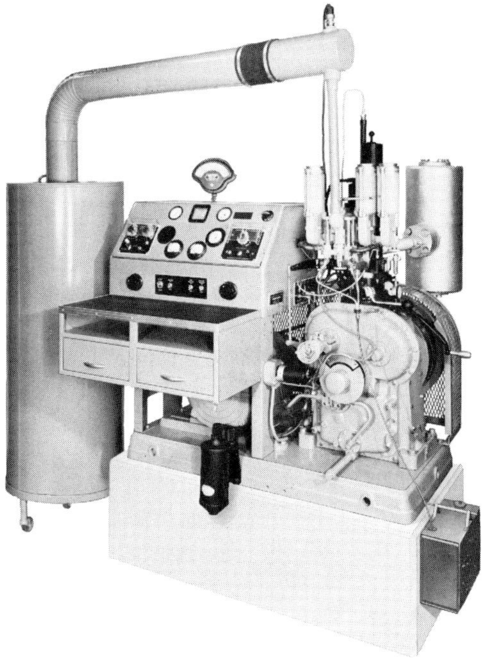

Fig. 10-3. Special engine for testing knock characteristics, or octane ratings, of fuels. (*Waukesha Motor Company*)

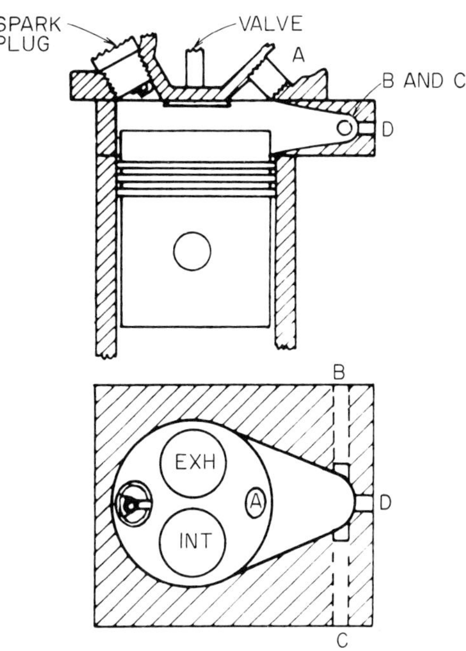

Fig. 10-4. Side and top schematic views of engine combustion chamber used to study knock. The four lettered holes (A, B, C, and D) provide receptacles for instruments. (*Shell Oil Company*)

During the test, the pressure sensor was placed in one or another of the probe holes (A, B, C, or D, Fig. 10-4), and the engine was operated on various fuels. The pressure sensor was connected to a high-speed oscilloscope so that the trace indicated the instantaneous pressure changes taking place. Figure 10-5 shows the traces of several individual knock events as displayed on the oscilloscope-tube face.

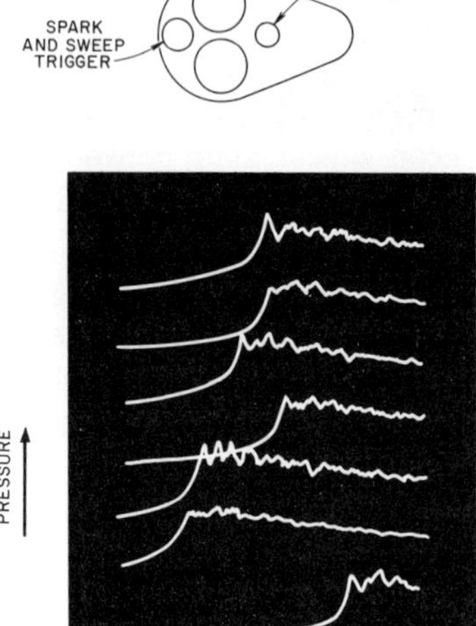

Fig. 10-5. Cycle-to-cycle variations in knock (sweep rate is 0.2 milliseconds per centimeter). (*Shell Oil Company*)

In addition, light detectors (photomultipliers) were placed at various probe holes (usually B or C) to measure light emission during the knocking phase of the combustion process. Also, ion gaps were placed at the various probe holes. (Ions are electrically charged atoms or molecules that have lost or gained electrons. In chemical reactions such as combustion, this loss or gain of electrons is a step in the chemical process.) The appearance of ions at the ion gap triggers impulses that produce traces on the oscilloscope-tube face.

With the above instrumentation, not only the pressures, but also the amount of light and the density of ions, can be displayed as traces on the tube face. For example, Fig. 10-6 shows the traces resulting from normal combustion. Note that the pressure rises in a long, smooth curve, with light and ions appearing later in the event. The reason for this, in the setup shown in Fig. 10-6, is that the photomultiplier (light detector) is placed at probe hole C, and the terminal ion gap is at probe hole D.

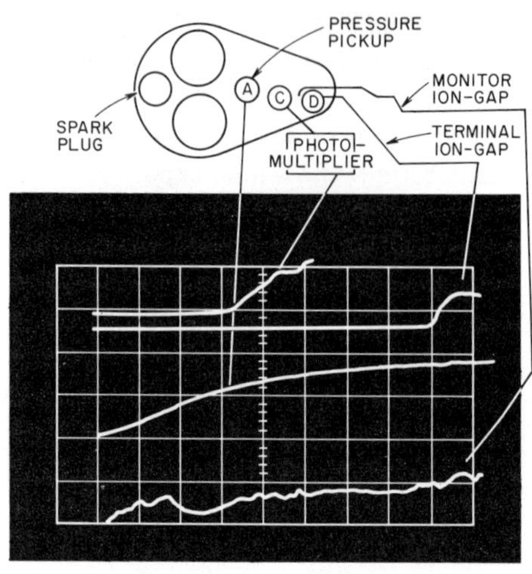

Fig. 10-6. High-resolution traces from pressure, ion-gap, and photomultiplier instrumentation located in combustion chamber in positions shown (sweep rate, 200 microseconds per centimeter). (*Shell Oil Company*)

The pressure pick-up is placed at probe hole A. This alignment picks up the pressure rise first, and, then, as the flame front moves toward probe hole D, the light is detected at probe hole C somewhat later, and the ions at probe hole D still later.

Figure 10-7 shows the pressure, ion, and light traces during knocking combustion. Notice now that the pressure rises abruptly, and that a series of pressure pulses of decreasing severity then follows. Notice also that the presence of light and ions were detected at probe holes C and D almost

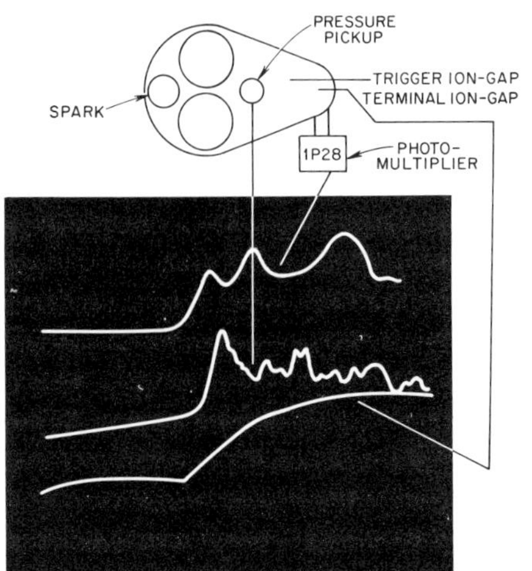

Fig. 10-7. High-resolution traces of knocking combustion (sweep rate, 100 microseconds per centimeter). (*Shell Oil Company*)

simultaneously with the sudden pressure rise. Contrast this with Fig. 10-6.

Analysis of many such traces permits certain deductions. The appearance of light emissions and the triggering of the ion gap at the same time that the sudden pressure rise occurs can be explained most logically by assuming that the last part of the air-fuel mixture exploded almost instantly. That is, this last part ignited as a unified mass because high pressure, light, and ions appeared in this area simultaneously.

§122. Control of knocking The urge to design engines of higher compression ratios and larger cylinder bores* for increased power and torque* has lead to the search for knock-free fuels and improved and more knock-free combustion-chamber designs for such engines. Increasing the compression ratio increases the knock tendencies of an engine. With a higher compression ratio, the air-fuel mixture at TDC is more highly compressed and is therefore at a higher initial temperature. Thus, it is nearer the explosion, or knocking, temperature. A smaller additional temperature increase will produce the almost instantaneous explosion of the last part of the air-fuel charge that produces knocking.

* The larger bore and shorter stroke design also reduces ring friction losses and bearing loads from inertia and centrifugal forces.

At the same time, a larger bore increases the distance that the flame front must travel to reach the end gas. This gives the end gas more time to react to the increasing pressure and thus increases the tendency for knocking to occur.

There are two general ways to control knocking. One relates to combustion-chamber design (Chap. 11), as some configurations are more knock-free than others. For example, a centrally located spark plug minimizes the distance that the flame front must travel. The second knock-control method relates to the chemical structure of the fuel itself, as well as the additives blended with the fuel. Before we describe these two approaches to knock control, let us first examine the methods used to measure the knock tendencies of fuels in engines.

§123. Measuring antiknock values of fuels Several methods have been developed[1] for testing fuels to determine their tendencies to knock in engines. Some fuels knock rather easily. Others have a high resistance to knock; that is, they have a high antiknock rating. The actual rating of a fuel for its antiknock value is made in terms of *octane* number, or ONR (octane number rating). A high-octane gasoline is highly resistant to knock; a low-octane gasoline knocks rather easily. There is a fuel called *isooctane* that is highly resistant to knocking; it is given an ONR of 100. Another fuel, called *heptane*, knocks very easily; it is given an ONR of 0. A mixture of half isooctane and half heptane (by volume) would have an ONR of 50. A mixture of 75 percent isooctane and 25 percent heptane would have an ONR of 75.

Actually, isooctane and heptane are reference fuels, used only to rate unknown fuels. One rating procedure makes use of a test engine (Fig. 10-3) which is built so that its compression ratio can be varied. A fuel that is to be rated is used to run the engine, and the compression ratio is increased until a certain intensity of knocking is obtained. Then, reference fuels of varying proportions of isooctane and heptane are used to run the engine. The octane rating of the reference fuel is decreased (by using smaller percentages of isooctane) until the same intensity of knocking results as obtained with the fuel to be rated. Then the fuel being rated is given the same octane number as the reference fuel, since both produce the same amount of knocking. If the reference fuel has 88 percent isooctane, for example, then both it and the fuel being tested are considered to have the same 88 octane rating.

1. *Laboratory-test method.* The laboratory-test method of measuring octane rating of a fuel has already been described. Essentially, the test engine is operated at a certain speed, with a certain ignition spark advance, and the compression ratio is varied until the test fuel causes knocking. Note that all conditions except compression ratio are kept constant through the test. This differs from actual over-the-road operation, where the compression ratio stays the same (being built into the engine) but most other conditions change (including speed, spark advance, temperature, carburetion, fuel distribution to cylinders, and so on). This difference between laboratory-test procedure and actual operating conditions has been apparent in the highway performance of laboratory-rated fuels. A fuel that knocks in one engine may not knock in another. A fuel that knocks at low speed may not knock at high speed. Another fuel may knock at high speed but not at low speed. However, despite the fact that the laboratory rating cannot pinpoint octane rating of a fuel for all kinds of performance, it is still of value, since it does give *comparative* ratings between different fuels.

2. *Road-test methods.* In order to determine more accurately how a fuel will act in normal highway operation, a number of road octane-rating tests have been developed. One of these, the Cooperative Fuel Research modified Uniontown road test (called the CFR Uniontown road test), rates fuels for knock intensity at wide-open throttle at various speeds. Octane is assigned by comparing knocking of the fuel being tested to reference fuels (isooctane and heptane mixtures) of known octane values.

Another method, called the *modified borderline procedure* (MBP) rates the fuel at various speeds and is considered to give much more information on fuel performance. This test is made by running a car at various speeds and then determining the amount of ignition spark advance the fuel can tolerate at each speed without knocking. If the spark is advanced too much at any speed, knocking will occur. Thus, the test results give us a curve that shows, at every speed, the knock characteristics of the fuel being tested (Fig. 10-8). Note, in Fig. 10-8, that the fuel tested permits an increasing spark advance with increasing speed. Any advance above the curved line causes knock.

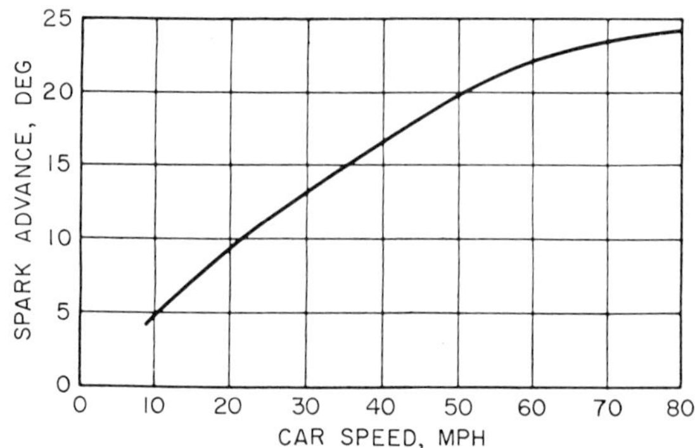

Fig. 10-8. Borderline knock curve. The fuel being tested will knock if the ignition spark is advanced to any value above the curve at any speed.

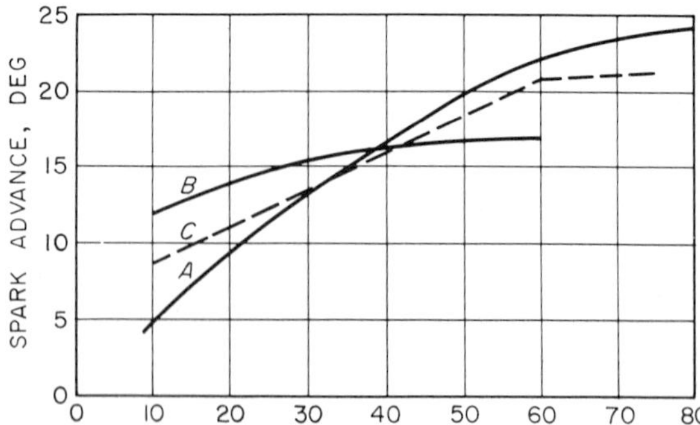

Fig. 10-9. Comparison of borderline knock curves of two fuels, A and B. Curve C is the spark advance actually provided by the ignition distributor on the engine.

To show how different fuels might act in the borderline knock test, see Fig. 10-9. This shows the curves of two fuels, *A* and *B*. Curve *C* is the amount of spark advance that the distributor provides on the engine used in the test. If, at any particular speed, the distributor advances the spark more than the fuel can tolerate, the fuel will knock. Thus, at low speeds, fuel *A* will knock, since the spark advance is more than the fuel can tolerate (that is, curve *C* is above curve *A* at low speeds). On the other hand, fuel *A* will not knock at high speeds, since the spark advance is not up to the amount the fuel can tolerate at high speeds. But fuel *B* gives a different story. It does not knock at low speeds, but it does knock at high speeds. These curves, which apply only to fuels *A* and *B*, emphasize the fact that different fuels act differently at different speeds and in different engines.

§124. Knock, preignition, and rumble Thus far, we have been discussing the type of knocking that results from detonation, or sudden explosion, of the last part of the fuel charge in the cylinder. This type of knocking is usually regular in character and is most noticeable when the engine is accelerated or is under heavy load, as when climbing a hill. Under these conditions, the accelerator is fully open, or nearly so, and the engine is taking in a full air-fuel charge on every intake stroke (that is, the volumetric efficiency is high). This means that the compression pressures are at the maximum; detonation pressures are more apt to be reached after the mixture is ignited.

There are other types of abnormal combustion, however.[3] Figure 10-10 outlines these abnormal combustion processes (surface ignition, wild ping, rumble, and so on). Surface ignition can originate from hot spots in the combustion chamber, such as on a hot exhaust valve or spark plug, or from combustion-chamber deposits. In some cases, particles of the deposit may float free and become hot enough to produce ignition. Surface ignition can occur before or after the spark occurs at the spark plug. Also, it can cause engine rumble and rough operation or mild to severe knocking. In some extreme cases, the hot spots act like glow plugs that substitute for the spark plug, so that the engine will continue to run even after the ignition switch is turned off. In severe runaway surface ignition, engine parts can be overloaded, and overheated, and the engine can be severely damaged.

Figure 10-11 shows pressure-time diagrams for normal combustion, rumble, and knock. Note that, with rumble, the pressure rises quickly to a peak, as opposed to knock, which commences somewhat later and is associated with a series of sharp pressure peaks.

Not only is the noise associated with rumble objectionable (Fig. 10-12), but also engine parts are severely stressed, as already mentioned. Figure 10-13 shows how rumble can greatly increase the deflection of the main-bearing caps.

Usually, preignition and rumble are service problems; that is, they result from inadequate maintenance of the engine, from the installation of the wrong spark plugs (a type that runs too hot), or from the use of incorrect fuels and lubricating oils for the engine and type of operation. With incorrect fuel or oil, engine deposits may occur so that preignition and rumble result.

To sum up, preignition and rumble are usually service problems in that they occur because of hot spots on surface deposits, valves, or spark plugs.* Knocking is a design problem, however, and is inherent in the combustion-chamber design as well as in the chemical structure of the fuel.

§125. Chemical control of knocking We have already mentioned that some fuels knock easily while others have considerable resistance to knocking. An examination of their chemical structures will help explain these characteristics. For example, the carbon skeleton of heptane, which knocks very easily (ONR of 0), is one long line, as shown in Fig. 10-14. Carbon has a valence of 4, which means that a carbon atom has, in effect, four bonds available with which it can attach to other atoms. In the linear arrangement shown in Fig. 10-14, most of these bonds are available, as it

* Of course, it is possible that poor design could allow surface deposits to form rapidly so that rumble would appear at low mileage.

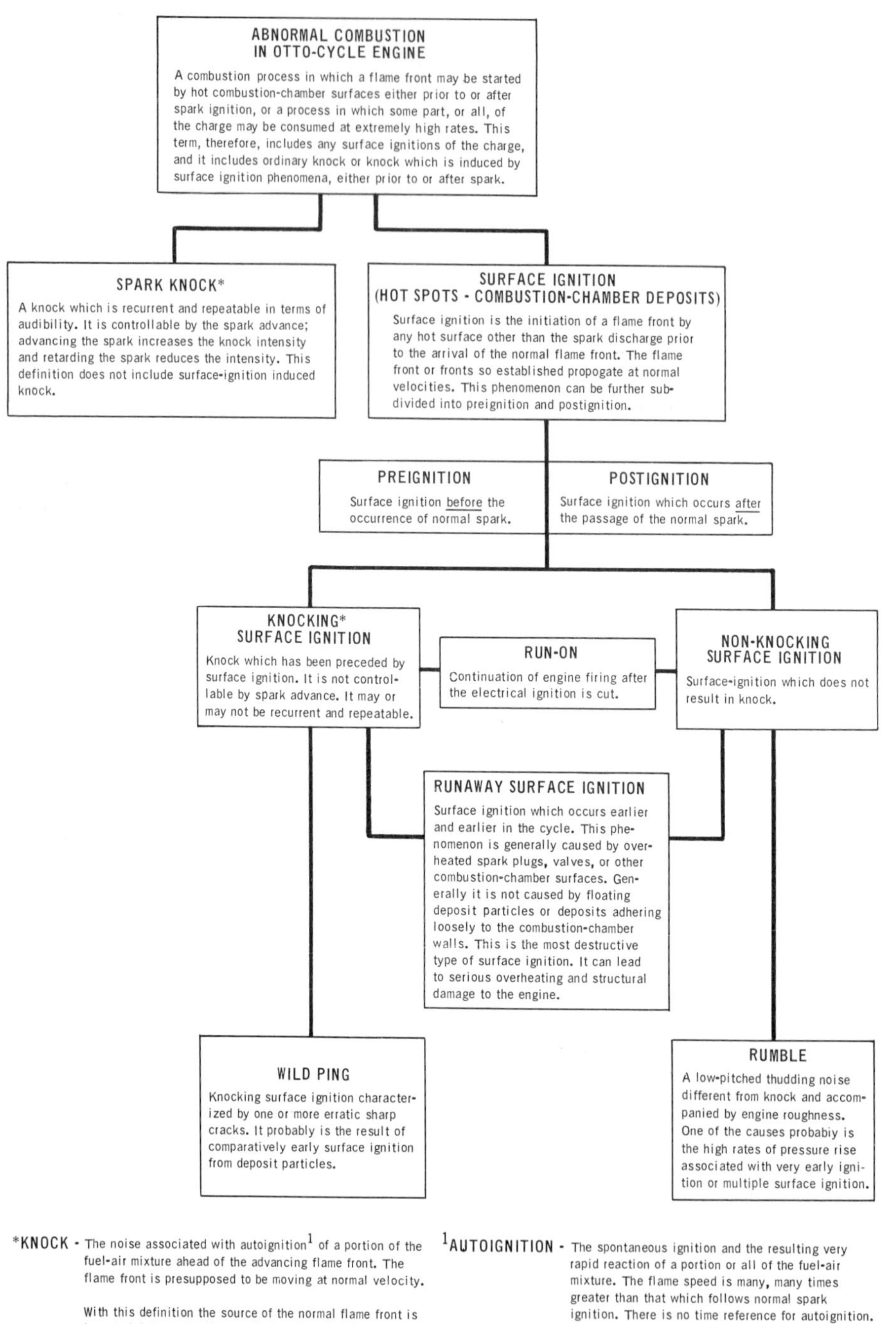

Fig. 10-10. Definitions of different types of abnormal combustion in the Otto-cycle engine. (*Pure Oil Company*)

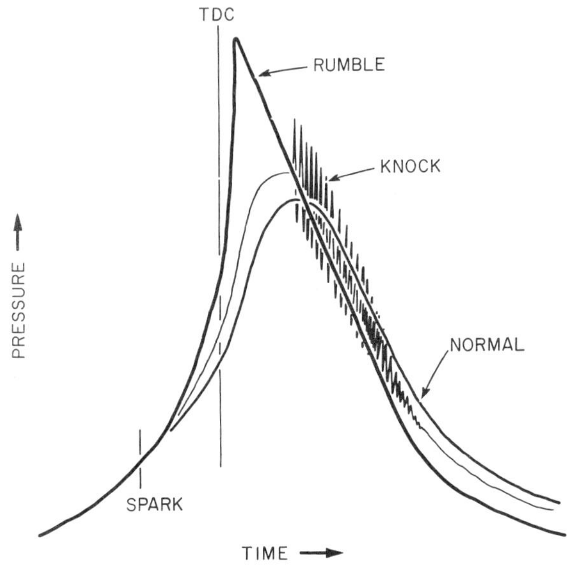

Fig. 10-11. Pressure-time diagrams for normal combustion, rumble, and knock. (*Pure Oil Company*)

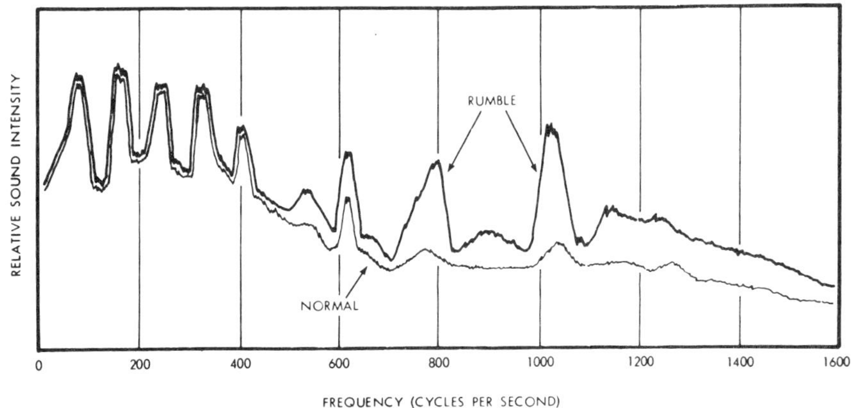

Fig. 10-12. Noise-frequency spectra for normal combustion and rumble. Note the marked increase of noise with rumble at 600, 800, and 1,000 cycles per second. (*Pure Oil Company*)

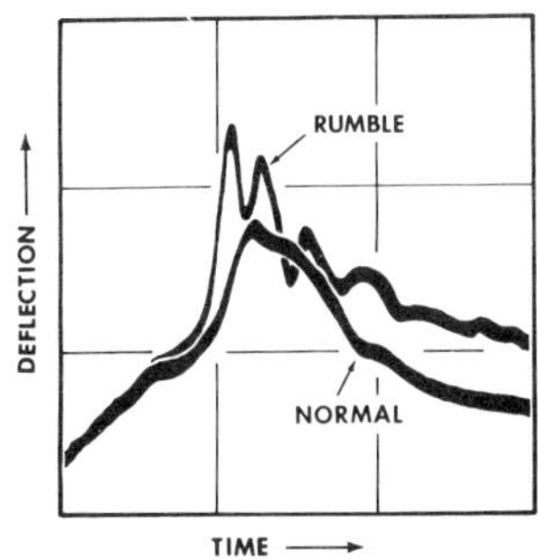

Fig. 10-13. Deflection of the main-bearing caps during normal combustion and during rumble. Note that the deflection, during rumble, is more sudden and remains higher through the early stages of the power stroke shown. (*Pure Oil Company*)

were, for instant attachment (only the single bonds between the carbon atoms need to be broken in a chemical reaction). These bonds can be broken quickly and at relatively low temperature.

C — C — C — C — C — C — C

Fig. 10-14. Carbon skeleton of heptane molecule.

On the other hand, isooctane has the carbon skeleton shown in Fig. 10-15. Note that one of the carbon atoms is bonded on four sides, and another on three. This means that these carbon atoms are more tightly locked together and it requires a higher temperature (or more time) to break them apart. In other words, isooctane has a higher antiknock, or octane, rating (an ONR of 100).

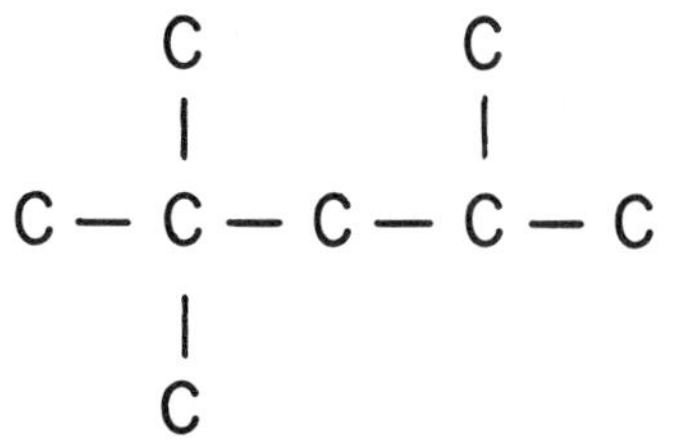

```
      C         C
      |         |
C  —  C  —  C — C — C
      |
      C
```

Fig. 10-15. Carbon skeleton of isooctane molecule.

The carbon skeleton of the benzene molecule (Fig. 10-16) illustrates another arrangement that gives benzene an ONR of 120. Note that the carbon atoms are bonded together in a ring. To break this ring down into separate atoms of carbon requires a still higher temperature (or longer time) than isooctane and thus benzene has a still higher ONR.

The carbon skeleton of the hydrocarbon molecule is thus closely related to the ONR of the fuel. In the refining process, different methods can be used to link the carbon atoms in various arrangements, producing fuels of different octane ratings.

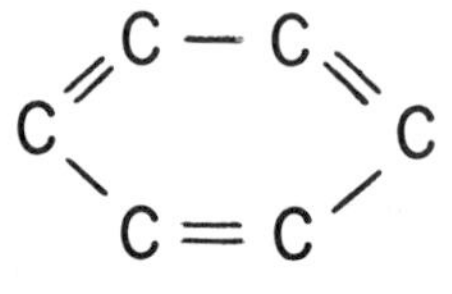

```
   C — C
 //     \\
C         C
 \       /
   C = C
```

Fig. 10-16. Carbon skeleton of benzene molecule.

The addition of antiknock agents to fuel can also raise its octane rating. The antiknock agent most widely used is tetraethyllead (*tel*). Within certain limits, the more *tel* added, the higher the octane rating of the fuel. Typically, about 2.5 ml (milliliters) of *tel* per gallon is used. The exact process by which *tel* inhibits knocking is not clearly understood. It is believed, however, that the *tel* molecules are decomposed into metals and oxides during the combustion process in the engine. These metals and oxides then momentarily interfere with the breaking of the carbon bonds in the hydrocarbon molecules and the forming of new bonds between the carbon atoms and oxygen atoms that are part of the air-fuel mixture. This increase of reaction time gives the flame front additional time to sweep on through the compressed air-fuel mixture, so that normal combustion continues through to the most remote part of the charge. Thus, the last part of the change does not explode and knocking does not occur.

To prevent the combustion products of the *tel* from depositing in the combustion chambers (on plugs, valves, walls, pistons, and rings), special *scavengers* are also added to the fuel. These compounds (ethylene dibromide and ethylene dichloride, for example) tend to change the lead compounds into forms which will vaporize and exit from the combustion chamber with the exhaust.

§126. Environmental factors affecting knocking A number of environmental factors influence knocking. Many tests have been made to establish the relationships between air temperature, humidity, ignition spark advance, engine deposits and knock tendency. Test results are usually given in terms of the octane-number increase necessary to eliminate knocking. For example, it is known that a hot engine knocks more easily than a cold engine. To obtain exact data on this, an engine is operated cold on the lowest-octane fuel it can use without knocking. Then it is operated hot on the lowest-octane fuel it can use without knocking. The difference in octane numbers is an indication of the increased octane requirements as the engine warms up. For example, one test showed that increasing the temperature of the cooling water in an engine from 100 to 190°F increased the octane requirements by 22 numbers (from 70 to 92, for instance). Other tests have shown the following:

1. A 20° rise in air temperature increases octane requirements by about three numbers.
2. An increase in humidity from 40 to 50 percent at 85°F reduces octane requirements by one number. This is laboratory proof of the common belief that the engine does run somewhat better and more quietly in damp weather.
3. Engine deposits increase octane requirements since they increase the compression ratio (part of the compression space is taken up by deposits). One series of tests showed that after about 10,000 miles of operation, engine deposits increased octane requirements by nine numbers.
4. Advancing the spark or leaning the mixture increases the octane requirements.
5. Higher altitudes (less dense air) reduce the octane requirements.

All these factors point up the need for good maintenance of the modern high-compression engine. Accumulation of scale in the cooling system, reducing cooling efficiency, deposits in the combustion chambers, clogged fuel lines or nozzles in the carburetor which lean out the mixture, improper ignition timing—all these increase the tendency to knock and require an increase of octane number to prevent knocking.

§127. Octane requirements The octane requirements of an engine are determined basically by the engine design. However, these requirements change with weather and driving conditions, as well as with the mechanical condition of the engine. We have noted in §126 how changing temperature and humidity change the octane needs of the engine. Engine deposits, reduced cooling-system efficiency, and carburetor or ignition troubles will also change octane requirements.

In addition to all these, the manner in which the driver operates the car has a marked effect on octane needs. If the driver is moderate and does not demand quick getaway and high speeds, he will seldom open the throttle wide, and his engine will be much less apt to knock (and thus have lower octane requirements). On the other hand, this type of operation tends to hasten engine deposits, which means an increase in octane needs. The driver who demands full engine power for rapid acceleration and high-speed operation will need a higher-octane fuel, even with a new engine.

It is interesting to note that automatic transmissions make a difference in octane needs. With an automatic transmission, the engine usually operates at part to full throttle at a fairly high engine rpm (revolutions per minute). There is very little low-engine-speed, full-throttle operation such as is found with manual transmissions. The difference here is, of course, in the manner of coupling. The manual transmission uses a mechanical clutch that connects the engine and rear wheels rigidly. But the automatic transmission uses a fluid coupling or torque converter which allows slippage; on acceleration the engine may turn at a high speed while the car is moving at a low speed. Thus, with an automatic transmission, there is less concern about knocking during low-engine-speed, wide-open-throttle operation. Consequently, a fuel such as is indicated by curve A in Fig. 10-9 would be more suitable than fuel B. Fuel A will tend to knock at low engine speeds, but not at high engine speeds (with spark advance indicated by curve C in Fig. 10-9). Fuel B will not knock at low engine speeds, but tends to knock at high engine speeds.

§128. Gasoline additives In addition to the antiknock compounds and their related lead-compound-vaporizing substances which are put into gasoline to raise its octane rating (§125), many other additives are used. Major additives include the following:

1. Oxidation inhibitors to help prevent the formation of gum while the gasoline is in storage.
2. Metal deactivators to protect the gasoline from the harmful effects of certain metals picked up in the refining process or in the vehicle fuel system.

3. Antirust agents to protect the vehicle fuel system.
4. Anti-icers to combat carburetor icing and fuel-line freeze.
5. Detergents to keep the carburetor clean.
6. Phosphorus compounds to combat surface ignition and spark-plug fouling.
7. Dye for identification.

In addition to having the proper volatility, antiknock properties, and additives discussed above, gasoline must be also treated so that it has minimum amounts of harmful chemicals and gum-forming substances. For example, sulfur compounds are often found in gasoline; when they are present in excessive quantities, they cause damage to engine parts. As the gasoline burns in the engine, the sulfur present tends to form sulfur acids. Sulfur acids attack metal parts and bearings and corrode them. Gum-forming substances may be dissolved in gasoline. As the gasoline evaporates, the gum solidifies in gasoline passages in the carburetor and intake manifold and on valves, pistons, and piston rings. Such gum formation can cause serious difficulty since it hinders the action of the fuel system and moving engine parts. Insufficient gasoline will be delivered, intake valves may hang open, and piston rings may stick. Gasoline manufacturers maintain rigid controls in their refineries to hold sulfur compounds and gum-forming substances to a minimum in their gasolines.

§129. Chemistry of combustion We have already discussed the combustion process in the engine and noted that gasoline is a hydrocarbon (composed of hydrogen-carbon compounds). The hydrogen and carbon atoms unite with oxygen atoms during combustion to form water (H_2O) and carbon dioxide (CO_2) *when enough oxygen is present.* However, in the gasoline engine sufficient amounts of oxygen may not be available, and the oxygen that is present may not "get to" the carbon. As a result, the carbon does not attain complete combustion. Some atoms of carbon are able to unite with only one atom of oxygen (instead of two). This produces carbon monoxide (CO). Carbon dioxide is a relatively inert and harmless gas, but carbon monoxide is dangerously poisonous. It has no color, it is tasteless, and it has practically no odor. A ratio of 15 parts of carbon monoxide to 10,000 parts of air is dangerous to breathe. Higher concentrations may cause quick paralysis and death. Consequently, an engine should never be operated in a closed space, such as a garage, without some means of exhausting the gas into the outside air. Remember this fact: Enough carbon monoxide can be produced in 3 minutes by an automobile engine running in a closed $10 \times 10 \times 20$ foot garage to cause paralysis and death! *Never operate an automobile engine with the garage doors closed!*

SUMMARY

Gasoline is a complex blend of hydrocarbons of different volatilities to satisfy different operating conditions, plus additives to increase octane number rating, combat formation of gum, rust, and ice, and so on.

The problem of knocking is a limiting factor in engine design because knock tendency increases with increasing compression ratios and cylinder-bore sizes. Knocking has been studied intensively. Knocking occurs when the end gas detonates before the flame front reaches it. This detonation occurs because the fuel is not sufficiently stable; the flame front does not reach the end gas in time, and the end gas temperature rises high enough to cause it to explode. Knocking can seriously damage engine parts.

Methods used to determine the knock resistance of fuel, or its ONR, include the laboratory-test method, in which compression ratio is varied, and the road-test methods, among which is the *modified borderline procedure* which uses spark advance as the test variable.

Knock is closely related to engine design; however, preignition and rumble are more likely to be service problems resulting from surface deposits in the combustion chamber.

Knocking can be controlled chemically by changing the carbon skeleton of the fuel, and by adding *tel*. Combustion-chamber design is also an important factor in the control of knocking.

REFERENCES

1. *Automotive Gasoline*, SAE Information Rep. J312a, 1965, in "SAE Handbook" (latest annual edition).

2. Haskell, W. W., and L. J. Bame, Engine Knock—an End-Gas Explosion, SAE (Society of Automotive Engineers) 650505, 1965 (paper).

3. Pless, L. G., Surface Ignition and Rumble in Engines, SAE (Society of Automotive Engineers 650391, 1965 (paper).

QUESTIONS

1. Explain volatility and list the different volatility requirements for various engine operating conditions.
2. Explain why increasing the compression ratio increases the tendency to knock.
3. What is the heat of compression?
4. Write a brief paper describing the process of knocking.
5. What are the three general methods of preventing knock?
6. Describe the experimental setup and procedure to study knocking reported in §121, and discuss the test results.
7. Describe the laboratory-test method of measuring the ONR of fuel. The CFR Uniontown road-test method. The MBP test method.
8. Write a brief paper explaining the differences between knock, preignition, and rumble, indicating causes of each.
9. Explain how the chemical structure of the fuel is related to its ONR.
10. List the environmental factors that affect knocking.
11. List various gasoline additives and explain their purposes.

Combustion-chamber Design

CHAPTER **11**

This chapter discusses many of the most important characteristics that an engine designer must consider when he turns his attention to the design of the combustion chamber. The combustion of the compressed air-fuel mixture takes place in the combustion chamber, and the characteristics of the combustion process are profoundly affected by the shape and size of the chamber as well as the position of the valves and spark plug.

§130. Combustion-chamber requirements In designing a combustion chamber, the engineer strives for a design that will have low knock tendencies, absence of rumble, high indicated horsepower, high thermal efficiency, high volumetric efficiency, adequate valve cooling and lubrication, and a low surface-to-volume ratio. Some of these are opposing characteristics. The engineer must move in one direction to improve one characteristic, but in a different direction to improve another. For example, increasing combustion-chamber-surface temperatures to increase thermal efficiency may result in engine roughness due to surface ignition. Thus, the engineer must make many compromises on his way to the final design.

It is very important, also, for the designer to arrive at a design that can be improved without major changes for subsequent model years. For example, if the compromises he selects puts the engine on the "ragged edge," as it were, then he has no place to go if further improvement in performance is requested by top management. On the other hand, if his design can be changed only slightly to significantly increase horsepower, torque, or efficiency (whichever is demanded), then he has an open-end design that is relatively easy and inexpensive to improve.

The designer of the combustion chamber, as well as of other engine components, must not only think about today, he must also think years ahead, as it were. If at all possible, his design must be subject to future improvements without major changes. Major changes and new designs cost a great deal to bring into production. It would be prohibitively expensive for an automotive manufacturer to bring out an "all-new" engine every year. A good design, from the manufacturer's standpoint, is one that can be modified year after year to repeatedly boost performance and increase engine efficiency and life.

The combustion chamber of an I-head engine is bounded at the top by the cylinder head, intake and exhaust valves, and the spark plug. It is bounded at the bottom by the piston head and top compression ring (Fig. 11-1). It is these various surfaces that the engineer must deal with when he designs a combustion chamber.

NOTE: The L-head engine is not considered in this chapter because it is no longer used in automotive engines. There are several reasons why the L-head engine has been abandoned. For one thing, the I-head engine can be designed to have a much higher compression ratio, and it has a shorter flame-travel path. Also, its surface-to-volume ratio is lower than the L-head engine, and this makes it a cleaner engine insofar as exhaust products are concerned (§139).

Certain dimensions and specifications are probably pretty well fixed for the engineer at an early

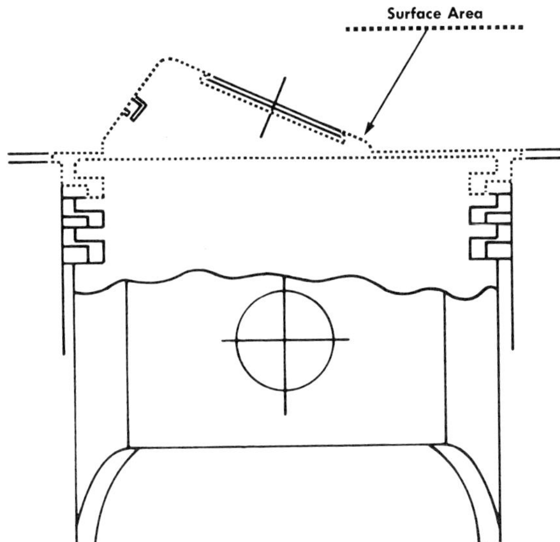

Fig. 11-1. Combustion-surface area in combustion chamber. Surface area is shown in dotted line.

stage. He probably knows, for example, what the approximate compression ratio, bore, and stroke of the new design will be. We have already mentioned that increasing the compression ratio and cylinder bore increase knock tendencies, and that knocking is a limiting factor in how far the engineer can go in increasing the compression ratio and bore. Of course, as higher-octane fuel is made available commercially, the engineer can increase compression ratios and bores. But aside from that, the engineer has a number of other tricks that help him design combustion chambers with relatively low knock tendencies. In this regard, it will be instructive to look at a specific example of design work on a combustion chamber.

§131. Designing a combustion chamber The shape of the combustion chamber has a considerable effect on its knock tendencies. For example, Fig. 11-2 shows a series of combustion-chamber shapes which were tested during design work on an early model of a Buick V-8 engine. Each of these was operated under identical conditions of speed, power output, compression ratio, and so forth. The only variation was in the ONR (octane-number rating) of the fuels used. Fuels were selected for each design as required to avoid knocking. It was found that design A required a 96-octane fuel to run without knocking, whereas design J required only 88-octane fuel. Thus, there is a difference of 8 octane numbers between fuel requirements for design A and design J. Reasons for the difference pertain to squish, quench, turbulence, and other factors, all of which are discussed in following sections.

It is desirable to have an engine design that will operate on the lowest possible octane number of fuel. For one thing, such an engine is apt to be less sensitive to accumulations of carbon (which raise compression and thus knock and rumble tendencies). For another, such a design is more adaptable to improvements in compression ratio without pushing octane requirements above the octane of fuels generally available in the market. In other words, if the design required 96-octane fuel, then increasing the compression ratio by further design modifications might push the requirements to a 110-octane fuel, and such a fuel might not be widely available. Such a design might be termed a "dead-end design" because it is not feasible to improve it further. On the other hand, if the design required only 88-octane fuel, then modifying the

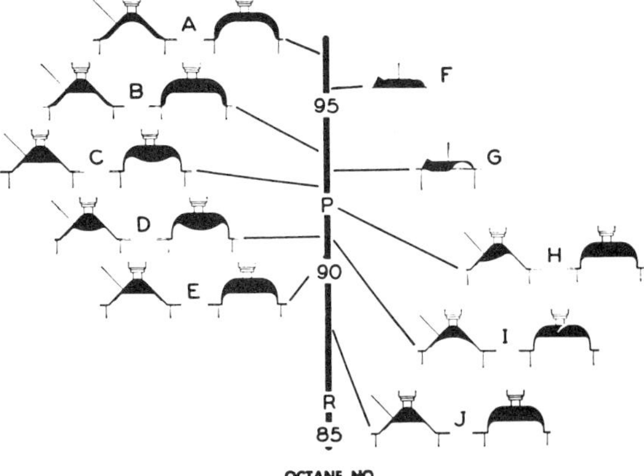

Fig. 11-2. Octane "tree" showing relationship between combustion-chamber design and octane requirements. Two views of the combustion chamber are shown for each design (end and side), except for designs F and G. (*Buick Motor Division of General Motors Corporation*)

design for a higher compression ratio would be perfectly feasible since this would not push the octane requirements beyond the range that is available at service stations. Also, this design would give a smoother-running engine since it would be less apt to knock or rumble under adverse operating conditions.

There are several ways to increase the compression ratio of a particular engine design without major alterations, provided the design has been well thought out. One method is to use pistons with a somewhat higher crown, or head. This reduces clearance volume and thus increases compression ratio. Sometimes an automobile company will supply two types of pistons for an engine—one with somewhat dished-out piston heads for a greater clearance volume and a lower compression ratio, and the other with "built-up" piston heads for lower clearance volume and a higher compression ratio (Fig. 11-3).

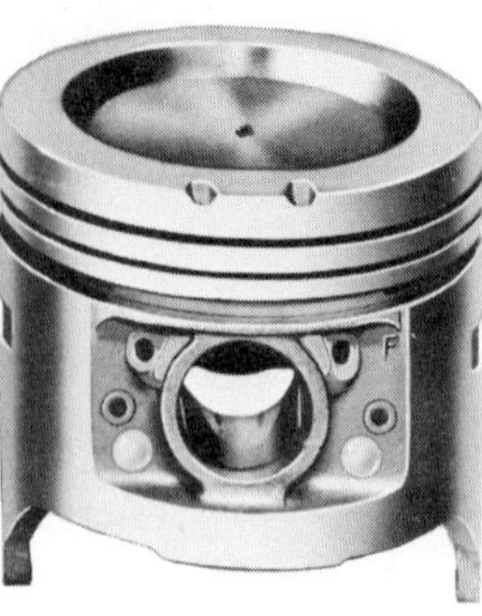

Fig. 11-3. Pistons for standard- and high-compression engines. The built-up section in the head of the piston on the right is called the "pop-up." (*Chevrolet Motor Division and Pontiac Motor Division of General Motors Corporation*)

A second method is to use the same block, but alter the cylinder-head design slightly so as to reduce the clearance volume. This can often be done by making a slight change in the cylinder-head pattern from which the head mold is made.

In any event, it is desirable to arrive at a combustion-chamber design that requires a comparatively low octane fuel, but that can be readily adapted for higher compression ratios in subsequent years as higher-octane fuels become available.

§132. Factors in combustion-chamber design Specific factors that the designer must cope with, in addition to the fundamental ones of compression ratio and bore, include turbulence, squish, quench, volumetric efficiency, placement and size of valves, position of the spark plug, and s/v (surface-to-volume) ratio. Several of the unfamiliar terms are explained in this section. Following sections discuss all of these factors in detail.

1. *Turbulence.* In the combustion chamber, turbulence pertains to the swirling motion of the compressed air-fuel mixture. When you stir your coffee, you impart turbulence to it so the cream and sugar mix with the coffee. In a similar manner, imparting turbulence to the air-fuel mixture assures more uniform mixing of the air and fuel so that combustion will be more uniform. Also, turbulence reduces the time required for the flame front to sweep through the compressed mixture (§133).

2. *Squish.* This word, which is similar in meaning to squash, refers to the way that pistons in some combustion chambers squash, or squeeze, a portion of the air-fuel mixture at the end of the compression stroke. Figure 11-4 shows the squish area in a combustion chamber. As the piston nears TDC (top dead center), the air-fuel mixture is pushed, or squeezed, out of the squish area. As it "squishes" out, it promotes turbulence and thus further mixing of the air-fuel mixture.

3. *Quench.* We have already noted that knocking results when the end-gas temperature goes too high and the end gas explodes before the flame front reaches it. However, if some heat is extracted from the end gas, then its temperature will not reach the detonation point. In the arrangement shown in Fig. 11-4, the squish area is also a quench area.[1,2] The closeness of the cylinder head to the piston and the relative coolness of these metallic surfaces cause heat to be extracted from the end gas. As a result, the tendency for detonation to occur is quenched.

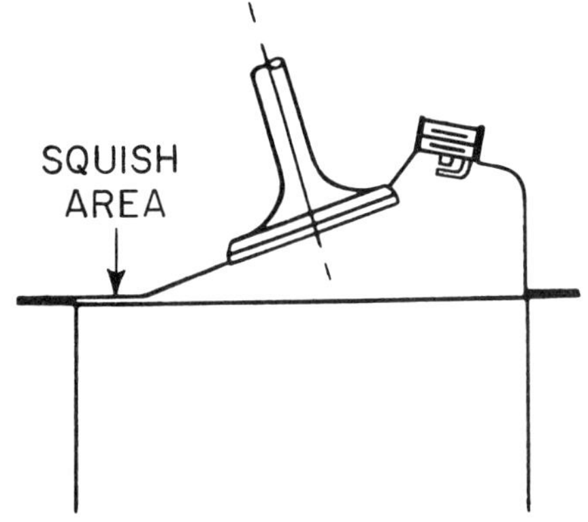

Fig. 11-4. Squish area in combustion chamber.

§133. Turbulence As already noted, good turbulence promotes good mixing of the air and fuel and thus makes for more uniform combustion of the mixture in all cylinders. Turbulence also reduces the time required for the flame front to pass through the compressed air-fuel mixture,[5] and this reduces knock tendencies. Turbulence will be imparted to the incoming air-fuel mixture if the intake valve is offset (not centered) in the combustion chamber, or if the intake valve is partly shrouded by adding metal at one side of the intake port. With this arrangement, the air-fuel mixture is given a swirling motion, or turbulence, as it enters the combustion chamber (Fig. 11-5). Viewed from the top of the cylinder, the motion would be as shown, with the lengths of the arrows designating the velocity of the gas.

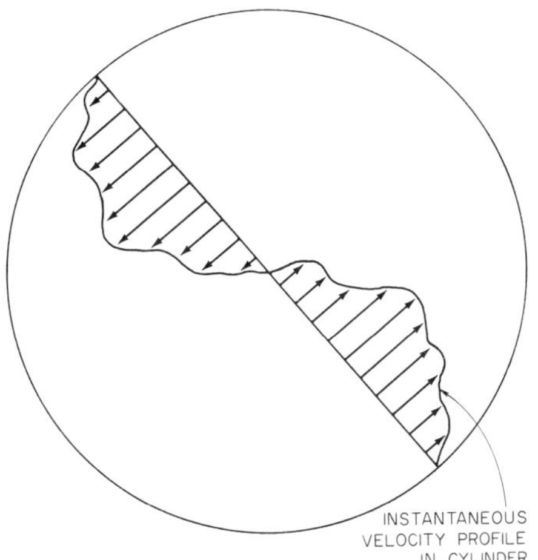

Fig. 11-5. Turbulent velocity of gas in combustion chamber, as seen from top. Lenghts of arrows indicate relative velocities of gas. (*General Motors Corporation*)

In one series of experiments, turbulence was induced by adding a scoop to the intake valve, as shown in Fig. 11-6.[3] A tang on the rocker arm mates with the slot in the valve stem to prevent the valve from turning. More or less swirl will be induced by the shape of the shroud and its orientation in the valve port.

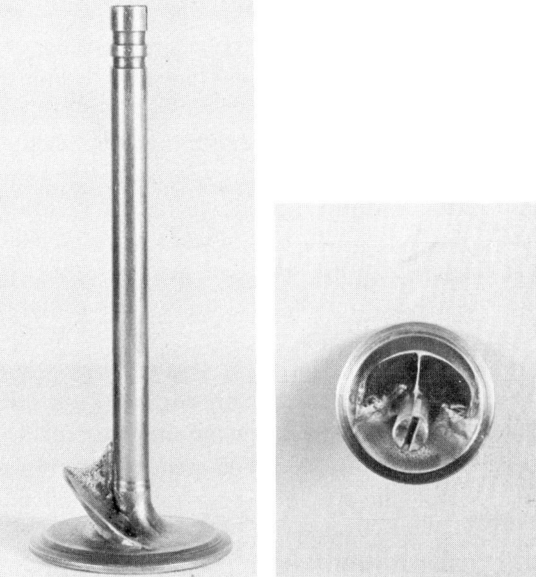

Fig. 11-6. Scoop added to intake valve in experimental installation to induce turbulence of the inflowing air-fuel mixture. (*General Motors Corporation*)

NOTE: A squish area, if present, imparts a somewhat different sort of turbulence since the gas squeezed out of the squish area squirts out into the combustion chamber more or less in straight lines, thus imparting a boiling motion to the air-fuel mixture.

Now, let us see how the turbulence imparted to the air-fuel mixture by the offset intake valve affects the combustion process. The flame, or combustion, is initiated at the spark-plug gap, and it grows in all directions like a soap bubble. Figure 11-7 shows how this would appear if the

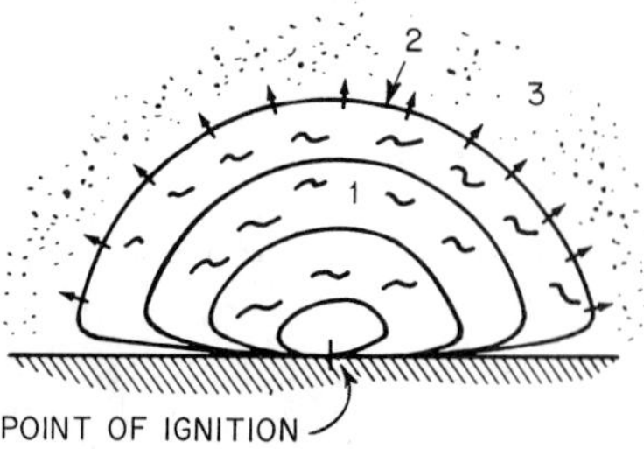

Fig. 11-7. Spherical flame propagation without turbulence: (1) flame kernel, consisting of combustion products; (2) flame front area; (3) unburned mixture. (*General Motors Corporation*)

gas were static, that is, if it had no turbulence. However, turbulence causes the gas to be in motion; it acts like a wind, "blowing" the bubble askew (Fig. 11-8). The effect of this is that the surface area of the bubble is increased.[3] With the larger surface area, the bubble, or flame front, passes through the air-fuel mixture more quickly. This means that the end gas has less time to detonate. Thus, one effect of turbulence is that it reduces knock tendencies.

The squish area (Fig. 11-4), also imparts turbulence to the end gases as they are squeezed out. These gases, moving rapidly into the approaching flame front, disturb it so that a somewhat more rapid completion of the combustion is produced.

§134. Volumetric efficiency High volumetric efficiency (§113) is desirable because, with more air-fuel mixture entering the cylinders, the engine will produce higher torque and horsepower. Combustion-chamber shape is one of several factors affecting volumetric efficiency. Others include manifold and valve-port configurations, valve size, shape, and placement, carburetor and air-cleaner design, and exhaust pipe and muffler.

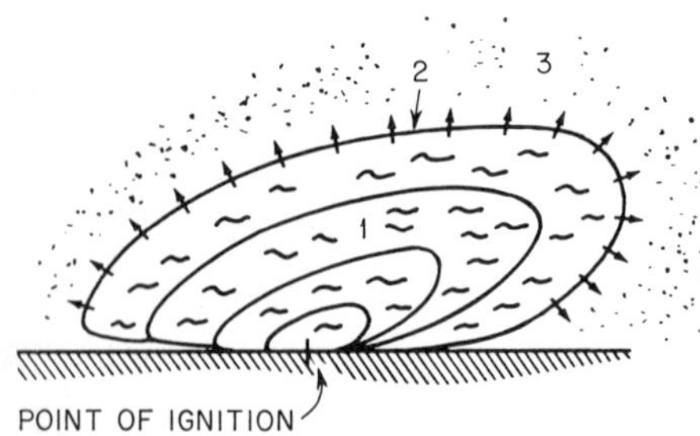

Fig. 11-8. Skewed flame propagation due to turbulence that produces movement of the unburned mixture from left to right: (1) flame kernel, consisting of combustion products; (2) flame front area; (3) unburned mixture. (*General Motors Corporation*)

Large valves, properly placed, and air-fuel induction and exhaust systems with minimum restrictions are essential for good volumetric efficiency. The easier the gas can flow in and out, the higher the volumetric efficiency.

Opposed to this, however, is the need for turbulence to improve the combustion process, as explained in §133. To impart high turbulence to the entering air-fuel mixture, the entering velocity must be high. This, in turn, requires an effective restriction through which the mixture must pass. That is, the intake valve and port should be comparatively small for high intake velocities. Once again, you will note, the designer must make a compromise. The compromise is normally in the direction of larger valves and higher volumetric efficiency because it is basic for the engineer to seek higher torque and power output.

And yet, there are limits to valve size. The spacing between the intake and exhaust valves must be great enough to allow adequate water jacketing around the valve seats and valve guides (§137). High valve temperatures lead to short valve and valve-seat life as well as the possibility of local hot spots and engine rumble.

Actually, excessive combustion-chamber-surface temperatures should be avoided, including valve heads, piston head, and cylinder head. If these surfaces become too hot, then the incoming gases being subjected to these temperatures will expand more. This will therefore reduce the amount of air-fuel mixture entering and thus lower the volumetric efficiency. Opposing this, however, is the need to keep the surface temperatures high enough to improve thermal efficiency. Again, a compromise.

§135. Hemispheric vs. wedge combustion chambers There are two general combustion-chamber shapes—wedge and hemispheric (Fig. 11-9). (See also Figs. 4-9 and 4-23 for illustrations of engines with the two types of chambers.) These are also known as the nonturbulent and the turbulent types.[1] The wedge chamber includes a squish area which, as already noted, imparts turbulence to the compressed mixture (§132). This is in addition to the turbulence of the mixture produced by its movement into the combustion chamber. The hemispheric chamber, not having a squish area, depends on the mixture movement into the chamber alone for turbulence. As a result, the mixture has relatively little turbulence. There are other differences between the two types.

In the hemispheric chamber, the spark plug is placed close to the center of the dome so that the flame front has a minimum distance to travel. This means rapid combustion and a rapid pressure rise. In contrast, the spark plug in the wedge chamber is normally located to one side so that the flame front has a longer distance to travel before it reaches the squish area. This means a slower and smaller pressure rise. Figure 11-10 shows the pressure-time curves in the two chambers, operating under similar conditions. Not only does the flame front have a greater distance to travel in the wedge chamber, but also, because of the longer time required, the piston is moving downward on the power stroke to provide increased volume into which the burning gases can expand.

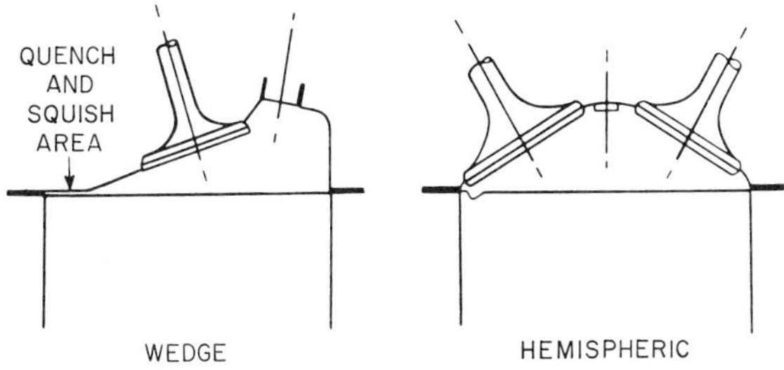

Fig. 11-9. Wedge and hemispheric combustion chambers. (*General Motors Corporation*)

With the longer time interval in the wedge chamber, the end gases have more time to react to the increasing heat of compression. The squish-quench area, however, reduces the tendency for detonation and knocking by extracting heat from the end gas.

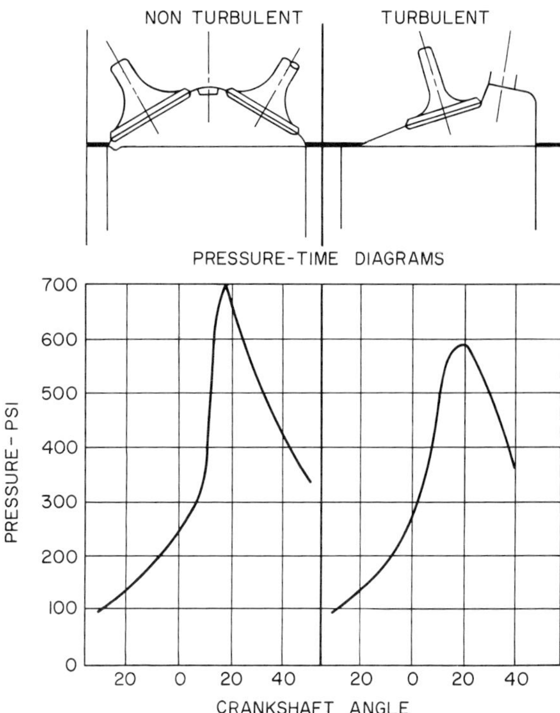

Fig. 11-10. Pressure-time curves in hemispheric (nonturbulent) and wedge (turbulent) combustion chambers. (*General Motors Corporation*)

The hemispheric chamber can accommodate larger valves because none of the head surface has to be devoted to a squish-quench area. This means that volumetric efficiency can be very good. Some hemispheric engines show a volumetric efficiency of over 85 percent at intermediate speeds and as much as 75 percent at 4,000 rpm (revolutions per minute). This means that high-speed power and torque of these engines is very good. Thermal efficiency is higher, too, because the surface area to which combustion heat can be lost is near the minimum. In addition, this type of combustion chamber, with its smaller surface area, burns a somewhat larger percentage of the fuel. The reason for this is that the layer of air-fuel mixture that lies on the combustion-chamber surfaces is relatively stagnant and cool so that it burns poorly or not at all. The smaller this surface area, the less unburned fuel. Thus, the hemispheric chamber emits exhaust gases that have a lower percentage of unburned hydrocarbons. Unburned hydrocarbons are a contributing factor to the formation of smog, and minimizing them in the exhaust gas reduces smog. (This is discussed further in §139.)

With high volumetric efficiency, high thermal efficiency, and quick burning of the charge (due to the short flame path), the hemispheric engine is a high-performance engine, particularly at high speeds. On the other hand, these very attributes tend to make the hemispheric engine rough and subject to detonation at low speeds. The short burn time produces a quick, high, pressure peak (Fig. 11-10). The high volumetric efficiency results in high compression pressures, particularly during open-throttle, low-speed operation; this further increases the possibility of detonation.

Comparison should also be made between the valve trains required for the two chambers. The wedge chamber is usually simpler because the valves can be arranged in a single row. The hemispheric chamber, with the two valves positioned on different sides of the dome and at two different angles, requires a more complex rocker arm, rocker-arm shaft, and push-rod arrangement. Some hemispheric engines use two rocker-arm shafts, one for intake valves and the other for exhaust valves (see Fig. 4-23).

§136. Hemispheric chamber with squish-quench A compromise hemispheric design with squish and quench areas is shown in Fig. 11-11. This might appear to include the best characteristics of the hemispheric and wedge chambers, but the design introduces other complications. In the first place, the locations of the valves in their relation to the piston requires a clearance of as much as 0.200 inch. Less clearance might result in the piston striking a valve in the event that the valve train misbehaves. However, laboratory tests have shown that with this much clearance there would be too little squish to be effective. It requires less clearance, somewhere in the neighborhood of 0.100 inch, to produce effective squish and good turbulence. Secondly, including the exhaust valve as part of the quench area reduces the quenching effect. The exhaust valve runs hot (red hot at times) and might well add heat to the compressed charge instead of removing it as the quench area should. This could increase detonation possibilities.

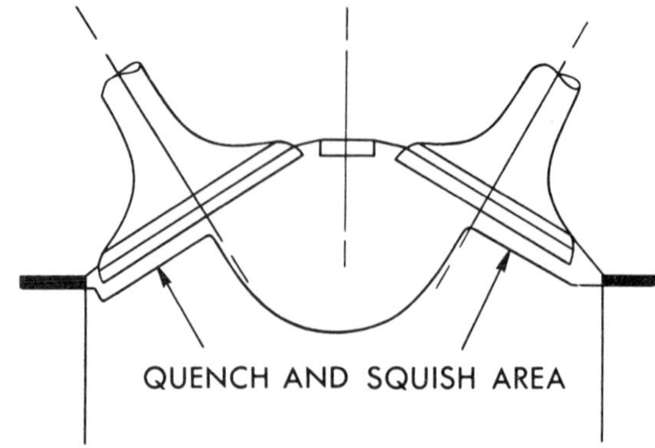

Fig. 11-11. Compromise hemispheric chamber with quench and squish areas. (*General Motors Corporation*)

Another, more successful, compromise combustion chamber is shown in Fig. 11-12. This chamber

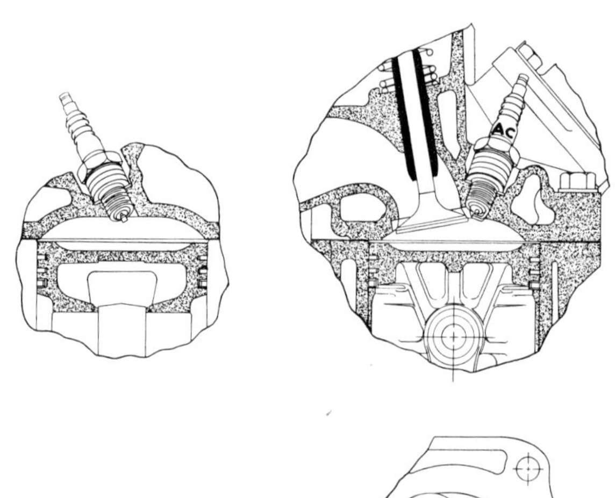

Fig. 11-12. Compromise combustion chamber somewhat hemispheric in configuration but with squish and quench areas. (*Buick Division of General Motors Corporation*)

consists of an elongated saucer shape in the cylinder head, matched with a shallow circular depression in the piston dome. The piston has a flat land around the edge of its head about 0.35 inch wide, and this is matched by flats on the two sides of the saucer in the cylinder head. The matching surfaces therefore provide squish-quench areas. Note that there is no valve interference with the flat surface of the piston head. The spark plug is centrally located to minimize flame-path travel. The chamber combines good features of the hemispheric chamber with those of the wedge. The valve locations permit an in-line arrangement, and the off-center position of the intake valve provides turbulence of the incoming air-fuel mixture.

§137. Valve cooling, size, and placement As already mentioned, it is desirable to have large intake and exhaust valves so as to achieve high volumetric efficiency, high torque, and good high-speed performance. The valve heads form part of the combustion-chamber perimeter, and thus their size is directly related to combustion-chamber design. For example, the hemispheric chamber can accept larger valves than can be used in the wedge chamber. But there are other factors involved in addition to size. The valves must be so located as to permit adequate cooling, good lubrication, and sufficient lift (or valve opening). This article discusses valves as they relate to combustion-chamber design. Chapter 15 is devoted to the various aspects of valve and valve-train design.

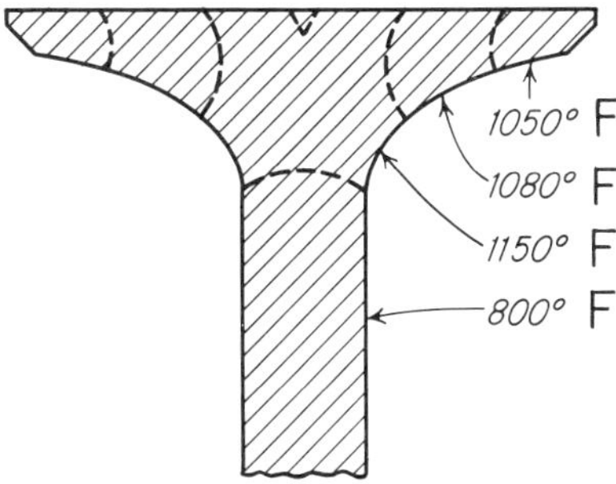

Fig. 11-13. Temperatures in an exhaust valve. The valve is shown in a sectional view. (*Eaton Manufacturing Company*)

1. Valve cooling. The valves, particularly exhaust valves, must be cooled adequately so their temperature will not rise too high. The exhaust valve passes the hot exhaust gases, and it may get red hot. Temperatures well above 1000°F are common. Heating of the exhaust valve is not uniform, however. Figure 11-13 shows a typical temperature pattern in an exhaust valve. Note that the center of the head is the hottest. The face of the valve is cooled by its periodic contact with the valve seat. The valve stem is cooled by passing heat to the valve guide. Excessive valve temperatures must be avoided. Not only do high temperatures burn the valves and valve seats, thus shortening their lives, but also hot valves promote engine rumble.

One interesting feature of high-compression engines is that they have higher thermal efficiencies; the exhaust gases are therefore cooler, and thus the exhaust valves run cooler.

2. Water jackets. In liquid-cooled engines, the combustion chamber is surrounded at the top and sides by water jackets. It is the function of the water flowing through these jackets to remove heat from the combustion-chamber surfaces, including the valve seat. The valve guide is also surrounded and cooled by the water jacket. [This is discussed further in the chapter on cooling systems (Chap. 18).]

3. Ports. Another factor of importance in the overall combustion-chamber design is the location of the valve ports. They must be so located as to permit adequate cooling, adequate breathing, and proper lubrication of the valve stem. It is sometimes rather difficult to find the right compromise. A port location and valve inclination that would give excellent breathing might not be best for adequate stem lubrication. Further, some positions are harder to cool than others. An added complication is the gear-train configurations demanded by some port and valve locations. For example, the hemispheric combustion chamber permits the use of larger valves and also allows the valves to be located on the two sides of the dome in the head (Figs. 4-23 and 11-9). However, this means a penalty in the increased complexity of the head and valve train required to operate the valves. (This is all discussed in detail in Chap. 15.)

§138. Spark-plug placement The placement of the spark plug is an important element in combustion-chamber design. The spark plug should be centrally located so that the flame front can sweep out in all directions through the compressed air-fuel mixture; that is, excessively long flame-front paths in any one direction should be avoided. As we have seen, this could cause excessive pressure and temperature rise in the last part of the charge so that detonation might result. But of course the squish-quench area, located at the place that the flame front reaches last, does provide cooling to reduce knocking tendencies.

It is also desirable to locate the spark plug somewhere near the intake valve, within the incoming stream of air-fuel mixture. This provides some measure of plug cooling. The tapped boss, in which the plug is mounted in the cylinder head, should be well jacketed so that adequate cooling from the water circulating in the cooling system is achieved. On the other hand, the plug must not be so close to either valve as to cause a shrouding effect which would interfere with the free flow of gases through the valve ports.

§139. The s/v ratio This is the ratio between the surface (*s*) areas in the combustion chamber and the volume (*v*) of the combustion chamber (Fig. 11-14). The s/v ratio has become of increasing importance in connection with the problem of smog.[4] Smog is the foglike haze that hangs over many of our larger cities. It is a menace to health, authorities say, and a major effort is being made to reduce it. Smoke and fumes from industrial processes, as well as the exhaust gases from automobiles, contribute to the formation of smog. It is the unburned portion of gasoline and other harmful chemicals in the exhaust gas that automotive engineers are trying to eliminate.

As previously noted (§135), during the combustion process in the combustion chamber, there are layers of stagnant air-fuel mixture adjacent to the combustion-chamber surfaces. The adjacent relatively cool metal surfaces inhibit combustion so these layers do not burn. If the surface area is relatively large, in comparison with the volume, then the percentage of unburned gasoline in the exhaust gases will be relatively large. However, if the surface area is relatively small (low s/v ratio), then the percentage of unburned gasoline, or hydrocarbons, in the exhaust gas will be relatively small.

Thus, it is desirable from the standpoint of smog reduction to use combustion chambers with minimum s/v ratios. A sphere is the shape that has the lowest possible s/v ratio. Combustion chambers, however, cannot, as a practical matter, assume this shape. But the closer the chamber approaches the shape of a sphere, the lower its s/v ratio. Figure 11-15 shows four different combustion-chamber shapes and their s/v ratios. Note that the double-hemisphere design, with a piston having a hemispheric head to match the hemispheric dome in the cylinder head, has the lowest s/v ratio (and thus the lowest percentage of unburned hydrocarbons in the exhaust gas).

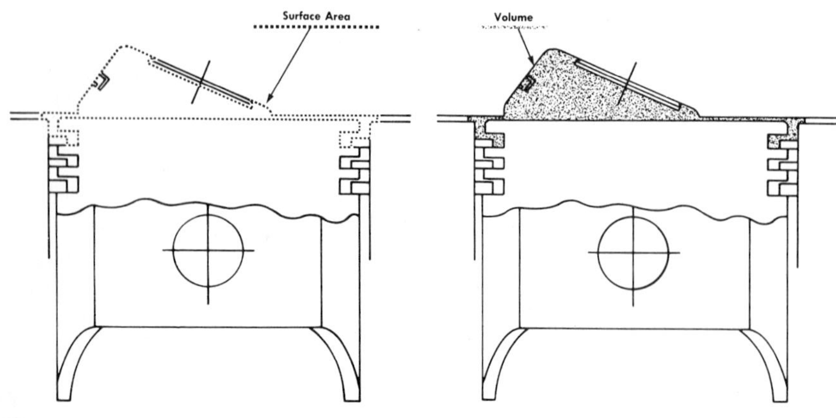

Fig. 11-14. Ratio of the surface area to the volume of the combustion chamber (or s/v) is an important factor in the amount of unburned hydrocarbons in the exhaust gas.

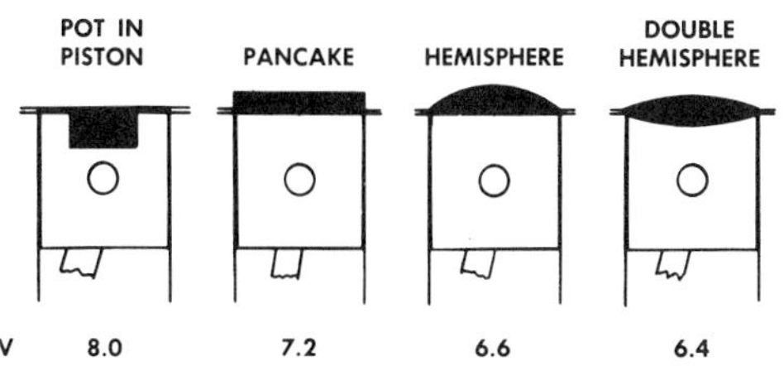

Fig. 11-15. Some s/v ratios of combustion chambers of different configurations.

Note also that the "pot-in-piston" design, which has a large quench area (between piston and head) has the highest s/v ratio. The quench areas add substantial amounts of surface areas with very little volume. This means that the combustion chamber will have a high s/v ratio and a higher rate of unburned hydrocarbon emission.

We have mentioned several times that the L-head engine has been abandoned for automotive use. Among the reasons for this is that it has limitations

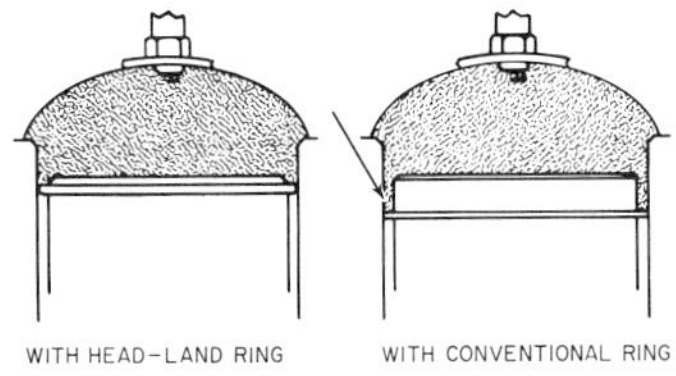

Fig. 11-16. Head-land piston-ring installation compared with conventional ring. Note that the head-land ring is located near the top of the piston, thus eliminating the surface area (arrowed) found in the conventional design. (*Sealed Power Corporation*)

on the possible maximum compression ratio. Also, the long flame-travel path increases detonation or knock possibilities. In addition, the high s/v ratio increases the amount of unburned hydrocarbons in the exhaust gas.

A method of reducing the s/v ratio of an engine without changing the shape of the combustion chamber is to use the recently introduced head-land piston ring and a special piston (see §158). This ring is L-shaped in cross section and is placed in a ring groove near the top of the piston. In this position, the surface area between the piston and the cylinder wall is much less than with the conventional piston ring (see Fig. 11-16).

SUMMARY

A good combustion chamber has low knock tendencies, absence of rumble, high indicated horsepower, high thermal efficiency, high volumetric efficiency, adequate valve cooling and lubrication, and a low s/v ratio. Also, the design should lend itself to repeated improvements year after year, so that engine performance can be repeatedly stepped up.

Factors that the engine designer must cope with in designing a combustion chamber include compression ratio, bore, turbulence, squish, quench, volumetric efficiency, placement and size of valves, position of the spark plug, and s/v ratio.

The hemispheric combustion chamber, with its large valves and no squish or quench area, has high volumetric efficiency but little turbulence. The spark plug can be placed near the center of the chamber, and this shortens the flame-front travel to a minimum. All this means a chamber that gives high performance at high speed. However, the hemispheric engine may be rough and tend to knock at low-speed, wide-open throttle operation. Its valve-train arrangement is also apt to be more complex than that for the wedge chamber.

The wedge chamber, with its squish-quench area, has better turbulence and, with a spark plug located to one side, a longer flame-front path. Thus, the pressure rise in the wedge chamber is somewhat lower and has a lower peak than in the hemispheric chamber. The wedge chamber is thus somewhat smoother in operation.

A modified hemispheric chamber with a squish-quench area is not particularly successful because the valve locations will not permit the small clearance that a good squish area needs. Also, including the exhaust valve in the quench area is not effective because it may run too hot to subtract heat from the end gas.

The valves must be so located in the chamber as to permit good cooling, good lubrication, and adequate lift. They should be large for good volumetric efficiency. However, for good turbulence the incoming air-fuel mixture should have high velocity, and this requires a restriction at the valve port which means relatively small valves.

The spark plug should be placed in a near-central position so that there will not be excessively long distances for the flame front to travel. The spark-plug boss should be adequately water-jacketed for good cooling. Additional cooling will result if the plug is located in the incoming air-fuel-mixture stream.

The s/v ratio is an important factor in clean burning of the fuel. With a high s/v ratio, there will be more smog-producing unburned hydrocarbons in the exhaust gas. The hemispheric combustion chamber has the lowest practical s/v ratio and thus low percentages of unburned hydrocarbons in the exhaust gas.

REFERENCES

1. Mantey, H. H. L., The Effect of Combustion-Chamber Shape on Smoothness of Power, Engineering Know-How in Engine Design, SAE (Society of Automotive Engineers), special publication SP-137, 1955.

2. El-Mawla, A. G., and W. Mirsky, Hydrocarbons in the Partial-Quench Zone of Flames: An Approach to the Study of the Flame Quenching Process, SAE (Society of Automotive Engineers) 660112, 1966 (paper).

3. Patterson, D. J., Cylinder Pressure Variations, a Fundamental Combustion Problem, SAE (Society of Automotive Engineers), 660129, 1966 (paper).

4. Scheffler, C. E., Combustion Chamber Surface Area, a Key to Exhaust Hydrocarbons, SAE (Society of Automotive Engineers) 660111, 1966 (paper).

5. Bolt, J. A., and D. L. Harrington, The Effects of Mixture Motion Upon the Lean Limit and Combustion of Spark-Ignited Mixtures. SAE (Society of Automotive Engineers) 670467, 1967 (paper).

QUESTIONS

1. List the major factors to be considered in combustion-chamber design.

2. Discuss the importance of arriving at an open-end design in the design of automotive engines.

3. Describe two ways to increase compression ratio of an engine without major alterations of the design.

4. Describe turbulence of the air-fuel mixture and two methods of obtaining it.

5. Define squish.

6. Define quench.

7. Does turbulence increase or shorten the burn time of the compressed air-fuel mixture?

8. Explain why the engineer may have to make a compromise between high volumetric efficiency and high turbulence. Between high volumetric efficiency and high thermal efficiency.

9. List advantages and disadvantages of the hemispheric chamber. Of the wedge chamber.

10. Explain what the s/v ratio is and its effect on smog.

11. What are three important factors to be considered in locating valves in the combustion chamber?

12. What are two important factors in the location of the spark plug in the combustion chamber?

Pistons and Rings

CHAPTER **12**

This chapter and the following one discuss pistons and piston rings—their function, operation, and design. While the piston and rings appear to be relatively simple parts in contrast to other engine components, their behavior in the engine is very complex. Thus, their design is not a simple matter, but requires much study and testing.

§140. Piston and piston-ring requirements The piston and top compression ring form the lower part of the combustion chamber (Fig. 11-1). Essentially, the piston and rings form a movable plug that slides up and down in the cylinder as the four strokes of the engine cycle take place. They hold pressure during the compression, power, and exhaust strokes, and they hold vacuum during the intake stroke. To perform properly, the piston and ring combination must have the following properties:

1. They must slide in the cylinder with a minimum of frictional loss.
2. They must be heavy enough to take the punishing pressures and temperatures of the combustion process.
3. They must have minimum weight so as to keep inertia losses down.
4. They must have a cross section sufficiently large to provide an adequate heat path so excessive piston-head temperatures will not occur.
5. They must be able to exercise adequate oil control.
6. They must have minimum clearance with the cylinder wall so as to minimize blow-by.
7. They must change in size or shape very little as a result of temperature changes.
8. They must resist adequately the bending forces imposed by combustion pressures.
9. They must be highly wear- and scuff-resistant for long life.

The piston undergoes great stresses during engine operation. With each power stroke, a pressure of several tons is suddenly applied to the piston head. At highway speeds, this suddenly applied pressure occurs 30 to 40 times a second. Combustion temperatures of thousands of degrees occur simultaneously with the high pressures. The piston must be able to take these heat and pressure stresses millions of times during its lifetime. A piston in an engine that has gone 100,000 miles will have made as many as 200,000,000 power strokes, and it will have traveled as much as 50,000 miles itself, moving up and down in the cylinder.

§141. Piston design As can be seen from the above list, the design of a piston for a particular engine is not an easy job.[1,2] Stresses, heat losses from the piston head, piston balance, and other factors can be analyzed mathematically, but in the ultimate analysis, the engine itself decides whether or not the piston design is correct. That is, no matter how well designed the piston is from the theoretical standpoint, the engineer will not know for sure whether the design is a good one for the engine until it is installed in the engine and tested in the laboratory and on the highway. (Figure 12-1 shows pistons with their standard nomenclature.)

A well-designed piston will handle all stresses (load and thermal), and it will be quiet under all operating conditions; it will not scuff or permit appreciable blow-by, and it will have a long service

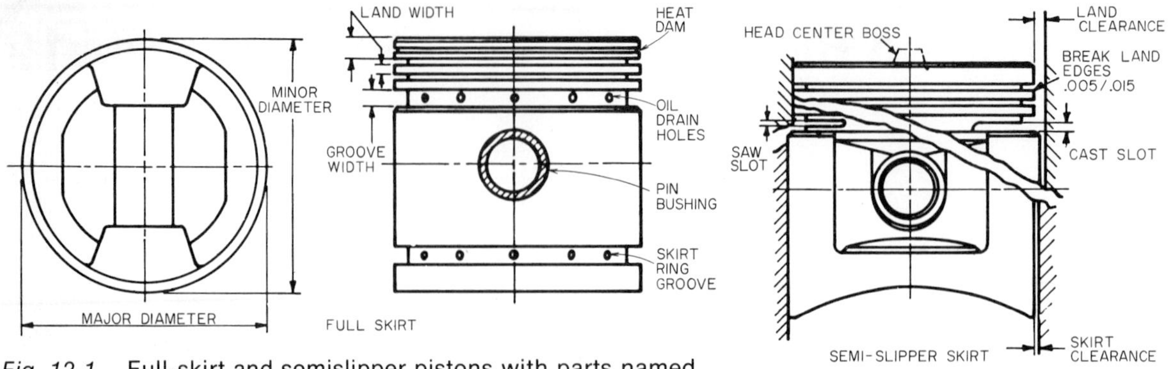

Fig. 12-1. Full-skirt and semislipper pistons with parts named.

life. It is especially important for the piston to be able to take the combustion-pressure and inertia loads without undue deflection or wear. Figure 12-2 shows the vertical and side-thrust loads on a piston during the power stroke. Note that the vertical inertia load is in the opposite direction to the combustion-pressure load at TDC (top dead center), where both are at their maximum values. However, Fig. 12-2 does not necessarily show the maximum loading on the piston. For example, the piston in a high-speed engine may be subjected to its maximum load at the end of the exhaust stroke at TDC. The gas pressure is essentially zero at this point, and thus the inertia load alone is acting. The piston-pin bosses must be heavy enough to carry this load (see §150).

It is difficult to generalize about piston design because, in a sense, each new engine design or variant may call for a new piston design. While the piston engineer can fall back on his previous experience and the standard design formulas, he must ultimately depend on laboratory and field testing to finalize his design. Sometimes this may require a number of piston changes, as the engineer "cuts and tries" until he achieves all the performance characteristics desired.

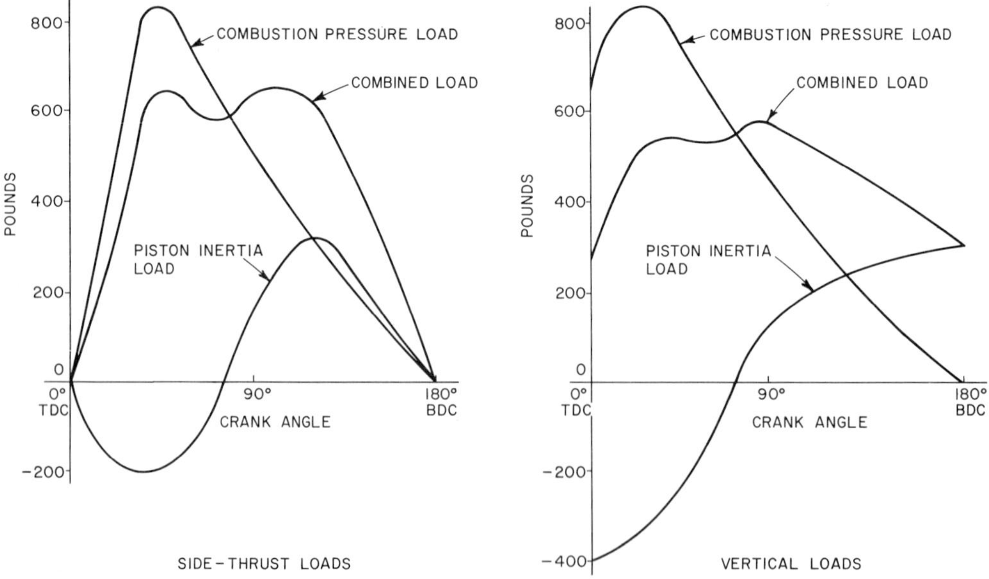

Fig. 12-2. Computed side-thrust and vertical loads on a piston during the power stroke under one specific operating condition. The loads will change with changing speeds, throttle openings, and other operating conditions. (*Thompson, Ramo, Wooldridge, Inc.*)

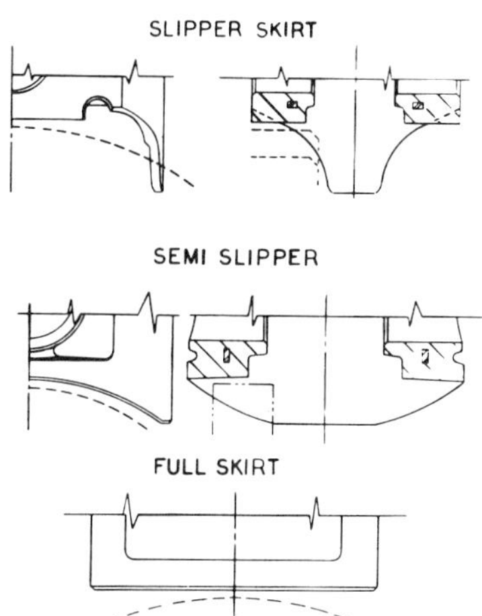

Fig. 12-3. With the shorter stroke, the piston skirt has to be cut away to provide room for the counterweights on the crankshaft to rotate. Dotted lines show movement of the counterweights under the pistons. (*Bohn Aluminum and Brass Company, Division Universal American Corporation*)

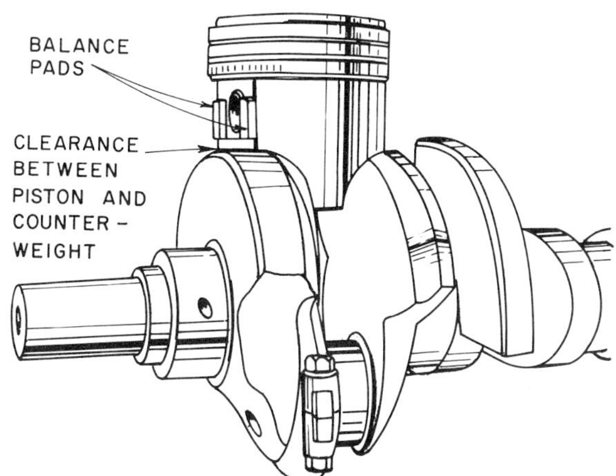

Fig. 12-4. Modern slipper piston and connecting rod assembled to crankshaft. Note small amount of clearance between the piston and counterweights on the crankshaft. (*Chevrolet Motor Division of General Motors Corporation*)

A basic problem for the piston designer is the matter of space. Earlier engines had a small bore and a long stroke. Modern automotive engines, however, trend toward a larger bore and a shorter stroke. In fact, many engines today are oversquare (bore diameter larger than stroke). This trend leaves less headroom for the piston. The earlier piston was of the full-skirt (or trunk) type (Fig. 12-1). As the stroke became shorter, however, there was less space for the skirt. The skirt had to be cut away to provide room for the counterweights on the crankshaft (Figs. 12-3 and 12-4). Thus, semi-slipper- and full-slipper-skirt pistons came into use (Figs. 12-1 and 12-5).

The following articles discuss some other important factors that the piston designer must consider.

§142. Piston-design considerations It often happens that the piston designer is handed an engine configuration and, in effect, told to design pistons to fit the engine. With the emphasis today on low hood lines, there is considerable pressure on engine designers to come up with lower and lower engine silhouettes. This means that the piston designer must follow along with shorter and shorter pistons.

However, the piston designer must be concerned with much more than just fitting his piston into the engine and making sure that it will live satisfactorily in the engine. He must also be concerned with manufacturing and cost factors. The piston should be easy to make and should incorporate all the locating, clamping, and chucking areas necessary to its manufacture. Also, it must have some excess metal, which can be removed as necessary during the process of balancing the piston-rod assemblies for an engine (all assemblies must weigh the same for smooth engine operation). Further, the piston designer should utilize, insofar as possible, the foundry and manufacturing equipment that his company or piston supplier already possesses. His new design should not require special machinery (except as a last—or next to last—resort). In addition to all this, it should be as inexpensive as possible, utilizing the least expensive materials and manufacturing methods compatible with the other piston requirements listed previously.

NOTE: In the following discussions, we will be referring to various parts of the piston as named in Fig. 12-6.

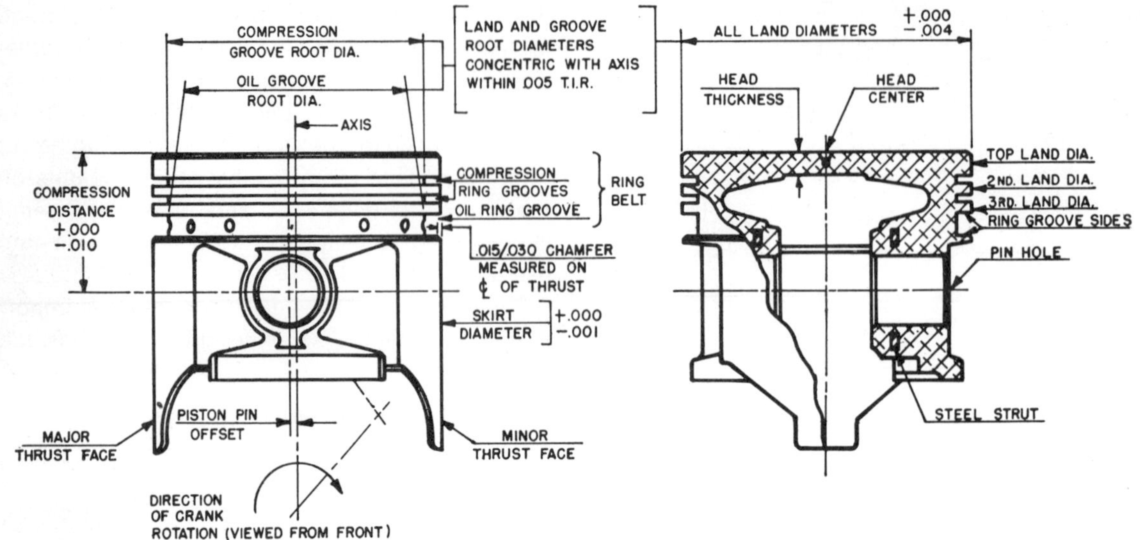

Fig. 12-5. Full-slipper piston.

After the piston designer has been handed a design job, he must make certain basic decisions. The general shape of the piston has already been set by the engine designers who, in turn, have been influenced by the car stylists. The decisions relate to piston material, skirt shape, head shape, the method of piston-pin attachment, whether or not the piston pin will be offset from the centerline, the method of controlling piston expansion as temperature goes up, controlling heat loss from the piston, and so on.

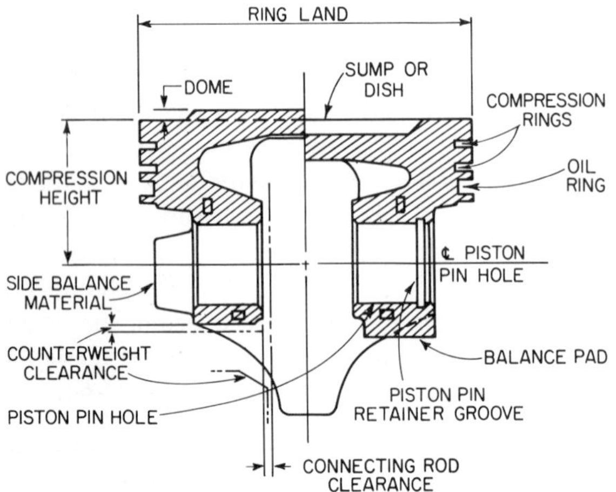

Fig. 12-6. Slipper piston with parts named.

§143. Piston material Earlier pistons were of cast iron. This material is satisfactory for low-speed, long-stroke engines. However, for the modern high-speed, high-compression, short-stroke, large-bore engine, a lighter metal with greater heat transfer is required. Thus, practically all automotive engines today use aluminum-alloy pistons. The most common alloys can be grouped into four categories:

1. Those containing about 10 percent silicon plus copper and other alloying agents.
2. Those containing silicon up to, or slightly be-

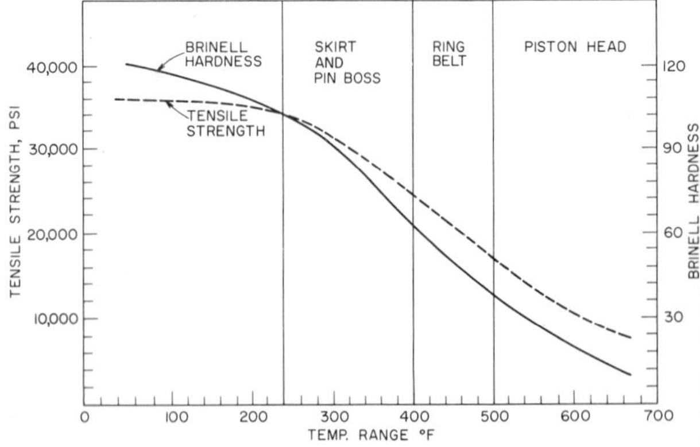

Fig. 12-7. Effect of temperature on the hardness and strength of an aluminum piston. (*Thompson, Ramo, Wooldridge, Inc.*)

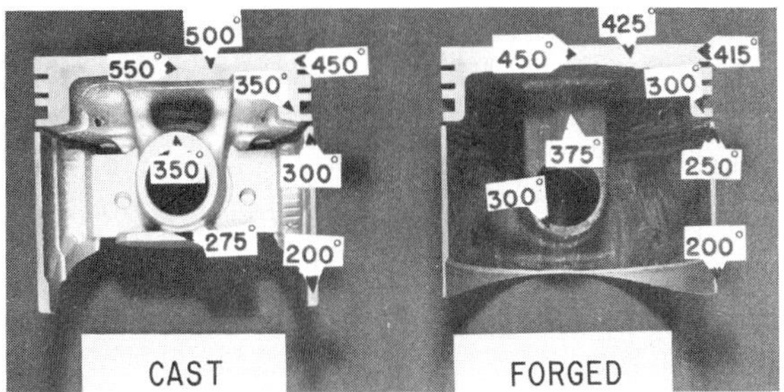

Fig. 12-8. Cast and forged pistons, cut in half to show operating temperatures at various comparable points in the two pistons. (*Thompson, Ramo, Wooldridge, Inc.*)

yond, the eutectic composition point (12 percent) plus other alloying elements.

3. Those containing copper, magnesium, and nickel, but no silicon.
4. Hypereutectic silicon-aluminum alloy, containing 17 to 22 percent silicon.

It must be remembered, however, that piston manufacturers may modify these standard alloys to suit their own manufacturing processes or to obtain special properties.

The use of aluminum for the piston results in a lighter piston and lower inertial loads which, in turn, permit higher engine rpm (revolutions per minute). Aluminum has higher thermal conductivity, and this permits higher compression ratios because the center of the head does not get so hot. The lower piston-head temperature reduces the possibility of preignition so that higher compression pressures can be used, thus permitting higher compression ratios.

However, aluminum, having a relatively high rate of thermal expansion (12.0×10^{-6} in./in./°F as opposed to 6.3×10^{-6} in./in./°F for cast iron), presents a problem in maintaining the proper clearance between the piston and the cylinder wall, which is of cast iron, throughout the temperature range encountered in engine operation. Various means of controlling the piston expansion have been used. (§147).

Another problem of which the designer must be aware is that all of the aluminum-alloy pistons show a considerable loss of strength, hardness, and resistance to wear at the temperatures they meet in operation. Figure 12-7 shows the tensile strength and hardness of a typical alloy at various temperatures. The data were obtained from samples heated to the various temperatures for 100 hours. The vertical lines show the range of temperatures experienced by the different parts of the piston in operation. Note that the hardness (solid line) in the ring-belt area drops at operating temperature to about one-fourth of the cold hardness. At the same time, the tensile strength drops to about one-half of the cold strength. This explains why high-performance pistons require special fortification of the ring grooves (§153).

In addition, the piston head is exposed to combustion temperatures twice as high as the melting point of the aluminum alloy. It is obvious, therefore, that the designer must include adequate heat paths for the heat to pass from the piston to the cylinder wall. Without adequate heat paths, operating temperatures in the head and ring areas could rise excessively, and this could weaken the piston so much that early failure would result. Note the difference that 50 or 100° makes in the strength and hardness of the alloy (Fig. 12-7).

Actually, the rate at which heat is transferred depends on several factors. The rate is inversely proportional to the length of the heat path and directly proportional to the temperature difference, the cross section of the heat path, and the coefficient of heat transfer.

NOTE: The above points up one limiting factor to larger cylinder bores. The larger the bore, the longer the heat path from the center of the piston head, and thus the higher the head temperature. The higher the head temperature, the greater the tendency for preignition. Passenger-car engines of today have cylinder bores of around 4.0 inches, and they may increase quite a bit over that in the future. However, some engineers set the outside limit of bore size as 6.0 inches, and this size would probably require some form of piston-head cooling —an oil jet under the piston crown, for example.

In addition to providing adequately large and properly located heat paths in the piston, the designer can also select alloys with high coefficients

Fig. 12-9. Forged aluminum piston, cut in half and etched to bring out the grain flow. The etched lines show the directions that the metal flowed during the forging process. (*Thompson, Ramo, Wooldridge, Inc.*)

Fig. 12-10. Appearance of a piston that has failed from scuffing. Note the scratch or scuff marks that run vertically on the piston skirt. (*Thompson, Ramo, Wooldridge, Inc.*)

of heat transfer (if such alloys also meet other design requirements). Also, the type of manufacturing process used (casting or forging) is of importance in heat transfer. Cast pistons are made by pouring the molten metal into molds. The forged piston is made from a slug of aluminum alloy which, when subjected to the high forging pressures, extrudes into the die to form the piston. Both types then require heat treating.

The forged piston has less porosity than the cast piston, and the denser metal provides a better heat path. This means the heat flows away faster from the hot areas in the forged piston than in the cast piston. The forged piston therefore runs cooler, as shown in Fig. 12-8. The flags indicate the temperatures at comparable points in the two pistons, with both operating under the same conditions.

The forged piston, in addition to its denser structure, also has a grain flow that improves its wear qualities and scuff resistance. Figure 12-9 shows the grain flow in a forged piston. Note that the flow is vertical in the skirt, that is, in the direction that the piston moves in the cylinder.

The forged piston is also lighter and thus imposes lower inertial forces. It also has greater tensile strength than the cast piston of similar composition (about 28 percent more). Finally, the forged piston has greater ductility, which permits it to sustain greater loads and to withstand higher thermal stresses.

Cast pistons are satisfactory for many automotive applications, but, for high-performance engines, the forged piston is recommended.

§144. Piston scuffing and its prevention Many pistons are given a tin coating, which helps them get a good start in life and resists scuffing. The mechanism of scuffing is as follows. The temperature between moving metal surfaces is sufficiently high, and the clearances are so small that the surfaces come into actual contact—not large-scale contact, but spot contact, here and there. The metal spots (high points on the metal surfaces) may rub together so heavily that small areas will momentarily melt. Small-area welds then occur. These welds may occur, for example, when the piston is momentarily at rest at TDC. Then, the welds are broken as the piston starts to move again, leaving rough spots in the areas of the former welds. Once started, scuffing progresses rapidly, with the surfaces becoming increasingly rough and engine failure rapidly approaching. The scuffing shows up as long gouges in the metal surfaces and discoloration in the areas of scuffing. (See Fig. 12-10.)

With a tin coating, the piston surface is much less apt to scuff during the initial wearing-in period of engine operation. The tin interposes a relatively soft surface of relatively low friction. If the oil film is momentarily broken so that actual contact between piston and cylinder wall results, there may be momentary melting at hot spots. But the tin tends to prevent actual welding from taking place

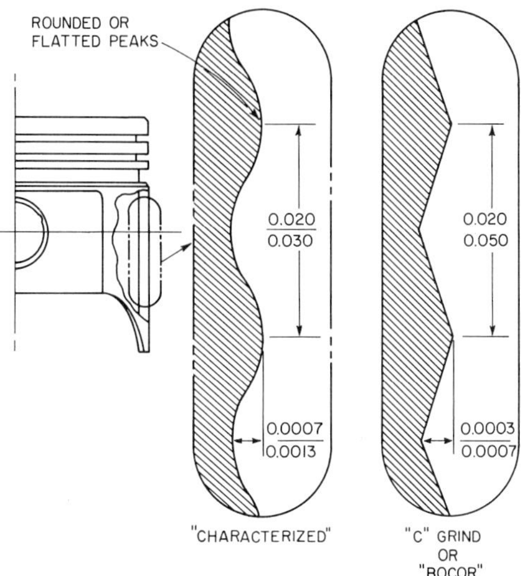

Fig. 12-11. Recommended skirt grinds to produce good antiscuff properties. "Characterized," "C" grind, and "BoCor" are names given to the process by different manufacturers. (*Thompson, Ramo, Wooldridge, Inc.*)

Fig. 12-12. Pistons used in modern spark-ignition engines.

because it is incompatible with the aluminum of the piston and the iron of the cylinder wall.

NOTE: Scuffing is usually more of a problem with piston rings than with pistons (see §160).

The type of finish on the piston skirt also has an important bearing on the piston life and antiscuff properties. A relatively rough piston-skirt finish has been found to have greater scuff resistance. This must be a controlled roughness, achieved by proper dressing of the grinding wheel used to finish the skirt. Figure 12-11 shows recommended grinds that produce a desired corrugated finish with good antiscuff properties. Apparently two factors are involved: First, the valleys can carry adequate oil to the moving surfaces so that a good oil film is maintained. Secondly, the high points tend to wear off so that the fit improves, and, in effect, the skirt becomes tailored to fit the cylinder bore.

§145. Piston-head design The simplest piston head is the flat head. It is easier to manufacture, it has the most uniform heat distribution across the head, the weight distribution can be so designed as to result in minimum distortion of ring grooves and piston-pin bosses, the weight itself can be reduced, and so on. However, the flat-head piston is falling into disuse in modern high-compression engines because it has become necessary to provide notches for adequate valve clearance with the piston at TDC and also quench and squish areas (in many engines). Further, some piston heads have a trough, or are dished, or are somewhat convoluted to improve turbulence or provide quench and squish areas around the head perimeter (Fig. 12-12). Also they may have a built-up section, or "pop up" as it is called, to provide for high compression (Fig. 11-3).

Such pistons are somewhat more difficult to manufacture. If the piston is being cast, then the trough, dish, or pop-up is usually cast into the head, and this requires very exact control of the mold and core so that all pistons will have the same head thickness and mass of material in the head (with a flat head, the head could be turned to achieve this uniformity). If the head is machined to produce the trough, dish, and so on, not only may the machining process require special tools, but also it must be performed with careful attention to head thicknesses and weight masses. These must be uniform with all pistons, of course.

§146. Heat control in piston The head of the piston should be hot, and the skirt should be comparatively cool.[3] If the head runs too cool, thermal efficiency is reduced, and the chilling effect of the cold metal on the combustion process will increase the percentage of unburned hydrocarbons in the exhaust gases (§139). On the other hand, the head should not run too hot because this could result in surface ignition with its related engine roughness and also short piston life.

The skirt of the piston should run comparatively cool so as to avoid excessive expansion of the skirt due to high temperatures. This is especially true of the full-skirt piston.

Figure 12-13 shows the operating-temperature pattern of a full-skirt piston. Various methods of reducing heat flow to the piston skirt are used. One method uses a heat dam just below the piston head. This is a groove that is cut circumferencially in the piston between the top ring groove and the head (Fig. 12-1). The heat dam reduces the path that the heat can travel from the head to the skirt. Part of the heat that does pass the heat dam is carried through the piston rings to the cylinder wall and therefore does not travel on down to the piston skirt to cause skirt expansion.

A second method of reducing heat flow is by cutting or casting horizontal slots in the piston (Figs. 12-1 and 12-14). This reduces the heat path from the head to the skirt.

§147. Expansion control in piston If the piston skirt expands too much, clearance between it and the cylinder wall will be reduced so much that loss of power from friction, severe wear, and possible seizure would occur. On the other hand, if the clearance is excessive, then piston slap will occur. Piston slap results from the sudden tilting of the piston in the cylinder as the piston starts down on the power stroke after combustion has started. The piston moves from one side of the cylinder wall to the other with sufficient force to produce a distinct, hollow, bell-like noise. Not only is the noise annoying, but also the slapping action can cause rapid wear of the piston and cylinder wall.

Recommended clearance between the piston and cylinder wall is in the neighborhood of 0.001

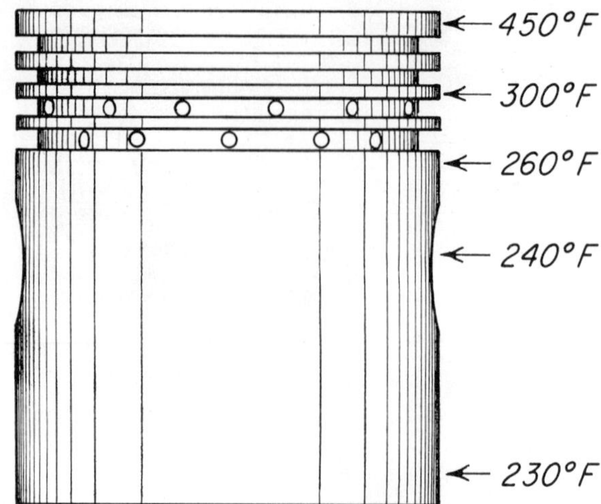

Fig. 12-13. Typical operating temperatures of various parts of a piston. (*Muskegon Piston Ring Company*)

Fig. 12-14. Piston with horizontal and vertical slots cut in its skirt. The horizontal slot reduces the path for heat travel, and the vertical slot allows for expansion without an increase in piston diameter.

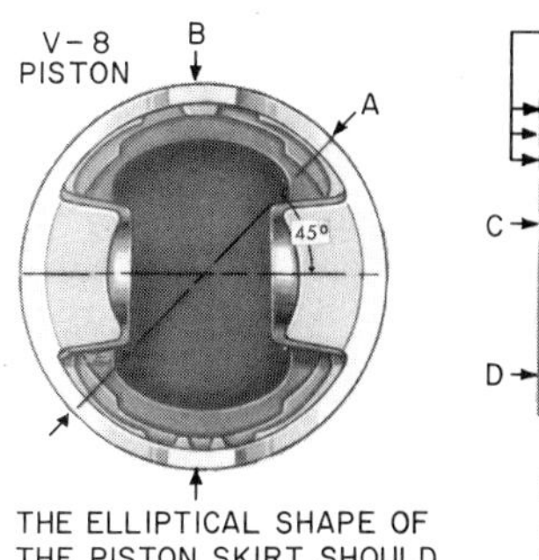

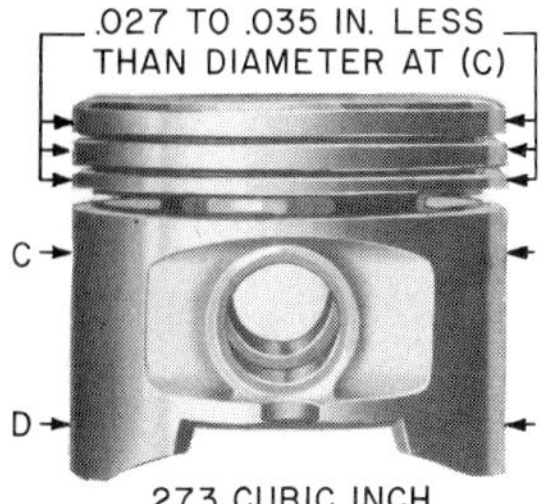

Fig. 12-15. Cam-ground piston. Piston skirt on the 273 cubic inch piston is also tapered (diameter at D is larger than at C). (*Chrysler-Plymouth Division of Chrysler Motors Corporation*)

to 0.004 inch. In operation, this clearance is filled with oil so that the piston and rings move on a film of oil. Specified clearance is different for different engines and must be held within narrow limits for optimum operation.

This is not an easy thing to do, however, because there is a temperature gradient in the skirt from the piston head to the lower end of the skirt. Figure 14-8 shows that the temperature in the cast piston, under operating conditions, drops from 450°F at the top of the skirt to 200° at the bottom. The design of the piston—locations of the metal masses and shape of the piston skirt—must take this into consideration. Many pistons have a tapered skirt to allow for the difference in expansion produced by the temperature differential (Fig. 12-15).

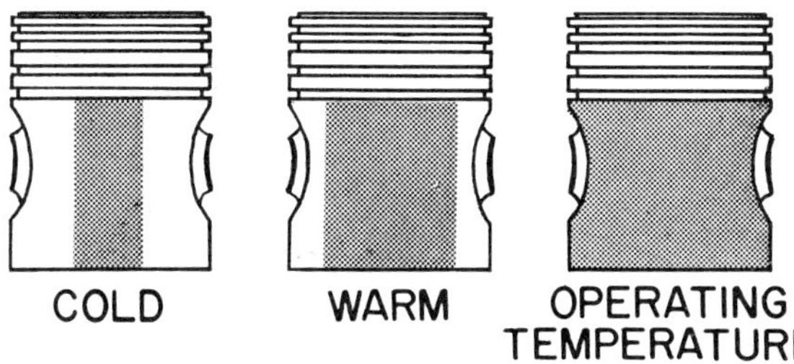

Fig. 12-16. As the cam-ground piston warms up, the expansion of the skirt distorts the piston from an elliptical to a round shape, so that the area of contact between the piston and the cylinder wall is increased.

One method of controlling the expansion of the piston skirt with increased temperature is to grind the piston to an elliptical shape. Another is to install, or cast in, carbon-steel bands or rings, or struts. In addition, the skirt may be barreled from the oil-control-ring groove to the piston-pin holes and tapered below that (Fig. 12-39).

When the piston is ground to an elliptical shape, it is called a *cam-ground piston* because the grinding machine employs a cam to move the piston toward and away from the grinding wheel as the piston revolves. When the cam-ground piston is cold, it is elliptical in shape, with the long axis (B in Fig. 12-15) perpendicular to the piston-pin bosses. The area of normal clearance of the cold piston is small and is at the thrust faces of the piston (Fig. 12-16). The clearance at the other areas is excessive. This changes, however, as the piston warms up. As this happens, the head of the piston expands equally in all directions. The relatively stiff piston-pin bosses are more effective in transmitting the outward forces than the thrust-face parts of the skirt. As the distance across the piston-pin bosses increases, the thrust faces tend to be

Fig. 12-17. Piston with cast-in belt to provide expansion control. (*Thompson, Ramo, Wooldridge, Inc.*)

drawn inward. This is called the "hoop-stretching" action because it is much like the action of a hoop that is pulled out in one direction. This causes the diameter of the hoop in the perpendicular direction to be decreased. The total effect is that the piston assumes a more nearly round shape as it reaches operating temperature, so that the area of normal clearance increases (Fig. 12-16).

Another method of controlling piston expansion is by use of struts, bands, or belts, made of carbon

Fig. 12-18. Piston with cast-in band to provide expansion control. (*Thompson, Ramo, Wooldridge Inc.*)

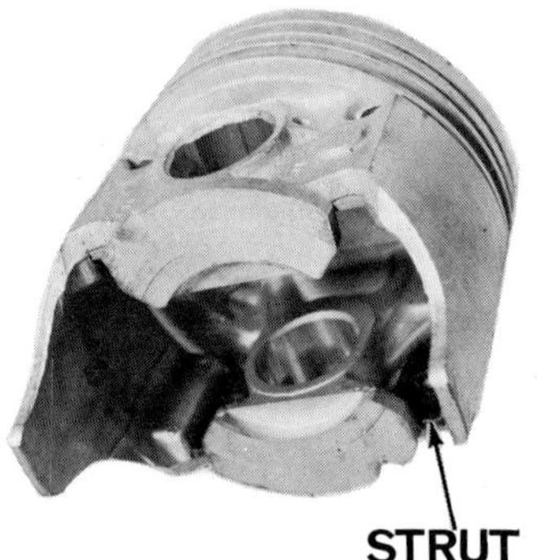

Fig. 12-19. Piston with cast-in strut to provide expansion control. (*Thompson, Ramo, Wooldridge, Inc.*)

steel which has a coefficient of expansion nearly equal to cast iron. Figure 12-17 shows a belted piston, partly cut away so that the belt can be seen. The belt is a ring, round in cross section, which is cast into the top of the skirt just below the horizontal slot. When the piston head expands with increased temperature, the band retards expansion along the thrust-face axis. The banded piston (Fig. 12-18) has a band, stamped from sheet steel and rectangular in cross section, cast into the top of the piston skirt. The band has a relatively large radial depth at the piston-pin boss locations and a relatively small radial depth at the thrust faces. The band stiffens the boss areas so they move out as the piston heats, thus producing a modified "hoop-stretching" action.

The most popular expansion-control element is the strut, a stamped steel plate cast into the piston-pin-boss sides of the skirt, as shown in Fig. 12-19. Figure 12-20 shows a similar arrangement in sectional view. The action is similar to that in belted or banded pistons as temperature increases. Pistons using struts, as shown, are called *strut pistons*, or Autothermic* pistons.

Another method of controlling piston-skirt expansion (no longer widely used) is to cut vertical

* Registered trade name.

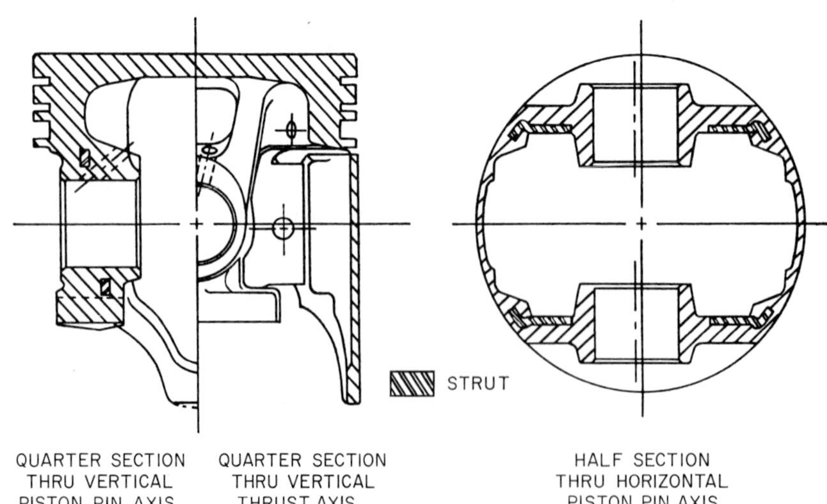

Fig. 12-20. Sectional views of a piston with a cast-in strut. This is known as an Autothermic piston.

Fig. 12-21. Piston with oval skirt. (*Thompson, Ramo, Wooldridge, Inc.*)

Fig. 12-22. Piston with undulated skirt. (*Thompson, Ramo, Wooldridge, Inc.*)

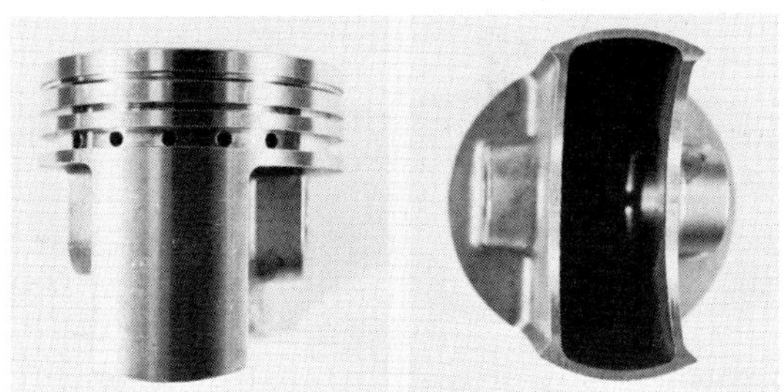

Fig. 12-23. Piston with outboard piston-pin bosses. (*Thompson, Ramo, Wooldridge, Inc.*)

slots in the skirt, as shown in Fig. 12-14. These allow the skirt to expand horizontally, without increasing greatly in size. However, not only do these vertical slots weaken the skirt, but also they do not provide for controlled expansion (as do the other methods already described).

§148. Piston skirts We have already noted (in §141) that the more compact, shorter-stroke engine requires a short piston. Furthermore, the space requirements for the counterweights on the crankshaft led to the slipper piston (Fig. 12-3 to 12-5). Also, expansion control is required in all pistons (as discussed in §147).

Figures 12-21 to 12-23 show other late-type pistons in which the skirts have been given special configurations for added strength and flexibility. The oval-skirt piston (Fig. 12-21) and the undulated-skirt piston (Fig. 12-22) were designed to provide both flexibility and high strength. These two pistons are for use in high-performance automobiles, but they are strong enough for use in competition engines. The outboard piston-pin-boss piston (Fig. 12-23) is designed for maximum strength and is used primarily in competition engines. Note that the piston-pin bosses are outside the walls of the piston, and also that the thrust faces in this piston are relatively small.

Piston skirts may also be barreled and tapered to allow for expansion and to provide adequate scuff and noise control (see §155).

§149. Piston weight Closely related to the piston material and method of manufacture is the piston weight. Heavier pistons are more apt to be more rigid, suffer less from heat of combustion, and live longer in the engine. On the other hand, heavier pistons are harder on engine bearings and put greater stresses on connecting rods, crankshafts, and other parts because of the higher inertia loads they impose. They also limit top engine speed and reduce the responsiveness of the engine. Impact-forged aluminum pistons (Fig. 12-8), with their thinner cross sections and lighter weight, make for a more responsive engine and permit higher engine speeds. They are more expensive, but the additional costs are justified for high-performance engines where a major consideration is the need for quick response and high rpm.

Pistons in modern automotive engines run, in weight, from about 10 ounces to about 30 ounces. All pistons in an engine must be of the same weight (and the piston-ring-rod assemblies also). Otherwise, an unbalanced condition may result that could cause serious engine vibration and even, under severe conditions, actual failure of engine parts. Another advantage of equal piston weights is that service pistons can be supplied in the same weight. Thus, if an automotive mechanic, during an engine-service job, finds that only two cylinders require service and new pistons, he can replace only the two pistons. He will not have to install a complete set of new, matched, pistons. (Pistons are also supplied in standard oversizes for service. Thus, the cylinder is finished to the correct larger size to take the proper oversize piston of the same weight as the other pistons in the engine.)

§150. Piston-pin attachment and lubrication The vertical loads imposed on the piston (Fig. 12-2) are transmitted to the piston pin, and both the pin and the piston-pin bosses must be rigid enough to carry the loads without appreciable deflection. Also, the piston-pin bushings must receive adequate lubrication.

Combustion pressures cause the ends of the piston pin to be deflected downward, and this tends to force the lower ends of the pin bosses closer together. Then, at the end of the exhaust stroke, the inertia load of the piston causes the ends of the piston pin to be deflected upward so the upper ends of the pin bosses are forced to move closer together. As a result of all this, if the deflections are sufficiently large, fatigue cracks may develop around the pin bosses, and piston failure then results.

The piston-pin deflection can be calculated by considering the pin as a simple beam if it is not press-fitted into the connecting rod. Or, if it is press-fitted into the connecting rod, each end of the pin may be considered as a cantilevered beam. The amount of deflection can then be calculated. It is obvious that the pin bosses should be as close together as possible so as to minimize the bending moment on the piston pin. Also, in highly loaded pistons it is desirable for the inner edges of the piston-pin bores to be provided with generous chamfers or radii that blend with the bores and permit deflection of the pin without excessively loading the edges of the bores.

Another type of pin deflection is also possible. When the vertical load is applied, the pin tends to be deflected, or squeezed, into a somewhat elliptical shape. This increases the horizontal dimension of the pin and loads the two sides of the piston-pin boss. This type of pin deflection has been known to split the piston-pin bosses. In some heavy-duty-engine pistons, the piston-pin bores are made elliptical in shape, with the large axis horizontal. This provides additional clearance for the pin in a horizontal direction so the pin can deflect horizontally without loading the pin bosses.

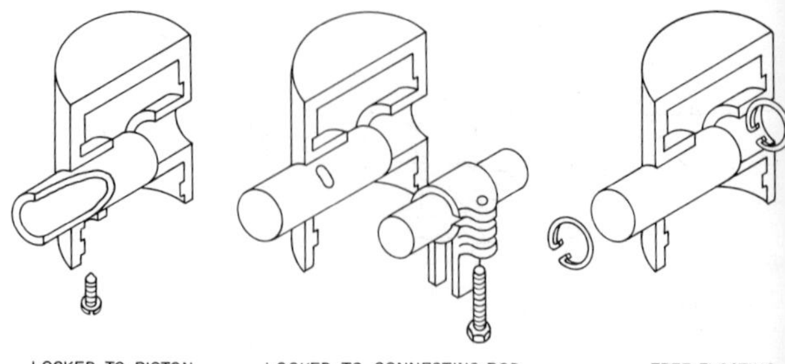

Fig. 12-24. Three piston-pin arrangements.

1. Methods of piston-pin attachment. There are three methods of attaching the connecting rod to the piston (Fig. 12-24). One method locks the piston pin to the piston by a lock bolt. The pin does not turn in the piston. The rod has a sleeve bearing that provides a bearing surface between the rod and pin as the rod rocks back and forth on the pin.

A second method locks the piston pin to the connecting rod, either by making the pin a press fit in the rod, or by using a lock bolt (Fig. 12-24). There are sleeve bearings in the piston-pin holes in which the piston pin can turn back and forth.

The third method uses a free-floating piston pin which is not locked to either the rod or the piston. Both the rod and piston have sleeve bearings in which the pin can turn. Lock rings are used at the two ends of the pin, in the piston, to hold the pin in position and prevent it from moving out and rubbing on the cylinder wall.

The third method is preferred by many engine designers because the bearing wear is distributed over three sleeve bearings, and the free movement of the pin reduces the tendency for the pin to wear out-of-round. On the other hand, the second method, by which the pin is locked to the connecting rod, is a less expensive design and has been widely used.

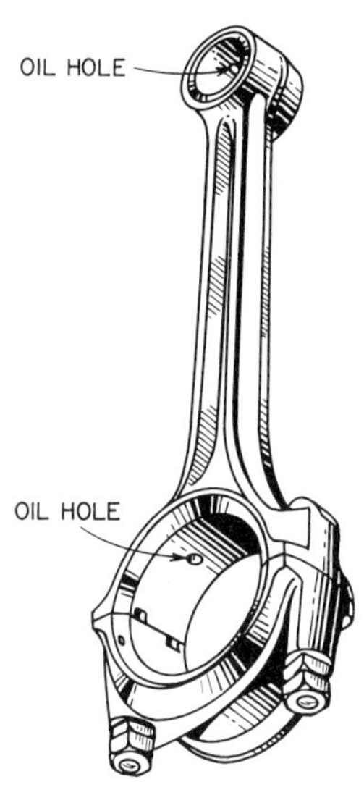

Fig. 12-25. Oil holes in assembled connecting rod, through which oil can feed from the rod big end to the rod small end to lubricate the piston pin.

2. *Piston-pin-bushing lubrication.* In the full pressure-fed lubricating system used in all modern automotive engines, lubricating oil under pressure is supplied to the various bearings and other surfaces where relative movement is taking place. On some engines using a sleeve bearing or bushing in the rod small end, a hole is drilled up through the connecting rod from the big end to the pin end. This hole is matched with holes in the rod upper bearing shell and in the piston-pin bearing (Fig. 12-25). With each revolution of the crankpin in the connecting rod, an oil hole in the crankpin indexes with the hole in the bearing shell and rod. There is oil under pressure in oil passages drilled in the crankshaft, and some of this oil surges into the bearing shell and rod holes when the crankpin and shell holes index. The oil passes up to the piston-pin bearing so that it is adequately lubricated.

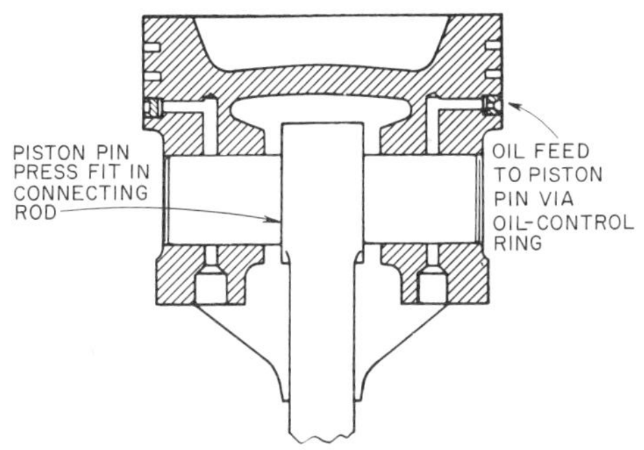

Fig. 12-26. One method of oiling piston-pin bushings in piston. (*Ford Motor Company, Limited*)

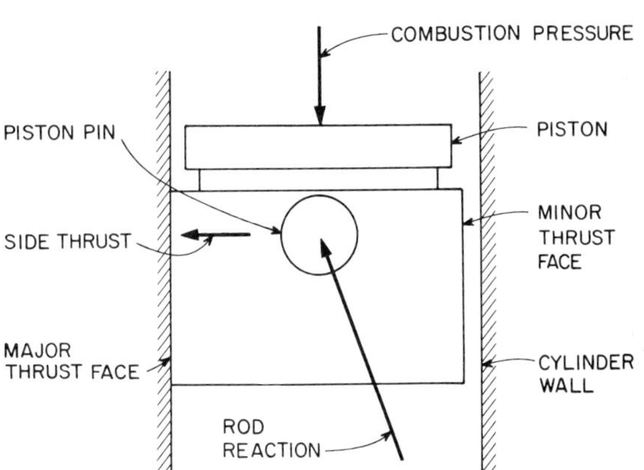

Fig.12-27. As combustion pressure is applied to the piston head and the connecting-rod angle changes from left to right, side thrust on the piston will cause it to shift abruptly toward the major thrust face.

On engines in which the piston pin is locked to the connecting rod (by a bolt or press fit), the piston pin rides in bushings in the piston-pin bosses of the piston. Lubrication of these bushings is from the cylinder wall. In these engines, the piston has grooves, holes, or slots to feed oil from the oil-control-ring groove, or from oil scoops on the piston, to the piston-pin bushings for adequate lubrication. One method of oiling piston-pin bushings in the piston is shown in Figs. 12-26 and 12-37.

§151. Piston-pin offset Some engine designs call for offsetting the piston pin from the centerline of the piston toward the major thrust face. This is the face that bears most heavily against the cylinder wall during the power stroke (Fig. 12-27). If the piston pin is centered, the minor thrust face of the skirt remains in contact with the cylinder wall until the end of the compression stroke. Then, as the piston goes up over TDC and starts down again on the power stroke, the rod angle changes from the left to the right (Fig. 12-27). This causes a sudden shifting of the side thrust on the piston from the minor thrust face to the major thrust face. The side thrust is proportional to the rod reaction and angle, as well as to combustion pressures. With any appreciable clearance, the sudden reversal of

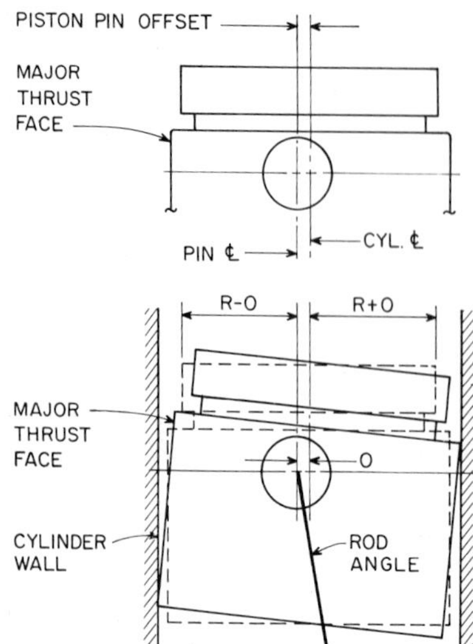

Fig. 12-28. If the piston pin is offset toward the major thrust face, combustion pressure will cause the piston to tilt to the right, as shown, to reduce piston slap. R = radius of piston; O = offset of piston pin. (*Bohn Aluminum and Brass Company, Division Universal American Corporation*)

side thrust will produce piston slap. This results from the sudden movement of the piston from one side of the cylinder to the other.

However, if the piston pin is offset (to the left in Fig. 12-28), the combustion pressures will cause the piston to tilt as the piston nears TDC (as shown), so that the lower end of the major thrust face will make contact with the cylinder wall. Then, after the piston passes TDC and the reversal of side thrust occurs, full major-thrust-face contact is made with less of a tendency for piston slap to occur.

The tilting action occurs because there is more combustion pressure on the right-hand portion of the piston (which measures $R + O$, or piston radius plus offset) than on the left-hand side of the piston (which measures $R - O$).

§152. Ring-groove stresses Another area where distortion cannot be tolerated is in the ring-groove region. If there is appreciable skirt deflection as the piston rocks back and forth in the cylinder and is subjected to the changing pressures in the combustion chamber, the oil-control groove will tend to change shape. In many pistons, the top of the skirt forms the bottom of the oil-ring groove. Thus, skirt distortion may distort the ring groove so much that some oil control will be lost. The skirt must be strong enough to prevent this.

The compression-ring grooves are less subject to distortion from skirt distortion, but the top ring groove encounters another sort of stress. With every power stroke, as the piston changes directions at TDC and combustion pressures rise, the ring is forced down hard against the lower side of the groove. In some cases, as in high-performance engines, the impact might approach 2,000 g's.* Then, during the exhaust stroke, the downward pressure is greatly reduced. Next, as the intake stroke starts and a vacuum results in the engine cylinder, the top compression ring will be lifted off the lower side of the ring groove and brought into contact with the upper side. Ring inertia also plays a part in this ring movement in the ring groove. The ring is in periodic motion relative to the ring groove, striking first the upper and then the lower sides of the groove. In engines where the combustion pressures are high, as for example in high-performance automotive and diesel engines, this ring movement tends to induce rapid wear of the sides of the ring groove. The higher the piston temperature, the more rapid this wear because, as

* One g is the force acting on a body due to the gravitational pull of the earth. This force, acting on a falling body, increases its velocity by 32.16 feet per second each second it falls.

Fig. 12-29. Piston with top-ring-groove cast-in fortification. (*Thompson, Ramo, Wooldridge, Inc.*)

we have seen (Fig. 12-7), aluminum loses strength and hardness as its temperature increases. Wear of the ring grooves reduces the effectiveness of the ring so that blow-by increases, with its accompanying loss of power and contamination of the engine oil in the crankcase.

§153. Ring-groove fortification To combat ring-groove wear, top ring grooves can be fortified with wear-resistant metal. In high performance engines, the fortification consists of a ring of cast iron or a nickel-iron alloy called Ni-Resist.* The ring forms an insert which is cast into the piston (Fig. 12-29). For cast pistons in medium-duty service, the inserts are stamped from steel sheets. They are highly configured for good mechanical anchorage to the piston. In forged pistons, a cast-in insert obviously cannot be used. However, groove fortification is possible in forged pistons. One method utilizes a spray process during which molten metal is sprayed into the groove area. Then, the groove is machined to the proper dimensions. Another design uses a mechanically anchored Ni-Resist insert, with a high area-to-mass ratio for adequate heat transfer from the piston to the insert.

§154. Piston tests As already mentioned, the final test of a piston design is in the engine. If the piston can live in the engine, and provide satisfactory service and long life, then the design is good. But if the piston shows poor performance and short life, then it is a bad design, no matter how theoretically perfect the design might be.

* Registered trade name.

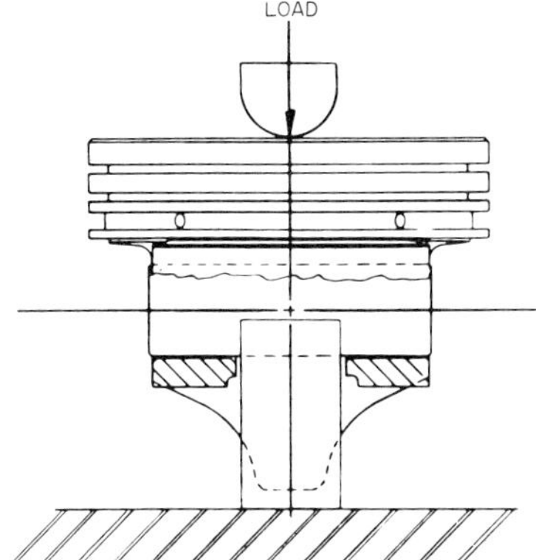

Fig. 12-30. Applying pressure on piston head to test its strength. (*Bohn Aluminum and Brass Company, Division Universal American Corporation*)

1. Preliminary tests. Before a piston design is tested in an engine, it is usually subjected to a series of static tests. For example, the strength of the piston head can be tested by applying pressure on it, as shown in Fig. 12-30. As the pressure is increased, the amount of diaphragming of the head and consequent distortion of the ring grooves can be measured. If the head is not sufficiently strong, then when the piston is installed in an engine, the ring grooves will distort enough in operation to cause the rings to lose compression and oil control, with possibly disastrous results to the engine. The static test can be carried to the actual crushing pressure of the head to determine its ultimate strength.

Another test determines the amount of expansion of the piston and skirt as temperature increases. To perform this test, a series of dial indicators are assembled to the piston by means of linkages and levers, and the piston is then immersed in a circulating oil bath. The oil is heated to several hundred degrees, and, during the consequent heating of the piston, its distortion, or the amount of expansion of its various parts, is noted.

Stress analyses of pistons may be made with stress coatings and strain gauges attached to the pistons while they are subjected to heavy pressures such as they would endure in the engine. Analysis of the stress patterns revealed by these tests often shows up serious weak points, for example, at a fillet or above a piston-pin boss. The design can then be revised slightly to strengthen these weak points. This work can be done before the piston is actually checked out in an operating engine, and often it saves much time and money.

Static loading of the piston in a test fixture such as shown in Fig. 12-31 permits measurement of side thrust on the minor and major thrust faces as well as deflection of the piston under varying loads and connecting-rod angularity.

2. Engine tests. During the operation of a new piston design in an engine, numerous tests can be

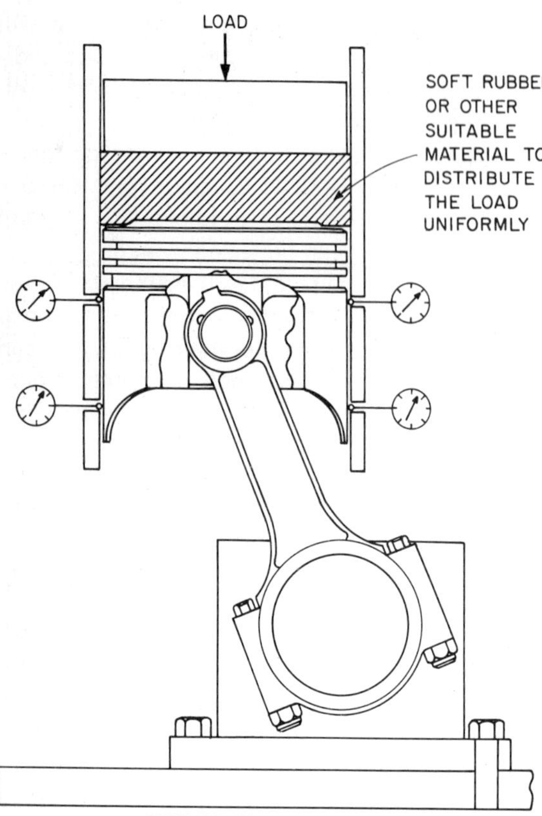

Fig. 12-31. Static loading of piston. (*Thompson, Ramo, Wooldridge, Inc.*)

made. Piston performance under varying operating conditions, different speeds, different compression ratios, different valve and ignition timing, and with different fuels, can be investigated. Evaluation of the following are usually included: resistance to hot scuff, resistance to cold scuff, high-load endurance capability, and noise level (piston slap) during both cold and hot operating conditions. These tests require operating the engine under a specified set of conditions for a specified time, and then tearing down the engine so the condition of the engine parts, including the pistons, can be noted.

Test engineers may also rig up special sensing devices to measure piston temperatures, stresses, and strains under various operating conditions. Pistons may be made of, or coated with, radioactive

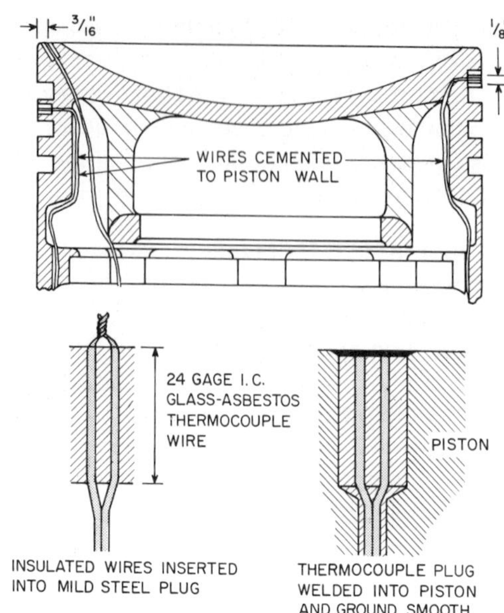

Fig. 12-32. Location of thermocouples in piston and method of installing them.

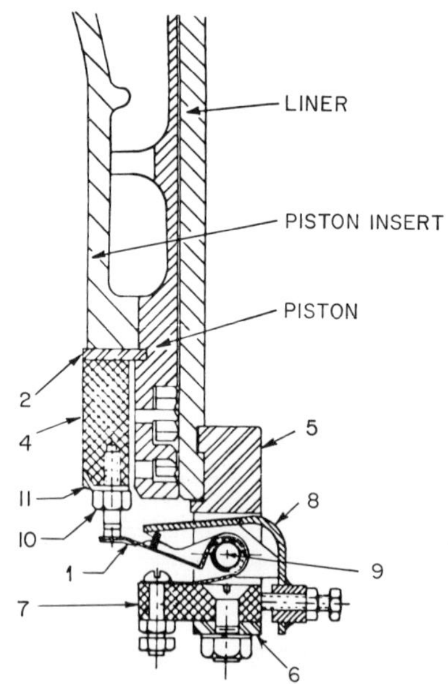

Fig. 12-33. Thermocouple contact arrangement to pick up current from thermocouple as piston reaches BDC:

1. Contact arm
2. Lock plate
4. Contact holder
5. Anchor ring
6. Bracket
7. Insulator
8. Adjusting bracket
9. Pin
10. Contact stud
11. Terminal lug

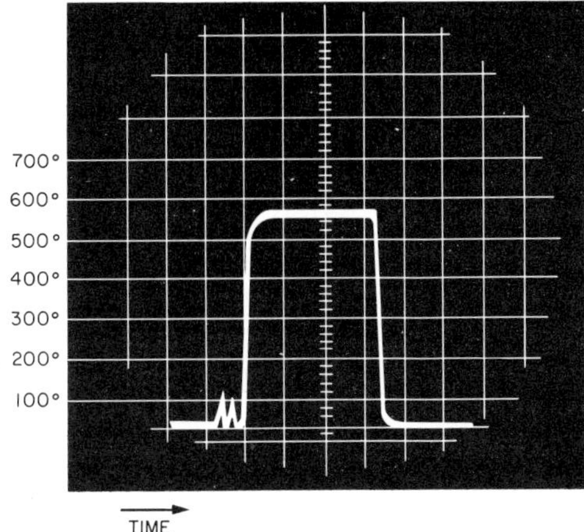

Fig. 12-34. Typical oscilloscope trace, with pulse indicating a temperature of about 575°F.

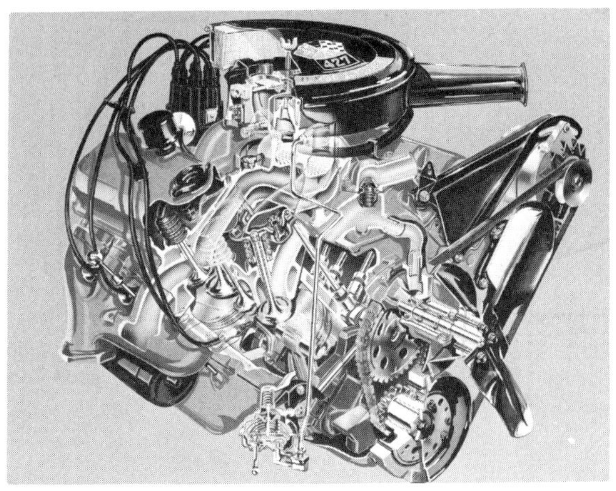

Fig. 12-35. Turbo-Jet engine cut away to show internal construction. (*Chevrolet Motor Division of General Motors Corporation*)

Fig. 12-36. Three piston designs for the Turbo-Jet engine. (*Chevrolet Motor Division of General Motors Corporation*)

materials, and then the lubricating oil can be monitored to determine how much of these materials is worn off. Any material that is worn off would be carried away in the oil; thus, testing the oil for radioactivity would disclose the wear. Actually this type of test is most often run on piston rings, not pistons (§163).

Thermocouples may be mounted in a piston, as shown in Fig. 12-32, with the couples located in different places to measure the temperature of various parts of the piston. The thermocouple produces an electric current that is proportional to temperature, so that a sensitive ammeter, or an oscilloscope, can be used to indicate temperature. Figure 12-33 shows one method of picking up the electric current as the piston reaches BDC (bottom dead center). The pulses of current, picked up in this manner, are sent to an oscilloscope which then displays a trace indicating the temperature. Figure 12-34 shows a typical trace, with a temperature of about 575°F indicated.

Less precise temperature measurements can be made with a simpler test setup by embedding small plugs of alloys of known melting temperatures at various places in the piston. Each plug has a different melting point. The operating temperature that the piston reaches can then be determined by noting which plugs melt during engine operation. A third method involves the time-temperature effect on an age-hardened aluminum alloy. Inasmuch as aluminum alloys change in hardness at known rates under various designated temperatures, a piston can be operated for a specified time, and sectioned for hardness tests of the varying parts. The change in hardness indicates the temperature that the part has reached.

All these methods are expensive and time-consuming and can be used only after pistons have actually been fabricated in a semifinal form. Therefore temperature tests are used less frequently than other tests noted above.

§155. The Chevrolet 427 piston—a case history During the development of the Chevrolet Turbo-Jet engine (Fig. 12-35),[4] three piston designs evolved (Fig. 12-36). The design on the left in Fig. 12-36 is for passenger-car engines using hydraulic valve lifters. It is cast aluminum, with cast-in struts

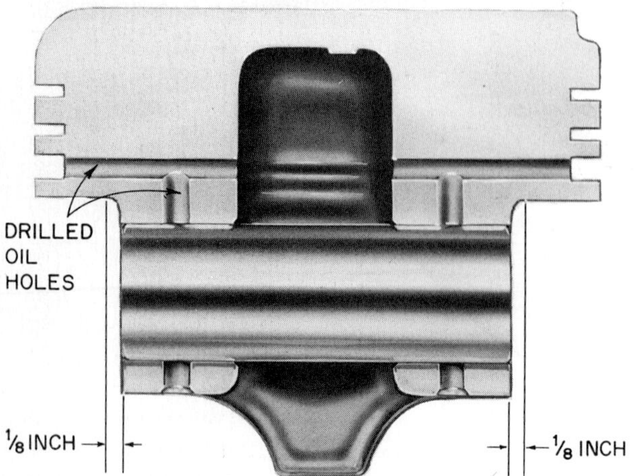

Fig. 12-37. Sectional view of piston showing how piston-pin bosses, as well as the oil holes, have been moved inward to lubricate the piston pin. (*Chevrolet Motor Division of General Motors Corporation*)

(Autothermic*) of the slipper type. The center piston is impact-extruded aluminum and is for the high-performance engine using solid or "mechanical" lifters, as they are sometimes called. On these, dome height is increased by a pop-up to achieve the high compression ratio of these engines (11 : 1). The piston on the right (Fig. 12-36) is for the truck version. It uses three compression rings and one oil-control ring to improve blow-by control, oil economy, and piston durability. This piston has a cast-in, alloy–cast-iron, top-ring-groove protector.

* Registered trade name

At an early stage, the decision was made to move the piston-pin bosses inboard 1/8 inch (Fig. 12-37). This shortened the piston pin by 0.32 inch and reduced the reciprocating weight. Also, with the bosses more inboard and the shorter piston pin, piston-pin deflection was reduced, thus reducing the possibility of pin scuffing. The design also provided for lubrication of the piston pin. Oil scraped from the cylinder wall by the oil-control ring passes through the drilled holes to the piston pin.

At an early stage in the engine development, some pistons in the high-performance engines were found to have the compression and oil-control rings stuck tight in their grooves. This was caused by collapse of the pistons at the oil slots. The slots were then replaced by six drilled holes, so that there was additional metal under the ring lands (Fig. 12-38). The strength of the piston at this point was increased satisfactorily.

The change to drilled holes, however, increased the heat path to the skirt as well as the rigidity of the piston. As a consequence, additional piston-to-cylinder-wall clearance was required to take care of the additional expansion and thus avoid scuffing. But this additional clearance allowed piston noise (piston slap) to become too noticeable. (You

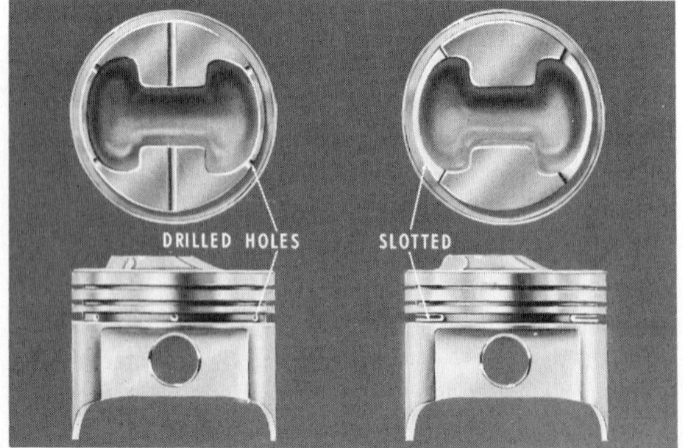

Fig. 12-38. During the development of the piston design, drilled holes were substituted for slots in the oil-control-ring groove to increase piston strength in this area. (*Chevrolet Motor Division of General Motors Corporation*)

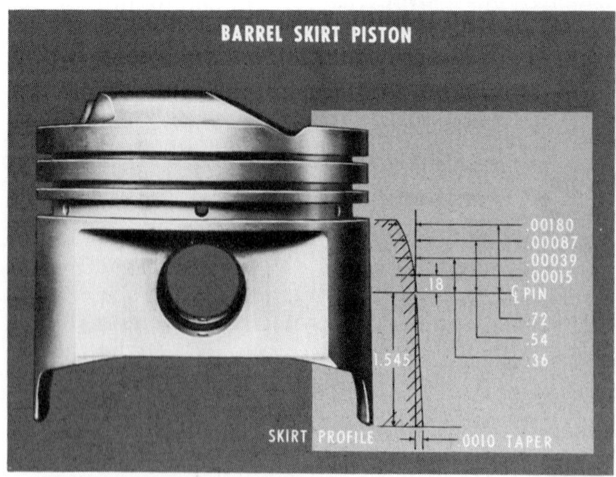

Fig. 12-39. Piston with barrel skirt and taper. (*Chevrolet Motor Division of General Motors Corporation*)

Fig. 12-40. Appearance of a piston that has failed due to preignition. Note how the ring lands, particularly the top one, appear to have been "nibbled" away. (*Thompson, Ramo, Wooldridge, Inc.*)

Fig. 12-41. Appearance of a piston that has failed due to detonation. Excessive pressure and temperature have caused a hole in the piston head. (*Thompson, Ramo, Wooldridge, Inc.*)

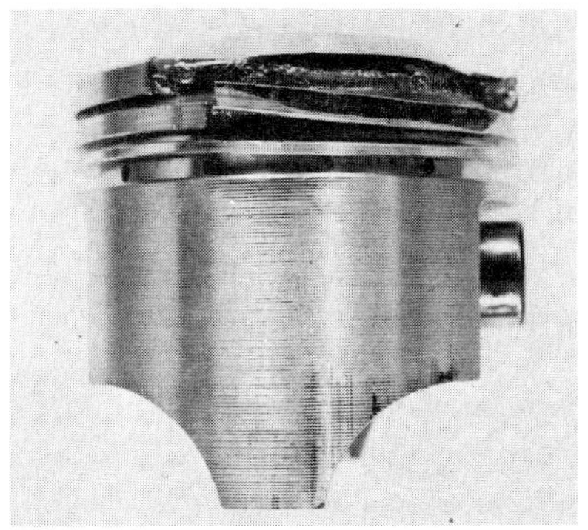

Fig. 12-42. Appearance of a piston that has failed in a spark-ignition engine with a compression ratio of 11:1. The pressure surge due to detonation was so severe that structural failure resulted even before thermal damage occurred. (*Thompson, Ramo, Wooldridge, Inc.*)

see how one "fix" can lead to other problems which must then be fixed?) After considerable laboratory work on different piston contours, the ultimate design was evolved (Fig. 12-39). The skirt above the piston-pin centerline is barreled, and it is tapered below the piston-pin centerline. This allows the piston-to-cylinder-wall clearance to be reduced enough to minimize piston noise without the danger of causing scuffing.

§156. Piston-failure analysis The final piston design depends to a large degree on accurate analysis of piston failures or incipient failures of prototype pistons operated under varying operating conditions. Identifying a cause of failure becomes increasingly difficult the longer the failing piston is operated. For example, initial failure may cause a rapid temperature increase throughout the piston. This, in turn, causes a loss of strength and hardness, abnormal expansion, and distortion. These could then produce distress in another part of the piston which could be confused with the initial problem.

Pistons can fail for a variety of reasons, including scuffing (Fig. 12-10), preignition and detonation, piston-pin lock-ring failure, other structural failure, and so on. Pin-pointing the basic cause of a failure is essential in piston design because the correct improvement must be made to eliminate the cause.

1. Scuffing wear. Scuffing has already been discussed in some detail (§144). Scuffing occurs when the oil film between the piston and cylinder wall is lost because of insufficient clearance due to a distorted cylinder bore, an overheated engine, contaminated oil, or improper piston design. If the scuffing has not progressed too far, the location of the scuffed area will provide a clue as to the cause. For example, a narrow scuffed area at the center of the major thrust face indicates an excessively elongated elliptical shape. Wide scuff patterns at the centers of both thrust faces indicate insufficient skirt-to-cylinder-wall clearance.

It is sometimes difficult to determine whether scuffing was initiated by the piston rings or by the piston skirt. When scuffing starts at the skirt, the faces of the rings do not become badly scored until the scuffing is well advanced. If the scuffing appears at all four 45-degree points (45 degrees off the centerline of the piston pin), tight piston pins could be the cause. Tight pins can restrict normal expansion and contraction of the skirt along the pin axis so that high skirt pressure and scuffing occur. This could also be caused by excessive "hoop-stretching" due to improper heat-expansion control in the design (§147).

Scuffing should not be confused with abrasive wear or corrosion damage on the thrust faces. These latter conditions are not encountered often in controlled laboratory or field tests, but can occur in normal over-the-road operation. The appearance of the damaged surfaces is quite different for each of the three types of conditions.

2. Preignition failure. Preignition can cause the type of failure shown in Figs. 12-40. Detonation can cause the types of failure shown in Figs. 12-41 and 12-42. These failures result from the excessively high temperatures and pressures reached during the abnormal combustion processes. In some cases, the pressure surge is great enough to produce structural failure before the temperature has a chance to cause thermal damage (Fig. 12-42). Except for sharp corners that could produce preignition, piston design does not cause abnormal combustion. If the pistons are expected to withstand abnormal combustion conditions, they will have to be made stronger in the head, with improved heat-flow paths from the head. However, it would be difficult to design a piston that could stand up under continuous preigniting or detonating conditions.

3. Piston-pin lock-ring failure. Piston-pin lock-ring failure can be readily identified because of the specific type of damage this failure causes (Fig. 12-43). Lock-ring failure involves the dislodgment or breaking up of the ring so that the side of the piston is damaged. Sometime the broken pieces of the ring work their way through the pin to the other side and cause similar damage there.

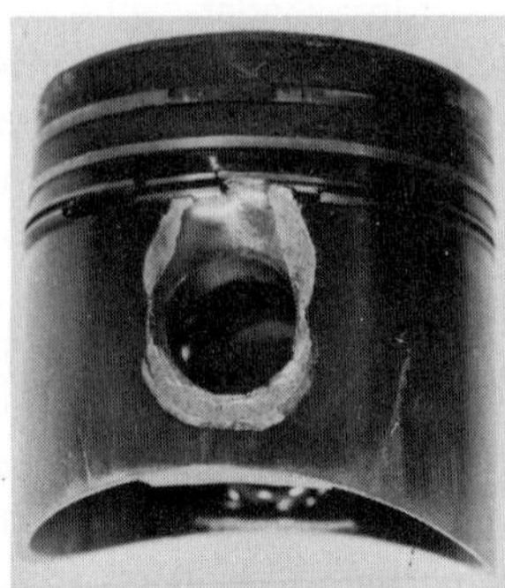

Fig. 12-43. Piston-pin lock-ring failure. (*Thompson, Ramo, Wooldridge, Inc.*)

Lock rings can become dislodged if a groove is not machined concentric with the piston-pin bore so that it is too shallow on one side, or if the grooves are machined oversize so the rings are loose. Improper groove spacing, which does not allow enough clearance with the piston pin, can also cause failure. A more common cause of lock-ring failure is the overcompression or distortion of the rings during assembly and the misalignment of parts, which cause the piston pin to be out of square with the cylinder bore. For example, if a connecting rod is bent or twisted, or if the centerline of the crankshaft is not perpendicular to the cylinder bore, then a considerable end thrust will be imparted to the piston pin, which could cause the lock ring to be broken or dislodged.

4. A piston-pin problem. During the development of the Mark II-427 GT engine,[5] Ford engineers had to solve a problem regarding the piston pins used in the engine. To start with, production piston pins were used. But the manufacturing tolerances for these pins permitted a variation of as much as 0.024 inch. During the testing program, several lock-ring failures occurred. It was thought that the failures were due to pounding of the piston pin against the lock rings. To prevent this, piston pins were select-fitted to achieve end play of only 0.001 to 0.005 inch. Failures still occurred. It was then decided that the failures were due to bending of the piston-pin bosses as maximum loading was applied to the piston. This action shortened the effective distance between the two lock rings and therefore caused the piston pin to be forced hard against the lock rings. It was the same as giving the piston pin a negative end play. The end play was therefore increased to 0.005 to 0.010 inch, and no further lock-ring failures occurred.

SUMMARY

The piston and ring assembly must be heavy enough to withstand the pressures and temperatures of the combustion process, and yet it must be as light as possible to keep the inertia loading of bearings and other parts down. The rings must seal compression, provide adequate oil control, and form an adequate heat path between the piston and cylinder wall. The piston must hold its shape sufficiently as its temperature changes. The piston and rings must be highly scuff resistant.

Piston design is a difficult procedure, involving many factors. Ultimately, however, the final test of a piston design is its ability to live in the engine. As engines have become shorter and oversquare, the piston has also become shorter, and this has produced the semislipper- and full-slipper-skirt pistons. Other factors to be considered include costs, casting and manufacturing procedures, head and skirt shape, method of piston-pin attachment, piston-pin-bushing lubrication, offsetting of the piston pin, method of piston-expansion control with increasing temperature, controlling heat loss from the piston, skirt finishes, possible use of ring-groove inserts, and methods of testing the piston after it is manufactured.

Piston tests can be either static or dynamic. Static tests include stress and strain testing and heat-expansion testing. Dynamic tests, performed in engines, include wear tests (pistons coated with radioactive material), running-temperature tests with thermocouples imbedded in the piston, endurance tests, and performance tests.

REFERENCES

1. *Winship, J. W., Engine Piston Design—Art or Science?, SAE (Society of Automotive Engineers) 660474, 1966 (paper); and Designing an Automotive Engine Piston, SAE 670020, 1967 (paper).*

2. *Cavileer, A. C., Piston Design Improvement Through Research Investigation; SAE (Society of Automotive Engineers) 636B, 1963 (paper).*

3. *Stotter, A., Heat Transfer in Piston Cooling, SAE (Society of Automotive Engineers) 660757, 1966 (paper).*

4. *Keinath, R. L., H. G. Sood, and W. J. Polkinghorne, Chevrolet Turbo-Jet Engine, SAE (Society of Automotive Engineers) 660340, 1966 (paper).*

5. *Macura, J. F., and J. Bowers, Mark II-427 GT Engine, SAE (Society of Automotive Engineers) 670066, 1967 (paper).*

QUESTIONS

1. *List nine requirements of the piston and ring combination.*
2. *List the most important factors that the piston designer must take into consideration.*
3. *What is piston scuffing, and what steps may be taken to prevent it?*
4. *What is the simplest piston head? Why?*
5. *Describe the various methods used to control the heat expansion of the piston skirt.*
6. *What are some of the problems associated with piston weight, and why do designers try to make the pistons as light as possible?*
7. *Describe the three methods of attaching the piston pin to the piston. Which is the method said to be preferred by many engine designers?*
8. *Describe the methods of lubricating the piston-pin bushing.*
9. *What is piston-pin offset, and why is it often used?*
10. *What could happen if the piston distorts enough from thermal and other stresses to change the bottom ring-groove shape?*
11. *What is a ring-groove insert, and what is its purpose?*
12. *Describe piston tests.*

Piston Rings

CHAPTER **13**

The preceding chapter discussed pistons in detail, outlined the requirements of the piston and ring combination, and described the essentials of piston design. This chapter deals with piston rings—their purpose, design, operation, and possible troubles.

§157. Purpose of piston rings A good seal must be maintained between the piston and the cylinder wall so that blow-by is prevented. "Blow-by" is a word used to describe the escape of burned gases from the combustion chamber, past the piston, and into the crankcase. In other words, the gases "blow by" the piston. It would be difficult to machine a piston accurately enough to prevent excessive blow-by. Even if this were possible, the differences in the amount of expansion between the cylinder and the piston due to changes in temperature would change the fit so it would be either too loose or too tight under different operating conditions.

Piston rings, assembled into grooves cut in the piston, as shown in Fig. 3-3, provide a good seal so that blow-by is kept at a minimum. Also, they seal in compression during the compression stroke. But the rings have more to do than this. Actually, piston rings have three basic jobs:

1. They must provide a good seal between the piston and cylinder wall, as already noted, to prevent excessive blow-by and maintain compression.

2. The rings must scrape oil off the cylinder wall on the downstrokes (power and intake). This prevents excessive amounts of oil from working up past the piston and getting into the combustion chamber. Oil in the combustion chamber burns, leaving a residue of carbon that fouls spark plugs, valves, and piston rings, thereby reducing their

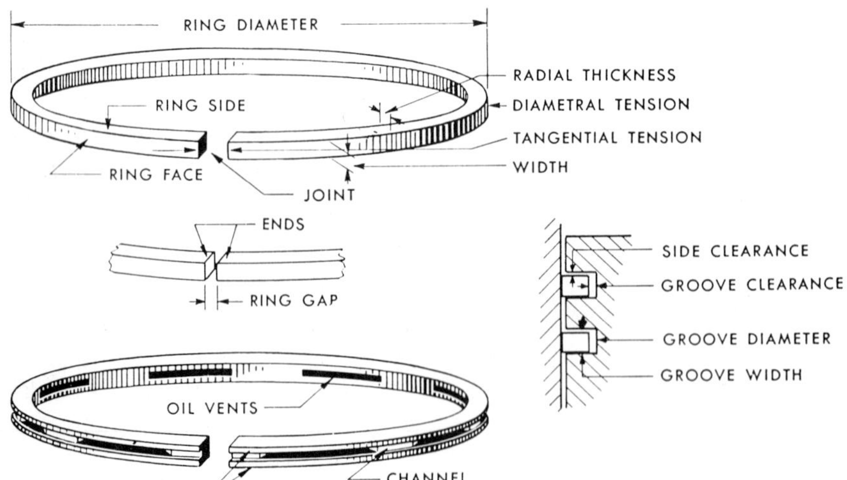

Fig. 13-1. A compression ring (top) and an oil-control ring (bottom) with the various parts named. (*Sealed Power Corporation*)

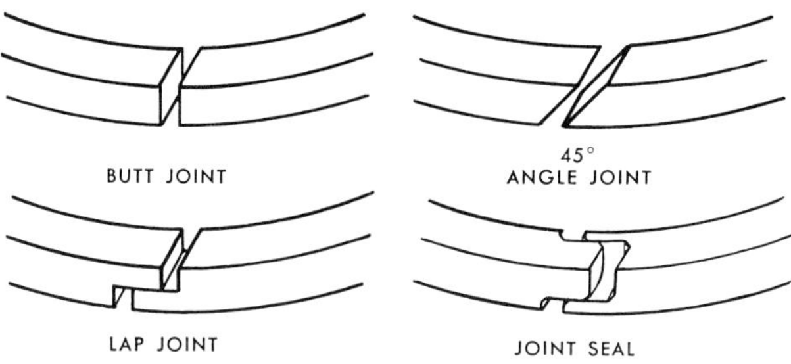

Fig. 13-2. Various types of ring joints. (*Sealed Power Corporation*)

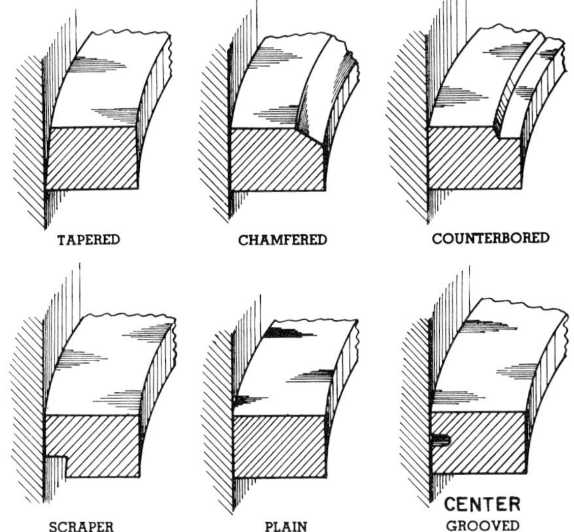

Fig. 13-3. Compression-ring shapes. (*Muskegon Piston Ring Company*)

effectiveness and thus reducing engine performance. These deposits can also cause engine rumble and knock, as noted in §124.

3. The rings must also help to cool the piston by transmitting heat from the hotter piston to the cooler cylinder wall.

Piston rings are of two types: compression rings and oil-control rings (Fig. 13-1). The basic purpose of compression rings is to provide the essential seal between the piston and cylinder wall. They also play a part in oil control. However, the major job of controlling the oil and preventing excessive amounts from reaching the combustion chamber is undertaken by the oil-control ring, or rings.

§158. Compression rings Compression rings[1,2] are usually made of gray cast iron. This material wears well and at the same time provides sufficient initial ring tension, or pressure, on the cylinder walls. Compression rings are usually coated with certain metals to improve their wearing qualities, as described in following paragraphs.

Fig. 13-4. Compression ring with counterbore. (*Perfect Circle Company*)

As already noted, the compression rings must hold blow-by to a minimum, and in order to do this, they must

1. Make good contact with the cylinder wall completely around the periphery of the ring.
2. Make good side contact with one or the other side of the piston-ring groove, entirely around the circumference of the ring.
3. Have a minimum gap at the ring joint, compatible with safe operation and avoidance of complete closure of the gap.

1. *Ring joints.* Most compression rings have butt joints (Fig. 13-2). Some heavy-duty engines use compression rings with angled, lap, or sealed joints. The ring is somewhat larger in diameter than it will be when it is compressed into the ring groove and installed in the cylinder. This gives the ring an initial tension that forces it outward into good contact with the cylinder wall.

The ring gap should be as small as possible, but it must not be so small that there will be danger of the ends of the ring coming into actual contact with each other. If this should happen, the ring probably would jam in the cylinder, causing the ring or piston to break and the cylinder wall to be damaged. On the other hand, if the gap is excessively large, then the blow-by through the gap will be too high. A typical specification for the ring gap in a modern engine is 0.010 to 0.020 inch.

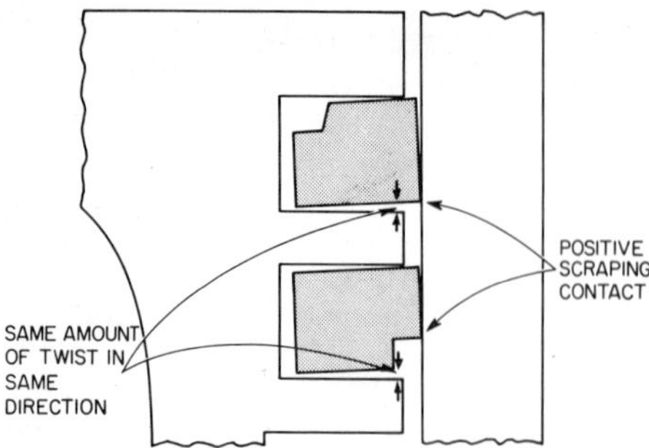

Fig. 13-5. Action of counterbored and scraper compression rings during the intake stroke. Internal forces of rings tend to twist them, so that a positive scraping contact is established between the rings and the cylinder wall. This helps to remove any excessive oil that has gotton past the oil-control rings. (*Perfect Circle Company*)

2. *Ring shapes.* Several different compression-ring shapes are shown in Fig. 13-3. The counterbored and scraper types have been most widely used for top and second compression rings. Figure 13-4 shows a counterbored ring. Cutting out the groove unbalances the internal tension forces in the ring. Then, when the ring is compressed for installation in the cylinder, it twists slightly because of this unbalance of internal tension forces. Note how this twist causes the ring to present a line contact with the cylinder wall during the intake stroke (Fig. 13-5). This induces a scraping action that scrapes down any excess oil that has been left on the cylinder wall by the oil-control and lower compression ring. Then, on the exhaust and compression strokes, when the ring is moving upward, it tends to "skate" over the film of oil on the cylinder wall so there is less tendency for the ring to carry oil up into the combustion chamber. The lower compression ring acts in a similar manner (Fig. 13-5).

As the power stroke begins, the combustion pressure is applied to the top and back of the ring (Fig. 13-6). This pressure overcomes the internal tension of the ring, causing it to untwist and apply full-face contact to the cylinder wall and full-side contact to the lower side of the ring groove. This action improves the sealing effect.

Combustion pressures that do get past the upper compression ring are applied to the top and back of the lower compression ring, as shown in Fig. 13-6. In effect, this provides a second barrier to the passage of combustion gases, or blow-by.

3. *Head-land ring.* This ring has a modified L-shaped cross section (Fig. 13-6*a* and *b*). Its name is derived from the fact that it covers, or shields, the head-land area of the piston. Several advantages are claimed for this design. First, because it is located only 1/16 inch down from the top of the piston (rather than the conventional 3/8 to 1/2 inch), it confines the gases in the combustion chamber,

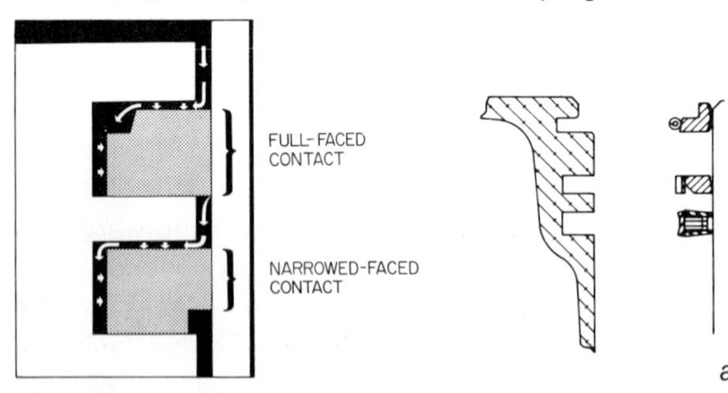

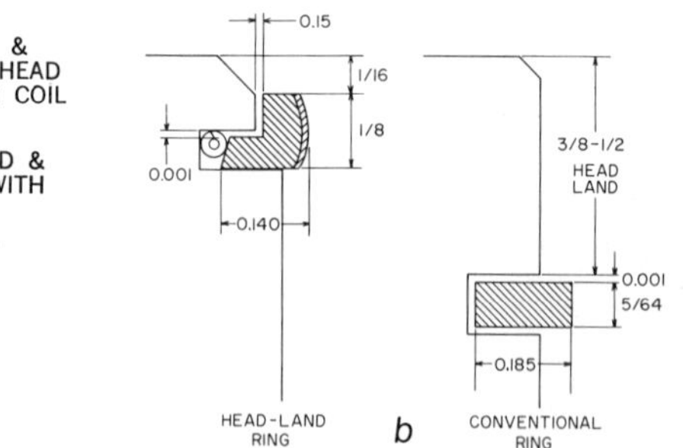

Fig. 13-6. Action of counterbored and scraper compression rings during the power stroke. The pressure of the burning charge in the combustion chamber presses the rings against the sides of the piston-ring grooves and the cylinder wall with full-face contact (white arrows), thus forming a good seal. (*Perfect Circle Company*)

Fig. 13-6a. Sectional view of piston and rings, showing (top) the head-land compression ring. (*Sealed Power Corporation*)

Fig. 13-6b. Head-land-ring installation compared with conventional ring. Note that with the head-land ring, there is no piston head land. The surface above the top ring groove is covered by the head-land ring up to the bevel. (*Sealed Power Corporation*)

thus promoting more complete combustion and reducing the percentage of unburned hydrocarbons in the exhaust gas. This is very desirable, of course, from the standpoint of reducing smog (see §139).

A second advantage claimed for the head-land ring is that it reacts swiftly to the build-up in combustion pressures. As combustion starts, the increasing pressure quickly acts upon the upper lip of the ring, forcing it outward and into a good sealing contact with the cylinder wall. With a conventional ring, the gas pressure must travel halfway around the ring before it gets behind the ring to force it outward. This quicker response of the head-land ring therefore reduces blow-by (by 50 percent or more, it is claimed). This, in turn, simplifies the closed-crankcase ventilating system (§256).

This more complete combustion, combined with reduction in blow-by, increases available engine horsepower (up to 10 percent, it is claimed). Further, the ring eliminates the head-land area of the piston (the area between the piston head and the conventional ring), which is one of the most common places in the engine for carbon deposits to form. Thus, the head-land ring makes for a cleaner engine, less wear of the cylinder wall, and better oil control by lessening the tendency of the rings to stick.

§159. Why two compression rings? The principle function of the lower compression ring is to reduce the pressure drop across the upper ring. With less pressure drop, the upper ring exerts less pressure on the cylinder wall and thus does not wear as rapidly. Also, the two compression rings seem necessary for adequate blow-by and oil control. Experiments with engines having pistons using two compression rings have indicated this. When the top ring was removed, leaving only the lower compression ring and the oil-control ring, relatively little oil control was lost, and blow-by control remained good *at lower speeds.* However, as speeds increased, oil consumption and blow-by went up far beyond acceptable limits. However, some odd relationships were found. For example, in one series of tests, it was found that, with the top ring removed, no oil control was lost up to 55 mph (miles per hour). But at 80 mph, 60 percent of the oil control was lost. With the top ring out, blow-by was 8 percent *less* at 2,500 rpm (revolutions per minute), but at 1,500 and 4,000 rpm blow-by increased 40 percent.

When the tests were run with the lower compression ring removed, different results were obtained. For example, with the top ring in and the lower compression ring out, 60 percent of the oil control was lost at 55 mph, but at 80 mph the oil control was satisfactory. Also, with the top ring in and the second ring out, blow-by increased by as much as 150 percent, and thus blow-by control was largely lost.

Satisfactory explanations of these phenomena await further tests and analyses. Such additional laboratory work may lead ultimately to a two-ring piston, that is, to a piston having but one compression ring and one oil-control ring. With this piston design, a further reduction in piston stroke, and thus a still lower cylinder block, could result.

§160. Compression-ring wear and materials As previously noted, most compression rings are cast from a gray cast iron (Fig. 13-7). A variety of coatings have been applied to piston rings to improve wearing qualities.[1-3] The type of coating selected by the piston-ring designer will depend upon the

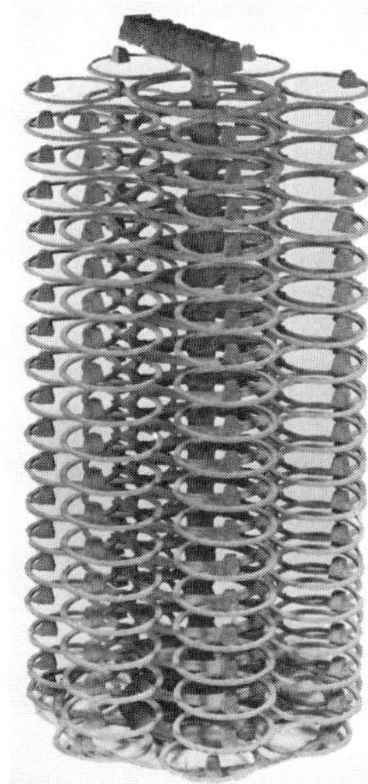

Fig. 13-7. This is how compression rings are cast by one manufacturer, 120 at a time, to form a casting "tree." After the mold is broken away to reveal the tree, as shown, the rings are separated and machined. (*Perfect Circle Corporation*)

type of wear that is to be expected in the operating engine. There are two general types of wear: abrasive wear and scuff wear.

1. *Abrasive wear.* Abrasive wear results mainly from abrasive particles that enter the engine through the air intake. These fine dust particles circulate throughout the engine in the engine oil and deposit on the cylinder walls to cause abrasive wear of the rings and pistons. The top compression ring, with its heavier ring pressure, wears most rapidly.

2. *Scuff wear.* The second type of wear is scuff wear. Some mention of scuffing has already been made in connection with pistons (§144). Let us now examine the phenomena of scuffing as it applies to piston rings. Scuffing is a sort of welding process, during which surfaces in contact become so hot that melting in small spots and welding take place. Scuffing usually starts near the top of the cylinder bore in the general area in which the top compression ring reaches the TDC (top dead center) position. At this point, the ring and cylinder-wall temperatures are highest, and lubrication is poorest. Further, the ring is momentarily stationary with respect to the cylinder wall. As the piston goes up over TDC, the ring completes its upward motion, stops, and starts downward again. It is during this momentary halt that the ring is most susceptible to scuffing. Scuffing is a self-feeding process. Once started, it progresses with increasing rapidity. Figure 13-8 shows scuffed compression rings. As scuffing proceeds, compression and oil control are lost, blow-by and oil consumption increase, and the scuffed areas become rougher and more widespread. In a short time, engine performance becomes so poor that a major service job is required. In addition, there is always the possibility that rings and pistons will be broken, with resulting major damage to the cylinder block.

Fig. 13-8. Scuffed compression rings. (*Perfect Circle Corporation*)

3. *Fighting ring wear.* To combat abrasive wear, piston-ring designers looked for harder ring coatings that would resist the wearing effect of the abrasive particles. The best material, because it is the hardest, is chromium. Thus, chromium plating of the top compression ring became common practice several years ago. The chromium plate is lapped to an extremely smooth finish, with surface irregularities of no more than 0.0001 inch. This hard, smooth finish stands up very well to abrasive wear and gives long service life.[3]

In recent years abrasive wear has become much less of a problem. Greatly improved air-filtering systems (carburetor air cleaners) have so reduced the intake of abrasive particles that there is much less abrasive wear of piston rings. However, at the same time, increased demands have been made on piston rings and other engine parts. These increased demands have resulted from higher engine outputs, which mean higher cylinder-wall, piston, and ring temperatures and pressures. These higher temperatures and pressures have increased the problem of scuff wear because the rate of scuffing of any particular metal is a function of pressure and temperature.

To combat this increased scuffing tendency, different ring-coating materials for the top compression ring have been tried. The most satisfactory material found to date is molybdenum. The iron from which compression rings are cast melts at about 2250°F. Chromium melts at about 3450°F. Molybdenum will not melt until it reaches a temperature of about 4800°F. Thus, it can be seen that the molybdenum coating will work to a considerably higher temperature without melting and thus scuffing. The molybdenum coating is somewhat porous and thus has some oil-retention ability; this improves its ability to fight scuffing. The

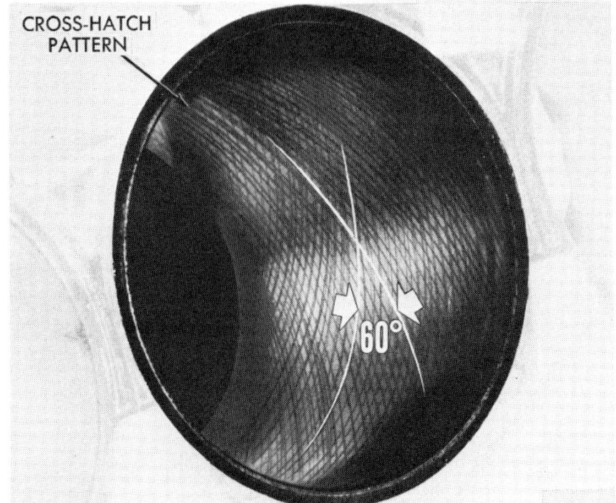

Fig. 13-9. Cross-hatch pattern recommended for final finish of cylinder bore after a honing operation. (*Chrysler-Plymouth Division of Chrysler Motors Corporation*)

molybdenum coating is not all to the good, however. Its rate of wear due to abrasives is about halfway between cast iron and chromium. Further, it has a somewhat adverse effect on cylinder-wall wear. However, where scuff wear is the problem, the molybdenum coating is the answer. But if the problem is abrasive wear, then chromium plating seems to be the best solution.

NOTE: Recent developments in plasma-thermal-application techniques[2] have made it feasible to apply coatings that were not possible previously. These include carbides of tungsten, titanium, and tantalum which, even though more expensive, show considerable promise as being highly resistant to both scuff and abrasive wear. Additional research with the plasma technique is proceeding, out of which may come still better ring coatings.

The lower compression ring, not subjected to such high temperatures and pressures, is worked much less hard than the top ring. Therefore, the lower compression ring is usually coated with a softer material such as ferrous oxide, or zinc or manganese phosphate. These materials have good antiscuff properties and are designed mainly to see the rings through the initial engine operation, or break-in, period.

NOTE: Scuff wear increases greatly if the cylinder bore is out-of-round or has bumps or high spots. The high spots will cause high localized ring pressures and resulting high local temperatures. Figure 13-9 shows a recommended cylinder-bore finish for good seating of new rings.

§161. Ring dimensions Standards tables have been published in the *SAE Handbook* and elsewhere, which specify piston-ring and piston-groove dimensions for various cylinder-bore diameters and operating conditions. As a rule, a piston designer selects one of the standard rings, and this determines the ring and groove dimensions that he will have to work with.

§162. Trends in compression-ring design The

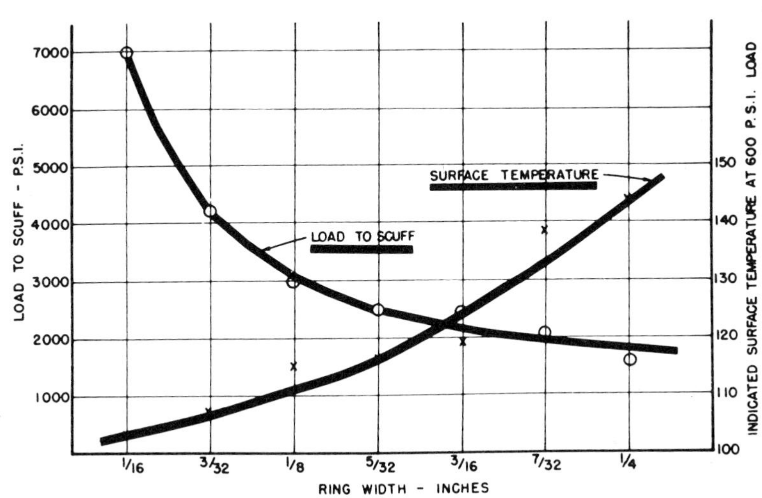

Fig. 13-10. Scuff resistance vs. compression-ring face width. (*Perfect Circle Corporation*)

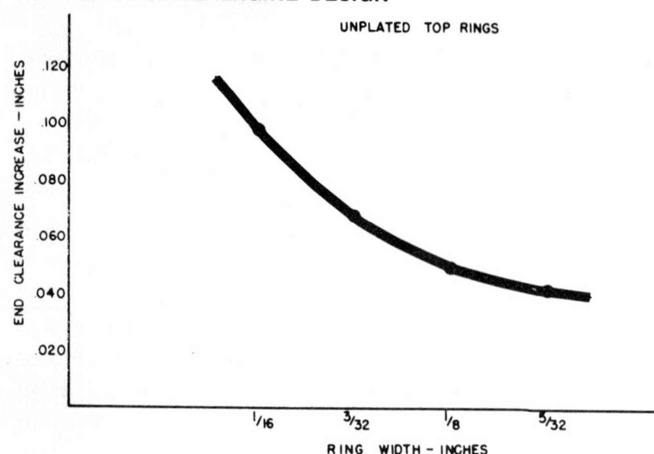

Fig. 13-11. Abrasive wear vs. face width. Curve compiled from standardized tests in which variable was width of compression-ring face. Increase of end clearance or ring gap is a measure of ring wear. (*Perfect Circle Corporation*)

trend toward high-compression, high-output, high-speed, oversquare engines has brought with it a lighter, narrower compression ring. This has improved ring performance in at least three ways.

1. The narrower ring face improves scuff resistance (Fig. 13-10). One reason for this seems to be that the surface temperature of the narrower ring does not go as high because there is less rubbing surface.

2. The lighter-weight ring has less tendency to flutter. Flutter is the up and down movement of the ring in the piston-ring groove. It is normal for the ring to move up and down as the piston passes from one stroke to another, for example, from intake to compression. But under certain critical conditions, the ring will move up and down in the groove with great rapidity. It may also vibrate radially so that the ring gap opens and closes. These phenomena are called *ring flutter.* Ring flutter allows greatly increased blow-by and can also cause rapid wear of the piston-ring grooves. Ring flutter is considered to be due to a balancing of the compression or combustion pressures with the mass inertia of the ring. This balancing of forces on the ring, which can occur at certain critical speeds and during certain phases of the compression or combustion stroke, permits the ring to momentarily float free so that it can "bounce" back and forth in its groove. The lighter ring, with its lower mass, is more susceptible to gas pressures and thus is more easily held against one or the other side of the ring groove. Therefore, It is less susceptible to flutter.

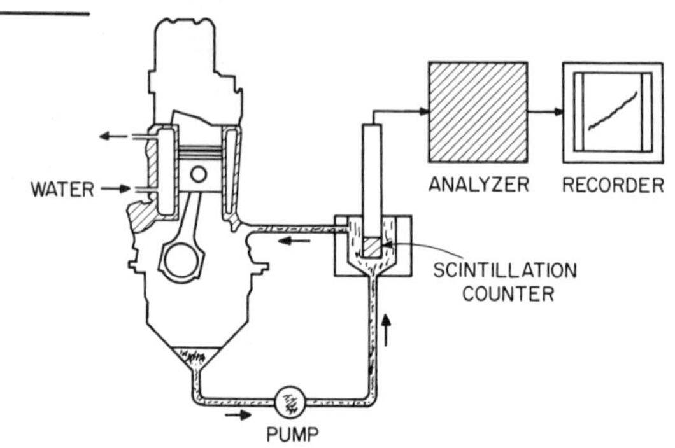

Fig. 13-12. Test setup to measure piston-ring wear with rings made of, or coated with, radioactive material.

3. The narrower ring makes it possible to have a shorter ring belt on the piston, with the result that the mean distance between the piston head and the crankshaft center line can be shorter. Thus, the engine height can be reduced.

However, the narrower ring does have certain drawbacks. For one thing, the narrower ring is more susceptible to abrasive wear (Fig. 13-11). Also, it is more susceptible to instability. If it is too narrow, it will buckle, or twist unevenly, when compressed to cylinder diameter. Further studies, including actual engine tests, are needed to evaluate the importance of this effect. A considerably wider top compression ring with an L-shaped cross section, called a *head-land ring*, has recently been introduced. It reduces exhaust pollutants by filling the head-land space above the top ring groove between the piston and the cylinder wall. Also, it reduces blow-by about 50 percent (see §139 and 158).

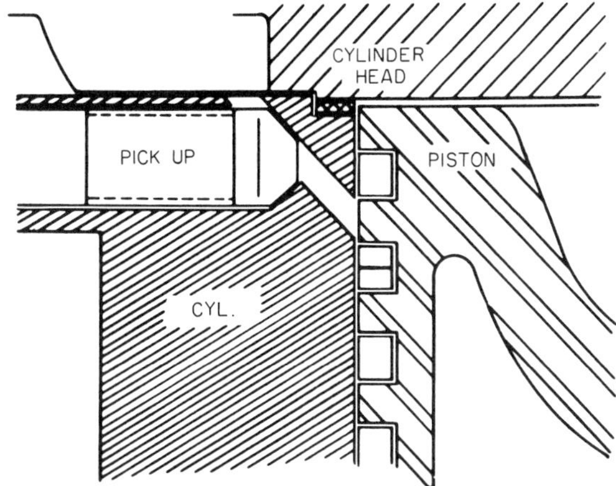

Fig. 13-13. Measuring the effectiveness of the top piston ring with a special pressure pickup connected by a hole to the space between the top and second rings when the piston is at TDC.

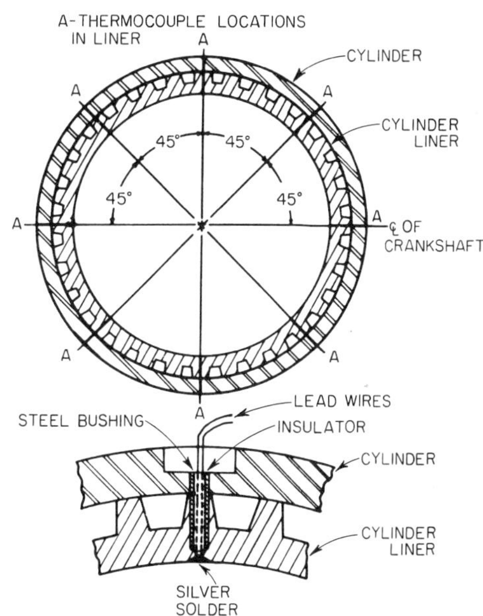

Fig. 13-14. Test setup to measure cylinder-wall liner temperature in the area where the top compression ring comes to rest at TDC. While this arrangement is for a cylinder with a liner, a somewhat similar arrangement could be made for other types of cylinders.

§163. Laboratory tests of compression rings Numerous tests can be made on piston compression rings in the laboratory, varying from the measurement of the face smoothness, hardness, and ring roundness, to actual wear in engine. Just as with pistons, the piston rings undergo their most severe tests in actual operating engines. A piston-ring design may appear to be theoretically correct, but until it can be proved to live satisfactorily in the engine, it cannot be considered to be an acceptable design.

One method of measuring wear of piston rings in an engine is illustrated in Fig. 13-12. In this engine, the piston rings are made of, or coated with, radioactive materials. As the rings wear during engine operation, the recirculating engine oil picks up the wear products and carries them through a scintillation counter. The counter is triggered by the radioactive particles of the rings that have been worn off, and the resultant counts are carried through an analyzer and then recorded. This method is quite accurate and is sensitive enough to detect and measure almost infinitesimal amounts of wear. Wear can be detected by this method even when it is too small to show any dimensional change or, indeed, any change of surface appearance.

Other tests measure the amount of blow-by and the rate of oil consumption. By installing different rings in a test engine and running them under identical test conditions, comparative performances of different ring designs can be evaluated. Two examples of test setups to measure piston-ring performance in operating engines follow.[4]

1. Compression test. To measure the effectiveness of the top compression ring in an engine, a special pressure pick-up was installed in the cylinder wall, with a hole drilled through the cylinder wall as shown in Fig. 13-13. Note that the hole is located between the top and second compression rings when the piston is at TDC. Thus, the pressure that leaks past the top ring is detected by the pressure pick-up. Naturally, the pressure pick-up will also report combustion pressures when the piston moves down enough so that the top ring clears the hole. It will report pressures during compression, intake, and exhaust also. However, the pick-up is attached to an electronic circuit which ignores all signals but the one desired. It then records this for future study.

2. *Cylinder-wall-temperature measurement.* This test was initiated to measure cylinder-wall temperature at the point where the compression ring comes to rest at TDC. It revealed, also, an unexpected result relating to ring action in the cylinder. To make the test, eight thermocouples were installed at 45-degree intervals around the circumference of the cylinder, as shown in Fig. 13-14. Holes were drilled through the cylinder wall and liner (this engine used cylinder liners), and the thermocouples were installed and silver soldered in place. The solder beads were then hand-finished to conform with the curvature of the cylinder wall. The thermocouples were then connected to electric meters to record the temperatures.

After the engine was reassembled and operated, temperatures were recorded around the circumference of the cylinder wall in the range of 250 to 300°F. (Other engines operating under different conditions might show different temperatures.) The engineers running the test were baffled, however, to note that a thermocouple might suddenly show a temperature increase of as much as 150°. Then, just as suddenly, the temperature would settle down again. Several thermocouples showed this eccentricity, but only one showed it at any time. It was not long, however, before the mystery was solved. The top compression-ring gap, moving around in the piston groove, would occasionally come into position opposite a thermocouple. At this instant, there would be blow-by through the gap that produced local heating of the thermocouple, which would respond by reporting the increased temperature.

§164. Life expectancy of compression rings A satisfactory compression ring will not wear excessively, and during its lifetime it will exhibit good blow-by and oil control without appreciable flutter. The mileage life of a ring varies with the type of operation and, to some extent at least, with the frequency of oil changes, as well as with the type of oil used. Obviously, dusty operating conditions, poor air-cleaner maintenance, and dirty engine oil will shorten ring life (and the life of other engine parts). But with the correct engine oil, good maintenance, and normal operating conditions, a service life of 50,000 miles for passenger cars is considered reasonable.

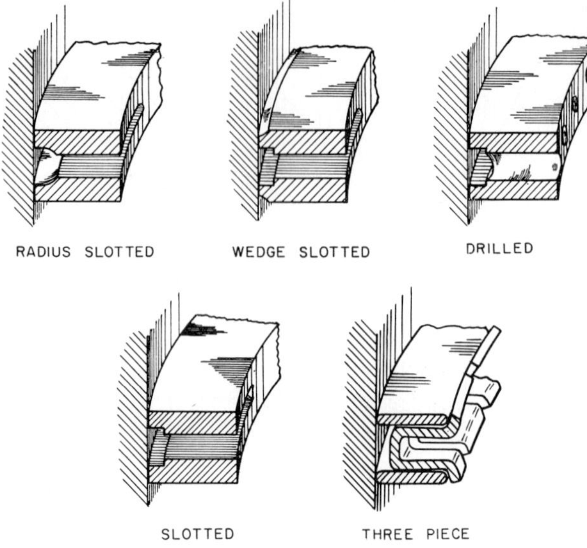

Fig. 13-15. Types of integral, or one-piece, oil-control rings compared with a three-piece type. (*Muskegon Piston Ring Company*)

Truck operators expect greater mileages. Some truck manufacturers, for example, advertise and even guarantee 100,000 miles of ring life. The truck operators, however, will accept a higher rate of oil consumption (a quart of oil every 500 miles, for example) than most passenger-car owners would tolerate.

§165. Oil-control rings[1-3] The oil-control ring helps to prevent excess oil from working up into the combustion chamber. The lower end of the engine, including the crankshaft, connecting rods, piston skirts, and cylinder walls, are bathed in lubricating oil. This oil comes from the lubricating system. It is pumped to the engine bearings in constant streams and is thrown off as it passes through the bearing clearances. This throw-off keeps the cylinder walls covered with lubricating oil. It is desirable to have lubricating oil on the cylinder walls to provide lubrication for the pistons and rings. However, far more oil is thrown on the

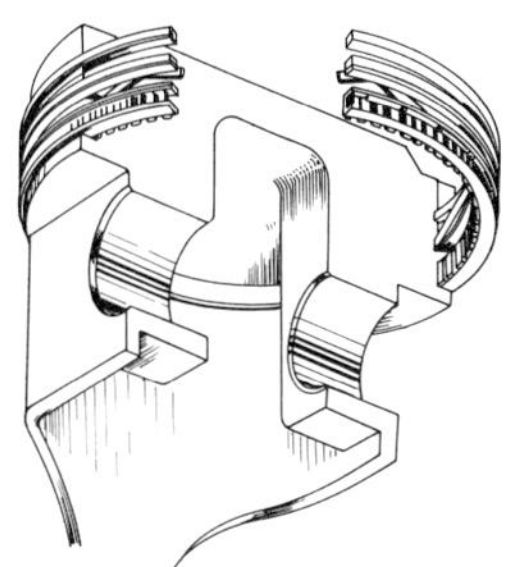

Fig. 13-16. Cutaway view of rings and piston to show construction. The second compression ring has an inner tension ring. The oil ring has an expander spacer and two rails. (*Thompson, Ramo, Wooldridge, Inc.*)

cylinder walls than is needed. Furthermore, the oil may not always cover the cylinder walls completely; some spots may be lightly oiled. It is the job of the oil-control ring, or rings, and the compression rings, to see that most of this oil is scraped off the cylinder walls and returned to the oil pan. Also, the oil-control ring, being open, can distribute the oil around its complete circumference so that no part of the cylinder wall is oil-starved.

The oil also helps to keep the engine clean, in addition to providing lubrication. As it circulates from the oil pan through the oil pump, through the bearing clearances, on and off the cylinder walls, it carries away with it particles of carbon that may have worked down past the rings, metal particles from wear of engine parts, and dust particles that have entered with the air-fuel mixture. Many of these particles are then removed from the oil by the oil filter. Smaller particles may continue to circulate in the oil, but they are generally so small as to represent no threat to the engine. The oil, in circulating thus, helps to clean the engine cylinder walls, pistons, rings, and bearings (see §272, item 9).

The oil circulation also has a cooling effect. The oil picks up heat from the engine parts as it circulates; then, after it returns to the oil pan, it is cooled somewhat because the oil pan, in the air stream from the car movement, is at a lower temperature. Tests have shown that in some engines, under certain operating conditions, the circulating oil may remove as much as 20 percent of the excess heat from the engine, with the engine cooling system removing the other 80 percent (not counting the heat lost in the exhaust gas).

The oil does another important job—it helps to seal between the rings and the cylinder walls and between the pistons and the rings. You can test this effect for yourself with an old engine that has lost compression and is subject to excessive blow-by because of tapered cylinder walls and worn rings. If you remove the spark plugs, test the compression with a gauge, pour a little heavy oil into the cylinders, and then test the compression again, you will find that the compression has gone up.

§166. Types of oil-control rings There are three general types of oil-control rings: the one-piece, slotted cast-iron type; the one-piece, pressed-steel type; and the three-piece, steel-rail type with expander (see Figs. 13-15 to 13-21). Figure 13-15 shows several of the one-piece type. These rings have holes or slots between the upper and lower faces, or surfaces, that bear on the cylinder wall. Oil scraped off the cylinder wall passes through these openings and through holes drilled in the

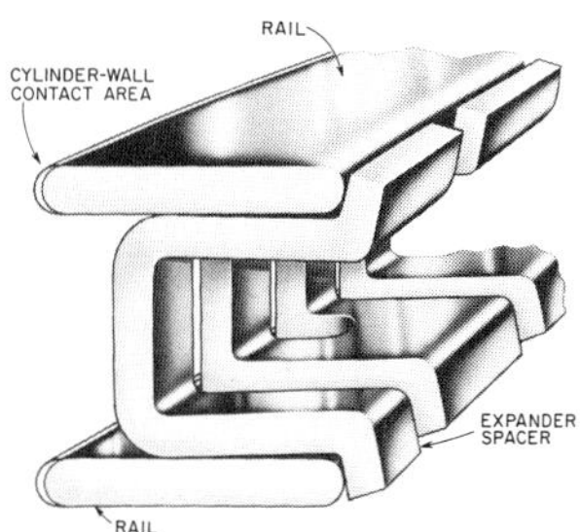

Fig. 13-17. Close-up of oil-control ring with two rails and an expander spacer. (*Perfect Circle Corporation*)

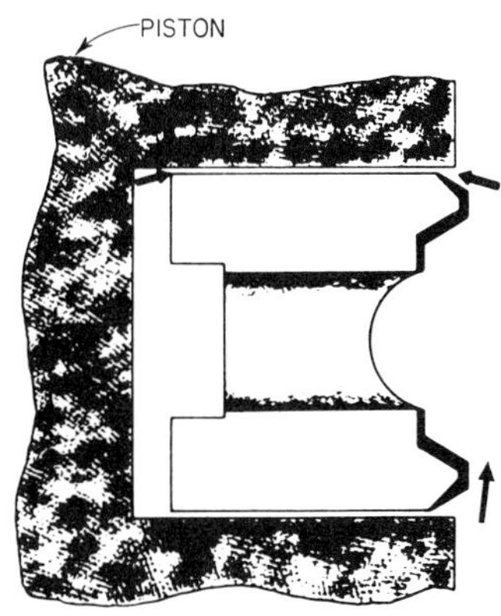

Fig. 13-18. Oil paths around and past one-piece oil-control ring. (*Perfect Circle Corporation*)

back of the oil-ring grooves in the piston. From there, it returns to the oil pan. The slots in the ring also tend to distribute the oil all around the cylinder wall so that no area will be oil-starved.

Some rings of the one-piece type are installed with expander springs, either of the hump or the coil-spring type. The expander spring increases the pressure of the ring on the cylinder wall and thus improves the oil-scraping effect.

In more recent years, the one-piece, oil-control ring has given way to the dual-rail and expander type (Figs. 13-16 to 13-20). One reason for this is that the one-piece ring became increasingly ineffectual as compression ratios and engine speeds increased. You can see why by referring to Fig. 13-18. Note that there are two paths by which oil can get past the oil-control ring and upward into the combustion chamber. One of these paths is past the ring face caused by the failure of the ring to do a complete job of scraping oil from the cylinder wall. The other path is between the upper side of the ring and the upper side of the ring groove in the piston. Both of these paths are shown by arrows in Fig. 13-18. This second path (between the sides of the ring and groove) exists only during the time that the ring is not resting against the upper groove side. At lower speeds and compression ratios, this condition is not present to any significant degree. However, at higher speeds and compression ratios, the second path exists a significantly larger part of the time so that oil consumption rises. One reason for this is that with higher compression there is a higher vacuum in the cylinder during intake. This increased vacuum then "pulls" more oil around the ring and upward into the combustion chamber. Also, at higher speeds, ring inertia prevents the ring from accelerating as rapidly as the piston, so that the oil path between the side of the ring and the ring groove is open a larger part of the time.

The dual-rail and expander type and the one-piece, pressed-steel type of oil-control rings (Figs.

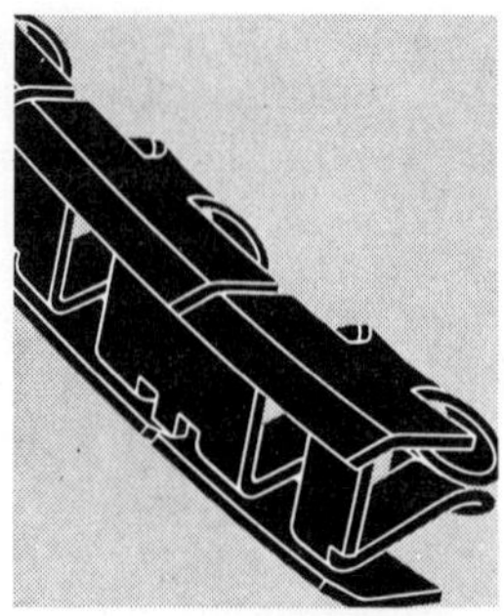

Fig. 13-20. One-piece, pressed-steel, oil-control piston ring. The segmental construction of this ring, with its three-way spring effect, provides pressure against the upper and lower sides of the ring groove, as well as against the cylinder wall. (*Muskegon Piston Ring Company*)

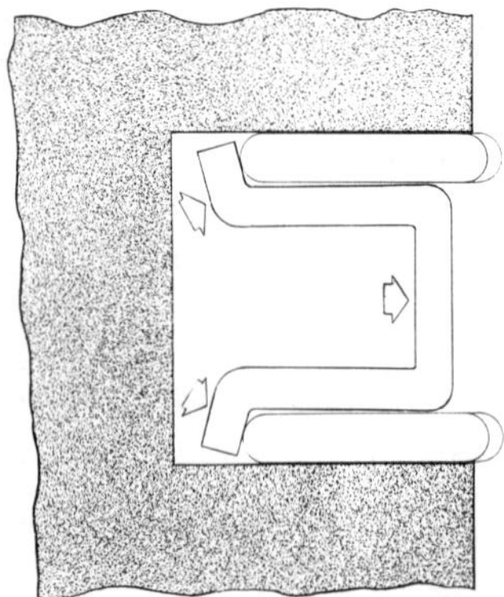

Fig. 13-19. Action of the expander spacer, as shown by arrows, forcing the rails out against the cylinder wall and up and down against the sides of the ring grooves. (*Perfect Circle Corporation*)

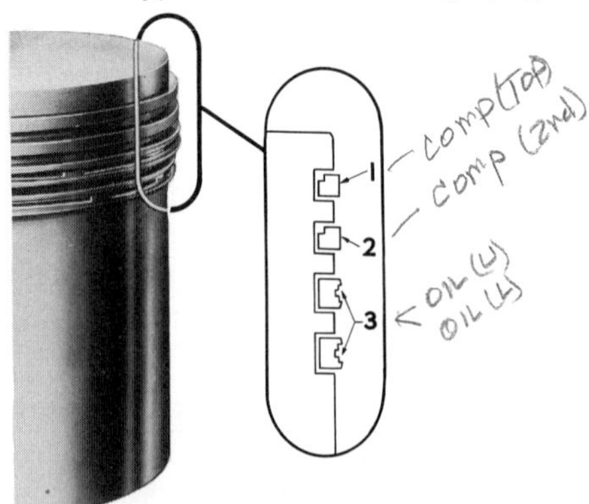

Fig. 13-21. External and sectional views of a piston with its four rings in place. 1 and 2 are top and second compression rings and 3 is upper and lower oil-control rings. (*Chrysler-Plymouth Division of Chrysler Motors Corporation*)

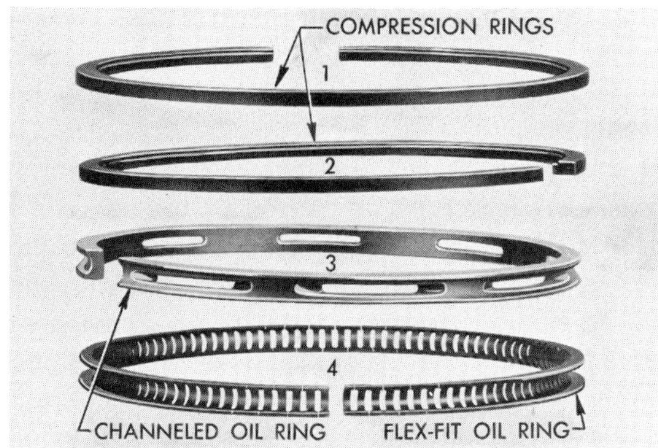

Fig. 13-22. Set of piston rings for one piston of an eight-cylinder engine of the mid-1950's. Note the construction of the two oil rings (3 and 4). (*Buick Motor Division of General Motors Corporation*)

13-16 to 13-20) are able to maintain contact with the sides of the ring groove in the piston under nearly all conditions. On the dual-rail and expander type, the expander not only forces the two rails outward and into contact with the cylinder wall, but also forces the two rails apart (Fig. 13-19) so that they rest against the two sides of the groove. This closes off the oil path around the back and up over the ring. The one-piece, pressed-steel ring works similarly.

§167. Why only one ring? On earlier engines using full-skirt pistons, it was customary to have two oil-control rings for each piston (Figs. 13-21 and 13-22). However, as engineers sought ways of shortening the piston stroke to reduce engine height, they adopted the slipper-skirt piston and eliminated one oil-control ring. It was possible to do this because rings had been improved so that three rings could do the job that formerly required four rings. It is possible that, someday, pistons will require only two rings (as noted in §159).

§168. What is good oil control? We have mentioned oil control and noted that some rings exert better control than others. What is considered good control? That is, how much oil consumption is acceptable?

In the first place, it is obvious that the piston rings operate very effectively to prevent excess oil from working up into the combustion chamber where it could burn. Consider this fact: If the engine burned as much as a single drop of oil on every power stroke, then the engine would burn a quart of oil *every two miles*! However, far less than this is burned, as every car owner knows. As a general rule, engineers consider that oil consumption is within limits if it falls between 0.0005 and 0.0020 pound per hp (horsepower) per hour, with the engine operating at rated maximum horsepower and speed.* This works out to varying mileages, according to the size of engine and the type of service (whether passenger car or truck, for example). Many passenger cars will run several thousand miles on a single quart of oil. Truck engines have a somewhat higher rate of oil consumption. Many truck operators, for example, are satisfied with only 500 miles per quart of oil during the early life of an engine. Further, they might become alarmed if the oil consumption dropped well below this. Very low oil consumption might mean that the oil rings are doing too good a job and not leaving sufficient oil on the cylinder walls for adequate lubrication of rings and pistons. In such a case, rapid ring and cylinder-wall wear would take place, and engine overhaul would be required at very low mileage. Of course, excessively low oil consumption could result from other conditions, for example, low oil pressure from a defective pump, or clogged oil lines that prevent adequate amounts of oil from reaching the cylinder walls.

§169. Speed and oil control As engine speed increases, the rings have a harder time controlling the oil, and oil consumption goes up. There are several reasons for this. For one thing, the engine and engine oil become hotter. This means the oil becomes thinner [unless it has a high viscosity index (see §272, item 3)]. Thinner oil can pass the rings more easily. Furthermore, at high speeds more oil is pumped, more oil is thrown off the bearings, and more oil gets onto the cylinder walls. In addition, at high speeds the rings have a greater tendency to flutter and skate over the oil films. All

* From a service bulletin of Buick Motor Division of General Motors Corporation.

this means that as speed increases, more oil gets up to the combustion chambers where it is burned. An engine may use several times as much oil at high-speed, full-power operation as during low-speed, part-throttle operation. One series of tests showed that one model of engine used seven times as much oil at 70 mph (miles per hour) as it did at 40 mph.

§170. Piston-ring-failure analysis As previously noted (§164), normal compression-ring life is considered to be 50,000 miles for passenger cars and 100,000 miles for trucks. The same mileage expectations hold true for oil-control rings also. Rapid ring wear, ring failure, or loss of oil control is seldom the fault of the rings but is caused by installation of the wrong rings for the job, incorrect installation procedures, unusual or improper operating conditions, or such engine conditions as worn cylinder walls or main bearings. For instance, preignition or detonation can damage the piston and rings. First, however, the piston would deteriorate, and this would carry over to the rings. A similar situation occurs with piston scuffing. If a piston begins to scuff, it will not be long before the damage to the piston and cylinder wall will begin to seriously deteriorate the rings (§156).

If a ring shows abrasive or scuff wear, a different type of ring finish should be specified, or improvements in the operating conditions should be made. For instance, with abrasive wear, better air-filter maintenance or more frequent oil changes might help. With scuff wear, lowering the cylinder-wall temperature by improved cooling-system action or by use of a higher-octane fuel that reduces detonation and thus lowers combustion temperatures might help. Cylinder wall and piston-skirt finish also play a part in possible ring wear, too.

If the rings fit the ring grooves in the piston incorrectly, then poor ring action, possibly undue groove wear, and ring breakage could result. Excessive side clearance between the ring and groove, for example, could allow too much ring movement relative to the groove, with consequent excessive pounding wear of the sides of the groove. Insufficient ring gap could allow the ends of the ring to abut when the ring is in action, moving up and down in the cylinder. This could lead to ring breakage and also to scoring of the cylinder wall and piston.

Loss of oil control and high oil consumption at low mileages could be caused by the use of the wrong rings, poor ring installation, excessive piston temperatures or combustion pressures that cause piston deformation in the ring-groove area, abrasive wear that has excessively worn cylinder walls and bearings, constant high-speed, full-power operation, and low-viscosity or diluted oil. If the oil is thin due to low viscosity or dilutants, more oil will be pumped and thrown on the cylinder walls, increasing the problem of oil control. Worn bearings will also throw off more oil. At high speed, the rings become less effective in controlling oil. Also, of course, if the cylinder walls are worn, the rings are less able to maintain effective contact through the full stroke.

There are other causes of high oil consumption, of course, including carboned rings, leakage past the intake-valve stem and valve guide, and, on older cars, leakage through a cracked vacuum-pump diaphragm. (This last condition applies only to cars having a vacuum pump for operating the windshield wiper.) Carbon in the combustion chamber and on the rings could come from an excessively rich air-fuel mixture, faulty combustion, or burning of oil in the combustion chamber.

SUMMARY

The piston rings must provide a good seal between the piston and cylinder wall; they must prevent excessive blow-by and also provide good oil control. They also serve as heat paths from the piston to the cylinder wall.

The two types of rings are compression rings and oil-control rings. Most compression rings have butt joints. The most common types of compression rings are the counterbored and the scraper. Counterboring a ring, or cutting out a groove, unbalances the ring so that it twists slightly when in place in the cylinder to provide line contact with the cylinder wall during the intake, compression, and exhaust strokes. On the power stroke, the combustion pressures force the ring to untwist so it lies flat against the cylinder wall and side of the ring groove, thereby providing a good seal.

Two compression rings are used to reduce the pressure drop across the top ring. One ring is not sufficient to hold the pressure differential between the combustion and crankcase pressures.

Compression rings suffer from two types of wear: abrasive wear and scuff wear. Abrasive wear is less of a factor today because of the improved air-filtering systems used on engines. Scuff wear is more important on the modern, high-performance engine where ring temperatures are high. One ring coating used to fight scuffing is molybdenum, which does not melt until it reaches a temperature of 4800°F. Where abrasive wear is a problem, rather than scuffing, chromium plating is used.

The trend in compression rings is toward a narrower, lighter ring. This type of ring has less tendency to flutter and scuff and permits a shorter ring belt on the piston. However, the narrower ring is more susceptible to abrasive wear and instability.

Rings are tested for smoothness, roundness, hardness, and performance in the engine. Rate of wear in operation can be checked by coating the rings with radioactive material. Other tests determine the amount of blow-by, rate of oil consumption, and ability to hold compression. Compression rings, under optimum conditions should give 50,000 miles of service for passenger cars, and up to 100,000 miles for trucks.

The oil-control ring scrapes excessive oil from the cylinder wall and returns it to the crankcase. Also, it helps distribute the oil around the circumference of the cylinder so that no part of the wall is oil starved. The oil not only lubricates, but it also cleans, helps seal the compression rings, and helps cool the engine. There are two general types of oil-control rings: the one-piece, and the steel rail with expander. That the rings do a good job of oil control is evident because of the small amount of oil burned in the modern engine. However, as engine speed increases, so does oil consumption.

REFERENCES

1. Binford, J. D., Piston Ring Designs—Have They Changed? SAE (Society of Automotive Engineers) 650483, 1965 (paper).

2. Anderson, R. D., H. E. McCormick, and H. F. Prasse, Automotive Piston Rings 1967 State Of The Art, SAE (Society of Automotive Engineers) 670019, 1967 (paper).

3. Charlesworth, W. H., and W. L. Brown, Wear of Chromium Piston Rings in Modern Automotive Engines, SAE (Society of Automotive Engineers) 670042, 1967 (paper).

4. Beadle, R. H., Pressure and Temperature Measurement in Engine Development, Engineering Know-how in Engine Design, SAE special publication SP-143, 1956.

QUESTIONS

1. What are the purposes of compression rings? Of oil-control rings?

2. Explain how the counterbored ring functions.

3. Why are two compression rings normally used?

4. Explain the difference between abrasive wear and scuff wear of compression rings. What are remedies for each?

5. Discuss trends in compression-ring design.

6. Describe tests of compression rings.

7. What are the two general types of oil-control rings?

8. What is good oil control? How does speed affect it?

Connecting Rods, Crankshafts, and Bearings

CHAPTER **14**

This chapter discusses connecting rods, crankshafts, and bearings—their function, operation, and design. These moving parts, with their associated bearings, accept the heavy loads imposed by the combustion process and inertia of the moving parts and translate the linear motion of the piston into the rotary motion that is carried to the car wheels.

§171. Connecting rod The connecting rod forms the link between the piston and the crankshaft. It is attached to the piston by the piston pin and to a crankpin on the crankshaft. The connecting rod must combine great strength with light weight. It must be strong enough to maintain its rigidity, while carrying the thrust of the piston during the power stroke. At the same time, it must be as light as possible so that the centrifugal and inertia loads on the bearings will be no greater than necessary. (Bearings and bearing loading are discussed later.)

Connecting rods (Fig. 14-1) are forged from high-strength alloy steel and carefully balanced so that all rods in an engine will be of the same weight. If they were of different weights, engine balance would be thrown off, and engine roughness would result. In the original factory assembly, rods and caps are individually matched to each other and usually carry identifying numbers so they will not be mixed if the engine is disassembled for service. They must never be mixed during any service job since this could result in poor bearing fit and bearing failure.

Some connecting rods have a hole drilled from the big end to the little end. In operation, oil passes up this hole to lubricate the piston-pin bushing (Fig. 12-25). Some connecting rods also have oil-spit holes (Figs. 14-2 and 19-8). As the crankpin rotates within the bearing, an oil-passage hole in the crankpin indexes with the hole in the bearing and rod. Oil feeds through for a moment so that oil streams, or spits, from the hole in the connecting rod. This oil is thrown against the cylinder wall to provide adequate cylinder-wall lubrication. The holes are arranged to index just as the piston approaches TDC (top dead center); thus, a large area of the cylinder wall is covered with oil.

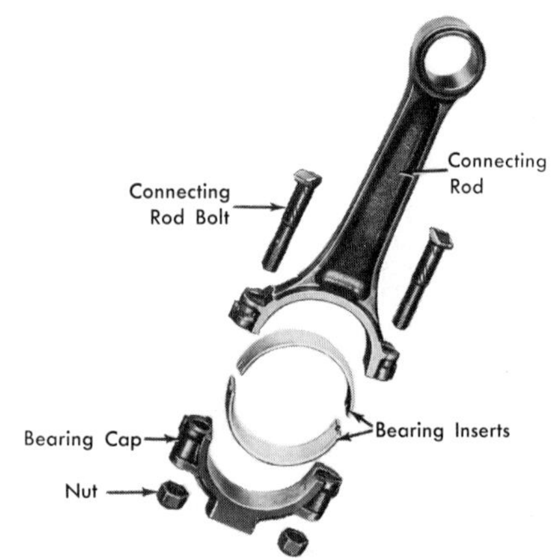

Fig. 14-1. Connecting rod and bearing assembly, disassembled. (*Cadillac Motor Car Division of General Motors Corporation*)

On many V-8 engines, cylinder walls and piston pins are lubricated by oil jets from opposing connecting rods. That is, each rod has a groove or hole that indexes with an oil-passage hole in the crankpin with every crankshaft revolution. When this happens, a jet of oil spurts into the opposing cylinder in the other cylinder bank.

§172. Engine bearings In the engine, there must be relative motion between the piston and the con-

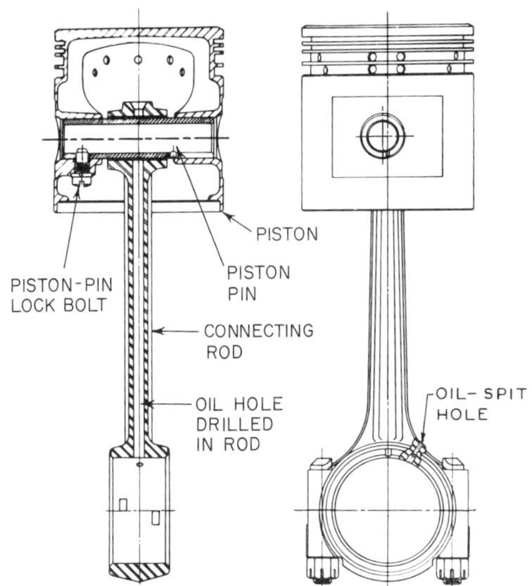

Fig. 14-2. Sectional view of a connecting rod and piston, showing the oil hole that lubricates the piston pin and the oil-spit hole that lubricates the cylinder wall. Note the lock bolt that locks the piston pin to the piston. (*Oldsmobile Division of General Motors Corporation*)

necting rod, between the connecting rod and the crankshaft, and between the crankshaft and the supporting bearings in the cylinder block. At all these points (as well as at other places in the engine), bearings must be installed (Figs. 14-3 and 14-4). The bearings are called *sleeve bearings* because they are in the shape of a sleeve that fits around the rotating journal. Connecting-rod and crankshaft (or main) bearings are of the split, or half, type; that is, the bearing is split into two halves. Figure 7-19 illustrates a typical sleeve-type-bearing half. With main bearings (Fig. 14-5), the upper half is assembled into the counterbore in the cylinder block, and the lower half is held in place in the bearing cap. Figure 14-3 shows the main-bearing caps, with bearing halves, for a V-8 engine. Figure 7-21 shows the bearings (Nos. 4 and 7), in disassembled and assembled views, used in a connecting rod. The rod-big-end bearing is the split type, but the piston-pin bearing is not; it is the full-round or *bushing* type.

Figure 14-5 shows a sleeve-type main bearing half, with the various parts named. Note that it has a back, to which a lining has been applied. It also has thrust faces (§173). The back, usually of steel or bronze, gives the bearing rigidity and strength. The lining is a thin layer of relatively soft material (the bearing material) only a few thousandths of an inch thick (Fig. 14-6). The bearing material usually is a mixture of two or more metals; lead, tin, copper, antimony, and aluminum are metals that have been used (see §177). The rotating journal is supported by this thin layer of bearing material. One reason for using a soft material is that when wear does take place, the bearing, rather than the more expensive engine part, will wear. When wear has gone beyond a certain point, the bearing, rather than the more costly engine part, can be replaced.

We noted previously that the bearing material "supports" the load of the rotating journal. Actually, the bearing surfaces are flooded with lubricating oil from the engine lubricating system so that the journals are, in effect, "floated" on films of oil. It can be said, however, that the bearings support the films of oil, which, in turn, support the journals. So the bearings do, of course, "carry the load."

The main bearings in most engines do not have the oil-distributing grooves shown in Fig. 14-5.

Fig. 14-3. Arrangement of the main, or crankshaft, bearings in a V-8 engine. The engine is shown from the bottom. The bearing caps with bearings have been removed and placed above the engine. The center bearing is an end-thrust bearing. (*Buick Motor Division of General Motors Corporation*)

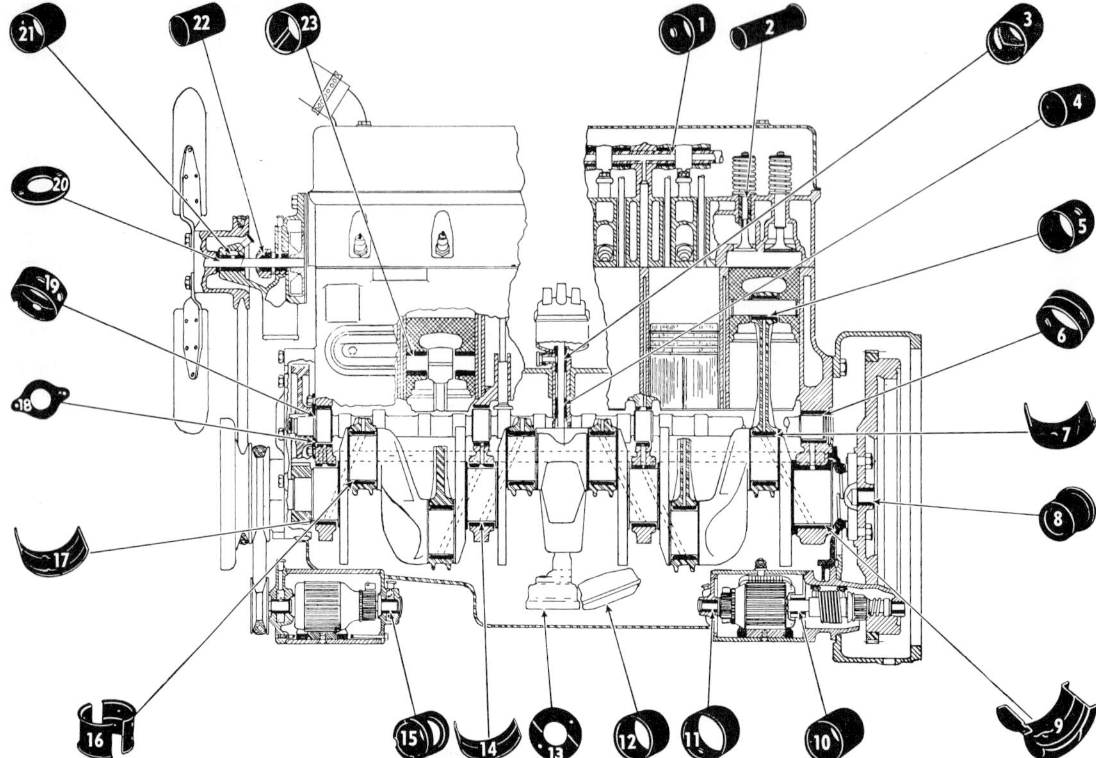

Fig. 14-4. Various bearings and bushings used in a typical engine. (*Johnson Bronze Company*)

1. Rocker-arm bushing
2. Valve-guide bushing
3. Distributor bushing (upper)
4. Distributor bushing (lower)
5. Piston-pin bushing
6. Camshaft bushing
7. Connecting-rod bearing
8. Clutch-pilot bushing
9. Main-thrust bearing
10. Cranking-motor bushing (drive end)
11. Cranking-motor bushing (commutator end)
12. Oil-pump bushing
13. Distributor thrust plate
14. Intermediate main bearing
15. Generator bushing
16. Connecting-rod bearing (floating type)
17. Front main bearing
18. Camshaft thrust plate
19. Camshaft bushing
20. Fan thrust plate
21. Water-pump bushing (front)
22. Water-pump bushing (rear)
23. Piston-pin bushing

They may or may not have the annular grooves. The main bearings on many engines do not have these grooves. On other engines, only the upper halves of the main bearings have them. On still other engines, both the upper and lower main-bearing halves have the annular grooves. Connecting-rod big-end bearings usually do not have oil grooves.

V-8 engines have five crankshaft bearings, one at each end and one on each side of every crank (Fig. 14-3). Six-cylinder in-line engines have either four or seven crankshaft bearings. Most in-line sixes today have seven main bearings. In the four-bearing arrangement, there is a bearing on each end of the crankshaft and a bearing between cranks 2 and 3 and between cranks 4 and 5. In the seven-bearing arrangement, there is a bearing on each end of the crankshaft and a bearing on each side of every crank. The engine shown in Fig. 14-7 has seven crankshaft bearings. Fig. 14-8 shows the location of these seven bearings in the engine. With seven bearings, there is less stress and vibration in the crankshaft and cylinder block, and the engine runs more smoothly.

NOTE: Some engines use ball bearings to sup-

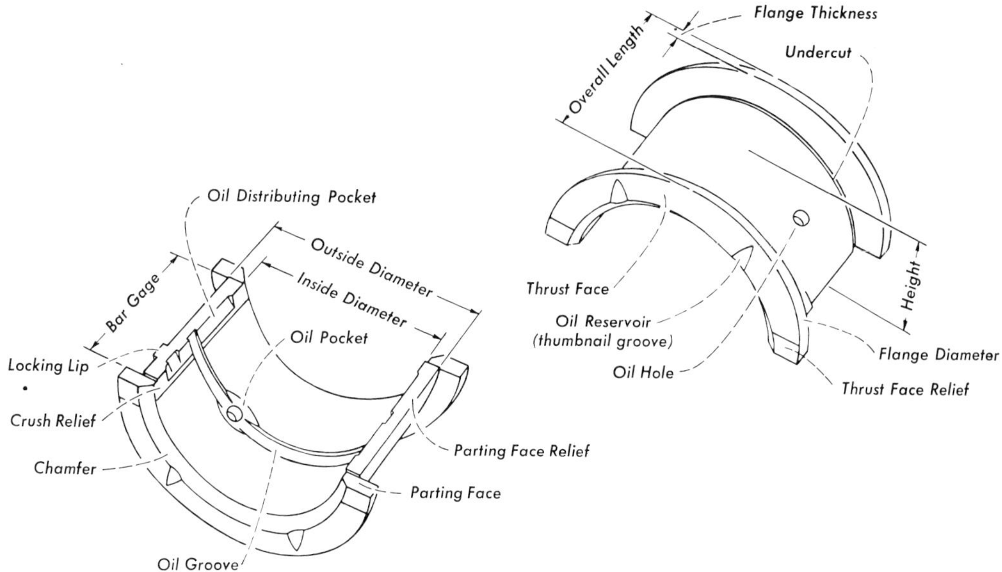

Fig. 14-5. Main-bearing nomenclature. The bearing shown is the thrust type. (*Federal-Mogul-Bower Bearings, Inc.*)

port the crankshaft and roller bearings at the crankpin and piston-pin ends of the connecting rod (Fig. 14-9). The engines in American cars and in most imports, however, use the type of bearing described in this section.

§173. Main-thrust bearing One of the main bearings is a thrust bearing, designed to prevent excessive end play of the crankshaft. Figure 14-3 shows an end-thrust bearing in place in the bearing cap of a V-8 engine. Figure 14-5 is a main-thrust bearing. Thrust bearings have thrust faces on their two sides. Flanges on the crankshaft ride against these thrust faces, thus holding the crankshaft in position so that it does not have excessive endwise movement. There is, of course, some clearance between the thrust faces on the bearing and the flanges on the crankshaft; these clearances permit oil to flow between the surfaces to provide for adequate lubrication. In V-8 engines, the intermediate or center main bearing is usually the thrust bearing. In in-line engines, the rear main bearing is usually the thrust bearing (Fig. 14-4).

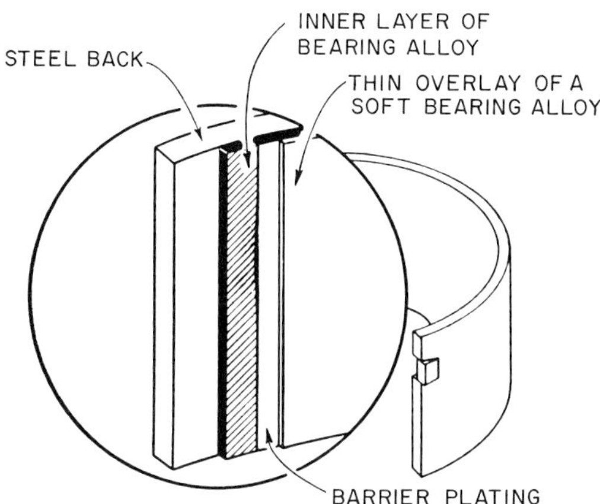

Fig. 14-6. Construction of a three-layer bearing. Some bearings have three layers, as shown; others have two layers. (*Federal-Mogul-Bower Bearings, Inc.*)

§174. Engine-bearing lubrication The engine bearings are flooded with oil by the lubricating system. For example, the bearing shown in Fig. 14-5 has an oil hole that aligns with an oil hole in the engine block. Oil feeds through this hole constantly, keeping the annular groove and the distributing grooves in the bearing filled with oil. Oil constantly feeds from these grooves onto the bearing surfaces. The oil works its way outward to the edges of the bearing. As it reaches the outer

Fig. 14-7. A late-model six-cylinder engine, partly cut away to show its internal construction. (*Ford Division of Ford Motor Company*)

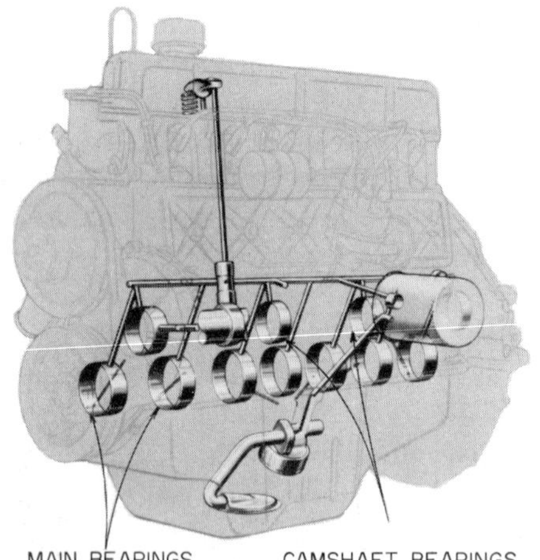

Fig. 14-8. Lubrication system of a six-cylinder, overhead-valve engine with seven crankshaft bearings. (*Ford Division of Ford Motor Company*)

edges, it is thrown off and falls back into the oil pan. Thus oil is constantly circulating across the faces of the bearings in the engine.

One function of the oil, of course, is to provide lubrication; that is, it keeps the bearing and rotating journal separated by a film of oil so that there is no actual metal-to-metal contact. In addition, the

Fig. 14-9. Sectional view of a three-cylinder, two-cycle engine. (*Daimler-Benz*)

oil helps to cool the bearing. The oil is relatively cool as it comes from the oil pan; as it spreads across the bearing and passes off the bearing edges, it warms up, thus removing heat from the bearing. This keeps the bearings at lower operating temperatures. A third function of the oil is to act as a flushing medium. It tends to flush out particles of dirt or grit that may have worked into the bearing (and on other engine parts). These particles either settle to the bottom of the oil pan or are removed from the oil by the oil filter (see Chap. 19).

Fig. 14-10. Shaft rotation causes layers of clinging oil to be dragged around with it, so that oil moves from the wide space A to the narrow space B, and thus supports the shaft weight W on an oil film.

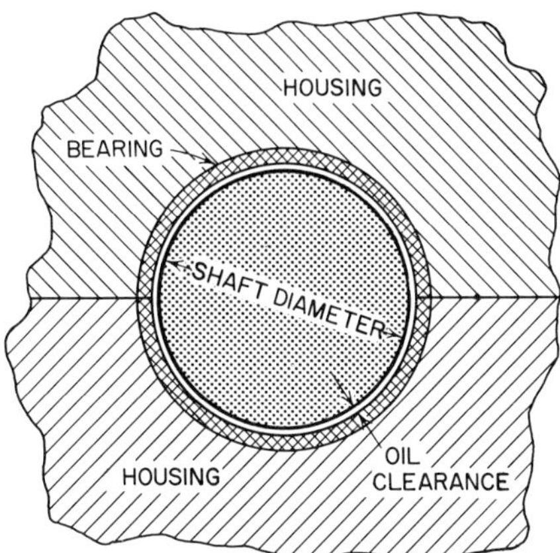

Fig. 14-11. Oil clearance between the bearing and the shaft journal.

In addition to these functions, the "throw-off" of oil from the engine bearings helps to lubricate other engine parts. For example, the cylinder walls, pistons, and rings are lubricated by the oil that is thrown onto the walls by the rotating crankshaft and connecting rods.

Of course, the primary purpose of the oil is to provide a lubricating film between the moving journal and the stationary bearing surface.[1,2] When the journal is stationary, the oil film is more or less squeezed out of the clearance so that the journal comes to rest almost directly on the bearing, with only a marginal film of oil between (high points may be in actual contact). But when the journal begins to rotate, it carries around with it layers of oil. These layers of oil act somewhat like wedges and lodge in between the shaft journal and the stationary bearing (Fig. 14-10). The wedging action lifts the journal off the bearing, as shown, and the journal is then supported on layers, or a film, of oil.

It is important to note that, in order to function properly, the oil must circulate *through* the bearing; it must flow. In order to permit this, the shaft-journal diameter is made somewhat smaller than the bearing diameter. The difference in diameters is called the *oil clearance* (Fig. 14-11). It is obvious that the greater the clearance, the faster the oil will flow through the bearing. Proper clearance varies somewhat with different engines, but 0.0015 inch would be a typical clearance. As the clearance becomes greater (from bearing wear, for instance), the amount of oil flowing through and being thrown off increases. With a 0.003-inch clearance (only twice 0.0015 inch), the oil throw-off increases as much as five times. A 0.006-inch clearance allows 25 times as much oil to flow through and be thrown off.

As bearings wear and oil flow-through and throw-off increase, more and more oil is thrown onto the cylinder walls. The piston and rings cannot handle this excess oil, and part of the oil works its way up into the combustion chambers, where it is burned, forming carbon on the piston, rings, and valves. This causes loss of power, increased engine wear, possibly engine rumble, and other troubles. It is also true that excess-oil clearance in some bearings may cause other bearings to be oil starved, so that they fail from lack of oil. The reason for this is that the oil pump can put out only so much oil. If the oil clearances of bearings are very large, most of this oil will pass through the oil clearances of the nearest bearings. An engine with this trouble usually has low oil pressure; the oil clearances are so great that the oil pump cannot build up normal pressures.

On the other hand, if oil clearances are not sufficiently great, the lubricating-oil films in the bearing may not be thick enough to prevent metal-

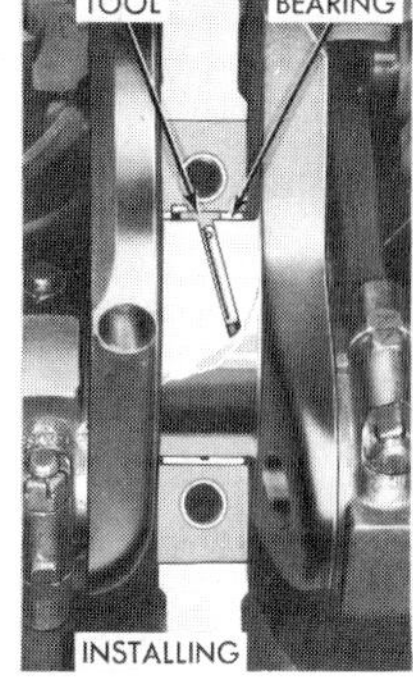

Fig. 14-12. Removal and installation of the upper main bearing. The crankshaft journal is shown partly cut away, so that tool can be seen inserted in the oil hole in the journal. (*Chrysler-Plymouth Division of Chrysler Motors Corporation*)

to-metal contact between the bearing and the shaft journal. Extremely rapid wear and early bearing failure would result. Furthermore, not enough oil will flow through, and therefore oil throw-off will be insufficient to provide adequate lubrication of such other engine parts as the cylinder walls, pistons, and rings.

§175. Engine-bearing types Early engines and some later-model heavy-duty engines used a "poured" bearing. This bearing was prepared by fitting a shaft-sized jig, or mold, into the counterbore where the bearing was to be, and then pouring molten bearing material into the space between the jig and counterbore. After the metal cooled, the jig was removed, and the metal was then scraped or machined down to the proper size to fit the shaft to be installed. This was a laborious process.

Today bearing installation is much simpler. In the first place, the bearings are supplied as replaceable shells (Fig. 14-5), consisting of a hard back coated with a layer of the bearing material. Secondly, in many engines these bearings are so precisely made that they can be replaced without any machining or fitting of the bearing, counterbore, or shaft journal (provided that the journal is not unduly worn). These bearings are called *precision-insert* or *precision-type bearings*. On many engines that use these bearings, main bearings can be replaced without removing the crankshaft; the old bearing is merely slipped out and the new bearing slipped in by use of a special roll-out tool (Fig. 14-12). The tool is inserted into the oil hole of the crankshaft. Then, when the crankshaft is rotated, the tool forces the bearing shell to move.

Some engines use *semifitted* bearings. These are approximately the correct size, but do have a few thousandths of an inch of extra bearing material that must be bored out after the bearings are installed; this establishes the proper fit and alignment with the shaft journals. The machining compensates for any slight irregularity in the alignment of the counterbores in the cylinder block and bearing caps. Figure 14-13 illustrates a semifitted crankshaft bearing of the thrust type. This illustration shows the "semifitted principle," which requires removal of bearing stock for proper fit.

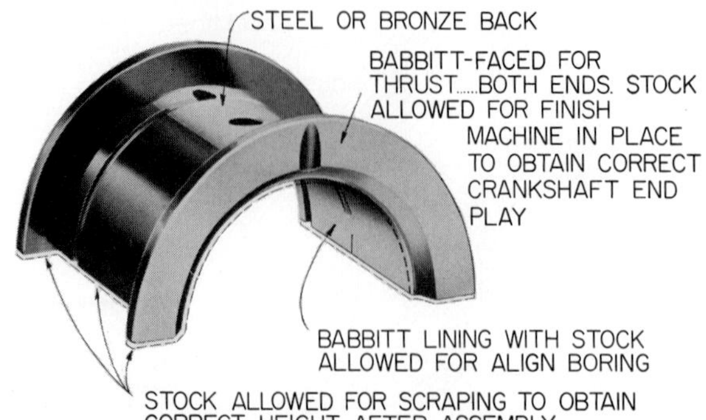

Fig. 14-13. Crankshaft thrust bearing of the semifitted type. (*Federal-Mogul-Bower Bearings, Inc.*)

Babbitt is a bearing material that is made of tin with small amounts of antimony, copper, and lead. It was widely used as a bearing material at one time, but in automotive practice it has been largely replaced by other materials (see §177).

§176. Bearing requirements Bearings must be able to withstand the varying loads imposed on them without being damaged or wearing with excessive rapidity. But bearings must have other desirable characteristics. Listed and described below (not necessarily in order of importance) are some of these characteristics.[2]

1. Load-carrying capacity. Modern engines are lighter and more compact, yet more powerful, than the engines of a few years ago. We have already noted that higher compression ratios and consequent higher combustion pressures have made it possible to step up horsepower output without increasing engine weight. These higher combustion pressures and horsepowers have brought with them greater loading of the engine bearings. For example, only a few years ago connecting-rod bearings on many passenger-car engines sustained loads of 1,600 to 1,800 psi (pounds per square inch). Today, connecting-rod-bearing loads of over 6,000 psi are not uncommon.

2. Fatigue resistance. When a piece of metal is repeatedly subjected to stress so that it flexes or bends (even slightly), it may harden and ultimately

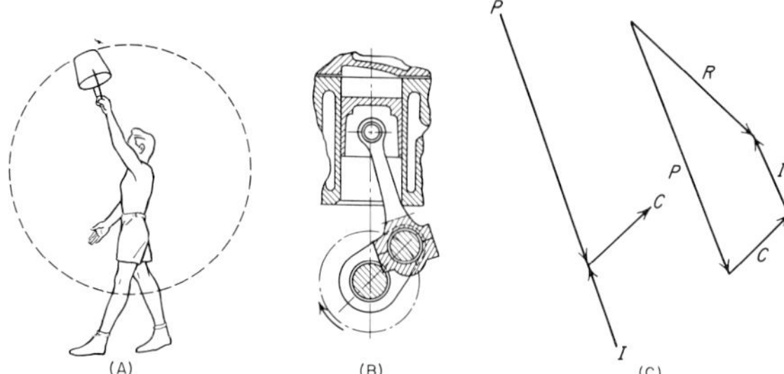

Fig. 14-14. The man swinging a pail of water in (*A*) illustrates one of the three forces acting on the connecting-rod bearing (*B*). This is centrifugal force, which keeps the water in the pail by pushing it outward, just as centrifugal force pushes the connecting rod outward away from the center of rotation. This imposes a centrifugal load on the bearing in the direction shown in (*C*) by arrow *C*. Arrow *P* represents combustion pressure acting along the connecting rod on the bearing. Arrow *I* is the inertia load, which is acting in the opposite direction to *P* in the piston and rod position shown. *R* is the resultant load. (*Federal-Mogul-Bower Bearings, Inc.*)

crack or break. An example of this is what happens when you repeatedly bend a piece of wire or sheet metal. Ultimately it will break. As far as bearings are concerned, they are subject to repeated and varying loads that tend to flex them. The bearing material must be able to stand this without any undue tendency to crack and break down.

3. *Embedability.* The term "embedability" refers to the ability of a bearing to permit foreign particles to embed in it. Despite air cleaners and oil filters and screens, particles of dirt and dust do get into the engine, and some of them find their way to the engine bearings. A bearing protects itself by permitting particles actually to embed in the bearing-lining material. If the bearing material were too hard to allow this, the particles would simply lie on the surface of the bearing. They would soon scratch the shaft journal turning in the bearing and also gouge out the bearing. This, in turn, would cause overheating and rapid bearing wear, so the bearing and the journal would soon fail. There is a limit to the number of particles that can be embedded in a bearing, however. If too many particles are embedded, the bearing will become overloaded with them and fail. Also, if particles are too large, they will not be completely embedded; they will scratch the shaft journal or gouge out grooves in the bearing. This also could lead to bearing failure.

4. *Conformability.* Conformability is associated with embedability. It refers to the ability of the bearing material to conform to variations in shaft alignment or journal shape. For example, suppose a bearing is installed under a shaft that is slightly bent (or that bends as it is loaded). This causes a certain area of the bearing to be heavily loaded, while other areas are very lightly loaded. If the bearing material has high conformability, it will "flow" slightly away from the heavily loaded area to the lightly loaded area. In effect, this redistributes the bearing material so that the bearing is more uniformly loaded. A similar action takes place when foreign particles are embedded in the bearing. As they are embedded, they displace material, thus producing a local high spot. However, the material flows away from the high spot, thus tending to prevent heavy local loading that could cause bearing failure.

5. *Corrosion resistance.* Certain acids appear in the oil as by-products of the combustion process and engine operation. Manufacturers of lubricating oils add certain compounds to their oils to combat the acids and prevent them from corroding engine bearings and other parts. Otherwise these acids would attack certain types of bearing materials and cause them to fail rapidly.

6. *Wear rate.* The bearing material must be sufficiently hard and tough so that it will not wear with excessive rapidity. At the same time, it must not be so hard as to have poor embedability and conformability or to cause undue wear of the shaft journal it supports.

§177. Bearing materials As has already been mentioned, the bearing back is usually steel or bronze. Steel is the more common backing material today; precision-insert bearings are steel-backed. The bearing material applied to the back is a mixture of several metals.[3,4] For example, one bearing material is made of lead, tin, antimony, and copper. Another bearing material is made of lead, tin, mercury, calcium, and aluminum. Other combinations include copper, antimony, and tin; silver, copper, and cadmium; copper, lead, and silver. A relatively new type of bearing uses a large percentage of aluminum. For example, one type uses 79 percent aluminum, 20 percent tin, and 1 percent copper. This alloy is held on a steel back. The base bearing material is sometimes given a microthin layer of babbitt (tin alloyed with copper, antimony, and lead). Bearings used in some models of the Chevrolet Turbo-Jet engine, for example, have an overlay of 0.0009 inch of babbitt.[6]

As can be seen, many possibilities exist. It is up to the bearing designer to compound a bearing material that will stand up under the specific stresses and conditions to which the bearing will be subjected in operation. What is satisfactory for one installation might not be good for another.

Corrosion, for example, might be a factor in some engines. Under certain operating conditions, acid appears in the engine oil, and this causes corrosion of some bearing materials. Also, the bearing-loading conditions change greatly with the type of engine operation (§178 and 179), and this factor must also be considered in the selection of bearing materials.

§178. Bearing loading We have already noted that the pressure in the engine cylinder varies from below atmospheric to several hundred pounds per square inch (Fig. 6-5). These varying pressures are transmitted through the piston and connecting rod to the crankpin; this imposes a varying load on the bearings. However, other forces are at work that also impose loads on the bearings.[5]

For example, let us analyze in detail the forces that act on the connecting-rod bearing (big-end bearing). In addition to the pressure loads, there are centrifugal loads and inertia loads. Centrifugal loads result from the centrifugal force on the rod big end that attempts to throw it outward from the center line of the crankshaft (Fig. 14-14). This imposes a load on that part of the connecting-rod bearing which is toward the center of the crankshaft. The centrifugal load is constant for any particular speed and increases as the speed in-

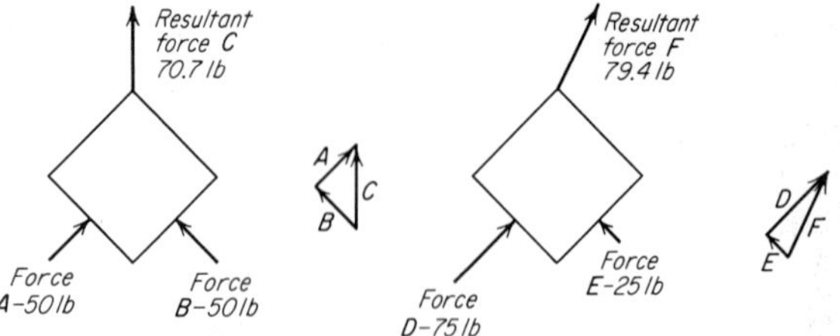

Fig. 14-15. Forces at angles to each other partly cancel each other out. At left, the two 50-pound forces give a resultant force of 70.7 pounds. At right, the 25- and 75-pound forces give a resultant force of 79.4 pounds. Lengths of arrows are proportional to the loads. Thus, arrow *D* (75 pounds) is three times as long as arrow *E* (25 pounds).

creases. It circles the bearing uniformly, and it can be quite large. For example, let us assume that the crankpin is offset 2 inches, and that the connecting rod weighs 2 pounds, of which 1 pound (at the big end) is effective in producing centrifugal force. With these assumptions, we can calculate that the centrifugal force acting on the connecting-rod bearing at 4,000 engine rpm (revolutions per minute) would be more than 900 pounds:

$$\text{Centrifugal force} = \left(\frac{W}{g}\right)\left(\frac{2\pi N}{60}\right)^2 (r)$$

$$= \frac{1}{32.16}\left(\frac{2\pi 4{,}000}{60}\right)^2 \frac{1}{6} = 914 \text{ lb}$$

This load is always on that section of the bearing which is toward the center of the crankshaft.

Now let us talk about inertia loads. Inertia is that characteristic of all material objects that causes them to resist any change of speed or direction of travel. The piston and upper part of the connecting rod are constantly changing speed and direction of travel. At the end of each stroke [at TDC (top dead center) and BDC (bottom dead center)] the piston is brought to a complete stop. Then it is accelerated to the high speed it attains in the middle of each stroke. At 4,000 engine rpm, for example, the piston will accelerate from a "standing start" to about 88 feet per second (a mile a minute) in 0.00375 second. Then, in the next 0.00375 second, it has to slow down and stop again. Even though a piston may weigh only about a pound (cast-iron pistons weigh a little more), it takes a considerable force to stop the piston, start it again, accelerate it to high speed, and then stop it once more. This force, remember, is imposed on the connecting-rod big-end bearing and produces what are known as *inertia loads*. Inertia loads vary greatly from a minimum toward the middle of the stroke to a maximum at around TDC and BDC when the maximum change of speed is taking place (or when the piston is brought to a stop and reversed in direction). For example, at 4,000 rpm, a 1-pound piston moving in a 4-inch stroke will impose a maximum inertia load of more than 700 pounds on the connecting-rod bearing.

Assume a uniform acceleration of 23,500 ft/sec^2, based on the formula

$$a = \frac{V_1 + V_2}{t}$$

Since V_1 is 0 and V_2 is 88 ft/sec, then $a = \dfrac{88}{0.00375}$ $= 23{,}500$ ft/sec^2.

$$\text{Force} = ma = \frac{1}{32.16} \times 23{,}500 = 733 \text{ lb}$$

There is an additional load due to the inertia effect of the connecting rod, which is also brought to a stop and then moved in the opposite direction. Remember that this maximum load occurs as the piston passes through TDC or BDC, or during the time that the piston is brought to a stop and then started moving in the opposite direction. Inertia loads increase with engine speed, just as centrifugal loads do.

§179. The effective bearing load The three different loads on the connecting-rod bearing sometimes add up and sometimes oppose each other, but generally they work at various angles to each other. You might compare this to two men pushing at angles on a box, as shown in Fig. 14-15. As they exert force *A* and force *B*, respectively, they work partly against each other, but part of their effort does add up to produce resultant force *C*. If they exerted different forces (as at force *D* and force *E*), then the resulting force would be to the right, as shown (resultant force *F*). Note that in the drawings the lengths of the arrows are proportional to the forces exerted.

In a similar manner, as the bearing loads work at different angles to each other, they produce a resultant loading force that is, in effect, the same as a single loading force. For example, in Fig. 14-14 the small drawings to the right show the power, inertia, and centrifugal loads on the bearing at one certain engine speed and piston position on the power stroke. Note that the pressure load opposes the inertia load; the inertia load partly cancels out the pressure load, since it is in the opposite direction to the pressure load. The centrifugal load is at an angle.

The small drawing to the right shows how to combine the three loads to find out the resultant

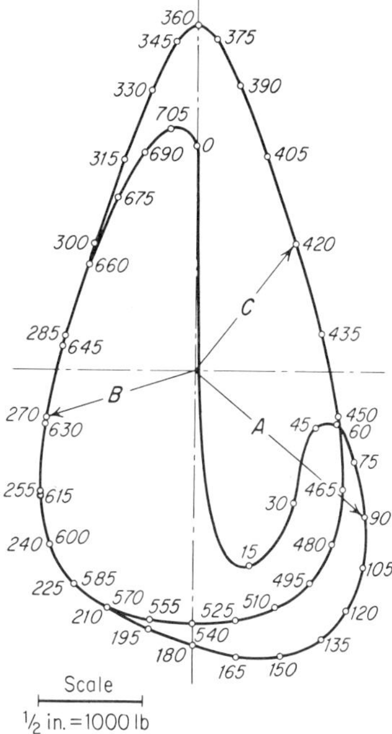

Fig. 14-16. Graph of resultant forces, or loads, on connecting-rod bearings, in a 3⅛ × 4⅜ engine, operating at 3,700 rpm. The figures represent degrees of crankshaft rotation: 0 to 180 degrees is the power stroke; 180 to 360 degrees is the exhaust stroke; 360 to 540 degrees is the intake stroke; and 540 to 720 (or 0) degrees is the compression stroke. (*Federal-Mogul-Bower Bearings, Inc.*)

load *R*. The arrows are proportional in length to the forces exerted, and they point in the directions in which the forces are exerted. After the three force arrows are drawn, the resultant arrow *R* is drawn in. Its length represents the strength of the resultant force, and its direction indicates the direction in which the force is exerted.

§180. The bearing-load graph Figure 14-16 is a graph of the resultant bearing loads (from pressure, centrifugal, and inertia loads) imposed on the connecting-rod bearing in a certain engine with a 3⅛ bore and a 4⅜ stroke operating at 3,700 rpm. The small figures represent the degrees of crankshaft rotation; 0 to 180 degrees of crankshaft rotation represents the power stroke; 180 to 360 degrees, the exhaust stroke; 360 to 540 degrees, the intake stroke; and 540 to 720 (or 0) degrees, the compression stroke. The distance from the intersection of the two straight lines to any point on the curved line represents the amount of bearing load imposed, and the direction in which the measurement is taken indicates the direction of loading. For example, at 90 degrees (or halfway through the power stroke), the bearing load is shown by arrow *A*, which scales at 2,100 pounds and is pointing down to the lower right. Then, at 270 degrees, which is halfway through the exhaust stroke, the bearing load is as shown by arrow *B*. This is almost horizontal to the left and scales about 1,470 pounds. Arrow *C* indicates the bearing load at 420 degrees, or at a point 60 degrees after the intake stroke has begun. This scales at 1,480 pounds and is toward the upper right.

The graph in Fig. 14-16 provides a great deal of interesting information. For instance, under the running conditions at which the graph was compiled, at the beginning of the power stroke there is an almost zero bearing loading for a few degrees of crankshaft rotation (because of pressure load canceling the centrifugal and inertia loads). Moreover, in a matter of 15 degrees of crankshaft rotation, the load changes from about 2,000 pounds on the upper part of the bearing (at 0 degrees) to about 1,800 pounds on the lower part of the bearing (at 15 degrees). Note also that the load de-

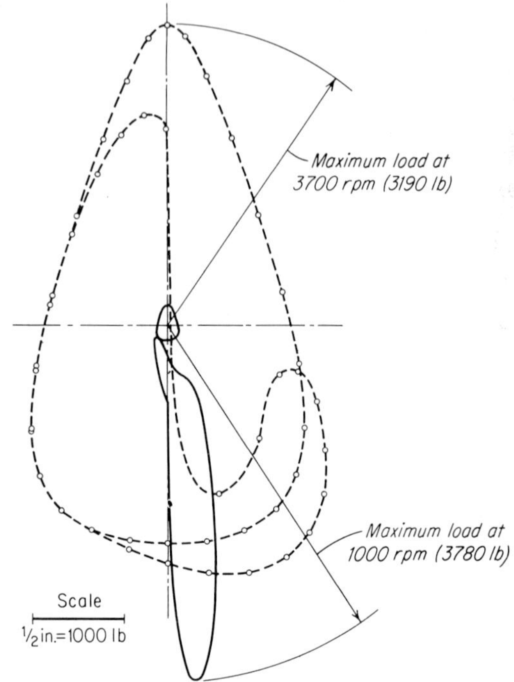

Fig. 14-17. Comparison graph of connecting-rod-bearing loads at 3,700 rpm (shown in the dotted line) with loads at 1,000 rpm at wide-open throttle (shown in the solid line). These graphs were compiled on the same engine. (*Federal-Mogul-Bower Bearings, Inc.*)

creases after this because of pressure drop and also swings up toward the right. Then, at about 45 degrees, the load again increases and swings downward. You might like to compare this graph of connecting-rod-bearing loading with the graph of cylinder pressures (Fig. 6-5).

It must be remembered that the graph (Fig. 14-16) shows only one set of conditions at one engine speed. The bearing loadings (and graph, of course) change with changed operating conditions. For example, Fig. 14-17 compares the bearing loads shown in Fig. 14-16 with bearing loads obtained at 1,000 rpm (with a wide-open throttle) on the same engine. Note that under these last conditions an entirely different set of bearing loads is imposed, with the maximum coming early in the power stroke and amounting to 3,780 pounds. Note also how small the inertia and centrifugal loads are

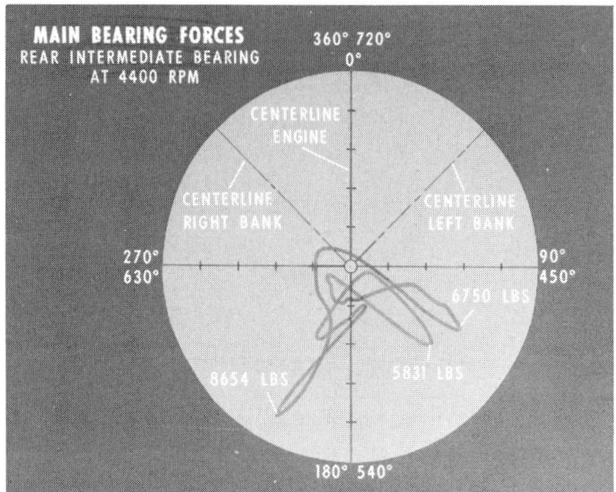

Fig. 14-18. Graph of maximum loads or forces exerted on the rear intermediate main bearing of a V-8 engine at 4,400 rpm. (*Chevrolet Motor Division of General Motors Corporation*)

at 1,000 rpm (upper part of graph). As is obvious from the graph, this sort of operation is very hard on the bearings; it subjects them to periodic heavy shock loads. Bearings will have a relatively short life under such conditions.

We should also note that we have been discussing only connecting-rod bearings. However, other engine bearings (main, or crankshaft, piston-pin, and so forth) also have varying loads imposed on them; somewhat similar bearing-load analyses could be made on these other bearings.

As a matter of comparison, refer to Fig. 14-18, which is a graph of the maximum loading of the rear intermediate main bearing of the Chevrolet Turbo-Jet V-8 engine, as reported in SAE (Society of Automotive Engineers) 660340 paper.[6] Note that the bearing is subjected to three heavy and suddenly applied loads of several tons.

§181. Bearing design This section is concerned entirely with the sleeve bearings and bushings used in automotive engines for crankshaft, connecting-rod, piston-pin, and camshaft bearings. Designing bearings for these and other moving members in the engine can be a complex job because so many different factors must be taken into consideration.

There are specification tables, published by the SAE and others, to which the designer can go for basic data on some specifications, such as type of material, shell and wall thickness for a given diameter of journal, relationship of journal diameter to bearing length, and so on. There are many other factors, however, that the bearing designer must consider. Some of the "do's" and "don'ts" of bearing design are listed here.

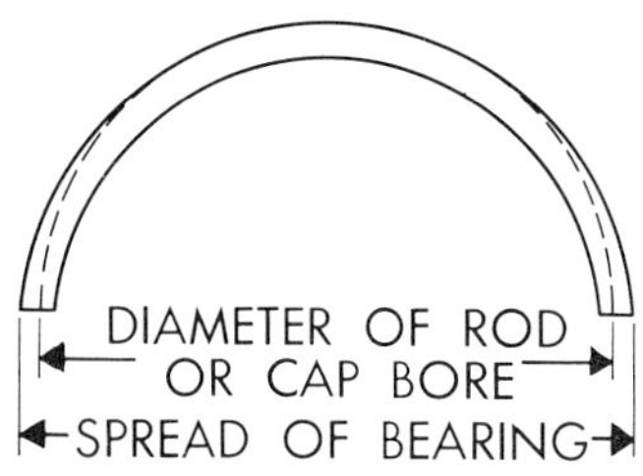

Fig. 14-19. Bearing spread.

1. *Bearing locking.* The bearing must "stay put" and not rotate in its mounting. Sleeve bearings, such as the piston-pin bushings, are usually held in place by making them a press fit. Split bearings, such as crankshaft or connecting-rod bearings, are usually held in place either by locking lips or tangs (Fig. 14-5), or by retaining dowels. One factor to be considered here is the relative expansion of the bearing itself and the case or housing in which it is installed. For example, experience with solid aluminum bearings in an iron housing showed that the bearings could work loose because of the differences in expansion rates. As the combination heated up, the bearing, expanding at a greater rate than the iron, would suffer deformation and take on a new set. Then, as it cooled, it would shrink more than the housing and thus become loose in the housing. Ultimately it would work free from the retaining dowel or locking lip and start to move. If it moved enough to cover up the oil hole, then the bearing would quickly fail.

2. *Bearing spread and crush.* Split-sleeve bearings, such as those used for main and connecting-rod big-end bearings, must fit snugly in the bearing bores (in cylinder block or connecting rod). To provide for this, bearing designers must provide for some bearing *spread* and *crush.* "Spread" means that the shell half has a somewhat larger diameter than the bore into which it will be in-

stalled (Fig. 14-19). Then, when the shell is installed, it will snap into place and hold its seat properly, making good contact all around (provided, of course, that the bore is clean).

Bearing crush provides a slight amount of height above the bore half into which the shell is to be installed (Fig. 14-20). That is, when the shell is first installed in the cap or half bore of the rod or cylinder block, its two edges will protrude slightly above the surface, as shown. Then, when the two bearing halves are brought together as the bearing cap is installed, this additional height will be crushed down. This crush, which is not great enough to cause bearing distortion, is just enough to force the two bearing shells into firm contact with the bore metal. Among other things, this assures that the heat conduction from the shell to the bore will be within the design limits.

3. Press-fit bushings. Where bushings are press-fitted into housings, the actual displacement of the bore, as well as the bushing, must be considered. A press fit means that the OD (outside diameter) of the bushing shell is somewhat larger than the ID (inside diameter) of the bore into which it is to be pressed. The interfering metal has to go someplace, either being pushed outward to make the bore larger or inward to make the OD of the bushing smaller. One series of tests showed that, when a steel-backed bushing was pressed into an aluminum housing, the outward displacement of the bore accounted for about 30 percent of the press fit. The remaining 70 percent was taken up by the inward displacement of the bushing. However, with a steel-backed bushing pressed into a steel housing, the steel housing gave only 10 percent, and the bushing had to give the other 90 percent.

It is obvious, therefore, that the designer must take this displacement of metal into consideration so that a proper fit can be established without damage to either the housing or bushing.

4. Journal geometry and finish. The journal geometry and finish have a profound effect on bearing life.[7] Various imperfections in journal geometry, greatly exaggerated, are illustrated in Fig. 14-21. Any of these, of course, will penalize

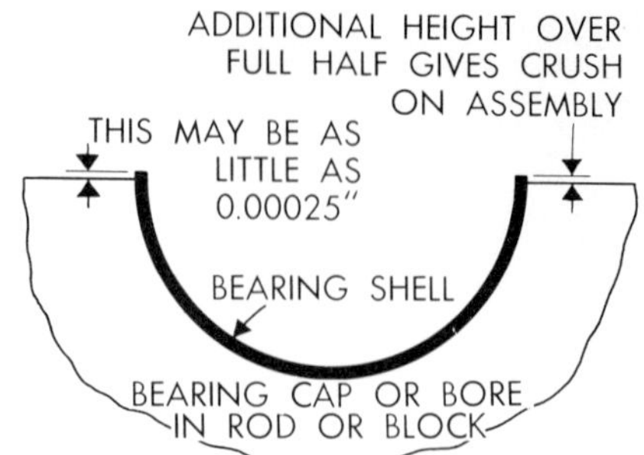

Fig. 14-20. Bearing crush.

bearing performance and shorten bearing life. It is obvious what most of these irregularities will do to bearings. They will cause the bearings to wear rapidly, with a resulting short bearing life.

Lobing has been studied intensively in recent years, and the relationships of different kinds of lobing with bearing life have been established. Lobing is identified with grinding-wheel "chatter." A series of lobes—hills and valleys—form around the circumference of the journal due to slight irregularities in the contact between the grinding wheel and journal. There may be only a few lobes, or there may be a dozen or more, irregularly spaced around the journal. Also, the height of the lobes may be slight, or it may be great enough to cause rapid bearing failure. Studies of the lobing effects on bearing life have revealed that the greater the amplitude of the lobes, the greater the bearing wear. Also, the more lobes there are, the greater the bearing wear.

Another aspect of journal grinding is that grinding leaves a microscopic "fuzz" of metallic edges that lay on the journal surface in the direction that the grinding wheel passes over the journal. This may become critical if the journal then turns in the bearing in the opposite direction to the lay of the fuzz. If this happens, the fuzz may dig into the bearing, resulting in a continuous scratching action. You might compare this with stroking the back of a cat in the wrong direction, which raises the hairs instead of laying them down.

To get rid of this fuzz, many engineers now recommend polishing the journals after the grinding operation. Polishing should be done in a direction opposite to the direction in which the journals

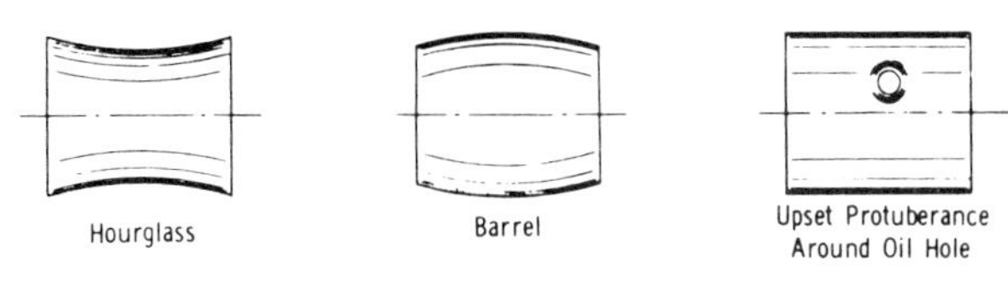

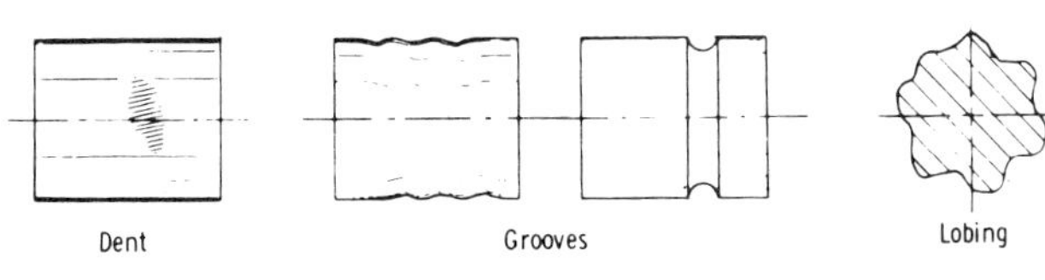

Fig. 14-21. Some typical defects in bearing journals. Defects are shown exaggerated. (*General Motors Corporation*)

were ground. Also, it is desirable to polish the journal in the direction in which it will turn in the bearing. This makes the remaining fuzz lay down in a nonharmful direction.

5. *Oil flow in bearings.* The bearing designer must be aware of the fact that it is just as important to get oil *out of* the bearing clearance as it is to get it *into* the bearing clearance. In other words, the oil must flow across the bearing, from the oil hole or groove to the edges. If the oil in the clearance is stagnant, the result will be overheating, fast bearing wear, and rapid bearing failure. One cause of oil stagnation could be *fillet ride*. That is, if the bearing is too wide for the journal, then the

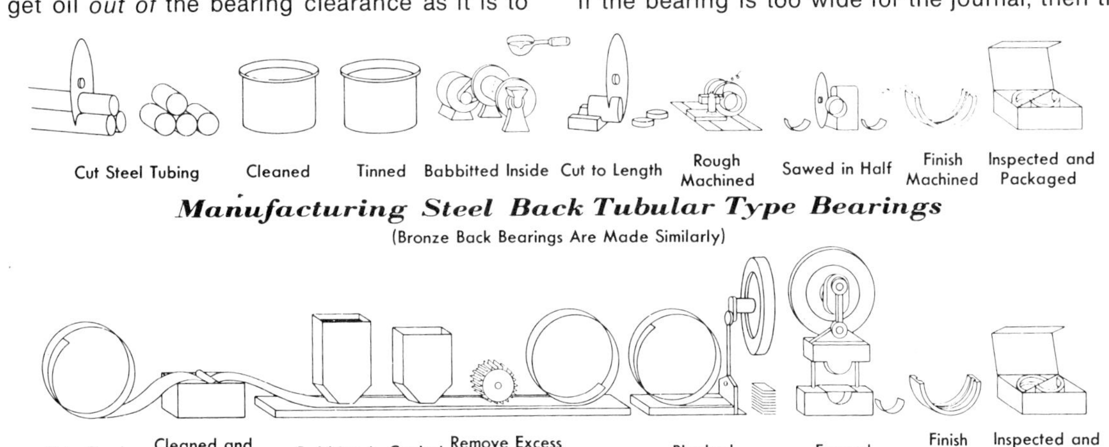

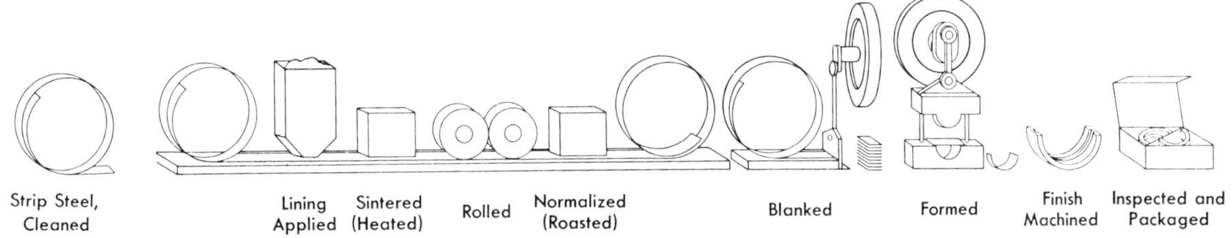

Fig. 14-22. Schematic drawings of manufacturing processes for different types of bearings. (*Federal-Mogul-Bower Bearings, Inc.*)

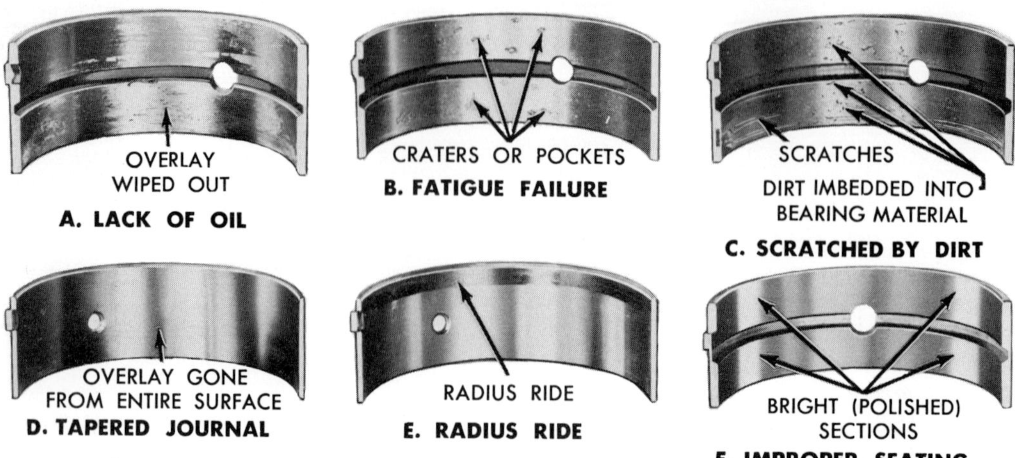

Fig. 14-23. Types of engine-bearing failure. The appearance of the bearing usually indicates the cause of failure. (*Ford Division of Ford Motor Company*)

edges of the bearing might ride too snugly on the journal fillets, thereby blocking oil flow off the edges of the bearing. Blocked oil flow could also occur in an engine having a worn main-thrust bearing. The worn thrust bearing could allow excessive endwise movement of the crankshaft so that fillet ride would occur on some main bearings.

6. *Oil-hole location.* The oil hole should never be placed in the area of maximum bearing loading. Not only does this reduce the available bearing surface, but also it reduces the oil flow into the bearing. That is, the area of maximum loading is the area with the thinnest oil film, and thus it is the smallest space into which oil can flow. If the oil hole is located in an area of minimum loading, there will be a greater clearance into which the oil can flow.

7. *Bearing eccentricity and maximum loading areas.* The main and rod bearings are subjected to great variations of loading (Figs. 14-16 to 14-18). Actually, some parts of the bearing are never subjected to anything like maximum loading. Thus, engineers are now discussing and testing bearings that are slightly eccentric to provide greater clearance in the nonloaded areas. This greater clearance does two major things: it permits more oil to flow in the nonloaded areas so that there will be adequate oil to feed into the loaded areas; and it reduces bearing friction in those areas where the clearance is greater.

Here is an example of what is being done in the way of testing this aspect of bearing design. In one heavy-duty engine, having a total projected bearing area of over 100 square inches, the effective bearing area (the area bearing the major load) was found to be about 69 square inches with standard bearings. Special eccentric bearings were then installed to reduce the effective bearing area to about 42 square inches. This was found to reduce bearing friction loss about one-third. Calculations indicated that the peak bearing loads under the effective bearing area were above 18,000 psi.

8. *Bearing manufacture.* Bearing manufacture is begun with either bronze or steel tubing, or strip steel (Fig. 14-22). Bearings that are lined with copper-lead alloy, for example, start out as a roll of strip steel. In a continuous process, the lining is applied, sintered, rolled, normalized (heated to relieve stresses), and then cut into blanks. These blanks are then formed, finish-machined, inspected, and packaged.

9. *Bearing life.* It is difficult to generalize about bearing life because there are many variables involved. However, engineers talk of 50,000 miles of service as being normal for bearings in engines that are well maintained and operated in average conditions. There are cases where bearing mileage has gone far beyond this, however. One study was made of 150 trucks equipped with special heavy-

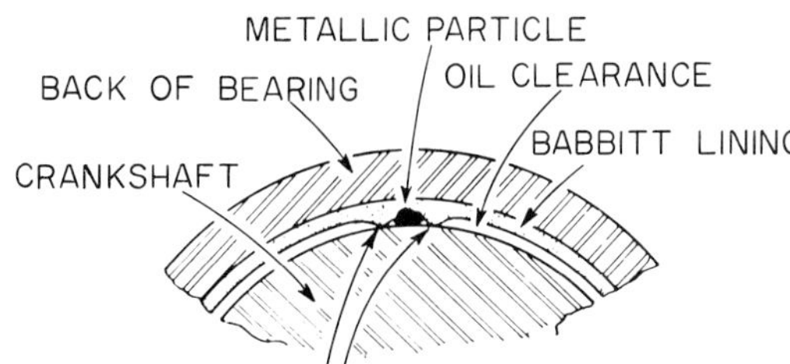

Fig. 14-24. Effect of a metallic particle embedded in bearing metal (the babbitt lining). (*Federal-Mogul-Bower Bearings, Inc.*)

duty bearings. Some trucks ran as much as 180,000 miles without excessive bearing wear.[4]

§182. Bearing failures An important part of a bearing designer's job is examining bearings that have failed in operation, either in the laboratory or out in the field. Quite often, the appearance of the bearing is a clue to the trouble; a number of the basic types of bearing failures and their causes are discussed and illustrated below. You will note that many of these failures are not due to a fault in the bearings.

1. *Bearing failure due to lack of oil* (*A* in Fig. 14-23). If the oil supply to a bearing fails for any reason, the protective oil film is lost. Actual metal-to-metal contact takes place, the bearing overheats, and the bearing metal then melts or is wiped out of the bearing shell. Further operation after this has happened usually results in welds forming between the rotating journal and the bearing shells. There is a good chance that the engine will "throw a rod"; that is, the rod will "freeze" to the crankpin and break, and parts of the rod will go through the engine block. Several conditions could cause loss of the oil supply to the bearing. If other bearings have excessive clearance, they may pass all the oil from the pump, thus starving one or more bearings, which then fail. In addition, oil lines may be clogged, the oil pump or pressure regulator may be defective, or there may be insufficient or the wrong kind of oil in the crankcase. Any of these could oil-starve bearings and cause them to fail.

2. *Fatigue failure of bearing* (*B* in Fig. 14-23). Repeated application of loads on a bearing will ultimately fatigue the bearing metal so that it

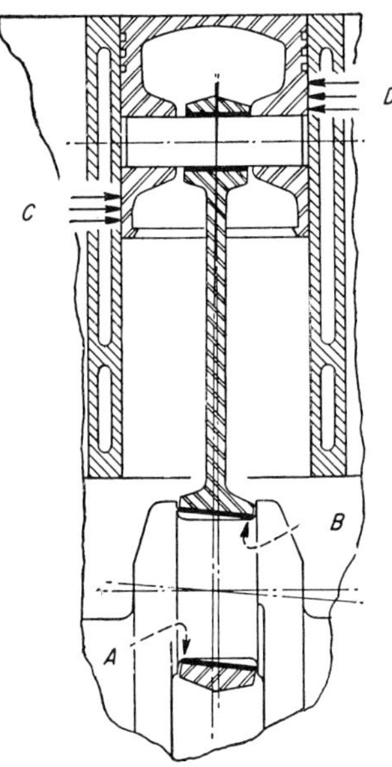

Fig. 14-25. Heavy-pressure areas caused by a bent rod. The bent condition is exaggerated. Areas of heavy pressure will wear rapidly, and so early failure results. (*Federal-Mogul-Bower Bearings, Inc.*)

starts to crack and flake out. Craters, or pockets, form in the bearing where metal has been lost. As more and more of the metal is lost in this manner, the remainder is worked harder and fatigues at an accelerated rate. Ultimately, complete bearing failure occurs.

Under normal operating conditions, fatigue failure of bearings is not a problem. However, there are certain operating conditions that hasten fatigue greatly. For instance, if crankpins or journals are worn out of round, bearings will be overstressed with every crankshaft revolution and will be short-

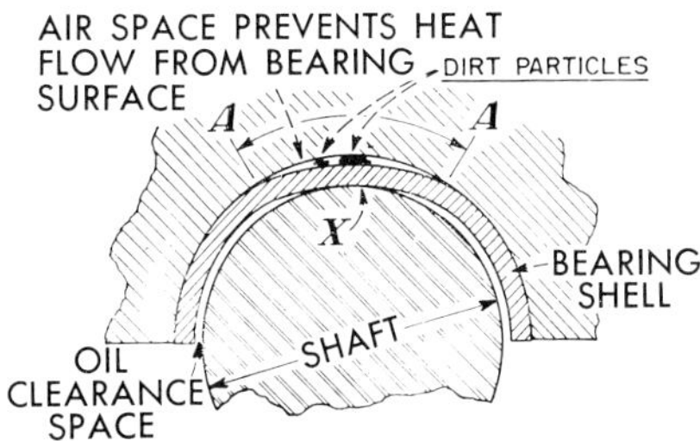

Fig. 14-26. Effect of dirt particles under the bearing shell due to poor installation. (*Federal-Mogul-Bower Bearings, Inc.*)

lived. Unusual operating conditions will produce unusual wear patterns on connecting-rod bearings. For example, if the engine is idled or operated at low speeds often, the center part of the upper connecting-rod-bearing half will carry most of the load and will "fatigue out," the lower half remaining in nearly perfect condition. However, if the engine is operated at maximum torque with wide-open throttle (that is, if the engine is "lugged"), then most or all of the upper connecting-rod-bearing half will fatigue out. If the lower bearing half fatigues, the engine has probably been operated at high speeds. Refer to §178-180 to see how the bearings are loaded under those different conditions.

3. Bearing scratched by dirt in the oil (*C* in Fig. 14-23). The property of embedability (§176) enables a bearing to protect itself by allowing dirt particles to embed so that they do not gouge out the bearing metal or scratch the rotating journal. However, when many particles are present (oil is dirty), the bearing becomes overloaded with dirt. And if dirt particles are too large to be embedded completely, they will be carried around (or roll around) with the rotating journal and will gouge out scratches on the bearing. In either case, loss of bearing surface and shortened bearing life result. Figure 14-24 shows, in an exaggerated view, what happens when a particle becomes embedded in the bearing metal. The metal is pushed up around the particle, reducing oil clearance in that area. Usually the metal can flow outward from the high spot, and fairly normal oil clearance can be restored. However, if too much dirt becomes embedded, then bearing failure will soon follow.

4. Bearing failure due to tapered journal (*D* in Fig. 14-23). If the journal is tapered, one side of the bearing will carry all or most of the load. The bearing metal will be overheated and will melt or be wiped from the bearing shell on the overloaded side. Short bearing life can be expected from a tapered journal.

NOTE: Bearing failure from a tapered journal should not be confused with bearing failure caused by a bent connecting rod. With a tapered journal, both bearing halves will fail on the same side; with a bent rod, however, failure will be on opposite sides (*A* and *B* in Fig. 14-25).

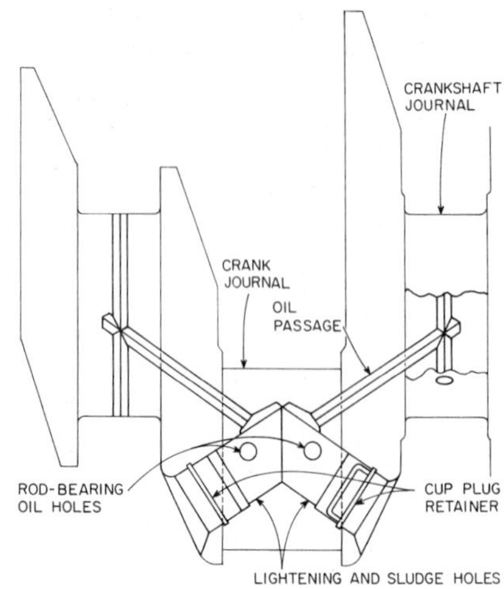

Fig. 14-27. V-8 engine crankshaft drilling for oil passages and sludge traps. (*Ford Motor Company*)

5. Bearing failure from radii ride (*E* in Fig. 14-23). If the radius on the journal, where the journal curves up to the crank cheeks, is not cut away sufficiently, the edge of the bearing will ride on the radius, causing cramming of the bearing, possible poor seating, rapid fatigue, and early failure. This sort of difficulty would be most likely to arise after a crankshaft-grind and bearing-replacement job where the radii were not relieved sufficiently when the crankpins or journals were ground.

6. Bearing failure from improper seating (*F* in Fig. 14-23). If the bearing is not properly seated in the counterbore, there will be high spots in the bearing where oil clearances will be too low. Figure 14-26 shows, in an exaggerated view, what happens when particles of dirt are left between the bearing shell and the counterbore. Not only is the bearing shell raised in the area so that oil clearance is reduced (as at *X*), but air spaces exist as well, which prevent normal cooling of the bearing. The combination can lead directly to quick bearing failure.

7. Bearing failure from ridging. Crankpin or main-journal ridging, or "camming," may cause

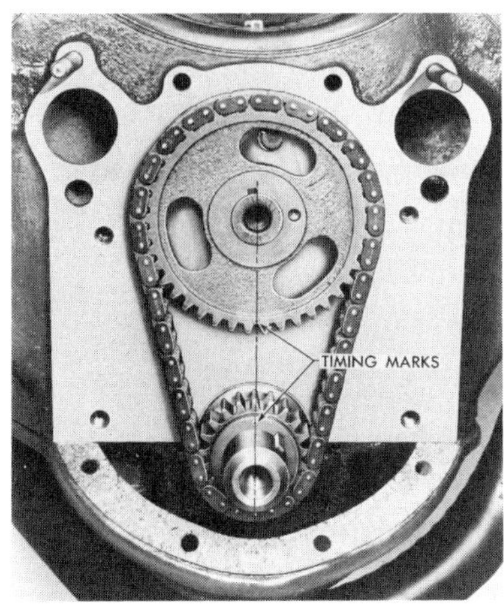

Fig. 14-28. Front of engine with timing-chain cover removed. (*Pontiac Motor Division of General Motors Corporation*)

failure of a partial-oil-groove-type replacement bearing installed without previously removing the ridge. The ridge forms on the crankpin, or journal, as a result of uneven wear rates between the part that runs on the solid bearing and the part that runs over the oil groove. The original bearing wears to conform to this change of contour. When a new bearing is installed, however, the center zone (at the ridge) will be overloaded and will soon fail. A ridge so slight that it can hardly be detected (except with a carefully used micrometer) may be sufficient to cause this sort of failure. Failures of this sort have actually been reported in engines having ridges of less than 0.001 inch.

§183. Crankshaft The crankshaft is a one-piece casting or forging of heat-treated alloy steel that is of considerable mechanical strength (Figs. 3-18 and 7-15). The crankshaft, it will be remembered, takes the downward thrust of the piston during the power stroke. Pressure exerted by the pistons through the connecting rods against the crankpins on the crankshaft causes the shaft to rotate. This rotary motion is transmitted through the power train to the car wheels. The problems of static and dynamic balance and torsional vibration must be considered in the design of a crankshaft. The cranks on the crankshaft, being offset from the center line of the shaft, have the connecting rods attached to them. This introduces an out-of-balance condition which would set up serious vibration during shaft rotation if it were not for counterweights. These place weights opposite the cranks which are equal to the unbalancing weights. The counterweights thus bring the assembly into practical balance (see §185).

Crankshafts generally have drilled oil passages (Fig. 7-15) through which oil can flow from the main to the connecting-rod bearings (see §174, on bearing lubrication). An improved method of drilling oil passages in the crankshaft is illustrated in Fig. 14-27. Here, the crankshaft and crank journals are both drilled straight through, with two holes being drilled in each crank journal (one for each connecting-rod bearing). Diagonal holes are then drilled to connect between the crankshaft and crank journals. The large holes drilled in the crank journals lighten the crankshaft and also serve as sludge traps. Cup plugs are used to seal these traps.

In the assembled engine the front end of the crankshaft carries three devices. One of these is a gear, or sprocket, that drives the camshaft (Fig. 14-28); the camshaft is driven at one-half the speed of the crankshaft. A second device is the torsional-vibration damper (see §190), which combats torsional vibration in the crankshaft. As part of the vibration damper, there is a pulley with one or more grooves. V belts fit these grooves and drive the engine fan and water pump, as well as the alternator. There is an additional groove in the pulley on cars equipped with power steering; this additional groove is fitted with a V belt that drives the power-steering hydraulic pump. There may also be another groove for belt-driving the compressor in cars equipped with air-conditioning.

As will be recalled (§88), the rear end of the crankshaft carries the flywheel. Its purpose is to smooth out the power impulses so the engine runs more evenly.

The purpose of the vibration damper has already been described (§89) and is considered in greater detail in §190.

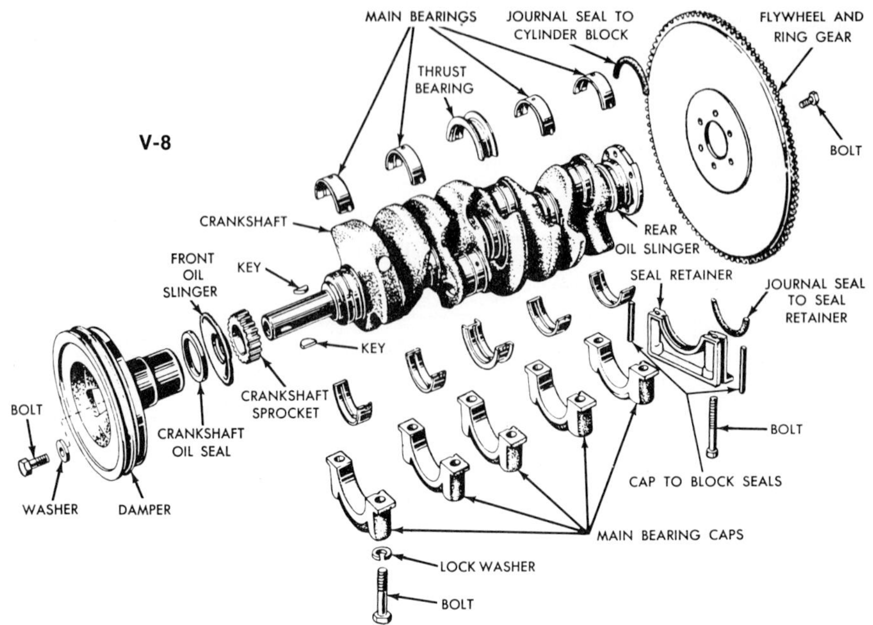

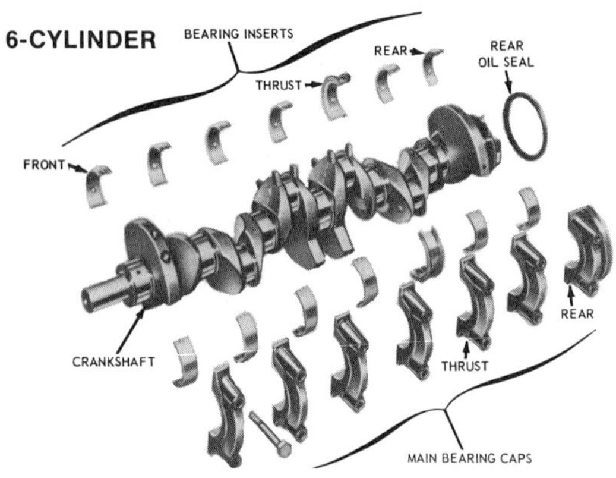

Fig. 14-29. Main bearing arrangements in six-cylinder and V-8 engines. (*Ford Motor Company*)

§184. Crankshaft design Basic considerations in the design of a crankshaft are strength, rigidity, and balance. It is comparatively easy to analyze mathematically the crankshaft stresses, based on the expected crankshaft loading, so that sufficient metal will be used for adequate strength. It is less easy to design balance into the crankshaft.

The overall configuration of the engine—height, length, number of cylinders, expected performance in terms of torque and horsepower, size, and number of bearings—determines the basic configuration of the crankshaft.

As a rule, after the basic specifications of the engine have been written, the cylinder-block design is started. At this stage, decisions already have been made as to the number of cylinders, whether or not the engine is to be the in-line or V type, the number of main bearings, the placement of the main-thrust bearing, and so on.

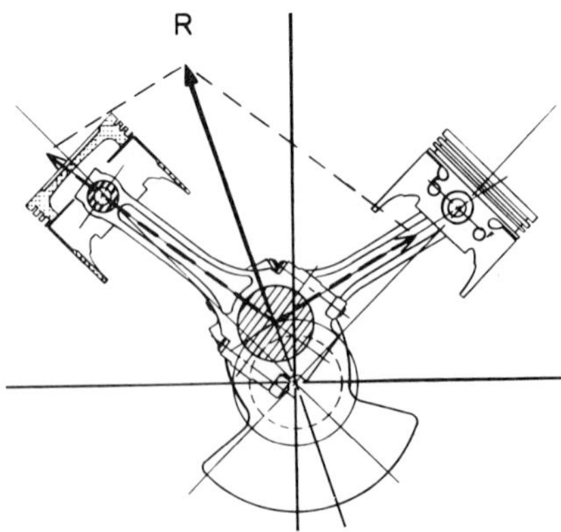

Fig. 14-30. Resultant of inertial and centrifugal forces from the rotating and reciprocating masses of crankshaft and connecting-rod and piston assemblies. (*Oldsmobile Division of General Motors Corporation*)

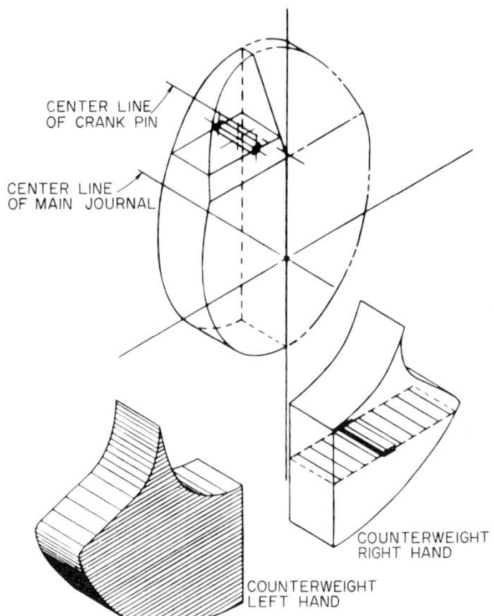

Fig. 14-31. Division of counterweight for purposes of anaylsis. (*Oldsmobile Division of General Motors Corporation*)

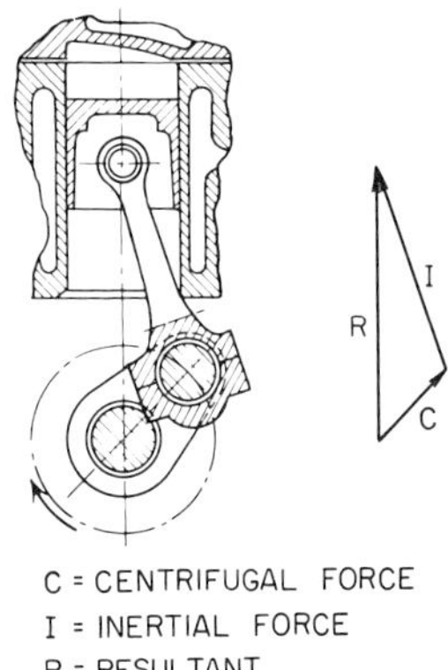

Fig. 14-32. Vector analysis indicates resultant at any position of crank.

In most modern engines, the maximum possible number of main bearings are used. For example, in a V-8 engine, five mains are used, one at each end, and the other three between the four crankpins (Fig. 14-29). Six-cylinder, in-line engines of modern design usually have seven main bearings, one at each end and one between each pair of crankpins (Fig. 14-29). With this construction, the load is distributed over more bearings. Also, each crankpin, in effect, is directly supported by main bearings on each side of it. There is less chance of crankshaft deflection or bending, and, likewise, there is less bending stress on the cylinder block.

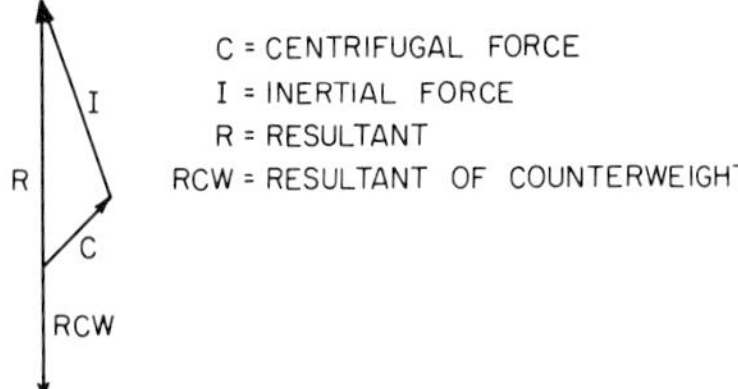

Fig. 14-33. Resultant of counterweight should equal resultant of centrifugal and inertial forces.

§185. Crankshaft-balance analysis After the basic dimensions of the crankshaft have evolved, including length, engine stroke, number and size of bearings, bearing journal diameters, oil holes, and so on, the crankshaft balance then receives attention.[8] This involves the determination of the size, weight, and location of the crankshaft counterweights. Figure 7-15 shows the counterweights on a crankshaft (see also Fig. 12-4).

The counterweights are required to balance the reciprocating and rotating motions of the piston and connecting-rod assemblies and cranks. Thus, the weights of these assemblies, as well as the stroke and the crank radius, must be established at this time. The designer must know what these weights are as well as what they will be doing during the rotation of the crankshaft.

Once these factors are established, vector anal-

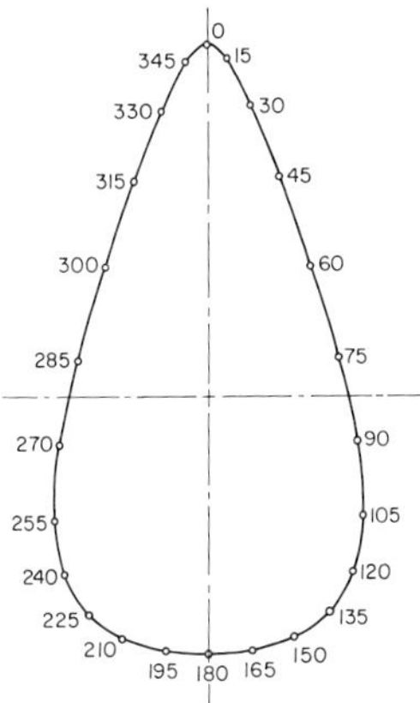

Fig. 14-34. Curve of resultant force due to inertial and centrifugal forces of crank and piston-and-rod assembly.

ysis can then be used to determine the resultant of the inertial and centrifugal forces from the reciprocating and rotating masses. For example, Fig. 14-30 shows the resultant force *R* in a V-8 engine, due to the motion of the two pistons and connecting rods attached to one crankpin of the crankshaft. It is this unbalanced force that must be corrected by the placement of counterweights on the crankshaft. Determining the position, shape, and weight of these counterweights is called *design balancing* the crankshaft.

A limiting dimension is the radius of the counterweights. If the radius is too large, the counterweights strike other engine parts—the piston skirt, for example. In many engines, the piston skirts are cut away to provide room for the counterweights to swing around under them at BDC as the crankshaft rotates (Fig. 12-3). The counterweights cannot be too thick through from front to back either. There must be clearance between the counterweights and the connecting rods. Also, there must be clearance between the counterweights and the cylinder-block webs supporting the crankshaft. These dimensions and clearances determine the maximum radius and thickness of the counterweights.

Two basic factors in designing a counterweight are the amount of weight (it must balance the piston and rod weight) and the placement and distribution of the weight (it must be so placed as to cancel out the opposing piston and rod weight). One procedure is to divide the counterweight into three parts for separate analysis: the arm, the left-hand half, and the right-hand half (Fig. 14-31). Each of the three parts is then subjected to an analytical routine that determines its volume (weight), center of gravity, and polar moment of inertia. The weight distribution is then determined. In effect, the distribution should be such that the unbalancing force of the piston and rod motion is countered exactly at any instant by a balancing mass from the counterweight, pulling in the opposite direction.

For example, suppose that at an angle of 45 degrees past TDC, the resultant force *R* of the inertia *I* and centrifugal force *C* is 1,200 pounds,

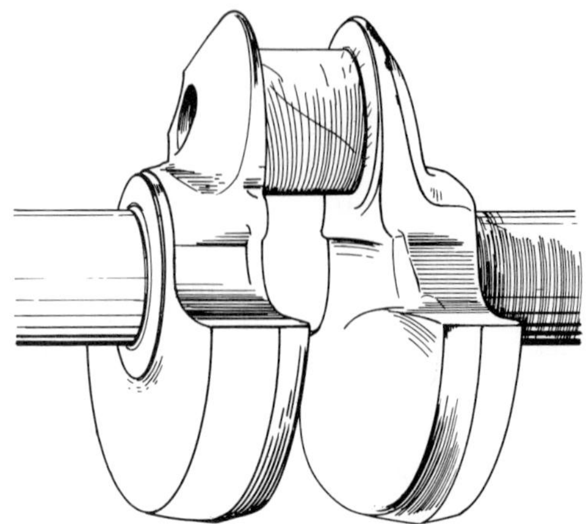

Fig. 14-35. Appearance of brittle lacquer coating on crankshaft of single-cylinder outboard marine engine after vibration test. Cracks in lacquer show stress. (*Outboard Marine Corporation*)

as shown in Fig. 14-32. This is the force that the counterweight must counterbalance. In other words, the centrifugal force of the counterweight must produce a resultant force that is of the same dimension and in the opposite direction (Fig. 14-33).

A graphical solution is possible here. Also, it is possible to program the problem for solution in a computer. Let us see briefly how the problem

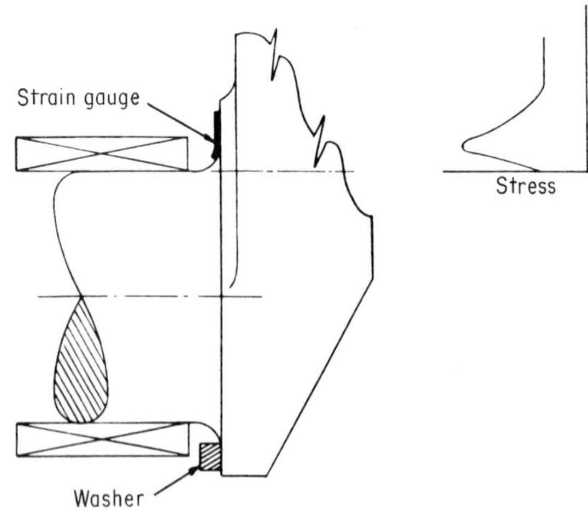

Fig. 14-36. Attachment of strain gauge on especially prepared crankshaft. (*Outboard Marine Corporation*)

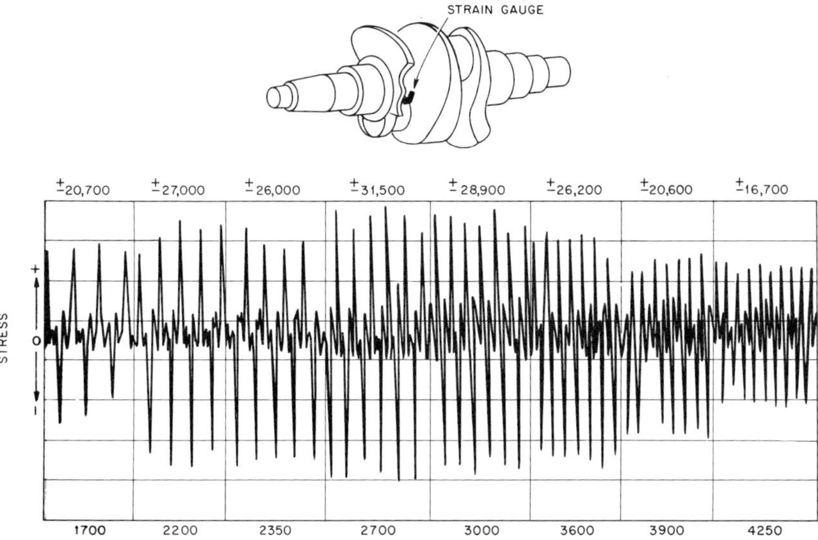

Fig. 14-37. Stress pattern at the point designated on a crankshaft, as indicated by traces on oscilloscope. (*Outboard Marine Corporation*)

may be solved graphically. First, the inertial and centrifugal forces and their resultant force due to piston and rod movement are determined at various positions as the crankshaft completes one revolution. From these determinations, a graph can be constructed. For example, suppose the resultant force is determined at 15-degree intervals. In this case, the graph might look as shown in Fig. 14-34. A properly designed counterweight to cancel the forces graphed in Fig. 14-34 would have to exert force just the reverse of what is shown. That is, the weight and center of gravity of the counterweight would have to be such as to cancel out the resultant force of the inertial and centrifugal forces of the crank and piston and rod combination.

By a series of vector drawings, the designer can determine the correct counterweight configuration. Also, if the problem is programmed, it can be fed into a computer, which will examine the counterresultant forces required and feed out a solution which indicates the amount of material needed for the counterweight as well as its placement in regard to the crankpin.

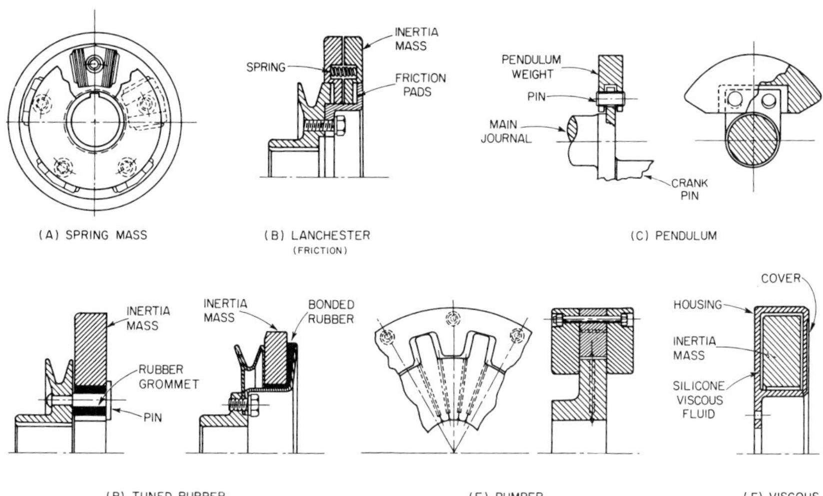

Fig. 14-38. Various designs of crankshaft torsional-vibration dampers. (*Houdaille Industries, Inc.*)

§186. Crankshaft-crankpin throw This is the distance between the main-journal center line and the crankpin center line. It is the distance that the crankpin is offset. This dimension is determined as a part of the overall engine design since it is related to piston stroke, connecting-rod length, and cylinder-bore diameter. A longer piston stroke demands a bigger crankpin throw.

In recent years, the trend has been to oversquare engines (§62). That is, the bore is greater than the stroke (see Fig. 6-2).

There are a number of reasons for this trend to the oversquare engine. With a smaller crankpin throw and a shorter stroke, the centrifugal and inertia forces are less. Maximum piston speeds at any given rpm are less with the smaller throw. Also, with the shorter stroke, the ring friction is lower, and this reduces friction horsepower (§74).

There are volumetric-efficiency and thermal-efficiency considerations, also. With the larger bore, valves can be made larger for improved engine breathing and higher volumetric efficiency. Also, the larger bore tends to reduce heat loss because of the greater distance from the center of the combustion chamber to the cooler cylinder walls.

§187. Crankshaft-journal size The size of the main and crankpin journals is determined largely by the overall dimensions of the engine. The crankshaft and bearing designers like to see large journals and bearings so that the load can be distributed over a larger area. Also, with larger journals, the crankshaft is less susceptible to distortion or deflection. On the other hand, the larger journals mean larger counterweights, and this is a limiting factor. Then, too, the cylinder-bore diameter limits the size of the crankpin journal because it is necessary for the big end of the connecting rod to pass through the cylinder during engine assembly and disassembly.

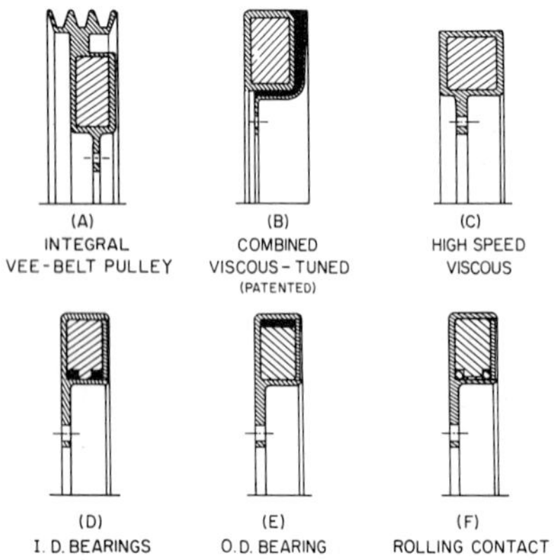

Fig. 14-39. The most commonly used crankshaft torsional-vibration dampers in sectional view, showing construction. (*Houdaille Industries Inc.*)

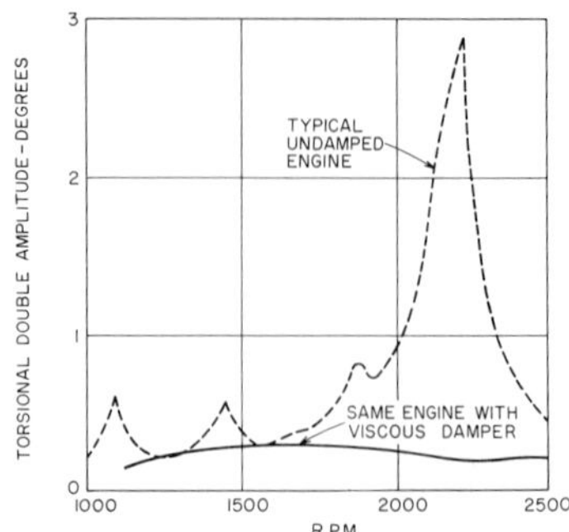

Fig. 14-40. Graph, showing effectiveness of viscous damper in quieting torsional vibration through the operating range of the engine. (*Houdaille Industries, Inc.*)

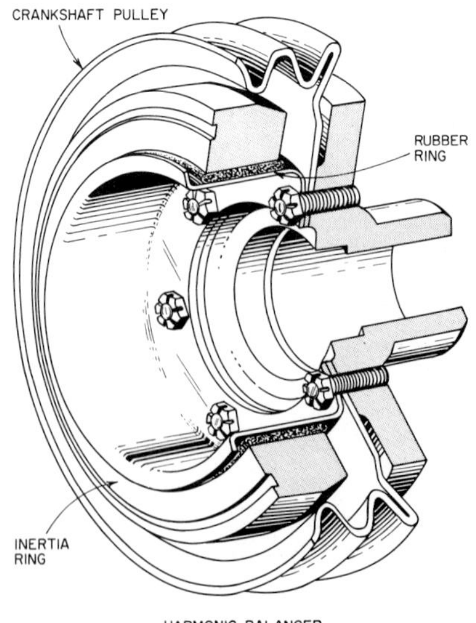

Fig. 14-41. Partial cutaway view of a torsional-vibration damper. (*Pontiac Motor Division of General Motors Corporation*)

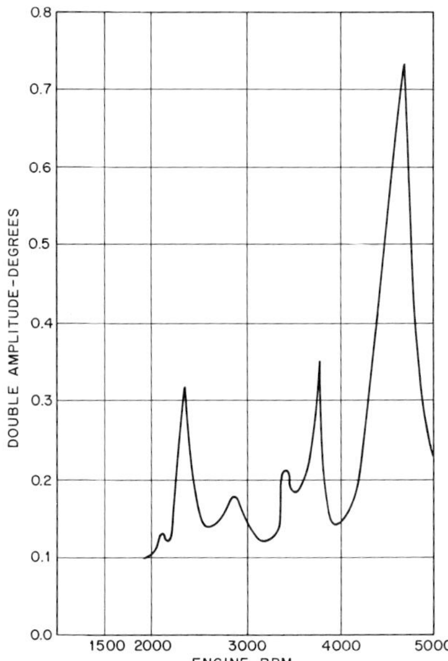

Fig. 14-42. Torsional vibration of crankshaft without vibration damper. (*Pontiac Motor Division of General Motors Corporation*)

With the overall length of the crankshaft established by the engine length, it is necessary to properly divide up this dimension so that both the main and crankpin journals "get their share" and still leave enough length for the arms connecting the two journals. The arms must have sufficient thickness for adequate strength and thus demand a certain minimum part of the total crankshaft length.

These factors are pretty much decided by standard practice based on accumulated experience, although variations from these standards are sometimes undertaken to meet special conditions.

§188. Crankshaft-journal geometry and finishes The relationship between journal geometry and finish and bearing wear has already been discussed (§181, 4). As already pointed out, for long bearing life, the journals, both main and crankpin, must be properly ground and polished for satisfactory bearing life. This is more a function of manufacturing procedures than of crankshaft design, but the crankshaft designer has a great interest in the manufacturing end. If crankshafts or bearings fail, he must be sure what the real cause is, and whether it is due to faulty manufacturing, design, materials, or operating conditions.

§189. Crankshaft tests The final testing of crankshafts, as with so many other engine parts, is done in actual operating engines, whether driven under test conditions or in normal, day-to-day service. Many preliminary tests are made on crankshafts of new designs, of course, before the new design is released for production.[9] Some of these are simple stress-loading tests during which varying loads are imposed so that deflections can be measured. For example, there is a brittle lacquer which can be sprayed on the crankpins and allowed to dry. Then, the crankpins can be loaded to simulate actual operating conditions, and this cracks the lacquer coating to disclose directions and magnitudes of stress in the crankpin (Fig. 14-35).

However, the brittle lacquer cannot be used on a crankshaft installed in an actual operating engine because it cannot stand up under heat and oil. For stress tests in an engine, a glazed ceramic

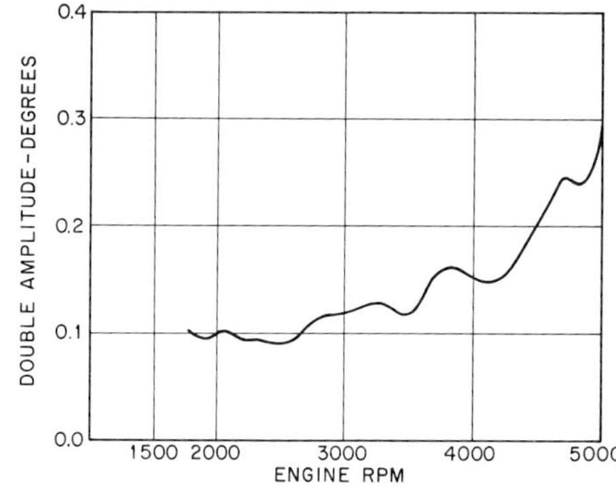

Fig. 14-43. Torsional vibration of crankshaft with vibration damper. Note marked reduction of torsional vibration. (*Pontiac Motor Division of General Motors Corporation*)

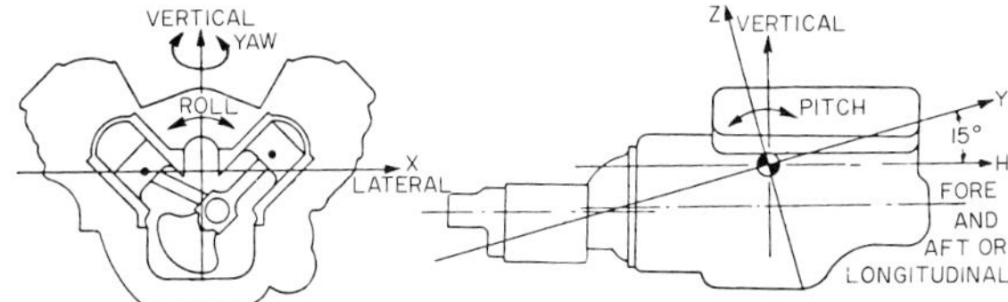

Fig. 14-44. Six modes of freedom of an automotive engine. (*Lord Manufacturing Company*)

coating can be used. This material is sprayed on and then fired at moderate heat (around 1000°F). The crankshaft can then be run in an engine under specified operating conditions and removed for inspection. Stress patterns will show up in the coating.

Another method of testing is to install strain gauges at strategic places on the crankshaft—at fillets where strain might be greatest, for example (Fig. 14-36). The strain gauges can be held in place by epoxy adhesive, and the wires can be run out through the crankshaft to slip rings. Brushes on the slip rings are attached to the electrical components of the test setup. Then, when the crankshaft is operated in the engine at varying speeds and loads, the strain gauges will report the amount of stress in the areas to which they are attached. For example, Fig. 14-37 is a typical stress trace at a designated point on a crankshaft operated in an engine with wide-open throttle and increasing load.

§190. Torsional-vibration dampers As already noted (§89), the crankshaft undergoes torsional vibration as a result of the repeated application of the power impulses to the cranks. Under some conditions, an undamped crankshaft will twist-untwist so much that ultimately it will break. A variety of damper designs have been used[10] (Fig. 14-38), but all have one thing in common. This is a metal mass that rotates and is driven through a flexible medium from the crankshaft. When the crankshaft attempts to twist, the rotating metal mass, because of its inertia, acts as a brake, reducing the amount of twist.

The most commonly used torsional-vibration dampers have a metal ring with the flexible medium being either rubber or a viscous-silicone liquid (Fig. 14-39). Some types combine the rubber and the viscous liquid (B in Fig. 14-39).

Figure 14-40 shows how effectively the damper kills off torsional vibration. The dotted line shows how much the crankshaft twists in one engine through the 1,000 to 2,500 rpm range. The twisting is shown in degrees of double amplitude. That is, at about 2,200 rpm, the total torsional vibration is about 3 degrees. This means that the crankshaft is twisting 1.5 degrees in one direction from the "no-twist" position, and then 1.5 degrees in the opposite direction. The solid line shows how effectively the damper damps out the torsional vibration.

Figure 14-41 is a partial cutaway view of a torsional-vibration damper used on a late-model, V-8 engine.[11] The inertia ring is mounted on a rubber ring inside the crankshaft pulley. Figures 14-42 and 14-43 show the torsional vibration of the crankshaft

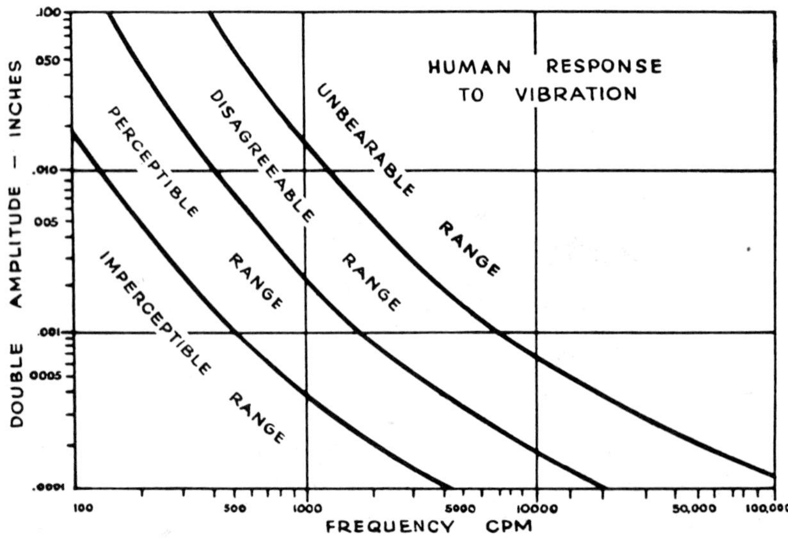

Fig. 14-45. Chart of human response to vibrations of different amplitudes and frequencies. (*Lord Manufacturing Company*)

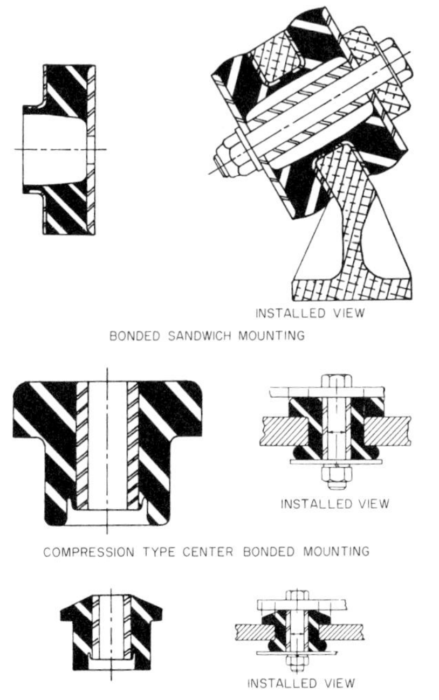

Fig. 14-46. Various types of engine mountings. (*Lord Manufacturing Company*)

without and with the torsional-vibration damper in use.

§191. Engine-vibration mountings[12] The crankshaft counterweights largely balance the inertial and centrifugal loads imposed by the piston and rod assembly. The torsional-vibration damper largely controls torsional vibration of the crankshaft. But there are other forces at work in and around the engine that produce vibrations of various frequencies and amplitudes (or intensities). A basic one, of course, is the periodic combustion pressure and its action in applying torque to the crankshaft. Also, as this torque is carried through the crankshaft to the transmission and power train, a countertorque is applied to the engine. Thus, the engine attempts to move in several directions.

To generalize, any body that is free to move in space has six degrees or modes of freedom: three linear or translational and three rotational. The three translational degrees of freedom permit the body to move in three axes: laterally, vertically, and fore and aft (longitudinally). The three rotational degrees of freedom permit the body to rotate about these same three axes (that is, to roll, yaw, or pitch). Figure 14-44 illustrates these six degrees of freedom on an automotive engine. Various forces acting on the engine will attempt to move it in some or all of these directions. The engine will thus vibrate in some or all of these directions.

If the engine were mounted rigidly to the car frame, these vibrations would be carried through the frame and cause several kinds of trouble. The driver would be subjected to various engine noises and vibrations, which would be both unpleasant and tiring. Various car components, such as the radiator core, relays, instruments, and so on, would be subjected to this vibration, and it could ultimately cause metal fatigue and failure of the part.

To prevent all this, the engine is mounted to the frame through flexible mountings that interpose a collar or pad of rubber or similar material between the engine and frame. These mountings are necessary or desirable for the following reasons.

1. The flexible mountings allow the car frame to twist (as it must when the car encounters irregularities in the road) without placing undue strain on the cylinder block. Without the flexible mountings, the cylinder block would be subjected to heavy twisting or bending loads as the frame

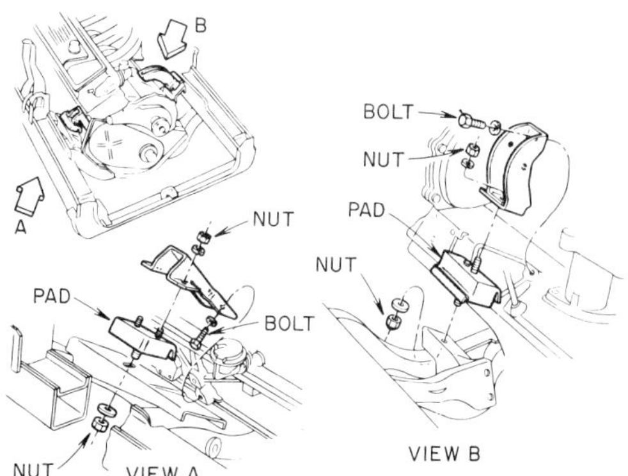

Fig. 14-47. Front engine flexible mounts used to support engine on frame. (*Chrysler-Plymouth Division of Chrysler Corporation*)

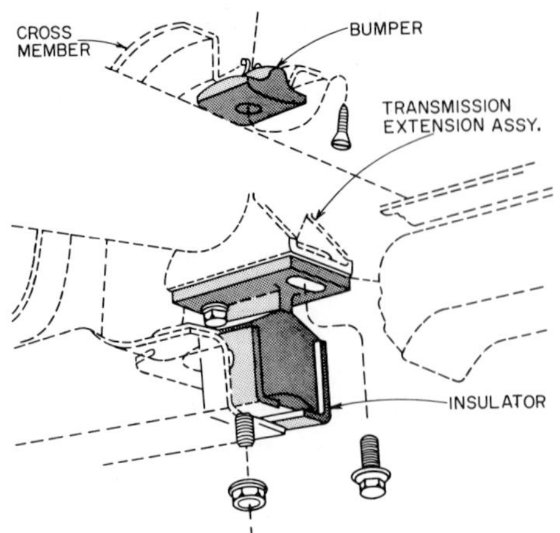

Fig. 14-48. Rear support for engine, showing insulator arrangement. (*Chrysler-Plymouth Division of Chrysler Corporation*)

twisted. This could break the engine-mounting lugs or otherwise damage the engine.

2. The flexible mountings reduce the noise from the engine by producing a damping effect that inhibits the sound from passing to the frame.

3. The flexible mountings damp out vibrations that would otherwise pass to the other components of the automobile, sometimes with damaging results.

4. The flexible mountings damp out vibrations and noise from the engine that otherwise would reach the driver and passengers. Such vibrations and noise can be very disagreeable and quite tiring. Figure 14-45 is a chart showing human response to vibration. Note that vibrations in the lower frequencies and of low amplitudes are not noticeable; with greater amplitudes and also higher frequencies (more cycles per minute), however, the vibrations pass from the perceptible range, through disagreeable, to unbearable.

The locations of the flexible mountings, as well as their design, are vitally important in their effective operation. It requires a considerable amount of mathematical analysis to determine the types of mountings needed and their optimum flexibility for any particular application. The mathematical solutions are apt to be only approximate, so that experimental mountings usually must be made and tested in operation to arrive at the final design.

Figure 14-46 shows several types of engine mountings. Figure 14-47 shows the front-engine mounts used for one engine. These mounts include rubber pads superimposed between the mounting brackets and car frame. Figure 14-48 shows the rear-mounting arrangement for the same engine.

SUMMARY

The connecting rods form the link between the piston and the cranks on the crankshaft, and the bearings provide the sliding surfaces on which the connecting rods, crankpins, and main journals can move. The bearings are lubricated by the engine lubricating system. The circulating oil also helps to cool the bearings and flushes away particles of dirt.

Several types of metal are used as bearing material. The bearing should have sufficient load-carrying capacity, and it should be fatigue and corrosion-resistant; also, it should have embedability, conformability, and long life.

Loading of bearings varies greatly. Connecting-rod and main bearings, for example, are subjected to loading from inertial and centrifugal forces caused by the crank and piston and rod movements plus combustion pressures.

Factors in bearing design include bearing locking, spread, crush, oil clearance, oil-hole location, and eccentricity. In press-fitted bushings, metal displacement must be considered. The journal geometry and finish, as well as oil flow over the bearing, have a great effect on bearing life.

Bearings may fail for many reasons, not all of which are due to a fault in the bearing. They will fail from a lack of oil, from fatigue, dirt in the oil, tapered journal, radii ride, improper seating, or ridging of the bearing.

The basic considerations in the design of a crankshaft are strength, rigidity, and balance. Achieving proper balance means locating masses of metal in the crankshaft counterweights that balance the inertial and centrifugal forces of the crank and piston and rod combination. Design balancing the crankshaft can be done by vector analysis or by computer.

A variety of torsional-vibration dampers have been used, but the purpose of all of them has been to damp out torsional vibration in the crankshaft that is induced by the power strokes. The modern damper consists of a metal ring suspended in the crankshaft pulley through a flexible medium such as rubber or a viscous-silicone liquid.

Vibration-inhibiting mountings are used to mount the engine. They prevent undue stresses on the engine block from the twisting of the frame. They largely prevent engine vibration from passing to the car frame and on to the driver and passengers.

REFERENCES

1. Willi, A. B., Jr., Bearings and Lubrication, Engineering Know-How in Engine Design, SAE special publication SP 122, 1954.

2. Engine Bearing Service Manual, 7th ed., Federal-Mogul Service Division of Federal-Mogul-Bower Bearing, Inc.

3. Willi, A. B., Jr., and R. F. Jacobs, Automotive Engine Bearings, Engine Bearings, SAE special publication SP 274, 1965.

4. Robertson, J. M., Aluminum-on-Steel Bearings Alter Design Practice, Engine Bearings, SAE special publication SP 274, 1965.

5. Gross, W., and A. W. Hussmann, Forces in the Main Bearings of Multicylinder Engines, SAE (Society of Automotive Engineers) 660756, 1966 (paper).

6. Keinath, R. L., H. G. Sood, and W. J. Polkinghorne, Chevrolet Turbo-Jet Engine, SAE (Society of Automotive Engineers) 660340, 1966 (paper).

7. DeHart, A. O., and J. O. Smiley, Imperfect Journal Geometry—Its Effect on Sleeve Bearing Performance, Engine Bearings, SAE special publication SP 274, 1965.

8. Crandall, J. G., Oldsmobile's Computer Application to V-8 Crankshaft Design, SAE (Society of Automotive Engineers) 660352, 1966 (paper).

9. Niles, D. E., Crankshafts Should be Broken in the Laboratory Instead of the Engine, Engineering Know-How in Engine Design, SAE special publication SP-256, 1964.

10. Rumsey, D. R., The Viscous Torsional Vibration Damper, Engineering Know-How in Engine Design, SAE special publication SP-163, 1959.

11. Charles, J. P., and M. R. McKellar, Pontiac's New Four-Cylinder Tempest Engine, SAE (Society of Automotive Engineers) 307E, January, 1961.

12. Sherrick, J. W., and B. A. Kindgren, Engine Mountings for Vibration Control, Engineering Know-How in Engine Design, SAE special publication SP-163, 1959.

QUESTIONS

1. *Describe the characteristics of a well-designed connecting rod.*
2. *Why do modern engines use as many main bearings as are technically feasible?*
3. *What three functions does the oil have in circulating through the bearing clearances?*
4. *What are advantages of the modern precision-insert bearing?*
5. *List six basic bearing requirements and explain them.*
6. *What would be the instantaneous centrifugal force acting on the crankpin bearing at 4,000 rpm if the effective weight of the connecting rod, acting centrifugally, were 12 ounces and the crankpin offset were 2 inches?*

7. What would be the inertial load imposed by a 2-pound piston moving in a 4-inch stroke at 4,000 rpm?

8. What is meant by bearing crush and spread?

9. In regard to journal geometry, explain lobing and fuzz and their effects on bearing life.

10. What would be the advantage of making bearings slightly eccentric?

11. Describe various types of bearing failure and their causes.

12. What are the basic considerations in crankshaft design?

13. What is the purpose of the counterweights on the crankshaft?

14. What are the two limiting dimensions of counterweights?

15. Explain, in a general way, how to design counterweights for a crankshaft.

16. Explain the advantages of the oversquare engine.

17. Describe different methods of testing crankshafts.

18. What is the purpose of torsional-vibration dampers as used on engine crankshafts?

19. Describe the construction of a typical torsional-vibration damper.

20. What are the six degrees or modes of freedom of a body free to move in any direction?

21. What are four good reasons for attaching the engine to the car frame with flexible mountings?

Valve Trains

CHAPTER **15**

We have already described L-head and I-head valve trains (§98 and 99); in this chapter we continue the discussion, with special emphasis on the design of the valve-train components. We will deal mainly with I-head valve trains because most automotive engines are of this type, and, furthermore, this valve train is more complex and thus more interesting. Also, this chapter will discuss overhead-camshaft (OHC, SOHC, and DOHC) engines and engines using three or four valves per cylinder.

§192. L-head vs. I-head We have mentioned previously that the I-head engine has displaced the L-head engine in the modern automobile. The major reason for this is that the I-head engine can be built to have considerably higher compression ratios than the L-head engine. Figure 15-1 shows why. The L-head engine has to have a certain minimum volume into which the two valves can move. There must be sufficient space around the valves when they are open to permit free passage of gas. This volume plus the necessary minimum volume above the piston are the total clearance volume of the cylinder. It cannot be reduced below a certain minimum, and this minimum fixes the ultimate compression ratio of the engine. The L-head engine also has the disadvantage of having a much longer flame-travel path, which increases the possibility of knocking and requires a large quench area (see §132). Also, the high s/v (surface-to-volume) ratio (§139) makes the L-head a dirtier engine insofar as the exhaust gas is concerned.

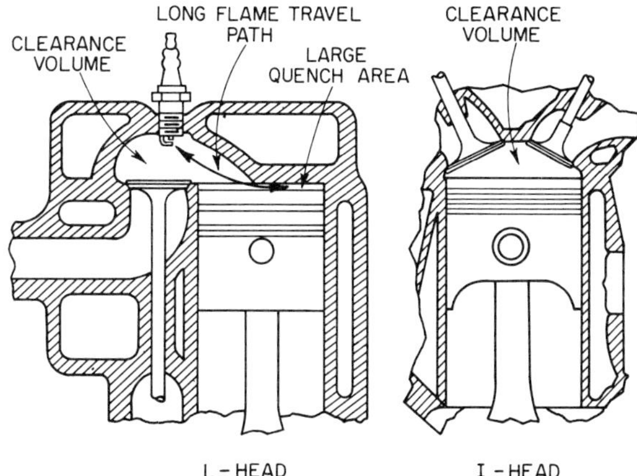

Fig. 15-1. Comparison of L-head and I-head combustion chambers and valve arrangements.

On the other hand, the I-head engine can be designed to have a much smaller clearance volume inasmuch as the valves and pistons are both working into the same general area. Many pistons have relief notches cut in their heads or are dished to give the valves space to move into when the piston is at or near TDC (top dead center) and one or the other valves is open (Fig. 12-12). With this smaller clearance volume, the compression ratio can be higher. (The advantages of higher compression ratios have been noted previously.)

In addition, because the valves can be made larger in the I-head engine, and because of the shorter paths that the incoming air-fuel mixture and the outgoing exhaust gases must travel, the volumetric efficiency of the I-head engine can be higher. Also, the s/v ratio of the I-head engine is lower than that of the L-head engine. As noted in §139, a large s/v ratio, as in the L-head engine, results in a larger percentage of unburned gasoline in the exhaust gases. Not only does this contribute to smog, but also the thermal efficiency of the engine is lower with a high s/v ratio.

Of course, one advantage of the L-head engine is its relative simplicity. This engine does not need push rods, rocker arms, and rocker-arm supports. Also, there is less possibility of oil passing up through the intake-valve-stem clearance into the combustion chamber. This is more of a problem in I-head engines, particularly those with high compression ratios, as will be discussed later.

§193. Valve and valve-train requirements[1] The valve train must open and close the valves in correct relationship to the events taking place in the engine cylinders. The valves must respond quickly to the valve-train actions, and they must seal against the compression and combustion pressures and temperatures. Also, they must continue to do this for millions of cycles. An exhaust valve in an engine that has successfully gone 100,000 miles, for example, is required to live through 150 to 200 million cycles of opening and closing, taking temperatures of up to 1400°F, seating and sealing satisfactorily with every closure, moving up and down in its guide as much as 3,000 miles, and taking high impact loading on the stem and on the valve head with every cycle.

Yet valves in a properly designed system can live through all this punishment. A good valve design will seal effectively on the valve seat, have sufficient stem rigidity to minimize stem flexure, have light weight for minimum inertia, be heavy enough in cross section for effective heat transfer, and be made of a material that can stand up under the pressures, temperatures, and impact pounding on the stem and head to which the valve is subjected.

Exhaust-valve temperature is one of the most critical factors in valve design and operation.[2,3] Figure 15-2 shows the heat input and output of an exhaust valve. Note that most of the heat enters through the top of the head, and most of it passes out through the valve seat. A smaller amount enters through the fillet under the head, and a smaller amount exits through the valve guide. A typical graph of the temperatures and heat flow in an exhaust valve is shown in Fig. 15-3.

Location, size, and shape of the valves are very important because these factors determine to a considerable extent the volumetric efficiency of the engine. The valves must be of adequate size for good gas flow past them and thus for good volumetric efficiency. But the valve ports also play a very important role in volumetric efficiency (§208). The relation of the valves to the valve ports, as well as the port configurations, must be carefully worked out to secure optimum operation.

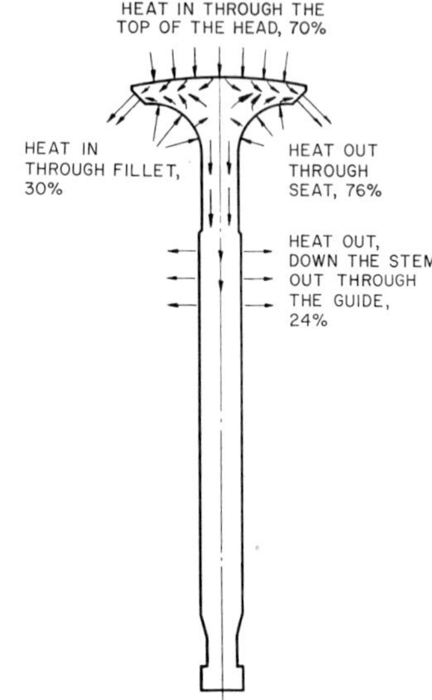

Fig. 15-2. Heat input and rejection of an exhaust valve. (*Eaton Manufacturing Company*)

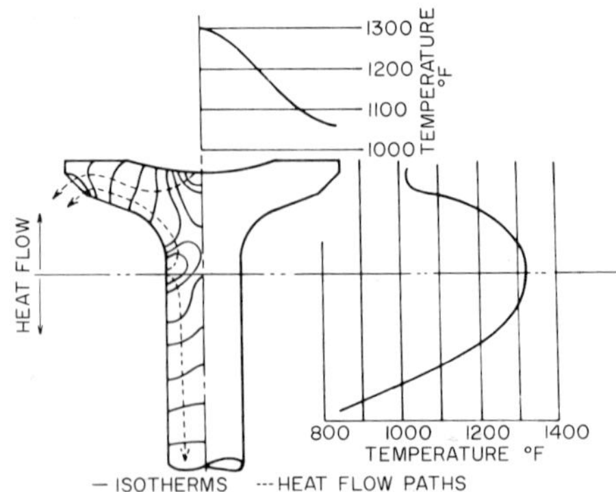

Fig. 15-3. Graph of temperatures and heat flow in an exhaust valve. Isotherms are lines joining points having the same temperature. (*TRW Valve Division, Thompson, Ramo, Wooldridge, Inc.*)

Some high-performance, heavy-duty engines have three or four valves per cylinder to improve engine breathing, volumetric efficiency (particularly at higher engine speeds), and thus engine output. With three valves per cylinder, two are intake valves and one is an exhaust valve. With four valves per cylinder, there are two intake valves and two exhaust valves. Figures 4-26, 4-42, 4-43, and 4-45 show different engines which have four valves per cylinder. Note that some of these have overhead camshafts.

Location of the intake valve plays a part in the turbulence of the compressed air-fuel mixture and thus in the type of combustion process that ensues after ignition.

§194. Valve and valve-train design[1] Probably the first thing the engine designer thinks about when he focuses his attention on the valve and valve ports for his new engine is to make them of sufficient size and to locate them properly so as to achieve high volumetric efficiency. Next, he must make sure that the valves will have the proper motion. Size, location, and motion determine to a great extent the efficiency of the engine. Also, of course, he must consider durability—the ability of the valves and valve train to live in the engine.

As with most other engine components, the final design of the valves and valve train depends to a considerable extent on engine operating tests. However, much preliminary work can be done prior to the operating tests. Generally speaking, the engine designer's past experience, laboratory tests of various valve-train components, and mathematical analysis provide adequate guidelines so that the prototype engines are usually fairly close to the optimum design.

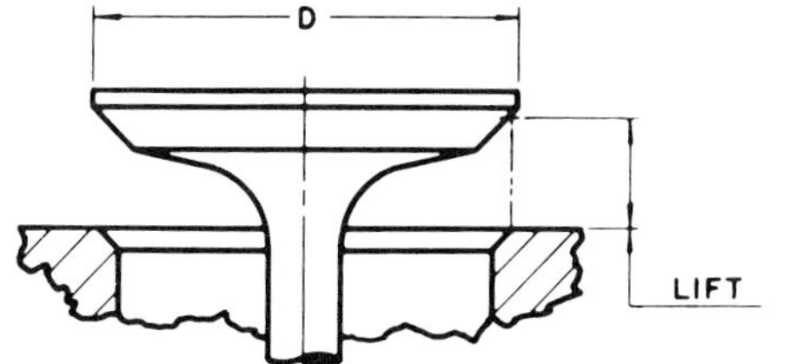

Fig. 15-4. Valve lift. (*TRW Valve Division, Thompson, Ramo, Wooldridge, Inc.*)

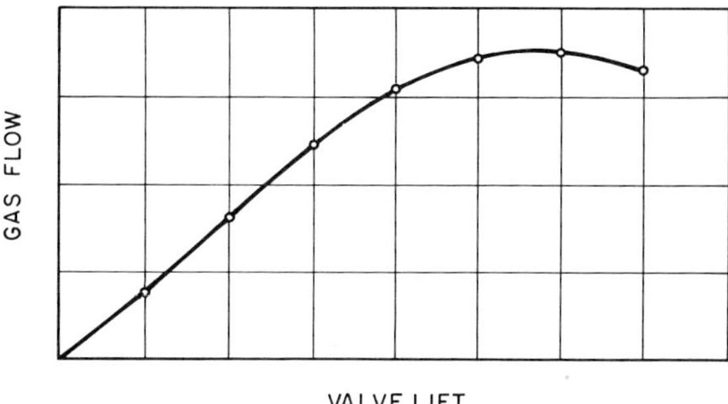

Fig. 15-5. Relationship between gas flow and valve lift. (*TRW Valve Division, Thompson, Ramo, Wooldridge, Inc.*)

At an early stage in the design work, layouts are made of the valves and valve ports so that their proper proportions and relative positions can be tentatively established. This work requires a knowledge of gas-flow behavior in complex passages, such as between the valve and valve seat. This, of course, is related to the amount of valve movement, or valve lift. The following articles examine this and other factors that must be taken into consideration by the valve-train designer.

§195 Valve lift Valve lift is the amount of movement that the valve undergoes as it moves from the closed to the opened position (Fig. 15-4). You might think that the greater the valve lift, the better the gas flow. Not so. The curve in Fig. 15-5 shows what happened during a typical test. At operating speeds, the gas flow improved as the valve lift increased, up to a point. Then, with further lift, the gas flow dropped off. Apparently, up to the critical point, the curvature of the fillet under the valve head helped to direct the gas through the port. With further lift, this effect, though slight, was lost, and gas flow decreased a little. Tests have shown that maximum flow occurs at the point where the lift is approximately 25 percent of the valve-head diameter. That this is generally recognized by engine designers is evident when we check the specifications of modern engines. In 1965 automotive engines, for example, lifts averaged 23 percent of the head diameter for intake valves and 26 percent of the head diameter for exhaust valves.

Changing the curvature of the fillet under the valve head will also influence gas flow (see Figs. 15-22 and 15-23).

An interesting confirmation of the importance of valve position in the valve port was made by Ford engineers in their design work on the 427GT V-8 high-performance engine. They found that many intake-port designs will allow more air flow with the intake valve in place and open between 0.500 and 0.600 inch than with the valve *completely removed.*

§196. Intake valve and gas flow The speed of gas flow as related to intake-valve size is also very important. The family of curves shown in Fig. 15-6 illustrates this. These curves were developed in tests of 10 different combinations of valve sizes and lifts at varying speeds. Note that the curves relate volumetric efficiency with *mach number.* In this case, mach number is the ratio of the speed of sound in the gas to the speed with which the gas moves through the port. As you know, the speed of sound varies with the density of the gas, and so the ratio, or mach number, is the valid figure to use here. The curves show that volumetric efficiency drops off sharply as the inlet mach number goes above 0.5. At mach 1.0, when the speed of the gas is equal to the speed of sound through the gas, the volumetric efficiency is down around 60 percent.

The lesson to be learned from Fig. 15-6 is that the intake valve should be of sufficient size so that the mach number will not exceed about 0.5 at the rated speed of the engine. In other words, if the valve is made smaller, the gas speed must be greater to achieve the same volumetric efficiency. However, as the mach number increases (gas speed approaches speed of sound in the gas), the gas has, in effect, greater difficulty in moving smoothly through the port. At mach 1.0, which is sonic speed (speed of sound through the gas), the gas no longer flows smoothly. As a result, at the higher gas speeds the volumetric efficiency falls off rapidly.

§197. Exhaust valve and gas flow Volumetric efficiency is much less affected by the size of the exhaust-valve port. The curves in Fig. 15-7 illustrate this. These three curves relate exhaust-valve-port volumetric efficiency and mach number for three different sizes of exhaust-valve ports. Here, the relationship shown is not direct, but is the ratio of the exhaust-port area to the intake-port area (or γ). You can see from the curves that varying the exhaust-flow area from 0.51 to 1.79 times the intake-flow area has little effect on volumetric efficiency for the lower mach numbers. Standard practice, however, is to make the exhaust valve large enough to give an exhaust-flow area at least 0.6 times the size of the intake-flow area, or larger.

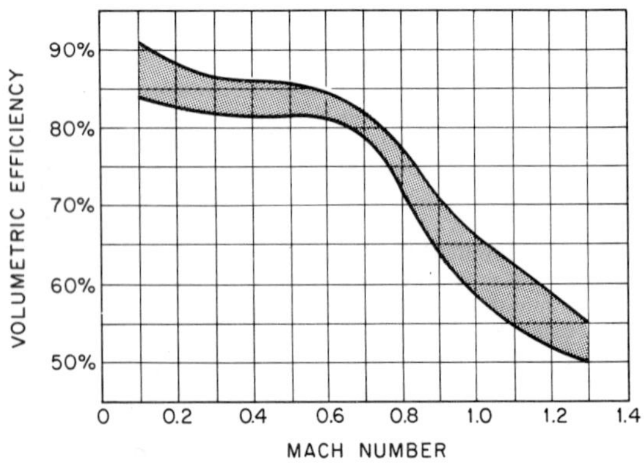

Fig. 15-6. Relationship between volumetric efficiency of intake-valve-port area and mach number. (*TRW Valve Division, Thompson, Ramo, Wooldridge, Inc.*)

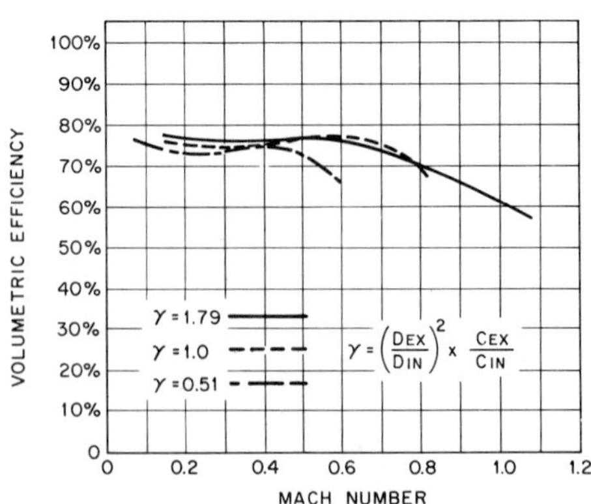

Fig. 15-7. Relationship between γ and volumetric efficiency. γ is the ratio of the exhaust-port area to the intake-port area. (*TRW Valve Division, Thompson, Ramo, Wooldridge, Inc.*)

The exhaust-port area is a much less critical factor in volumetric efficiency than the intake-port area and for a good reason. The maximum pressure on the gas flowing into the cylinder through the intake port is atmospheric, or about 15 psi (pounds per square inch), unless the engine is supercharged. But the pressure on the gas flowing out through the exhaust port is applied by the up-moving piston. Thus, the exhaust valve could be made quite small and still work. But this would not be desirable because higher pressures would be required to exhaust the gas, and this would result in some energy loss (termed in this case "pumping loss"). Furthermore, the smaller exhaust valve and valve seat would be worked much harder and at higher temperatures, resulting in short valve and seat life.

§198. Valve size The preceding discussion explains how to determine *minimum* valve sizes. As a practical matter, the valves are made as large as possible, consistent with other design factors. Let us again look at some averages for 1965 automobile engines. In these engines, the intake-valve-head diameters averaged 42 to 48 percent of the cylinder-bore diameter, and the exhaust valves averaged about 38 percent of the cylinder-bore diameter. Thus, exhaust valves averaged about 82 to 88 percent of the diameters of the intake valves.

We should like to repeat here that, as a general rule, increasing intake-valve size increases volumetric efficiency but decreases turbulence. The reverse is also true: decreasing intake-valve size decreases volumetric efficiency but increases turbulence. The designer must select the proper compromise between these two factors.

§199. Valve-face angle In the early or final stages of valve movement, as the valve begins to open or is nearing the closed position, the valve-face angle has a great influence on gas flow through the opening between the valve face and valve seat. During these early and late stages, the flow area is approximately proportional to the cosine of the valve-face angle (Fig. 15-8), or cos α. If the angle is

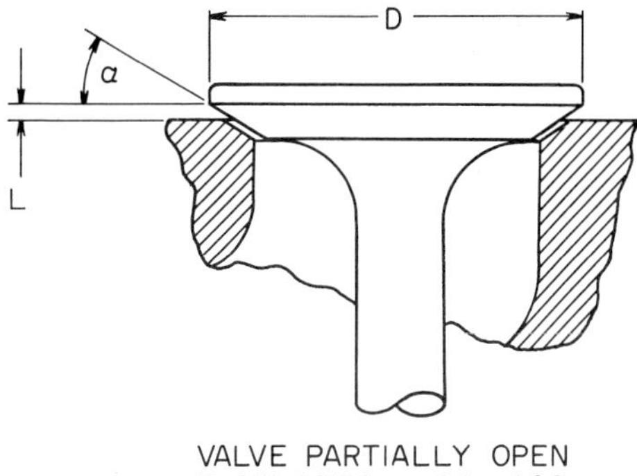

Fig. 15-8. During the early and late stages of valve opening and closing, the flow area is approximately proportional to the cosine of the valve-face angle. (*TRW Valve Division, Thompson, Ramo, Wooldridge, Inc.*)

large, the cosine and gas flow are small. But if the angle is small, the cosine is large and the gas flow greater. To say it another way, with a large angle, less space appears between the valve and valve seat for any given valve lift. But with a small angle, more space appears for the same valve lift.

Of course, after the valve lift has increased beyond a certain amount, the governing factor in gas flow is valve lift alone. That is, the valve face has moved so far away from the valve seat that it no longer has much influence in gas flow. In some critical applications, where gas flow is of great importance, face angles of intake valves may be as low as 15 to 30 degrees. Generally, however, other considerations are more important, and, thus, on most passenger cars, a valve-face angle of 45 degrees for both intake and exhaust valves is used.

One reason for standardizing on 45 degrees for both valves is that this simplifies manufacturing and servicing procedures. No extra tooling or procedures are required as would be the case if two different angles were used.

There are other factors to be considered in determining valve-face angles, however. These include seating pressure and cylinder-head distortion.

Seating pressure must be sufficient to provide a good seal and adequate heat transfer from the valve face to the valve seat. As already noted (see Fig. 15-2), about 75 percent of the valve-heat rejection takes place through the valve seat. Good seating is essential to prevent excessive and ruinous valve temperatures (exhaust valve). Seating pressure increases with increasing valve-face angle, other factors being the same. You can understand this by considering how a fairly large valve-face angle produces a sort of wedging action as the valve comes down on the valve seat. This also produces some wiping action, so that deposits on the valve face or seat, in effect, are wiped away to permit good seating. To visualize this, consider the action of a cork being put into a bottle.

Another problem is that of cylinder-head and thus valve-seat distortion, which arises from temperature and pressure changes, uneven cooling, differences in cylinder-head-bolt tightness, and other factors. [This is covered in more detail in the article on valve-seat design (§210).] The important point here is that a low valve-face angle is less sensitive to cylinder-head distortion than a large valve-face angle. At the extreme, a flat-faced valve would seat normally even though the valve seat was shifted to one side or the other, or if it went out of round. A 45-degree face, however, would be seriously affected by shifts or distortions of the valve seat. With a lateral shift, or deck tilt, one side of the valve face would strike the seat before the other (Fig. 15-9). In addition to producing poor seating, the lateral flexing, imposed on the valve stem as it bends in an effort to normalize seating, might ultimately cause the stem to break. Also, the valve face and seat could be damaged by the uneven loading. Of course, it is obvious that poor seating will result from out-of-round distortion of the valve seat. Poor seating, from whatever cause, can produce leakage erosion between the face and seat, which leads to exhaust-valve burning and rapid failure.

Thus, it can be seen that the valve-face angle is a compromise. A low angle improves gas flow as the valve starts to open or in the closing phase. A low angle also reduces the effect of seat distortion. But a large angle is desirable for high seating pressure and good valve seating.

§200. Interference angle To improve seating, some engine specifications call for an "interference angle" at the valve seat (Fig. 15-10). The valve seat is ground to an angle that is between 1/4 to 1 degree greater than the valve face. This gives a somewhat greater pressure at the outer edge of the seat for effective seating. However, with Stellite-faced exhaust valves and induction-hardened, exhaust-valve seats, the angles must be the same, as shown in Fig. 15-11.

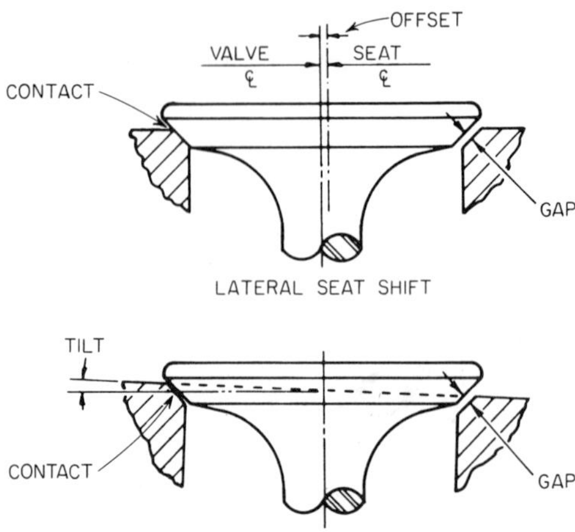

Fig. 15-9. If the valve seat shifts laterally, or if the deck tilts, the valve will not seat properly. (*TRW Valve Division, Thompson, Ramo, Wooldridge, Inc.*)

§201. Valve-head proportions With other factors determined as noted previously, the valve-head

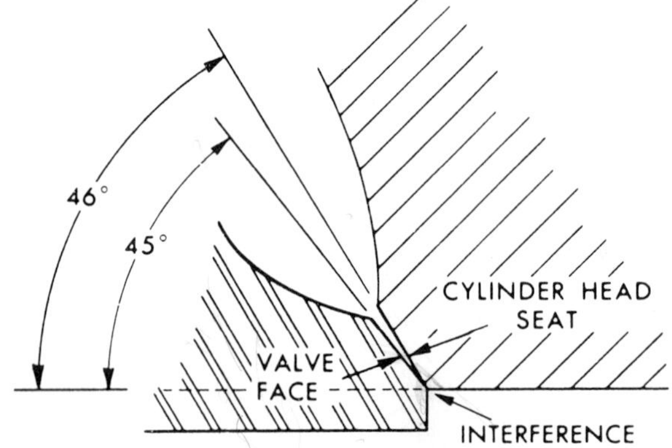

Fig. 15-10. Interference angle between valve face and valve seat. (*Chevrolet Motor Division of General Motors Corporation*)

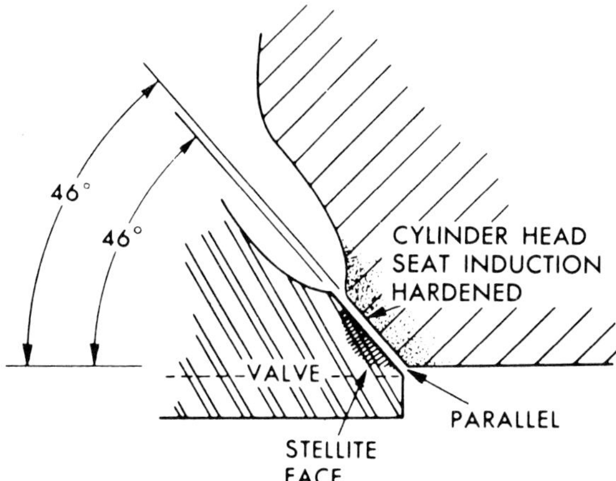

Fig. 15-11. For Stellite-faced exhaust valves and induction-hardened exhaust-valve seats, parallel faces are recommended. (*Chevrolet Motor Division of General Motors Corporation*)

proportions can be established (Fig. 15-12). Normal practice calls for making the diameter of the head about 1.15 times the port diameter, with approximately 0.015- to 0.030-inch overhang above and below the seat. This provides for full valve-face-to-seat seating. The margin and radius are also important because sharp edges should be avoided. Sharp edges will become hotter and could be the cause of preignition and rumble. The arrangement shown also provides some leeway for valve refacing in service in case an engine requires a valve job.

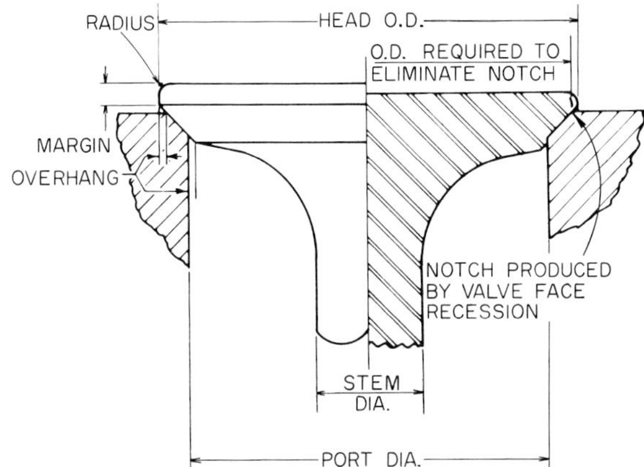

Fig. 15-12. Valve-head proportions. (*TRW Valve Division, Thompson, Ramo, Wooldridge, Inc.*)

The underside of the valve head should have proper curvature so that gas flows smoothly through the valve port and around the valve.

§202. Valve-stem size The diameter of the valve stem is determined by exhaust-valve-durability requirements. Usually, this diameter is made to be about 25 percent of the valve-head diameter. The intake-valve stem is given the same diameter so that the same tools can be used for valves in both manufacturing and service. Stem diameters have been standardized. For sizes from $1/4$ to $5/8$ inches, the sizes increase in $1/16$-inch steps. Larger sizes increase in $1/8$-inch steps.

§203. Valve-head shape There are two schools of thought regarding valve-head shape. Some engineers believe that the head section should be rigid and unyielding, with the head having a substantial thickness supported on a large fillet. Others believe that the head should be flexible, having a thin head and small fillet, with the head deeply cupped (Fig. 15-13). This shape, it is asserted, will conform to any seat distortion, so that good seating will be established even under very adverse conditions. A number of studies would seem to indicate that the most desirable shape, considering all factors, lies somewhere in between the rigid and the elastic. The most important factors include effective sealing, low stress, low temperature, and long life.

One series of tests was run with different types of valve heads and the two basic types of seat distortion (deck tilt and elliptical distortion). With deck tilt, the seat tilts out of perpendicular with

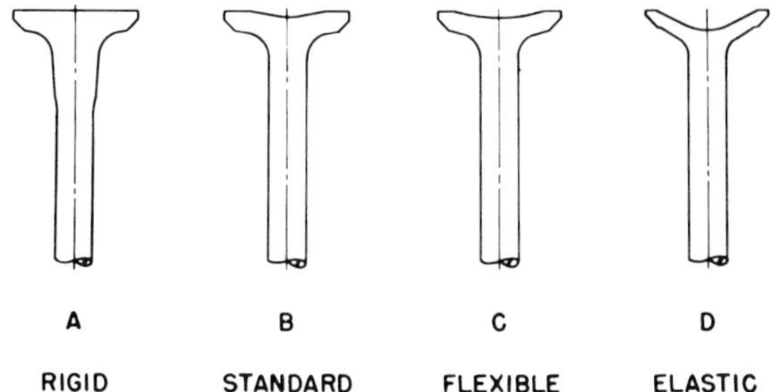

Fig. 15-13. Valve-head shapes. (*TRW Valve Division, Thompson, Ramo, Wooldridge, Inc.*)

the valve axis so that one side of the valve face strikes the valve seat first. What may happen here, if tilt is not great, is that the clearance of the valve stem in the valve guide is enough to allow the valve to tip and thereby achieve good seating without valve-head or stem bending. One test showed that, with a stem-to-guide clearance of 0.0015 inch, an eccentricity of 0.006 inch could be tolerated so that good seating still resulted. Then, the test was tried without clearance, and it was found that the stem bent sufficiently to allow good seating. In this case, head flexibility would not offer any seating improvement.

However, when the seat distorts elliptically, then the matter of head flexibility does become important. With an elliptical seat, the valve head makes contact at two diametrically opposite points first. If the head is flexible, then it will distort elliptically so that good seating results.

It should be remembered, however, that whenever metal is loaded enough to cause bending, then those areas where bending occurs come under high stress. Repeated stressing can cause fatigue cracks to start, so that a break will ultimately occur. Thus, the overall engine design, as well as the design of the valve head and seat, must be such as to minimize undue bending of the valve head or stem.

Another important aspect of valve-head shape is the matter of temperature. The thinner, elastic head, with less cross-section to carry away heat, runs hotter. Figure 15-14 relates head and upper stem temperatures for the standard (B) and the elastic (D) heads illustrated in Fig. 15-13. Note that the center of the head of the elastic valve runs above 1300°F while the fillet area below the head runs well over 1400°F. The higher temperatures are undesirable because they reduce the strength of the metal and shorten valve and seat life.

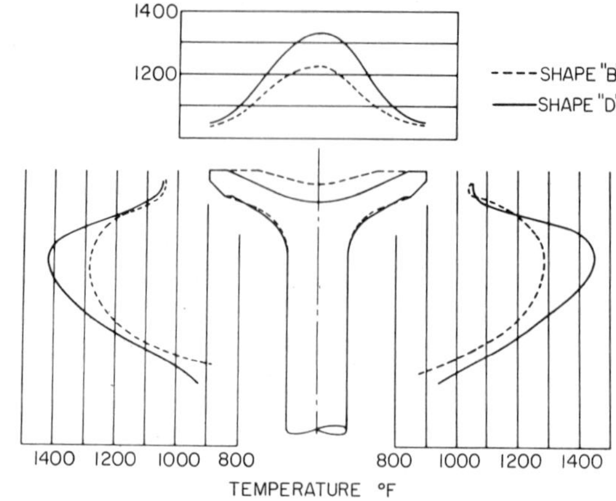

Fig. 15-14. Valve-head temperature profiles. (*TRW Valve Division, Thompson, Ramo, Wooldridge, Inc.*)

§204. Valve materials A variety of materials have been used for valves. Usually, the engine designer is called upon to select the least expensive material, from both the material- and the manufacturing-cost standpoints, that will operate satisfactorily in his engine. Various factors must be considered, including temperatures, impact loading (as valves close), stem-wear rate, tip-wear rate, and corrosion.

The exhaust valve, because it is worked much harder in terms of temperature and the corrosive effects of combustion products, has more critical material requirements than the intake valve.

All metals show a strength loss and a reduced resistance to corrosion with temperature rise. It is therefore desirable, in engine-design work, to take all reasonable steps to assure low exhaust-valve and valve-seat temperatures. If design or operating specifications are such as to make it likely that the exhaust valve and seat will have to withstand higher temperatures, then it will be necessary to select valve materials that will withstand these higher temperatures. As a rule, however, engineers are inclined to blame inadequate valve-seat cooling or seat distortion, whatever the cause, for valve temperatures that go above about 1500°F. Inadequate seat cooling or distortion could result from faulty design or from inadequate or improper service (accumulation of corrosion in water jackets, incorrect cylinder-head-bolt tightening, and so on).

Let us see what happens to valve materials at elevated temperatures. Figure 15-15 shows how the strength of a widely used exhaust-valve material drops off as its temperature goes up. The

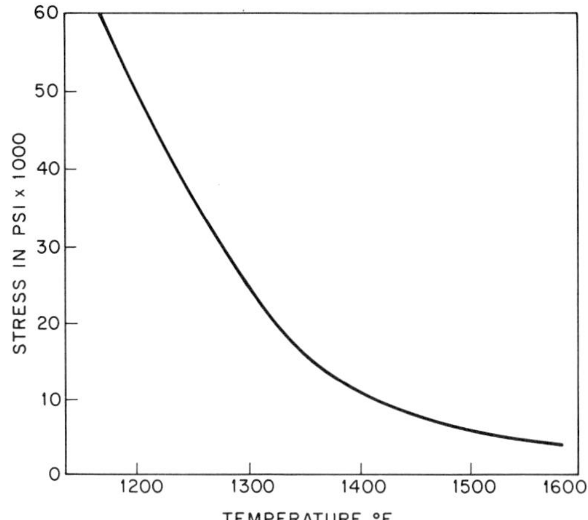

Fig. 15-15. Effect of temperature on strength of material. (*TRW Valve Division, Thompson, Ramo, Wooldridge, Inc.*)

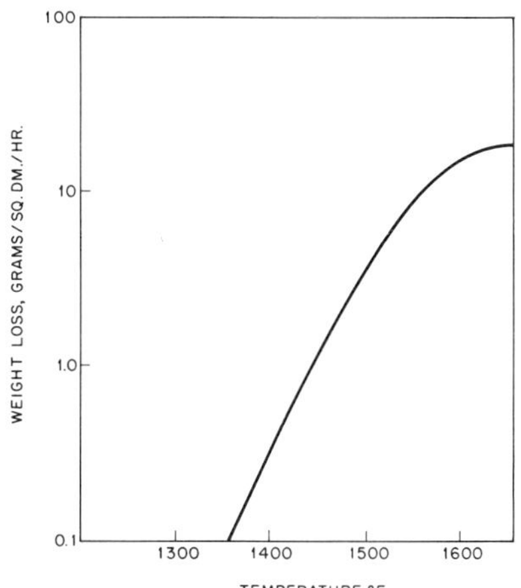

Fig. 15-16. Effect of temperature on PbO corrosion (*TRW Valve Division, Thompson, Ramo, Wooldridge, Inc.*)

curve is a plot of stress rupture at various temperatures, showing that the material will rupture under a stress of about 60,000 psi at 1200°F, but at 1400°F it will stress rupture at only about 15,000 psi. An exhaust valve of this material would give satisfactory service life if the valve temperatures never exceeded about 1300°F; however, as temperatures went above this, life expectancy would fall off sharply.

As to corrosion, Fig. 15-16 shows how PbO (lead oxide) corrosion increases with temperature. Lead, a constituent of tetraethyl lead, corrodes the exhaust valve when in the oxide form. At 1350°F, the curve shows a weight loss from one widely used valve material of 0.1 grams per square decimeter exposed per hour of exposure. An increase of only 25° in the temperature of the metal more than doubles the corrosion rate, while increasing the temperature to 1400°F increases the corrosion rate more than four times (to about 0.45 gram).

Obviously, then, temperature is a major limiting factor in the selection of valve material. If valves must live at higher temperatures, for example, in high-performance and truck engines, then metals that can withstand these higher temperatures must be used. For instance, exhaust valves in some high-performance engines are forged from high-chromium and manganese stainless steel and have, in addition, a tungsten-cobalt facing on the seating area.

Most automotive engines, however, use valves of austenitic steel, which gives an average life expectancy of more than 60,000 miles under normal operating conditions. This relatively long life has been achieved by careful attention to cooling of the valve seats and guides, improved oils and lubricating methods, and detailed valve-train-dynamics studies, out of which have come improved designs that reduce impact loading of the valve face and seat.

§205. Sodium valves For especially difficult applications, sodium-cooled exhaust valves may be used. This type of valve has a hollow stem which is partly filled with metallic sodium (Fig. 15-17). Sodium melts at 208°F. Thus, at engine operating temperatures, the sodium is liquid; it circulates between the head and stem, carrying heat from the head to the cooler stem area, from which it passes on to the valve guide and water jacket. Tests have shown, in some engines, a reduction of up to 350°F in valve-head operating temperatures with sodium-cooled valves.

§206. Valve facings As already noted, some exhaust valves for high-performance engines have facings of special alloys, such as tungsten-cobalt, which has the high-temperature properties needed

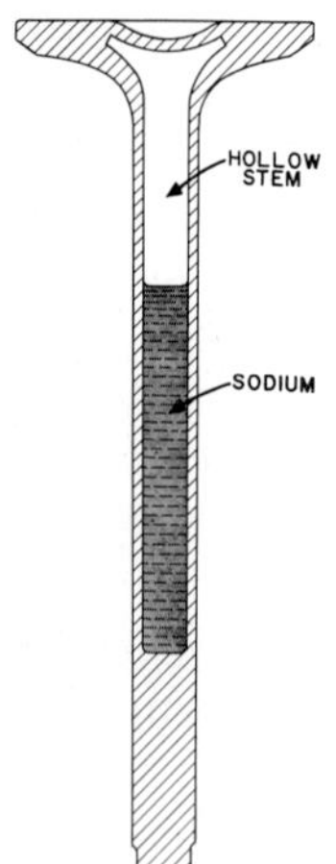

Fig. 15-17. Sectional view of a sodium-cooled valve. (*Eaton Manufacturing Company*)

in these engines. The facing is applied as a ring which is welded onto the valve head. This is much more satisfactory than making the entire valve out of the special alloy. Not only are these alloys more expensive, but also they may not have the correct properties to give normal wear in the valve-guide and valve-tip areas.

§207. Valve stems and tips High-performance valves may also have stems and tips of special alloys which are welded on. These special alloys are selected to withstand stem wear in the valve-guide area and scrubbing wear on the valve tip from the sliding motion of the rocker-arm tip moving across the valve tip (see §214).

§208. Valve-port design The valve-port design depends on several factors, including valve size and placement and cylinder-head and manifold configurations. Figure 15-18 illustrates some good design practices. There should be ample flow area for free passages of gas, but at the same time the throat depth should be no more than about 0.75 times the port diameter (in exhaust valves) to minimize the length of valve stem exposed to the hot exhaust gases. The flow passage in the cylinder head should be at least as large as that of the port so as to avoid restrictions that could reduce gas flow.

Some curious things have been found, however, regarding the intake-valve-port passages in the cylinder head. You might think that the passage should be as large as possible, with no restrictive

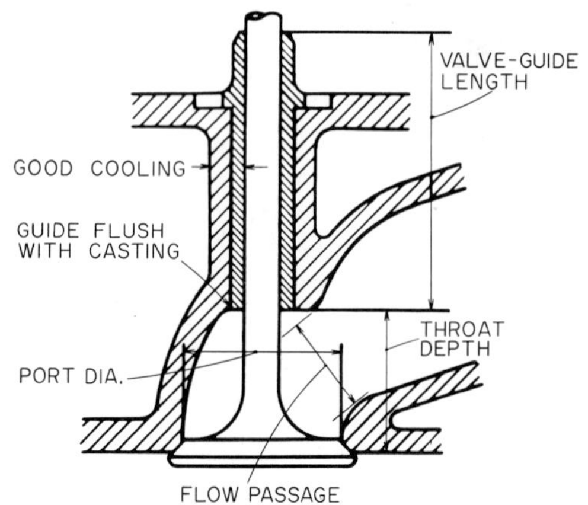

Fig. 15-18. Good practice in valve-port and valve-guide design. (*TRW Valve Division, Thompson, Ramo, Wooldridge, Inc.*)

humps. However, Fig. 15-19 shows how the manufacturer of one high-performance engine (Ford V-8) added a hump to the intake-port contour to improve gas flow and thus increase volumetric efficiency. Apparently, the hump throws the incoming gas (air-fuel mixture) toward the roof of the intake port so that it can more effectively "turn the corner" and flow evenly around the opened intake valve and into the cylinder.

1. *The Mark II-427 GT engine valve ports—a case history.* To give you an idea of how engineers often adopt new techniques in their design activities, let us look at how the Ford engineers set out to determine the best configuration for the intake- and exhaust-valve ports of their Mark II-427 GT engine.[4] The traditional method was to make drafting layouts of possible configurations and then transfer these drawings to patterns, and then to metal castings. The castings were then machined and tested on engines.

The engineers felt there was a quicker and more efficient way to design valve ports, which would be much more flexible and result in better engine performance. They started with the basic drafting layouts, as usual, but went from these directly to

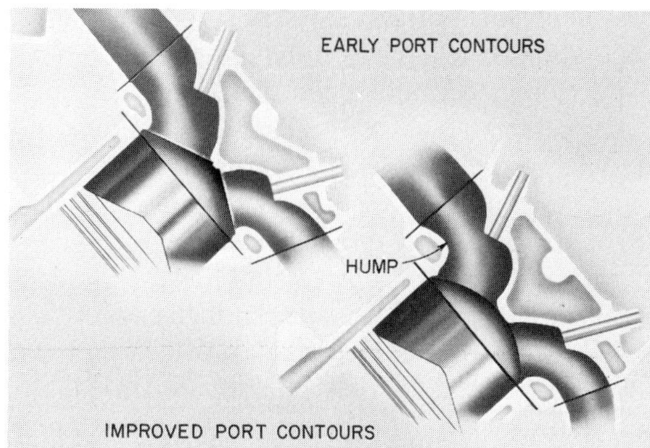

Fig. 15-19. Early and improved intake-port contours. Adding the hump improved volumetric efficiency. (*Ford Motor Company*)

a plastic flow box (Fig. 15-20). The flow box contained an intake port, an exhaust port, and a combustion chamber, all based on the drafting layouts. It was made in two parts which could be fitted together to form, in effect, the cylinder head for one cylinder, complete with valve seats, ports, and combustion chamber.

The two-part construction made it possible to add clay or grind away plastic to alter the configurations of the ports. Next, valves and valve springs were assembled in the flow box, and the assembly was mounted on a flow stand (Fig. 15-21). A dial indicator and adjusting screw were installed to permit the intake valve to be adjusted

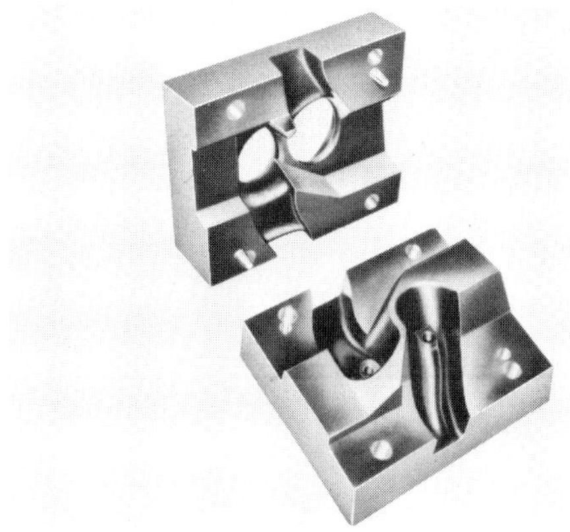

Fig. 15-20. Plastic partial-cylinder-head flow box to check air flow through valve ports. (*Ford Motor Company*)

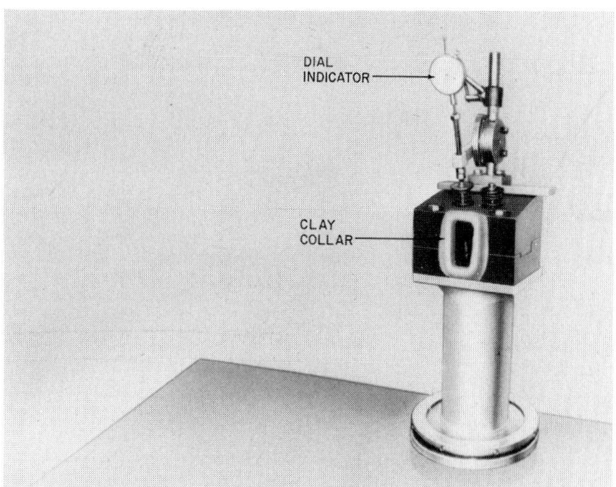

Fig. 15-21. Flow box mounted on flow stand to check air flow through valve ports. (*Ford Motor Company*)

for various openings. A collar of clay was fitted around the intake-port opening to provide for a smooth, nonturbulent air flow into the port. Then, vacuum was applied from the combustion-chamber side, and the efficiency of the intake port was measured with various valve openings.

Various changes in the port contours were tried, until finally the design shown to the right in Fig. 15-22 evolved. Note that, in this design, the floor of the port is raised, or humped, to throw the incoming air upward into the roof of the port. This design showed a great improvement over the original. But this change alone did not prove fully satisfactory, especially at high air velocities. The addition of a venturi-type ring just above the valve seat permitted a substantial increase in air flow at high air speeds. Thus, after considerable "adding to" and "taking off," the final design was reached.

At the same time that the various port contours were being tried out, engineers also tried various valve-head shapes. They took a basic valve design and ground down the back of the head. Then, they added clay to this area by putting the valve in a lathe and carefully applying the clay with a curved spatula [Fig. 15-22*a*]. By trying different shapes, the engineers were able to arrive at shapes that showed the best air flow. They were also able to

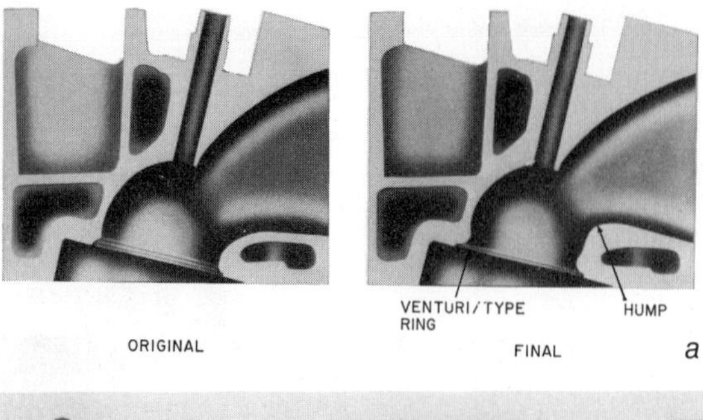

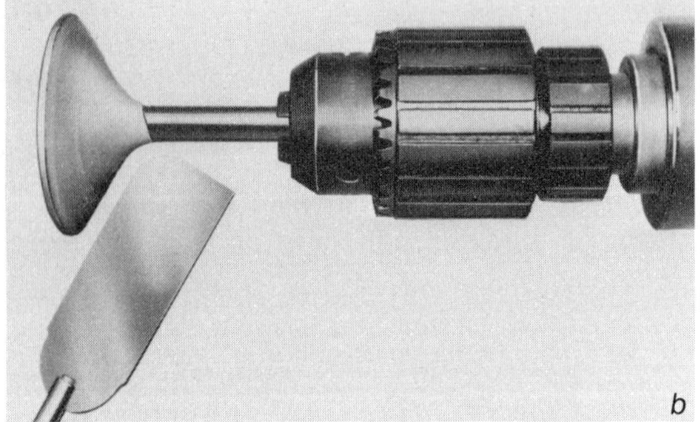

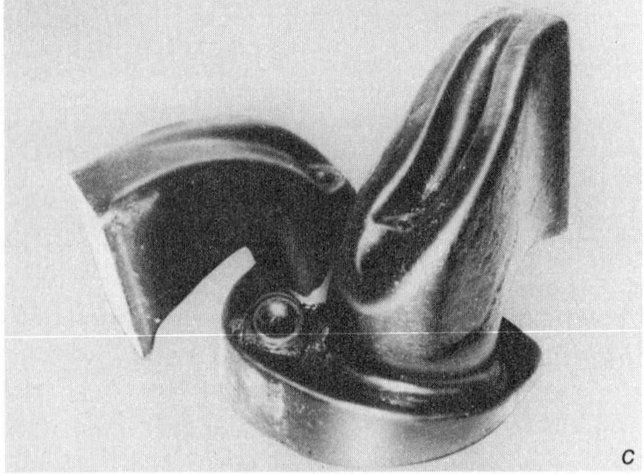

Fig. 15-22. (*a*) Original and final cylinder-head intake-port designs for the Mark II-427 GT engine; (*b*) shaping valve head for experimental testing; (*c*) rubber core made from flow box. (*Ford Motor Company*)

arrive at certain generalities about valve-head shapes. One of these was that, with a wedge combustion chamber, a relatively flat back face (back-face angle nearly 90 degrees with valve stem) was most suitable. With a hemispheric combustion chamber, an increased back-face angle flowed more air.

The exhaust port was studied in a similar manner and modified to provide optimum operation. After the two-port configurations had been finalized, a rubber compound was poured into the flow box and allowed to harden. The hardened rubber core [Fig. 15-22*b*] was then used to make the final layout of the ports. From this final layout, patterns, cores, and castings were made. Some slight loss in air-flow capacity was noted in the castings, and this loss was thought to be caused by drafting limitations in transferring the core contours to the layouts.

2. *The Chrysler solution.* The port design shown in Fig. 15-22 utilized properly located and shaped restrictions to improve air flow and volumetric efficiency. Chrysler Corporation, in the modifications their engine designers incorporated in their 1968 engines, removed restrictions to increase port areas, as shown in Fig. 15-23, and thus achieved better engine breathing and higher volumetric efficiency. To the left, modification of the intake port in the 340-cubic-inch displacement engine is shown. Note also that this modification included a change in the intake valve; the fillet under the valve head was given a considerably larger radius. Modification of the intake port for the 383- and 440-cubic-inch displacement engines is shown to the right.

In another Chrysler development—the intake and exhaust ports for their hemi-head, high-performance engine—it was found that a marked improvement in engine breathing and volumetric efficiency resulted from the addition of metal in the ports, as shown in Fig. 15-23*a*. It is obvious, from a comparison of Figs. 15-22, 15-23, and 15-23*a*, that there is no one approach to the problem of improving porting and engine breathing. Different engineers achieve their objectives by different methods. The best solution is apt to be unique, to some extent at least, for each model of engine. Note, for example, that the modifications shown in Fig. 15-23 are for a wedge-chamber engine; the modifications shown in Fig. 15-23*a* are for a hemispheric-chamber engine.

3. *Intake-valve location.* The location of the intake valve in the combustion chamber has a con-

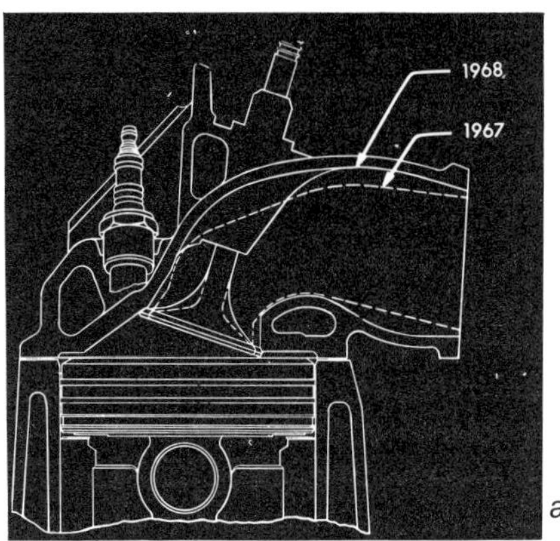

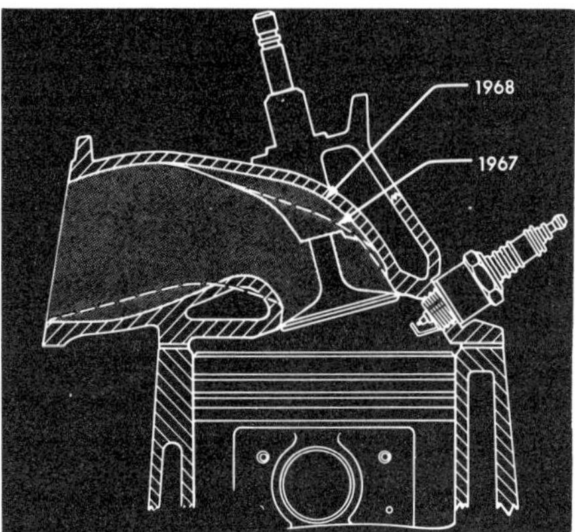

Fig. 15-23. (*a*) Cylinder-head modifications from 1967 to 1968 Chrysler-engine intake ports: *left,* 340 engine; *right,* 383 and 440 engines.

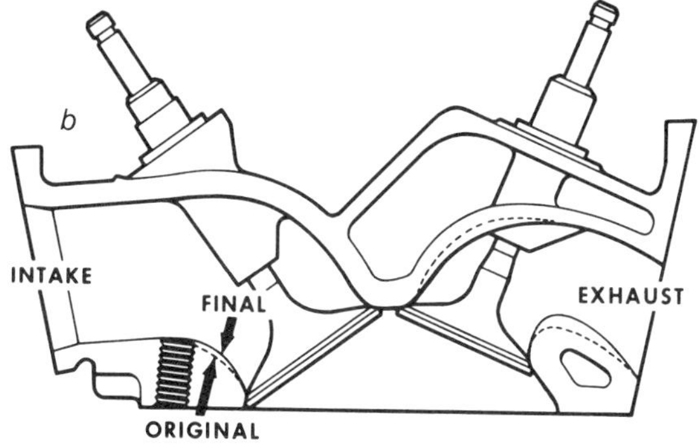

Fig. 15-23. (*b*) Development of intake and exhaust ports for the Chrysler hemi-head, high-performance V-8 engine. (*Chrysler Motors Corporation*)

siderable effect on the combustion process, as already noted in §133. If it is located so as to feed air-fuel mixture through the intake port toward the center of the combustion chamber, there will be little turbulence. But if it is located so the mixture flows in off center, then swirl and turbulence will result.

Valve ports must be so positioned as to be adequately cooled. Water jackets should be designed to surround the valve-seat areas and provide uniformly adequate water circulation around the seats. [This is discussed further in the article on valve cooling (§211).]

§209. Valve guide The valve guide is a round hole in the head (block in L-head engines) in which the valve stem moves up and down. In many engines, the valve guide is integral; that is, it is simply a hole drilled in the head. Other engines, however, use a separate valve-guide insert, which is essentially a tube press-fitted into a drilled hole in the cylinder head (Fig. 15-18). General practice is to make the guide as long as possible within design limits. It should be at least seven times the valve-stem diameter. This will minimize tipping of the valve in the guide due to the scrubbing action of the rocker-arm tip as it slides across the valve-stem tip. The valve-head end of the valve guide should be positioned as close to the valve head as possible. However, the boss projecting into the valve port, which surrounds the guide, must not be so close or so large as to obstruct the gas flow. Also, the guide should not project beyond the edge of the boss because the exposed end will either burn away (exhaust valve port) or become coated with deposits that would cause valve sticking.

It is also very important to provide adequate cooling in the valve-guide area, with the water jackets extending as far toward the valve-stem end of the guide as possible.

§210. Valve-seat design There are three interrelated factors of major importance to consider in the design of valve seats: distortion, cooling, and durability. Seat distortion reduces the area of contact between the valve face and seat, thereby raising the valve temperature and at the same time imposing bending loads on the valve stem. These conditions lead to short valve and seat life.

1. Valve-seat distortion. There are two general types of valve-seat distortion: temporary and permanent. The temporary or transient type results from combustion pressures and from temperature differentials arising from engine operation. The permanent type results from mechanical stresses that are imposed on the block and head during engine assembly, or from metal creep or permanent deformation of the engine parts.

It may sometimes seem to the engine designer that everything is working against him to cause seat distortion: stresses from temperature differentials and from combustion pressures or stresses set up by cylinder-head-bolt tightening or by uneven seat cooling. Careful design will minimize these distortions. For instance, it is important to position the valve seats in such a manner as to have adequate coolant flow all around the seat. This means that the intake and exhaust valves and

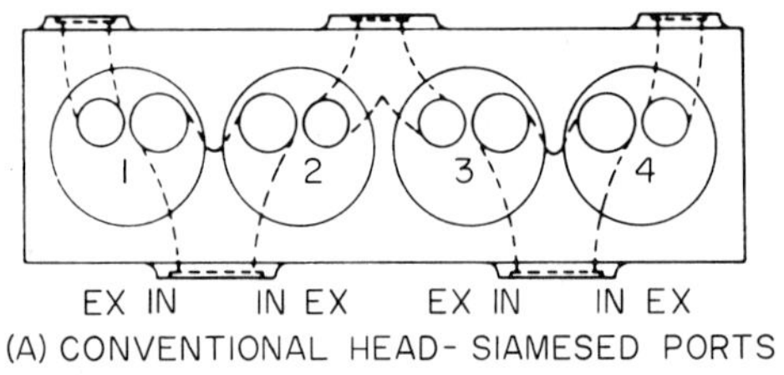

(A) CONVENTIONAL HEAD-SIAMESED PORTS

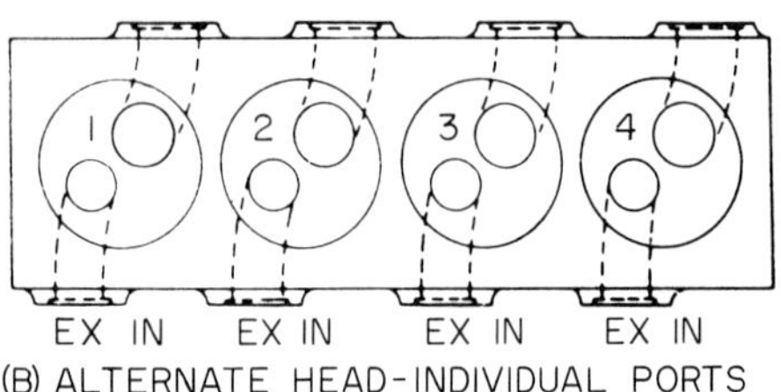

(B) ALTERNATE HEAD-INDIVIDUAL PORTS

Fig. 15-24. Two basic valve-seat arrangements: siamesed ports and individual ports. (*TRW Valve Division, Thompson, Ramo, Wooldridge, Inc.*)

the spark-plug boss must be sufficiently separated so that adequate water jacketing can be provided around each.

Two basic valve-seat arrangements are shown in Fig. 15-24. In some engines, the valve ports are "siamesed." That is, they are located so that two valves use the same manifold branch. (The word "siamese" comes from the Siamese twins who were born physically joined together.) The top half of Figure 15-24 illustrates siamesed valve ports. Note that intake-valve ports for cylinders 1 and 2 are connected to a common intake-manifold branch and ports 3 and 4 are connected to a second branch. Note also that, while the exhaust ports for cylinders 1 and 4 are connected to individual branches of the exhaust manifold, exhaust-valve ports 2 and 3 are siamesed. This arrangement, with two exhaust-valve ports being side by side, produces greater seat and valve cooling problems because there is less space between the two exhaust valves for coolant to pass through. For example, one series of tests on an engine showed that the exhaust valves for cylinders 2 and 3 ran from 42 to 67°F hotter than the exhaust valves for cylinders 1 and 4.

The lower half of Fig. 15-24 shows an arrangement wherein each valve has its own separate manifold branch so that each seat can be individually cooled. This permits more uniform valve and seat temperatures and also, temperatures lower than are found in the siamesed arrangement. One series of tests, for example, showed that with the alternately placed valve seats (lower half of Fig. 15-24), valves ran about 50°F lower on the average.

However, the alternate arrangement requires a more complex head and manifold, which may therefore be somewhat larger than those for the siamese arrangement. Also, the arrangement of the valves in two rows instead of one makes the valve train somewhat more complex.

For low-cost, standard-duty engines, the decision is often to siamese because the operating requirements are not so severe as to seriously affect valve durability. For higher-performance engines the alternately placed valve arrangement is preferred.

Distortion of valve seats can also result from variations in deck thickness in the seat area. Then too, it can result from variations in thickness of the metal surrounding the exhaust-port area, particularly around the valve-seat area. These variations could result in uneven seat cooling and seat distortion. The designer must avoid such variations. In addition, he must consider casting practices. Parting lines and casting tolerances must be such that shifting of the cores or casting pins will not jeopardize uniform cooling in the valve-seat area. [This is discussed further in the chapter on cylinder block and head design (Chap. 16).]

The block and head design and cylinder-head-bolt locations must be such as to minimize head and block deflections which would draw the valve seats out of line.

2. *Valve-seat cooling.* As previously noted, the valve head is cooled by periodic contact between the valve face and valve seat. Thus, it is very important for the seat to be maintained at a relatively cool temperature. Also, the seat must be cooled uniformly around its circumference.

The seat accepts heat, not only from the valve face, but also from the combustion process in the combustion chamber. About 75 percent of the heat rejection from the valve occurs through the valve seat; the other 25 percent occurs through the valve guide. It is obvious, therefore, that good contact must be made between the valve face and seat when the valve closes, and that this contact should be uniform around the entire circumference of the valve face. Further, the valve seat must not vary greatly in temperature at any point. Hot spots will tend to cause seat distortion and reduced seating contact. This could lead to localized hot spots on the valve face, valve and seat burning, and engine failure.

Good design practice calls for adequate water jacketing that will provide for sufficient water flow to keep the valve-seat areas within reasonable temperatures. In many L-head engines, for example, a water-distributing tube was placed in the cylinder-block water jacket (Fig. 15-25). The tube directed the water flow around the valve-seat and valve-guide areas for adequate cooling.

In I-head engines, some designs have included water nozzles that direct water flow around the valve-seat and valve-guide areas for adequate cooling (Fig. 15-26). Another design makes use of deflectors, cast into the cylinder head, which assure better water circulation around the critical areas (Fig. 15-27).

In the Chevrolet Turbo-Jet engine, the valves are splayed (rather than being parallel), as shown

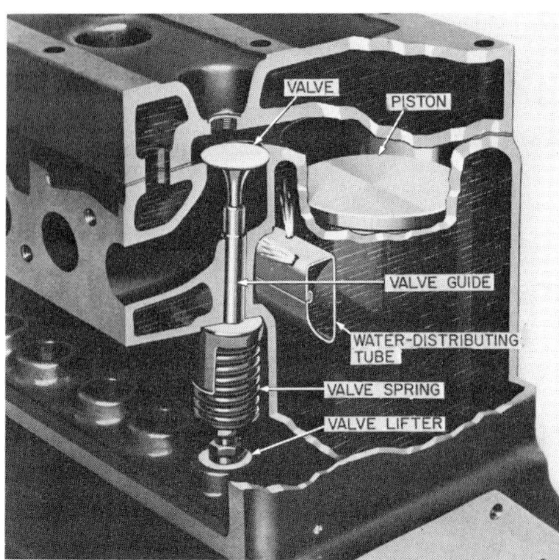

Fig. 15-25. Use of a water-distributing tube to cool a valve. (This is also a good view of the valve location in an L-head engine.)

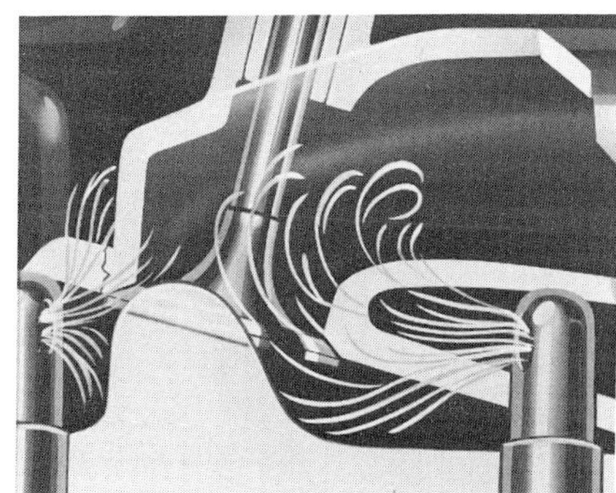

Fig. 15-26. Water nozzles used in the cylinder head of an overhead-valve engine to aid in valve-seat cooling. (*Chevrolet Motor Division of General Motors Corporation*)

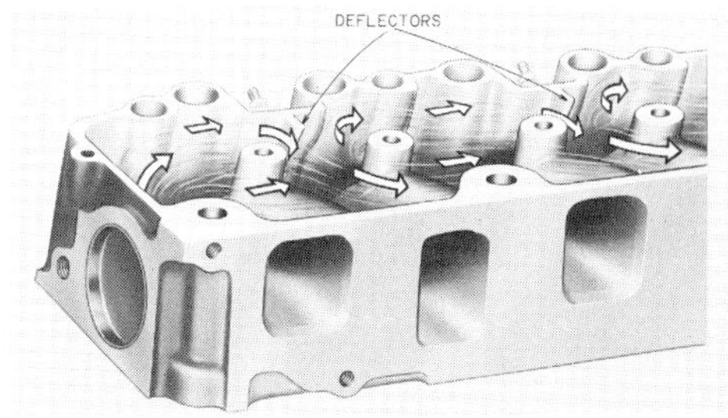

Fig. 15-27. Water circulation in the cylinder head of a late-model six-cylinder I-head engine. Arrows show direction of water flow. Note effect of the deflectors. (*Ford Division of Ford Motor Company*)

in Fig. 15-28. This has several advantages, as described in §218, one of which is that the water jacket could be extended downward between the valve seats, thus improving the cooling of the seats.

3. *Valve-seat durability.* Conventional cylinder-head materials, such as alloy-iron castings, usually are satisfactory for valve seats in engines in the standard-performance range. Such materials exhibit good wear and corrosion resistance if they are not subjected to excessively high temperatures and pressures. The engine designer usually prefers to use valve seats that are integral with the head. It is simple and relatively inexpensive.

If performance requirements are such as to cause rapid wear of the valve seats, then a more complex design is called for. In higher-performance engines, the temperatures and impact pressures (as the valve closes) may be higher than the integral seat can live with satisfactorily. One method of improving seat life under such conditions is to subject the valve seats to a hardening process. A typical process is to induction-harden the seat area (see Fig. 15-11).

The induction-hardening process uses a coil of wire through which high-frequency alternating current is passed. This produces an alternating magnetic field in the coil. Metal objects placed in this field are rapidly heated by the electromagnetic effect. In the case of induction-hardening of valve seats, the coil is positioned in the valve seat so that the seat area quickly reaches the desired temperature (which is above the transformation range). Then, the coil is removed, and the heated area is quenched, or cooled, in the manner required to produce hardening of the area.

Another method of improving valve-seat life is to use valve-seat inserts. The valve-seat insert is a ring of special metal, having the desired hardness and corrosion resistance. It is pressed into a counterbore in the cylinder head, as shown in Fig. 15-29. Note that the OD (outside diameter) of the insert is several thousandths of an inch larger than the ID (inside diameter) of the counterbore. It is extremely important for the fit to be very tight and yet not so excessive as to set up undue stresses in the cylinder head. A tight fit is necessary for full contact between the insert and head and good heat transfer through the interface. Note, also, the recommended proportions of the insert (Fig. 15-29). If the insert is made too thin, it might collapse from compressive stresses set up by thermal expansion of the ring. Collapse could also result from use of a material having a low yield strength.

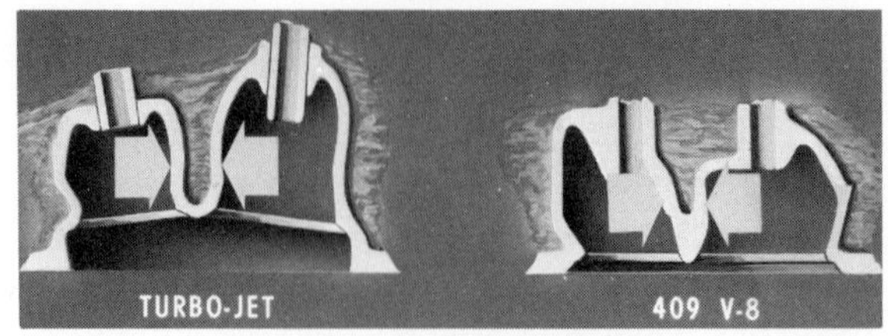

Fig. 15-28. Comparison of the valve ports and guides between the Chevrolet Turbo-Jet engine and the earlier 409 cubic inch engine. (*Chevrolet Motor Division of General Motors Corporation*)

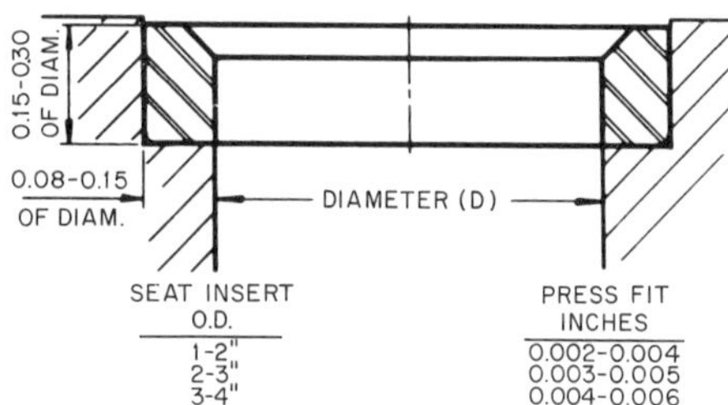

Fig. 15-29. Good design practice for valve-seat inserts. (*TRW Valve Division, Thompson, Ramo, Wooldridge, Inc.*)

While valve-seat inserts may seem to be the answer to high-performance requirements, they do have certain drawbacks. Many of the insert materials have rather low thermal conductivity, and this, combined with the heat barrier represented by the interface between the insert and counterbore, causes the valve seat to operate at a higher temperature. This, in turn, increases the valve temperature. Tests have shown that exhaust valves run as much as 150°F hotter in engines using valve-seat inserts. This means that, when valve-seat inserts are designed into an engine, the valves themselves may have to be redesigned so they will provide satisfactory life.

Valve-seat inserts also complicate engine manufacture. The inserts and counterbores must be machined to very close tolerances so that press fits will be within the design limits, and this of course adds to the cost of the engine. Further, if inserts are not properly installed, they may loosen in service and cause serious engine damage. The engine designer, therefore, makes use of integral valve seats if at all possible. Sometimes, a particular engine design may appear to require valve-seat inserts. However, the designer might be able to rework the design so that this need will be eliminated and the simpler integral valve seats can be used. For example, the designer might improve valve-seat cooling or valve-train dynamics so that valve-impact pressures are lowered (see §217). With these changes, the integral valve seat has a much better chance to survive normally in the engine.

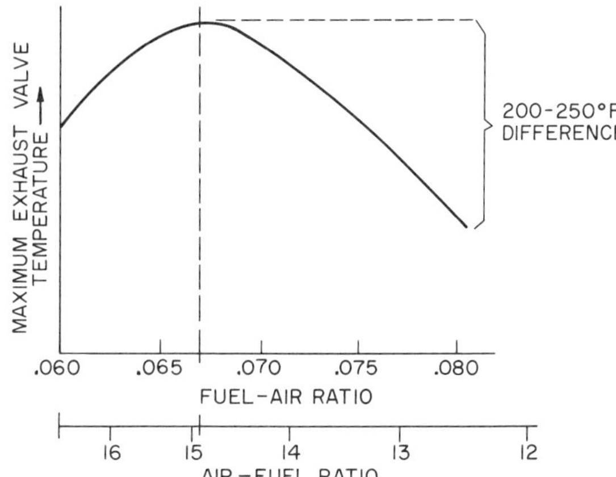

Fig. 15-30. Effect of air-fuel ratio on maximum exhaust-valve temperature. (*TRW Valve Division, Thompson, Ramo, Wooldridge, Inc.*)

§211. Valve temperature and cooling We have already mentioned several factors that influence valve temperature. These include seating pressure, effective valve-seating area, amount of seat distortion, adequacy and uniformness of seat cooling, valve-head shape, valve materials, valve-seat type (whether insert or integral), and valve-guide arrangement and cooling. All of these factors lie within the province of the engine designer, and he can balance them for optimum conditions or the best compromise.

There are other factors, however, which are not directly related to the valves themselves, but which can profoundly affect valve performance and life. The design engineer, therefore, must consider these factors. They include air-fuel ratio, speed, load, and compression ratio.

1. Effect of air-fuel ratio. Exhaust-valve temperature is directly affected by the air-fuel ratio of the mixture burned in the combustion chamber. Figure 15-30 is a curve showing this relationship (air-fuel ratio vs. exhaust-valve temperature). Note, in this typical example, that the exhaust valve reaches its maximum temperature with an air-fuel ratio of slightly above 15:1, and that it falls off sharply as the mixture is enriched above or leaned below this ratio. Inasmuch as exhaust-valve life is greatly shortened by high temperatures, it would seem that the designer would insist on a carburetor arrangement that would give him a mixture ratio that is well above or below 15:1 so that he could keep the exhaust valves cool. However, these other mixture ratios are not satisfactory for many engine operating conditions. As will be noted later in the discussions of fuel systems, a mixture ratio of around 15:1 is required for normal intermediate-performance engine operation. With a significantly leaner mixture, combustion will not take place normally, and engine performance will suffer. A richer mixture tends to increase the percentage of unburned hydrocarbons in the exhaust, thus reducing fuel economy and increasing the amount of smog-inducing components in the exhaust gases (§139).

Furthermore, the problem is not one of simply proportioning the fuel nozzles and venturis in the carburetor to secure the optimum air-fuel ratio. There are also other factors to be considered. The cylinders are located at different distances from the carburetor, and consequently the mixture travels further to get to the end cylinders than to get to the center cylinders. This can cause significant variations in the air-fuel ratio between cylinders. For example, tests of one engine, operating at full load and wide-open throttle, showed a variation in air-fuel ratios of from close to 15:1 (for the cylinder nearest to the carburetor) to about 12:1 (for the most distant cylinder). In terms of exhaust-valve temperature, this would mean a difference of as much as 200°F, with the valves in the cylinders using the leaner mixture (15:1) having the higher temperature. As a rule, the carburetor and fuel system are designed to supply the most distant cylinder with a satisfactory air-fuel ratio. This almost certainly means that the cylinder nearest the carburetor will get a leaner air-fuel mixture and thus will have lower exhaust-valve temperatures.

To understand why the variations in air-fuel ratios at the different cylinders exist, consider first that the fuel is not mixed perfectly with the air, and, in fact, some of it may be in the form of liquid droplets. Further, the intake manifold is somewhat like a straight pipe, with secondary pipes taking off at right angles and connecting to the intake ports. The air-fuel mixture with the greater density, and possibly containing droplets, has greater inertia. It thus has a greater tendency to continue straight along the intake manifold instead of "turning the corner" and entering the intake ports of the center cylinders. Thus, it travels to the end cylinders, thereby providing them with the richer air-fuel mixture. The intake manifold therefore acts somewhat as a sorting device, tending to deliver a leaner mixture to the center cylinders and a richer mixture to the end cylinders. Figure 15-31 shows an extreme example of this condition as experienced in a prototype engine under development.[5] Before the condition was corrected by changes in the manifold and unshrouding of the intake valve, the end cylinders were receiving a rich air-fuel mixture of below 13:1, while cylinders 3 and 4 were receiving a much leaner air-fuel ratio. Figure 17-55 shows the changes made, and Fig. 17-56 shows the improvements in distribution attained by the changes.

In addition to the above, changes in atmospheric pressure and temperature also cause variations in the air-fuel ratio and in the amount of air-fuel mixture ingested by the engine. Low air temperatures and high atmospheric pressures in-

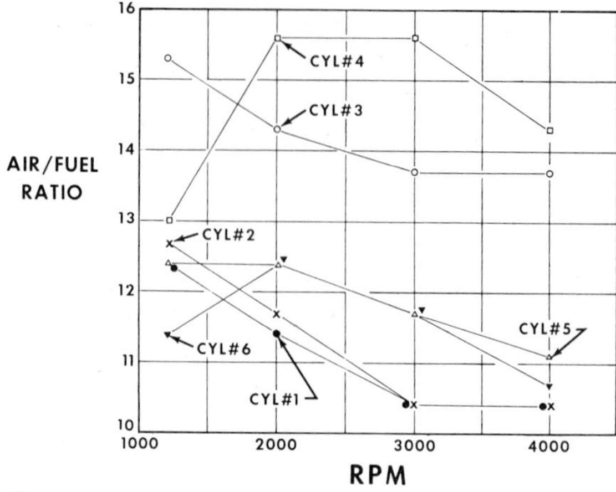

Fig. 15-31. Fuel distribution in a prototype engine under development. The intake manifold and ports were altered in the development work (as described in Chapter 17) so that there resulted more nearly uniform air-fuel ratios to all cylinders. (*Ford Motor Company*)

crease the amount of air-fuel mixture entering the cylinder and thus raise combustion pressures and temperatures. This increases exhaust-valve temperature.

2. *Effect of speed and load.* Higher speeds and increased loads require the combustion of greater amounts of fuel per unit of time, and naturally this increases the heat load on engine parts. Exhaust valves thus run hotter.

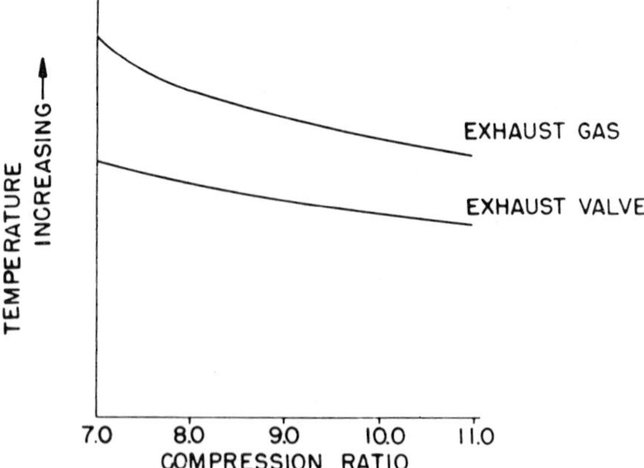

Fig. 15-32. Relationship between exhaust-gas and exhaust-valve temperatures and compression ratio. (*TRW Valve Division, Thompson, Ramo, Wooldridge, Inc.*)

3. *Effect of compression ratio.* We have already noted that the trend in compression ratios is upward (§64). Increasing the compression ratio increases engine thermal efficiency. This means that a greater percentage of the heat energy in the fuel is converted to work, and thus less heat escapes from the engine in the exhaust gases. In other words, the exhaust gases are cooler. Consequently, the exhaust valves operate at a lower temperature. Figure 15-32 shows how the temperatures of the exhaust gas and the exhaust valves drop off as the compression ratio increases.

§212. Valve lubrication In a later chapter we will describe in detail various engine-lubrication systems and the manner in which oil is supplied to the valves. There are two places at which the valve requires lubrication: at the tip, where it makes contact with the rocker arm, and in the valve-guide area of the stem, which moves up and down in the valve guide. Oil is supplied to these areas through either a hollow rocker-arm shaft or hollow push rods.

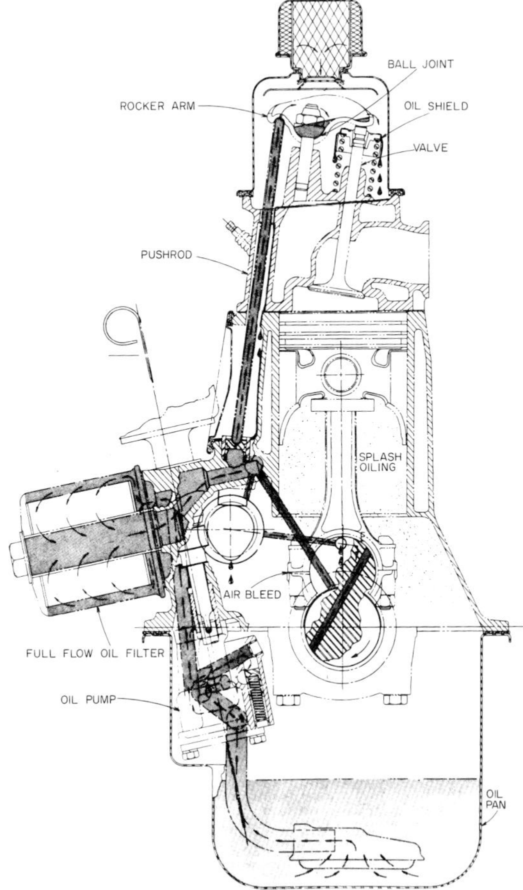

Fig. 15-33. Valve-train lubrication in six-cylinder, in-line engine. (*Chevrolet Motor Division of General Motors Corporation*)

Figure 15-33 shows the lubrication system for an in-line, overhead-valve engine using the hollow push rods. Note that the oil passes up the push rod, through holes in the top of the push rod and in the rocker arm, and fills the depression in the rocker arm. Here, it lubricates the ball joint on which the rocker arm moves. Excess oil spills over the valve end of the rocker arm to provide lubrication of the valve-stem tip and the valve-guide area. Then the oil runs back down past the outside of the push rods and is returned to the oil pan.

The positioning and inclination of the valve have a profound influence on its lubrication. For example, consider Fig. 15-34. This illustration shows an early design of a Chevrolet engine and a later modification which was adopted for production. The early design (Fig. 15-34*a*) was compact and permitted the use of a short, rigid rocker arm. Note that the center lines of the valve and push rod

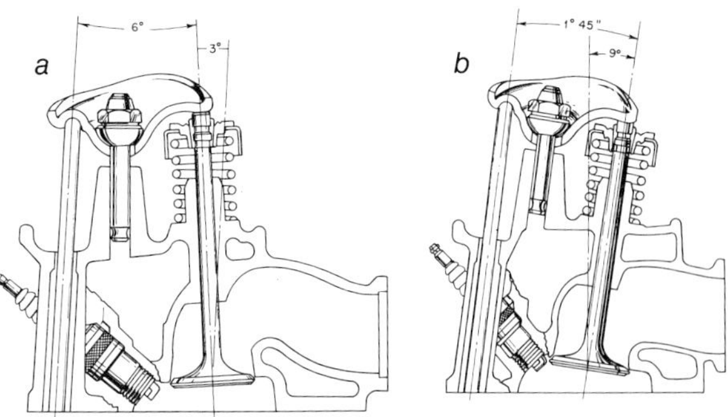

Fig. 15-34. Early and final arrangements of the valve train for the Chevy II engine. Even though the geometry of the prototype (*a*) was attractive, a change to the final design (*b*) was required to assure adequate valve-stem and tip lubrication. (*Chevrolet Motor Division of General Motors Corporation*)

converge at an angle of 6 degrees, while the valve itself is slanted toward the push rod at an angle of 3 degrees. At first, this design looked good. The short and rigid rocker arm improved valve-train dynamics (§217), and the combustion-chamber design (a modified bathtub-type) was satisfactory.

However, the design had an oiling problem. At low speeds, when there was little splash, oil would not spill over the valve end of the rocker arm in sufficient amounts to provide adequate lubrication of the valve tip and stem. The design was then modified, as shown in Fig. 15-34*b*. Here, the push rod and valve are practically parallel, and the valve stem is inclined from the vertical 9 degrees. This layout brought low-speed oiling of the valve stem and tip up to a satisfactory level. The layout also improved the combustion-chamber configuration since the wedge now slants away from the spark plug instead of toward it as in Fig. 15-34*a*. This reduces the chances of detonation, inasmuch as the combustion progresses from the larger area toward the smaller area instead of vice versa.

While inadequate oiling at low speeds can be a problem, excessive oiling at higher speeds can also be a problem. With the valves flooded with oil, there is a greatly increased tendency for oil to be pulled down into the combustion chamber past the valve stems during the intake stroke. This is much more of an intake-valve problem than an exhaust-valve problem. The intake valve is open during the entire intake stroke, while the exhaust valve is open during only a small part of the intake stroke. Some tests have shown that as much as 80 percent of the oil consumption in some engines is due to oil passing the valve stems and entering the combustion chambers. This condition becomes more critical as the compression ratio goes up. With higher compression ratios, the vacuum in the cylinder is higher during the intake stroke, and this increases the tendency for oil to pass the intake-valve stem.

To reduce oil consumption due to this condition, most overhead-valve engines are now equipped with valve-stem seals or shields.[6] Figure 15-35 shows one type of shield (see also Fig. 15-33), which covers the top two turns of the spring. The inner seal, which is a ring of Teflon or similar material, fits between the spring-retainer skirt and an undercut in the valve stem. The seal prevents oil from seeping down the valve stem past the locks and retainer. The shield prevents undue amounts of oil from being thrown through the spring onto the valve stem. A variation of this design is shown in Fig. 15-36. Here, the shield is on the inside of the valve springs rather than on the outside. The purpose of the shield is the same, however—to protect the valve stem from excessive oil.

Another type of seal to prevent oil seepage past

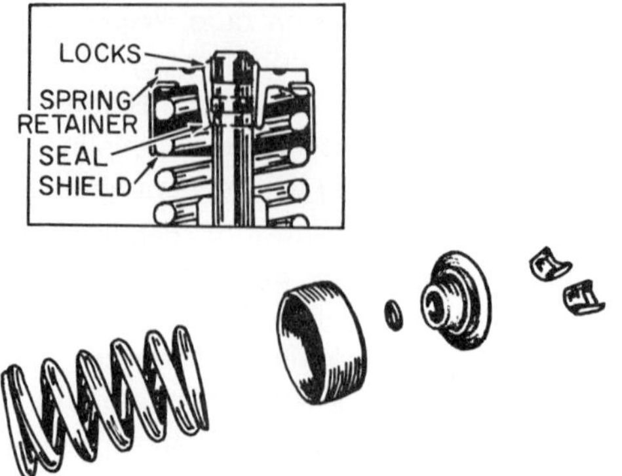

Fig. 15-35. Disassembled and sectional assembled views of a valve and spring assembly, with oil seal and shield. (*Chevrolet Motor Division of General Motors Corporation*)

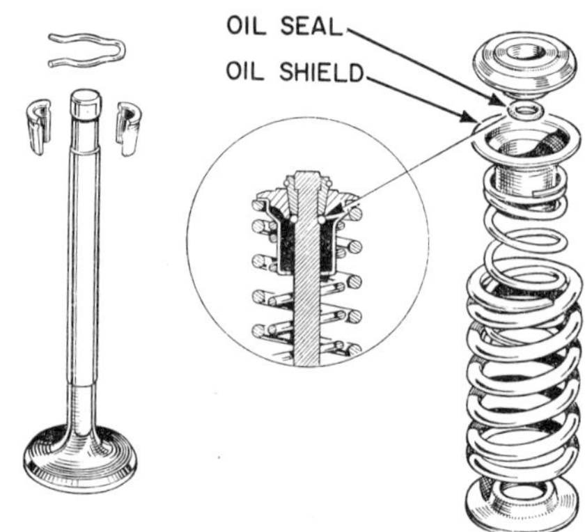

Fig. 15-36. Disassembled and sectional assembled views of a valve and spring assembly, with oil seal and shield. (*MG Car Company, Limited*)

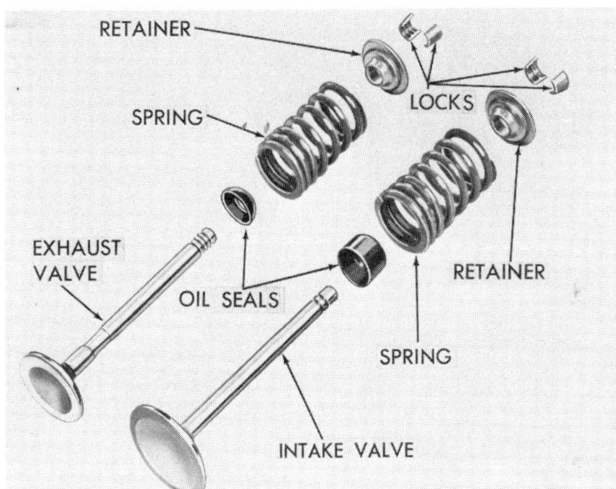

Fig. 15-37. Disassembled view of valves, springs, oil seals, and related parts. (*Dodge Division of Chrysler Motors Corporation*)

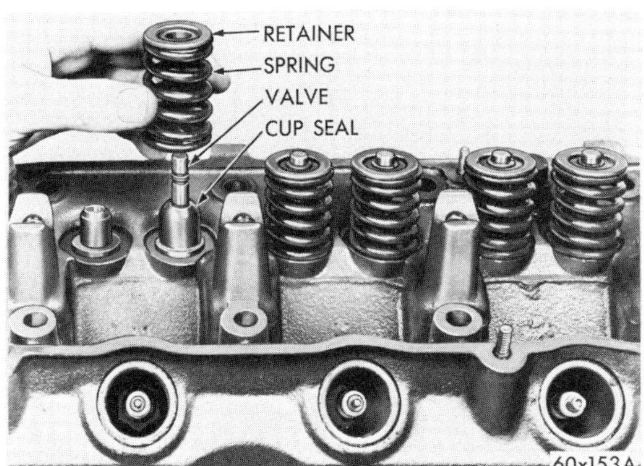

Fig. 15-38. Installation of a valve, spring, oil seal, and related parts. (*Dodge Division of Chrysler Motors Corporation*)

the valve stem is shown in Figs. 15-37 and 15-38. This oil seal fits down against the cylinder head and around the valve stem, as shown in Fig. 15-38. In this design, the valve stem moves up and down in the seal, and the seal wipes excessive oil off the valve stem, leaving only enough to provide satisfactory valve-guide lubrication.

§213. Valve rotation In the valve mechanisms thus far discussed, the valve simply moves up and down; it has little tendency to rotate. The valve-spring pressure, carried through the valve retainer and lock to the valve stem, tends to prevent any valve rotation in the valve guide. However, tests have shown that if the valve could be allowed to rotate a small amount each time it opened and closed, many valve troubles would be minimized. For example, one common cause of valve burning is the depositing of combustion products on the valve faces. Such deposits prevent normal valve seating, face-to-seat contact, and heat transfer. Soon, as the deposits collect, valves begin to overheat and burn. The poor seating also permits exhaust-gas leakage, which accelerates the burning process. Another cause of valve trouble is valve sticking. This condition usually results from accumulations of decomposed or carbonized oil (brought about by the high temperatures) on the valve stem. Ultimately, these deposits work into the clearance between the valve stem and valve guide; the valve sticks, or "hangs up," in the guide and does not close. Then, with poor or no seating, the valve soon overheats and burns.

Whenever a valve burns or does not seat properly, loss of compression and loss of combustion pressure will result. This means that the engine cylinder in which the offending valve is located will be "weak"; it will not deliver its share of the power.

If the valve is rotated as it opens and closes, there will be less chance of valve-stem accumulations causing the valve to stick. Also, there will be a wiping action between the valve face and the valve seat; this tends to prevent any build-up of face deposits. In addition, valve rotation results in more uniform valve-head temperatures. Some parts of the valve seat may be hotter than others; actual hot spots may develop. If the same part of the valve face continued to seat on a hot spot, that part of the valve face would reach a higher temperature and tend to wear, or burn, faster. But if the valve rotates, no one part of the valve face is subjected to this higher temperature; valve-head temperature is more uniform.

There are two general types of valve rotators: the "free-valve" type and the "positive-rotation" type. Details of a free-valve rotator are shown in

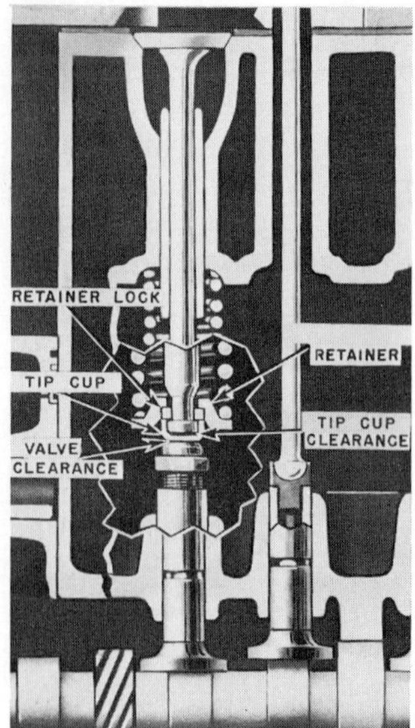

Fig. 15-39. Installation of a "free-type" valve rotator on an L-head-type valve. In this unit, the tip cup relieves spring pressure on the valve stem when the valve is opened, thus permitting the valve to turn when it is open.

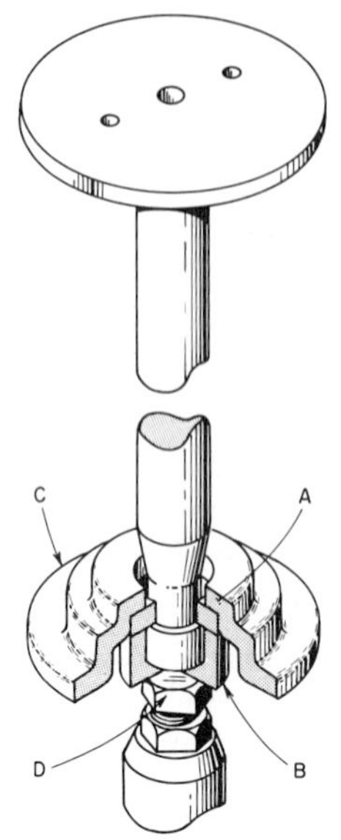

Fig. 15-40. Construction of a "free-type" valve rotator: (*A*) spring-retainer lock; (*B*) tip cup; (*C*) spring retainer; (*D*) lifter adjustment screw. (*Thompson Products, Inc.*)

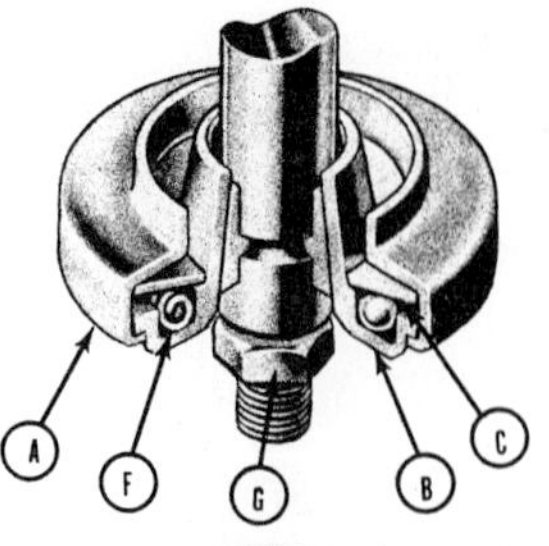

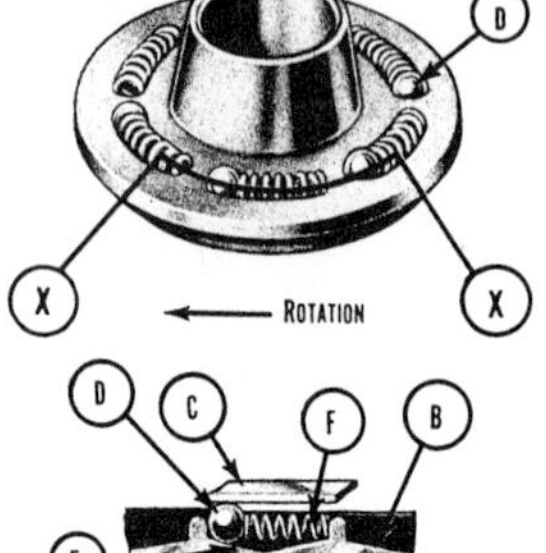

Fig. 15-41. Construction of the positive-rotation type of valve rotator: (*A*) seating collar; (*B*) spring retainer; (*C*) flexible washer; (*D*) balls; (*E*) inclined race; (*F*) ball-return springs; (*G*) lifter adjustment screw. (*Thompson Products, Inc.*)

Figs. 15-39 and 15-40. In this design the spring-retainer lock has been replaced by two parts: a washer-type lock (split) and a tip cup. As the valve lifter moves up, the adjustment screw presses against the tip cup, and the tip cup then carries the motion to the lock and valve retainer. The valve retainer is lifted, thereby taking up the valve-spring pressure. Then the bottom of the tip cup moves up against the end of the valve stem so that the valve is lifted. Note that the spring pressure is taken off the valve stem; the valve is free. Since it is free, it can rotate. Engine vibration causes the valve to rotate.

The free-valve type of rotator can be used on either an L-head or an overhead-valve engine. Figure 15-39 shows it installed on an L-head-type exhaust valve.

A positive-rotation type of valve rotator is shown in Figs. 15-41 and 15-42. This design contains a device that applies a rotating force on the valve each time it is opened, thereby assuring positive rotation. Figure 15-41 shows the details of the rotator, and Fig. 15-42 shows it installed on a

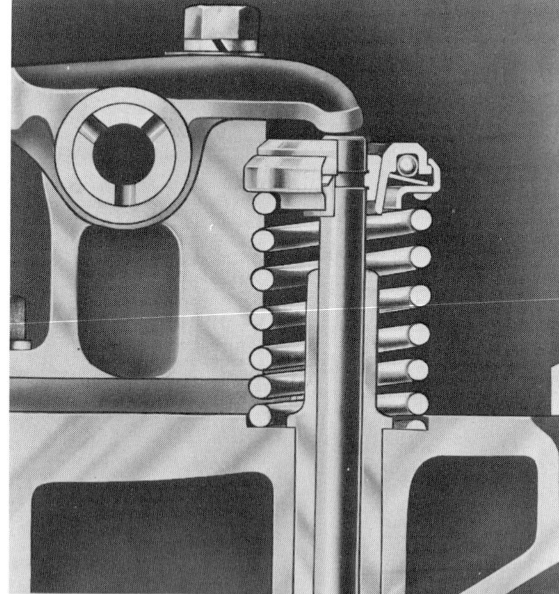

Fig. 15-42. Installation of the positive-rotation type of valve rotator on the valve in an I-head, or overhead-valve, engine. (*Thompson Products, Inc.*)

Fig. 15-43. Rocker-arm and shaft assembly on cylinder head of a V-8 engine. (*Chrysler-Plymouth Division of Chrysler Motors Corporation*)

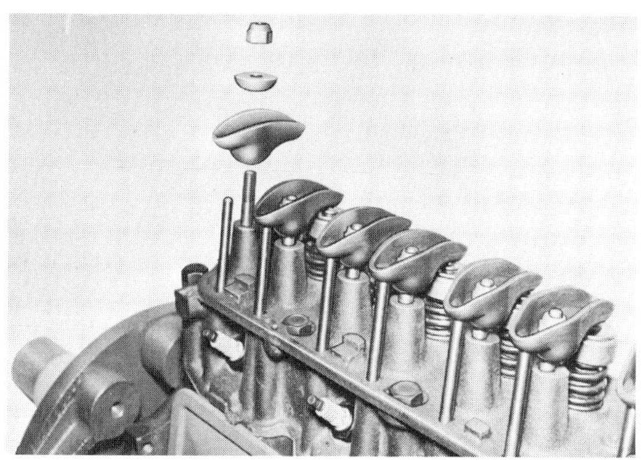

Fig. 15-44. Rocker arm of the type using a ball pivot, with associated parts shown. (*Chevrolet Motor Division of General Motors Corporation*)

valve in an I-head engine. A seating collar (*A* in Fig. 15-41) is spun over the outer lip of the spring retainer (*B*). The valve spring rests on the seating collar. The collar encloses a flexible washer (*C*) placed above a series of spring-loaded balls (*D*). The middle view in Fig. 15-41 shows how the balls and springs are positioned in grooves in the spring retainer. The bottoms of the grooves (or races) are inclined, as shown in the bottom view (*E* in Fig. 15-41), which is a section (*X-X*) cut from the middle view. When the lifter is raised, the adjustment screw (*G*) lifts the valve and applies an increased pressure (as the valve spring is compressed) on the seating collar. This flattens the flexible washer (*C*) so that the washer applies the spring load on the balls (*D*). As the balls receive this load, they roll down the inclined races. This causes the retainer to turn a few degrees, and this turning motion is applied through the retainer lock to the valve stem; the valve therefore turns. When the valve closes, the spring pressure is reduced so that the balls return to their original positions, ready for the next valve motion.

The positive-rotation type of valve rotator can be installed on the valves in either the L- or I-head engine. It can be installed at the tip end of the valve (as shown in Fig. 15-42) or at the valve-guide end, between the valve spring and the cylinder block, or head. In the latter installation, the turning motion would be carried from the rotator through the spring, spring retainer, and lock to the valve stem.

§214. Rocker arms There are two general types

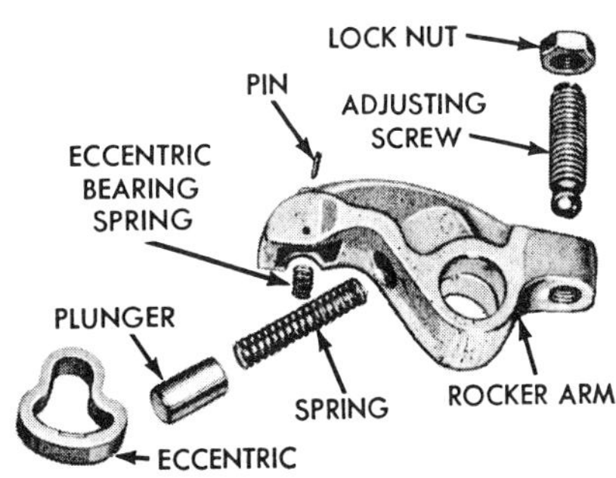

Fig. 15-45. Silent-lash rocker arm in disassembled view. (*Ford Division of Ford Motor Company*)

of rocker arms: the cast or forged type and the steel-stamping type. Rocker arms are supported on the cylinder head in either of two ways: by shafts or by studs. Figure 7-34 shows one shaft arrangement for supporting the rocker arms, and the cast rocker arm used in this arrangement is shown in Fig. 7-33. Figure 15-43 shows one type of steel-stamping rocker arm, mounted on a shaft. Figure 15-44 shows the steel-stamping type of rocker arm, mounted on a stud through a ball pivot or joint.

1. *Rocker arms for overhead camshafts.* A number of different rocker-arm arrangements are used in OHC engines. Many of these rocker arms are equipped with rollers (Fig. 15-56). The rollers rest against the cams on the camshaft and greatly reduce the friction and wear of the parts. (For a detailed discussion of OHC engines, see §221.)

2. *Silent-lash rocker arms.* Another type of rocker arm is shown in Fig. 15-45. This type is known as the *silent-lash rocker arm*, since the eccentric operates to take up any clearance be-

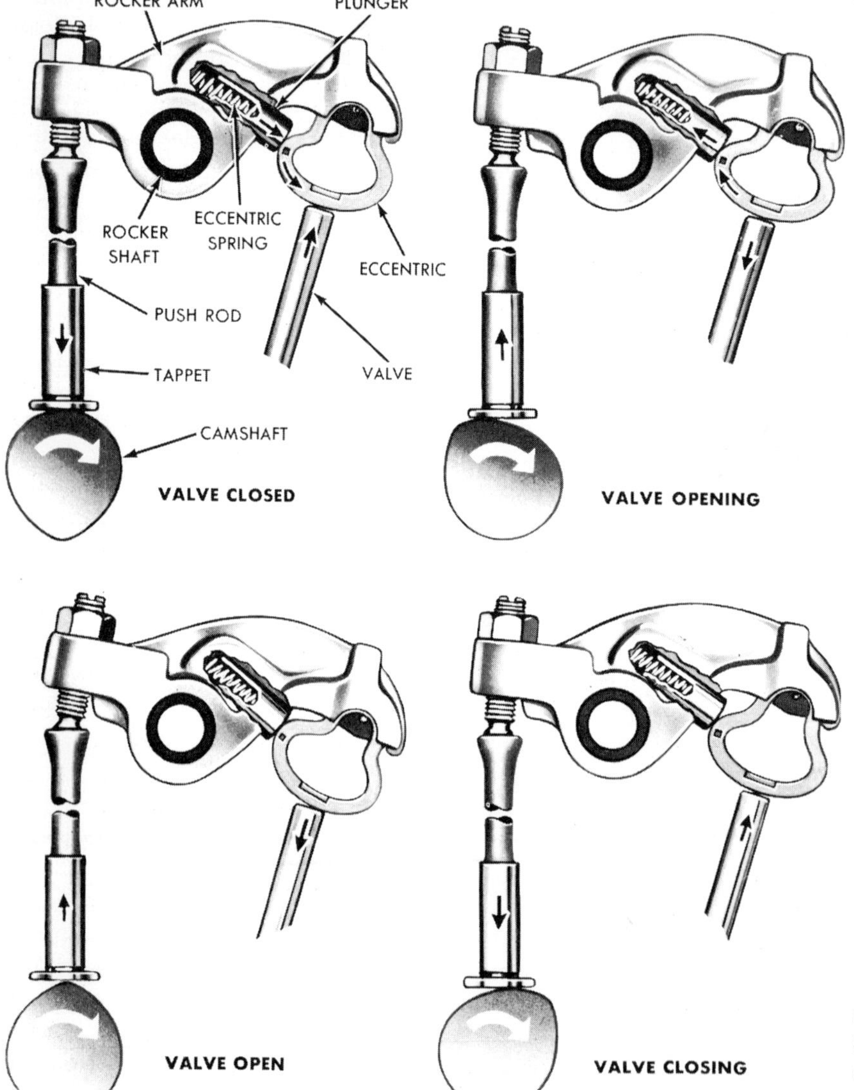

Fig. 15-46. Operation of the silent-lash rocker arm. (*Ford Division of Ford Motor Company*)

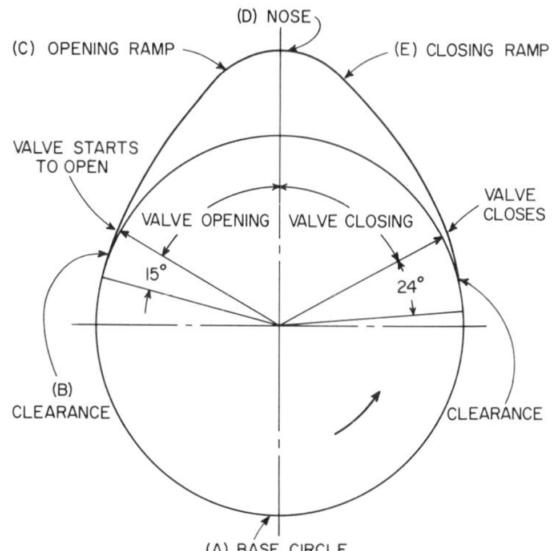

Fig. 15-47. Details of a cam contour for a solid valve lifter.

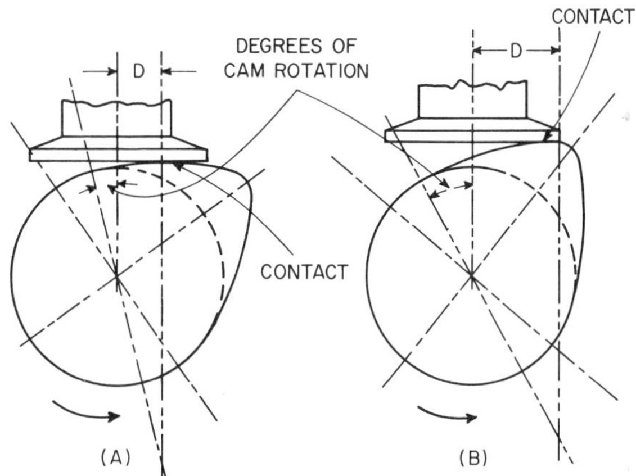

Fig. 15-48. The line of contact between the cam and the flat face of the valve lifter moves as the cam rotates.

tween the valve stem and the rocker arm. This eliminates any noise that would otherwise result because of the repeated clicks of the rocker arm moving down through the clearance and coming down against the end of the valve stem. The silent-lash rocker arm works as follows (Fig. 15-46): The eccentric pivots in the end of the rocker arm and rests on the end of the valve stem. If there is any clearance, or lash, between the eccentric and the end of the valve stem, then the spring-loaded plunger pushes the eccentric out to eliminate the clearance. Then, when the push rod moves up to operate the rocker arm, the rocker arm is already in contact, through the eccentric, with the valve stem. Therefore, there is no lash noise.

3. *Rocker-arm geometry.* On rocker arms without rollers, the motion between the valve-stem tip and the rocker arm is largely sliding (usually called scrubbing). There is only one point during valve movement at which the motion could be called rolling. This occurs at the point where a line drawn through the valve tip and the rocker-arm pivot is perpendicular to the axis of the valve stem. At all other points, the motion is sliding or scrubbing. It is this scrubbing motion that produces wear of the valve tip and rocker arm. To minimize this wear, the design should fix the valve-tip height, with the valve closed, in the proper relationship with the valve lift. If the valve-tip height above the point of roll is about one-third of the valve lift, then scrubbing will be minimized during the first third of valve opening, when acceleration loading in the valve train is highest. During the other two-thirds of valve lift, acceleration loads are much less, and even though much more scrubbing takes place during this time, less wear results.

§215. Cams We have described in some detail many of the design considerations of various components of the valve train. Now, let us look at the motions in the valve train, that is, valve-train dynamics.[7] For any specific layout of valve seat, valve, rocker arm, push rod, or valve lifter, the motion depends on three factors: cam contour, spring design, and speed. Ideally, the valve should open quickly, remain fully open for the proper number of degrees, and then close quickly. However, to avoid heavy loading of the valve-train parts during the opening phase, excessive acceleration must be avoided. Also, as the valve approaches the fully opened position, high deceleration must be avoided. Furthermore, as the valve approaches the closed position, deceleration must be great enough to permit relatively easy closing so that the closing impact load will not be excessive.

1. *Cam contour.* All these motions, accelera-

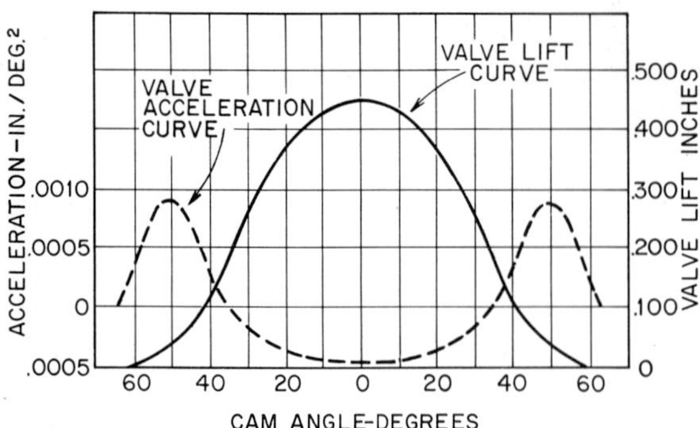

Fig. 15-49. Curves of desired valve lift and acceleration. (*TRW Valve Division, Thompson, Ramo, Wooldridge, Inc.*)

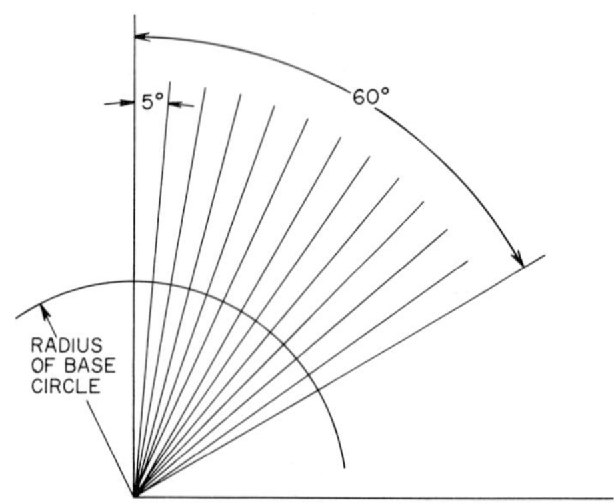

Fig. 15-51. Preliminary layout ready for designing the contour of cam.

tions, and decelerations are functions of the cam contour. Before we discuss cam-contour design, let us look at cam action and the various parts of a cam contour. Figure 15-47 shows the different components of a cam contour for a solid (not hydraulic) valve lifter. The base circle (*A*) is that part of the cam on which the lifter rides when the valve is closed. With the solid lifter, there must be some clearance (or valve lash) in the valve train to allow for dimensional changes as the engine warms up and the valve-train parts expand. Therefore, as the first part of the opening ramp comes around under the valve lifter, it raises the lifter enough to take up this clearance (*B*). Following that, the valve-train parts move as a unit, causing the valve to begin opening. The valve continues to open as the opening ramp (*C*) passes under the valve lifter. The shape of the opening ramp determines the acceleration, deceleration, and total amount of valve opening.

The valve reaches the fully opened position as the nose of the cam (*D*) comes under the valve lifter. The width of the nose (or number of degrees of cam rotation that nose is under lifter) determines the time that the valve remains wide open. After the nose passes from under the valve lifter,

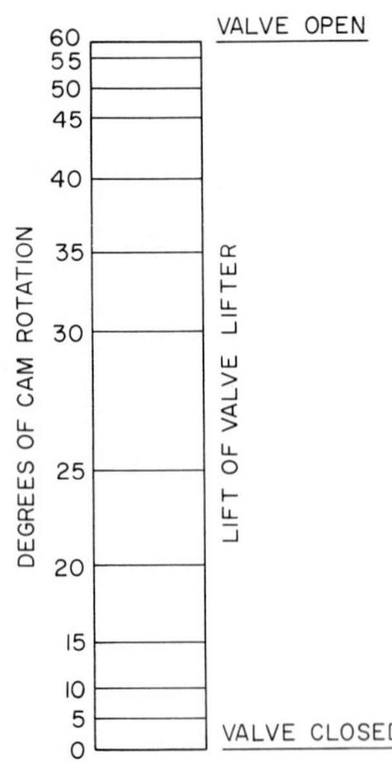

Fig. 15-50. Degrees of cam rotation, as related to lift of valve lifter to produce the curve of desired valve lift during opening of valve, as shown in *Fig. 15-49* (not drawn to same scale).

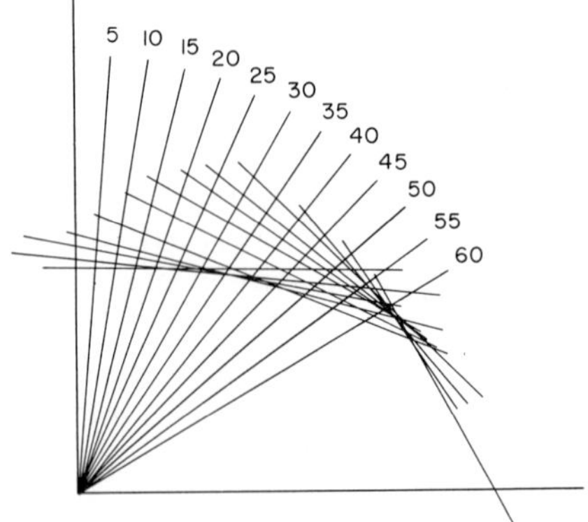

Fig. 15-52. Drawing lines perpendicular to 5-degree lines at correct distances (base circle plus lift) reveals cam contour.

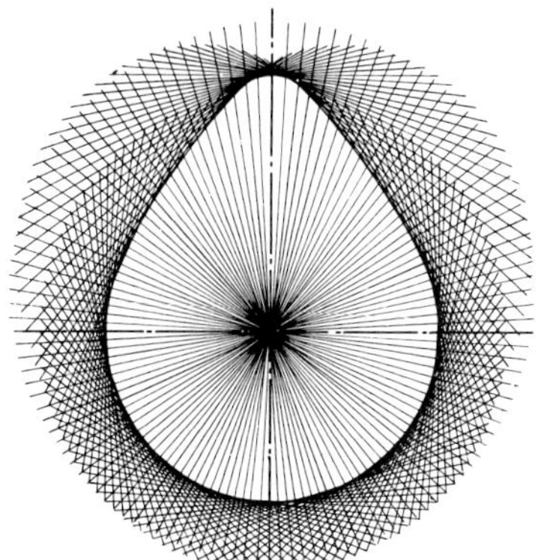

Fig. 15-53. Complete cam contour, as produced by method shown in *Fig. 15-52.*

the closing ramp (*E*) lets the valve spring move the valve-train parts toward the closed position. The acceleration and deceleration of the valve parts is determined by the shape of the closing ramp as well as the spring characteristics. Finally, after the valve reaches the closed position, the clearance reappears in the valve train as the base circle comes around under the valve lifter.

2. *Cam-contour layout.* The design of cams is a highly specialized activity, requiring many calculations, and various approaches can be used. One approach is vector analysis;[8] another makes use of a computer into which the required design data can be fed.

Before starting a cam design, we must first note that the line of contact between the curved cam and the flat base of the valve lifter moves from one to the other side of the lifter. Figure 15-48 illustrates this. In Fig. 15-48*a*, the opening ramp has begun to pass under the lifter. When the lifter is on the base circle, the line of contact is at the center of the valve lifter. However, in Fig. 15-48*a*, the line of contact has moved distance *D* from the center. Then, in Fig. 15-48*b*, the line of contact has moved much further, to the edge of the flat on the valve lifter. As the nose of the cam passes under the lifter, the line of contact will move back toward the center, through the center, and out to the other edge of the lifter.

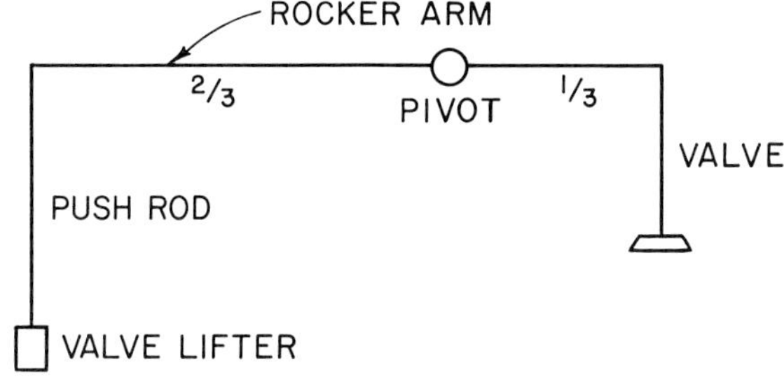

Fig. 15-54. If the rocker arm pivot is off center, then the cam contour must be modified to produce the proper valve lift.

You can see, therefore, that we are dealing with very complex motions. A primitive way of designing a cam contour would be to first prepare a curve showing the desired valve movement. Figure 15-49 is such a curve, showing both desired valve lift and preferred valve acceleration. Next, the motion of the valve lifter required to produce this valve movement is indicated on a large-scale drawing as a series of parallel lines, spaced at equal time intervals (this would be the same as equal degrees of cam rotation).

Figure 15-50 shows the movement of the flat on the valve lifter as parallel lines at intervals of 5 degrees of cam rotation (or 5 cam degrees). This drawing was developed from the valve-lift curve of Fig. 15-49. It shows where the valve lifter must be at 5-cam-degree intervals in order to produce the valve movement graphed in Fig. 15-49.

As a first step in designing the cam contour, the designer must select the proper base-circle radius. This radius is made as large as possible within the limits imposed by the camshaft-bearing diameters. In other words, the base-circle radius plus the lift must be less than the radius of the smallest camshaft-bearing radius. If it were larger, it would be impossible to slide the camshaft into place in the bearings.

Next, the designer starts to make a large-scale layout of the cam contour. For example, let us see how he would use the information in Fig. 15-50 to lay out the opening ramp. The ramp has a duration of 60 degrees, and the designer draws a series of radius lines 5 cam degrees apart (Fig. 15-51). To this he adds the base circle, as shown. Next, he measures off on each radius line the base circle radius plus the lift required at that cam angle (picking up this latter data from Fig. 15-50). Finally, from these established points, he draws perpendicular lines, as shown in Fig. 15-52. This develops the cam contour needed to produce the lift shown in Fig. 15-49. A complete cam contour developed by this method is shown in Fig. 15-53.

We must point out, however, that this is *valve-lifter* lift. In an L-head engine, this would approximate valve lift. However, in an I-head engine, push-rod and valve-stem angularity and rocker-arm geometry will require modification of the contour. To take an extreme example for illustrative purposes, let us say that the rocker arm is pivoted at a point two-thirds the distance from the push rod (Fig. 15-54). This means that the push rod would have to move ⅛ inch in order to move the valve 1/16 inch. It therefore follows that cam-contour measurements, as developed for the valve-lifter movement, would have to be doubled to obtain satisfactory valve movement.

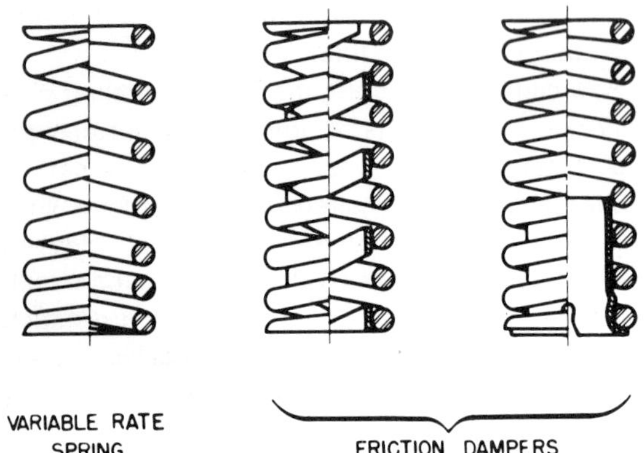

Fig. 15-55. Three methods for damping spring surges. (*TRW Valve Division, Thompson, Ramo, Wooldridge, Inc.*)

As a practical matter, consider that the line of contact of the rocker arm with the valve stem moves across the stem. This changes the effective distance between the pivot point of the rocker arm and the line of contact. This, plus the effects of push-rod and valve-stem angularity and the effect of the rocker-arm pivot being off center must be compensated for during the development of the final cam contour.

The above is a much simplified explanation of how the designer develops a cam contour. Furthermore, this is but the first step in arriving at the final design, for the cam must be made and tested in a running mechanism at varying speeds. Any deficiencies that show up must then be compensated for by modification of the contour.

Fig. 15-56. Laboratory setup to check valve-train dynamics on an overhead camshaft with roller-type rocker arms. (*Ford Motor Company*)

§216. Valve spring The valve spring must have sufficient tension to force the valve and other valve-train parts to follow the cam contour. At the same time, it must not have so much tension as to cause undue wear of the valve, seat, rocker arm, push rod, lifter, and cam. The spring must maintain its tension under greatly varying speeds and temperatures. Furthermore, it should have natural frequencies of vibration well above the top speed at which it will operate. If it does not, spring surge will develop at certain critical speeds. This shows up as high-frequency surging of the center coils of the spring. This action offsets the normal spring tension so much that the valve lifter and other valve-train parts no longer follow the cam contour. The results of this could be heavy impact pounding and rapid wear of valve-train parts and possibly serious engine damage.

A variety of procedures are used to minimize spring surge. The basic design can often be such that the natural frequency is high enough to avoid spring surge. This requires that the wire from which the spring is made will be as small in diameter as possible, consistent with the load requirements. There should be as large a number of coils as possible at maximum pitch diameter (distance between coils). Where space limitations do not permit realization of these ideals, the designer may use two or even three springs, nested inside each other, to obtain the required spring tension in the more limited space.

If space requirements are so severe as to require other methods of discouraging spring surge, the spring may be damped by any of a variety of means. Figure 15-55 shows three of these methods. The variable-rate spring has coils of varying pitch. The other two methods shown utilize dampers that damp out the surging by frictional action against the inside diameter of the spring.

§217. Valve-train dynamics[7] The complexities of the movements of the various parts in the valve train make it necessary to do much actual testing after all theoretical considerations have been applied in building prototype parts. For example, Fig. 15-56 shows a setup to check a newly designed valve train for an overhead-camshaft engine.[9] Note that the rocker arms in this engine have rollers. The camshaft was driven by a variable-speed electric motor, and proximity devices were used to indicate the valve motion at various speeds on an oscilloscope. This provides an accurate picture of valve action and helps the designer decide whether or not modification of valve-train parts is necessary. An endurance test was also run on the valve-train parts, with the same setup as shown in Fig. 15-56. This provided information on durability.

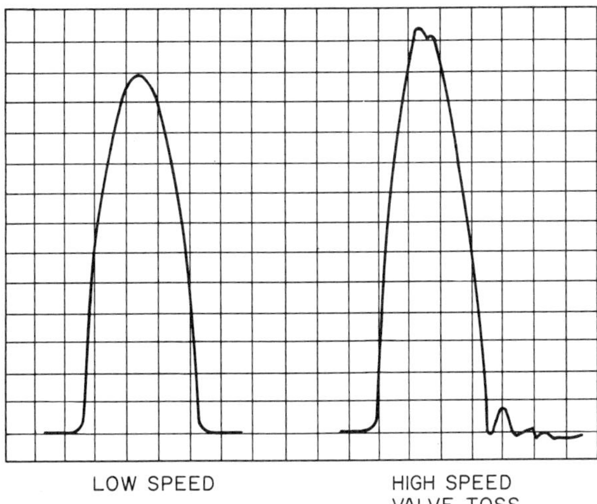

Fig. 15-57. Traces on oscilloscope showing valve motion at low speed and at high speed, during which valve toss is experienced. (*Ford Motor Company*)

One factor that may be difficult to predict during the design of a new valve train, particularly of the cam contour and spring, is the possibility of valve "toss." To understand what valve toss is, let us take another look at the actions of the components in the valve train. First, as the cam lobe starts to move around under the valve lifter, the valve lifter, push rod, rocker arm, and valve are all given an initial acceleration. Figure 15-49 shows a typical valve-lift curve and the acceleration curve necessary to achieve this lift curve. You will recall that we used this valve-lift curve to develop the cam contour shown in Fig. 15-52.

The slope of the valve lift curve is laid out by the designer to give the maximum acceleration possible without undue adverse effects. Suppose, for example, that the slope of the valve-lift curve were increased so as to get the valve opened in fewer cam degrees. This would increase the acceleration, perhaps excessively, and this could impose excessive shock loading on the valve-train parts. Not only would this wear the lifter, push rod, rocker arm, and valve rapidly, but it would produce undue deflections of parts, as well as improper operation.

The opening phase of the valve action can be divided into two parts. During part one, the valve-train parts are accelerated, or moved from a standing start to their maximum speed. During the second part, the valve-train parts are slowed down, or decelerated, from their maximum speed to the stationary, opened-valve position. During acceleration, the valve-train parts are following the cam contour as the opening ramp moves around under the valve lifter. During deceleration, the valve-train parts come under the influence of the valve spring.

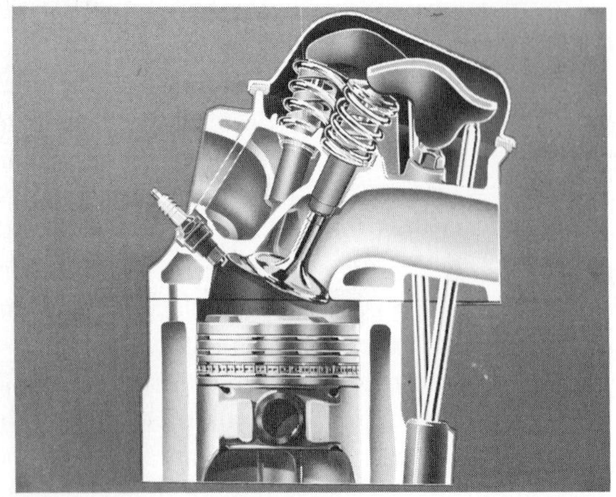

Fig. 15-58. Sectional and phantom view of one cylinder of the Turbo-Jet engine, showing valve, push-rod, and rocker-arm angles. (*Chevrolet Motor Division of General Motors Corporation*)

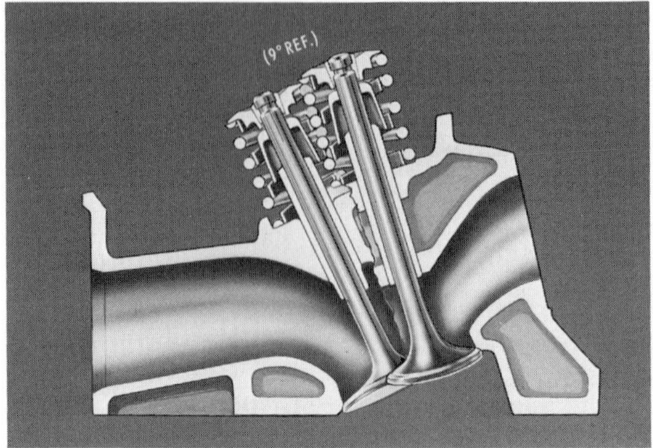

Fig. 15-60. Intake and exhaust valves and ports for the Turbo-Jet engine. (*Chevrolet Motor Division of General Motors Corporation*)

If the valve spring is not sufficiently stiff, then the inertia of the moving valve-train parts will momentarily overpower the spring. The result is valve toss; that is, the valve is "tossed" free from the direct influence of the cam contour. When this happens, valve control is lost. As the valve floats freely, clearances appear between the valve-train parts. Then, the spring recovers and takes up the slack. This produces a pounding effect between the parts, so that rapid wear and possibly breakage will result.

Valve toss is the result of the inertia of the valve-train parts momentarily overpowering the spring. It follows, then, that these two forces—inertia and spring tension—must be balanced so that, at the maximum-designed engine speed, valve toss will not occur. A faulty valve-train design may perform satisfactorily at low speeds, but at high speeds, where inertia becomes greater, valve toss will show up. Figure 15-57 shows curves displayed on an oscilloscope for low- and high-speed valve motions during which valve toss is experienced. The little squiggle at the top of the curve (right, Fig. 15-57) shows that the valve floats free momentarily. Note also that the valve closes with such impact that it bounces several times, opening and closing.

The two basic methods of relieving valve toss are to reduce acceleration and deceleration and to increase the valve-spring tension. The former

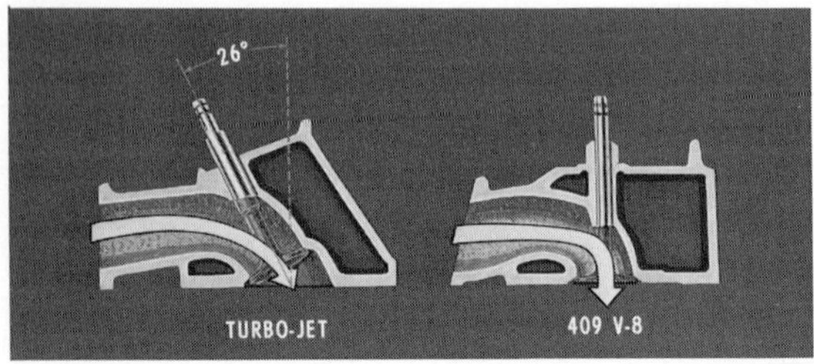

Fig. 15-59. Comparison of the intake-valve ports of the Turbo-Jet and 409 V-8 engines. (*Chevrolet Motor Division of General Motors Corporation*)

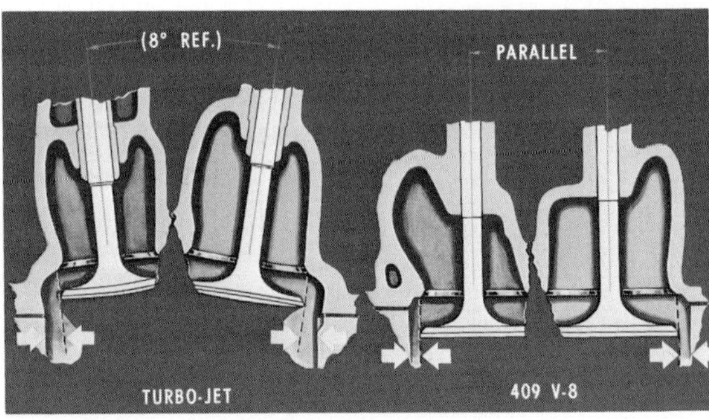

Fig. 15-61. Comparison of the valve locations and actions in the Turbo-Jet and 409 engines. (*Chevrolet Motor Division of General Motors Corporation*)

Fig. 15-62. Cylinder block for the Turbo-Jet engine, showing notches at the top of the block to improve intake-valve clearance. (*Chevrolet Motor Division of General Motors Corporation*)

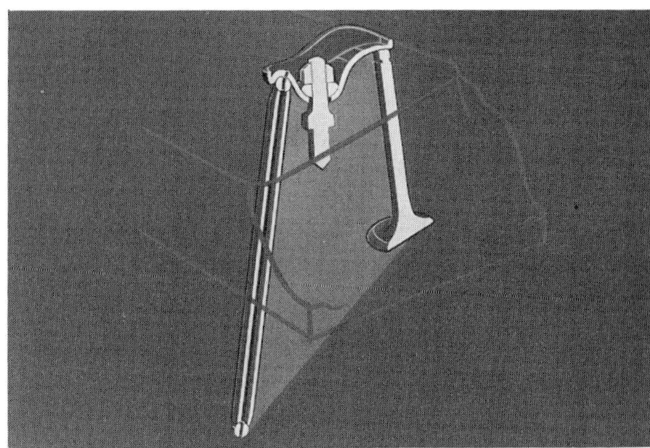

Fig. 15-64. The valve-train components lie in a single plane. (*Chevrolet Motor Division of General Motors Corporation*)

method involves changing the cam contour; the latter may excessively increase spring pressure and wear of valve-train parts. Thus, the final design must be a compromise. For high performance, the valves must open and close quickly so they can stay open for the longest possible time. This promotes better engine breathing and higher volumetric efficiency. But this added performance is achieved at the expense of valve-train life. For most purposes—the family car and light trucks, for example—the designer selects accelerations and decelerations and spring tensions that will not cause unduly rapid wear of valve-train parts.

It should also be remembered that the spring design, as well as tension, is important to the proper functioning of the valve train. The problem of spring surge, which produces a condition akin to valve toss, has already been discussed (§216).

§218. The Chevrolet Turbo-Jet engine valves—a case history The development of the valve train and ports for the Chevrolet Turbo-Jet engine[10] is very interesting; a number of difficult problems had to be solved. Figure 15-58 is a sectional view of one cylinder of the engine. Note that the valves are set at unusual angles with the push rods, and that the ball-pivot-mounted rocker arms also are set at angles.

The angled position of the intake valves and the wedge-shaped combustion chamber allow a more direct flow of air-fuel mixture into the combustion

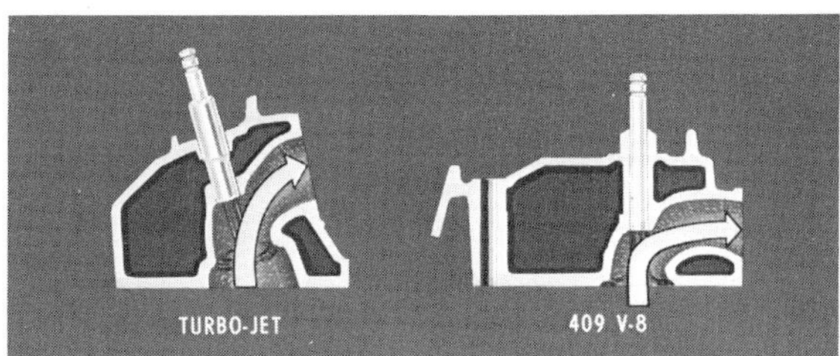

Fig. 15-63. Comparison of the exhaust-valve locations and ports between the Turbo-Jet and 409 V-8 engines. (*Chevrolet Motor Division of General Motors Corporation*)

Fig. 15-65. Push-rod guide plates are attached to the head by the rocker-arm studs. (*Chevrolet Motor Division of General Motors Corporation*)

chamber. Figure 15-59 compares the new intake-port design with the earlier 409 V-8 design. Note that the Turbo-Jet design provides a more direct passage with a smaller angle and less restriction through the intake-valve port; this, of course, allows better engine breathing and higher volumetric efficiency.

Another advantage of the angled intake and exhaust valves and ports is that the wedge-combustion chamber is somewhat rotated, in effect, from a straightahead position. This rotation moves the intake valve and port toward the intake manifold and moves the exhaust valve and port toward the exhaust manifold. Figure 15-60 shows how the valves are angled and moved toward their associated manifolds. In addition, the angling of the valves reduces the shrouding effect of the cylinder walls on the valves. In the 409 V-8 design, the valves are parallel and, when opening, move parallel to the cylinder wall so that one side of the valve remains close to the wall (Fig. 15-61). In the Turbo-Jet design, the valves move inward as they open, away from the cylinder wall. This reduces the shrouding effect of the wall and thus improves engine breathing. To further improve breathing, notches are cut in the top of the cylinder block on the intake side of the combustion chamber (Fig. 15-62). These notches increase intake-valve clearance and provide more room for the inflowing air-fuel mixture. Figure 15-62 also shows that the valve lifter bores are at different angles in the block to accommodate the angled valve trains.

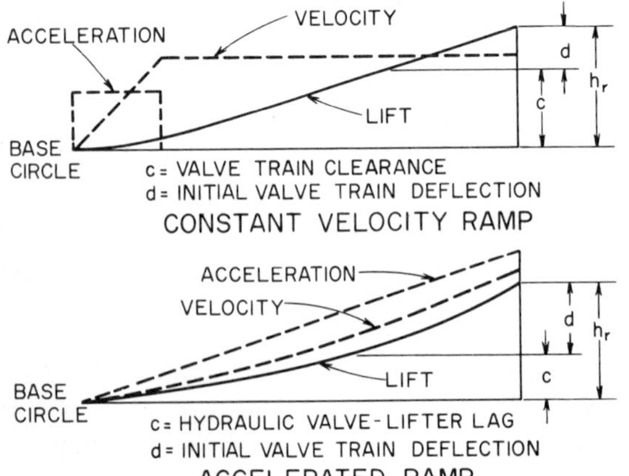

Fig. 15-66. Comparison of constant-velocity opening ramp for solid lifters with accelerated ramp for hydraulic lifters. (*TRW Valve Division, Thompsom, Ramo, Wooldridge, Inc.*)

The angling of the valves and ports also permits a more gentle exit angle for the exhaust gases through the exhaust ports (Fig. 15-63). Also, since the exhaust port is shorter, there is less exhaust-port surface area exposed to the engine coolant. This reduces the load on the cooling system.

Note that the valve train for any one valve is in a single plane (Fig. 15-64), with the center lines of the push rod, rocker-arm stud, rocker arm, and valve lying in a common plane. This eliminates any side thrust that would occur if the parts were at angles to each other. The push rods are held in place by special guide plates which are attached to the cylinder head by the rocker-arm studs (Fig. 15-65). The guides hold the push rods in proper position for good alignment and thus good rocker-arm stability.

Another plus value in the angling of the valves is that it allows the water jacket to be extended downward between the valve seats, thus improving the cooling of the seats (Fig. 15-28).

§219. Cams for hydraulic lifters We have already described (§215), cam contours for solid or mechanical valve lifters. The first part of the opening ramp, coming off the base circle, takes up the clearance, or valve lash, in the valve train. There is no need for this clearance in the system using hydraulic valve lifters. However, the hydraulic valve lifter does have a certain amount of "lag" which, in effect, is simply the looseness with which the lifter parts have settled during the closed-valve phase. To state this another way, when the valve closes, oil pressure from the engine lubricating system enters the hydraulic valve lifter and extends the plunger to take up clearance in the system (see §101). However, the pressure imposed on the oil entering the lifter during this phase is small compared with the pressure imposed when the valve lifter enters the opening phase of valve action.

The pressure increase must first be absorbed by the hydraulic valve lifter before motion is trans-

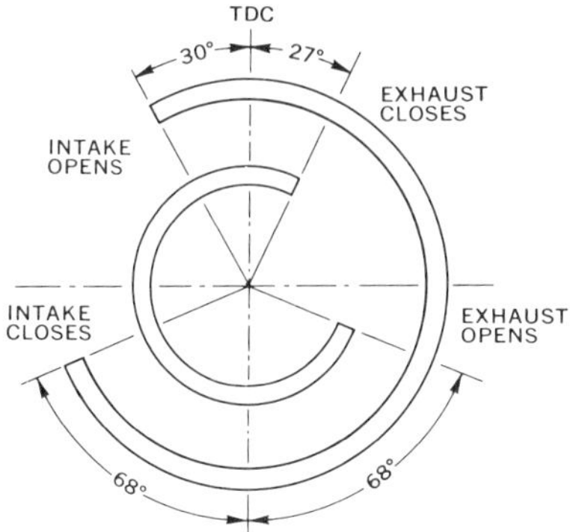

Fig. 15-67. Intake- and exhaust-valve timing for cams of a "road and drag" high-performance camshaft.

mitted from the lifter body (already in motion) to the plunger. This produces a slight lag which amounts to only a few thousandths of an inch or a few degrees of cam rotation.

Now, after this preliminary explanation, let us compare the first parts of the opening ramps for solid lifters and hydraulic lifters. As the opening ramp moves under the solid lifter, the first movement of the lifter takes up the clearance in the valve train, as already noted. Then, some additional motion is required to take up the initial valve-train deflection. It must be recognized that the valve-train parts (on I-head engines especially) are compressed slightly by the load imposed due to spring tension and inertia loading. After all this takes place, the valve begins to move. Figure 15-66 (top) illustrates this. This type of ramp, used with all solid valve lifters, is called a *constant-velocity ramp*. There is first a short acceleration period at the junction of the ramp with the base circle. Then, the ramp imparts a constant velocity to the valve lifter for the rest of the initial phase, during which the valve-train clearance and initial valve-train deflection are taken up. After this phase, at the moment when all play is eliminated from the system and the valve begins to open, acceleration is again imparted to the valve lifter and train. This type of ramp avoids undue impact loading on valve-train parts during the initial phase.

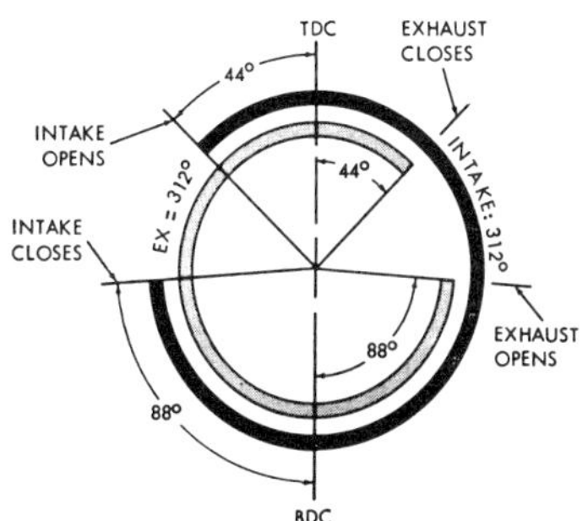

Fig. 15-68. Valve timing for a V-8 competition engine. (*Chrysler-Plymouth Division of Chrysler Motors Corporation*)

The ramp for the hydraulic valve lifter starts out differently and is called an *accelerated ramp* (bottom, Fig. 15-66). This ramp immediately introduces acceleration, which continues throughout the initial phase (take-up of hydraulic valve-lifter lag and initial valve-train deflection). Thus, the valve-train parts have already received some acceleration before the valve starts to move. This allows the valve to be opened more quickly. The take-up of the lifter lag provides a cushioning effect which permits this arrangement without undue shock loading.

The last part of the closing ramp for hydraulic valve lifters must be higher than the opening ramp by an amount equal to the leakdown rate of the lifter during the open-valve phase. This allows the lifter to come down onto the base circle without undue deceleration.

§220. High-performance cams For high-performance engines, such as those used in racing and drag-strip cars, the cams are contoured to give a longer duration of valve opening and thus greater overlap between intake- and exhaust-valve opening. (Refer to §102 for a discussion of valve timing.)

Figure 15-67 shows valve timing for a road-and-drag cam. Note that the intake valve opens 30 degrees before TDC (top dead center), and that the exhaust valve does not close until 27 degrees after TDC, giving an overlap of 57 degrees. The exhaust valve opens at 68 degrees before BDC (bottom dead center), and the intake valve does not close until 68 degrees after BDC, giving a total overlap of 136 degrees. The long duration of valve

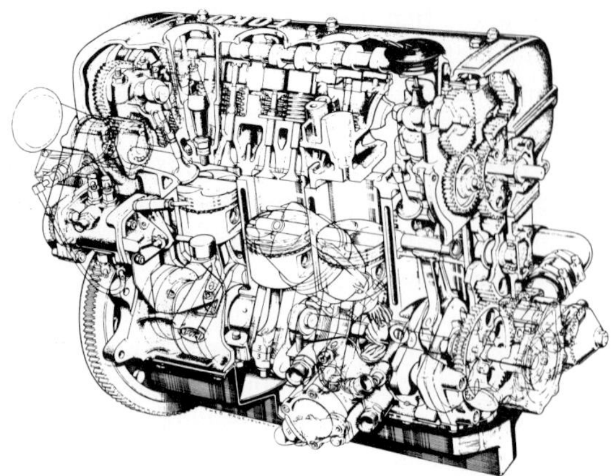

Fig. 15-69. Partial cutaway view of a four-cylinder, in-line DOHC engine. (*British Ford*)

opening gives the engine a much better chance to breathe at high speeds. However, low-speed and idling characteristics become very poor because of the great overlap. Thus, to eliminate rough low-end operation, the idle speed must be increased considerably. Of course, to achieve this high performance, economy must be sacrificed. An engine with this type of camshaft would not give very good fuel economy.

Figure 15-68 shows the valve timing for a high-performance competition engine. This timing is even more radical than that shown in Fig. 15-67; the intake and exhaust valves are both open 312 degrees.

Another method of improving engine performance at the higher end is to use a higher-lift cam, that is, a cam that lifts the valve farther and thus opens it wider. As an example, a typical standard cam for a modern engine provides a total lift, or valve opening, of slightly less than 0.400 inch. A high-performance cam for the same engine provides a lift of about 0.450 inch. The difference of 0.050 inch allows a greater amount of gas to pass in a given time and thus improves engine breathing and high-speed performance. However, there

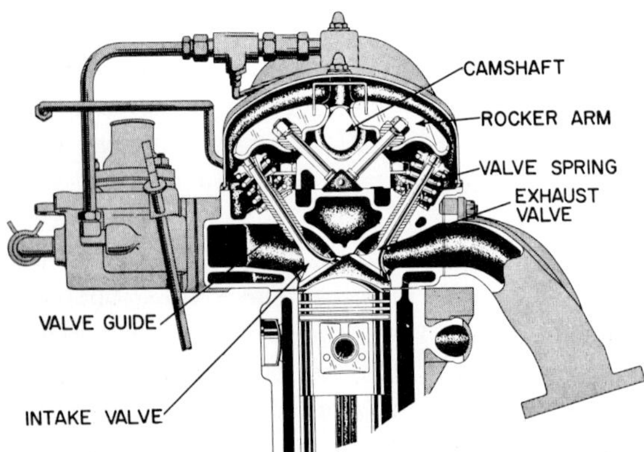

Fig. 15-70. Sectional view from the end of the upper part of a six-cylinder, in-line, SOHC engine. (*Kaiser-Jeep Corporation*)

Fig. 15-71. External view of an SOHC V-8 engine, showing chain and sprocket arrangement to drive the camshafts. (*Ford Division of Ford Motor Company*)

Fig. 15-72. Partial cutaway view of a six-cylinder SOHC engine with camshaft driven by a toothed belt. (*Pontiac Motor Division of General Motors Corporation*)

Fig. 15-73. Sectional view of an SOHC in-line engine, using a toothed belt to drive the camshaft. (*Pontiac Motor Division of General Motors Corporation*)

is a limit to the amount of lift that cams can provide because of the close clearances between valves, when open, and the pistons at TDC. If the lift is too great, then the piston could strike the valves and cause severe damage. Also, with close clearances, any carbon build-up on the piston head could result in the same situation.

We have already mentioned the effects of increasing the opening and closing ramp slopes to increase acceleration and deceleration and thus improve engine breathing (§217).

Actually, according to automotive engineers, there are four general classifications of racing camshafts: road, road and drag, super road and drag, and track and drag. Each has special cam contours designed for the specific type of operation to which the engine will be subjected. Also, there are many modifications and special cam grinds developed by racing-engine specialists.

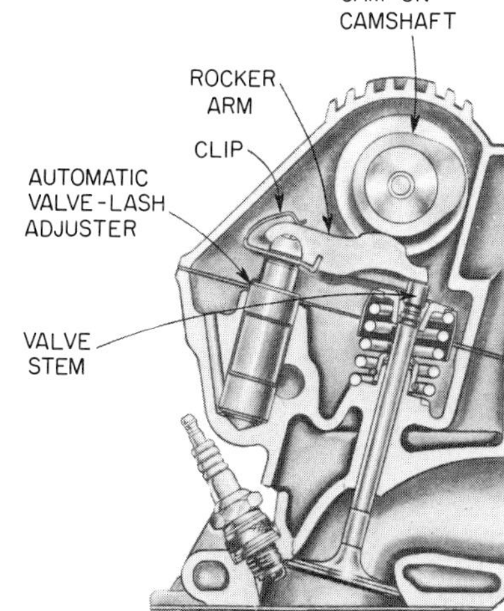

Fig. 15-74. Sectional view of valve mechanism in SOHC engine, using a toothed belt to drive the camshaft. (*Pontiac Motor Division of General Motors Corporation*)

§221. Overhead camshaft We have already mentioned overhead-camshaft engines (§40). These engines may have one camshaft per cylinder bank (SOHC) or two camshafts per cylinder bank (DOHC). Figure 15-69 is a partial cutaway view of a four-cylinder, overhead-valve, DOHC engine. One camshaft operates the intake valves, and the other the exhaust valves.

Figure 15-70 shows the valve arrangement of a six-cylinder, in-line, SOHC engine. Figure 15-71 shows the chains and sprockets used to drive the camshafts in a V-8 SOHC engine. Figure 15-56 is a closeup of the camshaft and roller-type rocker arms used in this engine. (See Chap. 4.)

Most OHC engines use chains and sprockets to drive the camshafts. One relatively new engine that uses a neoprene belt to drive the camshaft is shown in Figs. 15-72 to 15-74. The belt is reinforced with fiber glass cords and has a facing of woven nylon fabric on the toothed side. The teeth in the belt fit teeth on the two drive pulleys. Figure 15-73 is a sectional view of the engine. Note that there is no midpoint support of the rocker arm. Instead, the rocker arm floats. It is attached at one end by a clip to the automatic valve-lash adjuster (which corresponds in some ways to the hydraulic valve lifter). The other end of the rocker arm rests on the tip of the valve stem. Midway, a hump on the rocker arm rests against a cam on the camshaft.

The automatic valve-lash adjuster (Fig. 15-74) is very similar in construction to hydraulic valve lifters (§101). It has a hollow cylinder in which a small piston fits. Oil under pressure from the engine oiling system flows into the hollow cylinder, lifting the piston. One end of the rocker arm is attached to the piston by a clip. The upward movement of the piston raises the rocker arm so it moves up into contact with the cam. This reduces valve lash to zero. Now, when the cam lobe comes around against the rocker arm, the rocker arm is forced down. It pivots on the piston in the valve-lash adjuster, and thus the valve stem end of the rocker arm moves down, forcing the valve to move down and open.

As soon as the lobe passes the rocker arm, the valve spring moves the valve upward to the closed position, forcing the rocker arm upward. Any oil that may have leaked out of the valve-lash adjuster is now replenished by the engine oiling system, and the piston pushes upward to bring the rocker arm into contact with the cam. It is then ready for the next opening cycle.

One advantage of the OHC engine is that, with the elimination of the push rod and (in some engines) the valve lifter, the inertia of the valve train is reduced; also, there is less deflection in the system. With lower inertia, there is less tendency toward valve toss.

Another advantage of the OHC design is that cam contours can be sharper to provide more rapid accelerations and decelerations.[11,12] With less mass to move (no push rod or lifter), the valve train can be accelerated at a higher rate. The practical effect of this is that the valve can be opened and closed more quickly so that it will remain wide open for a larger part of the total cycle. As a consequence, the engine can breathe better, and volumetric efficiency is higher. This improves engine performance, particularly at the high-speed end.

Fig. 15-75. Valve burning due to seat distortion. (*TRW Valve Division, Thompson, Ramo, Wooldridge, Inc.*)

Considering these advantages, it might be natural to ask, "Why aren't all automotive engines OHC?" It is possible that they will be, someday. For the present, however, most OHC engines are designed for high performance—racing engines, for example. The gain in performance is largely at the higher speeds, and the majority of car owners have no need of this high-speed performance. Also, changing over an engine from a camshaft-in-block design to a camshaft-in-head design would be a very expensive procedure, requiring many millions of dollars to prove out the new design and tool up a factory to make it. Nonetheless, there has been some movement in this direction, with the Pontiac six-cylinder OHC engine, the Ford OHC high-performance V-8, and several foreign makes. Even so, it would appear that the push-rod engine will be with us for some time to come.

Fig. 15-76. Effects of valve leakage caused by failure of the valve to fully seat. (*TRW Valve Division, Thompson, Ramo, Wooldridge, Inc.*)

§222. Valve-failure analysis In a new engine design, it sometimes happens that valve life is shortened by valve burning or breakage. A number of conditions could cause these failures.

1. Valve burning. There could be many causes for valve burning, and thus it is very important to pin-point the basic cause so it can be corrected. Most often, the trouble comes from valve-seat distortion or deposit accumulations. However, burn-

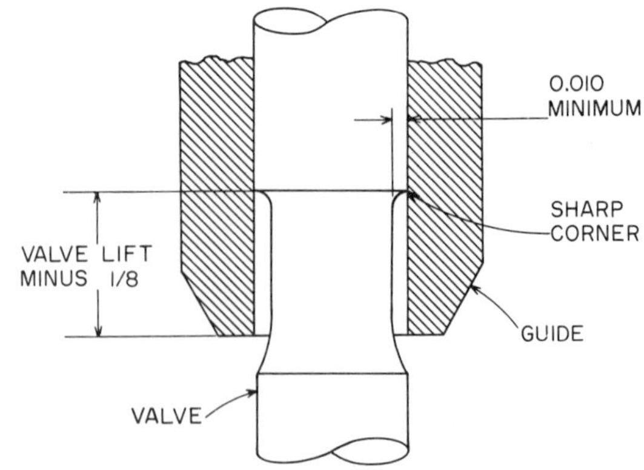

Fig. 15-77. Carbon-relief groove in valve stem, which reduces sticking due to stem deposits. (*TRW Valve Division, Thompson, Ramo, Wooldridge, Inc.*)

ing cloud also come from cracking, thermal stresses, improper valve clearance, or unduly fast

Seat-distortion failures usually can be identified because the valve face has large burned areas (Fig. 15-75). These areas may extend around the face from 45 to 180 degrees. Sometimes two burned areas are found opposite each other. Seat distortion prevents uniform seating so that heat transfer is poor at some points, and these points then overheat. Seat distortion will also cause heavy bearing pressure at some points on the seat, and these points will show up on the seat. Sometimes the valve face will be grooved at these points, showing some sliding motion. If there is only a single heavy-bearing area, the seat has shifted laterally or has tilted. If there are two heavy-bearing areas opposite each other, the indication is that the seat is distorting elliptically.

Uniform burning all the way around the valve face (Fig. 15-76) usually means that the valve is

Fig. 15-78. Face guttering caused by deposits flaking off from the valve face and seat. (*TRW Valve Division, Thompson, Ramo, Wooldridge, Inc.*)

not seating fully. This could result from insufficient clearance (valve-tappet clearance) in the valve-train or valve-stem sticking or stretching. It is possible for there to be sufficient clearance in the valve train when the engine is cold, but thermal expansion of the valve train as the engine heats up could more than take up this clearance so the valve cannot close. More clearance is needed.

Valve-stem sticking is relatively rare on modern engines, partly because of recent improvements in fuels and lubricating oils. Sticking can result from inadequate stem-to-guide clearance or deposit accumulations at the hot end of the valve guide. If the trouble is from deposits, valve-stem seals should be used to reduce the amount of oil passing the stem-to-guide clearance. A carbon relief groove can also be incorporated in the valve stem (Fig. 15-77). The sharp edge of the groove is designed to scrape deposits from inside the guide. Positive valve rotation (§213) is usually effective in combatting deposits because it continually repositions the valve stem, thus wiping away the deposits.

Valve-stem stretching would be a rather rare phenomonen. It could result from excessively strong valve springs, excessive valve-guide temperatures, or use of incorrect valve-stem metal.

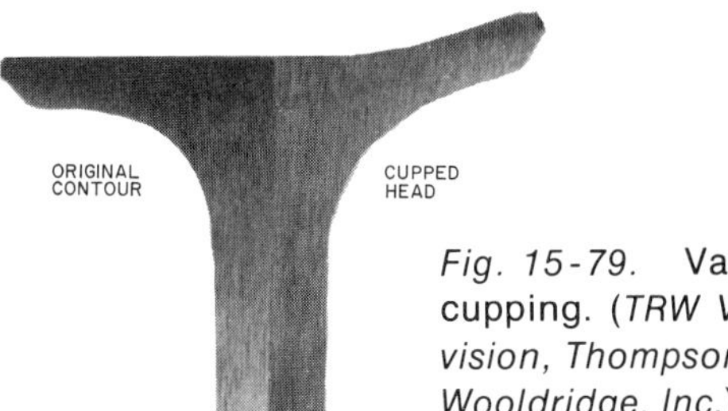

Fig. 15-79. Valve-head cupping. (*TRW Valve Division, Thompson, Ramo, Wooldridge, Inc.*)

Another cause of valve burning is the accumulation of deposits on the valve face and seat. When this happens, parts of the deposits break off, and this forms a path through which exhaust gases can pass when the valve is closed. Then, after a time, these places overheat, and channels burn in the valve face. This action is called *face guttering* (Fig. 15-78), and once it is started, valve failure soon occurs. Positive valve rotation minimizes this type of failure because of the wiping action that tends to remove deposits as they form.

NOTE: Excessive deposit formation and subsequent burning most often occur in engines having large combustion-chamber *s/v* ratios (§139) and in engines operated at constant speeds and loads. This latter condition allows deposits to accumulate because there are no significant changes in temperature or pressures. In other engines, variations in operating characteristics tend to loosen deposits and prevent their formation.

Head cupping can also cause valve-burning failures (Fig. 15-79). Cupping is caused by use of a valve metal that lacks creep strength at operating temperatures, high-combustion pressures, strong valve springs, and high impact pressures. The usual remedy here is to use a valve material with

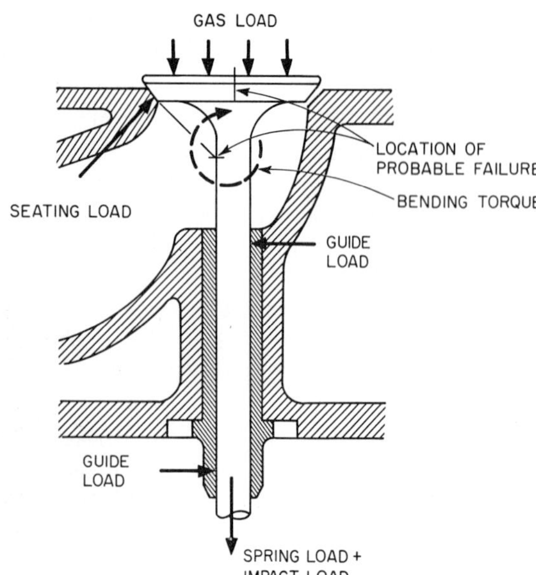

Fig. 15-80. Bending load on the valve stem can cause stem breakage. (*TRW Valve Division, Thompson, Ramo, Wooldridge, Inc.*)

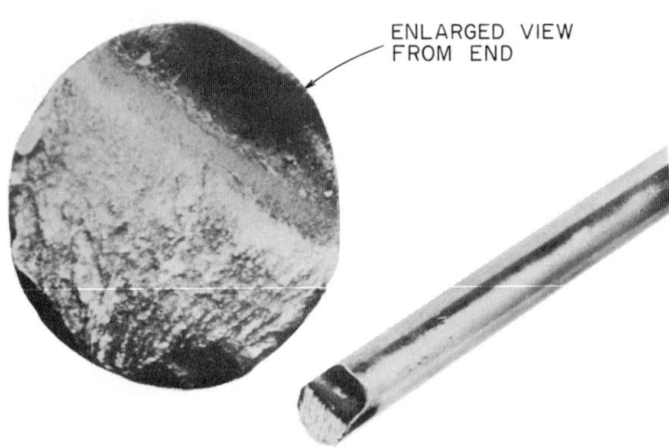

Fig. 15-81. Impact failure of valve. (*TRW Valve Division, Thompson, Ramo, Wooldridge, Inc.*)

greater hot-creep strength. If the cause is excessive impact stresses, then perhaps valve-train dynamics require restudy, and possibly a different cam contour is needed (§217).

2. *Valve breakage.* Valve breakage can result from such things as bending stresses due to seat distortion, high impact stresses due to faulty valve-train dynamics, high thermal stresses, excessive valve temperatures, and piston interference. High

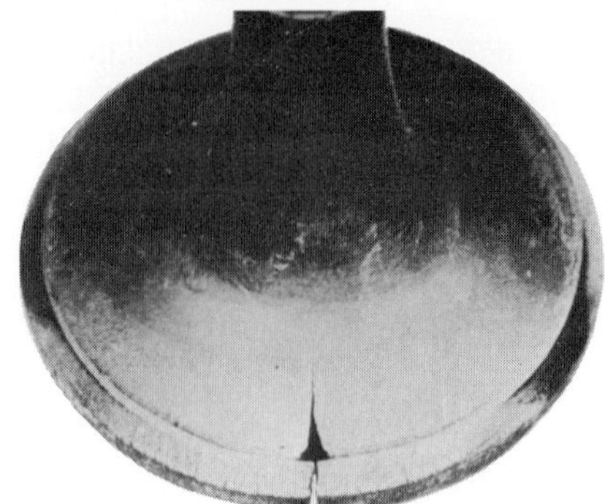

Fig. 15-82. Valve failure caused by thermal fatigue. (*TRW Valve Division, Thompson, Ramo, Wooldridge, Inc.*)

valve temperatures are often due to valve-seat distortion, so distortion is really the cause of failure. Piston interference could result from carbon build-up on the piston head or from valve-train misbehavior (which could cause valve toss, for example —see §217).

Bending loads on the valve stem and under the head of the valve originate from seat distortion (Fig. 15-80). Usually, the head, being hottest, is where the break occurs, as indicated.

Valve-train misbehavior, which allows the valve to seat at excessive speeds, produces heavy impact stresses on the valve and can cause either head or stem breakage. Figure 15-81 shows a stem that has broken due to excessive closing speeds. Note the fracture lines radiating from the failure origin and the shear wedge on the opposite side. Conditions which can cause excessive impact loads include valve-train vibrations and resultant valve bounce, excessively large valve-tappet clearance, and a heavy valve spring.

Another type of valve breakage can occur from thermal stresses set up in the valve head. The center of the head becomes hotter than the valve face and therefore tends to expand more than the valve-head rim. In extreme cases, this can cause the valve to crack radially (Fig. 15-82). Sometimes, there will be several cracks, and occasionally two cracks will intersect and a piece of the head will break off. The remedy is to select a metal of greater strength and lower coefficient of thermal expansion.

SUMMARY

Valves must seal effectively, have minimum stem flexure and inertia, have sufficient cross section for effective heat transfer, and withstand the pressures, temperatures, and impact pounding they meet in service.

Temperature is a critical item in exhaust-valve performance, and this is affected by seat and guide cooling, effective seating of the valve, amount of distortion of the seat, head shape, valve materials, air-fuel ratio, speed, load, compression ratio, and other factors.

In designing a valve train, factors to be considered include the following: size and location of the valves; valve lift; configuration of the valve ports; valve-face angle; valve-head proportions; valve-stem size; valve-head shape; valve materials; desirability of high-performance valve facings, valve stems, and valve tips; valve-port design; valve-guide material and proportions; valve-seat design, angle, and material; valve-seat cooling; valve cooling and lubrication; rocker-arm type and material; type of valve lifter; cam contour; valve-spring design and material; and valve-train dynamics. This last item embraces the entire valve train and its varied and intricate motions. Valve accelerations and decelerations must be high enough to open and close the valves rapidly and thus improve volumetric efficiency. But they must not be so high as to cause excessive impact loading of the valve-train parts. The spring must be strong enough to prevent valve toss, but not so strong as to cause excessive loading of the valve-train parts. Spring surge is another condition to be avoided, and this requires proper spring design.

The overhead camshaft, while somewhat complicating the engine configuration, requires fewer valve-train parts and can lead to a higher-performance engine.

REFERENCES

1. Giles, W. S., Fundamentals of Valve Design and Material Selection, SAE (Society of Automotive Engineers) 660471 (paper), 1966; Engineering Know-How in Engine Design, SAE special publication SP-283, 1966.

2. Analog Study of Valve Heat Flow, Eaton Manufacturing Company, 1961 (booklet).

3. Cherrie, J. M., Factors Influencing Valve Temperatures in Passenger Car Engines, SAE (Society of Automotive Engineers) 650484, 1965 (paper).

4. Rominsky, A. O., Mark II-427 GT Engine Induction System, SAE (Society of Automotive Engineers) 670067, 1967 (paper).

5. Smith, W. R., Ford's New 240 I-6 Engine, SAE (Society of Automotive Engineers) 966C, 1965 (paper).

6. Controlling Overhead Valve Lubrication, Perfect Circle Paper C2484, Perfect Circle Division, Dana Corporation.

7. Brinson, L. T., Jr., Techniques in Evaluating Valve Train Dynamics, Engineering Know-How in Engine Design, SAE special publication, part 8, SP-178, 1960.

8. Timpner, F. F., How to Use Vectors to Compute Engine Cams, SAE (Society of Automotive Engineers) 660349, 1966 (paper).

9. Faustyn, N. W. and J. Eastman, The Ford 427 Cubic Inch Single Overhead Cam Engine, SAE (Society of Automotive Engineers) 650497, 1965 (paper).

10. Keinath, R. L., H. G. Sood, and W. J. Polkinghorne, Chevrolet Turbo-Jet Engine, SAE (Society of Automotive Engineers) 66340, 1966 (paper).

11. McKellar, M. R., Pontiac's New Overhead Camshaft Six Cylinder Tempest Engine, SAE (Society of Automotive Engineers) 660126, 1966 (paper).

12. Meeusen, H. J., Overhead Cam Valve Train Design Analysis with a Digital Computer, SAE (Society of Automotive Engineers) 660350, 1966 (paper).

QUESTIONS

1. What are the basic requirements of a good valve-train design?

2. What is valve lift, and what is its significance in regard to volumetric efficiency?

3. What does mach number 0.5 have to do with the size of the intake valve?

4. Why is the size of the exhaust valve much less a critical factor in engine volumetric efficiency than the intake valve?

5. Why is the valve-face angle important? What is the most widely used valve-face angle?

6. Explain what interference angle means, as related to valves.

7. What are some factors to be considered when establishing valve-head proportions?

8. What are the two schools of thought regarding valve-head shape? What are advantages and disadvantages of using a flexible head?

9. What are the major factors to be considered in selecting a material for a valve?

10. Explain the purpose of sodium valves and how they work.

11. What is the purpose of valve facings?

12. What are the important factors to be considered in designing valve ports for an engine?

13. What are the factors to be considered in designing valve guides?

14. Describe valve-seat distortion, its causes, and the troubles that can result from this condition.

15. What are the advantages and disadvantages of siamesed ports?

16. Describe heat input to, and heat rejection from, a typical exhaust valve, giving percentages.

17. Describe the induction-hardening of valve seats.

18. What are advantages and disadvantages of using valve-seat inserts?

19. What are the major factors that influence valve temperatures?

20. Describe the effects of the air-fuel ratio on valve temperature. Why is it possible for the ratio to vary from cylinder to cylinder in an engine?

21. What is the effect of compression ratio on valve temperature?

22. What are valve-stem shields, and what is their purpose?

23. Describe the two general types of devices that produce valve rotation. What is the purpose of valve rotation?

24. What is the best rocker-arm geometry to minimize scrubbing?

25. Explain the basic requirements for a good cam-contour design.

26. Describe the basic procedure of designing a cam contour.

27. What are the basic requirements for a good valve-spring design?

28. What is valve-spring surge? What is valve toss? How do the two differ?

29. In what ways does the cam for a hydraulic lifter differ from that for a solid lifter?

30. Describe the special characteristics of a high-performance cam.

31. Describe some of the advantages of the overhead camshaft.

Cylinder Block and Head

CHAPTER **16**

We have already discussed several aspects of cylinder-block and cylinder-head design, such as combustion-chamber configurations, valve locations, intake- and exhaust-port shapes, provisions for optimum heat withdrawal from the valves and pistons, and so on. In this chapter, we will examine the design problems relating directly to the block and head—their manufacture and operation.

§223. Basic considerations The purpose of the cylinder head and cylinder block is to provide a structure that will contain and support the moving parts of the engine, permit them to move in their prescribed paths or orbits, retain compression and combustion pressures and intake vacuums, and reject the proper amount of heat to the circulating water in the cooling system. They must do all this without undue distortion as the varied pressures, stresses, and strains are applied during the course of engine operation. Figure 7-2 shows various parts that are attached to the cylinder block or assembled in it.

The block and head designer must not only have all of the above requirements in mind, but also must produce a design which can be cast and machined in the simplest and most efficient manner. The designer must have an intimate knowledge of foundry practices, the making and placing of cores, the forming of the drag and cope, and the actions of molten metal as it pours into the mold. He must also know machining practices and the stresses set up in the block and head as various machine tools are brought to bear on the castings. Further, he must be able to foresee the stresses produced in the castings by the tightening of the assembling bolts—particularly head bolts—and by the combustion processes and loading applied through the pistons, connecting rods, and crankshaft to the block and head assembly.

This latter point may be elementary, but it is important to note that, when pressure is applied to the piston by the combustion process, this pressure is also applied to the head (Fig. 16-1). This places the head, head bolts, cylinder block, and main-bearing-cap attaching studs in tension. Figure 16-2 is a greatly exaggerated view of what the applied load does to the crankshaft and main-bearing supports at the lower end of the block.

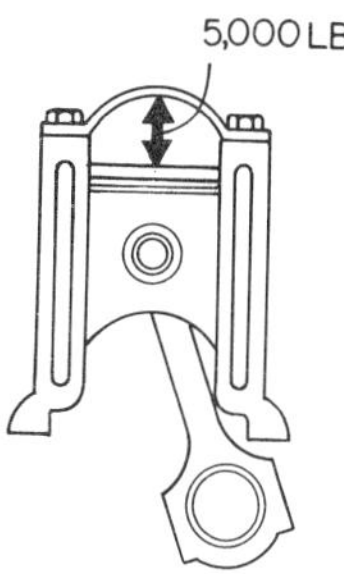

Fig. 16-1. The combustion pressure is applied to both the piston and cylinder head.

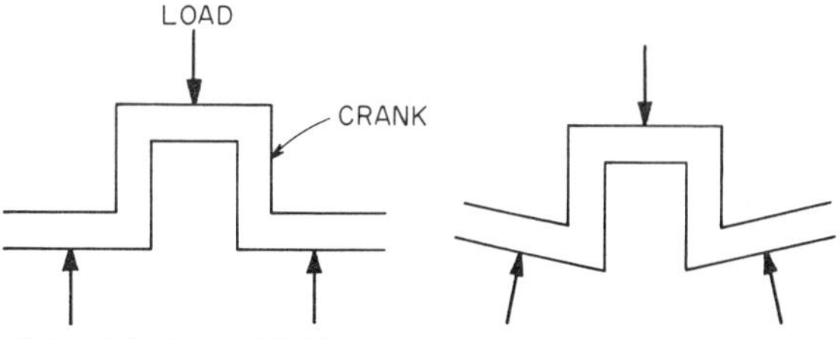

Fig. 16-2. The load applied to the crank tends to bend the main-bearing supports off horizontal. (Bending effect is greatly exaggerated.)

The load, in effect, bends the supports off horizontal. This load is applied during every power stroke. Actually, the load applied is the resultant of the combustion pressures and the inertial and centrifugal forces acting on the piston, connecting rod, and crank, as shown in Fig. 14-16 and 14-17. Figure 14-18 shows the actual loads imposed on the rear-intermediate main bearing of a V-8 engine running at 4,400 rpm (revolutions per minute).

As a consequence of all this, the block and head are continuously subjected to a barrage of forces that act in different directions and constantly change directions and magnitudes. These forces repeatedly try to twist, bend, and otherwise distort the head and block. In addition, there are the distorting effects of thermal stresses due to uneven heating and thus uneven expansion of the various parts of the head and block.

All of these factors must be taken into consideration by the designer. A tabulation of some of the basic design factors might run somewhat as follows:

1. The head and block must provide the proper combustion-chamber, valve, and valve-port configuration.
2. Metal masses must be well distributed to avoid excessive temperature gradients and possible hot spots.
3. The block and head should be as light as possible, with cylinder walls and other sections as thin as possible, consistent with strength requirements and foundry practices.
4. Water jackets should be made large enough—but not too large—for adequate heat rejection and proper engine cooling.
5. The block and head must be strong enough to take the loads imposed by machining processes.
6. There must be adequate metal to permit boring of oil galleries for the lubrication system.

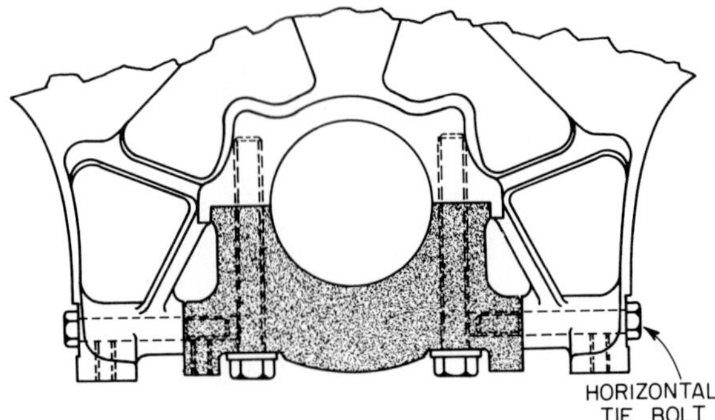

Fig. 16-3. Location of horizontal tie bolts used on intermediate main-bearing caps. (*Chrysler-Plymouth Division of Chrysler Motors Corporation*)

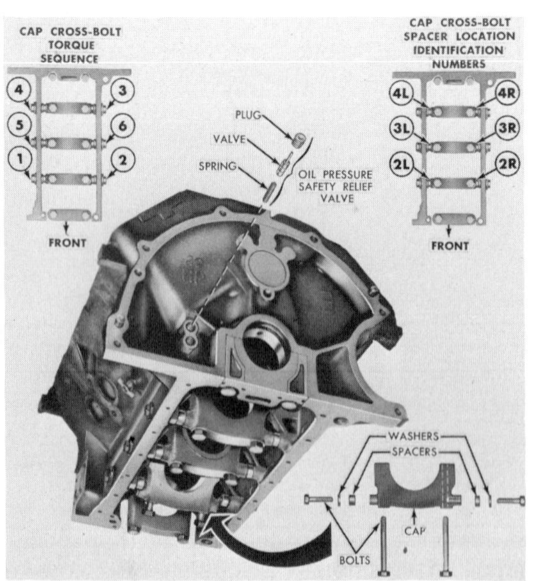

Fig. 16-4. Cylinder-block details, showing locations of horizontal tie bolts on intermediate main-bearing caps. (*Ford Division of Ford Motor Company*)

Fig. 16-5. Cylinder block, showing location of additional main-bearing-cap attaching bolts. (*Pontiac Motor Division of General Motors Corporation*)

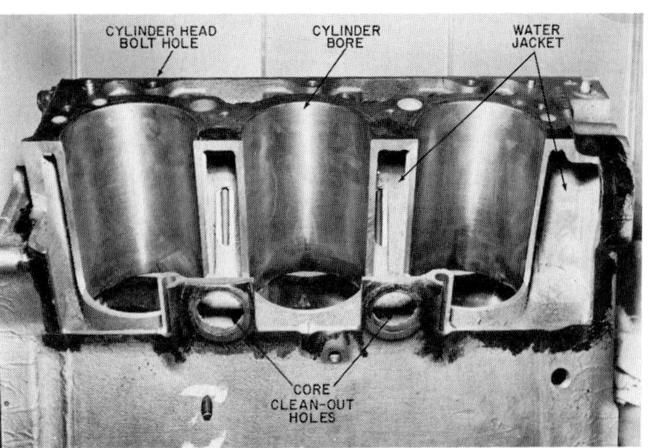

Fig. 16-6. One bank of a V-6 engine block partly cut away so that the internal construction can be seen. (*Truck and Coach Division, General Motors Corporation*)

7. The head-attaching bolts should be so located as to minimize block and head distortion as they are tightened.

8. The main-bearing caps must be rigidly supported and tied in solidly to the block. This is necessary to minimize stresses and distortion of the supporting webs as a result of the heavy loading of the main bearings (see Fig. 14-18). In some high-performance engines, the intermediate main-bearing caps are tied in to the sides of the block with two additional bolts (Fig. 16-3). This gives additional support and rigidity to the caps. Figure 16-4 is a bottom view of a cylinder block, showing the details of the horizontal tie bolts. In some engines, the additional bolts are vertical and tie the caps into the bearing supporting webs (Fig. 16-5).

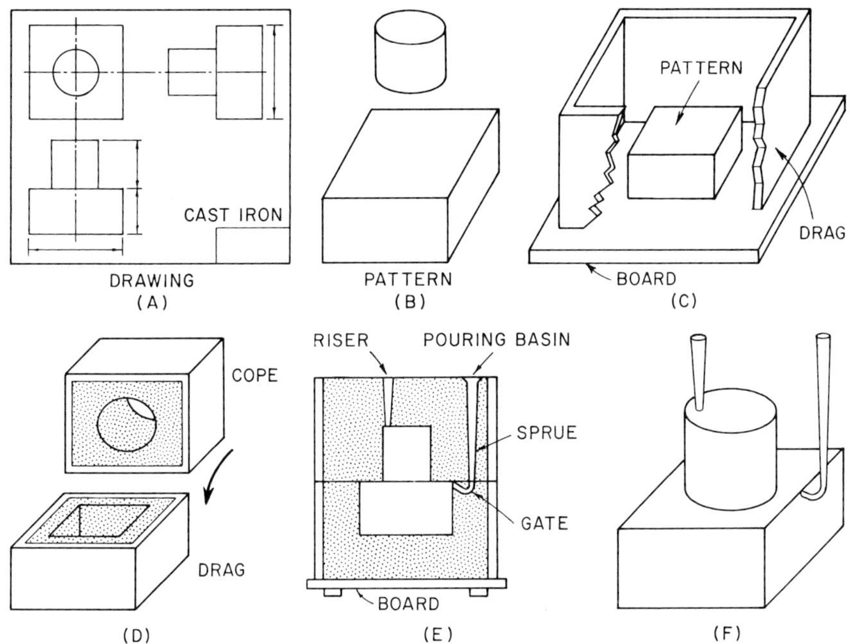

Fig. 16-7. Making a casting, from drawing to final casting. (See text for explanation of A to F.)

9. The head and block must be designed so they can be cast in conformity with good foundry practice. This means a number of things, as follows: Sharp edges and fillets must be avoided if possible because these may cause casting problems. The cores should be as simple and as few in number as possible. Cores must fit firmly and snugly together to avoid shifting with consequent formation of fins in the water jackets, or uneven thickness of cylinder or block walls. There should be an adequate number of core clean-out holes to assure complete elimination of cores. Sprues, gates, and risers must be so located as to assure solid castings, with minimum occlusions or voids.

10. The head and block must be so designed as to permit the use of the most modern automated block and head processing and assembling equipment.

§224. Foundry practice A brief review of foundry practice and an explanation of how the cylinder block is cast follow. As a first step, after the drawings for the block have been completed, the patterns must be made. There are two types of patterns —one which defines in three dimensions the outside surfaces of the casting, and the other from which the cores must be made. The cores define in three dimensions the cavities or openings inside the casting. For example, Fig. 16-6 shows a cylinder block for a V-6 engine which has been partly cut away. The water jackets and core clean-out holes are formed in the casting by cores. Later, the cores are broken up and cleaned out through the clean-out holes.

The cores usually are made from sand mixed with a binder, and, after forming, they are baked. They may include strengthening wires or bolts by which several subcores are assembled.

A simple example may clarify the casting process (Fig. 16-7). First, a drawing is made (A). This drawing goes to the pattern shop so the patternmakers can make a pattern. In the example shown, two subpatterns are required (B). The patterns may be made of wood or metal. Metal is used if the casting is to go into big production.

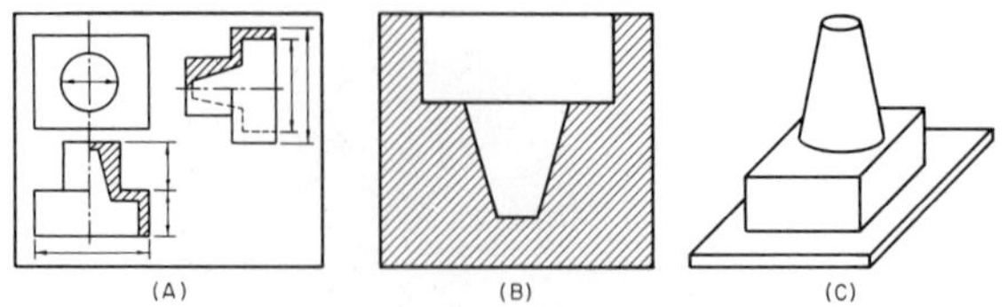

Fig. 16-8. Making a core.

The lower pattern half is positioned on a board, and the drag is placed around it (C). The drag is like a box without a top or bottom. Next, sand is packed firmly into the drag. Then a second board is placed on the top, and the drag is inverted. Now, the pattern is at the top, and it can be removed to leave a cavity in the sand filling the drag (D).

The other half of the pattern is used to form the cavity in the cope (D). The placement of the patterns in the drag and cope must be done exactly so that when the cope is set on top of the drag, the cavities in the two will match properly.

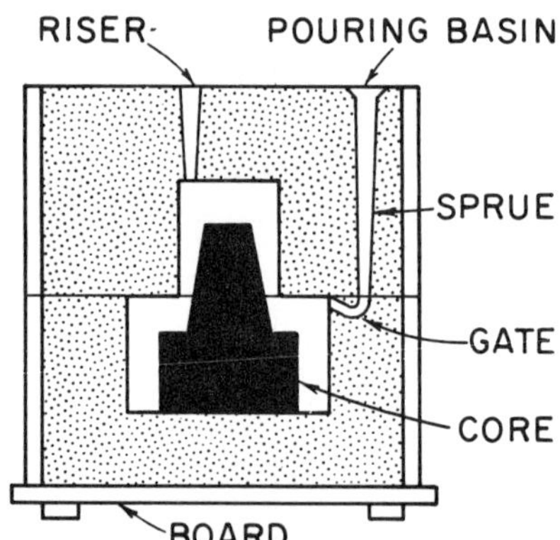

Fig. 16-9. Placing core in mold in preparation for pouring the metal.

The sand normally used for making molds is called *green sand*, which is a mixture of sharp sand (sand in which the particles have sharp edges), a binder, and some water.

The mold, when completed and ready for pouring, also contains a pouring basin, a sprue, a gate, and a riser (E). These are necessary to allow the molten metal to run down into the cavity without changing the shape of the cavity and thus the final casting. The gate takes the impact of the molten metal as it runs down the sprue and allows it to

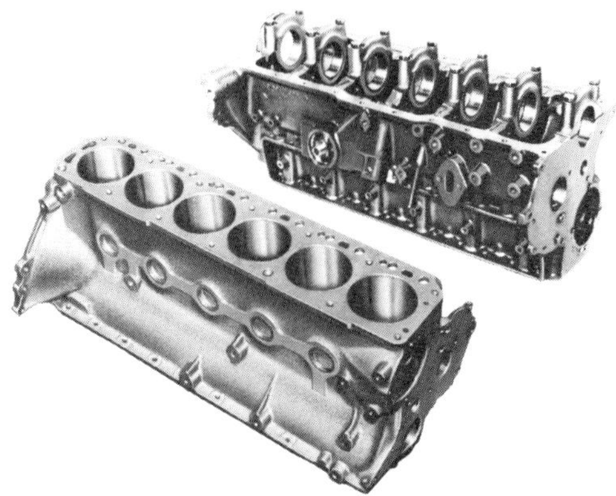

Fig. 16-10. Bottom and top views of a cylinder block for a six-cylinder, in-line engine. Note that the main-bearing caps are installed. *(Ford Motor Company)*

run into the bottom of the cavity. Usually, there is steam from the mold and entrapped gases in the molten metal, and, as the metal rises in the cavity, these can escape through the riser hole. At the end of the pour, the metal rises up into the riser, carrying with it any particles of sand or other impurities that might have been included in the molten metal. Actually, the appearance of molten metal in the riser is the signal for the foundryman to stop pouring because this means that the cavity is filled.

After the casting has cooled, the cope and drag are removed, and the sand mold is broken away. This leaves the casting with the riser and sprue still attached. Later, these are broken off, and the points of attachment are ground down. The rough casting then remains, ready for further machining as called for by the manufacturing process.

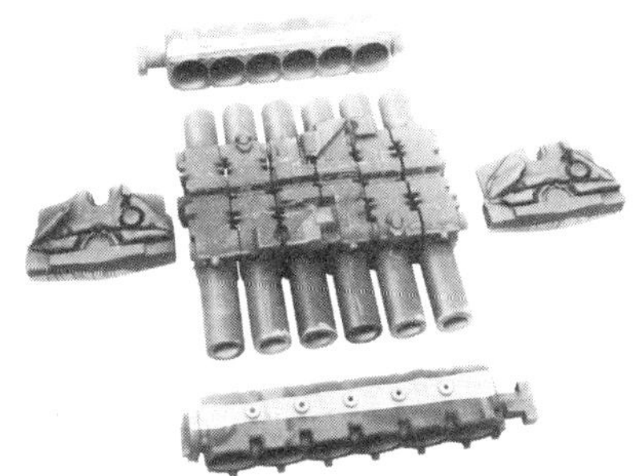

Fig. 16-11. Coring for two six-cylinder blocks. *(Ford Motor Company)*

Fig. 16-12. Cores placed in drag mold. *(Ford Motor Company)*

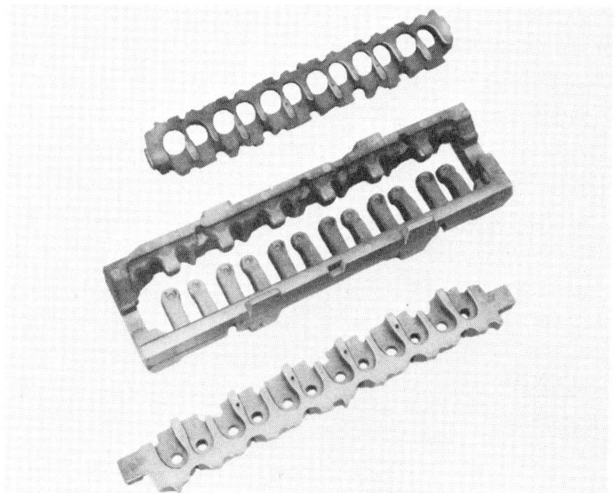

Fig. 16-13. The three cores required for the cylinder head of a six-cylinder, in-line engine. *(Ford Motor Company)*

Now what happens if the drawing calls for the inside of the casting to be hollow (Fig. 16-8)? This requires the making of a pattern mold for a core. The patternmaker produces, in wood or metal (if many castings are to be made), the core pattern (B). This is then filled with core sand, which is sharp sand with a binder. The core mold is then inverted on a board so the core stands alone. Uusually, the core is baked in an oven so that it will be strong enough to resist breaking up when the molten metal is poured around it.

After the core is ready, it is set into the drag just before the cope is put into place (16-9). Now, when

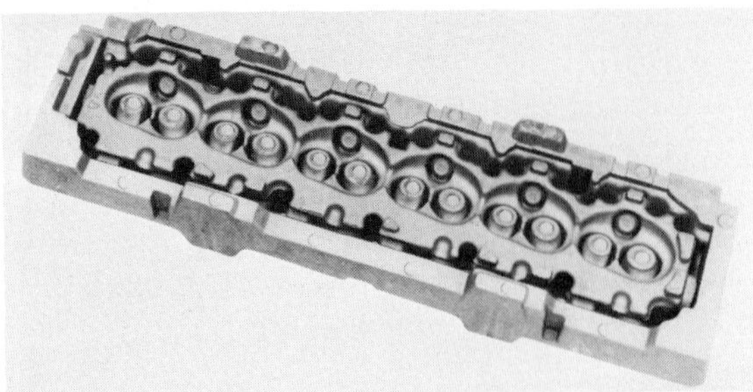

Fig. 16-14. The cores assembled in preparation for being placed into the cylinder-head mold. (*Ford Motor Company*)

the metal is poured, it will fill the cavity between the mold and the core to form the hollow casting that the drawing called for in Fig. 16-8.

§225. Casting a cylinder block When casting anything as complicated as a cylinder block or cylinder head, the procedure, the molds, and the cores are much more complex than described in the previous section. For example, consider the cylinder block shown in Fig. 16-10, which is for a six-cylinder, in-line, overhead-valve engine. The engineers decided that it would be feasible to cast two blocks in the same mold, positioned crankcase to crankcase. The coring for this is shown in Fig. 16-11. The central-core assembly is formed from two crankcase cores and two water-jacket cores. Each of these is formed from several smaller subcores. Figure 16-12 shows how the cores look when placed in the drag mold.

Figure 16-13 shows the three cores required for a cylinder head used in a six-cylinder, in-line, overhead-valve engine. Figure 16-14 shows these three cores assembled in readiness to be placed in the cylinder-head mold.

Cores for cylinder heads and blocks must be very accurately made, and the process calls for metal core molds that are at fairly high temperatures. The core sand is rammed into these molds, and the molds are then put into ovens so the cores are baked. The cores are then removed from the molds. This process prevents dimension changes during the baking process.

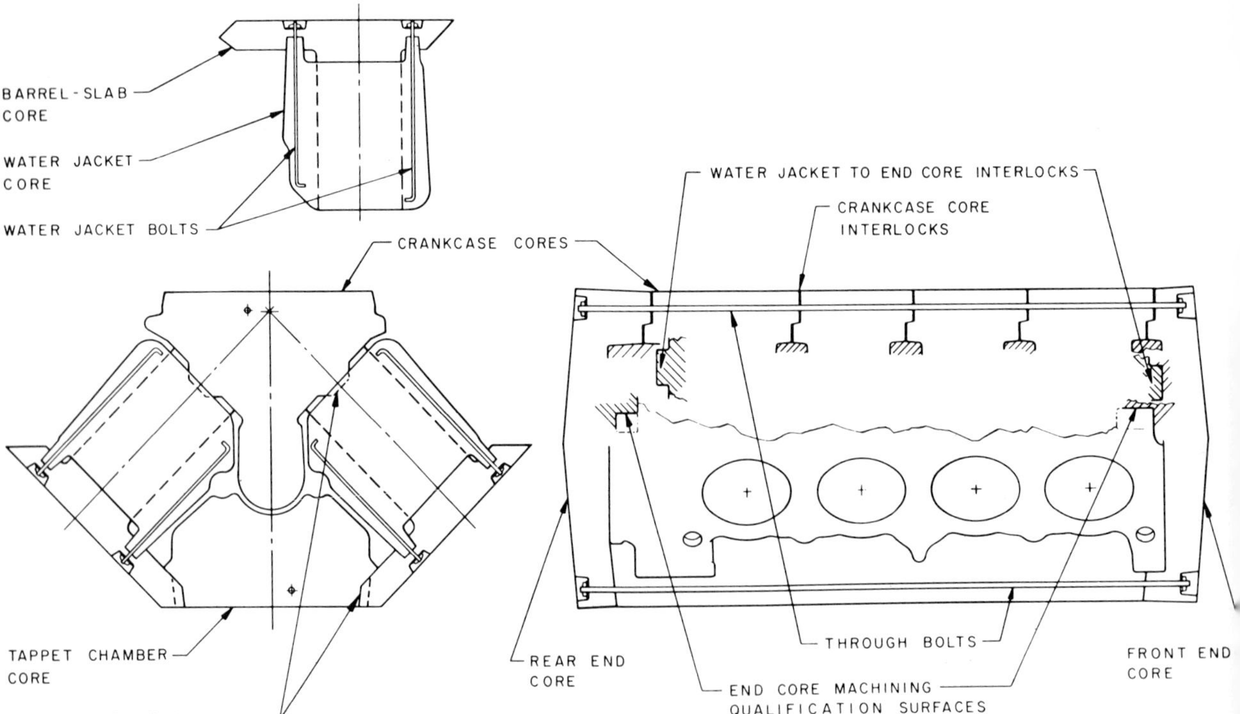

Fig. 16-15. Cylinder-block core assembly. (*Chrysler Motors Corporation*)

Cores are often assembled by pasting the various subparts together. For example, the three cores shown in Fig. 16-13 are pasted together to form the assembly shown in Fig. 16-14.

Cores may also be held together by bolts or wires, as shown in Fig. 16-15. This shows the cores for a V-8 engine cylinder block.[2] It is cast with the crankcase up, in the position shown. Note the bolts and interlocks used to position the cores.

An essential reason why the cores must be accurately dimensioned and located is that the surfaces they form in the finished casting may become the reference points by which the casting will be positioned when the machining operations start. Note, in Fig. 16-15 (lower right), how the end cores form the machining-qualification surfaces from which the entire machining procedures will start. An automated cylinder-block-machining setup is described in §227. In this setup, the machine has locating spindles that are inserted through the core-clean-out holes in the sides of the cylinder-block casting to press against the inner surfaces of the cylinder water jackets. These inner surfaces are, of course, the outer surfaces of the cylinders and were formed by the water-jacket cores.

You can understand, then, that if the cores are only slightly off in final dimensions or are assembled slightly off position in the mold, then the final casting would have cylinder walls or other wall sections of uneven dimensions. If such a block were actually used to build an engine, the engine might very well give poor service and could even fail in a short time. In practice, however, inspection procedures would disclose such defective castings, and they would be scrapped—melted down to make new castings.

§226. Designing Ford's 240 engine cylinder block—a case history It might be interesting to take a look at some of the problems and their solutions encountered during the design of a cylinder block for the Ford 240, six-cylinder, in-line, overhead-valve engine.[1] This is similar to the block shown in Fig. 16-10. To start with, experimental, or test, blocks were cast, machined, and built-up into test engines for laboratory investigation. The block configurations were based on the experience gained by the engineers from other engines their company had produced which had proven successful in operation. The engineers did try, however, in their design work on the new block, to eliminate metal and therefore weight wherever possible. It was considered probable, during the early design work, that they had gone too far in this direction.

Completed engines using the new block were tested in many ways. This provided thorough testing, not only of the block itself, but also of other newly designed or modified engine parts. One such test required the installation of a series of strain gauges on the engine block. The engine was then operated at various speeds and loads on a dynamometer so that the stresses applied to the block could be determined under all operating conditions. The strain gauges showed several interesting conditions—some were expected and others, perhaps, were unexpected. For one thing, the gauges showed stress reversals with each revolution of the crankshaft, with stresses going from tensile to compressive. Further, the stresses increased exponentially with engine speed. It was

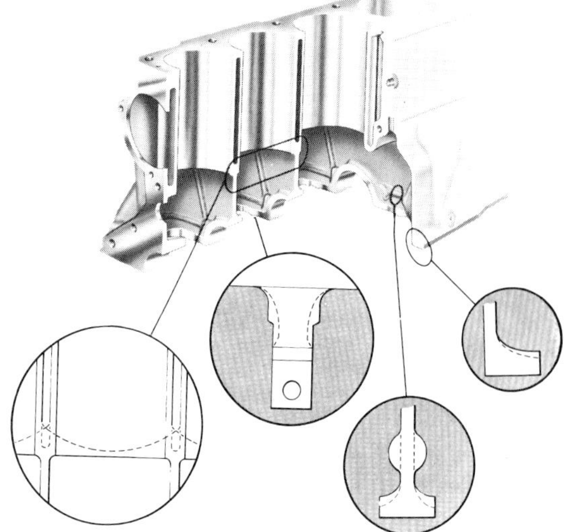

Fig. 16-16. Areas strengthened by addition of metal in six-cylinder, in-line engine block. Dotted lines show original configurations. (*Ford Motor Company*)

also instructive to note that all strain gauges peaked at the same time, regardless of their location on the cylinder block, with half showing tension and half showing compression. The peak occurred with the No. 1 crankpin 120° after TDC (top dead center). These data indicated that the cylinder block was bending as a loaded beam bends. Further testing with stroboscopic light and photoelastic stress analysis confirmed this finding.

The rotating forces acting on the crankpins, consisting of combustion pressures, inertia, and centrifugal force, attempt to bend the crankshaft and the cylinder block, as already noted (§223). It was found that these forces tended to lag behind the No. 1 crankpin by 30 degrees. Thus, at 120 degrees after TDC, the forces were acting in a horizontal direction. The same thing occurred with the crankpin at 300 degrees after TDC, but the forces were in the opposite direction. The result was that the cylinder bores tended to distort into an elliptical shape. In other words, the forces were trying to stretch the block horizontally.

The comprehensive studies of the cylinder block, as outlined above, pointed the way to what had to be done to eliminate the distortions. Insofar as the block was concerned, it was reinforced in the proper places to provide the added strength needed. Also, crankshaft balancing was improved to reduce some of the rotating forces.

Figure 16-16 shows the changes that were made in the block to add strength where it was needed. The dotted lines show the original design. Note how only minor additions of metal—to thicken some cross sections or to add ribs—were required. One of the changes was made to strengthen the main-bearing webs. This change was required because it was found that these webs sometimes failed during the broaching operation, that is, during the finishing of the main-bearing surfaces. This emphasizes once again the importance of designing for the manufacturing process, as well as for performance in the assembled engine.

It becomes obvious, in considering all the design factors discussed above, that the design of a cylinder block is an extremely complex matter. Engineers may utilize their prior experience and the backlog of knowledge built up by their company when starting on a new design, but the final design takes shape empirically, at least to some degree.

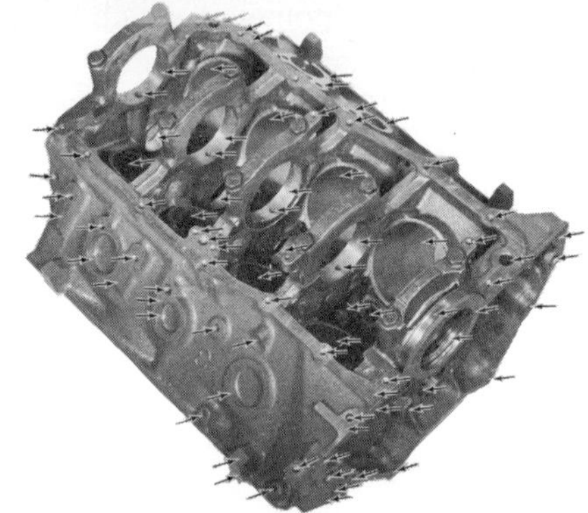

Fig. 16-17. Cylinder block for V-8 engine with various machining operations indicated by arrows. (*Buick Motor Division of General Motors Corporation*)

Fig. 16-18. Horizontal broaching machine which rough-finishes flat surfaces on block in preparation for other machining operations. (*Cincinnati Milling Machine Company*)

Fig. 16-19. Transfer machine for finishing V-8 engine cylinder blocks. It consists of many automatic machine tools plus transfer mechanisms that move the cylinder blocks automatically from one machine tool to the next. (*The Cross Company*)

That is, prototypes must be built and subjected to laboratory analysis so that possible weaknesses can be ferreted out and eliminated.

It is also true that cylinder-block design has become increasingly difficult because horsepower requirements continue to rise while pounds per horsepower continue to go down. To achieve these opposing aims, engineers focus their attention on every part of the engine, thinning cylinder walls, bulkheads, and top decks, and removing metal wherever possible. At the same time, they place strengthening ribs or thicken cross sections where necessary to provide adequate rigidity and strength.

In earlier engines, say of 30 years ago, speeds, combustion pressures, and loads were much lower. The major aims then were to make the block good and strong, without too much concern about weight, and with enough jacketing to assure adequate cooling.

Today, however, every ounce possible must be eliminated without overweakening the block. Thin-wall casting techniques, with precision-made cores precisely placed, have made it possible to take out unneeded metal while still providing the strength needed.

Another way to eliminate the weight is by using a lighter metal, such as aluminum. Thus, in recent years, several companies have produced engines with aluminum blocks. (These are discussed in §230.)

§227. Finishing a cylinder block After the block has been cast, the cores are broken up and removed. This is done on a shaker. Also, rods can be poked into the core-clean-out holes to help break up the cores. Core bolts and wires must also be removed. The casting is then cleaned in preparation for its progress through the machining process. Figure 16-17 shows the cylinder block for a V-8 engine, with the various required machining operations indicated.

In our description of the machining operations performed on the V-8 block, we will take as an example a modern automated block-machining line (Fig. 16-19). As a first step, the block is sent through a horizontal broaching machine (Fig. 16-18), which rough-machines flat surfaces on the block (such as the surfaces on which the cylinder heads will mount). Next, an automatic-transfer machine receives the block casting and performs certain initial and important operations on it. The term "transfer" relates to the functioning of the machine as it moves the workpiece from one station, or operation, to the next. The machine automatically *transfers* the workpiece from operation to operation. In the automatic-transfer machine, the casting is first properly positioned. This is essential because the operations that follow include drilling and reaming of manufacturing, or locating, holes that will be used subsequently as reference holes for the later machining operations on the casting. To assure this, the machine has locating spindles that are inserted through openings in the sides of the casting (the core-clean-out holes) to press against the inner surfaces of the water jackets. These inner surfaces are, of course, the outer surfaces of the cylinders. Thus, everything that is done to the casting from this point on is directly related to the locations of the cylinders.

Once the casting has been properly located, a series of machining operations are performed on it as it moves down the line from station to station. The manufacturing holes are drilled and reamed; half-rounds are milled in the transverse members or webs which will later take the main bearings, and so on. Then, the casting passes on to other complex groupings of machines which perform all of the following operations:

1. Cylinders are rough-bored.
2. Front and back faces of block are milled.
3. Series of holes are drilled, chamfered, and reamed, in the top and bottom faces of the block.
4. Series of holes are bored, drilled, chamfered, and reamed in the front and rear faces.
5. Oil galleries are drilled, core holes are bored and finish-reamed for welch plugs, mounting holes are drilled, and mounting pads are milled on both sides of block.

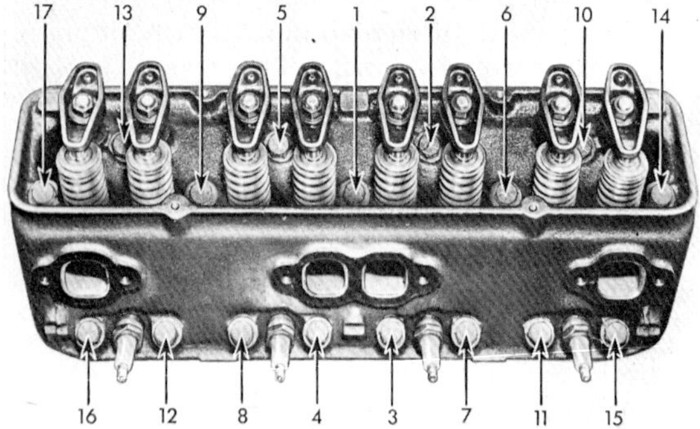

Fig. 16-20. Sequence chart for tightening cylinder-head bolts on a V-8 engine. (*Chevrolet Motor Division of General Motors Corporation*)

6. Holes are drilled, reamed, countersunk, and counterbored in the top, or head, ends; oil holes are drilled, and the pads on sides of block milled.

NOTE: These various pads that are milled are for mounting such parts as distributor, oil pump, manifolds, and so on.

7. Holes in which valve tappets are assembled are drilled, chamfered, and reamed.
8. Holes to be threaded are tapped and blown out.
9. There are check points all along the line. The various operations are automatically checked by inspecting devices that provide an instant warning to the attendant if some operation does not meet manufacturing specifications.

At this point, most of the "minor" operations on the cylinder block have been completed. Now, such major machining operations as finishing the cylinders and the camshaft and crankshaft bores are required. For these operations, the main-bearing caps must be installed, and the cap bolts must be tightened to the proper tension. This is important because tightening the bolts changes the block dimensions slightly; machining must be done so that the final dimensions will approximate those required in the assembled engine. Now, the casting enters still another complex transfer machine. One view of this complex is shown in Fig. 16-19. In succession, the block casting goes through the following machining operations:

1. First, a semifinish pass is made on the camshaft and crankshaft bores, chamfer-camshaft bores, face and chamfer crankshaft thrust-bearing

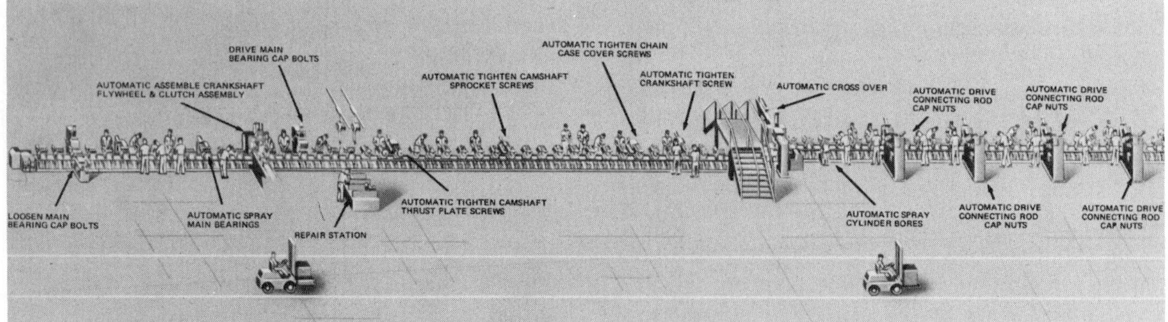

Fig. 16-21. Birds-eye view of automated V-8 engine assembly line. Engines pass from left to right.

surfaces, chamfer rear-camshaft bore; and the oil-seal diameter is bored. A second semifinish pass is made on the camshaft and crankshaft bores; then the camshaft bore is finish-bored, and a third semifinish pass is made on the crankshaft bores. The rear dowel holes are semifinish-reamed, and the distributor body and distributor-shaft bores are semifinished.

2. Next, the block enters another phase of machining, during which an assembling operation is performed. The camshaft bushings are pressed in and finish-reamed, the crankshaft bore is final-finished, dowel holes are final bored, and the rear face of the block is finish-milled.

3. Next, the two cylinder-head-mounting faces are final-broached in preparation for the cylinder-boring operation. Cylinders are bored in two stages: semifinish and final-finish boring. In separate operations, the cylinder bores are chamfered, top and bottom.

4. Then, the casting moves on to a honing machine, and all cylinders are honed to final-finish (see Fig. 13-9).

5. Following this operation, the block passes through an automatic inspecting machine which checks and grades each cylinder bore as to diameter. This information is appended to the block so that pistons and rings can be matched to the bores during the assembly operation.

6. Next, the block enters the assembly line. The bearing-cap bolts are automatically loosened in preparation for installation of the main bearings. Then, on the assembly line, a mix of attendant operators and automatic machines install the main bearings, crankshaft, camshaft, timing chain, piston-ring-rod assemblies, oil pump and pan, heads, manifolds, and other parts that go to make up the completed engine. The completed engine then passes through an automatic paint-spray station and finally to the testing station. Each engine is then given a series of actual running tests. (See §229 for more details on this assembly line.)

As can be seen by a study of the above list of machining operations, most of the steps are automatic, with the transfer equipment moving the casting from one station to the next automatically. As the block reaches a station, it is locked into position, and the machining operation is performed on it. The block may be turned or rotated by the transfer equipment to bring it into position in the proper relationship to the machine tools that are to be brought to bear it.

Note, also, that the complete series of operations is not accomplished on a single transfer machine. There are several located in series so that the block passes from one transfer machine, with its grouping of special automatic machine tools, to the next. All of the machining operations are required to prepare the cylinder block for the assembly procedures.

§228. Designing a cylinder head Many of the problems associated with cylinder-head design have already been discussed. These include port, valve, and valve-seat locations and configurations, combustion-chamber design, types of valve seats and valve guides (whether integral or insert), and methods of valve and seat cooling. All of these

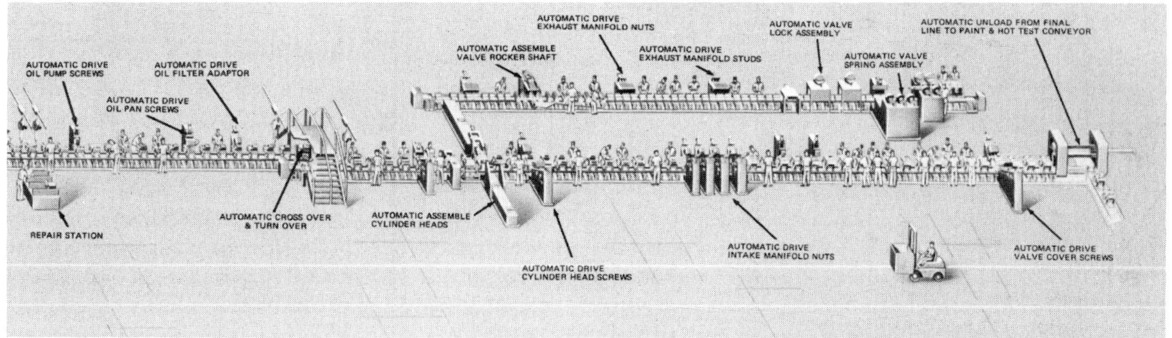

(*The Cross Company*)

Fig. 16-22. Automated assembly line for V-8 engine cylinder heads. Cylinder heads pass from left to right during assembly. (*The Cross Company*)

are important considerations, but the designer must also think about casting and machining procedures, removal of cores from the casting, and so on.[1,2] For example, the cores shown in Figs. 16-13 and 16-14 are easily broken up and removed from the casting because the designer positioned the water-outlet connection at the front and the core-clean-out hole at the rear in such a way that clean-out rods can be inserted through these holes for the entire length of the casting.

The designer must also keep in mind the desirability of a design that may be easily adapted to more than one engine. For example, the cylinder-head design, for which the cores shown in Figs. 16-13 and 16-14 are used, can fit more than one engine insofar as the cores and the cope are concerned. Use of different drags (which form the combustion chambers) adapts the design for engines with different compression ratios and outputs.

Many of the comments made about weight and machining problems of the cylinder block also apply to the cylinder head. The head must have adequate strength and rigidity, and at the same time useless metal must be eliminated. In this connection, the location of the cylinder-head bolts is of great importance. When the head bolts are tightened, the shape of the head and block will change. If the bolts are properly located and are drawn down to the proper tension in the correct sequence, this change will be at a minimum. As a

Fig. 16-23. Cylinder head for a V-8, overhead-valve engine, with parts assembled into the head on the automated assembly line shown in *Fig. 16-22*. (*The Cross Company*)

Fig. 16-24. Machine for automatically loosening main-bearing-cap bolts (center). Cylinder block moves from right to left. Operator, at left, takes bearing caps off and places them in the pans provided on the moving jig to which the block is temporarily attached. (*The Cross Company*)

rule, specifications call for tightening the center bolts first and then working away from the center to the ends of the head, as shown in Fig. 16-20.

§229. Engine assembly After the cylinder block and head (or heads) have been machined, they are carried to the engine assembly line. A bird's-eye view of a modern, automated assembly line is shown in Fig. 16-21. Notice that there are operators all along the line, but notice, also, that there are numerous automatic assembling processes being carried out on the line.

Figure 16-22 is a closer look at one part of the total setup. This is the subassembly line that assembles cylinder heads. Figure 16-23 shows the various parts that go into the cylinder head. First, of course, the cylinder head is subjected to a long series of machining operations that prepares it for the final assembly process. Then, on the subassembly line, the springs, valves, oil seals, spring retainers, and spring-retainer locks are installed in the heads. The assembled heads are then brought to the main assembly line. Prior to the installation of the heads on the block, however, many other assembly operations are required.

If you will study Fig. 16-21 from left to right, you will note that numerous automatic operations are performed on the cylinder block. First, the main-bearing caps are loosened (Fig. 16-24), which permits installation of the main bearings and crankshaft. The bearings are spray oiled as they are installed. Next, the flywheel and clutch assembly are installed, followed by the camshaft, timing sprockets and chain, and chain cover. The block is now rotated, the cylinder bores oil-sprayed, and the rod-piston-ring assemblies (see Fig. 7-23) are installed. The rod caps are then installed, and the rod bolts are automatically driven down to the proper tightness. As the engine moves along on the assembly line, other parts are added until the engine assembly is complete, and it is automatically unloaded from the line to be conveyed to the spray booths and final test area.

§230. Aluminum cylinder blocks Experimental work on aluminum cylinder blocks has gone on for a long time, and a number of automotive manufacturers have brought out aluminum-block engines.[3-7] There are several advantages in using aluminum in engines. It is light, strong, and has a high heat conductivity. However, it also presents several problems. For one thing, aluminum is not a satisfactory material for cylinder walls. Also, its coefficient of expansion is greater than cast iron. In addition, aluminum requires different treatment from cast iron in the foundry and in the manufacturing plant.

There is also the problem of cylinder liners. Cast-iron cylinder liners, or sleeves, are required because aluminum would wear rapidly from the action of the piston, rings, and combustion pressures and temperatures. There are two general types of cylinder liners: the cast-in, permanent type and the replaceable type. The replaceable type can be either wet or dry. With the wet type, the liner is in contact with the cooling water and is sealed at top and bottom. With the dry type, the liner is in contact its full length with the cylinder-bore hole in the casting.

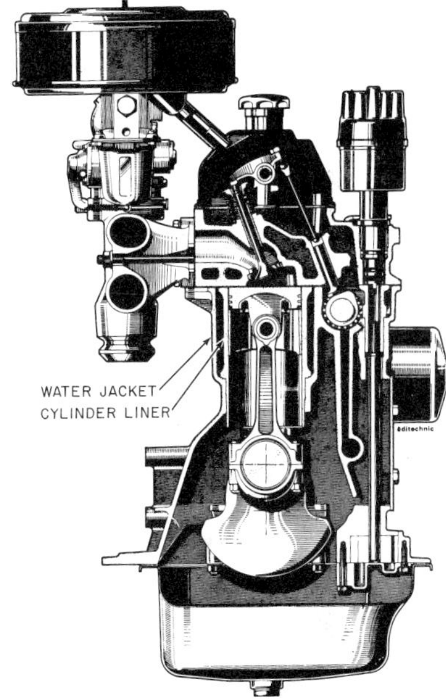

Fig. 16-25. Engine using removable wet cylinder liners. (*Renault*)

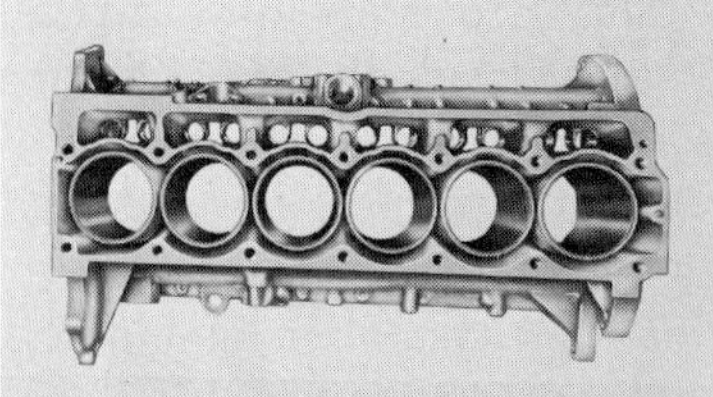
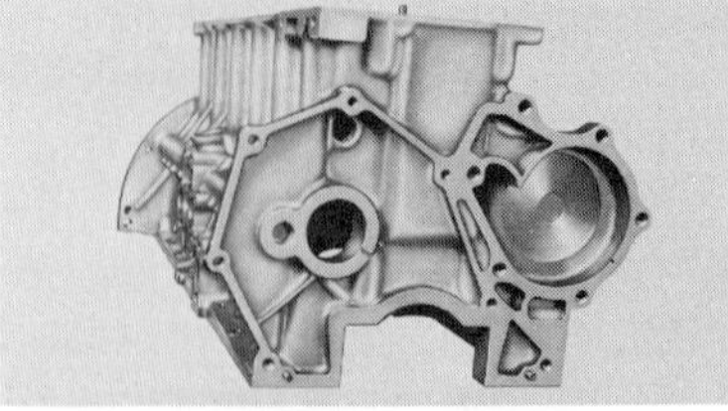

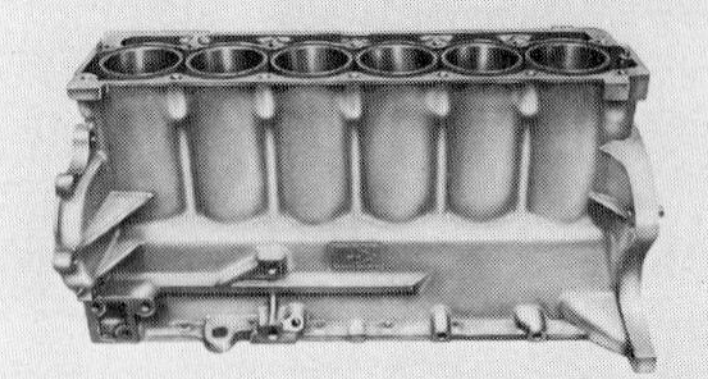
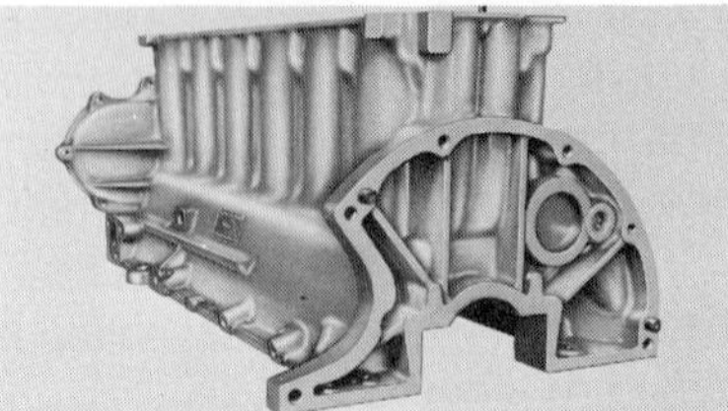

Fig. 16-26. Various views of aluminum die-cast cylinder block for six-cylinder, in-line engine. (*Chrysler Motors Corporation*)

In addition, there is the problem of corrosion in the water jackets, brought about by the action of the hot water circulating in the cooling system. Of course, it requires new foundry and manufacturing facilities to go from cast iron to aluminum blocks.

However, in the late 1950s, several automobile manufacturers decided to bring out aluminum engines—engines with aluminum blocks and, also, in some engines, aluminum heads. Prior to that, aluminum had been used for a number of engine parts such as pistons, water-pump bodies, rocker-arm-shaft supports, and so on. There were three different paths that designers could follow: (1) They could cast blocks and heads of aluminum, using sand molds and sand cores, in much the same manner that iron blocks and heads were cast. (2) They could use permanent steel molds with sand cores. (3) They could take advantage of the important characteristic of aluminum, which is that it can be cast in permanent movable dies, and that such die-cast castings are considerably cheaper to make (not considering the costs of the dies and

Fig. 16-27. Stationary half of die for aluminum die-cast cylinder block, assembled on die-casting machine. (*Chrysler Motors Corporation*)

Fig. 16-28. Movable or ejector half of die, with die slides for aluminum die-cast cylinder block, assembled on die-casting machine. (*Chrysler Motors Corporation*)

casting machine). Further, with this latter method, core-making and removal is eliminated. Also, the accuracy of die-cast aluminum castings greatly reduces machining time and costs.

In 1961, several aluminum engines appeared. Even though most of these engines are no longer being produced, it is interesting to look into their design and manufacture. A few companies still supply aluminum engines, and there is always the possibility that aluminum engines will have a major comeback.

Several combinations of cast-iron and aluminum were brought out. For example, the 1961 Buick Special had an aluminum engine with the cylinder block cast with permanent molds and sand cores. Exterior surfaces were all formed by metal die sec-

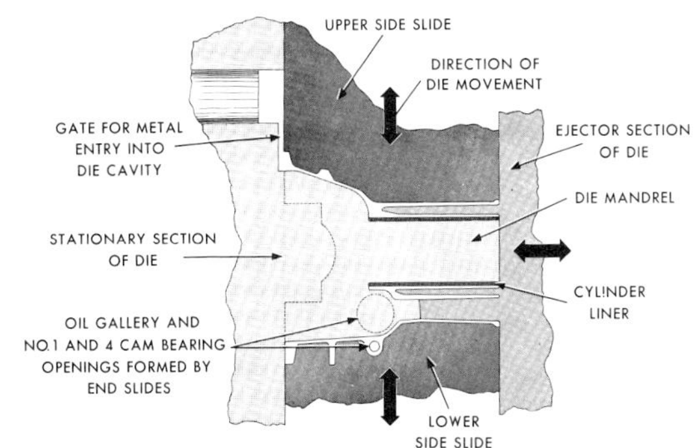

Fig. 16-29. Sectional view of cylinder-block die in closed position. (*Chrysler Motors Corporation*)

tions, with the water jackets and lower crankcase areas formed by sand cores. The head was also cast by the same method, with metal dies used for the external surfaces and sand cores used to form the water jackets. The cylinder walls were made of cast-iron liners, which were cast into the aluminum block to become integral parts of the block.

An alternative to cast-in liners is to use removable liners, either wet or dry. The dry type, requiring careful machining of the block so the liner will fit snugly, is not considered feasible by most engine manufacturers using removable liners. Instead, a wet liner is preferred, even though this may pose a sealing problem at the top and bottom of the liner. One solution of this problem is shown Fig. 16-25, which is a sectional view of a late-model Renault 16 engine. The liner fits down into the cylinder-block casting and the cavity between it, and the block forms the water jacket. The top is sealed by the head gasket.

Another example is the slant-six, in-line engine shown in Fig. 4-20. The engine had a completely die-cast aluminum block but a cast-iron head. The block design and manufacturing process deserve some analysis. Several views of the die-cast block are shown in Fig. 16-26. As you study this illustration, several things will become obvious. First, note that this block has no top deck, as with cast-iron blocks. Instead, the upper ends of the water jacket are sealed by the cylinder-head gasket. Note also that this means, of course, that the mold must consist of six different die sides, each of which can be pulled directly away from the block after it is cast. In addition, there are six cast-iron cylinder liners which are cast in place in the block.

Figures 16-27 and 16-28 show the stationary and movable parts of the die. The heavy posts on the stationary half (Fig. 16-27) serve as guides to align the movable half as it is brought into position against the stationary half. The movable half consists of five separate die parts, one each for the top, two sides, front, and back of the block. The two side, front, and back die parts have slides so arranged that the die parts slide, swing into place, and lock as the movable half reaches the closed or "ready-to-cast" position. Note, in Fig. 16-27, the eight heavy metal posts surrounding the stationary die half. The two side, front, and back die parts slide on these heavy posts as the movable half moves into the closed position. The posts are slanted so these four sides slide and swing inward into place as the die closes. Before this action, however, six cast-iron cylinder liners are placed on the six cylinder mandrels in the stationary half of the die. (The manufacture of the liners is described in a following paragraph.)

Figure 16-29 is a sectional view of the cylinder-block die assembly in the closed position, ready to receive the molten aluminum. This illustration will help you visualize the movements of the die sides as they slide into position. After the six sides of the

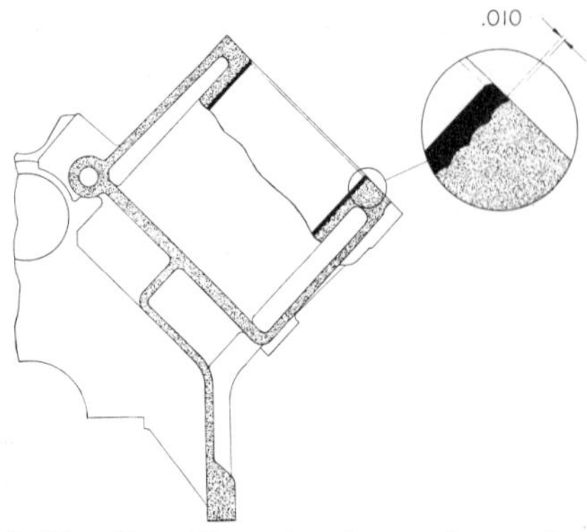

Fig. 16-30. Grooving of outer surface of cylinder sleeve that forms a lock with aluminum. (*Buick Motor Division of General Motors Corporation*)

Fig. 16-31. Aluminum cylinder block with bearing caps installed. (*Chrysler Motors Corporation*)

die are locked into place, mandrels move in from the front and back sides to form the oil gallery and cam bearings (see lower left of Fig. 16-29). Now, everything is in readiness for the hot metal.

The molten aluminum is forced, or injected, into the die mold under a pressure of up to 8,000 psi (pounds per square inch). This high pressure greatly reduces the possibility of casting porosity and "cold shuts" (cavities produced by setting up of metal before mold is completely filled). The resulting dense casting is strong and without weak spots. After the metal has set up, the oil gallery and cam-bearing mandrels are withdrawn (they are attached to hydraulic cylinders), and the movable half is slid away from the stationary half. The side dies back off from the casting in four directions as the movable half moves away.

Because of the pressures involved, the die assembly must be heavy and rigid, and the die-casting machine itself must be very strong so as to produce locking forces great enough to hold under the pressure of the molten metal as it is injected into the mold. The die itself (Figs. 16-27 and 16-28) weighs 44,000 pounds, while the complete press weighs 2,000 tons. The dies operate at a temperature of several hundred degrees. This aids in preventing cold shuts and porosity and also reduces the thermal shock to the die as the hot metal enters.

The aluminum used is alloyed with other materials to obtain good castability and strength. The alloy used for the blocks described above, for example, has from 10.5 to 12 percent silicon and 3 to 4.5 percent copper. The V-8 block for the 1961 Oldsmobile aluminum engine also contained iron, zinc, manganese, magnesium, and titanium. The formulas for these and other aluminum alloys are given in the SAE (Society of Automotive Engineers) *Handbook*.

Cylinder liners are made of cast iron, as previously mentioned. They are cast centrifugally in steel molds. That is, the mold is spinning when the molten iron is poured into it. This produces a strong, dense casting. Two different methods of providing a good lock between the sleeve and the surrounding aluminum shell are used. It is necessary to have a good bond at the iron-aluminum interface, not only for strength, but also for good heat transfer. One method requires that the outer surface of the sleeve be machined with circumferential grooves, having a pitch of 8 per inch and a depth of 0.010 inch. The grooves form a good lock (Fig. 16-30). The second method makes use of a fine coating of ceramic slurry on the outer face of the mold. The slurry is sprayed into the spinning mold just before the molten iron is poured. Then, when the iron is poured, the water in the slurry evaporates, leaving tiny porous openings in the outer surface of the sleeve. Next, when the sleeve is put into the block mold or die and the aluminum is poured, it enters these small voids to produce an excellent interlock between the iron and aluminum.

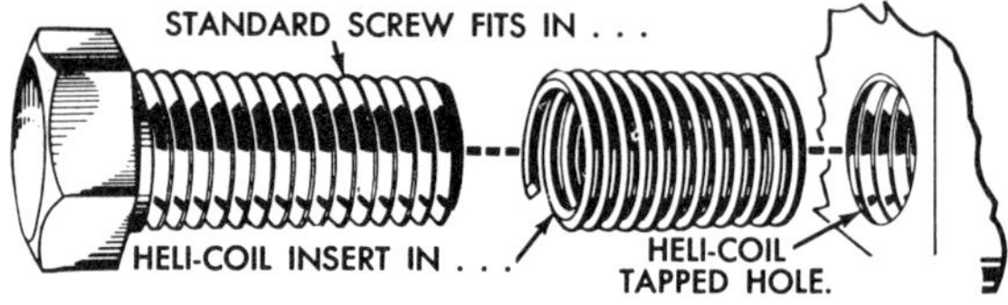

Fig. 16-32. Heli-coil installation. *(Chrysler-Plymouth Division of Chrysler Motors Corporation)*

The cylinder liners used in the die-casting machine (Figs. 16-27 and 16-28) are preheated to 600°F before they are loaded onto the mandrels in readiness for the aluminum pour. This reduces the residual tensile stresses set up in the aluminum resulting from the difference in expansion rates of the two metals to below 10,000 psi.

Another problem that the designers of the aluminum cylinder block had to solve related to the main bearings. As you know, in the cast-iron block, the upper bearing-shell halves fit directly into the half bores in the block. Further, the lower bearing-shell halves are held into place by bearing caps (see Fig. 14-3). This arrangement would not be satisfactory in the aluminum block, however, because the bearing shell is not compatible with the aluminum. The bearing shell expands at a different rate than the aluminum, and, in addition, the aluminum is comparatively soft so that the shell would begin to work loose.

A different arrangement is therefore required with the aluminum block (Fig. 16-31). Here, cast-iron upper and lower bearing caps are used. The upper caps are press-fitted into the recesses provided in the bearing webs of the block. Both the lower and upper caps are attached by cap bolts that enter threaded holes in the bearing webs. Drilled holes feed oil from the oil gallery along the side of the block to the bearings.

Thread fastenings presented another problem for the aluminum-cylinder-block designers. Aluminum, being softer and weaker than the steel cap screws used to attach main-bearing caps, cylinder head, and other parts, made it necessary to develop new threading specifications. First, it was found necessary to increase the threaded engagement of the screw in the aluminum beyond what was normal for cast iron. Also, the screw bosses had to be made large enough so they would be sufficiently strong to withstand the hoop stresses resulting from the tightening of the screws. These hoop stresses are due to the outward push of the sides of the screw threads on the surrounding aluminum, and there must be enough aluminum around the threaded hole to withstand this stress.

Aluminum threads, being softer than the steel screws threaded into them, tend to gall much easier than threads in cast iron. Cross-threading also is more likely to occur with aluminum threads. Where thread failure is a problem, special steel inserts are available for making repairs in tapped holes. One such insert is shown in Fig. 16-32. The repair is made by drilling out the worn threads, tapping the hole with a special tap, and then threading the insert into position in the new enlarged threads.

SUMMARY

The cylinder block and head must contain and support the moving engine parts with minimum distortion, providing the proper combustion-chamber configuration and rejecting the proper amount of heat to the cooling system. In addition, the block and head must be cast and machined without undue problems.

Most cylinder blocks and heads are cast of iron alloy in sand molds with sand cores. In designing a cylinder block, the engineers take off from previously successful designs, modifying them to suit new requirements. Prototype blocks are cast and tested in various ways, including operation in completed engines. Results of these tests are evaluated, and further design modifications are made as required.

In the modern engine factory, engine blocks are finished on transfer lines, which include the various machine tools required as well as automatic transfer devices to move the blocks from one machining station to the next. The raw casting enters at one end and comes out the other end completely machines and ready for final engine assembly.

The cylinder-head design must have the proper combustion chamber, valve and seat configuration, water-jacket arrangement; also it must be cast and machined with normal procedures. In addition, a good head design is subject to modification to fit different engines by changing the combustion-chamber shape for different compression ratios.

The final assembly of engines in modern plants is automated as much as feasible so that many of the assembling operations are done by machine.

Aluminum cylinder blocks and heads have been used for production runs of different engines. Aluminum is light and has high heat conductivity. Its relatively poor wearing quality, especially at higher temperatures, requires the use of cast-iron cylinder liners, either of the dry or wet type.

Aluminum blocks can be cast with sand molds and cores or permanent molds and sand cores; or they can be die-cast with permanent molds and cores. With any of these, cast-in cylinder liners are usually used, although some engines have removable liners which are installed separately after the block has been cast.

REFERENCES

1. Smith, W. R., Ford's New 240 I-6 Engine, SAE (Society of Automotive Engineers) 966C, 1965 (paper).

2. Beckman, E. W., and W. L. Weertman, Chrysler Corp.'s New 273 cu. in. V-8 Engine, SAE (Society of Automotive Engineers) 826A, 1964 (paper).

3. Adamson, J. F., C. E. Burke, D. V. Potter, and W. J. Zechel, The American Motors New Die Cast Aluminum Engine, SAE (Society of Automotive Engineers) 307A, 1961 (paper).

4. Holtzkemper, E. H., C. G. Studaker, and J. D. Turlay, The New Buick Aluminum Engine, SAE (Society of Automotive Engineers) 307B, 1961 (paper).

5. Eriksen, H. E., E. G. Moeller, and W. L. Weertman, Chrysler Corporation's Die-Cast Aluminum Slant Six Engine, SAE (Society of Automotive Engineers), 1961 (paper).

6. Ball, F., and G. Burrell, The Oldsmobile F-85 Aluminum Engine, SAE (Society of Automotive Engineers) 307D, 1961 (paper).

7. Johnson, H. R., Jr., E. M. Sabo, and T. A. Scherger, The New Lark VI Overhead Valve Engine, SAE (Society of Automotive Engineers) 307F, 1961 (paper).

QUESTIONS

1. List the most important items to be taken into consideration in designing a cylinder block and head.

2. Describe briefly the procedure followed in carrying a casting from drawing to finished product.

3. Describe the procedure of casting a cylinder block.

4. List the machining operations required on a cylinder block.

5. What are the machining qualification surfaces on a cylinder block and how are they formed?

6. List the major items to be considered in designing a cylinder head.

7. Describe briefly the procedure of assembling an engine.

8. What are the major advantages and disadvantages to the use of aluminum for cylinder blocks?

9. What are the three methods of casting a cylinder block from aluminum?

10. What are cylinder liners and why are they used in aluminum cylinder blocks?

11. Describe the different types of cylinder liners.

12. What is hoop stress as regards threaded holes?

Automotive Fuel Systems

CHAPTER **17**

This chapter discusses in detail the carbureted fuel system, its design and operation. This system consists of the fuel tank, fuel lines, filter, pump, carburetor, and intake manifold, which were all discussed briefly in Chap. 8. The fuel pump (described in §103) is driven by an eccentric on the camshaft (Fig. 19-10). (Chapter 10 discusses engine fuels in detail.) The carburetor and intake manifold, together with the intake valves and ports, are generally referred to as the induction system. *This chapter also describes the* exhaust system, *which includes the exhaust manifold, connecting exhaust pipe, muffler, and tail pipe.*

§231. Fuel-system requirements The induction system must supply an air-fuel mixture of the correct ratio and density to the engine cylinders, with high volumetric efficiency. The air and fuel should be a homogeneous mixture, without liquid fuel droplets or mist. For starting and full-performance operation, the mixture should be rich (have a higher percentage of fuel). For intermediate, low-performance operation, the mixture should be leaner.

§232. Carburetor requirements The carburetor is the mixing device that supplies the engine with the air-fuel mixture. There are two aspects to this requirement.[1] First, the carburetor must regulate air-fuel consumption and thus engine-power output, *without significant curtailment* of the maximum air flow. That is, the pressure drop through the carburetor must be at a minimum when full power is required. Second, the carburetor must prepare the air-fuel mixture, mixing the two in the right proportions to suit operating requirements. The mixture must be homogeneous as it is delivered to the intake manifold. From this point on, the fate of the mixture is up to the remainder of the induction system—the intake manifold, intake valves, ports, and valve seats.

While carburetor efficiency is, in part, a function of carburetor design, its operation is to a considerable degree at the mercy of other components. The air cleaner must supply clean air at practically atmospheric pressure. The fuel pump must supply clean, liquid fuel at sufficient inlet pressure. Also, the intake manifold, valves, and ports must not unduly restrict the flow of the air-fuel mixture from the carburetor to the combustion chambers.

In addition to these basic requirements, the ever-smaller space available under the hood poses still another requirement. As hood lines have come down, the carburetor has had to follow suit, so that the top-to-bottom dimensions of the carburetor have been reduced in recent years. A late-model four-barrel carburetor measures 3.20 inches from manifold to air-cleaner gasket-mounting faces (Fig. 17-47). This contrasts with the 5- or 6-inch height of carburetors of years past. In addition to this, there is often less room side to side or front to back under the hood because of the installation of other accessories, such as power steering, air-conditioning, and so on.

There is also the requirement to reduce unwanted fuel evaporation from the carburetor. Higher-output engines with more under-the-hood accessories increase the temperature around the carburetor. Figure 17-1 shows what happens to the fuel stored in the float bowl of a carburetor

Fig. 17-1. Temperature reached in the carburetor under various operating conditions, and the percentage of fuel evaporated from the carburetor. (*Rochester Products Division, General Motors Corporation*)

under various conditions. With an ambient temperature of 92°F, the carburetor will be at a temperature of around 100 to 125° during cruising, up to around 160° during idling, and can reach 175 to 200° during the hot-soak period (this is the period immediately after the engine has been shut off after a drive, when there is no cooling effect and the retained heat is radiated from the engine). The right half of Fig. 17-1 shows the percentage of fuel evaporated by the heat. During hot soak, the heat will cause about 25 percent of the fuel to evaporate. There are three ways to reduce the total amount lost by evaporation: (1) by insulating the float bowl to reduce the heat going into the bowl; (2) by reducing the amount of fuel stored in the float bowl; and (3) by capturing the evaporates. However, it is almost impossible to insulate the float bowl. The only alternative, insofar as the carburetor itself is concerned, is to reduce the fuel stored. However, there are devices in the developmental stage that are designed to control evaporation (§257).

§233. Fuel gauge Two types of fuel gauges are used: the balancing-coil gauge (Fig. 17-2*a*) and the thermostatic gauge (Fig. 17-2*b*). Each has a tank unit and an instrument-panel (or dash) unit. The tank unit has a float that moves up and down as the fuel level changes, thereby providing a signal to the dash unit.

1. *Balancing-coil fuel gauge.* The balancing-coil gauge uses a variable resistance, or rheostat, in the tank and two coils of wire placed at 90-degree angles to each other in the dash-indicating unit (Fig. 17-2*a*). The movement of a float up or down in the tank as the tank is filled or emptied causes a sliding contact to move around to various positions on the resistance. This allows the resistance to pass more or less electric current, passing more as the tank empties and less as the tank fills. As the tank empties, more and more of the electric current passing through the "empty" coil from the battery then flows through the resistance instead of through the "full" coil. Consequently, the magnetic strength of the "full" coil is

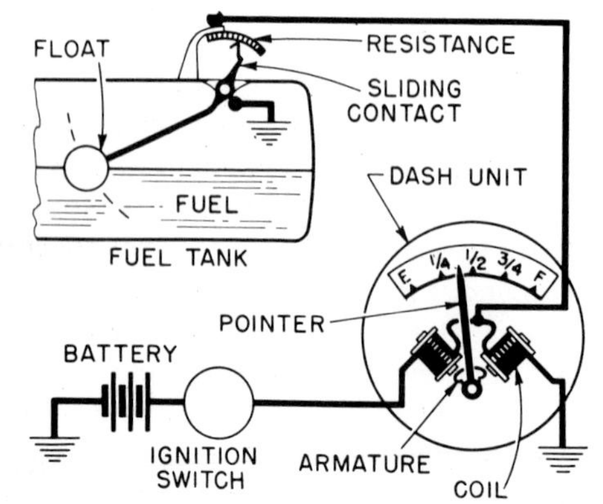

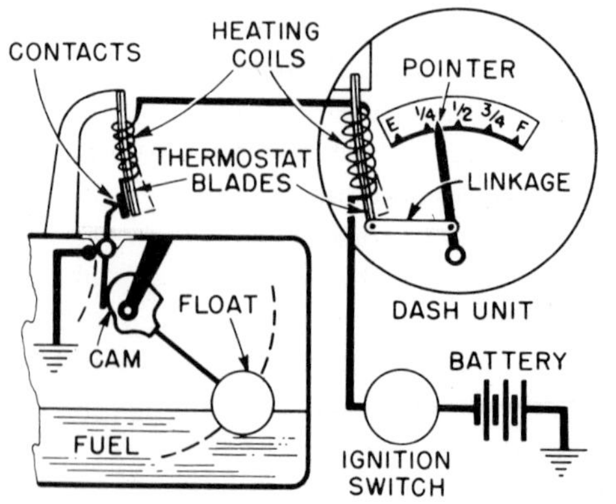

Fig. 17-2. Two types of fuel gauge: *a*, balancing-coil gauge; *b*, thermostatic gauge.

weakened, allowing the armature to which the indicating needle is fastened to be pulled around by the magnetic force toward the "empty" coil. But when the tank is filled, the sliding contact moves around so that resistance is increased. Most of the current passing through the "empty" coil then passes through the "full" coil. This produces a different magnetic pattern which turns the armature and needle toward the "full" coil. Note that the fuel-gauge indicator is connected to the battery through the ignition switch. This prevents any drain on the battery when the ignition switch is turned off and the engine is not running.

2. *Thermostatic fuel gauge.* The bimetal-thermostat type of fuel gauge depends upon the heating and bending of two bimetal-thermostat blades, one in the tank unit and one in the dash-indicating unit (Fig. 17-2*b*). Each bimetal-thermostat blade consists of two strips of different metals, welded together. When heated, the two metals expand at different rates, causing the blade to bend. Around each blade is a heater wire. Both wires carry the same amount of current, and thus each blade is heated the same amount. Consequently, each blade will bend the same amount. When the tank is filled, a cam attached to the float in the tank moves a contact button that imposes an initial distortion on the tank-unit blade. This blade must then heat considerably before it bends enough to move away from the contact button. While it is heating, the blade in the dash unit also heats, bending so that the indicating needle is moved toward "full." When the tank-unit blade has bent enough to move away from the contact button, current stops flowing, and the blade cools and moves back to the button. Current again flows; the blade heats and bends away again. As the tank empties, the float drops, and the cam moves around so that it imposes less initial distortion on the blade. Thus, the blade does not have to heat quite as much to bend further and move away from the contact button: less heating is required to keep the tank-unit blade vibrating and opening and closing the circuit. Consequently, the dash-unit blade is heated less and does not bend so much, so that the needle moves back toward "empty."

§234. Carburetor fundamentals The carburetor must vary the air-fuel ratio to meet varying operating requirements. Figure 17-3 illustrates this. For starting, the mixture must be rich, that is, have a high proportion of fuel; a ratio of 9:1 would be typical (9 pounds of air for each pound of fuel). During starting, with the engine cold, the fuel does not evaporate very well, and the rich mixture assures that enough will evaporate for initial starting. During idle, the mixture leans out to around 12:1. Then, during normal, part-throttle running, the mixture further leans out to about 15:1. For high-speed operation, or acceleration, the carburetor supplies a richer mixture, as shown.

Generally speaking, the mixture is kept as lean as possible for the various operating conditions. For example, on idle, the carburetor should supply the least amount of fuel possible without causing rough idle or missing. Likewise, at part-throttle operation, the mixture should be as lean as possible without compromising engine performance or jeopardizing engine parts. For example (as noted in §211, 1), air-fuel ratios have a profound effect on exhaust-valve temperature and life. Leaning out the mixture ratio from 12:1 to 15:1 will increase exhaust-valve operating temperature as much as 200°F. On the other hand, it is necessary to keep the ratio up near 15:1 for good fuel economy, good exhaust-valve life (§211), low unburned-hydrocarbon emission in the exhaust gases, and minimum carbon formation in the combustion chambers. However, even though the carburetor may deliver a

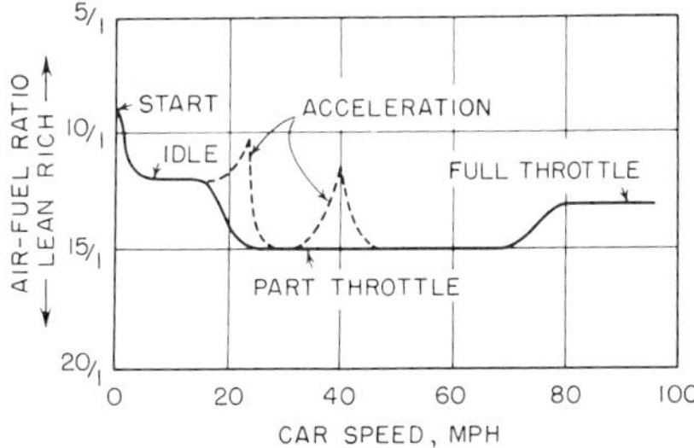

Fig. 17-3. Graph of air-fuel ratios for different car speeds. The graph is typical only; car speeds at which the various ratios are obtained may vary with different cars. Also, there may be some variation in the ratios.

15:1 mixture, this mixture undergoes changes in the intake manifold. As previously noted, the intake manifold acts somewhat as a sorting device, supplying the end cylinders (or cylinders most distant from the carburetor) with a richer mixture (see §211, 1). Reduction of this differential can be made by altering the design of the intake manifold (as explained in §251).

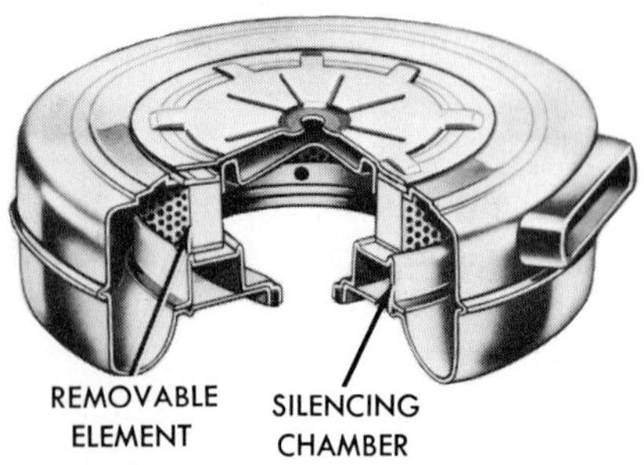

Fig. 17-4. Typical air cleaner, partly cut away so that the filter element can be seen. (*Ford Division of Ford Motor Company*)

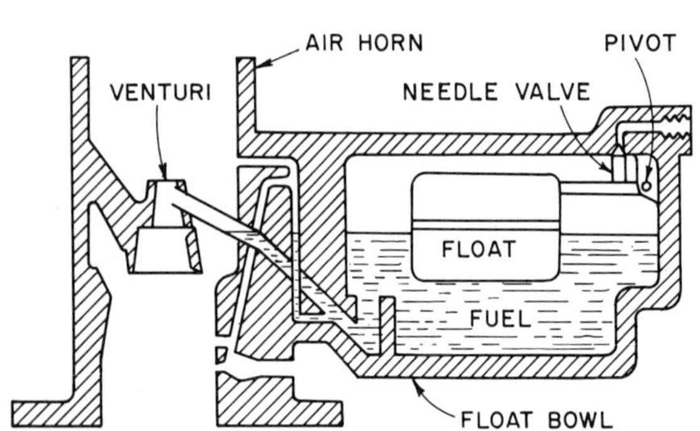

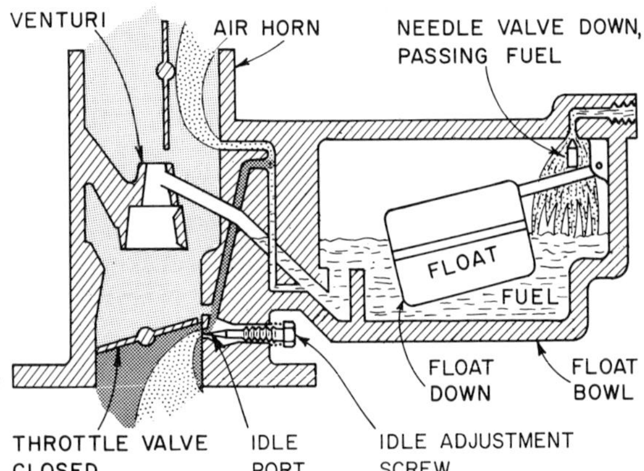

Fig. 17-5. Carburetor float circuit: *left,* float bowl filled to proper level, float up, needle valve closed; *right,* fuel level low, float down, needle valve open, fuel entering float bowl.

§235. Carburetor circuits In order for the carburetor to vary the air-fuel ratio as required by different operating conditions, the carburetor has several circuits, each "specializing" in one operating condition. These circuits are the following:

1. Float circuit
2. Idling and low-speed circuit
3. High-speed, part-load circuit
4. High-speed, full-power circuit
5. Accelerator-pump circuit
6. Choke

These are described in following articles.

§236. Air cleaner Before describing the carburetor circuits, let us look at the air cleaner which sits atop the carburetor and filters the air that enters. A great deal of air passes through the carburetor and engine—as much as 100,000 cubic feet of air every 1,000 car-miles. This is a great volume of air, and it is likely to contain a great amount of floating dust and grit. The grit and dust, if it entered the engine, could cause serious engine damage. Thus, an air cleaner is mounted on the air horn, or air entrance, of the carburetor to keep out the dirt (Fig. 17-4). All air entering the engine through the carburetor must first pass through the air cleaner. The upper part of the air cleaner contains a ring of filter material (fine-mesh metal threads or ribbons, special paper, cellulose fiber, or polyurethane) through which the air must pass. This material provides a fine maze that traps most of the dust particles. Some air cleaners have an oil bath. This is a reservoir of oil past which the incoming air must flow. The moving air picks up particles of oil and carries them up into the filter. There the oil washes accumulated dust back down into the oil reservoir. The oiliness of the filter material also improves the filtering action.

The air cleaner also muffles the noise resulting

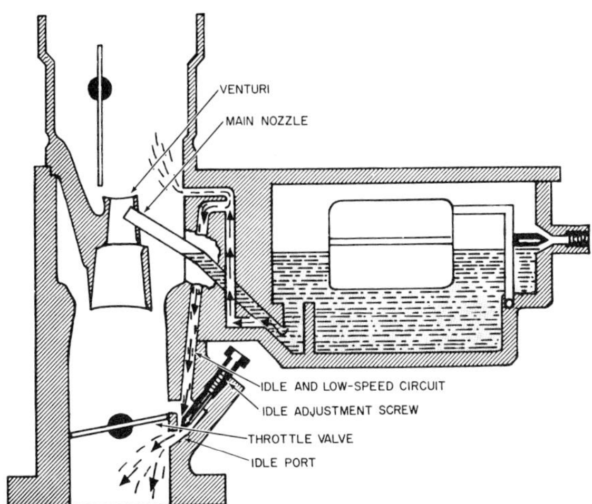

Fig. 17-6. Idle and low-speed circuit in a carburetor. Throttle valve is fully closed, and all gasoline is being fed past the idle adjustment screw. Lines indicate air; arrows indicate gasoline.

from the intake of air through the carburetor, muffler, and valve ports. This noise would be quite noticeable if it were not for the air cleaner. In addition, the air cleaner acts as a flame-arrester in case the engine backfires through the carburetor. Backfiring may occur at certain times as a result of ignition of the air-fuel mixture in the cylinder before the intake valve closes. When this happens, there is a momentary flashback through the carburetor. The air cleaner prevents this flame from erupting from the carburetor and possibly igniting gasoline fumes outside the engine.

§237. Float circuit The float circuit includes a float bowl or fuel reservoir, a float, and a needle valve and seat (Fig. 17-5). When the carburetor is delivering air-fuel mixture to the engine and thus withdrawing fuel from the float bowl, the float drops. This allows the needle valve to move off the valve seat so that the fuel pump can deliver fuel to the float bowl. In actual operation, the needle valve assumes a position that allows the fuel inflow to balance fuel outflow.

§238. Idling and low-speed circuit When the throttle valve is closed, only a small amount of air can pass around it. Thus, there is little air flowing through the venturi, and the vacuum in the venturi is slight—too slight to produce fuel delivery through the main discharge nozzle centered in the venturi.

With this condition, the idling circuit delivers the fuel necessary to supply the engine with the air-fuel mixture it needs to idle. Pressure differential between the intake manifold and the upper part of the air horn provides the motivating force. Air flows through a passage that bypasses the venturi and throttle valve, picking up fuel as it does so, as shown in Fig. 17-6. The richness of the mixture may be varied by turning the idle-mixture adjustment screw opposite the idle-port or discharge hole. Idle speed is adjusted by another screw which positions the throttle valve in the idle position. Turning this screw changes the closed-throttle position so that more or less air can pass between the edge of the throttle plate and the carburetor body.

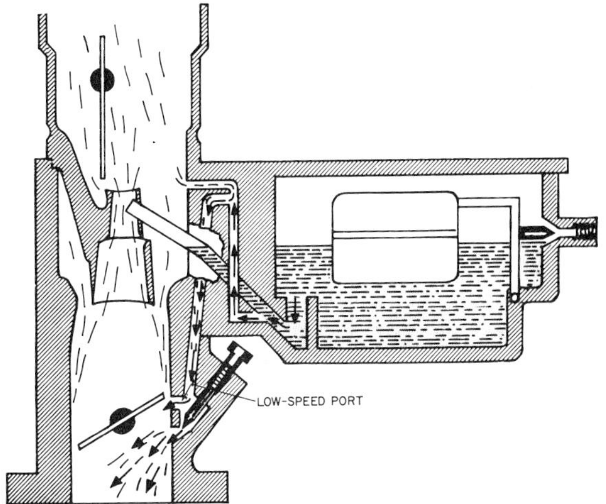

Fig. 17-7. Idle and low-speed circuit in a carburetor. Throttle valve is slightly opened, and gasoline is being fed through the low-speed port. Lines indicate air; arrows indicate gasoline.

§239. Off-idle or low-speed circuit This circuit comes into play as the throttle is opened slightly from the idle position. When this happens, the edge

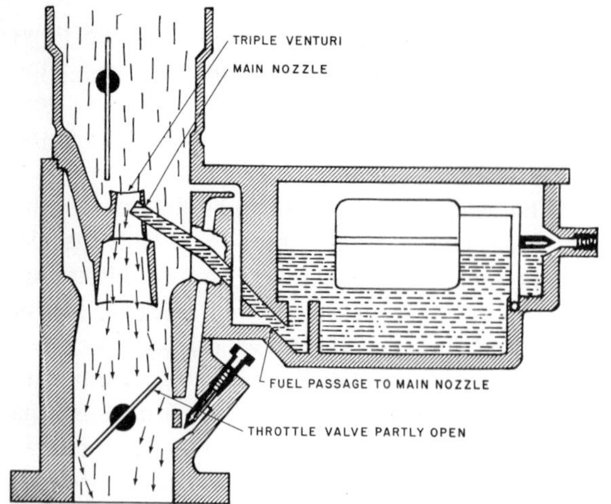

Fig. 17-8. High-speed circuit in a carburetor. Throttle valve is fairly well open, and gasoline is being fed through high-speed nozzle. Lines indicate air; arrows indicate gasoline.

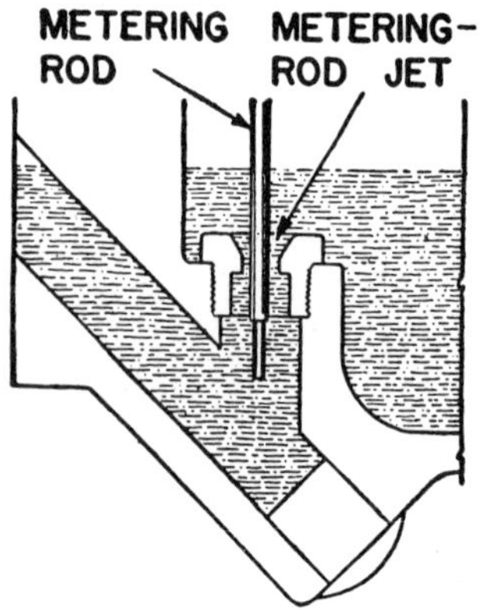

Fig. 17-9. Metering rod and metering-rod jet for securing added performance at full throttle.

of the throttle plate passes a low-speed or off-idle port that is located just above the idle port (Fig. 17-7). As a result, more air can pass the throttle plate, and more fuel can discharge from the idle and off-idle ports. This provides a satisfactory mixture for low-speed operation.

§240. High-speed, part-load circuit As the throttle is opened beyond the low-speed position, the pressure differential between the upper air horn and intake manifold is no longer great enough to cause the air-fuel mixture to discharge from

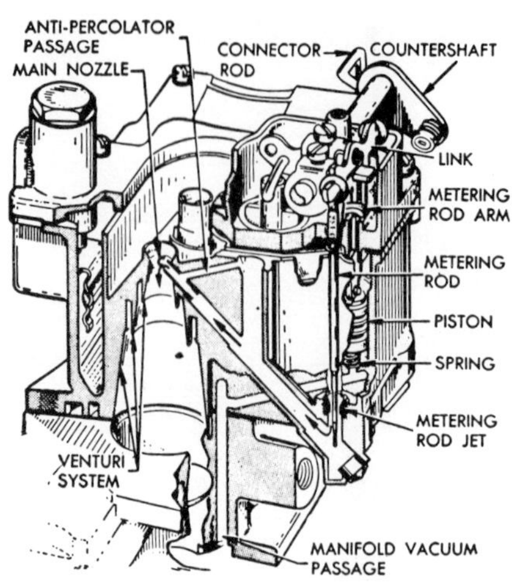

Fig. 17-10. Carburetor that is partly cut away so that the high-speed circuit of one barrel can be seen. Fuel flow is shown by arrows. The carburetor is a dual, or two-barrel, unit. (*Buick Motor Division of General Motors Corporation*)

the idle port. However, more air is now passing through the venturi, and a vacuum has developed there, which causes the main nozzle to discharge fuel (Fig. 17-8). The motivating force here is the pressure differential between the top of the float bowl (atmospheric) and the vacuum in the venturi. The more air that passes through (as a result of increased throttle opening and engine speed), the greater the vacuum and the greater the amount of fuel that discharges.

§241. High-speed, full-power circuit The air-fuel mixture supplied by the high-speed circuit just described is satisfactory through the operating range from off-idle to nearly wide-open throttle. However, when additional power is desired, as during wide-open-throttle operation, the carburetor must supply a richer mixture. The enrichment is produced by an auxiliary mechanism which, in effect, increases the size of the main metering jet in the passage from the float bowl to the main discharge nozzle. This mechanism includes a metering rod that is centered in the main metering jet, or metering-rod jet as it is also called, as shown in Fig. 17-9. The rod is of a smaller diameter on the lower end, and, when it is lifted, this smaller

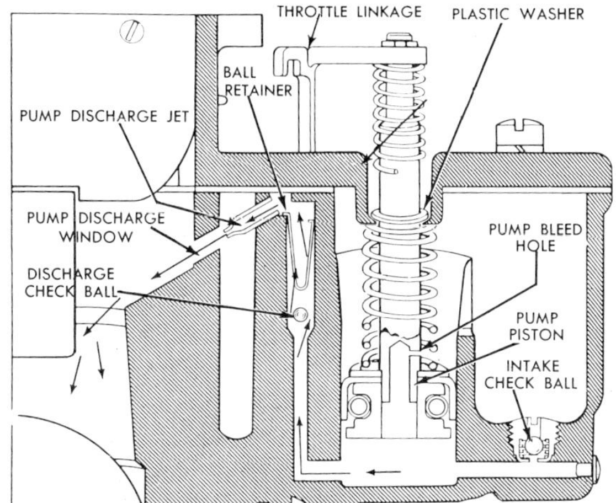

Fig. 17-11. Accelerator-pump system in a carburetor. When the piston moves down, fuel is sprayed from the pump jet, as shown by the arrows.

diameter moves up into the jet, thereby increasing the effective size of the jet and permitting more fuel to flow through it. The mixture is thus enriched.

Two basic methods of producing movement of the metering rod are used: mechanical and vacuum from the intake manifold. Figure 17-8 shows the mechanical method, which is simply a linkage that lifts the metering rod as the throttle is moved to the wide-open position. Figure 17-10 is a cutaway view of a carburetor using both mechanical linkage and vacuum. Vacuum from the intake manifold is applied to a piston in the carburetor, which is connected by an arm to the metering rod. During part-throttle operation, when the intake-manifold vacuum is comparatively high, the piston is held down by the vacuum so that the larger diameter of the rod is positioned in the jet. However, when the throttle is opened wider so that the vacuum drops, then the piston spring moves it up so that the smaller diameter of the rod is brought into position in the jet. More fuel is delivered, and a richer mixture results. This action also takes place during the time that the engine is operating at low speed with an open throttle. With this condition, the air movement through the venturi is comparatively low, so that the vacuum is small. The increased clearance through the main metering jet, however, permits added fuel to flow so that the mixture richness is maintained.

§242. Accelerator-pump circuit When the throttle valve is suddenly opened, for example, when passing another car, the main nozzle requires a moment to respond to the suddenly increased flow of air through the venturi. This could cause a momentary hesitation of the engine if it were not for the accelerator-pump circuit. This circuit delivers a "squirt" of fuel into the passing air when the throttle valve is moved to the opened position.

Figure 17-11 is a simplified schematic drawing of an accelerator circuit in a carburetor. It consists of a pump piston connected by a lever to the throttle linkage. When the throttle is opened, the linkage forces the piston to move down in the pump cylinder, and this action discharges a jet of fuel through a special jet in the side of the carburetor body, as shown.

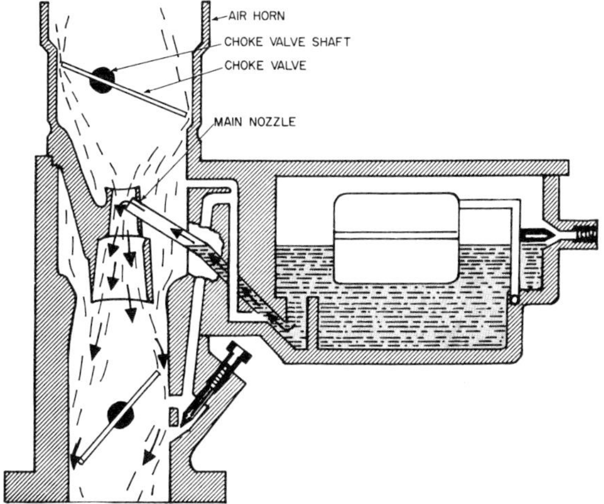

Fig. 17-12. Operation of the choke when starting an engine.

§243. Choke When the engine is cranked for starting, a very rich mixture must be delivered by the carburetor. Normal cranking speeds are around 100 rpm (revolutions per minute), so that air speed through the carburetor is low. Also, with the engine cold, the fuel will not evaporate readily. Thus,

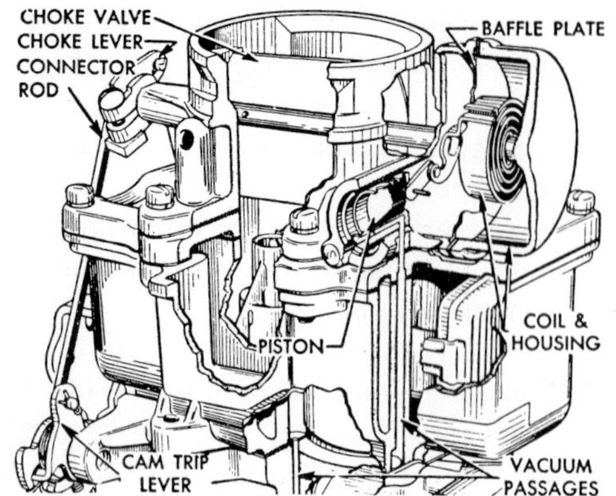

Fig. 17-13. Carburetor that is cut away so the automatic-choke construction can be seen. (*Buick Motor Division of General Motors Corporation*)

more than normal amounts of fuel must be delivered to the air stream through the carburetor. The choke produces this increased fuel delivery. It consists of a choke valve in the top of the air horn (Fig. 17-12). When the choke is closed, only a small amount of air can get past it. Then, as the engine is cranked, a fairly high vacuum is produced in the intake manifold and air horn; this causes the main fuel nozzle to discharge a heavy stream of fuel. The mixture thus delivered by the carburetor is sufficiently rich for starting the engine.

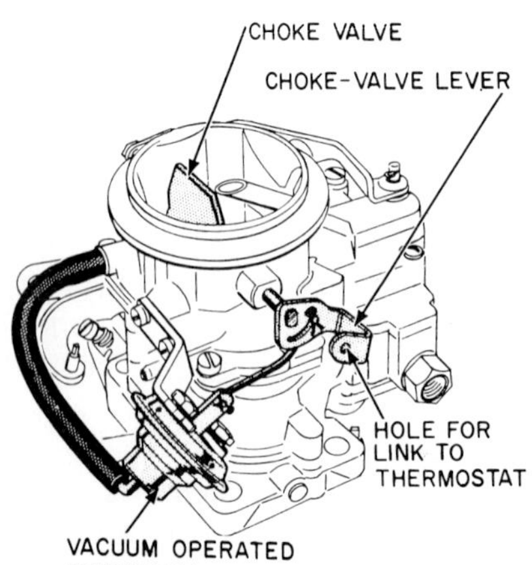

Fig. 17-14. Automatic choke, using a vacuum-operated diaphragm (*Chrysler-Plymouth Division of Chrysler Motors Corporation*)

The choke system includes a spring or a spring-loaded section of the choke valve. The spring holds the choke valve closed during cranking, but as soon as the engine starts, the increased engine speed causes the choke valve, or valve section, to open (due to the increased vacuum produced by increased engine speed).

In most carburetors, the choke valve is positioned by a thermostatic coil and a vacuum-operated piston or diaphragm (Fig. 17-13). When the engine is stopped and cools off, the thermostatic coil increases its tension and moves the choke valve to the closed position. Then, after the engine starts, warm air from a passage in the exhaust manifold is drawn through the thermostatic-coil housing, warming the coil. This causes the coil to lose its tension so that over a period of several minutes the choke valve is moved to the opened position. If the throttle valve is opened during this warm-up period, the loss of intake manifold vacuum, which acts on the vacuum piston, causes the piston to move. This action moves the choke toward the closed position so that more fuel is delivered by the main fuel nozzle. The mixture is therefore enriched to produce smooth engine operation during the transitional period.

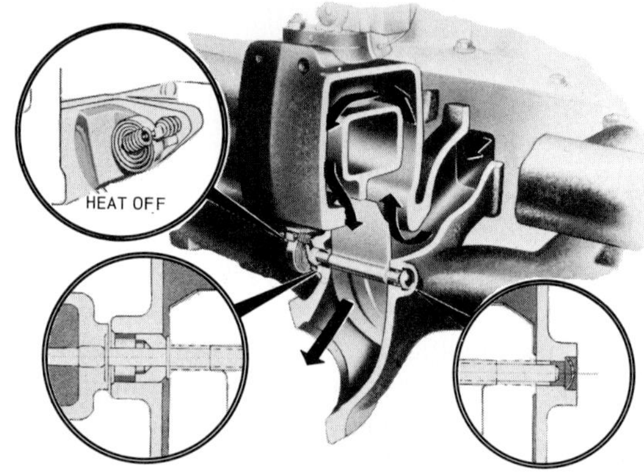

Fig. 17-15. Intake and exhaust manifolds of a six-cylinder, in-line engine that is cut away so that the location and action of the manifold heat control can be seen. The heat-control valve is in the "heat on" position, directing hot exhaust gases up and around the intake manifold, as shown by the arrows. (*Ford Motor Company*)

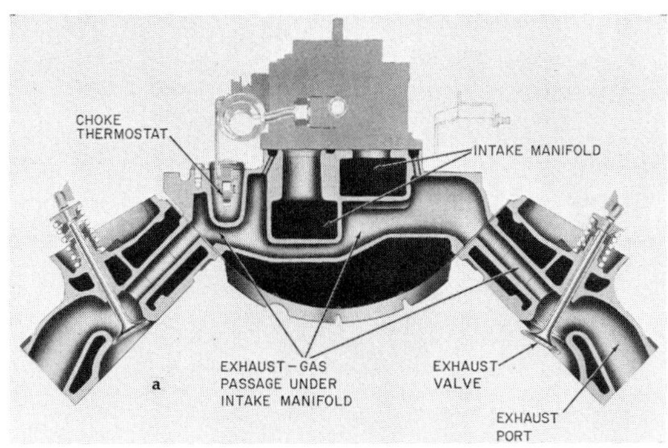

Fig. 17-16a. Exhaust-gas passage under the intake manifold in a V-8 engine. Note the well in which the carburetor-choke thermostat is located. (*Buick Motor Division of General Motors Corporation*)

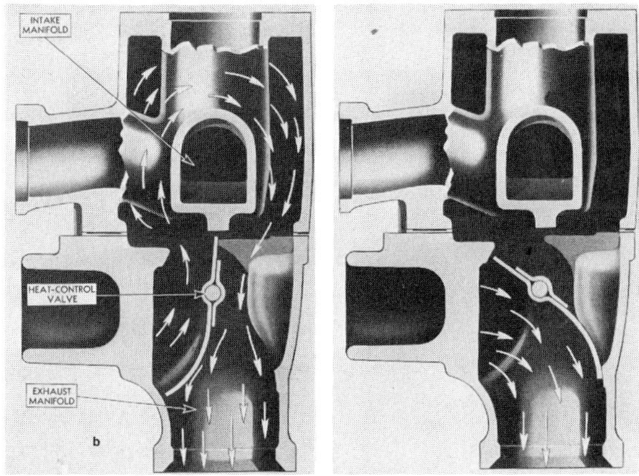

Fig. 17-16b. The two extreme positions in the exhaust manifold of the manifold heat-control valve that controls the flow of exhaust gases through the intake-manifold jacket. (*Chevrolet Motor Division of General Motors Corporation*)

A variety of automatic chokes are used. Some are similar to the type shown in Fig. 17-13. Others use a thermostatic coil mounted on the exhaust manifold (Fig. 17-21). Also, instead of a vacuum piston, some carburetors use a flexible diaphragm sealed in a metal case (Fig. 17-14).

§244. Manifold heat control As a further means of obtaining smooth engine operation during warm-up, a manifold heat control is used. This device causes considerable heat transfer from the warming exhaust manifold to the cold intake manifold. The heat added to the intake manifold assures better fuel vaporization and thus better engine operation during the critical warm-up period. A typical arrangement for a six-in-line engine[3] is shown in a cutaway view in Fig. 17-15 and in a sectional view in Fig. 17-16. The intake manifold is positioned above the exhaust manifold. When the engine is cold, a thermostatic spring coils up to rotate the heat-control valve into the position shown to the left in Fig. 17-16*b*. The hot exhaust gases must pass upward through a jacket in the intake manifold so that heat enters the intake manifold and improves vaporization of the fuel. As the engine warms up, the thermostatic spring uncoils to rotate the heat-control valve into the position shown to the right in Fig. 17-16*b*. Now, the exhaust gases pass directly down from the exhaust manifold into the exhaust pipe. Extra heat is no longer needed to help vaporize the fuel after the engine reaches operating temperature.

The manifold heat-control arrangement for a V-8 engine is shown in Fig. 17-16*a*. An exhaust-gas passage is located under the central part of the intake manifold. When the engine is cold, the heat-control valve is closed, blocking off the exhaust manifold of one cylinder bank. The exhaust gas from this bank must therefore pass under the intake manifold—through the passage shown—to heat the intake manifold. As the engine warms up, the heat-control valve opens so that the exhaust

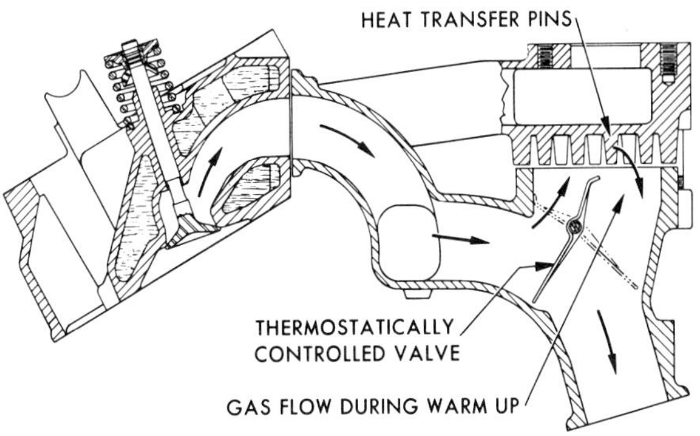

Fig. 17-17. Manifold heat control, using heat-transfer pins under intake manifold. (*Chrysler Motors Corporation*)

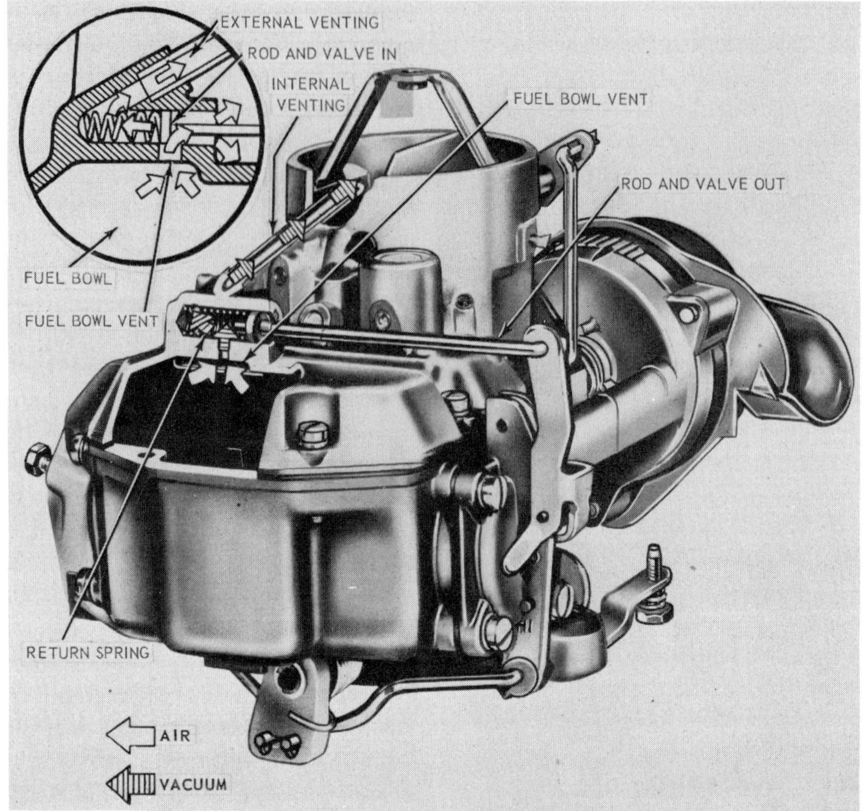

Fig. 17-18. Mechanically operated float-bowl venting system. (*Lincoln-Mercury Division of Ford Motor Company*)

gas can exhaust through the exhaust pipe, instead of through the exhaust-gas passage shown in Fig. 17-16*a*.

Instead of a special jacket in the intake manifold, some engines use a series of heat-transfer pins,[4] positioned just above the heat-control valve, as shown in Fig. 17-17.

§245. Other carburetor devices The past several articles have constituted a quick tour of the basic circuits of automotive carburetors. There are also numerous "add-on" devices to take care of specific operating situations or to provide control of other automotive components. Several of these are dealt with in following paragraphs.

1. *Float-bowl vents.* The float bowl must be vented to the atmosphere so that atmospheric pressure can force fuel flow through the carburetor circuits. If the vents open into the upper air horn, the carburetor is said to be *balanced.* If the vents open to the atmosphere directly, and not through the air cleaner, the carburetor is said to be *unbalanced.* With unbalanced vents, any clogging of the air cleaner can lead to increased fuel delivery and a richer air-fuel mixture. This is because a clogged air cleaner increases the vacuum in the induction system and thereby imposes a higher vacuum on the main fuel nozzle.

Some carburetors are equipped with a special mechanical valve which vents the float bowl externally during idling or hot soak. With either of these conditions, the fuel in the float bowl is subjected to excessive heating and thus high evaporation. The vapor forming during this time, if it entered the carburetor through the float-bowl vents, could unduly enrich the mixture, causing the engine to load up and stall when idling. One type of valve which prevents this condition is shown in Fig. 17-18. The valve is linked to the throttle-valve shaft. When the throttle is opened, the linkage moves the valve to the right (in Fig. 17-18) so that the fuel vapors can pass up into the carburetor (that is, the carburetor is *balanced*). When the throttle is closed, the linkage moves the valve to the left so that the float bowl is vented into the atmosphere. Now, fuel vapors can pass into the atmosphere where they will not cause an excessively rich mixture and engine stalling.

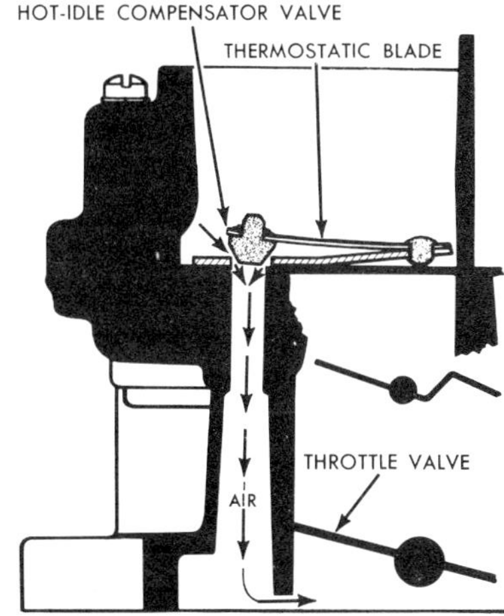

Fig. 17-19. Thermostatically operated float-bowl venting system, using a hot-idle air valve. (*Pontiac Motor Division of General Motors Corporation*)

Another device that prevents excessive enriching of the air-fuel mixture is operated by a thermostatic blade (Fig. 17-19). When the temperature increases sufficiently, the thermostatic blade warps and lifts the valve so that additional air can now flow through a bypass passage around the throttle valve. This compensates for the increased richness of the mixture from the idle circuit. The valve is called a *hot-idle compensator valve.*

2. *Carburetor icing.* The formation of ice in the carburetor is due to the vaporization of the higher-volatility fractions of the fuel, combined with certain atmospheric conditions.[6] The condition is most likely to occur during the warm-up period following the first start-up of the day, with the ambient air temperatures in the range of 40 to 60°F and the air fairly humid. There have been reports, however, of icing with fully warm engines operating at normal driving speeds.

The most volatile fractions of the fuel require about 160 Btu (British thermal units) per pound to evaporate. This heat is extracted from the air and the carburetor parts in the venturi and throttle-valve area. If enough heat is removed, the moisture gathering on the throttle valve and air horn will freeze. Once started, the process may continue rapidly and soon cause the car to stall.

There are two methods of preventing icing: to supply additional heat to the carburetor, or to alter the formulation of the fuel. Heat can be added to the area around the throttle valve by providing passages in the carburetor body through which hot exhaust gases, or water from the cooling system, can circulate (Fig. 17-20). However, supplying additional heat in this manner can lead to other difficulties, such as vapor lock, increased evaporation losses (§232), and reduced volumetric efficiency.

The fuel must have good starting and warm-up characteristics, and this requires the addition of fractions with high volatility. But excessive

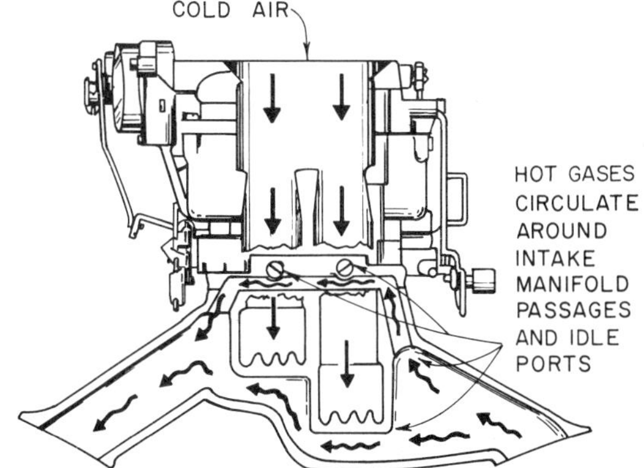

Fig. 17-20. Intake-manifold and carburetor idle-ports heating passages. Hot exhaust gases heat these areas as soon as the engine starts. (*Cadillac Motor Car Division of General Motors Corporation*)

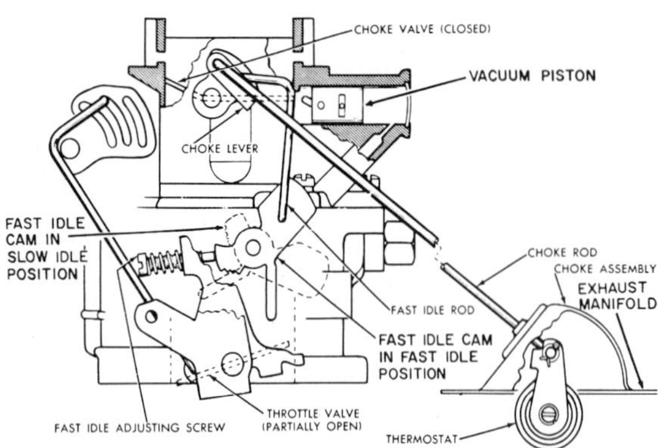

Fig. 17-21. Vacuum- and thermostatically operated choke with the thermostat located in the exhaust manifold. (*Chrysler-Plymouth Division of Chrysler Motors Corporation*)

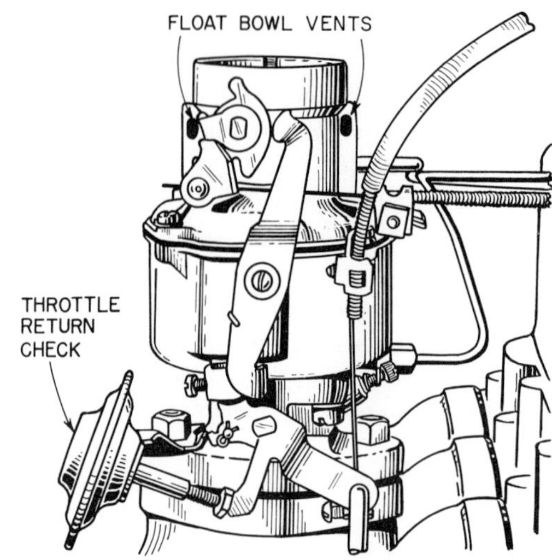

Fig. 17-22. Throttle-return check on a carburetor. (*Chevrolet Motor Division of General Motors Corporation*)

amounts of these high-volatility fractions can produce icing. Thus, the fuel producer must supply a carefully balanced fuel that will not ice but will allow easy starting and warm-up. Often, anti-icing additives are used, such as isopropyl alcohol or surface-active additives, which combat ice formation on the cold metallic surfaces.

3. *Fast idle.* When the engine is cold, some throttle opening must be maintained so that it will idle faster than it would when warm. Otherwise, the slow idle with the engine cold might cause the engine to stall. With fast idle, enough air-fuel mixture gets through and air speeds are great enough to produce adequate vaporization and mixing of the air-fuel mixture. Fast idle is obtained by a fast-idle cam which is linked to the choke valve (Fig. 17-21). When the engine is cold, the automatic

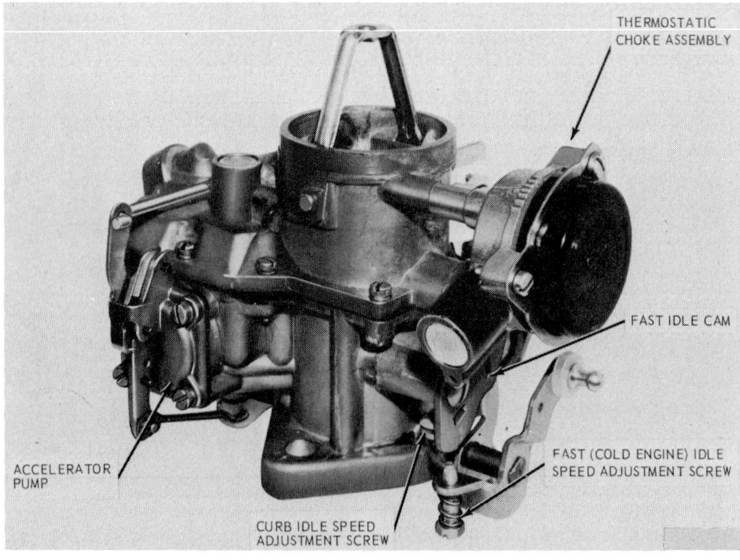

Fig. 17-23. One-barrel carburetor, exterior view. (*Ford Motor Company*)

choke holds the choke valve closed. In this position, the linkage has rotated the fast-idle cam so that the adjusting screw rests on the high point of the cam. The adjusting screw therefore prevents the throttle valve from moving to the fully closed position. The throttle is held partly open for fast idle. As the engine warms up, the choke valve opens. This rotates the fast-idle cam so that the high point moves around from under the adjusting screw. The throttle valve can then close for normal hot-engine slow idle.

4. Ignition vacuum advance. Ignition systems include a device that advances the spark as vacuum increases in the intake manifold (Chap. 20). This vacuum is tapped in the carburetor body, close to the throttle valve. The opening is just above the throttle valve when the throttle valve is closed. Thus, vacuum advance does not occur when the throttle is closed, but comes into action when the throttle is moved past the idle position.

5. Other carburetor devices. These include a throttle-return check which retards throttle closing, kick down switches, and governors. The throttle-return check slows throttle movement when the driver takes his foot off the throttle, which prevents stalling that might otherwise occur if the throttle closed quickly at intermediate or high speeds. Figure 17-22 shows a throttle-return check mounted on a carburetor. It contains a spring-loaded diaphragm which traps air behind it when the throttle is opened. The air escapes slowly when the throttle is closed so that the throttle closes slowly.

Electric kickdown switches have been used in connection with some types of transmission to provide a means of downshifting the transmission when the throttle is opened wide.

Governors are largely confined to heavy-duty vehicles. They prevent excessive engine speeds and rapid engine wear. One type of governor ap-

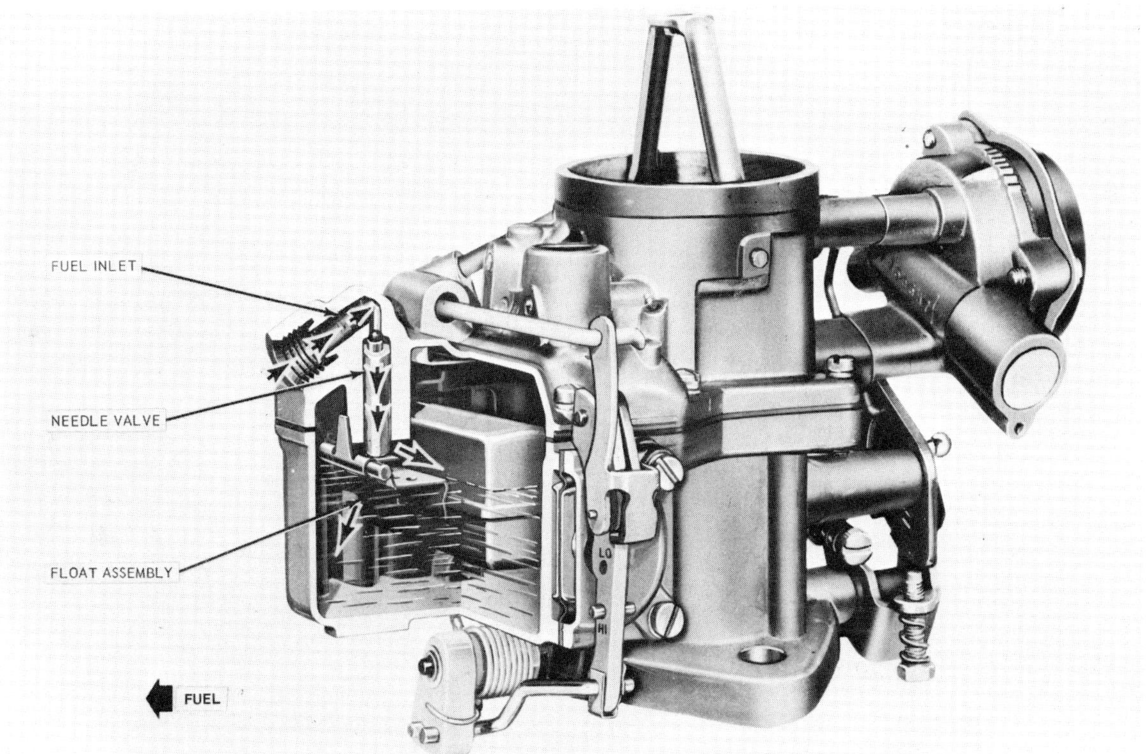

Fig. 17-24. Fuel inlet system of a one-barrel carburetor. (*Ford Motor Company*)

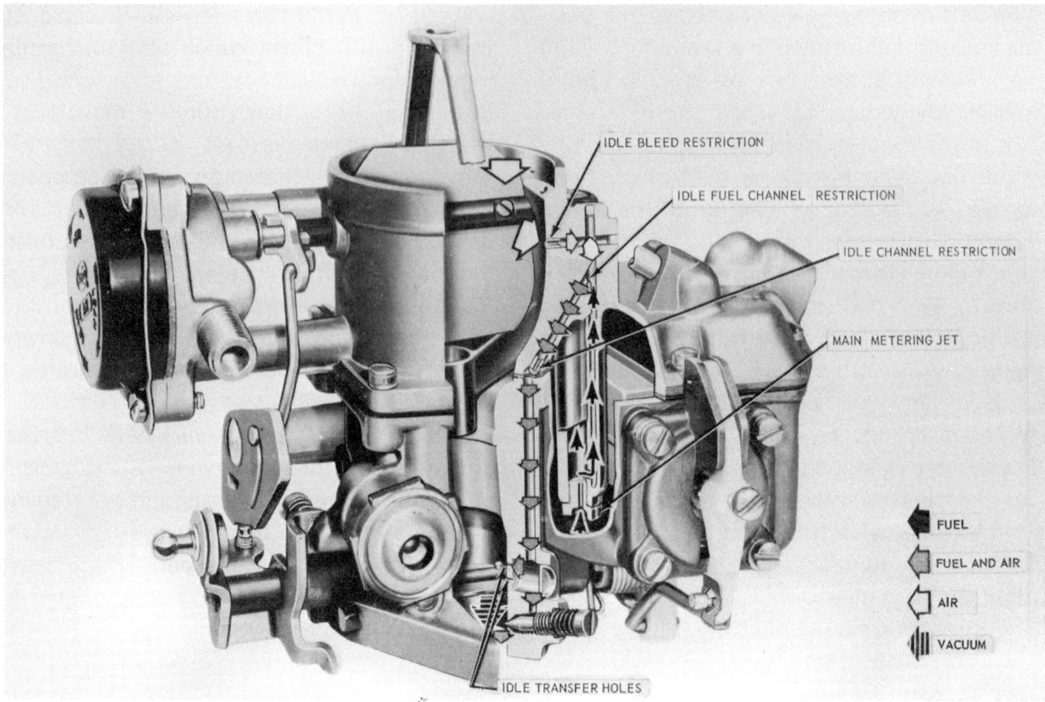

Fig. 17-25. Idle system of a one-barrel carburetor. (*Ford Motor Company*)

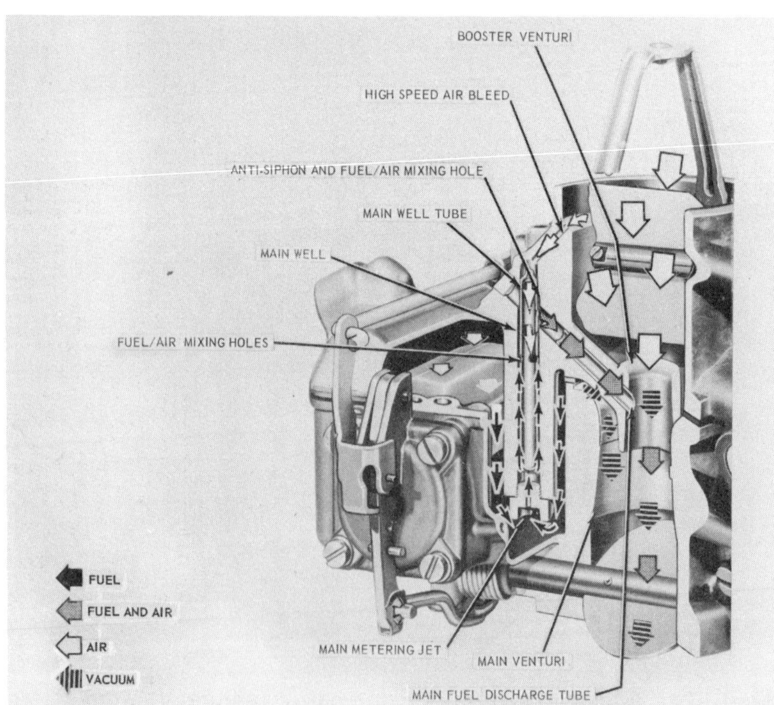

Fig. 17-26. Main-metering system of a one-barrel carburetor. (*Ford Motor Company*)

plies control directly to the throttle valve; it tends to close the valve as the engine approaches rated maximum speed. Another type interposes a throttle plate between the carburetor throttle valve and the intake manifold. The throttle plate moves toward the closed position as rated speed is approached.

§246. Typical carburetors A great variety of carburetors has been used on automotive engines. Each carburetor is tailored to meet the requirements of the engine with which it is to work. This is a matter of adjusting the sizes of the fuel nozzles and jets, metering rod, and so on. In addition, some installations may require special devices to satisfy special operating requirements. Several typical carburetors are described in the following articles, including one-barrel, two-barrel, and four-barrel, or quadrijet, carburetors.

§247. One-barrel carburetors Figure 17-23 is an exterior view of a one-barrel carburetor. Figures 17-23 to 17-29 show the various operating circuits in the carburetor. These illustrations are self-explanatory. (Refer to §236 to 243 for discussions of the various circuits in carburetors.)

§248. Two-barrel, or dual, carburetors To improve breathing of the engine, particularly during intermediate- and high-speed operation, many engines are equipped with two-barrel, or dual, carburetors. The dual carburetor is essentially two single-barrel carburetors in a single assembly (Fig. 17-30). Each barrel handles the air-fuel require-

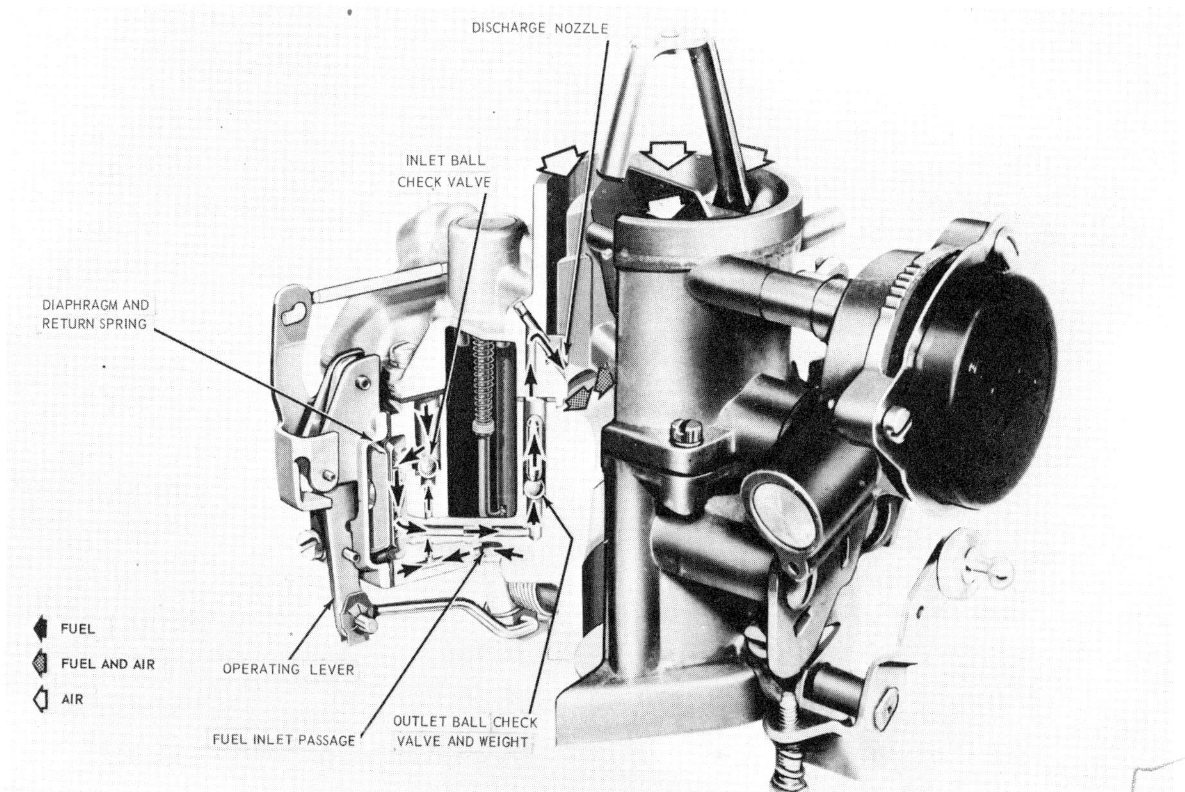

Fig. 17-27. Accelerating-pump system of a one-barrel carburetor. (*Ford Motor Company*)

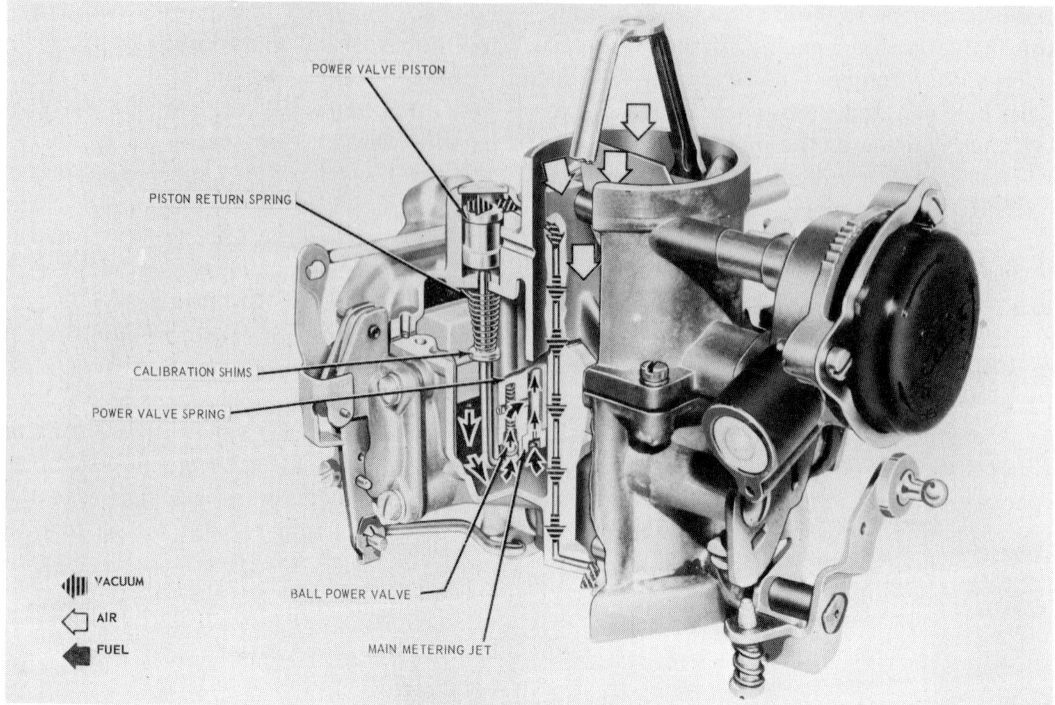

Fig. 17-28. Full-power circuit of a one-barrel carburetor. (*Ford Motor Company*)

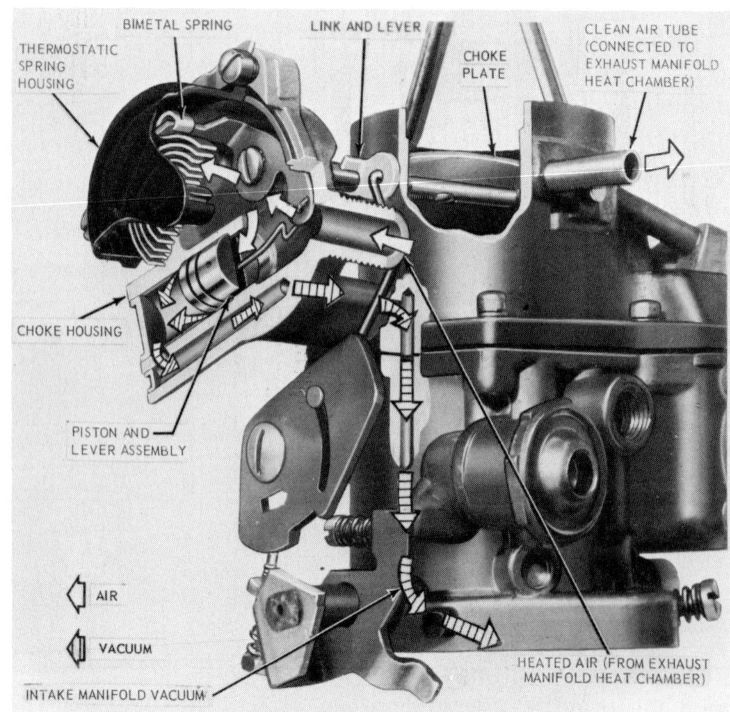

Fig. 17-29. Choke system of a one-barrel carburetor. (*Ford Motor Company*)

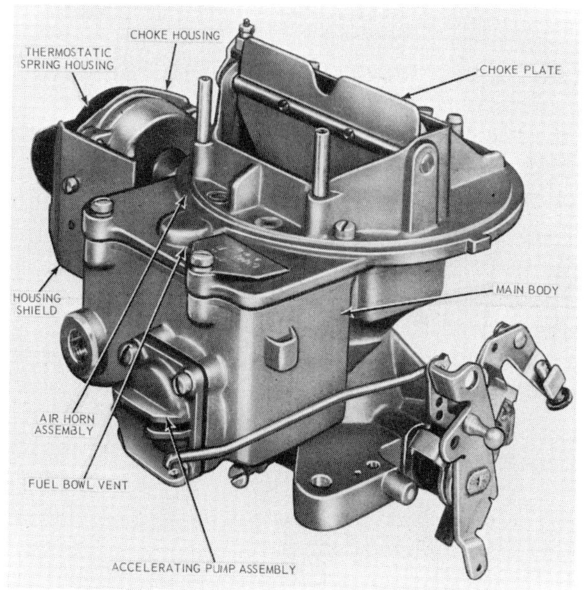

Fig. 17-30. Two-barrel, or dual, carburetor. (*Ford Motor Company*)

Fig. 17-31. Intake manifold for a dual carburetor. Arrows show flow of air-fuel mixture from two barrels of the carburetor to cylinders. The central passage connects the two exhaust manifolds; exhaust gas flows through this passage during engine warm-up.

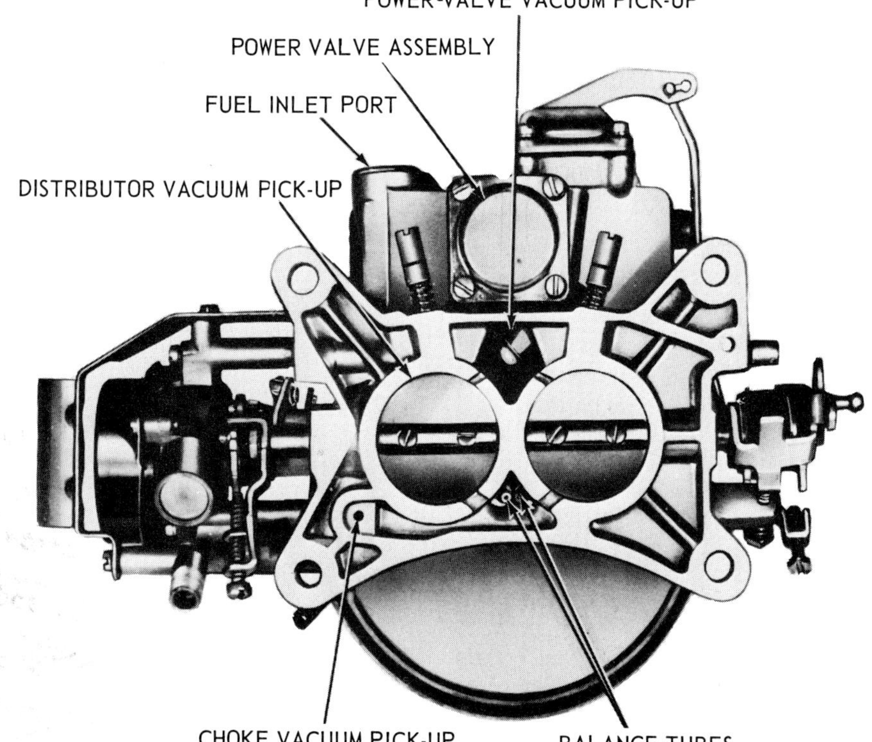

Fig. 17-32. Bottom view of a dual carburetor. (*Ford Motor Company*)

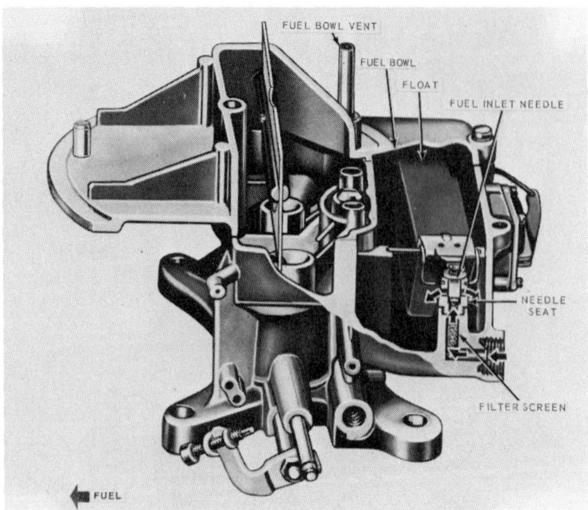

Fig. 17-33. Fuel-inlet system of a dual carburetor. (*Ford Motor Company*)

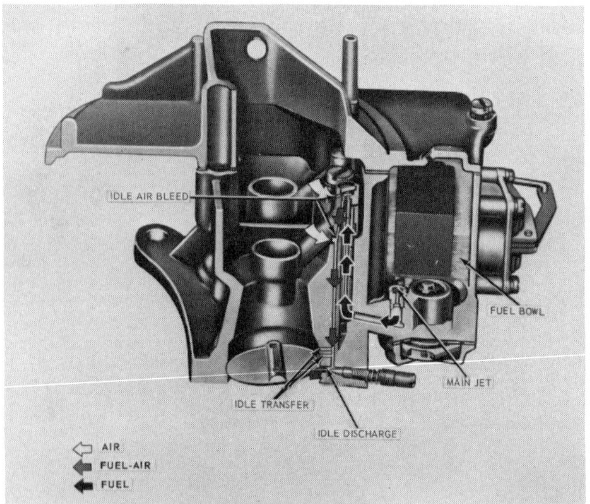

Fig. 17-34. Idle fuel system for a dual carburetor. (*Ford Motor Company*)

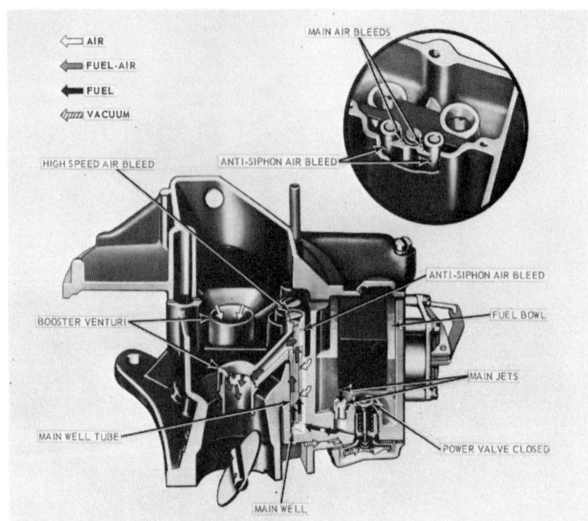

Fig. 17-35. Main fuel system for a dual carburetor. (*Ford Motor Company*)

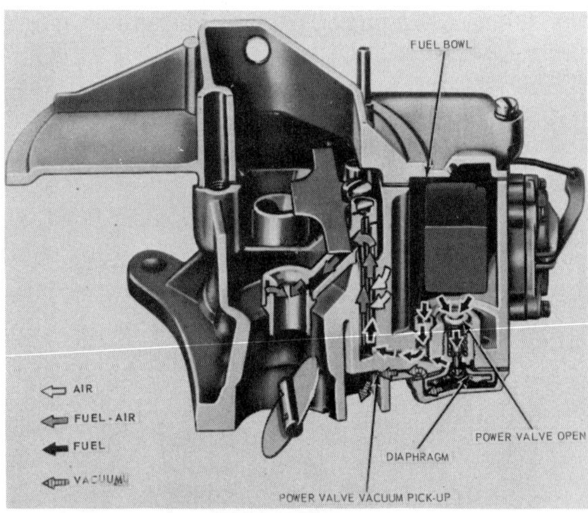

Fig. 17-36. Full-power system for a dual carburetor. (*Ford Motor Company*)

ments of half the engine cylinders. Figure 17-31 is a top view of the intake manifold for a V-8 engine, showing how each barrel supplies four cylinders. Each barrel has a complete set of circuits. The two throttle valves are attached to a single shaft so that both open and close together. Figures 17-32 to 17-38 show the various circuits in the carburetor.

Some people may wonder why engineers decided to use two barrels, with the added complications required by doubling the number of circuits, instead of simply increasing the size of the barrel. Increasing the barrel and venturi size, of course, would improve engine breathing and volumetric efficiency. However, the larger venturi would not function satisfactorily. It would be unstable and erratic at some speeds so that the air-fuel ratio would be unsatisfactory. The venturi must be relatively small to produce accurate metering of the fuel from the main fuel nozzle and thus good air-fuel ratios throughout the operating range.

§249. Four-barrel, or quadrijet, carburetors The four-barrel carburetor consists essentially of two dual carburetors combined into a single assembly. One pair of barrels makes up the primary side, the other two make up the secondary side (Figs. 17-39 and 17-40). The primary barrels are responsible for delivery of air-fuel mixture under most operating conditions. The secondary barrels come into operation when the throttle is moved toward the wide-open position for full engine power. The secondary barrels then contribute air-fuel mixture to improve engine breathing, or volumetric efficiency. At all other times, only the primary barrels supply air-fuel mixture.

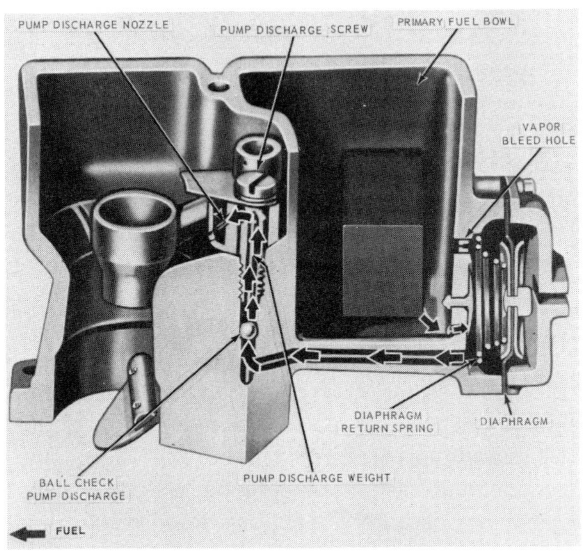

Fig. 17-37. Accelerating-pump system for a dual carburetor. (*Ford Motor Company*)

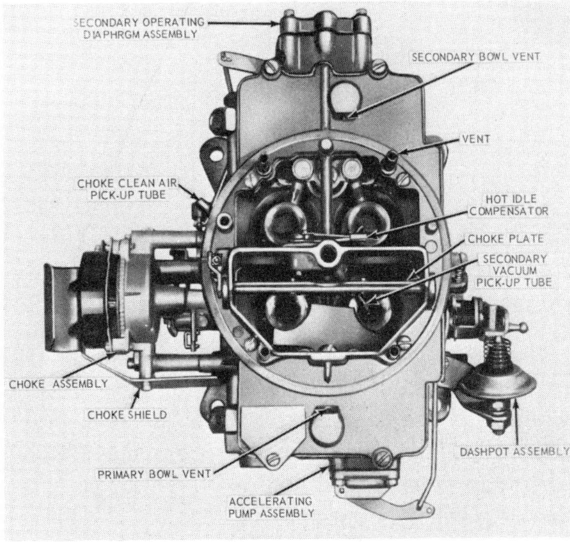

Fig. 17-39. Top view of a four-barrel, or quadrijet, carburetor. (*Ford Motor Company*)

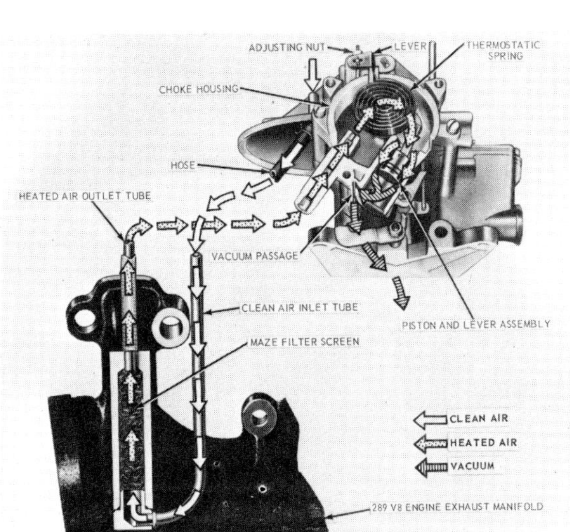

Fig. 17-38. Automatic choke for a dual carburetor. (*Ford Motor Company*)

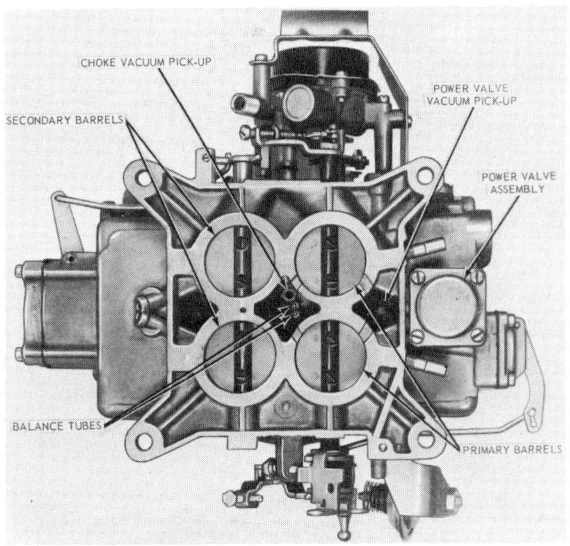

Fig. 17-40. Bottom view of a four-barrel carburetor. (*Ford Motor Company*)

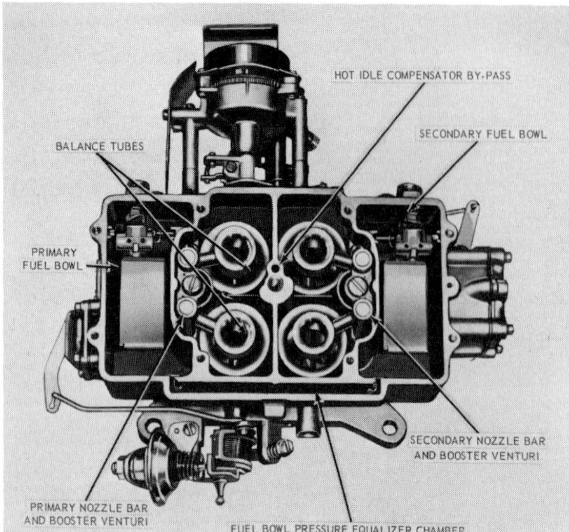

Fig. 17-41. Top view of a four-barrel carburetor with air horn removed. (*Ford Motor Company*)

The primary barrels have a full complement of circuits, including float bowl, choke, idle, off-idle, high-speed, high-speed full-power, and accelerator. Thus, the primary barrels compare almost exactly in construction and operation to the two-barrel, or dual, carburetor.

The secondary barrels have only main-fuel nozzles for high-speed, full-power work. In some carburetors, the secondary barrels have their own float bowl (Fig. 17-41). In others, a centrally located float bowl provides a single reservoir which feeds both sets of barrels (Fig. 17-42).

Figure 17-43 is a top view of a V-8 intake manifold used with a four-barrel carburetor. The two primary barrels divide the eight cylinders between them, as do the two barrels of a dual carburetor (see Fig. 17-30). When in operation, the two secondary barrels parallel the primary barrels, as shown in Fig. 17-43.

Figure 17-44 will give you an idea of how much the two added secondary barrels can improve engine performance. The four-barrel carburetor shows a gain, on the engine tested, of about 50 hp (horsepower), or from 260 to 310 hp. Torque also improved with the use of the four-barrel carburetor, increasing about 20 pound-feet, or from about 390 to 410 pound-feet. Note also that the torque curve with the four-barrel carburetor held up much better at higher speeds, giving 340 pound-feet at 4,800 rpm, as compared with about 290 pound-feet for the dual carburetor. The engine is much more responsive at higher speeds with the four-barrel carburetor because it can produce as much as 50 pound-feet more torque at 4,800 rpm.

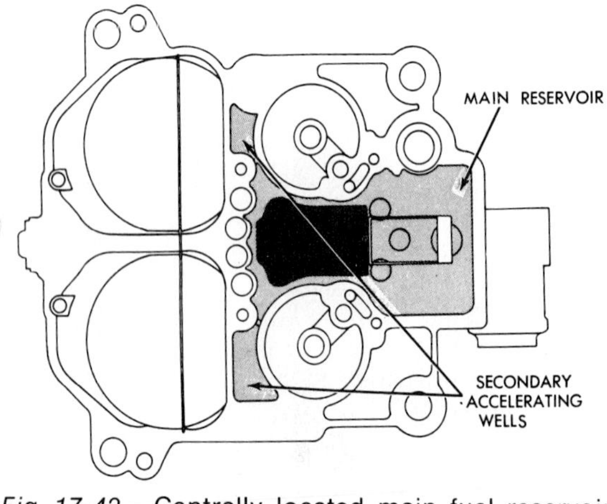

Fig. 17-42. Centrally located main fuel reservoir in a four-barrel carburetor. (*Cadillac Motor Car Division of General Motors Corporation*)

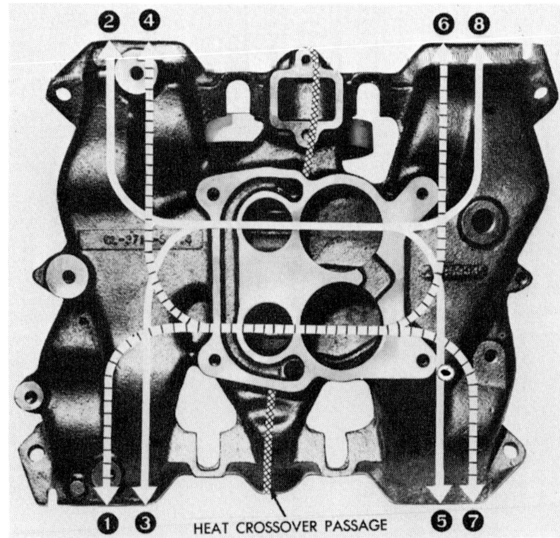

Fig. 17-43. Intake manifold for a four-barrel carburetor. (*Cadillac Motor Car Division of General Motors Corporation*)

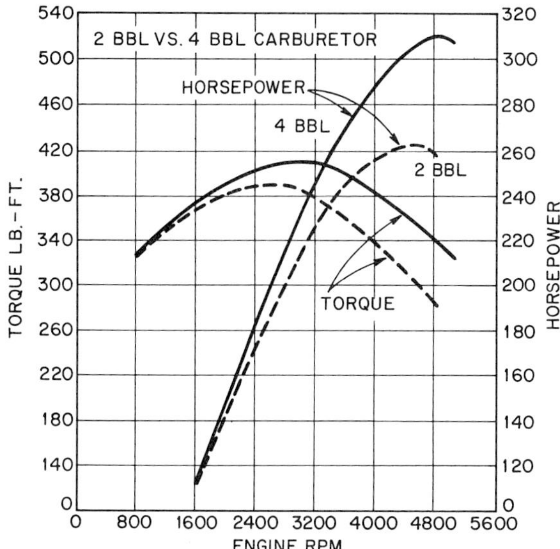

Fig. 17-44. Torque and horsepower output curves of an engine operated first with a two-barrel carburetor and then with a four-barrel carburetor. (*Oldsmobile Division of General Motors Corporation*)

There are two general systems of controlling the secondary-barrel action: by mechanical linkage from the primary-throttle-valve shaft to the secondary-throttle-valve shaft, or by a vacuum device. Figure 17-45 is a sectional view of a carburetor using mechanical linkage. During part-throttle operation, only the primary-throttle valves in the two primary barrels are opened. Whenever the throttle is opened wide for additional power, the linkage from the primary-throttle valves to the secondary-throttle valves causes the secondary-throttle valves to swing open. There is a spring-loaded air valve in the upper end of the air horn on the secondary side. Normally this valve is held closed by the spring. But when the secondary-throttle valves open, the vacuum below the air valve causes it to swing open and admit air into the secondary barrels. As this happens, the air passing through causes the secondary-barrel main-fuel nozzles to discharge fuel. The air-fuel mixture thus produced passes into the intake manifold to augment the mixture from the primary barrels, thereby improving volumetric efficiency and high-speed performance.

If the primary-throttle valves are opened wide at low engine speeds, the intake-manifold vacuum is not sufficient to overcome the air-valve spring tension in the secondary side. The secondary barrels therefore do not come into operation at low engine speeds. If the air valve somehow did improperly open at low engine speed, the air flow through the secondary barrels would be too low, because of the low engine speed, to produce appreciable fuel discharge from the secondary main-fuel nozzles. The result would be excessive

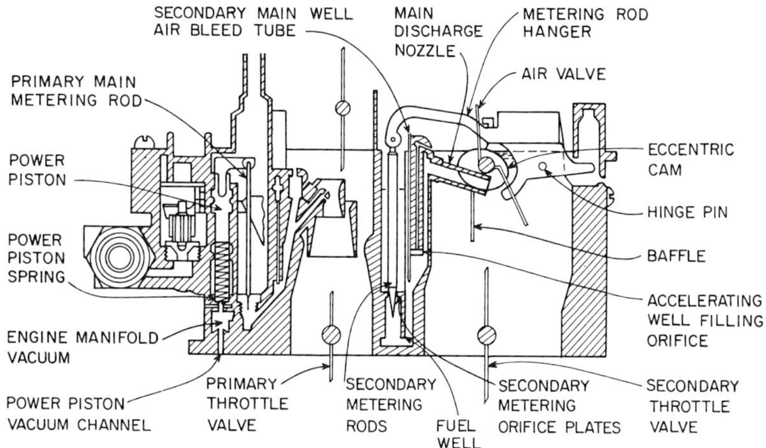

Fig. 17-45. Sectional view of a four-barrel carburetor with mechanical-linkage control of secondary throttle valves. (*Cadillac Motor Car Division of General Motors Corporation*)

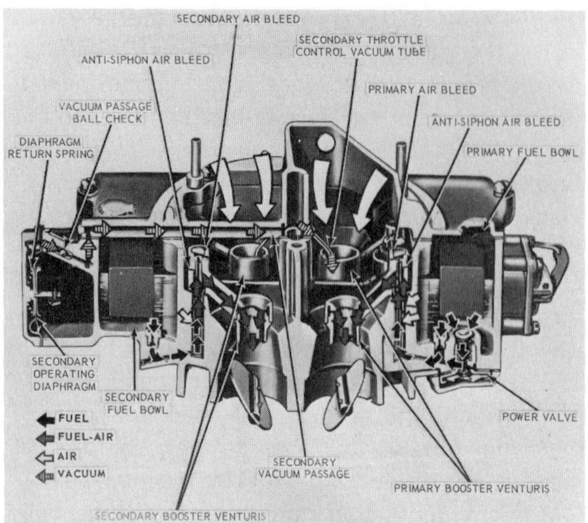

Fig. 17-46. Cutaway view of four-barrel carburetor, using a vacuum diaphragm to operate the secondary throttle valves. (*Ford Motor Company*)

leaning-out of the air-fuel mixture delivered to the engine cylinders and a resultant stalling, or at least stuttering, of the engine.

Let us go back now to the point where the air valve starts to open at high engine speed in response to the opening of the secondary-throttle valves and the consequent development of vacuum in the secondary barrels. As the air valve opens, its edge moves past an opening, or port, that connects to the accelerator-circuit well. When this happens, the vacuum causes the fuel in the accelerator-circuit well to be fed into the passing air stream in the secondary barrels. This additional fuel, immediately available, prevents any momentary leanness and possible engine stuttering during the short interval it takes the secondary main-fuel nozzles to start delivering fuel.

In four-barrel carburetors having a vacuum device to control the secondary barrels, there is no air valve in the upper end of the secondary barrels. Instead, the secondary-throttle valves are controlled by a vacuum-operated diaphragm, which is linked to a lever on the secondary-throttle-valve shaft (Fig. 17-46). The vacuum is picked up from one of the primary-barrel venturis. As the primary-throttle valves are opened, the air speed through the primary venturis increases. When the vacuum reaches a predetermined amount—indicating a rather high engine rpm—the vacuum is

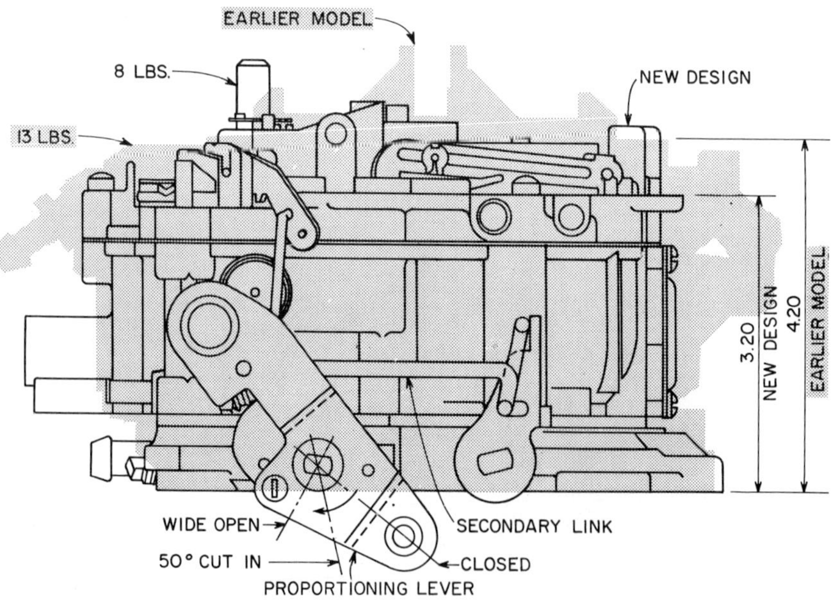

Fig. 17-47. Weight and height comparisons between an earlier and a new design of a four-barrel carburetor. (*Rochester Products Division of General Motors Corporation*)

great enough to actuate the secondary-throttle-valve operating diaphragm. Now, the secondary-throttle valves open and the secondary barrels begin to supply air-fuel mixture. A ball check, located in the vacuum passage in the diaphragm housing, controls the rate at which the secondary-throttle valves can open. Any rapid increase in vacuum which would tend to make the secondary-throttle valves open too quickly causes the ball to seat tightly. A small air bleed that bypasses the ball then allows the vacuum to actuate the operating diaphragm with comparative slowness. The purpose of all this is to prevent sudden opening of the secondary-throttle valves and a consequent sudden influx of raw air before the secondary main-fuel nozzles begin delivering fuel. If this should happen, the mixture delivered to the cylinder would become momentarily too lean, and the engine would hesitate, or stutter.

§250. Carburetor design The demand for higher volumetric efficiency and smaller size today has placed a heavy burden on the carburetor designer. Complicating the design task is the fact that the designer has little control over the air and fuel that go into the carburetor, or the air-fuel mixture after it leaves the carburetor. He must assume that the air cleaner will deliver adequate amounts of clean air at practically atmospheric pressure, and that the fuel pump will deliver adequate amounts of clean fuel at sufficient pressure to keep the float bowl filled. The designer must also assume that the engine designer will design an intake manifold, intake ports, and valves, that will permit easy and uniform flow of the air-fuel mixture to all cylinders, with all cylinders getting an even share of the mixture, and further, that the air-fuel ratio at all cylinders will be nearly the same.

But these are ideals. The design engineer knows, for example, that some cylinders will receive more air-fuel mixture than others, and that the air-fuel ratio will differ for different cylinders (see §211, 1). He knows also that it is practically impossible to prove out a design by bench tests. The final test is on an actual operating vehicle. Also, the results of this type of test are not clear-cut because many other variables, due to transmission, drive line, and other components, obscure the effect of carburetor-design changes. It is also true that an engine will operate fairly satisfactorily on enormously poor metering and distribution. That is, it will still run, even though the air-fuel ratio is far from ideal and the distribution of the mixture to the cylinders varies greatly. Thus, almost any sort of carburetor design could "work" to some extent. But developing a carburetor that will supply nearly ideal air-fuel mixture ratios for all operating conditions is another matter. It is not too difficult to achieve the first 90 percent, but achieving the final few per cent of operating perfection is the most difficult part of the design program; it is this that the design engineer focuses on.

Now let us look at some problems that were encountered by carburetor engineers in developing a new carburetor design.[1] Preliminary considerations indicated that the venturi type of metering system, used for many years in numerous variations, would be applicable to the new design. The new carburetor was to be a four-barrel unit of the type already described (§249). Lower hoods and larger engines designated a shorter carburetor, and the indication was that it would be desirable to reduce carburetor height from the 4.20 inches of earlier types to 3.20 inches (Fig. 17-47).

This posed the problem of venturi size and signaling ability. With a shorter carburetor, the venturi length would be shorter, and this dictated a venturi of a smaller diameter. The L/D (length-to-diameter) ratio of the venturi must be maintained within certain limits if an adequate signal is to be produced. That is, the vacuum in the venturi must have a proportional relationship to the air-flow volume, and this vacuum must produce a proportional fuel flow from the fuel nozzle so that the desired air-fuel ratio is maintained through the operating range. All this is summed up by the term "metering reliability." That is, the metering of the fuel from the main nozzle must provide the correct air-fuel ratio.

1. Float bowl. In considering the new design, it was decided to locate the float bowl, or fuel reservoir, in a central position, as shown in Fig. 17-48.

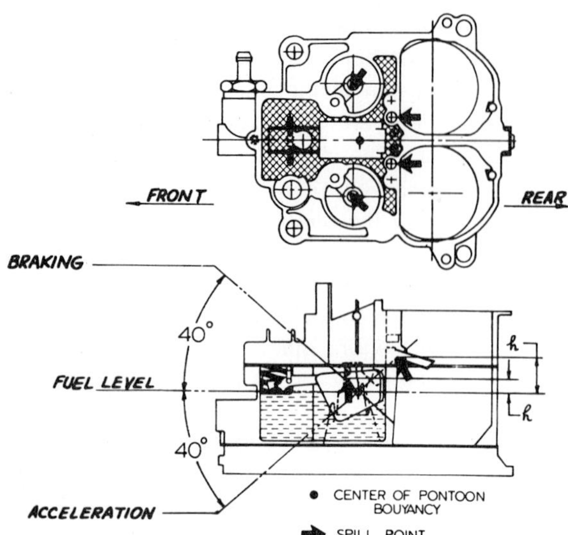

Fig. 17-48. The central location of the main nozzles permits a 40° forward or backward tilt of the carburetor, or the equivalent in accelerating or braking, before the spill point is reached. (*Rochester Products Division of General Motors Corporation*)

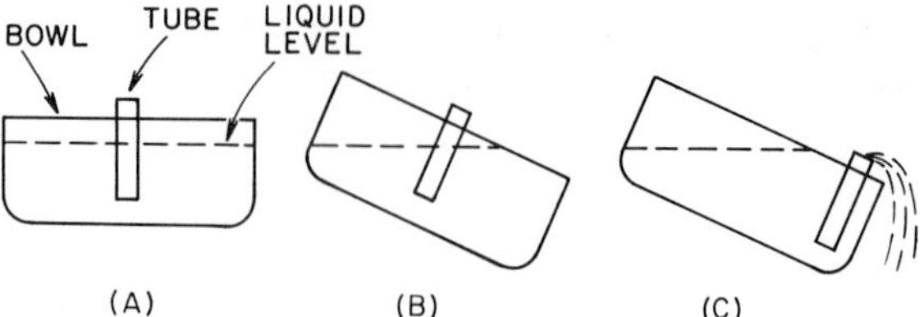

Fig. 17-49. If the tube is located in the center of the bowl, as at (*A*) and (*B*), tilting of the bowl will not change the level of the liquid in the tube to any great extent. However, if the tube is at one end of the bowl, then tilting of the bowl, as shown at (*C*), may cause the liquid to spill out of the tube.

This had several advantages. It reduced the external envelope of the carburetor (Fig. 17-47). It eliminated a secondary-float system, thus simplifying carburetor design, manufacture, and service. Also, it permitted putting the nozzle spill points (or openings) of the two main nozzles (in the primary bores) close to the center of gravity of the stored fuel and the float (Fig. 17-48).

This last point is of particular significance. If the spill points of the two main nozzles were far off center, then tilting of the car, as on upslopes or downslopes, or accelerating and braking, could have a marked effect on mixture richness. Fig. 17-49 illustrates this. In Fig. 17-49*a* the tube is centered in the bowl. When the bowl tilts, as in Fig. 17-49*b*, the liquid level remains at the same height in the tube. However, if the tube were at one end of the bowl as Fig. 17-49*c*, then tilting of the bowl would bring the liquid level nearer the top of the tube. In the carburetor, this condition would cause additional fuel to feed from the tube, or nozzle, so that the mixture could become overly rich. On the other hand, if the bowl were tilted in the opposite direction from that shown in Fig. 17-49*c*, then the liquid level would be much lower in the tube. In the carburetor, this would cause excessive leaning-out of the mixture.

The central location of the nozzles, as shown in Fig. 17-48, permits a tilt of 40 degrees forward or backward without disturbing the metering of the fuel and the air-fuel ratio. This is equivalent to heavy braking or accelerating. With either of these, the inertia of the fuel, as it moves forward in the bowl during braking, or backward during acceleration, produces the same effect as actual tilting of the carburetor.

The central location of the float is also important because it acts through the center of gravity of the fuel in the bowl. If the float were at one end of the bowl, then when the bowl tilted it would either shut off the fuel flow or permit too much fuel to enter, depending on which way the bowl were tilted.

2. Sizes and proportions of primary and secondary throttles. For good high-speed, full-power operation, the four carburetor barrels must allow a heavy air flow with very little pressure loss. If the carburetor were to offer appreciable restriction to air flow, then engine volumetric efficiency will be low, and engine performance will suffer. In consideration of the size of engine with which this carburetor would be used (up to 400 cubic inches displacement), the carburetor was required to permit an air flow of 50 pounds of air per minute at 1-inch Hg (mercury) pressure loss.

Figure 17-50 indicates why the figure of 1 inch Hg was selected. It shows the hypothetical effect of induction-system losses on horsepower, based on the intake-stroke mean-effective pressure (or average pressure in the cylinder during the intake stroke). The illustration indicates that there is a 3-inch Hg loss and that, if this loss could be eliminated, 10 percent more horsepower could be obtained.

Actually, the carburetor is responsible for only part of the pressure loss in the induction system. The air cleaner and the intake-manifold—intake-valve-port complex are responsible for much of this pressure loss. In the theoretical example shown, the 1-inch Hg pressure loss allowed the carburetor represents only about 3 percent more horsepower and is about the minimum at which the carburetor could function.

Having arrived at the 50 pounds of air per minute at 1-inch Hg pressure loss figure, it was now time to decide upon the sizes and proportions of the throttle valves (or carburetor-barrel throats). We have already noted that the primary-barrel venturi

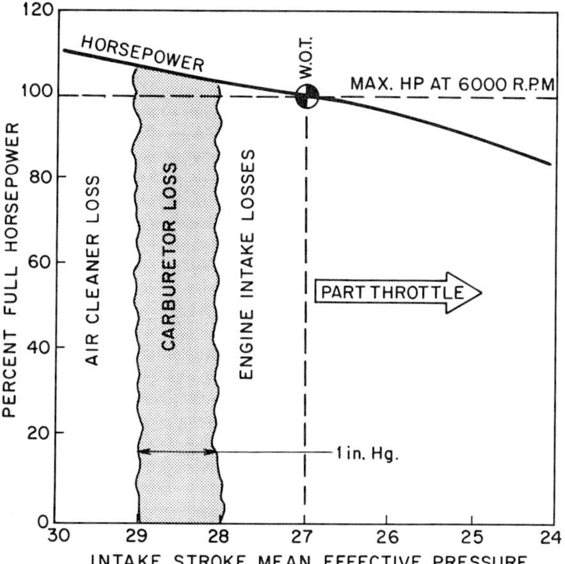

Fig. 17-50. Horsepower of engine related to intake-stroke mean-effective pressure. (*Rochester Products Division of General Motors Corporation*)

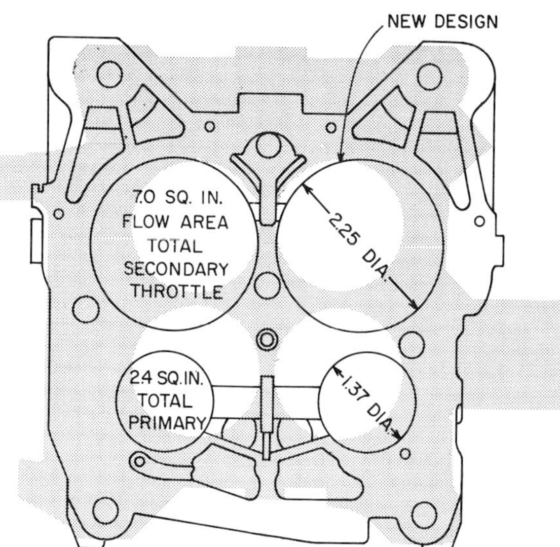

Fig. 17-51. Sizes of primary and secondary throttle bores in an earlier model and in a new design of a four-barrel carburetor. (*Rochester Products Division of General Motors Corporation*)

systems must be relatively small in diameter in order to achieve strong metering signals and proper air-fuel ratios during the primary-barrel operating range. This meant that the secondary barrels would have to be made comparatively large in order to achieve the air flow desired at minimum pressure loss. Based on these considerations, the following decisions were made:

a. The primary side would be tailored exclusively for maximum economy and reliability.

b. The secondary side would be tailored exclusively for maximum power.

c. The primary side would be totally responsible for metering fuel most of the time.

Air-flow studies through prototype or test-throttle bodies permitted the selection of throttle sizes that would achieve the design aims. The ultimate selection is shown in Fig. 17-51, which compares the new design with the old. Note that the primary-throttle area is smaller than the prior design, but that the secondary-throttle area is larger.

3. Throttle control. With throttle sizes and proportions established, it was now necessary to work out control linkage that would bring the secondary throttles into action at the correct time.

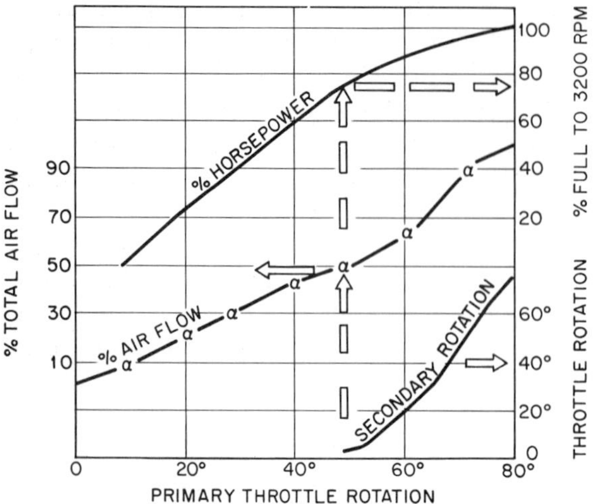

Fig. 17-52. Relationship of horsepower output with percentage of total air flow and action of secondary throttles. (*Rochester Products Division of General Motors Corporation*)

It was decided that the secondary throttles should not start to open until the primary throttles had reached a throttle rotation of 50 degrees from the closed position (Fig. 17-52). In the early stages of primary-throttle opening, a small increase in flow area (or a few degrees of throttle rotation) will produce a marked increase in air flow. During later stages, it takes a much larger increase in flow area (or more degrees of throttle rotation) to achieve significant increases in air flow. By the time the primary throttles have rotated 50 degrees, most of their throttling effect is gone. That is, opening from 50 degrees to wide open will not permit a proportionally greater air flow.

Thus, the 50-degree figure was selected and linkage designed to cause the secondary throttles to start opening at this point. It was necessary to arrange the linkage to the secondary throttle so that no marked increase in pedal pressure would be noticed by the driver as he advanced the throttle past the 50-degree primary-throttle position. This was achieved by using a proportioning-lever arrangement (Fig. 17-47), which permits the driving link from the primary throttle to contact the secondary lever as a long lever arm for sufficient force to break the secondary throttles from their bores and start them moving. Further movement of the driving link shortens the lever arm so that the secondary throttles open proportionally faster the farther they open.

4. Air-valve design. The purpose of the air valve is to provide a vacuum, or signal, that will produce fuel discharge from the secondary-main nozzles. The air valve must therefore be responsive to the air flow through the secondary barrels so that the proper air-fuel ratio is maintained during all phases of secondary-throttle-valve opening. Note that the same objective could be achieved with a venturi, but the venturi would demand a penalty of pressure loss.

The air valve, in its final design, was shaped as shown in Fig. 17-53 and was offset in the top of the air horn. A spring was used to hold the air valve closed when the secondary throttles were closed. The spring was offset as shown to allow a variable lever arm to work on the air valve. The purpose of these arrangements was to cause the air valve to open in proportion to the air flow. A flat offset valve, spring-loaded directly on the valve shaft, will open rapidly as a result of a small signal; however, it takes an increasingly stronger signal (or higher vacuum) to get the valve to move from partly open to wide open. This is contrary to what the air valve should actually do. The air valve, as actually formed (Fig. 17-53), has a bent short section that moves upward as the main offset part

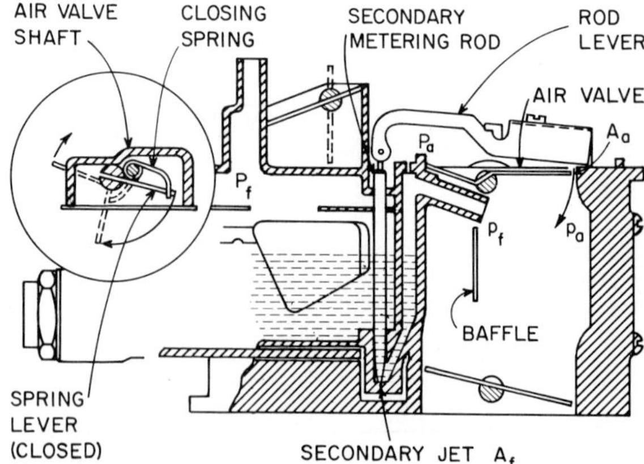

Fie. 17-53. Details of the secondary, side air valve and spring. (*Rochester Products Division of General Motors Corporation*)

moves downward. The bent short section thus becomes a controlling factor as the valve nears the wide-open position. An aid in keeping the valve opening proportional to air flow is the off-center spring (as already noted).

5. *Designing for manufacturing.* During the developmental work on the carburetor, the designer must keep in mind the fact that the carburetor not only must work properly, but it must also be manufactured. For example, the throttle body and the bowl cover are die cast as separate items, machined separately, and then assembled, with other parts, into the completed carburetor. To assure mating of parts, the designer must make provision for work holes that will permit proper location of the parts during machining. Figure 17-54 shows, for example, how the designer has indicated the center line of the reamed work hole as being a dimensioned distance from the assembly dowel which is cast in to the part.

6. *Assembly and testing.* The designer is also interested in assembly and testing of the carburetor. The various parts must also be tested as part of the quality-control program. Testing includes not only visual inspection for surface defects, but also checking of dimensions and measuring the calibration of jet, bleed, and idle tube orifices in the float bowl, for example. The carburetor engineer is still not through, however, after the carburetor has been given its final testing and is shipped from the factory. He is still interested in how it will perform in service, what service problems arise, how servicing is handled, and what service parts are needed. For example, if replacement float-needle valves or seats were sent out from the factory to service carburetors, the engineer would want to know why they were needed. He would want to know if the trouble was due to some defect in design or manufacture, or if the parts themselves were at fault.

§251. Intake manifold The intake manifold essentially is a series of tubes leading from the carburetor to the intake-valve ports. However, as we have previously noted, the proportioning of the passages to the different cylinders is extremely important. Without proper proportioning, the air-fuel mixture ratios and the amount of mixture delivered to the different cylinders will vary greatly. Figure 15-31 shows the fuel distribution in an unbalanced prototype intake manifold for a six-cylinder, in-line engine. Note that the end cylinders were receiving an air-fuel mixture as rich as 10.5 : 1, whereas the center cylinders had lean mixtures of around 15.5 : 1. Relatively minor changes in the cross sections of the intake manifold and in

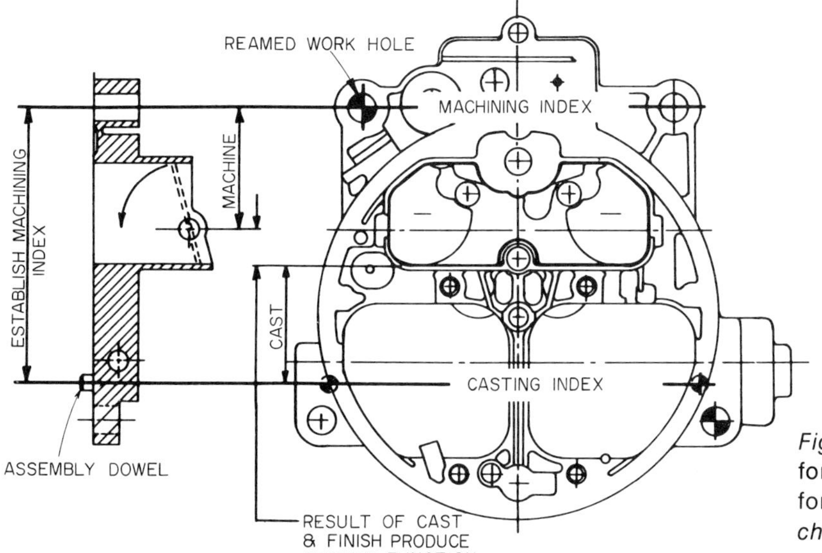

Fig. 17-54. Location of indexes for positioning of carburetor part for machining operations. (*Rochester Products Division of General Motors Corporation*)

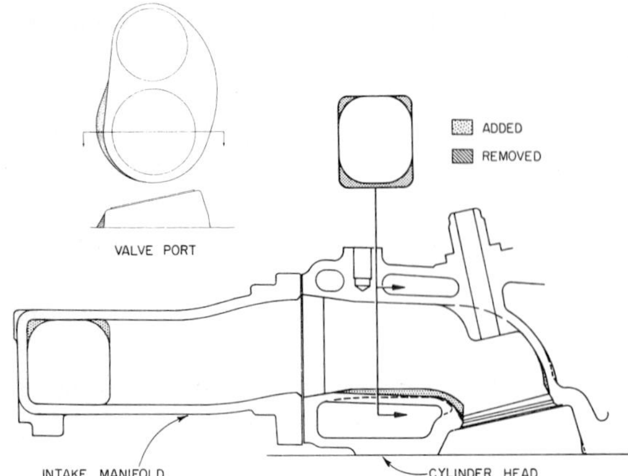

Fig. 17-55. Changes made in the intake manifold and valve ports to improve balance of air-fuel ratios to various cylinders. (*Ford Motor Company*)

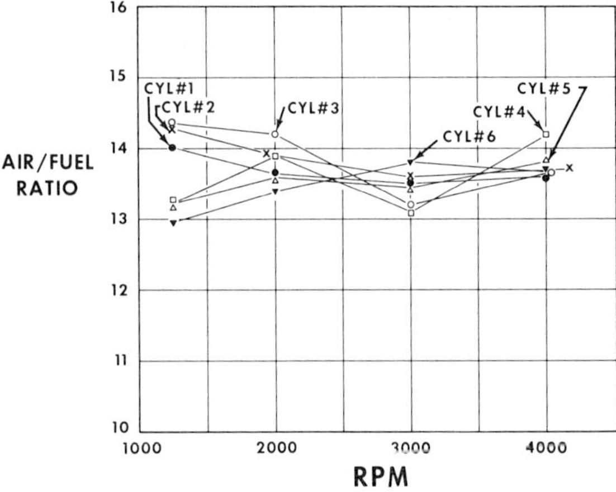

Fig. 17-56. Air-fuel ratios to different cylinders, after changes were made as shown in *Fig. 17-55.* (*Ford Motor Company*)

the intake-valve port[3] (as shown in Fig. 17-55) improved the air-fuel ratio balance between cylinders greatly (Fig. 17-56). (See also §209.)

During the development of their 427 GT V-8 engine, Ford engineers found that some of the intake-manifold contours were so extremely critical that the addition or removal of as little as 0.010 inch of thickness in certain areas changed the air flow 5 percent. This emphasizes again the extreme importance of careful studies of prototypes in the laboratory.

§252. Tuned intake manifold For high volumetric efficiency, valves and ports are made as large as possible, and the passages in the intake manifold and exhaust manifold are also made as large as feasible.

Another method of improving volumetric efficiency in high-performance engines is to tune the intake and exhaust systems. "Tuning," in this case, means selecting the proper length of manifold, for example, between the carburetor and intake ports. Tuning a manifold is similar to tuning a pipe organ. In the pipes of a pipe organ, air is set into vibration. As the air in a pipe vibrates, high-pressure waves pass rapidly up and down the pipe, and this action produces the sound. (Sound is nothing more than high-pressure waves passing through air.) In a tuned intake manifold, the incoming air-fuel mixture is made to vibrate, not to produce sound, but to ram more of the mixture into the cylinder. Under ideal circumstances, a high-pressure wave in the mixture will reach an intake-valve port just as the intake valve opens.

The high-pressure waves in the mixture are initiated by the sound of the intake valve closing. The waves pass back and forth in the tube, or manifold branch. If the branch is of the correct length, the waves will resonate, or pass back and forth, without loss of significant energy. Then, when the valve opens again, the high-pressure wave will arrive at the valve port in time to produce the ramming effect. It is obvious, however, that a manifold cannot be tuned for effective action at all speeds. The velocity of the sound waves through the mixture will not vary a great deal. Thus, varying the time interval between valve action will throw valve opening out of phase with the high-pressure waves. As a rule, the intake manifold will be tuned to be in phase when the engine is operating near or at top speed. This is the time when volumetric efficiency begins to drop off and the ramming effect would be most needed.

Chrysler was a pioneer in the development of tuned manifolds, and they termed the process "ram charging," or "ram induction," because the use of sound waves does have a ram effect on the ingoing air-fuel mixture. An early configuration

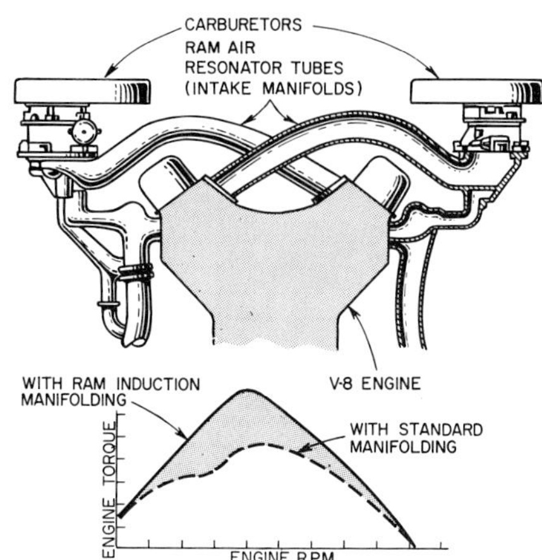

Fig. 17-57. Tuned, or ram, induction system, using long intake-manifold passages (or resonator tubes). (*Chrysler Motors Corporation*)

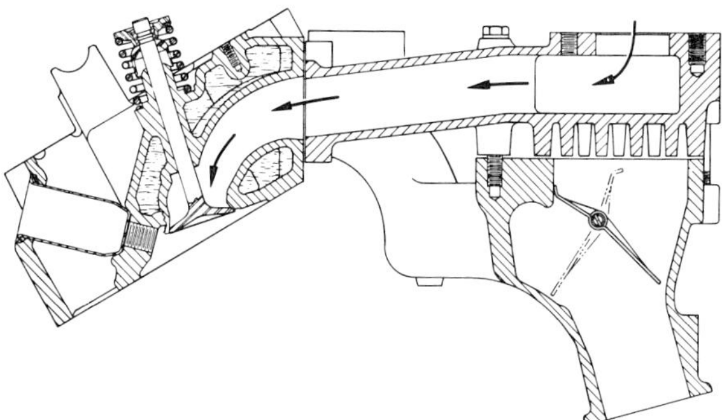

Fig. 17-58. Modified tuned induction system. (*Chrysler Motors Corporation*)

using two carburetors is shown in Fig. 17-57. It used intake branches 36 inches long for maximum high-speed performance.

Figure 17-58 is a modification of the tuned system, with longer than minimum individual passages from the carburetor to the intake ports.[4]

§253. The Ford Mark II-427 GT intake manifold During the development of the Mark II-427 GT engine, Ford engineers started with a basic intake-manifold design which they modified extensively. The design was the four-venturi, over-and-under type (Fig. 17-59). That is, it was for a four-barrel carburetor (§ 249), with half the runners or passages over, and half under. Figure 17-60 shows the runner system for the manifold. There are two independent sets of runners, one set at the intake-port level, the other slightly above. Note that the arrangement shown in Fig. 17-60 separates the firing pulses by alternating them from one runner system to the other. Thus, no two cylinders are fed successively from the same runner system. This increases the uniformity of the air-fuel flow to the cylinders.

At any early stage in the development program, the cylinder-head flow box was installed on the

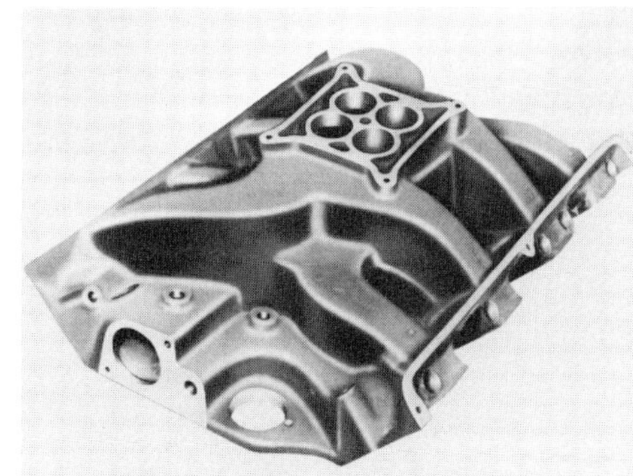

Fig. 17-59. Four-venturi intake manifold for a V-8 engine. (*Ford Division of Ford Motor Company*)

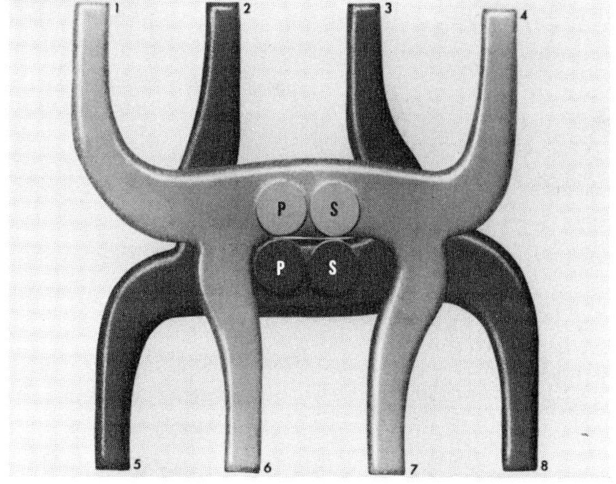

Fig. 17-60. Runner system for a four-venturi intake manifold. The forms shown represent the actual cavities or passages within the manifold. *P* and *S* indicate the primary and secondary barrels of the quadrijet carburetor used with the manifold. (*Ford Division of Ford Motor Company*)

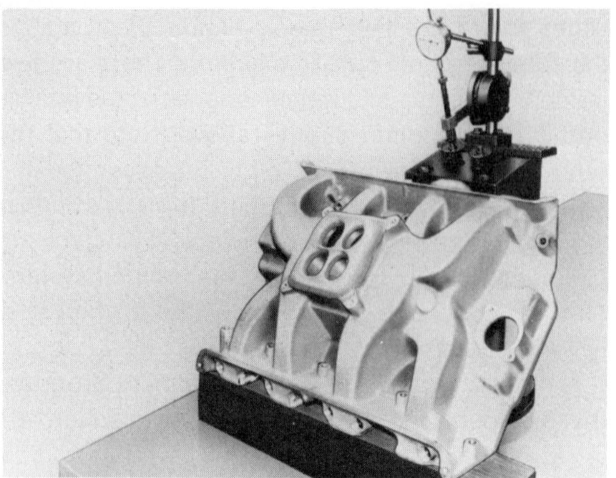

Fig. 17-61. Prototype intake manifold in place on flow stand, ready to check air flow through one runner. (*Ford Division of Ford Motor Company*)

flow stand (Fig. 15-21), and the intake manifold was then placed in position (Fig. 17-61). This arrangement simulated the actual condition for one cylinder in an engine.

Air flow through each runner of the intake manifold was then measured with this setup under varying intake-valve openings. This enabled engineers to determine the degree of unbalance between runners.

The intake manifold was then sliced into three sections, one cut being made through the lower-plenum section, the other cut through the upper-plenum section (Figs. 17-62 and 17-63). Then engineers added clay or ground-away metal in various areas to determine the effect on air flow. After each "add-to" or "take-away" session, the three sections were put together again and rechecked on the flow stand. Note the ground and clay areas in Figs. 17-62 and 17-63. These modifications not only balanced the air flow in the runners, but also increased the amount of air flow.

Next, wood patterns were made of the modified intake manifold, and metal castings made. These castings were machined and checked on the flow stand and also on actual engines. The results are shown in the curves (Fig. 17-64). These curves show the improvement in air flow, torque, and horsepower achieved by the modifications.

Later, a dual four-venturi intake manifold was developed by a similar technique. This intake mani-

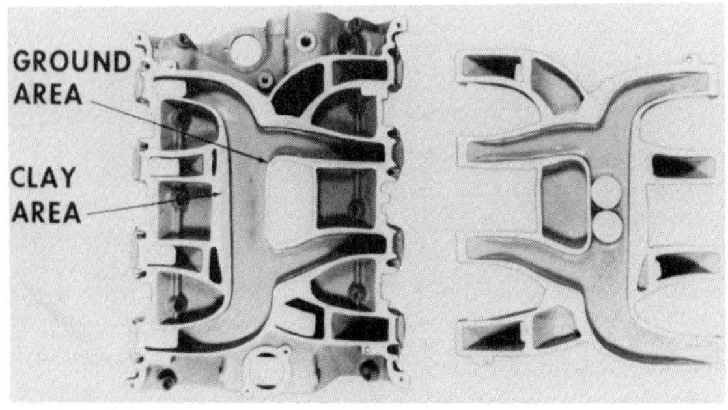

Fig. 17-62. Intake manifold sectioned through the lower plenum. (*Ford Division of Ford Motor Company*)

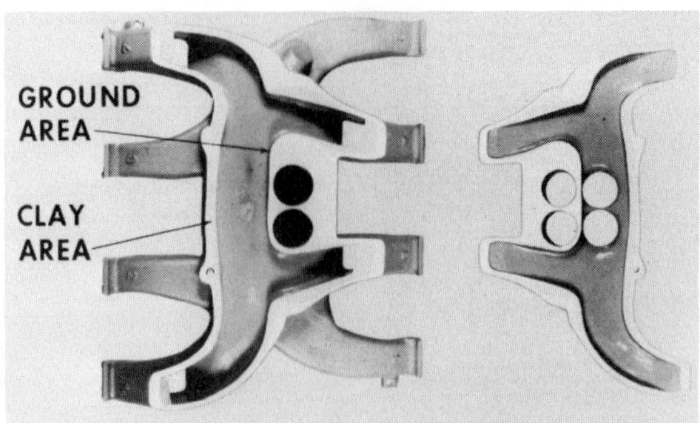

Fig. 17-63. Intake manifold sectioned through the upper plenum. (*Ford Division of Ford Motor Company*)

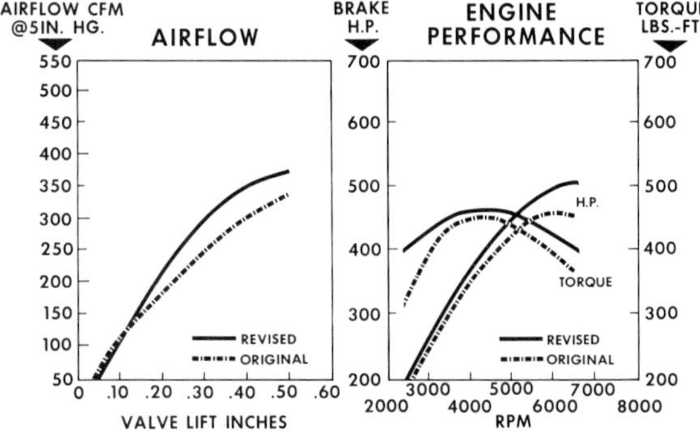

Fig. 17-64. Comparisons of air flow and engine performance with the original and revised intake manifold. (*Ford Division of Ford Motor Company*)

Fig. 17-65. Dual four-venturi intake manifold for a high-performance V-8 engine using two quadrijet carburetors. (*Ford Division of Ford Motor Company*)

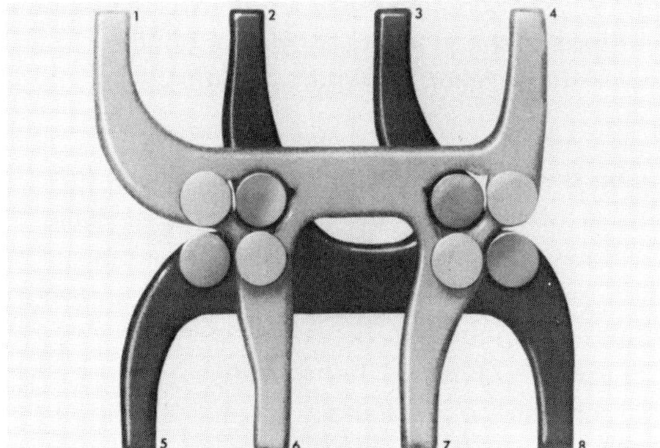

Fig. 17-66. Runner system for a dual four-venturi intake manifold. (*Ford Division of Ford Motor Company*)

fold (Figs. 17-65 and 17-66) is for two four-barrel carburetors and a high-performance engine.

§254. The Chevrolet Turbo-Jet engine intake manifold—a case history Three manifolds were developed for use in late-model Chevrolet engines. Figure 17-67 shows these—or at least one set of runners for each. The tuned runner gives a ram or partial supercharging effect, as explained in §252.

The intake manifold for the high-performance engine is cast from aluminum and has larger ports and an enlarged plenum area (Fig. 17-68). Also, a series of ribs was added to the intake-manifold floor (Fig. 17-69 and 17-70). These ribs improve the uniformity of fuel distribution to the cylinders. Part of the fuel is held in a liquid state in the ribs

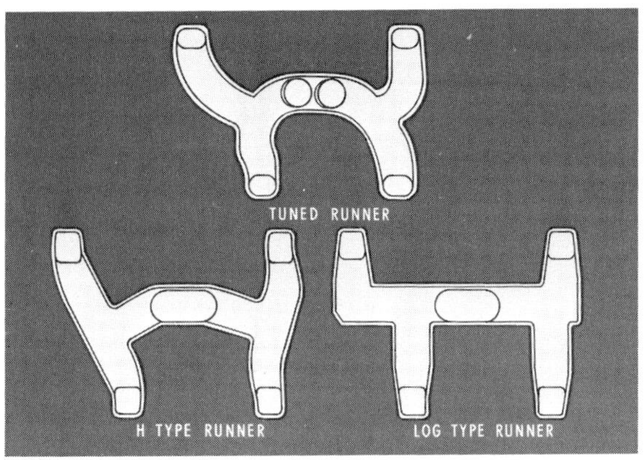

Fig. 17-67. Manifold runners used in various Chevrolet engines. Each runner set shown represents only half the total used in an intake manifold. (*Chevrolet Motor Division of General Motors Corporation*)

and tends to follow the ribs. Thus, by changing the shapes and lengths of the ribs, any combination of fuel delivery to the cylinders can be achieved. The final design shown in Fig. 17-69 achieved uniform fuel delivery within an air-fuel ratio spread of only 2 through the engine-speed range (from 14:1 to 16:1, for example).

The plenum floor is heated by exhaust gases passing through the cross-over passage during the engine warm-up period, when the manifold-heat-control valve is closed. The intake manifold

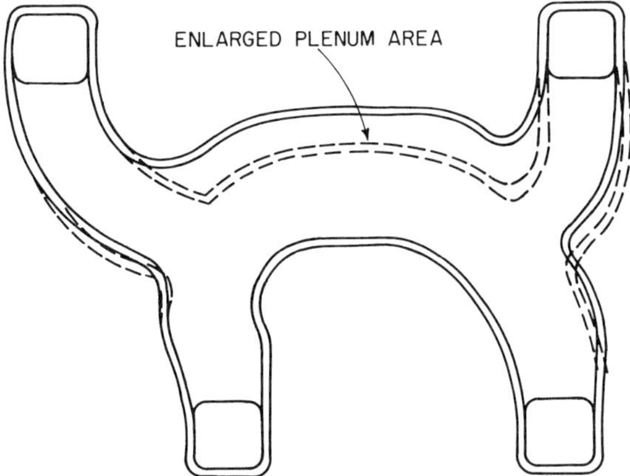

Fig. 17-68. Modifications of one of the two runner sets in the intake manifold for a high-performance engine. (*Chevrolet Motor Division of General Motors Corporation*)

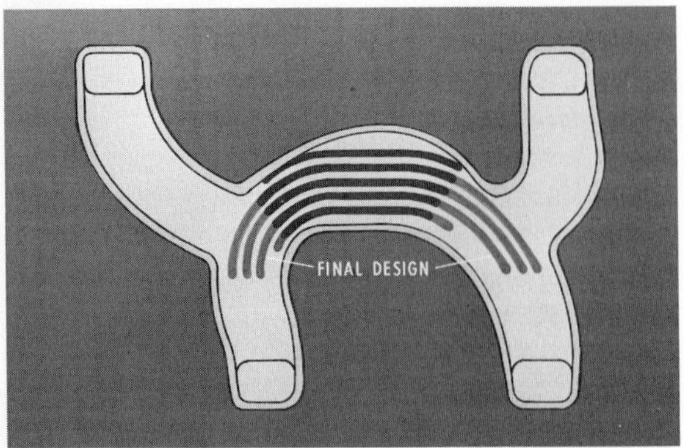

Fig. 17-69. Design of ribs in one of the two intake-manifold runner sets for a high-performance engine. The early design is shown in dark gray; the final design extended the ribs, as shown in light gray. (*Chevrolet Motor Division of General Motors* Corporation)

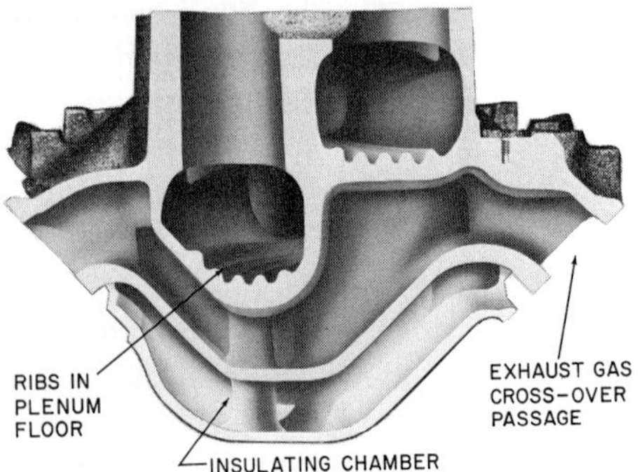

Fig. 17-70. Sectional view of an intake manifold for a high-performance engine, taken through the centers of the carburetor primary-barrel passages. (*Chevrolet Motor Division of General Motors Corporation*)

also includes an insulating chamber (Fig. 17-70) which insulates the underside of the hot exhaust cross-over passage by interposing dead air space. This is designed to prevent oil that splashes up on the underside of the manifold from burning and coking to the manifold.

§255. Supercharging Another way to get more air-fuel mixture into the engine cylinders, and thus improve volumetric efficiency and engine performance, is to apply pressure to the ingoing air-fuel mixture. The supercharger is a form of air

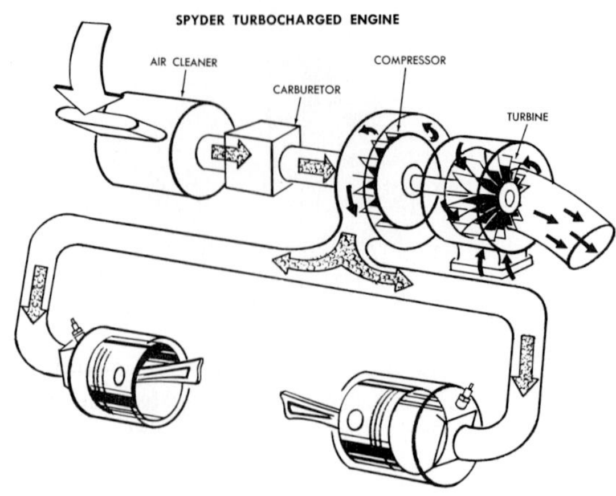

Fig. 17-71. Schematic layout of a turbo supercharger system on a flat six-cylinder engine. (*Chevrolet Motor Division of General Motors Corporation*)

pump, driven by either mechanical means or by a turbine operated by the exhaust gases. Because it "blows" air-fuel mixture into the engine, it is often called a blower, and the engine is known as a "blown" engine.

Figure 17-71 is a schematic layout of a supercharger used on a flat-six engine. It contains a compressor and a turbine which are mounted on a common shaft. The turbine rotor is rotated when the exhaust gases are directed against the rotor blades and the compressor rotor is thereby turned. The compressor rotor then pressurizes the ingoing air-fuel mixture, adding as much as 6 psi (pounds per square inch) above atmospheric pressure.

§256. Exhaust manifold The exhaust manifold includes a heat-control valve, as already described in §244. Exhaust manifolds may also be tuned for improved action. In the case of the exhaust manifold, however, the tuning should be such as to cause a low-pressure wave to appear at the exhaust port as the exhaust valve opens. The low-pressure wave, at below atmospheric pressure, produces improved exhausting action.

Some exhaust systems for V-8 engines use a crossover pipe to connect the two exhaust manifolds to a single exhaust system. Others use two separate exhaust systems, one for each bank (Figs.

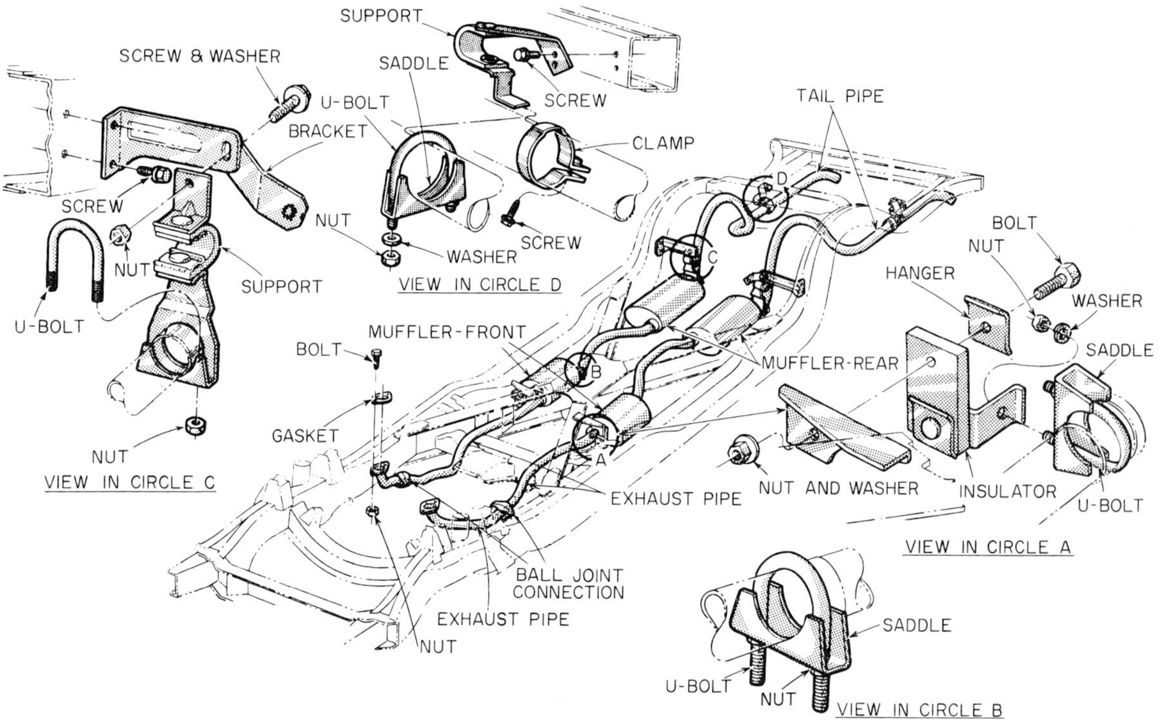

Fig. 17-72. Dual-exhaust system for a V-8 engine. Each bank of cylinders has its own exhaust system. (*Chrysler-Plymouth Division of Chrysler Motors Corporation*)

7-13 and 17-72). The use of a dual-exhaust system, by reducing the back pressure in the exhaust line, permits more efficient elimination of the exhaust gases with less pumping loss. This can significantly improve high-speed engine performance, as shown in Fig. 17-73.

§257. Smog control In recent years, considerable engineering work has been done in an effort to reduce the amount of unburned gasoline and harmful chemicals coming from the engine (see §139). These substances are being blamed as being partly responsible for the smog conditions in many of our larger cities. These substances leave the engine by two paths: (1) through the crankcase ventilating system, and (2) through the exhaust system. In addition, fuel evaporates from the carburetor and fuel tank.[2]

1. *Positive-crankcase ventilating (PCV) system.* During the operation of the engine, some blow-by occurs, which puts some products of combustion into the crankcase. In addition, when the engine is cold, a certain amount of moisture will condense on the engine parts (H_2O or water is a product

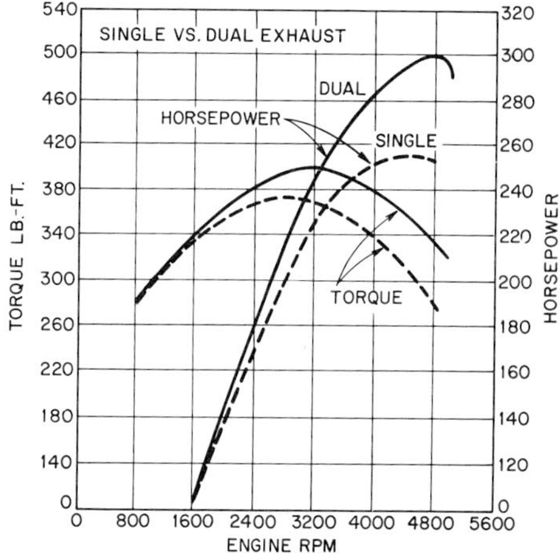

Fig. 17-73. Comparison of horsepower and torque of engines with single and dual exhausts. (*Oldsmobile Division of General Motors Corporation*)

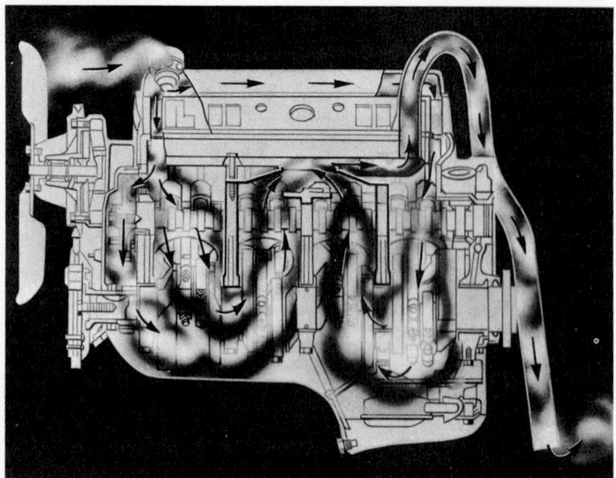

Fig. 17-74. Flow of ventilating air through the crankcase of a V-8 engine. (*Pontiac Motor Division of General Motors Corporation*)

of combustion), and particles of unburned gasoline will also collect in the combustion chamber. The water and unburned gasoline, if present in sufficient quantities, will pass the piston rings and enter the combustion chamber. Water in the oil pan can produce trouble. It mixes with the oil, and, under certain circumstances, the churning effect of the rotating crankshaft can whip it into a thick, gummy sludge. This sludge can clog oil passages and prevent normal engine lubrication, thereby leading to early engine failure.

Gasoline entering the oil pan can thin the oil and reduce its lubricating ability.

After the engine reaches operating temperature, the water and gasoline will evaporate. There must be a means of getting these vapors as well as any blow-by gases out of the crankcase. The crankcase ventilating system does this. Earlier crankcase ventilating systems (Fig. 17-74) had an air entrance (the oil-filler pipe) through which air entered the crankcase. It passed through the crankcase, picking up water and gasoline vapors and discharging them into the atmosphere through a vent tube. However, in recent years, the smog problem has brought about the necessity of preventing the crankcase vapors from discharging into the atmosphere. Today, cars are equipped with closed-crankcase ventilating systems (Figs. 17-75 and 17-76). The air enters through the oil-filler cap (passing through an air filter in the cap), circulates through the crankcase as shown, and then passes through a connecting tube into the intake manifold. From there, it passes through the engine as part of the air-fuel mixture and exits through the exhaust system.

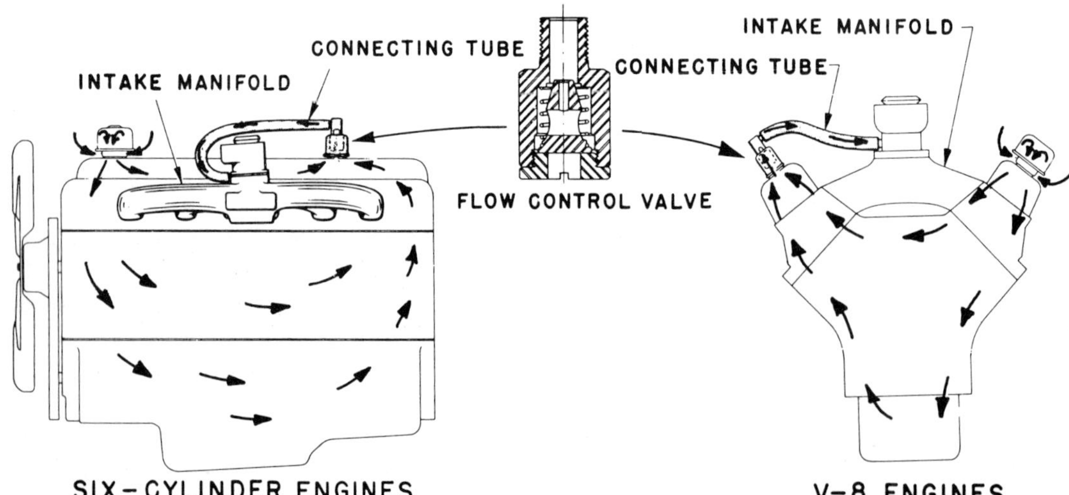

Fig. 17-75. Positive crankcase ventilating system on six-cylinder and V-8 engines. On the V-8 shown, the air circulates from one rocker-arm cover, through the crankcase, and out the other rocker-arm cover to the intake manifold. (*Chrysler-Plymouth Division of Chrysler Motors Corporation*)

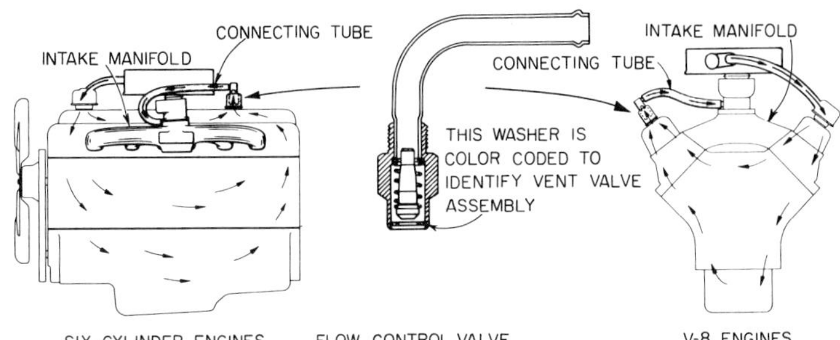

Fig. 17-76. Positive crankcase ventilating system on six-cylinder and V-8 engines of the type with sealed filler cap. (*Chrysler-Plymouth Division of Chrysler Motors Corporation*)

In the so-called "California system" (Fig. 17-75), there is an additional tube connecting from the carburetor air cleaner to the oil-filler cap. The oil-filler cap is sealed, and thus all air passing into the engine ventilating system must first go through the carburetor air cleaner. With this system, if any restrictions develop that could cause a backflow of crankcase gases, the backflow will vent into the air cleaner.

The *flow-control valve,* also called the *crankcase-ventilator valve* (Fig. 17-77), is required to prevent excessive air flow during idling and low-speed operation. Excessive air flow would upset the air-fuel mixture ratio and result in poor engine idling and stalling. When the engine is operating at low speed, the high-intake-manifold vacuum holds the valve in the closed position. In this position, there is only a small opening for crankcase vapors to pass through, and not enough can get through to upset the air-fuel ratio. But at higher speeds, when the intake-manifold vacuum is reduced, the valve spring pushes the valve off its seat so that more crankcase vapors can pass through. The two positions are shown in Fig. 17-77. In either position, there is adequate circulation through the valve to take care of crankcase vapors.

This valve must be checked periodically. Some manufacturers recommend checking the valve action every engine oil change; others say every six months. It is important to keep this valve working freely. If it sticks, not only will poor idling and stalling result, but products of combustion and blow-by will be retained in the crankcase. These products will cause sludge, acids, and varnish to form in the engine. Engine corrosion, poor lubrication, and serious damage to the engine may result. If the valve sticks, it should be cleaned or replaced. Some manufacturers recommend cleaning, others suggest replacement.

2. *Cleaning up the exhaust gases.* Cleaning up the exhaust gases from the exhaust system can be done in different ways. One method is to install a special afterburner or catalytic device in or adjacent to the muffler to process the exhaust gases passing through. The catalytic device is not effec-

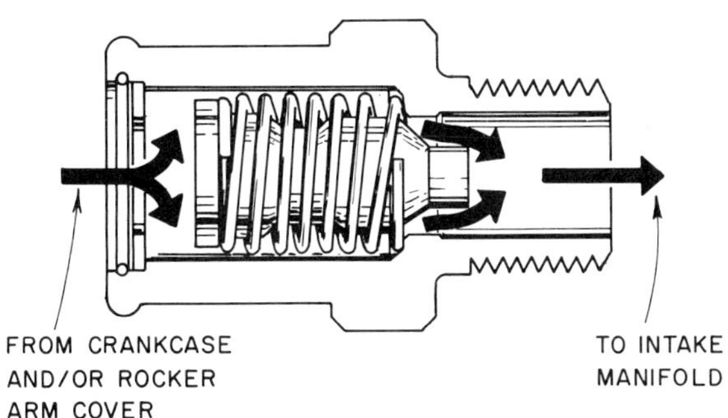

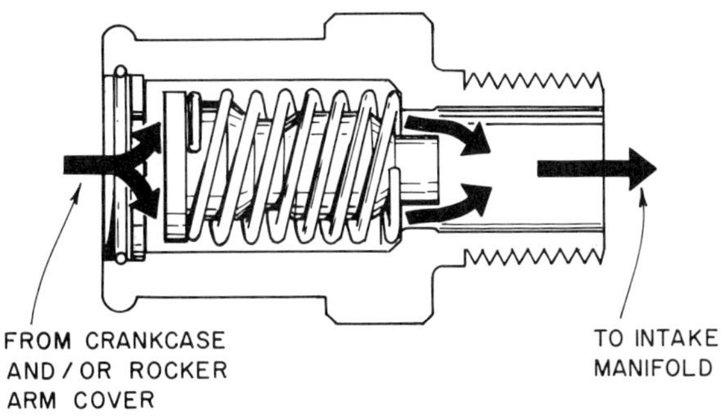

Fig. 17-77. Two positions of a crankcase ventilation valve. (*Ford Division of Ford Motor Company*)

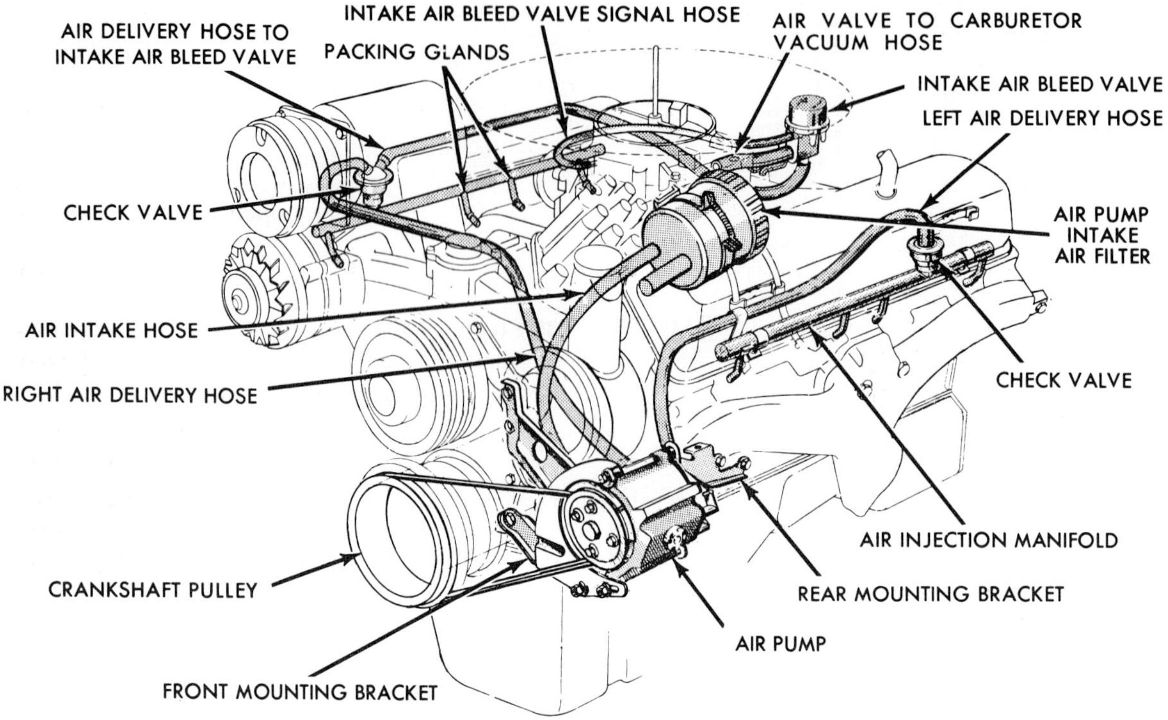

Fig. 17-78. Air-injection system. (*Cadillac Motor Car Division of General Motors Corporation*)

tive for any long period of time because it soon becomes clogged, particularly with lead when leaded gasoline is used.

A second method is to inject extra fresh air into the very hot gases coming out of the exhaust ports (Fig. 17-78). This extra air completes the combustion process that started in the engine cylinders, so that almost all of the unburned gasoline is burned, and any harmful gases are converted largely into carbon dioxide and water. This second method requires a belt-driven air pump mounted at the front of the engine and a series of tubes from the air pump to the exhaust manifold. These air tubes blow fresh air directly into the exhaust ports so that the combustion process can be completed. Ford and General Motors have used this method.

A third method is the Chrysler CAP (cleaner air package). This is shown in Fig. 17-79. The main feature of this system is a vacuum-operated sensing valve. The basic idea is that the operation of the engine is modified slightly so as to avoid incomplete combustion of the gasoline in the engine cylinders. Incomplete combustion is most common during idle and especially when the accelerator is returned to idle from an open position. In operation, the sensing valve advances the ignition timing during closed-throttle deceleration and during acceleration. This gets the combustion started sooner in the engine cylinders so that more complete combustion is assured.

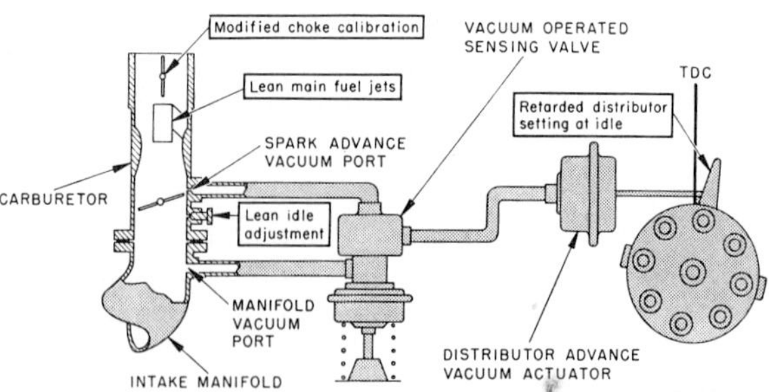

Fig. 17-79. Schematic view of the Chrysler CAP, or cleaner air package. (*Chrysler Motors Corporation*)

Fig. 17-79a. Cutaway view of a four-cylinder, overhead-valve engine, using two carburetors and a preheating chamber to reduce unburned hydrocarbons in exhaust gas. (*Volvo*)

In addition, engines equipped with the CAP have chokes that open sooner to avoid an overrich mixture which will only partly burn. Also, carburetors operate close to the lean limits to assure more complete combustion. A fourth method of cleaning up the exhaust gas and thus reducing smog is to provide a means of injecting extra heat into the ingoing air-fuel mixture during part-throttle, city driving. Figures 17-79*a* and *b* illustrate the way in which Volvo does this. The engine uses two carburetors and a preheating chamber inside the intake manifold, as shown. There are two secondary valves in the intake manifold that, during part-throttle operation, are closed. When in the closed position as shown in Fig. 17-79*b*, the ingoing air-fuel mixture from the carburetors must pass through the preheating chamber. In the chamber, they receive added heat from the exhaust manifold, which assures improved vaporization of the fuel. The air-fuel mixture that enters the combustion chambers therefore undergoes more complete combustion. This reduces the amount of unburned hydrocarbons in the exhaust gas. When the throttle is opened wide for acceleration and high-speed performance, the secondary valves are opened. Now, the air-fuel mixture can pass directly from the carburetors into the combustion chambers, bypassing the preheating chamber.

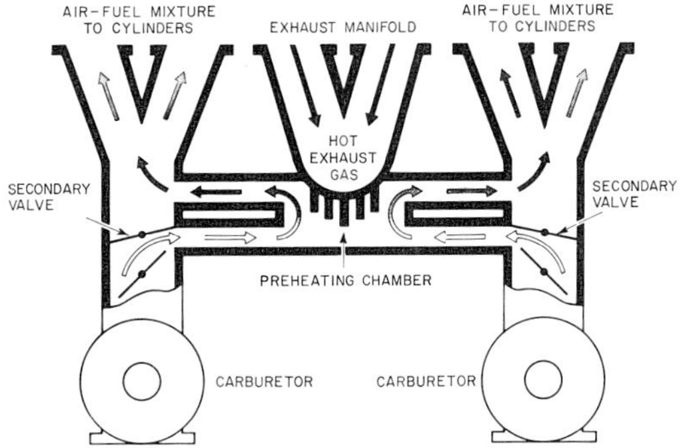

Fig. 17-79b. Schematic view of the Volvo smog-control system. The preheating chamber injects additional heat into the ingoing air-fuel mixture during part-throttle operation when secondary valves are closed. This improves fuel vaporization. (*Volvo*)

What might be considered a fifth method of cleaning up the exhaust gases relates to certain engine-design details that reduce unburned hydrocarbons. For example, some engines in 1969 came out with longer strokes than their predecessors. One Ford six-cylinder engine had a stroke of 3.91 inches as compared with 3.13 inches for the previous year. The longer stroke reduces the s/v (surface-to-volume) ratio (§139). Another design improvement was the introduction of the head-land piston ring, a ring with an L-shaped cross section that also reduces the s/v ratio and thus reduces exhaust pollutants (§139 and 158). The head-land ring, because of its better sealing properties, also reduces blow-by about 50 percent.

3. *Fuel-evaporation control.* Experimental work has been done on special systems that will capture the fuel evaporating from the float bowl and fuel tank and prevent its loss to the atmosphere. The purpose of this work is not so much to improve gasoline mileage of the automobile, but to keep the smog-inducing hydrocarbons from contaminating the air. One device that has been tested is shown in Fig. 17-80.[2] The canister is filled with activated charcoal. During a hot-soak period, just after the engine has been turned off and heat is penetrating the carburetor, gasoline vapors from the float bowl pass through the canister and are adsorbed by the charcoal. Then, when the engine starts, air passes through the canister in the opposite direction, picking up the adsorbed gasoline and carrying it to the intake manifold. Note that the vapors from the fuel tank are also captured

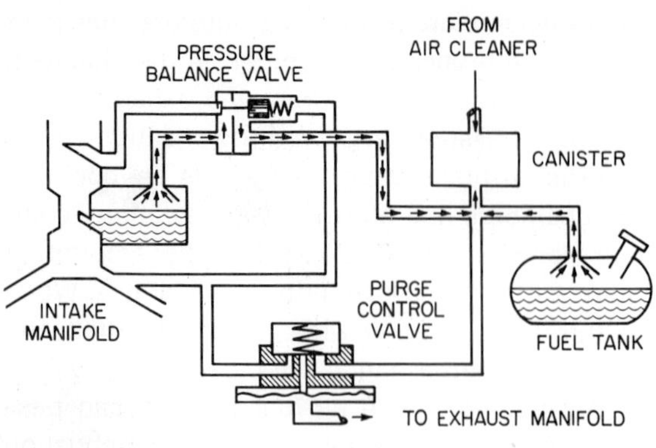

Fig. 17-80. A fuel-evaporation-control system. (*Esso Research and Engineering Company*)

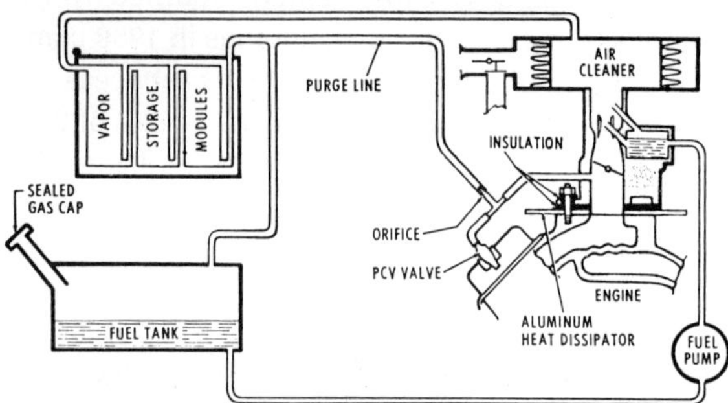

Fig. 17-80a. Fuel-evaporation-control system. (*Chevrolet Motor Division of General Motors Corporation*)

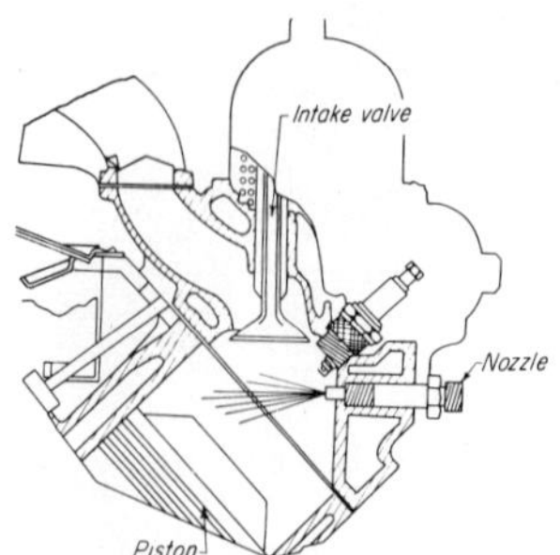

Fig. 17-81. Simplified view of a method of injecting fuel directly into the combustion chamber of an engine.

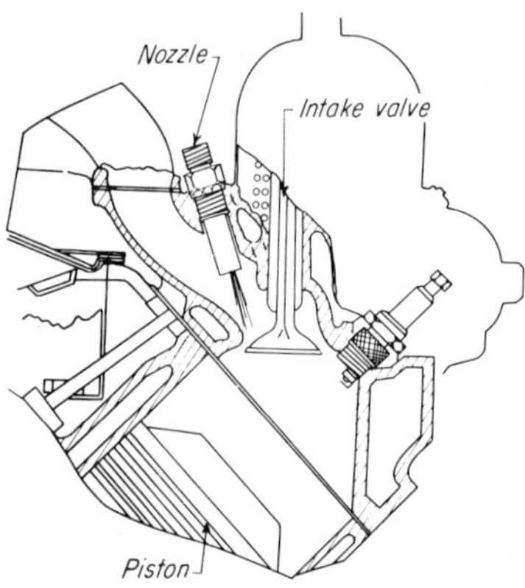

Fig. 17-82. Simplified view of a method of injecting fuel into the intake manifold located just behind the intake valve.

in this same manner. The pressure-balance valve has the job of closing off the vents from the float bowl to the outside so that no gasoline vapor can exit to the atmosphere. Then, when the engine starts, the pressure-balance valve opens the vents for normal carburetor action. The purge-control valve, operating from exhaust-manifold pressure, opens to allow air to pass from the canister to the intake manifold when the engine is running.

An evaporative control engineered by Chevrolet is shown in Fig. 17-80*a*. The purge line is connected into the line from the positive-crankcase-ventilation valve to the carburetor. The carburetor is protected from engine heat by insulation and an aluminum heat dissipator.

§258. Fuel injection The fuel-injection system[5] uses, instead of a carburetor, a series of injection nozzles and a high-pressure fuel pump to spray the fuel either into the cylinder directly or into the intake port just behind the intake valve (Figs. 17-81 and 17-82). The end effect is the same: a properly proportioned mixture of air and fuel appears in the cylinder, ready for compression and ignition.

The layout of one fuel-injection system is shown in Fig. 17-83. The major parts include an air-intake and air-meter assembly, a fuel pump and meter, and an intake manifold with eight fuel nozzles (one for each cylinder). The air-intake assembly has a throttle valve which is linked to the accelerator pedal. When the driver depresses the accelerator pedal, more air is admitted to the intake manifold.

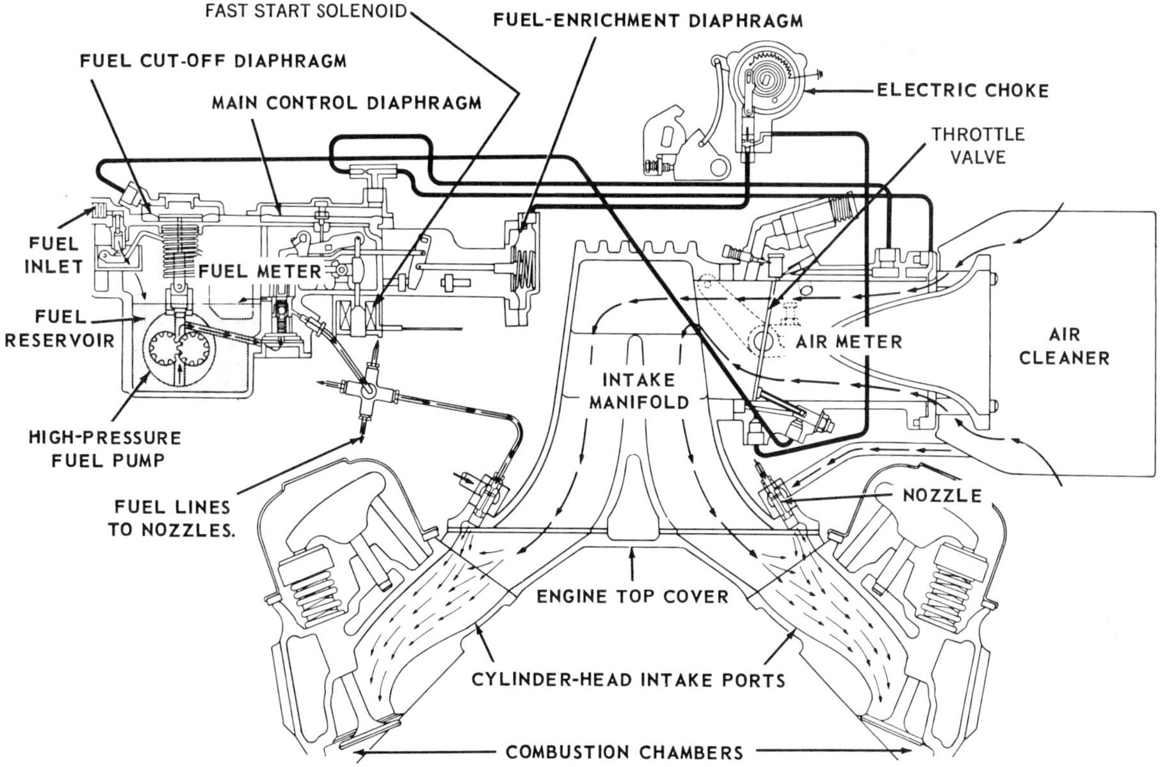

Fig. 17-83. Sectional view of the fuel-injection system used in a V-8 engine. (*Chevrolet Motor Division of General Motors Corporation*)

Interconnected controls then actuate the fuel meter so that more fuel is sprayed from the fuel nozzles into the manifold.

Some of the details of the fuel-delivery system are shown in Fig. 17-84. Fuel is delivered to the reservoir by a standard fuel pump, just as in other fuel systems. The high-pressure fuel pump in the reservoir, driven off the ignition distributor, delivers fuel to the metering chamber. From there, it can pass on to the fuel nozzles or flow back into the reservoir. The amount that is delivered to the fuel nozzles depends on the requirements of the engine, that is, on the engine operating conditions. For instance, if the engine is cold, a choke system comes into operation to enrich the mixture for cold starting and initial running. Likewise, the mixture is enriched for acceleration and high-speed performance. The controls to accomplish this are based on the vacuum in the air-meter venturi, which actuates a diaphragm in the fuel

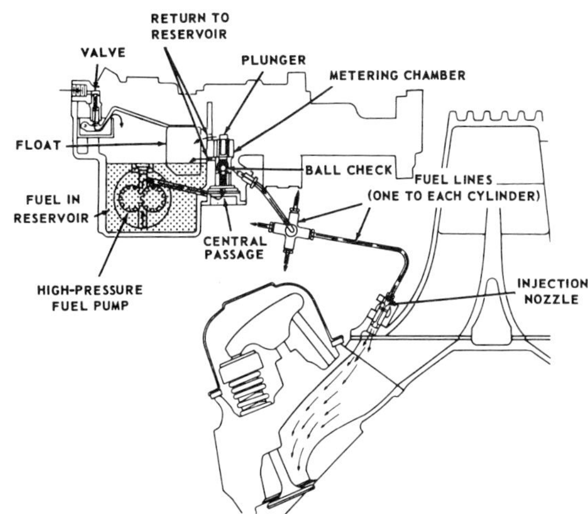

Fig. 17-84. Fuel intake and injection of a fuel-injection system. (*Chevrolet Motor Division of General Motors Corporation*)

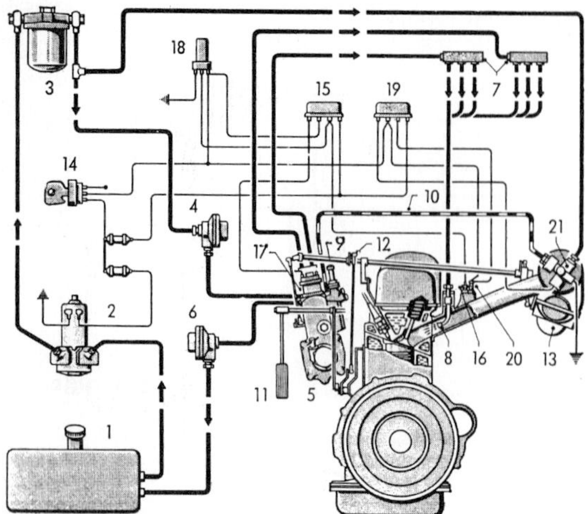

Fig. 17-85. Schematic layout of a fuel-injection system used on a six-cylinder engine. (*Mercedes-Benz, Daimler-Benz Aktiengesellschaft*)

1. Fuel tank
2. Fuel-feed pump
3. Fuel filter
4. Damper container (inlet)
5. Injection pump
6. Damper container (outlet)
7. Fuel-metering units
8. Injection valves
9. Cooling-water thermostat
10. Additional air duct
11. Accelerator pedal
12. Control linkage
13. Throttle connector
14. Ignition-starter switch
15. Relay
16. Thermo switch in cooling-water circuit
17. Magnetic switch for mixture control
18. Time switch
19. Relay
20. Thermo-time switch in cooling-water circuit
21. Electromagnetic starter valve with atomizing jet

meter. This diaphragm positions the plunger in the metering chamber to change the amount of fuel being delivered to the injection nozzles, in accordance with engine and operating requirements.

Figure 17-85 is a schematic view of another fuel-injection system that differs in many respects from the system illustrated in Figs. 17-83 and 17-84. This system has a two-plunger pump, each plunger feeding three cylinders through a metering unit. Fuel is injected into the intake ports of the cylinders. The metering units are controlled by a link-

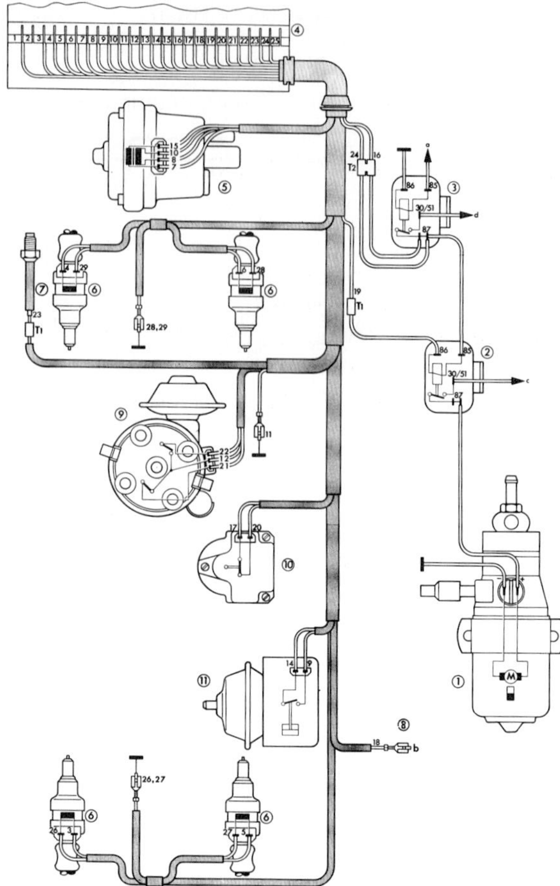

Fig. 17-86. Schematic layout of the control system for the Volkswagen electronic fuel-injection system. The electronic control unit (4) receives signals from various sensors and integrates them to determine the amount of fuel to be injected. (*Volkswagen*)

1. Fuel pump
2. Pump relay
3. Main relay
4. Control unit
5. Intake-manifold pressure sensor
6. Injector
7. Cylinder-head temperature sensor
8. Crankcase sensor
9. Ignition distributor
10. Throttle switch
11. Full-load pressure switch

age to the accelerator pedal, while the amount of fuel delivered by the pump is controlled by a centrifugal governor. Other controls are included to increase the richness of the air-fuel mixture for starting, cold operation, and high-speed full-power running. There are also pressure cells built into the diaphragms of the injection pump, which alter the amount of fuel delivered in accordance with the altitude and the density of the air. At higher altitudes, the air is less dense, and therefore less fuel is required to achieve the normal air-fuel-mixture ratio. The pressure cells take care of this adjustment automatically.

§259. Volkswagen electronic fuel injection For their 1968 models, Volkswagen introduced a new type of electronically controlled fuel-injection system. The Volkswagen engine, you will recall (Figs. 4-16 and 4-17), is a flat-four, air-cooled unit. The fuel is injected into the intake manifolds behind the intake valves, and the injection is timed to coincide with valve opening by triggering contacts in the ignition distributor. The amount of fuel injected is controlled by the length of time the fuel injectors are opened. This, in turn, is determined by a number of sensors which send electrical signals to the transistorized control unit, as shown in Fig. 17-86. Figure 17-87 illustrates the air-supply system and its controls. Figure 17-88 illustrates the fuel-supply system.

§260. Binder fluidic carburetor—an experimental unit This unit, proposed in 1967 by Alan M. Binder, uses a proportional fluid amplifier (PFA),

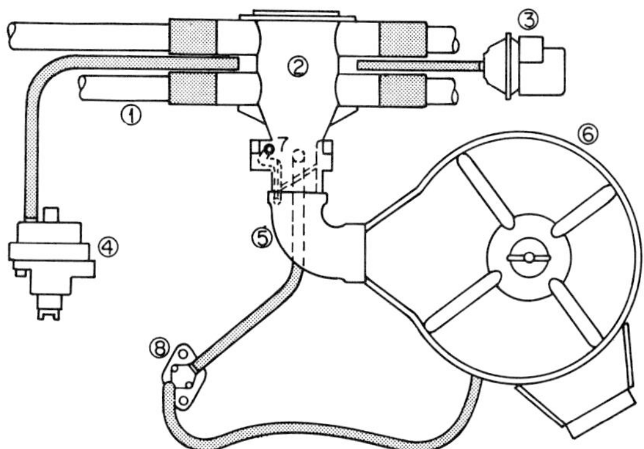

Fig. 17-87. Air-supply control for the Volkswagen electronic fuel-injection system: (1) air pipes to cylinders; (2) air distributor; (3) pressure switch; (4) pressure sensor; (5) idling circuit; (6) air cleaner; (7) adjusting screw; (8) air flow valve. (*Volkswagen*)

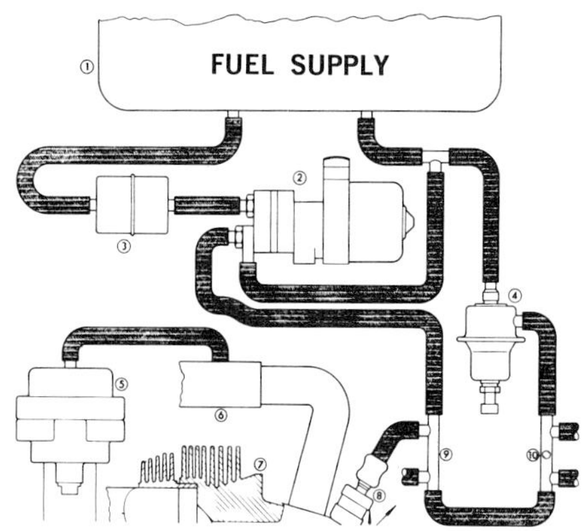

Fig. 17-88. Fuel-supply system for the Volkswagen electronic fuel-injection system. (*Volkswagen*)

1. Fuel tank
2. Electric fuel pump
3. Filter
4. Pressure regulator
5. Intake-manifold pressure sensor
6. Air pipe
7. Cylinder head
8. Fuel injector
9. and 10. Distribution pipes to injectors

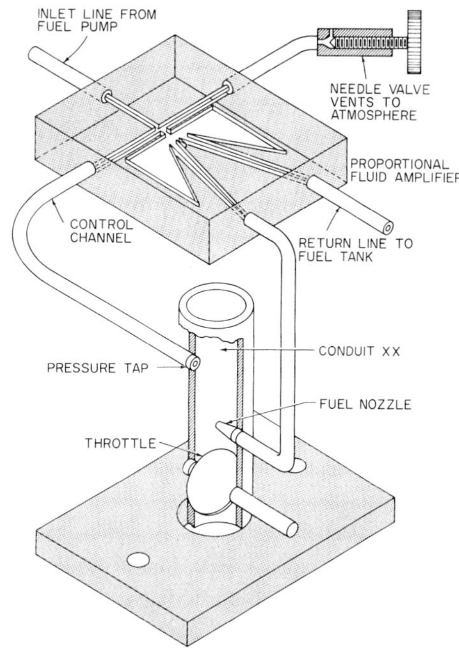

Fig. 17-89. Schematic view of the Binder fluidic carburetor. The proportional fluid amplifier has three circuits through it: two for fuel (inlet to return line and inlet to carburetor line), and one for air (needle valve to pressure tap).

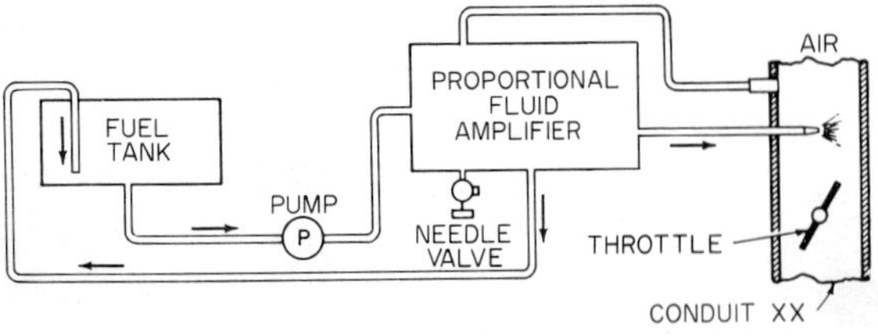

Fig. 17-90. The Binder fluidic carburetor.

amount of fuel delivered to the carburetor depends on the amount of air flowing through the PFA which, in turn, depends on the amount of throttle opening. At wide-open throttle, the air stream through the PFA would be at maximum so that the condition shown at the bottom of Fig. 17-91 would result.

The unit shown and described is a basic unit.

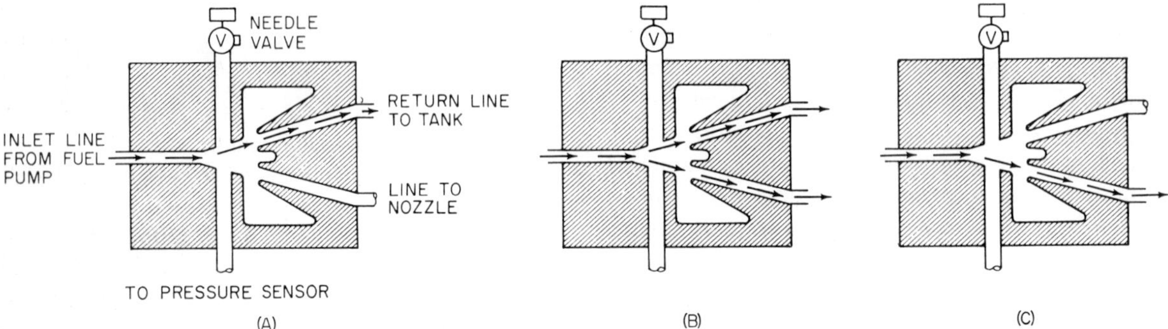

Fig. 17-91. Three operating phases of the Binder fluidic carburetor: *a*, throttle closed; *b*, throttle partly opened; and *c*, throttle wide open.

and the only moving part in the system is the throttle. Figure 17-89 is a schematic layout of the system. Figure 17-90 diagrams the system. Figure 17-91 illustrates the operation of the PFA, which is the heart of the system. Refer to these three illustrations as we describe the system.

Fuel is delivered from the fuel tank to the PFA by the fuel pump. As it enters, it is subjected to a stream of air that flows from a needle valve, through a passage in the PFA, to the upper part of the carburetor. The amount of air that flows in this stream is proportional to the amount of air flowing through the carburetor, which in turn is proportional to the amount of throttle opening. When the throttle is closed, no air flows through the PFA, and the condition shown at the top of Fig. 17-91 results. That is, the fuel flowing in from the fuel pump is directed into the return line to the fuel tank. However, if the throttle is partly opened, then air will flow from the needle valve to the carburetor through the PFA. This air flow diverts part of the fuel entering so that some of it flows into the line to the carburetor fuel nozzle. This is the situation shown in the center of Fig. 17-91. The However, engineers believe that additional sensing devices could be incorporated that would automatically vary the controls to compensate for variations in altitude, temperature, humidity, and summer and winter operation.

SUMMARY

The fuel system must supply an air-fuel mixture of the correct ratio for every operating condition with high volumetric efficiency. Delivery of air-fuel mixture should be uniform to every cylinder. The carburetor is the most complex component of the fuel system. It should provide the correct air-fuel ratio for each operating condition and regulate air-fuel consumption and thus engine output without significant curtailment of maximum air flow.

There are two types of fuel gauges: the balancing-coil gauge and the thermostatic gauge.

The carburetor has six basic circuits: float, idle and low-speed, high-speed part-load, high-speed full-power, accelerator-pump, and choke. The manifold heat control supplies heat to the intake manifold during engine warm-up for better cold-engine performance. The two methods of preventing carburetor icing are to change the gasoline formulation and to provide additional heat to the carburetor. Three types of carburetors are one-barrel, two-barrel, and four-barrel. The two-barrel carburetor is much like two one-barrel carburetors in a single assembly, with each barrel taking care of half of the engine cylinders. The four-barrel carburetor has two barrels that are very similar to the two-barrel unit, and an additional two barrels that come into operation only for full-power, high-performance operation. These additional or secondary barrels are controlled either mechanically, by linkage to the primary throttles, or by intake-manifold vacuum.

Carburetor design is complicated by a number of factors, including the necessity for reduced height to fit under the lower hoods of modern cars. It is fairly easy to design for the first 90 percent of the ideal, but it becomes increasingly difficult to achieve the last 10 percent. The shorter carburetor means that the venturi is shorter and thus must be smaller to achieve metering reliability. Many other factors must be considered in the design of a carburetor, including the location of the float bowl, sizes and proportions of the primary and secondary throttles, method of throttle control, and designing for manufacturing, assembling, and testing procedures.

Design of the intake manifold is extremely critical. Very slight changes in the internal configurations have a large effect on air flow. Tuning the manifold improves the volumetric efficiency due to the ram effect achieved at certain speeds. Supercharging is another method of getting more air-fuel mixture into the engine cylinders. Using dual exhausts also improves volumetric efficiency.

In the interest of smog control, engines are being equipped with closed-crankcase ventilating systems and with devices to clean up the exhaust gases. In addition, experimental work is being done on devices to control fuel evaporation from the system.

In fuel injection, pumping devices are used to inject fuel as a spray into the intake manifold or engine cylinders.

REFERENCES

1. Stoltman, D., The Design Evolution of the Quadrajet Carburetor, SAE (Society of Automotive Engineers) 660127, 1966 (paper).

2. Clark, P. J., J. E. Gerrard, C. W. Skarstrom, J. Vardi, and D. T. Wade, An Adsorption-Regeneration Approach to the Problem of Evaporation Control, Esso Research and Engineering Company, 1966 (paper).

3. Smith, W. R., Ford's New 240 I-6 Engine, SAE (Society of Automotive Engineers) 966C, 1965 (paper).

4. Eriksen, H. E., E. G. Moeller, and W. L. Weertman, Chrysler Corporation's Die-Cast Aluminum Slant Six Engine, SAE (Society of Automotive Engineers) 307C, 1961 (paper).

5. Miller, S. E., Automotive Gasoline Injection, SAE (Society of Automotive Engineers), special publication SP-143, 1956.

6. Brewster, B., and R. V. Kerley, Automotive Fuels and Combustion Problems, SAE (Society of Automotive Engineers) 725C, 1963 (paper).

QUESTIONS

1. *What are the major induction-system requirements?*
2. *What are the major aims of good carburetor design?*

3. *What are the two types of fuel gauges? Describe their operation.*
4. *Describe what is being done to reduce fuel evaporation from the carburetor.*
5. *Name several reasons why it is desirable to operate the carburetor on the lean side.*
6. *Name and describe the action of the six circuits in the typical carburetor.*
7. *Describe the purpose and operation of the manifold heat control.*
8. *What is the difference between a balanced and an unbalanced carburetor?*
9. *What is carburetor icing, and what are two ways to combat it?*
10. *Describe the construction and operation of a one-barrel carburetor. Of a two-barrel carburetor. Of a four-barrel carburetor.*
11. *Describe the two systems of controlling the operation of the secondary barrels in a quadrijet carburetor.*
12. *What is metering reliability as related to the fuel nozzle?*
13. *Why should the spill points of the fuel nozzles be near the center of the fuel reservoir?*
14. *Describe some of the important considerations that design engineers entertained during the design of the quadrijet carburetor described in the chapter.*
15. *What are some of the things that have been done to improve air flow in the intake manifold?*
16. *Describe intake-manifold tuning and how it works.*
17. *Explain what supercharging is and how it is achieved.*
18. *What is the basic purpose of dual exhausts on a V-8 engine?*
19. *What is the purpose of the closed-crankcase ventilating system, and how does it work?*
20. *Describe methods used to clean up the exhaust gases from internal-combustion engines.*
21. *Describe the Esso fuel-evaporation control.*
22. *Describe a typical fuel-injection system.*

Engine Cooling Systems

CHAPTER **18**

This chapter discusses the function, design, and operation of internal-combustion-engine liquid-cooling systems, from the standpoints of both the engine designer and the user.

§261. Purpose of cooling system The purpose of the cooling system (Fig. 18-1) is to keep the engine at its most efficient operating temperature at all speeds under all driving conditions.[1] During the combustion of the air-fuel mixture in the engine cylinders, temperatures as high as 4500°F may be reached in the burning gases. Some of this heat is absorbed by the cylinder walls, cylinder head, and pistons, which, in turn, must be provided with some means of cooling so that their temperatures will not reach excessive values. Cylinder-wall temperatures should not increase beyond 450 to 500°F. Higher temperatures will cause the lubricating oil to break down and lose its lubricating properties. In liquid-cooled engines, the combustion chamber is surrounded at the top and sides by water jackets. Water flowing in these jackets removes heat from the metal shell that forms the upper part of the combustion chamber. The heat-transfer process is very complex. First, the heated gases must give up heat to the cylinder walls, and then the walls must give up heat to the water. All three modes of heat transfer occur: radiation, conduction, and convection. A complicating factor is the flow of heat through the stagnant layer of gas adjacent to the metal walls of the combustion chamber. This thin layer of stagnant gas has more resistance to the flow of heat than all the other parts of the heat path combined.

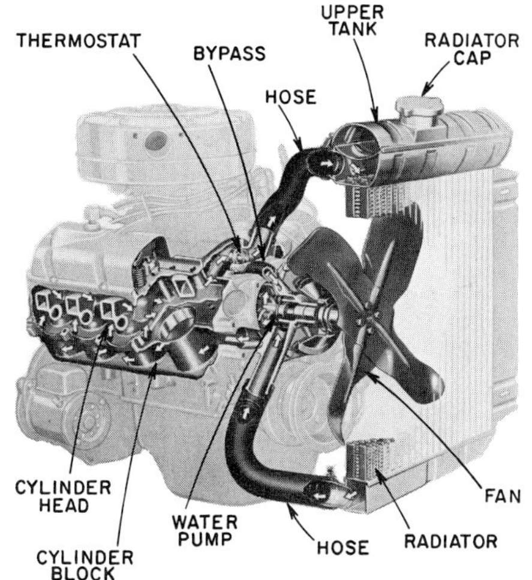

Fig. 18-1. Cutaway view of a V-8 engine, showing its cooling system. (*Lincoln-Mercury Division of Ford Motor Company*)

High cylinder-wall temperatures will cause the film of lubricating oil on the cylinder wall to break down so that lubrication is lost. In addition, operating the engine at excessively high temperatures will increase oil oxidation and varnish, lead to sticking of piston rings and hydraulic-valve lifters and ultimately serious loss of engine power. Also, the excessive temperatures in the combustion chamber can cause abnormal combustion such as rumble or preignition and serious engine damage.[2]

On the other hand, operating an engine at insufficient temperatures lowers thermal efficiency (§59), reduces fuel economy, increases oil dilution, can cause the formation of sludge and rust, and hastens piston-ring and cylinder-wall wear. Figures 18-2 to 18-5 show the results of various tests relat-

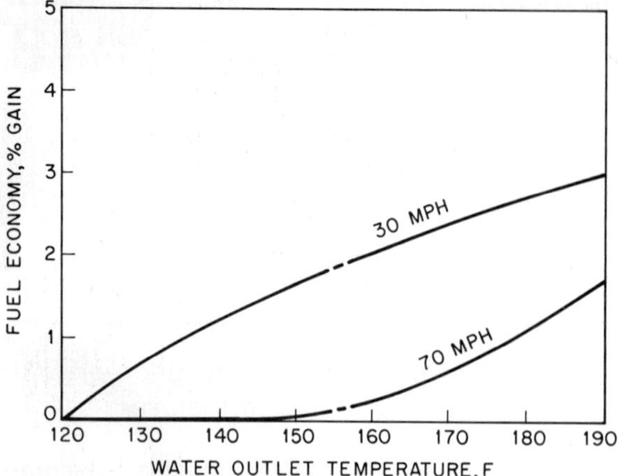

Fig. 18-2. Effect of engine temperature on fuel economy. Increasing water jacket temperature from 120 to 190°F can increase economy as much as 3 percent. (*Chevrolet Motor Division of General Motors Corporation*)

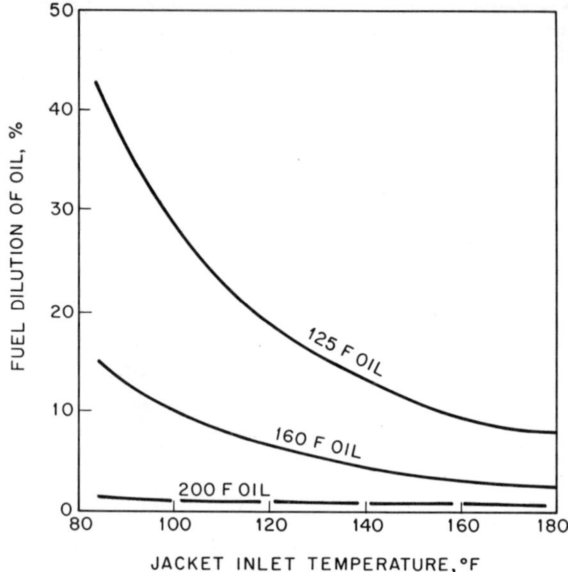

Fig. 18-3. Dilution of oil by fuel increases with lower temperatures. (*Chevrolet Motor Division of General Motors Corporation*)

ing temperature to fuel economy, oil dilution by fuel and water, and cylinder-wall and top-piston-ring wear. If the engine is cold, the fuel will not evaporate readily, and some of it, in the form of droplets or as condensate, will appear on the cylinder walls and bypass the piston rings to drop into the crankcase and dilute the oil (Fig. 18-3). For every gallon of gasoline burned, about 1 gallon of water will be formed within the combustion chambers. If the engine is at operating temperature, this water will pass out of the combustion chamber in the form of vapor with the remainder of the exhaust products. But if the engine is cold, some of it will condense on the cylinder walls and work its way down past the piston rings to dilute the crankcase oil (Fig. 18-4). Not only will this water tend to form sludge when whipped with the oil by the rotating crankshaft, but also the water will cause rusting of the engine parts.

Water and fuel in the crankcase can be eliminated by the crankcase-ventilating system [§257(*1*)] after the engine reaches operating temperature. It is important, therefore, for the engine to be brought to operating temperature as quickly as possible after first starting, and then maintained at that temperature throughout the operation of the engine. In other words, the cooling system should cool slowly or not at all when the engine is warming up or cold. Then, it should cool rapidly when the engine is hot. The cooling system removes about 30 to 35 percent of the heat produced in the combustion chambers by the burning of the air-fuel mixture. Another third of the heat is lost

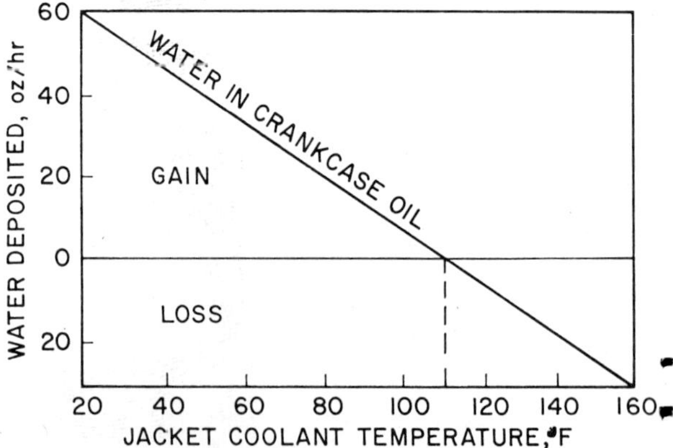

Fig. 18-4. With low temperatures, water accumulates in the crankcase oil. As water-jacket temperature rises above about 110°F, this water begins to evaporate, so that water in the crankcase decreases. (*Chevrolet Motor Division of General Motors Corporation*)

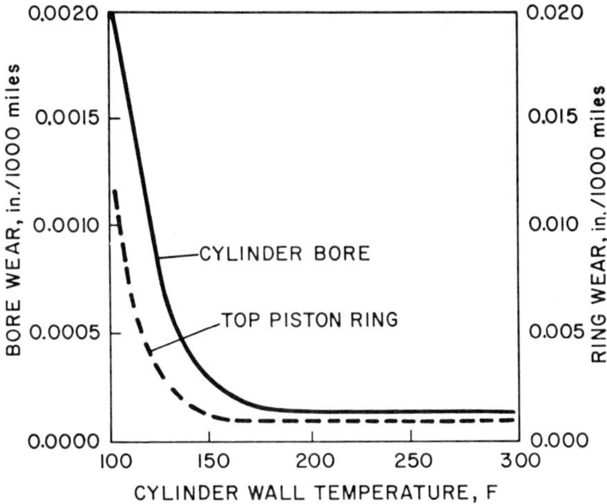

Fig. 18-5. Wear of the cylinder bore and top piston ring is very rapid at low temperatures, but as cylinder-wall temperature increases beyond 150°F, wear falls off to almost nothing. (*Chevrolet Motor Division of General Motors Corporation*)

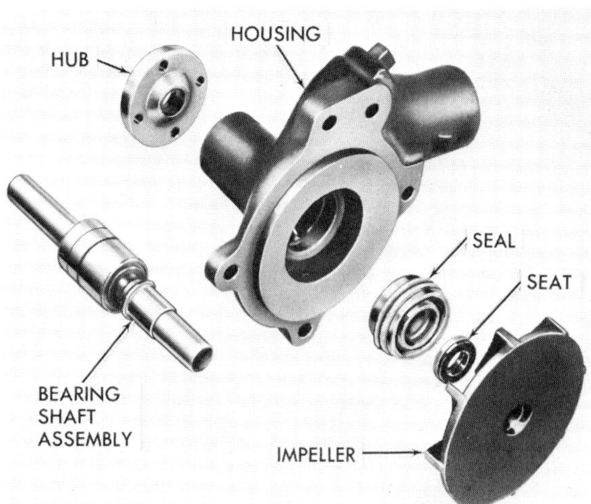

Fig. 18-6. Disassembled view of a water pump. (*Pontiac Motor Division of General Motors Corporation*)

in the exhaust gases. Some of the heat is lost to engine friction, leaving only about 20 percent of the fuel energy left to produce power (§80).

Two general types of cooling systems are used: air cooling and liquid cooling. Most automotive engines now employ liquid cooling, although engines for airplanes, motorcycles, power lawn mowers, and so on, are all air-cooled. Air-cooled engines have metal fins on the heads and cylinders to help radiate the heat from the engine. Cylinders are usually partly or completely separated to improve air circulation around them. Special shrouds and blowers are used on many air-cooled engines to improve air circulation around the cylinders and heads. Figures 4-16 and 4-22 illustrate air-cooled engines.

§262. Water jackets Just as we might put on a sweater or a jacket to keep warm on a cool day, so water jackets are placed around the engine cylinders. There is this difference: water jackets are designed to keep the cylinders cool. The water jackets are cast into the cylinder blocks and heads (§225 and 228). Since the valve seats and valve guides may need additional cooling (as noted in 210, 2), it is often the practice to install water-distributing tubes, deflectors, and nozzles in the water jackets (Figs. 15-25 to 15-27). These direct cooling water to critical areas for adequate cooling.

§263. Water pumps Water pumps are usually of the impeller type and are mounted at the front end of the cylinder block between the block and the radiator (Fig. 18-1). The pump (Figs. 18-6 and 18-7) consists of a housing, with a water inlet and outlet, and an impeller. The impeller, which is mounted on the pump shaft, is a flat plate, having a series of flat or curved blades, or vanes. When the impeller rotates, the water between the blades is thrown outward by centrifugal force and is forced through the pump outlet into the cylinder block. The pump inlet is connected by a hose to the bottom of the radiator, and water from the radiator is drawn into the pump to replace the water forced through the outlet.

The impeller shaft is supported on one or more bearings; a seal prevents water from leaking out around the bearing. The pump is driven by a belt to the drive pulley mounted on the front end of the engine crankshaft.

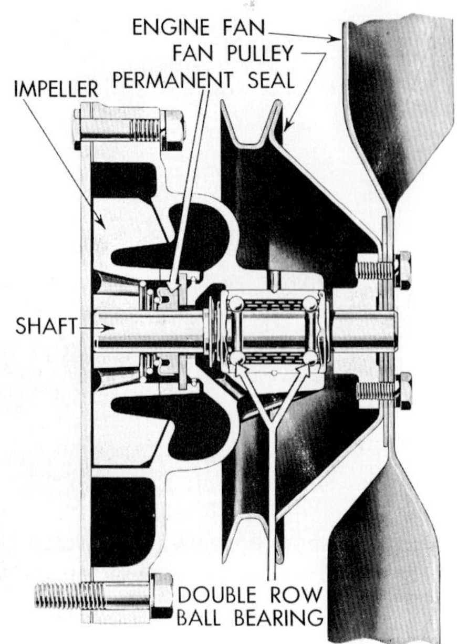

Fig. 18-7. Sectional view of a water pump, showing the manner of supporting the shaft on a double-row ball bearing and the method of mounting the fan and pulley on the shaft. (*Studebaker Corporation*)

§264. Engine fan The engine fan usually mounts on the water-pump shaft and is driven by the same belt that drives the pump and the alternator (Fig. 18-7). The purpose of the fan is to provide a powerful draft of air through the radiator. Some applications are equipped with a fan shroud that improves fan performance. The shroud increases the efficiency of the fan by ensuring that all air pulled back by the fan must first pass through the radiator.

1. *Fan belt* Most of the belts are of the V type. Friction between the sides of the belt and the sides of the grooves in the pulleys causes the driving power to be transmitted through the belt from one pulley to the other. The V-type belt provides a substantial area of contact so that considerable power may be transmitted; the wedging action of the belt as it curves into the pulley grooves aids in preventing belt slippage.

2. *Variable-speed fan drive* Many engines use a variable-speed fan drive which reduces fan speed to conserve horsepower at high engine speeds and also when cooling requirements are low. At high speeds, a typical engine fan might use up several horsepower and, in addition, produce some noise. The variable-speed fan drive (Fig. 18-8) contains a small fluid coupling partly filled with a special silicone fluid. When engine cooling requirements are severe, as during high-temperature, high-speed operation, more fluid is injected into the fluid coupling; this causes more power to pass through the coupling. Fan speed therefore increases. When cooling requirements are low, as during cool-weather intermediate-speed operation, fluid is withdrawn from the fluid coupling;

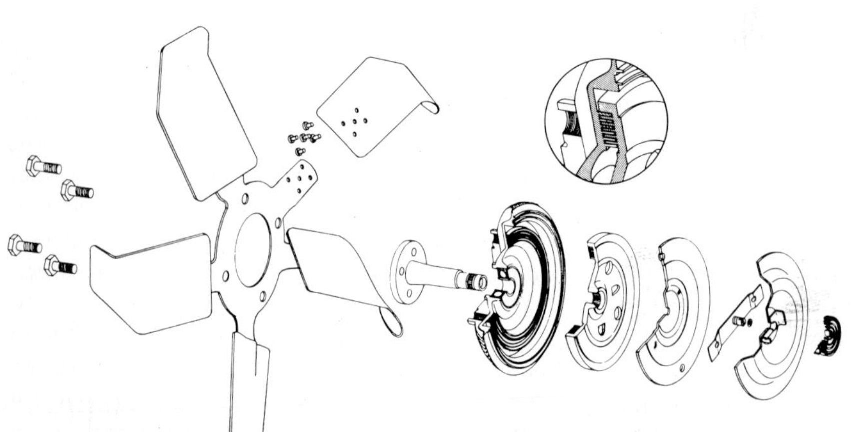

Fig. 18-8. Fan-drive assembly. The fan drive contains a small fluid coupling which varies fan speed according to driving requirements. (*Ford Motor Company*)

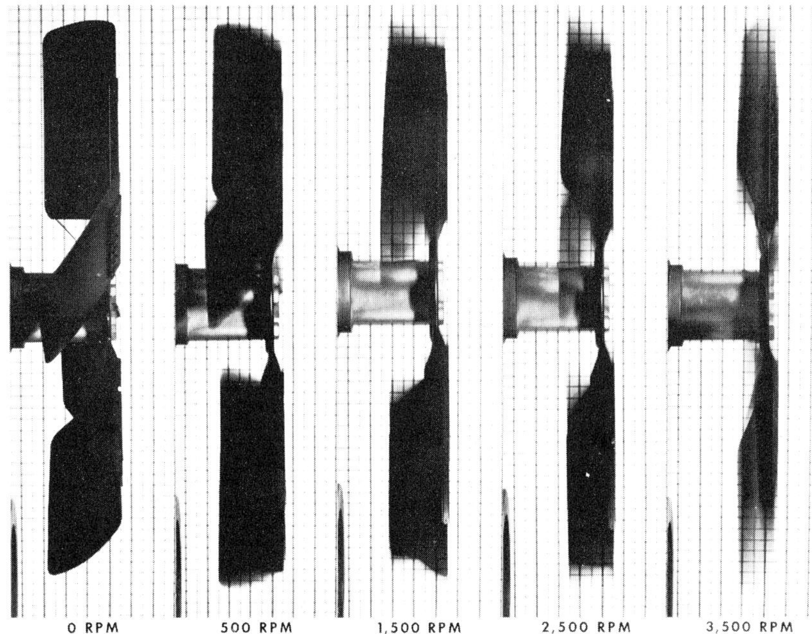

Fig. 18-9. Change of pitch of fan blades as fan speed increases. (*Ford Motor Company*)

Fig. 18-10. Flexible-blade fan mounted on engine. (*Ford Motor Company*)

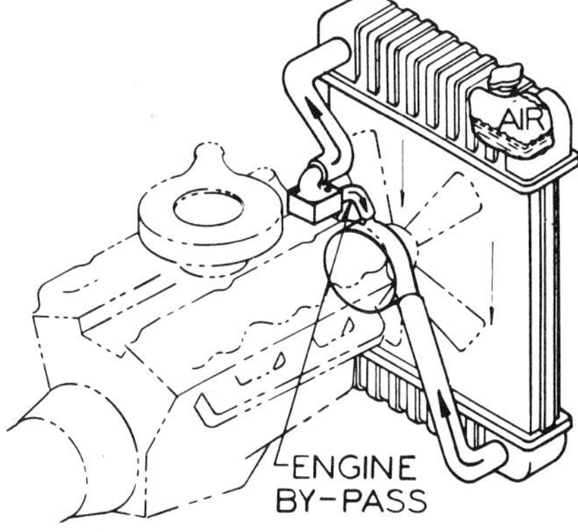

Fig. 18-11. Cooling system using a down-flow radiator. (*Harrison Radiator Division of General Motors Corporation*)

therefore, less power passes through, and fan speed decreases.

The amount of fluid in the fluid coupling and thus fan speed are controlled by a thermostatic strip (Fig. 18-8) which is held at its two ends by clips to the face of the fan drive. The strip bows outward with increasing under-the-hood temperatures, and this motion allows a control piston centered in the fan drive to move outward. The outward-moving piston causes more fluid to flow into the fluid coupling, and this speeds up the fan for improved cooling. As under-the-hood temperatures drop, the thermostatic strip straightens, forcing the control piston in. This action causes fluid to leave the fluid coupling, so fan speed decreases.

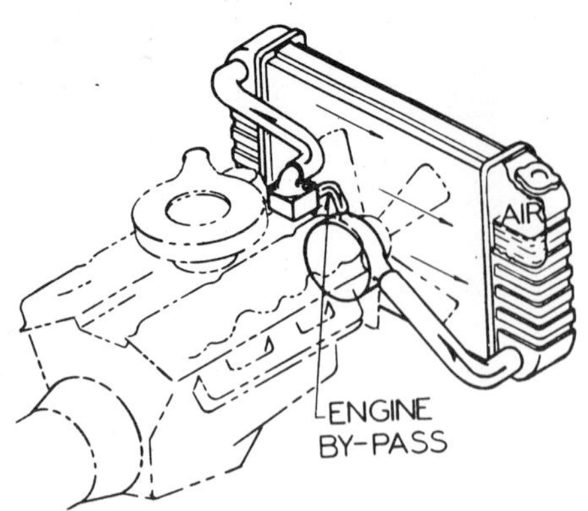

Fig. 18-12. Cooling system using a cross-flow radiator. (*Harrison Radiator Division of General Motors Corporation*)

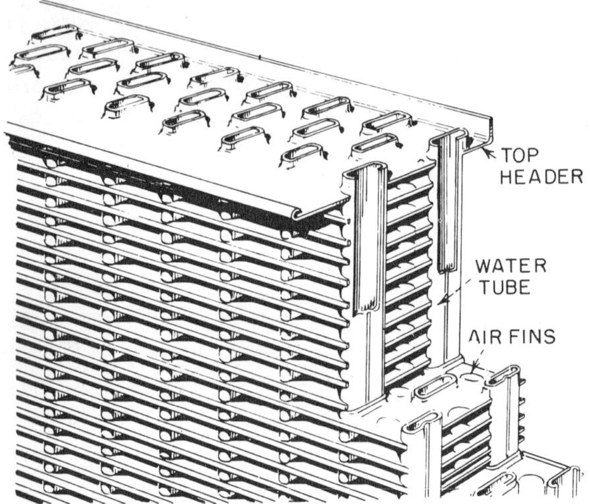

Fig. 18-13. Construction of a tube and fin radiator core.

3. Flexible fan. Another method of reducing power requirements to drive the fan and fan noise at high speeds is to use a fan with flexible blades. With this design, the pitch of the blades decreases as fan speed increases due to centrifugal force. The result is that each blade pushes less air per revolution, and thus power needs and noise are reduced at higher speeds. Figure 18-9 shows how the fan blades change pitch as speed increases, and Fig. 18-10 shows a fan of this type mounted on an engine.

§265. Radiator The radiator is a device for holding a large volume of water in close contact with a large volume of air so that heat will transfer from the water to the air. The radiator core is divided into two separate and intricate compartments: water passes through one, and air passes through the other. There are two basic types of radiators: the down-flow and the cross-flow. In the down-flow type, the water flows from the top of the radiator to the bottom (Fig. 18-11). This radiator has a supply tank at the top and a collecting tank at the bottom. In the cross-flow type of radiator, the water flows across the radiator, from the supply tank along one side to the collecting tank along the other side (Fig. 18-12). Note that this type of tank is considerably shorter from top to bottom and thus can fit more easily under the lower hoods of late-model cars.

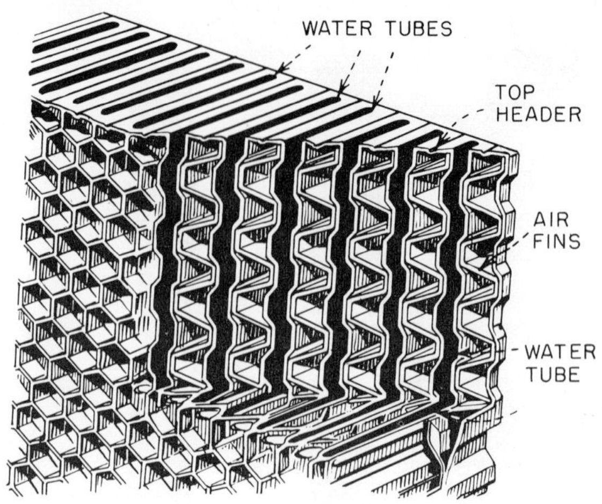

Fig. 18-14. Construction of a ribbon-cellular radiator core.

1. Core construction. Two of the more common types of core construction are the tube and fin type (Fig. 18-13), and the ribbon-cellular type (Fig. 18-14). The tube and fin type consists of a series of long tubes extending from the top to the bottom of the radiator (or from upper to lower tank). Fins are placed around the tubes to improve heat transfer. Air passes around the outside of the tubes between the fins, absorbing heat from the water in passing.

The ribbon-cellular radiator core (Fig. 18-14) is made up of a large number of narrow water passages, formed by pairs of thin metal ribbons

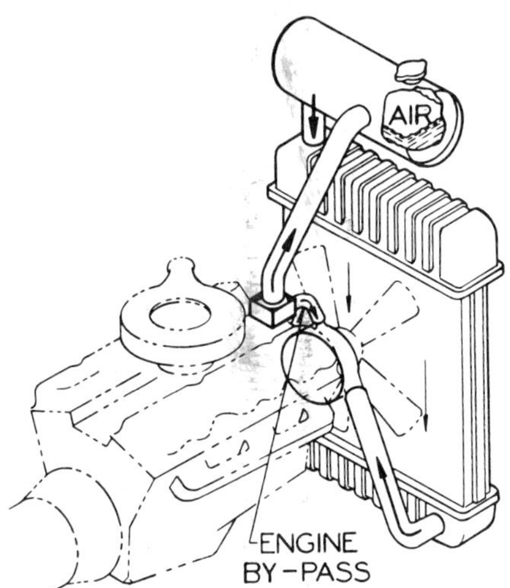

Fig. 18-15. Cooling system, using a down-flow radiator and a separate full-flow supply tank. (*Harrison Radiator Division of General Motors Corporation*)

soldered together along their edges and running from the upper to the lower tank. The edges of the water passages, which are soldered together, form the front and back surfaces of the radiator core. The water passages are separated by air fins of metal ribbon, which provide air passages between the water passages. Air moves through these passages from front to back, absorbing heat from the fins. The fins, in turn, absorb heat from

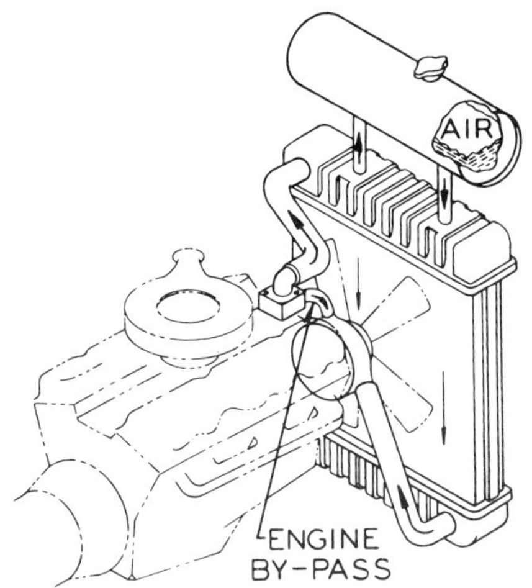

Fig. 18-16. Cooling system, using a down-flow radiator and a separate partial-flow supply tank. (*Harrison Radiator Division of General Motors Corporation*)

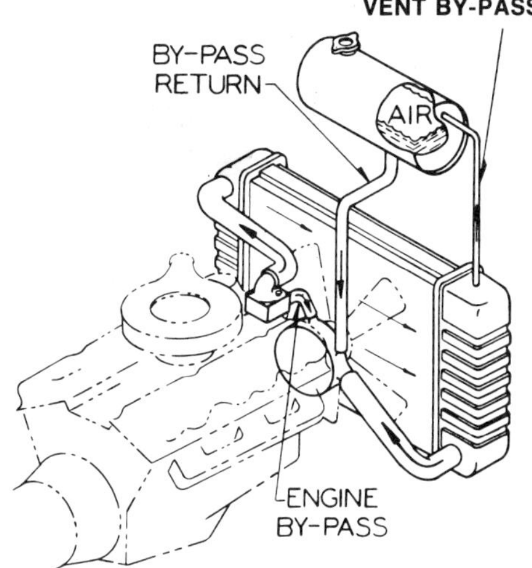

Fig. 18-17. Cooling system, using a cross-flow radiator and a separate partial-flow supply tank. (*Harrison Radiator Division of General Motors Corporation*)

the water that is moving downward through the water passages. As a consequence, the water is cooled.

2. *Air separation.* It is important for the cooling system to eliminate any air that might be circulating with the coolant. The thermostat (§266) usually has a small air bleed which allows air that is trapped in the water jackets to escape when the system is filled (after having been flushed out, for example). Any air is then delivered to the supply tank in the radiator, where it is separated by gravity from the coolant. Baffling is often used in the supply tank to assist in the separation and to prevent water from being thrown upward into the air in the top of the tank. This keeps the air from mixing with the coolant as the coolant passes through the radiator and then reenters the engine water jackets.

3. *Separate supply tanks.* When the design requires additional reserve volume for coolant expansion and air separation, a separate supply tank is used. There are several arrangements (Figs. 18-15 to 18-17). The full-flow arrangement, as used with a down-flow radiator, is shown in Fig. 18-15. Here, the return from the engine empties into the separate supply tank, and water then flows from this tank into the radiator supply tank. The partial-flow arrangement, shown in Fig. 18-16, uses

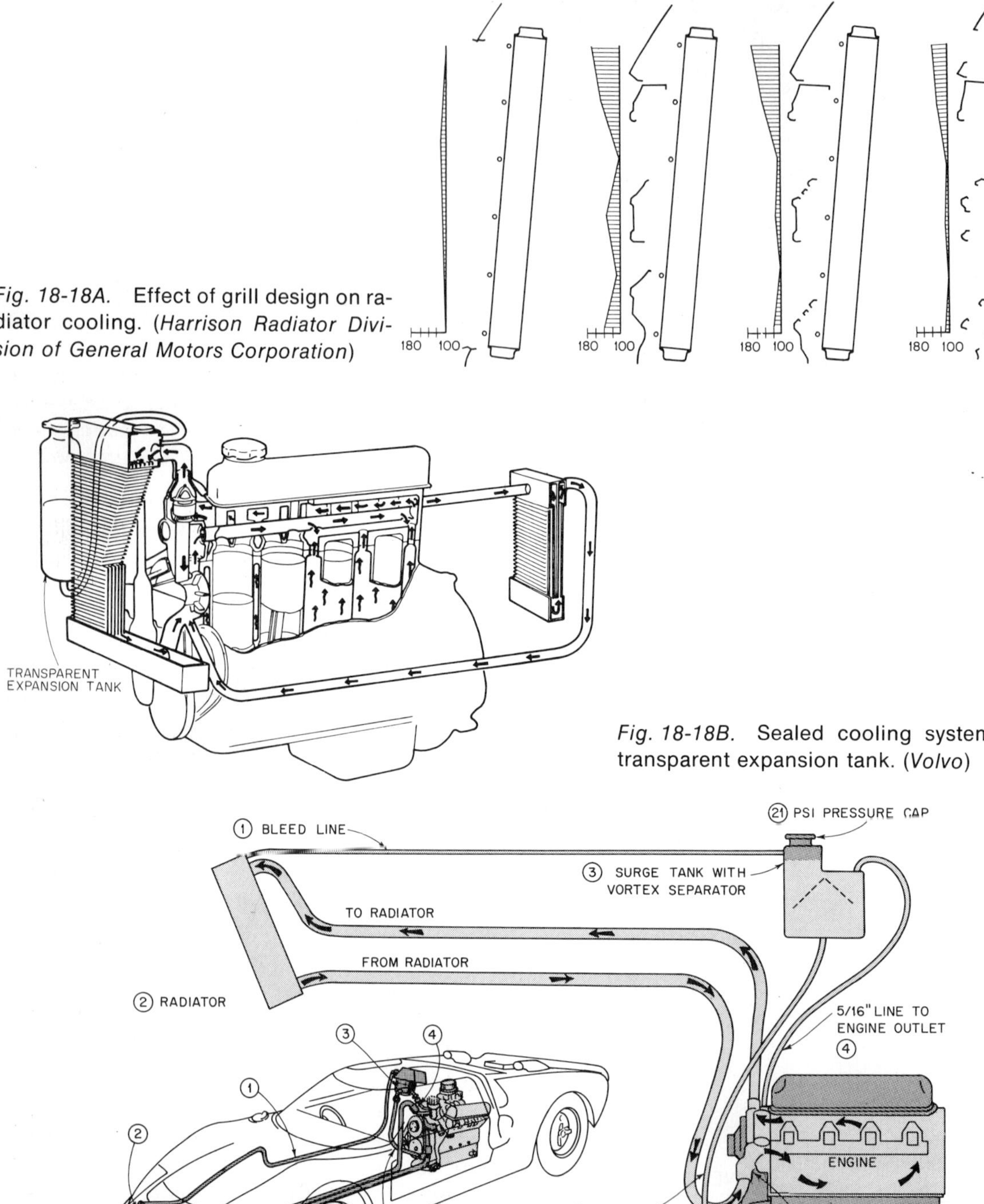

Fig. 18-18A. Effect of grill design on radiator cooling. (*Harrison Radiator Division of General Motors Corporation*)

Fig. 18-18B. Sealed cooling system with transparent expansion tank. (*Volvo*)

Fig. 18-19. Cooling system for Ford Mark II-427 GT engine. (*Ford Motor Company*)

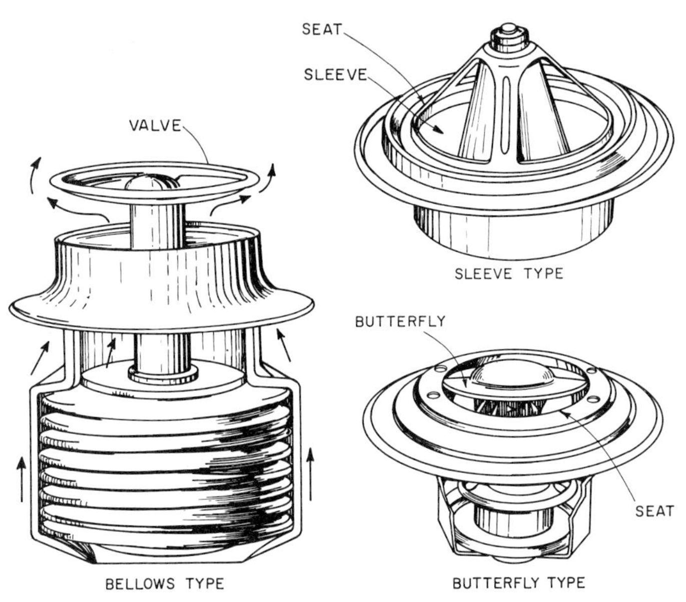

Fig. 18-20. Various thermostats for engine cooling systems. The bellows type is shown open, with arrows indicating water flow past the valve. (*Chrysler-Plymouth Division of Chrysler Motors Corporation*)

a separate supply tank with two lines between it and the radiator supply tank. A partial-flow supply tank used with a cross-flow radiator is shown in Fig. 18-17. Air from the collecting tank in the radiator is vented into the separate supply tank, and this effectively eliminates air from the cooling system.

4. *Grill design.* The grill design must be carefully worked out in order to prevent hot spots from developing in the radiator and thus reducing cooling efficiency. Fig. 18-18a shows, in profile, the effect of various grill configurations on uniform cooling in the radiator. The graphs to the left of each configuration show the temperatures at the radiator. Note that in the original proposal there were hot areas in the center and at the lower end of the radiator. Revision 2 gave almost as efficient cooling as was obtained with no grill.

5. *Sealed system.* Some cooling systems are sealed with a permanently installed cap on the upper radiator tank. A transparent expansion tank alongside the radiator permits checking of coolant level and condition without removing the filler cap. The filler cap is located on top of this tank (Fig. 18-18b). If the system ever requires additional coolant, this cap can be removed. The advantage of the sealed system is that it keeps additional oxygen from entering and thus reduces oxidation in the system. With other systems, every time the filler cap is removed to check the coolant level, some oxygen enters. Further, if the filler cap is removed when the engine is hot, some boil-over may result. This requires the addition of water and the fresh water will probably contain some dissolved oxygen in it. The sealed system eliminates unnecessary filler-cap removal.

6. *Special designs.* In some cooling-system designs, the radiator is located far from the engine. Some rear-engine cars have the radiator up front where it can have relatively unobstructed access to the air stream. Figure 18-19 illustrates the cooling system for the Ford Mark II-427 GT engine.[4] The engine is located behind the driver in the vehicle, as shown, with the radiator being up front in the region of maximum air flow. Note that the system uses a separate surge tank with a bleed line to the top of the radiator.

§266. Thermostat The thermostat is placed in the water passage between the cylinder head and the top of the radiator (Fig. 18-1). Its purpose is to close off this passage when the engine is cold so that water circulation is restricted, causing the engine to reach operating temperature more quickly. The thermostat consists of a thermostatic device and a valve (Fig. 18-20). Various valve arrangements and thermostatic devices have been used. The bellows type contains a liquid that evaporates with increasing temperature, so the internal

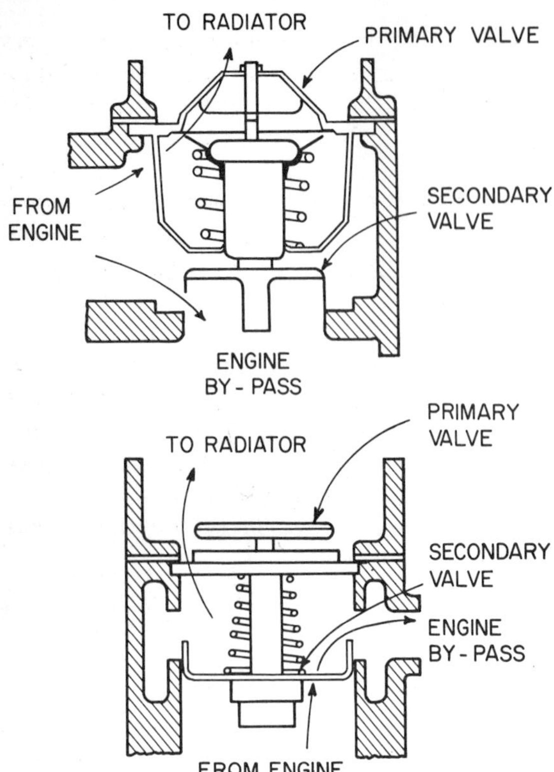

Fig. 18-21. Blocking by-pass thermostats. (*Harrison Radiator Division of General Motors Corporation*)

pressure causes the bellows to expand and raise the valve off its seat. This permits water to circulate between the engine and radiator. Instead of a liquid, many thermostats are powered by a petroleum-base wax pellet which expands with increasing temperature to open a valve. The sleeve and butterfly thermostats shown in Fig. 18-20 both use the wax pellet.

Thermostats are designed to open at specific temperatures. For example, a thermostat designated as a 180°F unit will start to open between 177° and 182°F and will be fully open at 202°F. A 160°F thermostat will operate at 20° below these figures. Thermostats of proper characteristics are selected to suit the operating requirements of the engine, as well as the kind of antifreeze used. For example, with permanent-type (glycol) antifreeze, a 180°F thermostat is recommended by the automotive manufacturers.

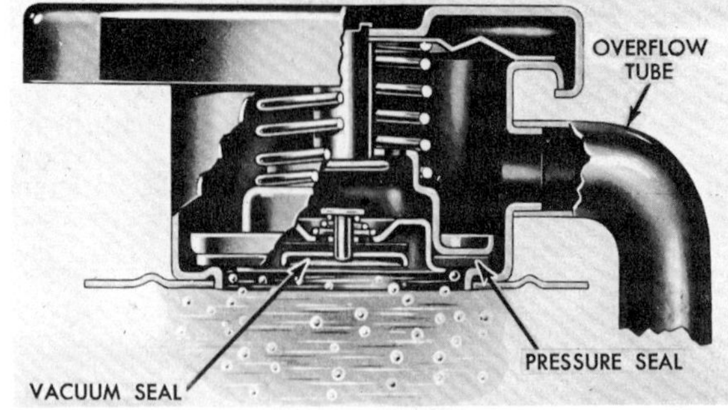

Fig. 18-22. Radiator pressure cap.

With alcohol-type antifreeze, a 160°F thermostat is recommended.

When the engine is cold and consequently the thermostat is closed, water cannot pass between the engine and radiator. It must continue to circulate in the engine, however, for three very good reasons:

1. To provide for a uniform rate of warm-up throughout the engine.
2. To prevent excessive coolant-system pressures from building up when the cold engine is operated at high speeds.
3. To eliminate hot spots, steam pockets, and excessive thermal stresses.

If the water did not circulate in the engine, serious damage could result due to high-pressure build-up and local hot spots. To permit circulation, some engines have a small spring-loaded bypass valve which is forced open by the water pressure from the pump so that the water can circulate through the engine water jackets.

Another widely used arrangement has a secondary valve in the thermostat (Fig. 18-21). When the primary valve is closed, thus blocking circulation to the radiator, the secondary valve is open, permitting coolant to circulate through the engine bypass. But when the primary valve opens, permitting the coolant to flow to the radiator, the secondary valve closes, thus blocking off the engine bypass.

Restriction of water circulation between the engine water jackets and the radiator by closure of the thermostat, as described above, prevents the removal of heat from the engine itself by the cooling system. The engine consequently reaches operating temperature more rapidly. Then, when

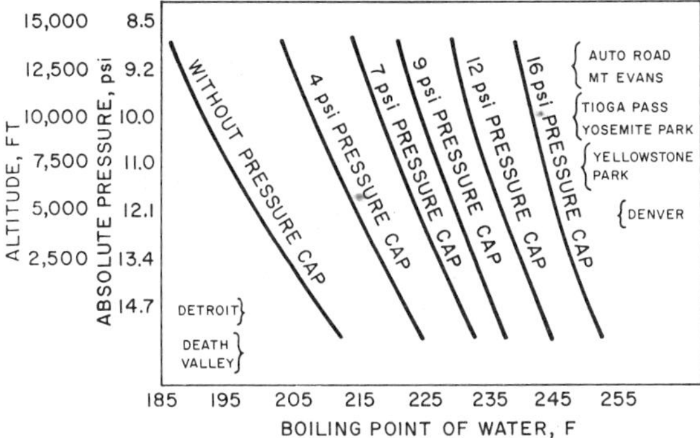

Fig. 18-23. Relationship between pressure and boiling point of water, showing how pressure caps of various capacities can increase the boiling point. (*Chevrolet Motor Division of General Motors Corporation*)

the engine reaches operating temperature, the thermostatic valve begins to open. The water can then begin to circulate between the water jackets and the radiator, and the cooling system operates in the hot-engine condition, as already described.

§267. Radiator pressure cap To improve cooling efficiency and prevent evaporation and surge losses, many late-model automobiles use a pressure cap on the radiator (Fig. 18-22). At sea level, where atmospheric pressure is about 15 psi (pounds per square inch), water boils at 212°F. At higher altitudes, where atmospheric pressure is less, water will boil at lower temperatures (Fig. 18-23). Higher pressures increase the temperature required to boil water. Each added pound per square inch increases the boiling point of water about 3¼°F. The use of a pressure cap on the radiator increases the air pressure within the cooling system by several pounds per square inch. Thus, the water may be circulated at higher temperatures without boiling. The water therefore enters the radiator at a higher temperature, and the difference in temperature between the air and the water is greater. Heat is therefore more readily transferred from the water to the air, thus improving cooling efficiency. Evaporation of water is reduced by the higher pressure, inasmuch as the boiling point of the water is higher. The pressure cap also prevents loss of water caused by surging when the car is quickly braked to a stop.

The pressure cap fits over the radiator filler tube and seals tightly around the edges. The cap contains two valves: the blow-off (or pressure) valve and the vacuum valve. The blow-off valve consists of a valve held against a valve seat by a calibrated spring. The spring holds the valve closed so that pressure is produced in the cooling system. If pressure is obtained above that for which the system is designed, the blow-off valve is raised off its seat, relieving the excessive pressure. Pressure caps are designed to provide as much as 15 psi in the cooling system; this increases the boiling point of the water to almost 250°F (at sea level). The higher temperature at which a system operating at 15 psi can safely attain increases the cooling efficiency considerably (33 percent in one specific test).

The vacuum valve is designed to prevent the formation of a vacuum in the cooling system when the engine has been shut off and begins to cool. If a vacuum forms, atmospheric pressure from the outside causes the small vacuum valve to open, admitting air into the radiator. Without a vacuum valve, the pressure within the radiator might drop so low that atmospheric pressure would collapse it.

It is important to remember that a system designed for pressurization and using a radiator pressure cap could suffer perhaps fatal overheating if the cap is defective or lost. Without the cap, the water could boil under severe operating conditions, with a resulting very rapid rise in engine temperature.

§268. Antifreeze solutions and temperature indicators

1. Antifreeze. Antifreeze solutions are required to prevent the water from freezing when temperatures drop below 32°F. When water freezes in the engine, the resulting force of expansion is often sufficient to crack the cylinder block and the radiator. Antifreeze solutions added to, and mixed with, the water prevent freezing of the mixture. A good antifreeze material must mix readily with water, prevent freezing of the mixture at the lowest temperatures encountered, and circulate freely. It must not damage the cooling system by corrosive action or lose its antifreezing properties after extended use. The most commonly used antifreeze materials now are either alcohol, an alcohol base, or ethylene glycol. The alcohol-base materials make only temporary antifreeze solutions since they evaporate at temperatures below the boiling point of water and thus are gradually lost. Such materials require periodic additions to maintain an antifreeze solution of adequate strength. The ethylene glycol antifreeze materials are of the so-called "permanent" type; they remain liquid at the boiling point of water. In fact, adding ethylene glycol raises the boiling temperature of the mixture several degrees (Fig. 18-24).

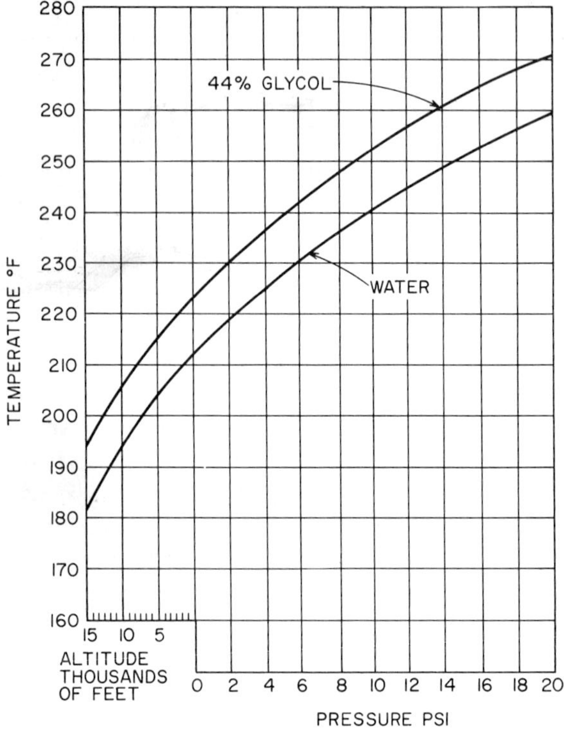

Fig. 18-24. Boiling points of water, as compared with a mixture of 56 percent water and 44 percent ethylene glycol at various pressures. (*Harrison Radiator Division of General Motors Corporation*)

Antifreeze materials are mixed with water in various proportions, according to the expected temperature. The lower the temperature, the higher the percentage of antifreeze material necessary in the solution to prevent freezing of the mixture.

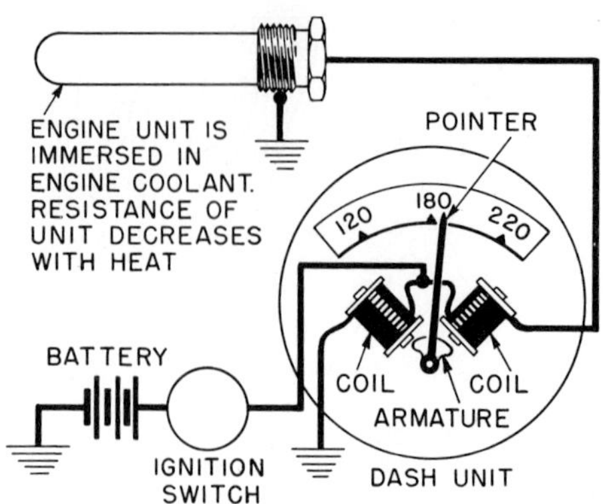

Fig. 18-25. Circuit diagram of an electric-resistance temperature-indicator system.

2. *Temperature indicators.* In order that the operator will know the water temperature in the cooling system at all times, a temperature indicator is installed in the car. An abnormal heat rise is a warning of abnormal conditions in the engine. The indicator thus warns the operator to stop the engine before serious damage is done.

The typical temperature indicator (Fig. 18-25) consists of an engine unit and a dash, or instrument-panel, unit. As the engine unit becomes hotter, its resistance is reduced. This allows more current to flow through the right-hand coil in the dash unit, thus strengthening the magnetic field of the right-hand coil. This in turn, attracts the armature of the pointer, moving the pointer to the right to indicate the higher engine temperature.

§269. Cooling-system design Cooling-system requirements have already been spelled out (§261). In designing a cooling system, the engineer must provide water jackets of the proper size and configuration to permit uniform water circulation through the engine. Certain engine areas may need extra cooling, for example, the valve-seat area. To achieve this, the design may call for deflectors or distributing tubes to assure added water circulation around the critical areas (§210, 2).

The radiator must be of adequate size and design to provide adequate heat rejection under the most adverse circumstances. Likewise, the water pump must provide for more than adequate water cir-

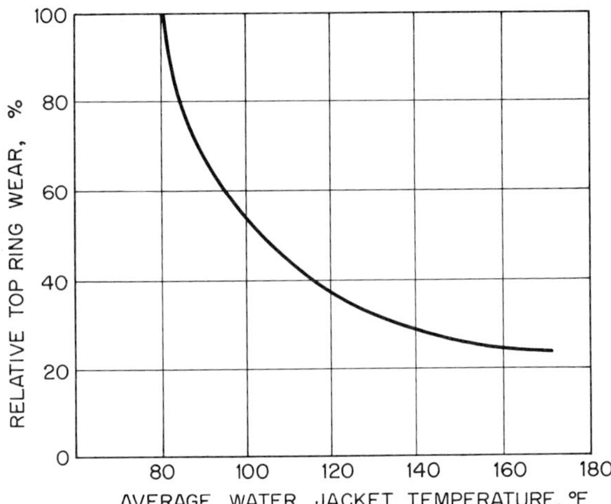

Fig. 18-26. Water-jacket temperature vs. top ring wear.

culation. The heat load that the cooling system must handle can be calculated once the engine displacement, compression ratio, and expected top speed and output are established. As a rule, the cooling system is provided with an adequate factor of safety, so it can still function satisfactorily even through the water jackets or radiator have become partly clogged so that circulation is reduced. On the other hand, it is not desirable to make the water jackets too large; this would mean that a larger volume of water would have to be heated during the engine warm-up period. It would therefore take longer for the engine to warm up and the engine would be operating longer in the cold, high-wear, sludging condition (Figs. 18-2 to 18-5). The relationship between water-jacket temperature and wear rate of engine parts is shown in Fig. 18-26. Obviously, the faster the engine reaches operating temperature, the less the wear of the engine. This is especially important for vehicles used in city, start and stop driving. As noted in the chapter on lubricating systems (Chap. 19, §283), studies have shown that a majority of all trips are short—too short to allow the engine to warm up adequately (Fig. 18-27). Thus, the design engineer must seek a compromise between water jackets that are large enough for adequate cooling under the most adverse conditions and water jackets that are small enough to permit quick warm-up of the engine.

The selection of the correct thermostat and radiator-pressure cap must be governed by maximum temperature considerations (§266 and 267).

§270. The Chevrolet Turbo-Jet engine cooling system[5] This system is conventional in design, but considerable work went into improving the efficiency of the system so as to reduce the horsepower requirements of the water pump. Water jackets and passages were enlarged and simplified somewhat. The greater freedom of flow that resulted allowed the engineers to reduce the

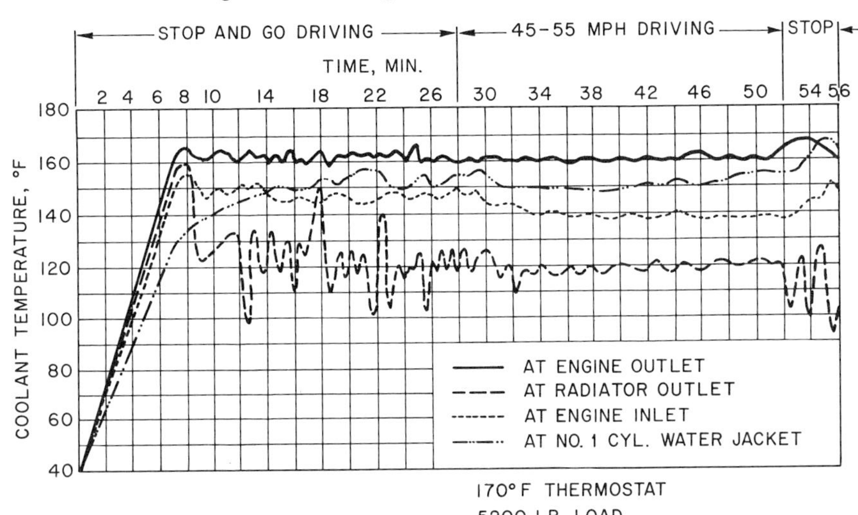

Fig. 18-27. Coolant temperature in a light-truck engine under actual driving conditions.

water-pump-rotor diameter. These modifications reduced the power requirements of the water pump without any sacrifice of cooling-system efficiency. The graph (Fig. 18-28) shows the horsepower requirements of the water pump in the 409 V-8 engine as compared to the Turbo-Jet. The earlier engine required as much as 17 hp (horsepower) at high speeds, whereas the Turbo-Jet water-pump requirements are much less all along the line.

Another problem encountered by Chevrolet engineers at an early stage in the development of the Turbo-Jet engine was that, even though the water jackets in the two cylinder banks were of identical design, the left bank had considerably better cooling (Fig. 18-29). The left bank flowed from 20 to 60 gpm (gallons per minute), while the right bank flowed only about 14 to 45 gpm. Engineers believed the difference was due to the fact that, even though the water jackets in the two banks were of the same design, one, in effect, was the mirror image of the other. Thus,

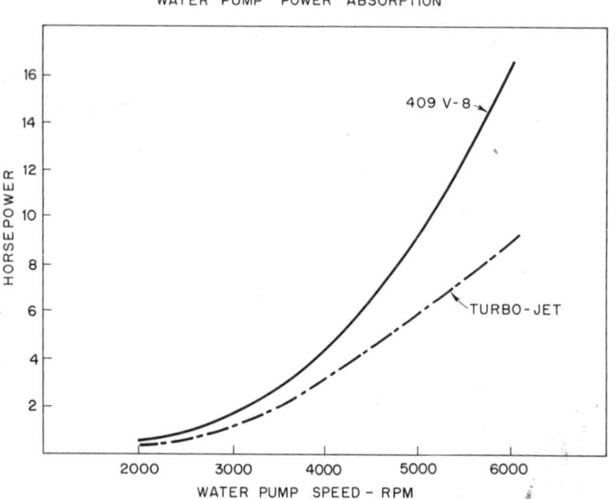

Fig. 18-28. Comparison of the power requirements of the water pumps in the 409 V-8 engine and the Turbo-Jet engine. (*Chevrolet Motor Division of General Motors Corporation*)

one bank (the left) just happened to offer less restriction to water flow. The problem was solved by adding a diverter in the water pump, which is of the correct size and shape to equalize the flow (Fig. 18-29).

SUMMARY

There are two general types of cooling systems for internal-combustion engines: air cooling and liquid cooling. In the air-cooled engine, radiating fins surrounding the cylinders, and cylinder heads radiate heat into the passing air. In liquid-cooled engines, water circulates in water jackets surrounding the combustion chamber and cylinders and the radiator, thus removing heat from the engine.

The liquid cooling system consists of the water

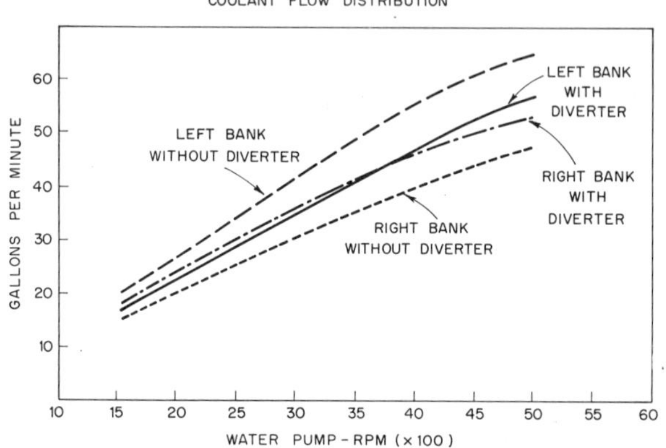

Fig. 18-29. Coolant flow in the left and right banks of the Turbo-Jet engine, without and with a diverter in the water pump. (*Chevrolet Motor Division of General Motors Corporation*)

jackets, a water pump, thermostat, water hoses, and radiator. The water pump is driven by a belt from the crankshaft, and the engine fan mounts on the water-pump pulley. When the water pump is in operation, impellers on the pump rotor force the water to circulate.

The engine fan produces a draft of air through the radiator so that heat is extracted from the water circulating through the radiator. Some engine fans have a variable-speed device to reduce fan load at higher engine speeds. The flexible fan also produces a similar effect, but by centrifugal action.

The thermostat prevents water circulation between the engine and radiator when the engine is cold. This assures rapid engine warm-up. The radiator pressure cap holds pressure in the cooling system, and the increased pressure raises the boiling point of the water in the system. This improves the cooling efficiency of the system.

A main objective in the cooling-system design is to provide ample capacity for adequate cooling under the most adverse operating conditions. On the other hand, cooling must be minimal when the engine is cold, so as to permit rapid engine warm-up and thus minimum cold-engine wear.

REFERENCES

1. Brabetz, J. C., and D. S. Pike, Engines Like to be Warm, SAE (Society of Automotive Engineers) 640583 (891A), 1964 (paper).

2. Ferris, D. R., D. D. Forester, W. R. Herfurth, P. P. Kazlauskas, W. J. Kovelan, and C. L. Moon, Coolant Temperature Effects on Engine Life and Performance, SAE (Society of Automotive Engineers) special publication SP-194, 1961.

3. Beatenbough, P. K., Engine Cooling Systems for Motor Trucks, SAE (Society of Automotive Engineers), special publication SP-274, 1966.

4. Macura, J. F., and J. Bowers, Mark II-427 GT Engine, SAE (Society of Automotive Engineers) 670066, 1967 (paper).

5. Keinath, R. L., H. G. Sood, and W. J. Polkinghorne, Chevrolet Turbo-Jet Engine, SAE (Society of Automotive Engineers) 660340, 1966 (paper).

QUESTIONS

1. What is the purpose of the engine cooling system?
2. Why is it undesirable to operate an engine at too low a temperature?
3. Explain how water can appear in the crankcase.
4. Describe the path of water circulation in a hot engine.
5. Explain how a water pump operates.
6. Describe how the variable-speed fan drive works.
7. Explain how the flexible engine fan works.
8. Describe two types of radiators.
9. Explain the purpose of the thermostat and how it works.
10. Explain the purpose of the radiator pressure cap and how it works.
11. What is meant by the term "antifreeze solution?" What is its purpose?
12. Explain how the temperature indicator works.
13. Why must water continue to circulate in the engine even though the engine is cold and there is no circulation to the radiator?
14. What are some of the basic considerations of cooling-system design?
15. What are several reasons why cold-engine operation should be avoided?

Engine Lubricating Systems

CHAPTER **19**

This chapter discusses the function, design, and operation of engine lubricating systems, as well as the properties and characteristics of engine oil.

§271. Purpose of engine lubricating systems The engine lubricating system provides a flow of lubricating oil to all moving parts in the engine, thus reducing to a minimum possible wear and frictional losses due to surfaces moving against each other. However, the lubricating oil performs other jobs, also, as follows:

1. Lubricates moving parts to minimize wear
2. Lubricates moving parts to minimize power loss from friction
3. Removes heat from engine parts by acting as a cooling agent
4. Absorbs shocks between bearings and other engine parts, thus reducing engine noise and extending engine life
5. Forms a good seal between piston rings and cylinder walls
6. Helps keep engine parts clean by carrying away dirt and other foreign matter

1. Minimizing wear and power loss from friction. Since the lubricating oil interposes a film of oil between moving engine parts, actual metal-to-metal contact is prevented. This minimizes wear and frictional power losses (see §70 to 74 on friction). However, it must be recognized that even though only viscous friction is present in the engine during normal operation, it can cause considerable power loss, especially at high speeds. Figure 8-11 is the frictional horsepower curve of an engine. Note that 40 hp (horsepower) is used up at 4,000 rpm (revolutions per minute) by engine friction. Figure 19-1 shows the three types of frictional surfaces in an engine that require lubrication. It is true that greasy friction may exist in a cold engine and during early engine warm-up. Since greasy friction is far less effective than viscous friction in preventing engine wear, it is obvious that the wear rate will be much greater for the first few minutes after the engine is started (Fig. 18-5). This is the reason that the engine should not be raced or heavily loaded before it has had a chance to run several minutes and get warmed up. After the engine has started to warm up, the lubricating system has circulated oil to the moving parts so that viscous friction, rather than greasy friction, exists. Wear is much less with viscous friction.

2. Removing heat from engine parts. We have already noted several times that the engine oil, as it passes through the engine, picks up heat and carries it back to the oil pan. Air passing around and under the oil pan cools the oil. Thus the oil acts as a cooling agent and is an important factor in preventing excessive engine temperatures.

3. Absorbing shocks between bearings and other engine parts. As the air-fuel mixture is ignited toward the end of the compression stroke, combustion pressures in the cylinder quickly increase to several hundred psi (pounds per square inch). This means that a heavy load of as much as several tons is suddenly imposed on the piston, piston pin, and connecting rod and on their bearings. This load, carried through the bearings, attempts to "squeeze out" the oil in the bearing oil clearance. The oil must resist the shock load which attempts to penetrate the oil film and

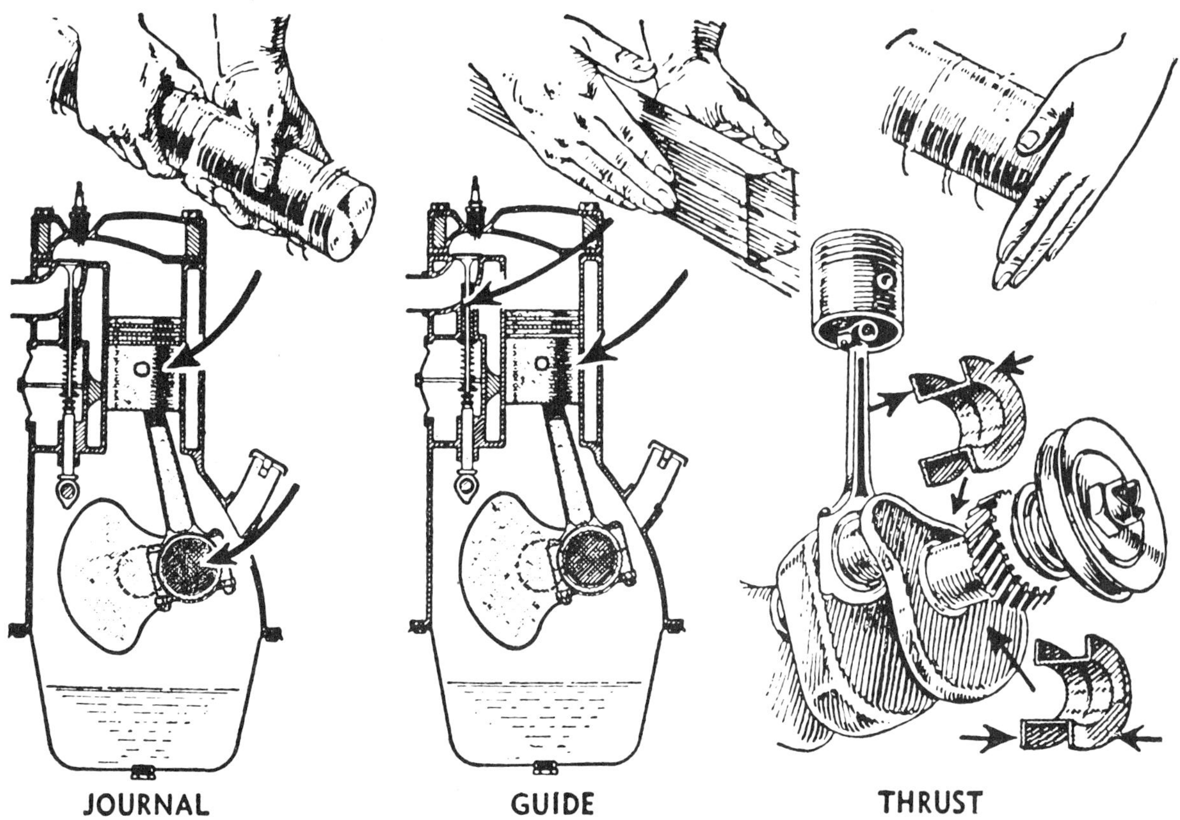

Fig. 19-1. Three types of frictional surfaces in an engine.

squeeze it out. As it does this, the oil helps quiet the engine and prevents metal-to-metal contact, which would greatly increase wear.

4. *Forming a seal between piston rings and cylinder walls.* Piston rings must form a gas-tight seal between the pistons and the cylinder walls; the oil helps the rings do this job (see §165). The oil film on the cylinder wall, rings, and piston helps to compensate for any small irregularity and, in effect, fills in the gaps through which gas might escape. Also, since the oil clings to the metal surfaces, it resists any attempt for gas to blow by, or pass through, the oil film between the metal surfaces.

5. *Cleaning the engine.* Since the oil is in constant circulation between the oil pan and the engine parts, it tends to wash away any foreign material that may enter the engine. For example, particles of dust may pass the air filter and enter the engine with the air-fuel mixture. Particles of carbon may form in the combustion chambers and then work down onto the cylinder walls or rings. The oil tends to flush such particles back into the oil pan. Helping the oil in this job are the cleaning agents, or *detergents*, that are now added to many brands of lubricating oil (see §272, *9*).

§272. Source and properties of oil Geologists and petroleum scientists are not sure how crude oil, or petroleum, was originally formed, or how it came to collect in pools underground. But it is known that petroleum is a very versatile substance, and that many grades and kinds of engine fuel and engine oil can be made from it by various refining procedures.[1] During that part of the refining and manufacturing process that results in engine oil, the petroleum chemists make sure that the lubricating oil has the proper viscosity (body and fluidity) and resistance to oxidation, carbon formation, corrosion, rust, extreme pressures, and foaming. Also, oil must act as a good cleaning agent, pour at low temperatures, and have good viscosity at extremes of high and low temperatures.

Any mineral oil, by itself, does not have all these properties. Lubricating-oil manufacturers therefore, during the manufacturing process, put into the oil a number of additives. An oil for severe service may have many additives, as follows:[2]

1. Pour-point depressants
2. Oxidation inhibitors
3. Corrosion inhibitors
4. Rust inhibitors
5. Extreme-pressure agents
6. Detergent dispersants
7. Foam inhibitors
8. Usually a viscosity-index improver

All these will be discussed in following paragraphs.

1. Viscosity (body and fluidity). Primarily, viscosity is the most important characteristic of lubricating oil. "Viscosity" refers to the tendency of oil to resist flowing. In a bearing and journal, layers of oil adhere to the bearing and journal surfaces. These layers must move, or slip, with respect to each other, and the viscosity of the oil determines the ease with which this slipping can take place. Viscosity can be divided for discussion into two parts, body and fluidity. Body has to do with the resistance to oil-film puncture, or penetration, during the application of heavy loads. When the power stroke begins, for example, bearing loads sharply increase. Oil body prevents the load from squeezing the film of oil out from between the journal and the bearing. This property cushions shock loads, helps maintain a good seal between piston, rings, and cylinder walls, and maintains an adequate oil film on all bearing sufaces under load.

Fluidity has to do with the ease with which the oil flows through oil lines and spreads over bearing surfaces. In some respects, fluidity and body are opposing characteristics, since the more fluid an oil is, the less body it has. The oil used in any particular engine must have sufficient body to perform as explained in the previous paragraph, and yet must have sufficient fluidity to flow freely through all oil lines and spread effectively over all bearing surfaces. Late types of engines have more closely fitted bearings with smaller clearances, and consequently they require oil of greater fluidity so that it will flow readily into the spaces between bearings and journals. Such engines use oils of lower viscosity.

Temperature influences viscosity. Increasing temperature reduces viscosity. That is, it causes oil to lose body and gain fluidity. Decreasing temperature causes oil viscosity to increase. The oil gains body and loses fluidity. Since engine temperatures range several hundred degrees from cold-weather starting to operating temperature, a lubricating oil must have adequate fluidity at low temperatures so that it will flow. At the same time, it must have sufficient body for high-temperature operation.

2. Viscosity ratings. Viscosity of oil is determined by use of a viscosimeter, a device that determines the length of time required for a specified amount of oil to flow through an opening of a specified diameter. Temperature is taken into consideration during this test, since high temperature decreases viscosity and low temperature increases viscosity. In referring to viscosity, the lower numbers refer to oils of lower viscosity (thinner). The SAE (Society of Automotive Engineers) rates oil viscosity in two different ways: for winter and for other than winter use. Winter-grade oils are tested at 0 and 210°F. There are three winter grades: SAE5W, SAE10W, and SAE20W, the "W" indicating winter grade. For other than winter use, the grades are SAE20, SAE30, SAE40, and SAE50, all without the "W" suffix. Some oils have multiple ratings, which means they are equivalent in viscosity to several single-rating oils. An SAE10W-30 oil, for example, is comparable to SAE10W, SAE20W, and SAE30 oils. This oil has a high viscosity index (see next paragraph).

3. Viscosity index. When oil is cold, it is thicker

and runs more slowly than when it is hot. In other words, it becomes more viscous when it is cooled. On the other hand, it becomes less viscous when it is heated. In normal automotive engine operation, we do not have to be too concerned about this change of oil viscosity with changing temperature. We recognize that the engine is harder to start at low temperature because the oil is thicker, or more viscous. But until the engine is cooled to many degrees below zero, we do not have to take any special steps to start it.

Some oils change viscosity a great deal with temperature changes. Other oils show a much smaller change of viscosity with temperature changes. In order to have an accurate measure of how much any particular oil will change in viscosity with temperature changes, the viscosity-index scale was adopted. Originally, the scale ran from 0 to 100. The higher the number, the less the oil viscosity changes with temperature changes. Thus, an oil with a VI (viscosity index) of 100 will change less in viscosity with temperature changes than an oil with a VI of 10. In recent years, special VI-improving additives have been developed which have stepped up viscosity indexes to as much as 300. Such an oil shows relatively little change in viscosity from very low to relatively high temperatures. You could especially appreciate the significance of VI if you were operating automotive equipment in a very cold climate (say, in northern Alaska). You would have to start engines at temperatures of as much as 60°F below zero (92° below freezing). However, once started, the engines would soon reach operating temperatures that heat the oil to several hundred degrees. If you could select an oil of a relatively high VI, it would be fluid enough to permit starting but would not thin out (or lose viscosity) so much that lubricating effectiveness would be lost. On the other hand, an oil with a low VI would probably be so thick at low temperatures that it might actually prevent starting. But if you could start, it might then thin out too much as it warmed up.

Oil companies make sure that their oils have a sufficiently high VI to operate satisfactorily in the variations of temperatures they will meet. Also, they supply oil with multiple viscosity ratings. For example, an oil may be designated SAE10W-30, which indicates that it is comparable to SAE10W, SAE20W, and SAE30 oils. This oil has a relatively high VI.

4. *Pour-point depressants.* At low temperatures, some oils become so thick they will not pour at all. Certain additives can be put into oil which will depress, or lower, the temperature point at which the oil will become too thick to flow. Such additives keep the oil fluid at low temperatures for adequate engine lubrication during cold-weather starting and initial operation.

5. *Resistance to carbon formation.* Cylinder walls, pistons, and rings operate at temperatures of several hundred degrees. This temperature, acting on the oil films covering walls, rings, and pistons, tends to cause the oil to break down or burn, producing carbon. Carbon formation can cause poor engine performance and damage to the engine. Carbon may pack in around the piston rings, causing them to stick in the ring grooves. This prevents proper piston-ring operation, so blow-by, poor compression, excessive oil consumption, and scoring of cylinder walls may result. Carbon may build up on the piston head and in the cylinder head. This fouls spark plugs, excessively increases compression so that knocking occurs and reduces engine performance. Carbon may form on the underside of the piston to such an extent that heat transfer will be hindered and the piston will overheat. Pieces of carbon may break off and drop into the oil pan, where they may be picked up by the lubrication system. They could then clog oil channels and lines so that flow of lubricating oil to engine parts would be dangerously reduced. A good lubricating oil must be sufficiently resistant to the heat and operating conditions in the engine to exhibit a minimum amount of carbon formation.

6. *Oxidation inhibitors.* When oil is heated to fairly high temperatures and then agitated so that considerable air is mixed with it, the oxygen in the air tends to combine with oil, oxidizing it. Since this is the treatment that engine oil undergoes (that is, it is heated and agitated with, or

sprayed into, the air in the crankcase), some oil oxidation is bound to occur. A slight amount of oxidation will do no particular harm; but if oxidation becomes excessive, serious troubles may occur in the engine. As the oil is oxidized, it breaks down to form various harmful substances. Some of the products of oil oxidation will coat engine parts with an extremely sticky, tarlike material. This material may clog oil channels and tend to restrict the action of piston rings and valves. A somewhat different form of oil oxidation coats engine parts with a varnishlike substance that has a similar damaging effect on the engine. Even if these substances do not form, oil oxidation may produce corrosive materials in the oil that will corrode bearings and other surfaces, causing bearing failures and damage to other parts. Oil chemists and refineries control the refining processes and may add certain chemicals known as *oxidation inhibitors* so that engine lubricating oils resist oxidation.

7. Corrosion and rust inhibitors. At high temperatures, acids may form in the oil which can corrode engine parts, especially bearings. Corrosion inhibitors are added to the oil to inhibit this corrosion. Also, rust inhibitors are added. These function in two ways: They displace water from metal surfaces so that oil coats them, and they have an alkaline reaction to neutralize combustion acids.

8. Foaming resistance. The churning action in the engine crankcase also tends to cause the engine oil to foam, just as an egg beater causes an egg white to form a frothy foam. As the oil foams up, it tends to overflow or to be lost through the crankcase ventilator (§257). In addition, the foaming oil is not able to provide normal lubrication of bearings and other moving parts. Foaming oil in hydraulic valve lifters will cause them to function poorly, work noisily, wear rapidly, and possibly break. To prevent foaming, antifoaming additives are mixed with the oil.

9. Detergent dispersants. Despite the filters and screens at the carburetor and crankcase ventilator (§257), dirt does get into the engine. In addition, as the engine runs, the combustion processes leave deposits of carbon on piston rings, valves, and other parts. Also, some oil oxidation may take place, resulting in still other deposits. Then, too, metal wear in the engine puts particles of metal into the oil. As a result of these various conditions, deposits tend to build up on and in engine parts. The deposits gradually reduce the performance of the engine and speed up wear of parts. To prevent or slow down the formation of these deposits, some engine oils contain a detergent additive.

The detergent acts much like ordinary hand soap. When you wash your hands with soap, the soap surrounds the particles of dirt on your hands, causing them to become detached so that the water can rinse them away. In a similar manner, the detergent in the oil loosens and detaches the deposits of carbon, gum, and dirt. The oil then carries the loosened material away. The larger particles drop to the bottom of the crankcase, but smaller particles tend to remain suspended in the oil. These impurities, or contaminants, are flushed out when the oil is changed.

To prevent the particles from clotting and to keep them in a finely divided state, a dispersant is added to the oil. Without the dispersant, the particles would tend to collect and form large particles. These large particles might then block the oil filter or reduce its effectiveness. They could also build up in oil passages and plug them, thus depriving bearings and other engine parts of oil. The dispersant prevents this and thus greatly increases the amount of contaminants the oil can carry and still function effectively.

Lubricating-oil manufacturers now place more emphasis on the dispersant qualities of the additive than on its detergent qualities. If the contaminants can be kept suspended in the oil as small particles, they will not deposit on engine parts, and there is less need of detergent action.

10. Extreme-pressure resistance. The modern automotive engine subjects the lubricating oil to very high pressures, not only in the bearings, but also in the valve train. Modern valve trains have heavy valve springs and high-lift cams. This means that the valves must accelerate and decelerate more rapidly and move farther against heavier spring opposition. To prevent the oil from squeezing out, extreme-pressure additives are put into the oil. They react chemically with metal surfaces to form very strong, slippery films which may be only a molecule or so thick. Thus, they supplement the oil by providing protection during moments of extreme pressure, when the oil itself is likely to be squeezed out.

§273. Service ratings of oil We have already mentioned that the viscosity of lubricating oil is rated by number. Lubricating oil is also rated in another way, by what is called *service designation.* That is, it is rated according to the type of service for which it is best suited. There are five service ratings: MS, MM, and ML, for gasoline or other spark-ingition engines; and DG and DS, for diesel engines. The oils differ in their characteristics and in the additives they contain.

1. MS oil. This oil is for severe service and unfavorable conditions. It is to be used where there are special lubricating requirements for bearing-corrosion and engine-deposit control because of operating conditions or engine design. This includes the following:

a. Low operating temperature and short-trip, start-stop driving conditions, as found in city operation
b. High-speed highway driving, where oil will become unusually hot, as during a summer-vacation trip
c. Heavy-load operation, such as is typical of highway truck service

2. MM oil. This oil is for medium service such as the following:

a. High-speed but fairly short trips
b. Long trips at moderate speeds and summer temperatures
c. Operation at moderate cold-air temperatures, where the car is used for both long and short trips

3. ML oil. This oil is for comparatively light service, where most of the trips are longer than 10 miles, and where no extremes of air temperature are encountered.

CAUTION: Do not confuse *viscosity* and *service* ratings of oil. Some people think that a high-viscosity oil is a "heavy-duty" oil. This is not necessarily so. Viscosity ratings refer to the thickness of the oil; thickness is not a measure of heavy-duty quality. Remember that there are two ratings —viscosity and service. Thus, an SAE10W oil can be an MS, MM, or ML oil. Likewise, an oil of any other viscosity rating can have any one of the three service ratings, MS, MM, or ML.

4. DS oil. This is an oil for lubricating diesel engines operating under the most severe service conditions, as follows:

a. Continuous low temperatures and light loads
b. Continuous high temperatures and heavy loads
c. Operation on fuels of high sulfur content or abnormal volatility

5. DG oil. This is an oil for lubricating diesel engines operating under comparatively light to normal conditions, such as are typical of most trucking and farm-tractor operations.

§274. Testing engine oil Engine lubricating oil must undergo a series of tests, both outside and inside engines, in order to make sure that it qualifies and will do a satisfactory job.[3] The tests may be divided into two catagories: laboratory tests and road tests.

1. *Laboratory tests.* Properties to be evaluated in laboratory tests include wear, corrosion, rust, cleanliness, viscosity-temperature relationship, oxidation stability, effect on combustion, resistance to foaming, effect on engine seals, effect on packages, and compatability.

a. Wear. Three types of wear of special interest to oil engineers include: wear due to corrosion; wear due to scuffing, welding, and surface disintegration; and wear due to abrasion from abrasive contamination.

b. Corrosion. The oil must be checked with all the various types of materials used in the engine —babbitt, silver, aluminum, iron, steel, bronze, and so on—to make sure it will not produce undue corrosion.

c. Rust. The oil must have adequate rust-inhibiting properties. This is particularly important during the winter months, when the car is used in start and stop driving (§283).

d. Engine cleanliness. This includes studies of the effectiveness of the oil in holding down the formation of piston varnish and lacquer, oil-ring sludge, ring-groove carbon, filter deposits, oil-pan sludge, and hydraulic-valve-lifter deposits.

e. Viscosity-temperature relationship. The oil should have a satisfactory VI for acceptible performance in the extremes of temperature (cold and hot) that the oil will meet in service. Also, the oil must have viscosity stability; that is, it must retain its viscosity even after being subjected to heavy shearing stress, as occurs when a heavily loaded shaft is turning at high speed.

f. Thermal and oxidation stability. Thermal stability refers to the ability of the oil to resist degradation, or "cracking," due to temperature. Products of thermal degradation may be corrosive or carbonaceous and thereby promote wear as well as engine deposits. Oxidation stability refers to the ability of the oil to resist oxidation at high temperatures. The adverse effects of oxygen instability are similar to those due to thermal degradation.

g. Effect on combustion. Poor oil formulation can result in combustion-chamber deposits and consequent combustion problems such as rumble, preignition, and knock.

h. Foaming. As previously noted, special additives are required to prevent foaming of the oil (§272).

i. Effect on engine seals. A variety of natural and synthetic sealing materials in the form of rings, gaskets, and so on, are used in the engine, transmission, and other automotive components. Oil must be checked against these materials to make sure they will not cause such adverse effects as swelling or disintegration.

j. Effect on packaging materials. The oil is marketed in a variety of containers, and it must be tested to make sure the containers will hold the oil satisfactorily. For example, a special cement is used to seal the side seam of the cans in which oil is packaged. If the oil tends to dissolve this cement, not only would it tend to cause oil leakage, but the oil itself might be damaged from the cement dissolved in it.

k. Compatability. This is a very important property because the oil will probably be mixed in the crankcase with other types and grades. That is, when the motorist needs to have oil added, the service attendant will add the oil that he has on hand, without reference to the oil already in the crankcase. Thus, a new oil must be tested to make sure it will be compatable with oils that are already on the market.

2. Road tests. Road tests of engine oil vary greatly, from testing oil performance in a number of cars operated by an oil company to the use of the oil in a taxicab fleet of hundreds of vehicles. Two general types of tests are made: high-temperature, high-speed tests; and low-temperature tests.

a. High-temperature, high-speed tests. These are primarily oil-endurance tests, run at temperatures and speeds higher than would be expected in normal service. Such tests might be conducted on a proving ground, for example, where cars could be operated around the clock at speeds above 100 mph (miles per hour). At the end of such tests, the engines are completely disassembled so that each part can be carefully inspected for wear, deposits, or other damage.

b. Low-temperature tests. The objective of the low-temperature tests is to simulate winter, start and stop driving. Such tests are usually conducted under adverse weather conditions so as to subject the engine and oil to the worst possible driving conditions. At the end of the tests, the engine is disassembled so all parts can be inspected.

3. Manufacturer's approval. There is an additional hurdle that an oil must clear—it must pass the engine manufacturer's tests. Most engine manufacturers use most or all of the standard MS test procedures, as outlined in the report of the Section G-IV Technical Committee B of ASTM.

4. Military qualification. It is also necessary to qualify the oil for use in military vehicles, as outlined in military specifications, if the oil is expected to be sold for that purpose.

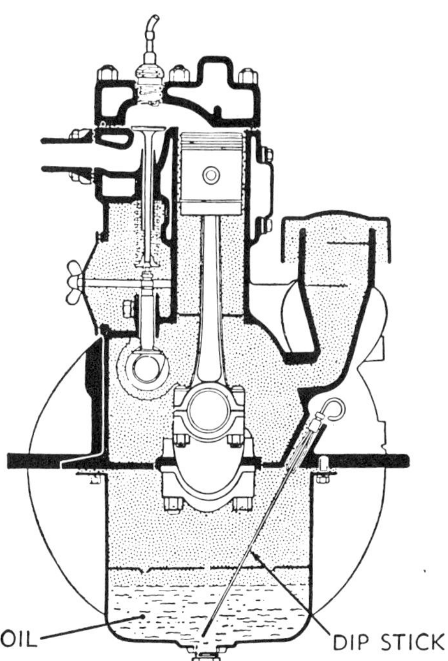

Fig. 19-2. Location of the oil-level stick, or dip stick, in the engine.

§275. Automotive lubricants In addition to engine oil, many other lubricants are required for the automobile. Wherever one part slides on or rotates in another part, you will find some kind of lubricant at work protecting the parts from undue wear. The steering system, axles, differential, transmission, brakes, alternator, ignition distributor, and so on, all use special types of lubricant.

1. *Gear lubricants.*The gears in transmissions and differentials must be lubricated with special heavy oils that have sufficient body to resist oil-film puncture and thereby prevent actual metal-to-metal contact between the moving gear teeth. On the other hand, the oil must flow readily even at low temperatures so that it does not "channel" as the gears begin to rotate. Channeling of the oil takes place when the oil is so thick that the teeth cut out channels in it, and it does not readily flow to fill these channels.

The lubricant used in hypoid-gear differentials is subjected to very severe service since hypoid gears have teeth that not only roll over one another, but also slide over each other. This combined rolling and sliding action puts additional pressure on the lubricant. So that the lubricant will stand up under this service, it is especially compounded and contains certain added chemicals that enable it to withstand much greater pressure than oil alone would withstand. Such lubricants are called extreme-pressure, or EP, lubricants. There are actually two classifications of these lubricants: powerful extreme-pressure lubricants, for use on heavy-duty applications; and mild extreme-pressure lubricants, for use on applications with less severe requirements.

2. *Grease.* Essentially, lubricating grease is oil to which certain thickening agents have been added. The oil furnishes the lubricating action; the thickening agents simply function to hold the oil in place so that it does not run away. The

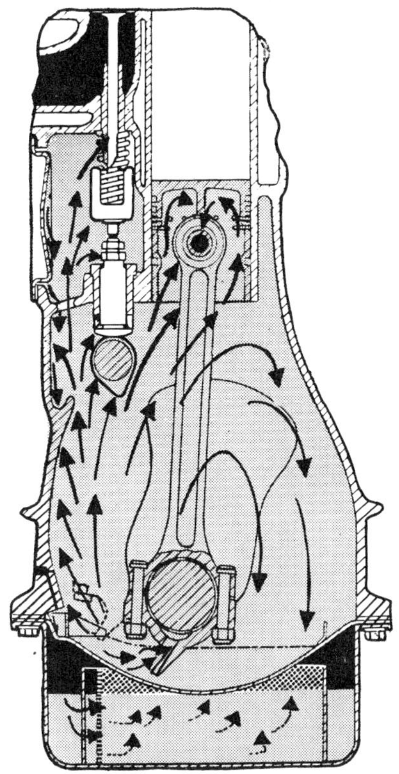

Fig. 19-3. Splash lubrication system of a six-cylinder, L-head engine. Arrows show oil splash to the moving parts in the engine.

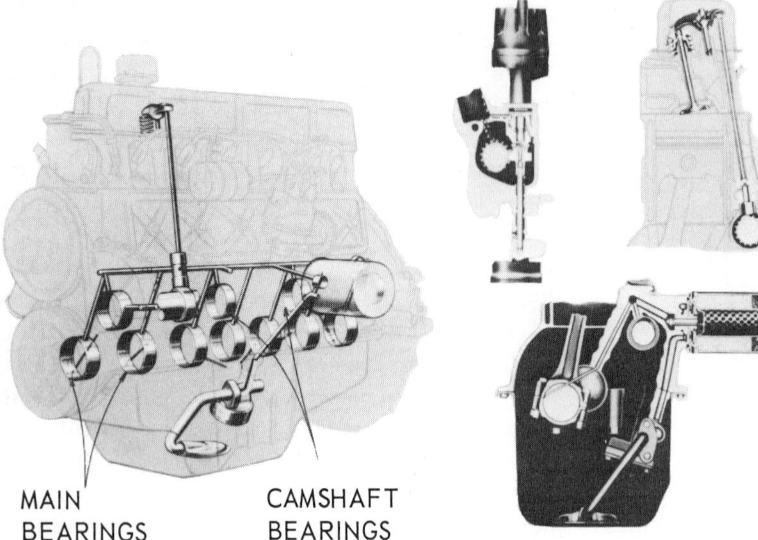

Fig. 19-4. Lubrication system of a six-cylinder, overhead-valve engine with seven crankshaft bearings. (*Ford Division of Ford Motor Company*)

thickening agents are usually called *soap.* This is not the kind of soap used in washing, but any one of several metallic compounds; the type used depends on the service required of the grease. This is also true of the viscosity grade (or thickness) of the oil that goes into the grease. For some services, a relatively light oil is used. For others, a heavy oil is used.

a. Aluminum grease. Aluminum grease contains aluminum compounds as thickening agents. This grease has good adhesive properties and is widely used for chassis lubrication. While it will not withstand extreme temperatures, it is highly resistant to moisture and is therefore valuable for lubricating springs and other chassis parts that are subjected to road splash.

b. Soda grease. Soda grease contains sodium compounds as thickening agents, which give the grease a thick, fibrous appearance, even though the grease contains no actual fiber. This grease is often called *fibrous grease,* or *fiber grease.* While it is less resistant to moisture than some other greases, it is very adhesive and clings tightly to rotating parts. It is therefore valuable for rotating parts such as wheel bearings and universal joints.

c. Calcium grease. Calcium grease uses calcium compounds as thickening agents. This grease is often known as *cup grease* and is used in lubricating parts supplied with grease cups. It has a tendency to separate into liquid oil and solid soap at high temperatures.

d. Mixed greases. Each of the various greases mentioned above has special valuable characteristics. Mixed greases are blends of these different greases. This blending produces greases that can better meet the requirements of certain

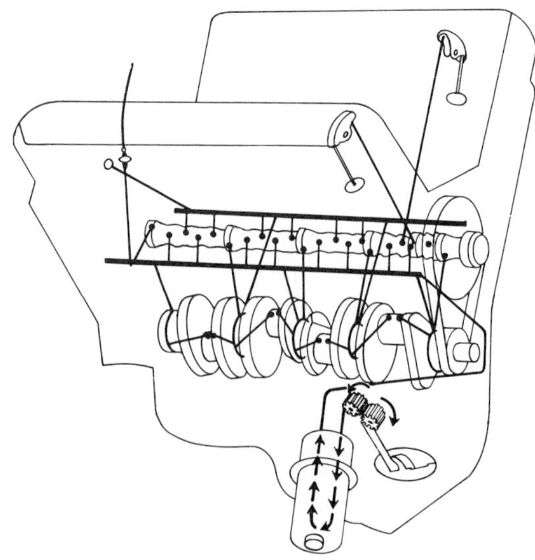

Fig. 19-5. Simplified lubricating system for a V-8 engine. (*Cadillac Motor Car Division of General Motors Corporation*)

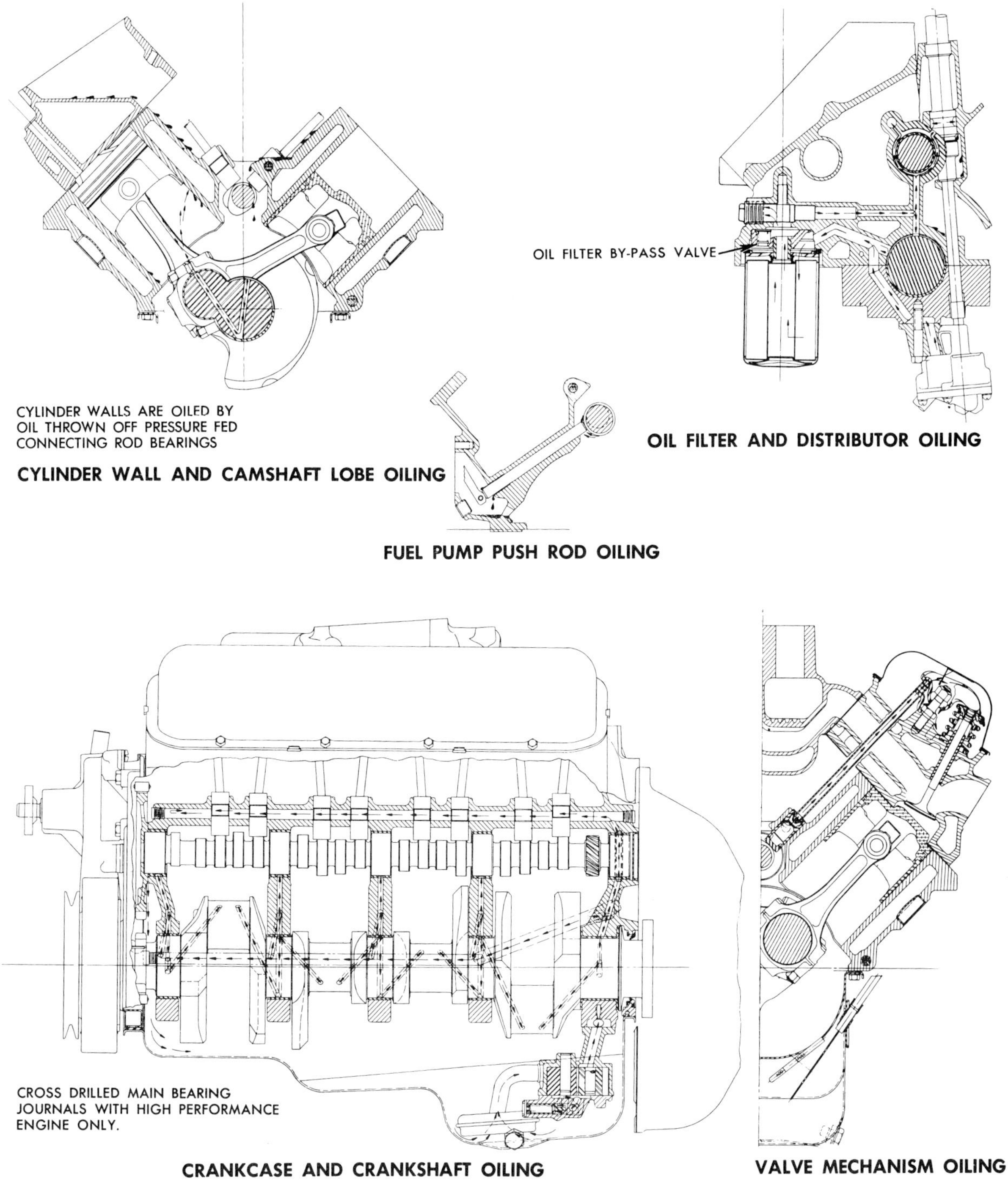

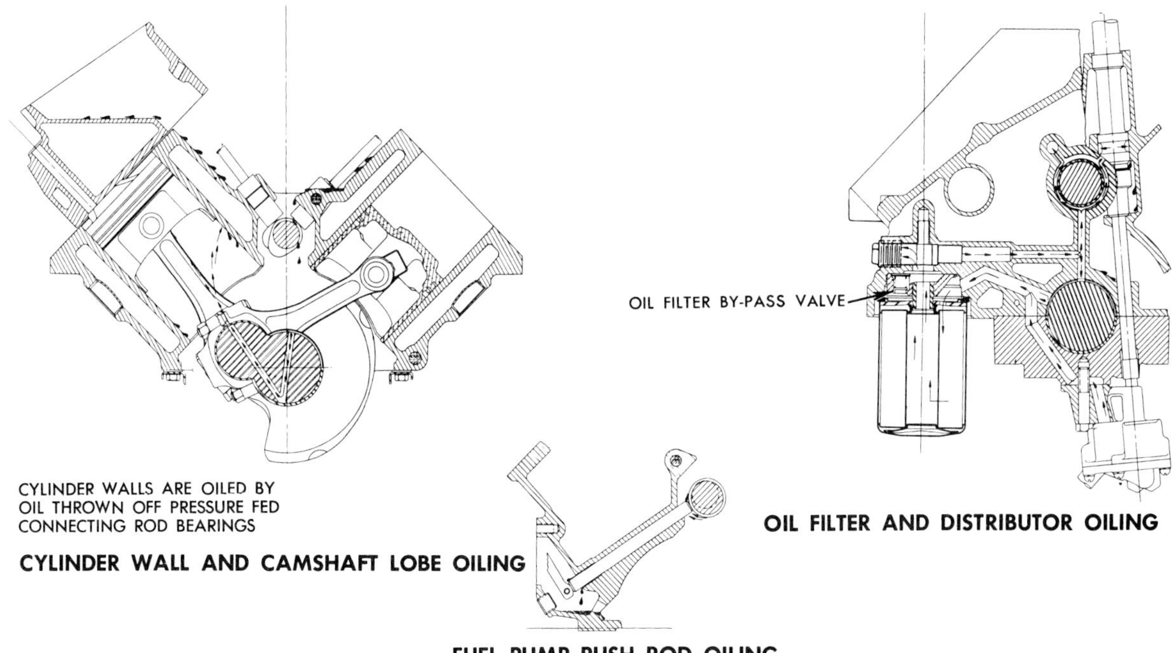

CYLINDER WALLS ARE OILED BY OIL THROWN OFF PRESSURE FED CONNECTING ROD BEARINGS
CYLINDER WALL AND CAMSHAFT LOBE OILING
OIL FILTER BY-PASS VALVE
OIL FILTER AND DISTRIBUTOR OILING
FUEL PUMP PUSH ROD OILING
CROSS DRILLED MAIN BEARING JOURNALS WITH HIGH PERFORMANCE ENGINE ONLY.
CRANKCASE AND CRANKSHAFT OILING
VALVE MECHANISM OILING

Fig. 19-6. Lubrication system of a V-8, overhead-valve engine. Arrows show oil flow to the moving parts in the engine. (*Chevrolet Motor Division of General Motors Corporation*)

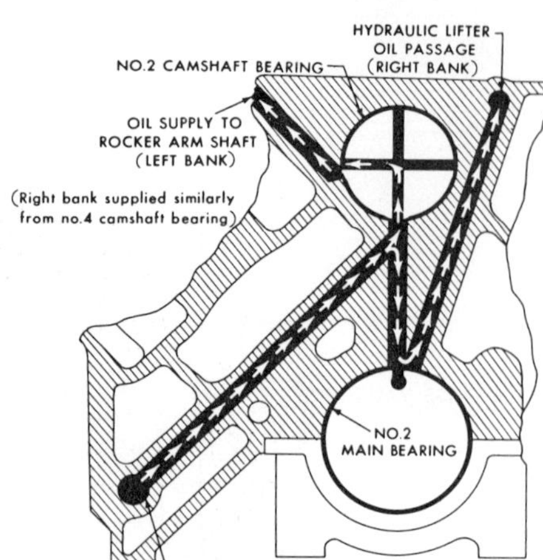

Fig. 19-7. Oil passages in the engine block carry the oil to the crankshaft main and the camshaft bearings. The oil passages in the block connect with oil passages in the head, so that the valve mechanisms are lubricated. (*Lincoln-Mercury Division of Ford Motor Company*)

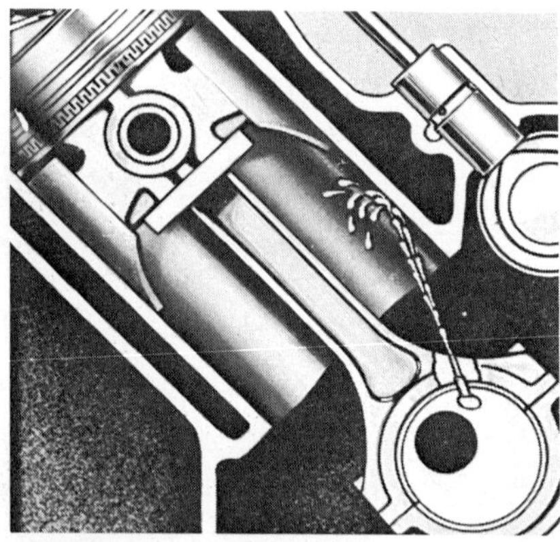

Fig. 19-8. When a hole in the connecting rod aligns with a hole in the crankpin, oil is sprayed onto the cylinder wall, as shown, providing lubrication of the piston and rings. (*Lincoln-Mercury Division of Ford Motor Company*)

specific applications. Actually, the automotive technician does not have to worry about the composition of the various greases since the automotive manufacturer and the petroleum company have worked together to produce oils and greases exactly suited for the various parts and places that require lubrication on the automobile. As long

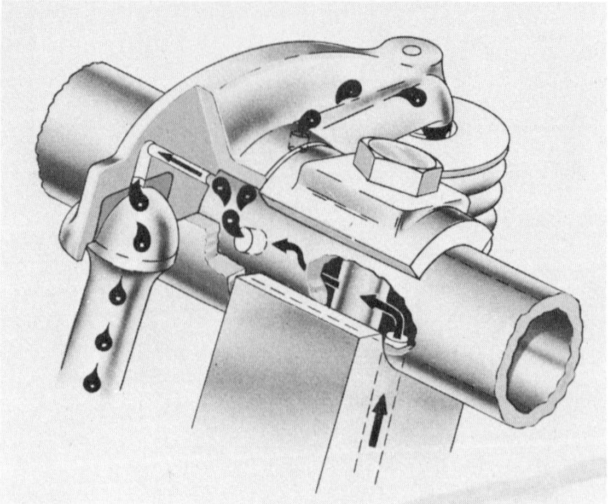

Fig. 19-9. Lubrication of push-rod end and valve-stem tip in an engine, using shaft-mounted rocker arms. Rocker arm is partly cut away to show oil holes. (*Buick Motor Division of General Motors Corporation*)

as the automotive technician follows the automobile manufacturers' recommendations, he is sure of putting the right lubricant in the right place on the car.

§276. Types of lubricating systems The lubricating system, no matter what type, has the job of supplying adequate amounts of oil to all moving engine parts, as previously noted. The oil does a variety of jobs (§271). In some heavy-duty engines, where the oil has a harder and hotter job to do, an oil cooler is included in the lubricating system. The oil cooler has a radiator much like the cooling-system radiator, and the oil passes through it; this cools the oil. All engines have some sort of oil-level indicator, which usually consists of a *dip stick*, or oil-level stick, that enters the crankcase from the side of the block. A dip stick is shown in Fig. 19-2 in the sectional view of an engine. To check the oil level in the oil pan, the dip stick can be pulled out and the height of the oil on the stick noted. Oil can then be added if the level is too low for adequate engine protection.

Engine lubricating systems are divided into three types: splash systems, pressure-feed systems, and

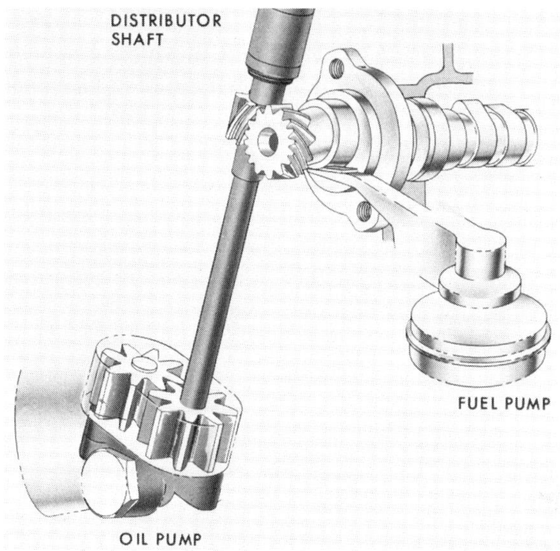

Fig. 19-10. Oil pump, distributor, and fuel-pump drives. The oil pump is the gear type. A gear on the end of the camshaft drives the ignition distributor, and an extension of the distributor shaft drives the oil pump. The fuel pump is driven by an eccentric on the camshaft. (*Buick Motor Division of General Motors Corporation*)

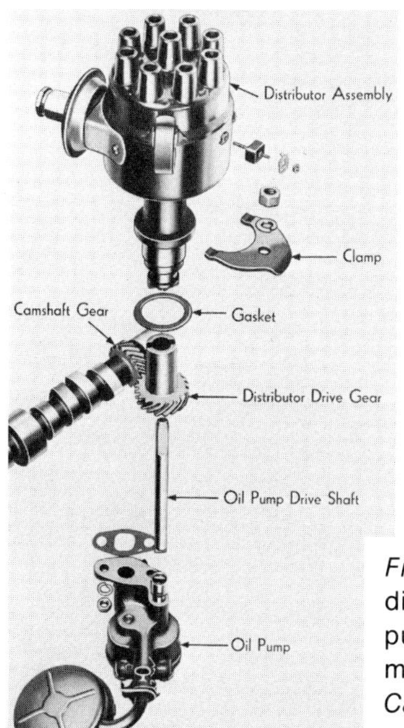

Fig. 19-11. Ignition distributor and oil-pump-drive arrangement. (*Cadillac Motor Car Division of General Motors Corporation*)

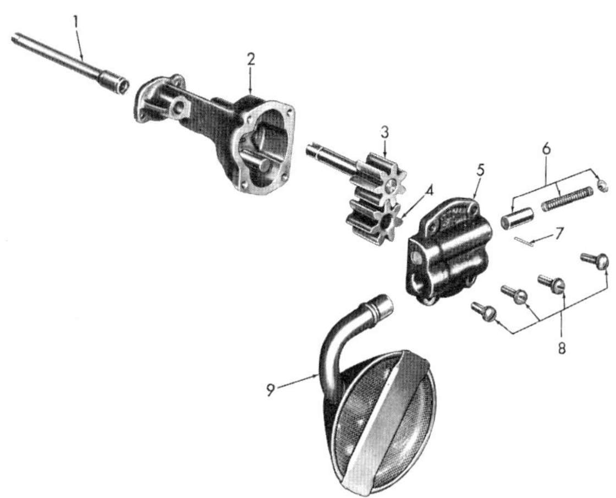

Fig. 19-12. Disassembled view of a gear-type oil pump: (1) shaft; (2) pump body; (3) drive gear; (4) idler gear; (5) cover; (6) regulator valve; (7) pin; (8) screws; (9) intake pipe and screen. (*Chevrolet Motor Division of General Motors Corporation*)

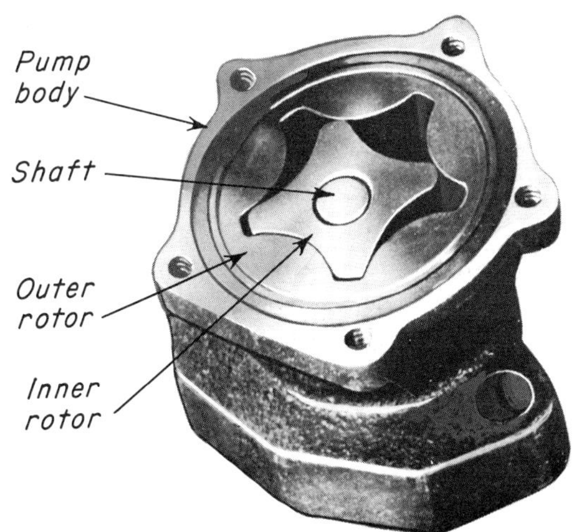

Fig. 19-13. Rotor-type oil pump, with its cover removed to show how the inner and outer rotors fit each other. (*Chrysler-Plymouth Division of Chrysler Motors Corporation*)

combination splash and pressure-feed systems.

1. *Splash system.* In the splash lubricating system (Fig. 19-3) there are dippers on the lower part of the connecting-rod-bearing caps; these dippers enter oil trays in the oil pan with each crankshaft

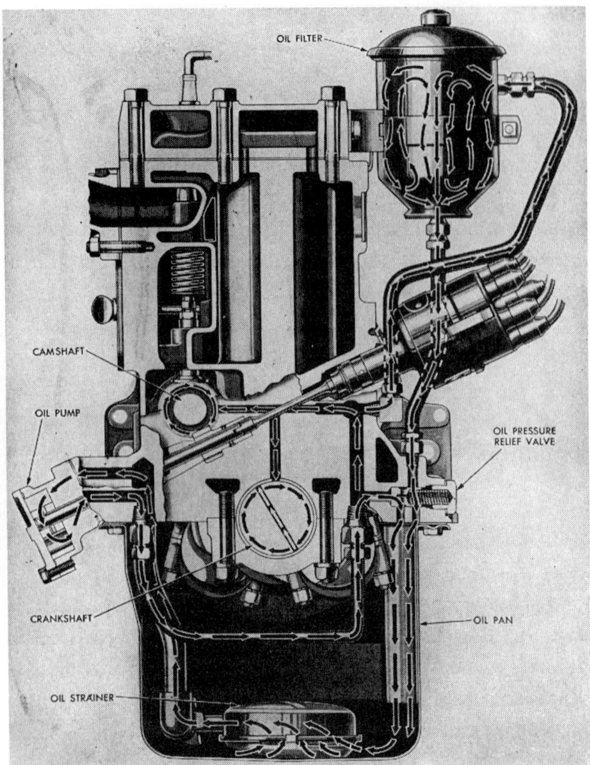

Fig. 19-14. End sectional view of an L-head engine, showing the location of the oil pump, oil filter, and oil-pressure-relief valve. The direction of the oil flow is shown by arrows. (*Dodge Division of Chrysler Motors Corporation*)

revolution. The dippers splash oil to the upper part of the engine. The oil is thrown up as a fine oil spray which provides adequate lubrication to valve mechanisms, cylinder walls, piston rings, and bearings. An oil pump is used to maintain a constant level of oil in the oil trays.

2. *Pressure-feed system.* In the pressure-feed lubricating system (Figs. 19-4 to 19-6) the oil is forced by the oil pump through holes drilled in the crankshaft and connecting rods to the connecting-rod and piston-pin bearings. Valve mechanisms are lubricated by oil galleries in the cylinder block or by oil lines. Cylinder walls are lubricated by oil thrown off from the connecting-rod bearings and, in some engines, by spit holes in the connecting rods. (Lubrication of bearings, cylinder walls, and piston rings is discussed in some detail in §171 and 165 to 168.) The pressure-feed lubricating system is used in practically all modern automotive engines.

3. *Combination splash and pressure-feed system.* The combination splash and pressure-feed lubricating system depends on oil splash to lubricate some engine parts and on pressure feed to lubricate other engine parts.

4. *Oil passages.* Oil passages in the engine block and head permit circulation of oil to bearings and moving parts (Fig. 19-7). Many engines have holes drilled in the connecting rods and crankpins, as shown in Fig. 19-8, to lubricate the cylinder walls and pistons. These are often called *oil-spit holes.*

5. *Valve-train lubrication.* The points of contact between the upper ends of the push rods, the rocker arm, and the valve stem, as well as the rocker-arm pivot, must be adequately lubricated (I-head engines). On some engines, the push rod is hollow and feeds oil up to the rocker arm. It lubricates the ball pivot and also spills over to lubricate the point of contact between the rocker

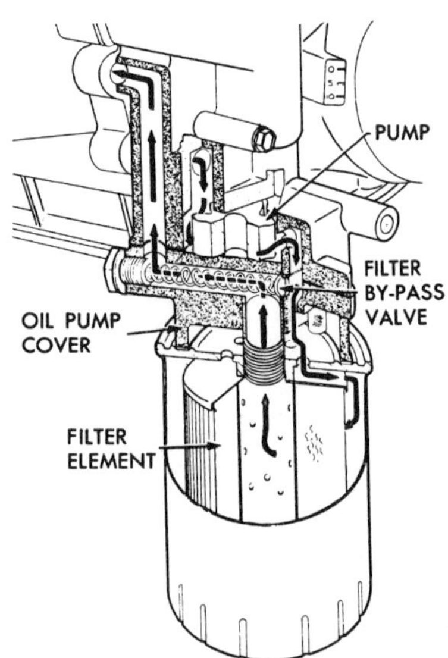

Fig. 19-15. Cutaway view of a full-flow oil filter with by-pass valve. (*Buick Motor Division of General Motors Corporation*)

arm and the end of the valve stem (see Fig. 15-33). Engines having the rocker arms supported on a shaft (Fig. 7-34) are lubricated by another system. One method uses passages drilled in the cylinder block and cylinder head to the end rocker-arm-shaft brackets. Drilled holes in the hollow rocker-arm shaft distribute oil to each rocker arm. The oil flows through holes in the rocker arm to the push-rod and valve-stem tips as shown in Fig. 19-9.

§277. Oil pumps The oil pump is usually driven from a gear on the camshaft (the same gear that drives the ignition distributor), as shown in Figs. 19-10 and 19-11. Oil pumps may be located in the crankcase, as shown in Fig. 19-4, or externally, as shown in Fig. 19-6.

One type of oil pump is shown in Figs. 19-10 to 19-12. This is a gear-type pump. As the gears rotate, the spaces between the gear teeth become filled with oil from the oil pan. The oil is then carried around to the oil outlet, and here the gear teeth mesh to force the oil out through the outlet. It then flows to the various engine parts.

Another type of oil pump, with the cover removed, is shown in Fig. 19-13. This pump has an internal rotor and an external rotor. The internal rotor is driven, causing the external rotor to turn with it. The action is much like that in the gear-type pump. Oil enters at one side, where the spaces between the rotors are increasing, and is carried around to the other side, where the spaces are decreasing. There the inner rotor lobes move into the spaces and force the oil out.

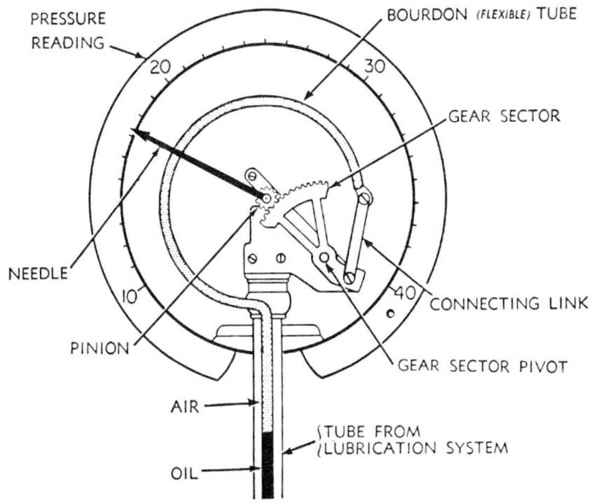

Fig. 19-16. Bourdon tube and linkage to indicating needle used in pressure-expansion oil-pressure-expansion oil-pressure indicator.

§278. Relief valve In any pressure-feed system

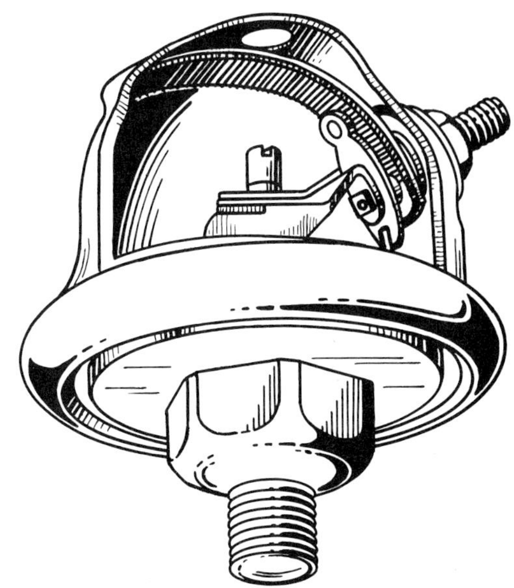

Fig. 19-17. Engine unit of electric-resistance oil-pressure indicator. Housing has been cut away so that resistance and movable contact can be seen. (*AC Spark Plug Division of General Motors Corporation*)

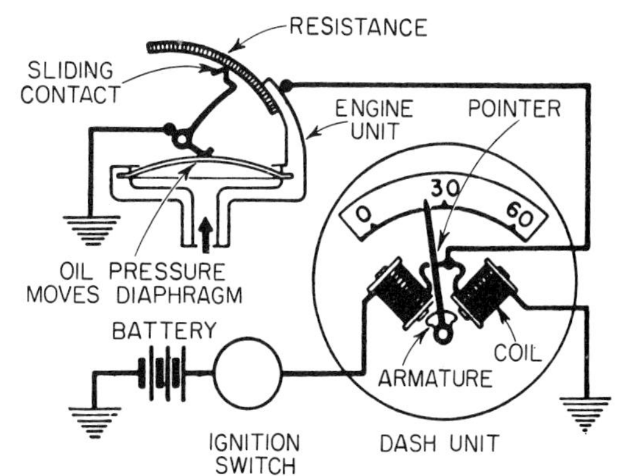

Fig. 19-18. Electric circuit of electric-resistance oil-pressure indicator.

a relief valve must be incorporated to prevent excessive pressure build-up. Without a relief valve, pressures could go so high at high speeds, for example, that the oil-control rings would be utterly unable to cope with the quantity of oil thrown onto the cylinder walls. The relief valve usually consists of a spring-loaded ball or plunger, which opens when the pressure exceeds the specified amount, and which then allows some of the oil to return to the oil pan. The relief valve may be incorporated into the oil pump, or it may be in a separate location (Fig. 19-14).

§279. Oil filters As we have already mentioned, one of the jobs that the oil has in the engine is to flush dirt, dust particles, and other foreign matter from the engine parts and carry it to the oil pan. There most of it settles out and drops to the bottom of the oil pan, where it remains until the oil is drained. Some of the smaller particles, however, may remain in suspension in the oil and thus could be carried back to the engine bearings and other parts. There they could embed and cause rapid wear. In order to clean these smaller particles from the oil, the oil is passed through a filter. The filter contains porous cellulose material, metal mesh, or a similar substance which passes the oil but retains most of the solid impurities in the oil. Filters are of two types: bypass filters and full-flow filters.

The bypass filter filters only part of the oil from the oil pump. That is, the line is so connected that oil is fed to the engine through one line and to the filter through another. Although only part of the oil from the pump is filtered, some oil is always going through the filter and being cleaned.

The full-flow filter (Fig. 19-15) is directly in the line from the oil pump, and all oil from the pump goes through the filter. This type of filter contains a bypass valve, which opens if the filter becomes clogged. This permits lubrication of the engine when the filter has become too clogged with impurities to pass an adequate amount of oil.

Since oil filters are effective only as long as they are sufficiently clean to pass oil, it is obvious that the filter elements should be changed periodically or before they have become completely clogged.

§280. Oil-pressure indicators The oil-pressure indicator, or oil gauge, provides the driver with an indication of the oil pressure in the engine. This gives warning if some stoppage occurs in the lubricating system that prevents delivery of oil to vital parts. Oil-pressure indicators are of two general types: pressure-expansion indicators and electrical-resistance indicators. The latter is the more commonly used. Instead of a gauge, many cars now use a warning light. The light comes on when the pressure is low, but as pressure increases to a normal value, a pressure switch opens the light circuit, and the light goes out.

1. Pressure-expansion indicator. The pressure-expansion indicator uses a hollow Bourdon (curved) tube that is fastened at one end and free at the other. The oil pressure is applied to the curved tube through an oil line from the engine and causes the tube to straighten out somewhat as pressure increases (Fig. 19-16). This movement is transmitted to a needle by linkage and gears from the end of the tube. The needle moves across the face of a dial and registers the amount of oil pressure.

2. Electrical-resistance indicators. Electrically operated oil-pressure indicators are of two types: the balancing-coil type and the bimetal-thermostat type. The balancing-coil type makes use of two separate units, the engine unit and the indicating unit (Figs. 19-17 and 19-18). The engine unit (Fig. 19-17) consists of a variable resistance and a movable contact (Fig. 19-18) that moves from one end of the resistance to the other, in accordance with varying oil pressure against a diaphragm. As pressure increases, the diaphragm moves inward, causing the contact to move along the resistance so that more resistance is placed in the circuit between the engine and indicating units. This reduces the amount of current that can flow in the circuit. The indicating unit consists of two coils that balance each other in a manner similar to electrically operated fuel gauges (§233). In fact, this type of indicator operates in the same manner as the fuel indicator, the only difference being that the fuel indicator uses a float that moves up or down as the gasoline level changes in the gasoline tank, while, in the oil-pressure indicator, changing oil pressure operates a diaphragm that causes the resistance change.

The bimetal-thermostat type of oil-pressure indicator is similar to the bimetal-thermostat fuel gauge (§233). The dash units are practically identical. The engine unit of the oil-pressure indicator, while somewhat different in appearance from the tank unit of the fuel gauge, operates in a similar manner. Varying oil pressure on a diaphragm distorts the engine-unit thermostat blade by varying amounts, and this distortion produces a like distortion in the dash-unit thermostat blade, causing the oil pressure to be registered on the dash unit.

§281. Oil changes From the day that fresh oil is put into the engine crankcase, it begins to lose its effectiveness as an engine lubricant. This gradual loss of effectiveness is largely due to the accumulation of various contaminating substances. For example, water sludge may accumulate, as noted in §283. In addition, during engine operation, carbon tends to form in the combustion chamber. Some of this carbon gets into the oil. Gum, acids, and certain lacquerlike substances may also be left by the combustion of the fuel, or may be produced in the oil itself by the high engine temperatures. In addition, the air that enters the engine (in the air-fuel mixture) carries with it a certain amount of dust. Even though the air filter is operating efficiently, it will not remove all the dust. Then, too, the engine releases fine metal particles as it wears. All these substances tend to circulate with the oil. As the mileage piles up, the oil accumulates more and more of these contaminants. Even though the engine has an oil filter, some of these contaminants will remain in the oil. Finally, after many miles of operation, the oil will be so loaded with contaminants that it is not safe to use. Unless it is drained and clean oil put in, engine wear will increase rapidly.

Modern engine oils are compounded to fight contamination. They contain certain chemicals (called *additives*) which deter corrosion and foaming and help to keep the engine clean by detergent action (§272). Yet they cannot keep the oil in good condition indefinitely. As mentioned in the previous paragraph, after many miles of service, the oil is bound to become contaminated, and it should be changed. The actual mileage varies with the type of operation.

Until about 1960, the recommendations were these: For dusty or cold-weather, start and stop driving, the oil should be changed every 500 miles or 60 days. For "average" operation, that is, short-run, start and stop service on paved roads with moderate temperatures, mixed with longer trips, the oil should be changed every 1,000 miles. For open-highway driving on paved roads, the oil should be changed every 2,000 miles.

With the development of improved lubricating oils and more efficient oil and air filters, automotive manufacturers have liberalized their recommendations as follows: With favorable operating conditions, some manufacturers recommend that the oil should be changed every two months or 4,000 miles of operation, whichever occurs first. Other manufacturers put the change intervals at every two months or 6,000 miles, whichever occurs first. All recommend, however, that for more adverse driving conditions, such as start and stop driving, cold-weather, or dusty conditions, the oil be changed more frequently.

NOTE: Automobile manufacturers recommend changing the oil (along with the oil filter) and cleaning the air filter whenever the car has been subjected to a spell of dusty driving or has encountered a dust storm. When dusty conditions are encountered in driving, the air and oil filters are likely to become clogged with dust rather quickly. This means that the oil takes on an excessive amount of dust. This dust must be removed from the engine by draining the oil, cleaning the air filters, and replacing the oil filter.

NOTE: With the universal adoption of positive-crankcase ventilation and exhaust-emission-control systems (§257), some engineers are questioning the advisability of the longer periods between oil drains.[4] Some oil engineers, for example, suggest that, as the engine accumulates mileage, the length of time between oil changes be reduced. An older engine (50,000 miles), for example, should have the oil changed every 2,000 miles, according to their suggestion.

§282. Oil consumption Oil is lost from the engine in three ways: by burning in the combustion chamber, by leakage in liquid form, and by passing out of the crankcase through the crankcase ventilating system in the form of vapor, or mist. The piston rings are designed to prevent excessive amounts of oil from working up into the combustion chambers where it will burn (§168 to 169). Excessive oil consumption is not difficult to detect, since the necessity for frequent additions of oil to maintain the proper oil level in the crankcase makes the condition obvious. The actual amount of oil consumption can be accurately checked by filling the crankcase with oil, to the correct level, operating for several hundred miles, and then measuring the additional oil that must be added to bring the oil back to the original level.

External leaks can often be detected by inspecting the seals around the oil pan, valve-cover plate, timing-gear housing, or at oil-line and oil-filter connections. Presence of excessive amounts of oil indicates leakage. Some authorities suggest that a white cloth attached to the underside of the engine during a road test is helpful in determining the location of external leaks, although this is generally an impractical procedure.

The burning of oil in the combustion chamber usually produces a bluish tinge in the exhaust gas. Oil can enter the combustion chamber in three ways: through a cracked vacuum-pump diaphragm when the car is equipped with a combination fuel and vacuum pump; through the clearance between the intake-valve guides and stems; or around the piston rings.

When the exhaust smoke has a bluish tinge and the car is equipped with a combination fuel and vacuum pump, the vacuum pump should be checked to see if the diaphragm is cracked. This can be easily done by operating the windshield wiper and then quickly accelerating the engine. If the windshield wiper stops during acceleration, it indicates that the vacuum-pump diaphragm is cracked. Oil can pass through the crack into the combustion chamber. If the windshield wiper continues to operate at normal speed during acceleration, the vacuum-pump diaphragm is not the cause of excessive oil consumption. (This test does not apply, of course, to a car without a combination fuel and vacuum pump.)

A second means by which oil can enter the combustion chamber is through clearance caused by wear between the intake-valve guides and stems. When clearance is excessive, oil will be sucked into the combustion chamber on each intake stroke (§212). The appearance of the underside of an intake valve provides a clue to the condition of its stem and the guide. If the underside of the intake valve has excessive amounts of carbon, the valve guide and possibly the valve stem are excessively worn. Part of the oil that passes around the valve remains on the underside to form carbon. When this condition is found, it is usually necessary to install valve seals or a new valve guide. A new valve may also be required.

Probably the most common cause of excessive oil consumption is passage of oil to the combustion chamber between the piston rings and the cylinder walls. This results from worn, tapered, or out-of-round cylinder walls, or from worn or carboned piston rings. In addition, when the bearings are worn, excessive amounts of oil are thrown on the cylinder walls, so that the piston rings, unable to control all of it, allow too much oil to work up into the combustion chamber.

Another factor that must be considered in any analysis of oil consumption is engine speed (§169). High speeds produce high oil temperatures and thin oil. This combination causes more oil to be thrown on the cylinder walls. The piston rings, moving at high speeds, cannot function so effectively, and more oil works up into the combustion chamber past the rings. In addition, the churning effect on the oil in the crankcase creates more

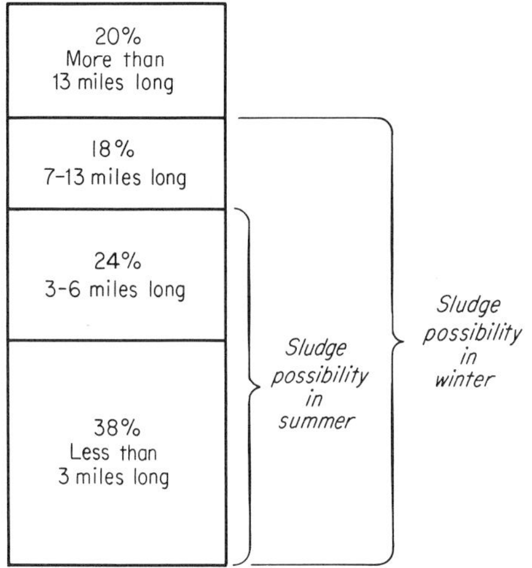

Fig. 19-19. Car-trip mileages, showing percentage of short, medium, and long trips (percentages are only approximate).

oil vapor at high speeds, and more oil is lost through the crankcase ventilation system. Tests have shown that an engine will use several times more oil at 60 mph than at 30 mph.

There is one misleading aspect of this matter of high-speed operation and oil consumption. For example, take the case of a car that is driven around town in start and stop driving, where the engine never really gets warmed up. With this condition, some oil will circulate, but the remaining oil may be diluted with water and unburned gasoline (see §257). Thus, even though some of the oil is gone, the crankcase will still measure full, due to the addition of the dilutes. However, suppose the car is now taken out onto the highway and driven at high speed. The dilution elements will boil off rapidly and the car will appear to have lost a quart or two of oil in 100 miles or less.

§283. Water-sludge formation As already mentioned in §257 and 261, water will form sludge when mixed with the oil in the engine crankcase. Sludge is a thick, creamy, black substance that can clog oil screens, filters, and lines, thus preventing normal circulation of lubricating oil to the engine parts. This can result in engine failure from oil starvation.

1. How sludge forms. Water collects in the crankcase in two ways. (1) Water is one of the products formed during combustion. Hydrogen in the fuel unites with oxygen in the air to form H_2O, or water. Most of this water is exhausted from the engine as vapor in the exhaust gases. But when the engine is cold, some of it condenses on the cold engine parts. It then works its way past the piston rings and drops into the crankcase. (2) Another way that water gets into the crankcase is through the crankcase ventilating system. When the engine is cold, moisture in the air drawn through the crankcase by the ventilating system is apt to condense on the cold engine parts and thus stay in the crankcase.

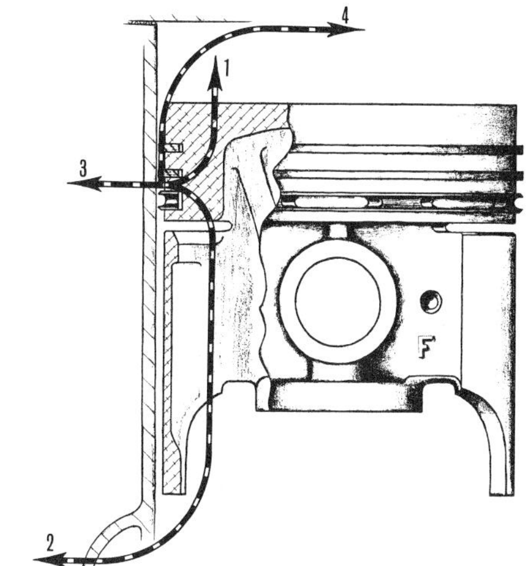

Fig. 19-20. Four paths by which blow-by may be diverted so it does not enter the crankcase.

The water that accumulates is churned up with the lubricating oil by the action of the moving parts, particularly the crankshaft. In effect, the crankshaft is a super egg beater that whips the oil and water together to form the thick, black, mayonnaiselike "goo" called *water sludge.* The black color comes from dirt and carbon in the oil.

2. Sludge-forming operation. If you drive your car for fairly long distances each time you start it, you will have little trouble with water sludge. It is true that water will collect in the crankcase for the first few miles, before the engine warms

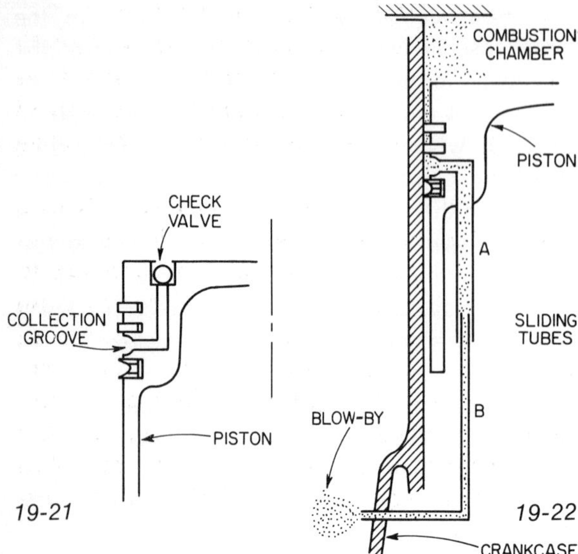

Fig. 19-21. One method of diverting blow-by. A collecting groove in the piston collects blow-by and returns it to the combustion chamber via a check valve, when the power stroke is completed.

Fig. 19-22. A method of diverting blow-by in which a blow-by tube connected to a collecting groove in the piston conducts blow-by to the outside of the engine.

Fig. 19-23. A method of diverting blow-by which uses a blow-by passage in the piston that bypasses the oil-control ring. An opening in the cylinder wall allows the blow-by to discharge into the atmosphere.

Fig. 19-24. A method of diverting blow-by which uses a collection groove and compression rings that will allow gas to flow upward but not downward. The collection groove is large enough to hold considerable blow-by, and, when the power stroke is finished, the blow-by passes upward by the compression rings into the combustion chamber.

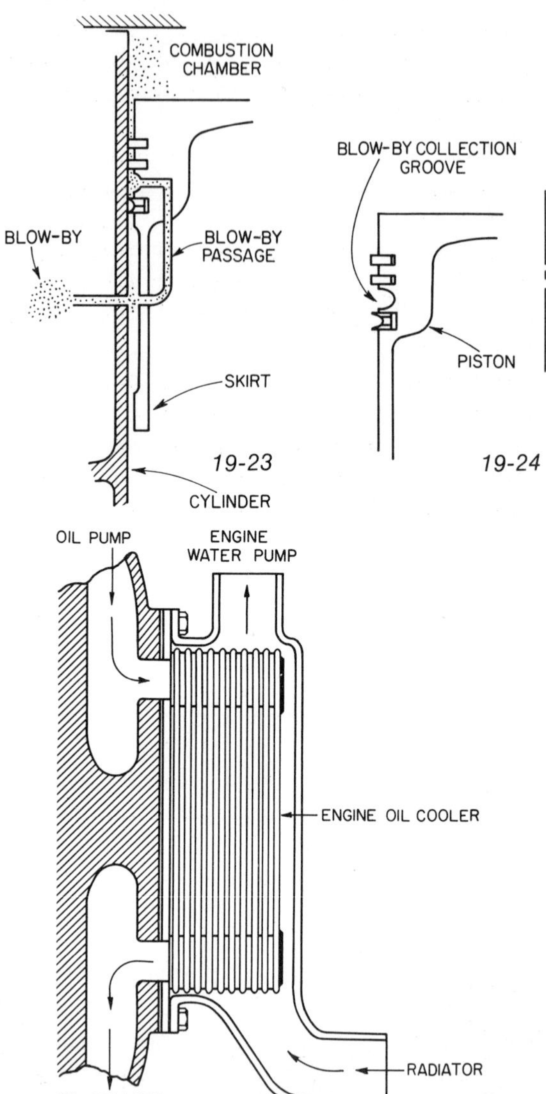

Fig. 19-25. Integral engine oil cooler. (*Harrison Radiator Division of General Motors Corporation*)

up. But as soon as the engine reaches operating temperature, the water evaporates and is cleared from the crankcase by the crankcase ventilator. However, if you drive your car only a few miles each time you start it and allow it to cool off between trips, then the engine will not get warm enough to throw off the water it has collected in the crankcase. With each short trip, more water collects. And as the water collects, it is whipped with the oil into water sludge.

Note that it is the short-trip, start and stop type of operation that produces sludge, and this type of operation is far more common than you might think. Studies of car operation in the United

States have shown that about 38 percent of all trips are less than 3 miles in length. Another 24 percent are from 3 to 6 miles long. An additional 18 percent are from 7 to 13 miles long, and only 20 percent are more than 13 miles in length (see Fig. 19-19).

3. Getting rid of water. As we mentioned, if the car is driven long enough, the engine will warm up, and the water will be evaporated and carried out of the crankcase by the ventilating system. The number of miles required for this varies from car to car, and also with the weather. During winter months, the engine is colder and takes longer (more miles) to warm up. Studies have shown that during the summer it takes from 3 to 6 miles, on the average, for the engine to reach operating temperature and begin to rid itself of water. But during the winter it takes about 14 miles. When you compare these figures with the average length of trips, as noted in the previous paragraph, you can see that as many as 60 percent of car trips are too short in summer to rid the engine of water. In winter as many as 80 percent of car trips are too short to rid the engine of water (Fig. 19-19).

4. Preventing sludge accumulations. Sludge can lead to engine failure by blocking oil circulation to engine parts. Thus, it is important to prevent accumulation of sufficient sludge to cause poor oil circulation. One way of doing this, as noted above, is to take longer trips in your car. Another way is to drain the crankcase oil frequently. With frequent oil drains, the sludge never has a chance to accumulate in such quantities as to cause engine failure. (Oil changes are discussed in §281.)

§284. Blow-by diversion If a means were found

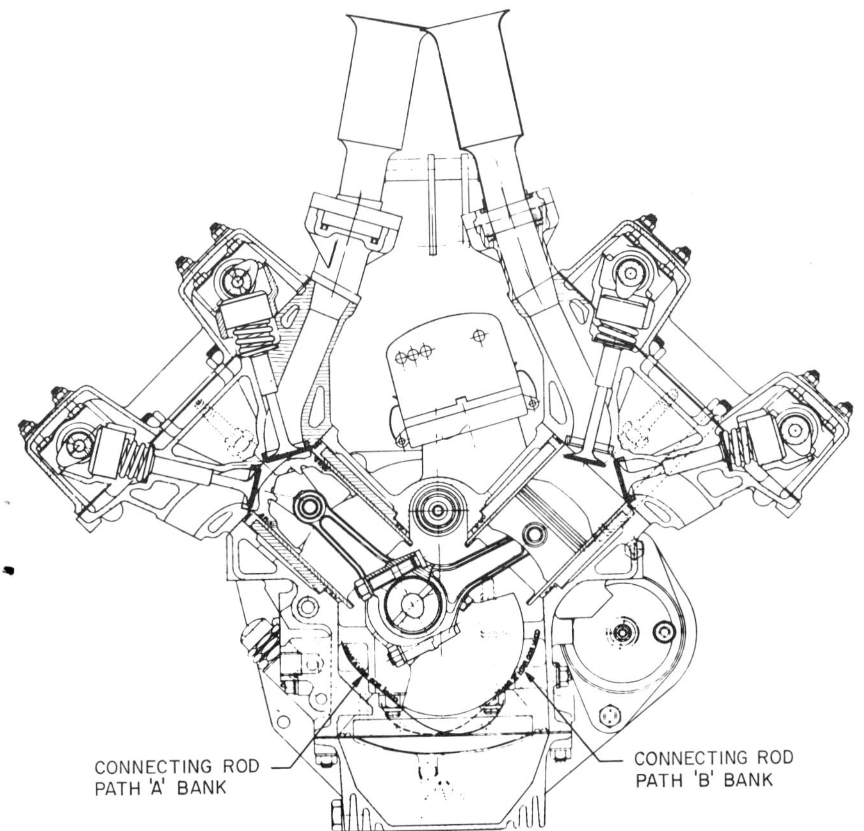

Fig. 19-26. Installation of a copper gauze screen below the connecting rod path to reduce oil churning. (*Coventry Climax Limited*)

to prevent blow-by from passing into the crankcase, then sludge formation would be greatly reduced.[5] Engineers have devised four experimental methods of diverting blow-by so it does not get down into the crankcase (Fig. 19-20): Blow-by can be diverted through a passage back into the combustion chamber, to the outside of the engine via an isolated crankcase passage, to the outside of the engine via a passage through the cylinder wall, or by a passage from below the compression rings back into the combustion chamber. Figures 19-21 to 19-24 illustrate the four methods. These are basically experimental methods and are not in actual use in automotive engines today.

§285. Lubricating-system design Lubricating-system design is really engine design because the lubricating system is such an integral part of the engine. As we have seen in past chapters, engine designers, as they study bearings, valves, pistons, piston rings, crankshafts, and other moving parts, spend a great deal of time in providing for the flow of adequate amounts of oil to all moving surfaces. In the case of the piston rings and cylinder walls, as well as intake-valve stems and guides, they then must make sure that excessive amounts of oil do not get into the combustion chambers.

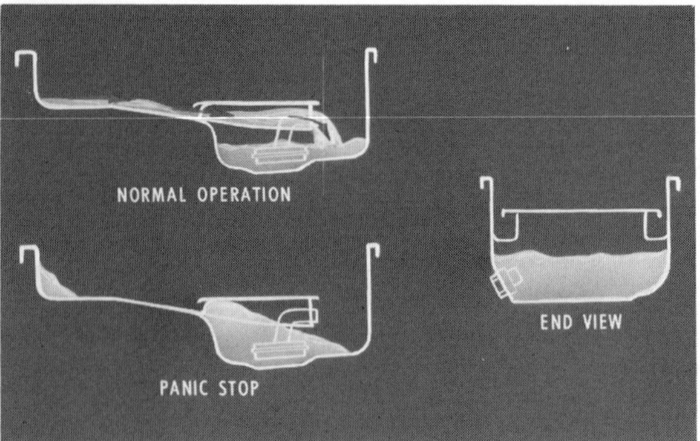

Fig. 19-27. Sectional views of the oil pan of the Turbo-Jet engine. At top, during normal operation, the oil from the forward part of the engine drains down into the sump. The slosh baffle prevents the oil from being thrown forward during a panic stop, as shown at lower left. At right, adding troughs permits fast drainback even at high engine speeds. (*Chevrolet Motor Division of General Motors Corporation*)

High-performance and special-duty engines may require special equipment or design modifications in the lubricating system. For example, some of these engines are equipped with a special oil cooler which is much like the cooling-system radiator. Oil passes through this radiator and is thereby cooled. Figure 19-25 shows an engine oil cooler that is positioned in the cooling system in a special passage from the radiator to the water pump.

1. *Oil-pan capacity.* Most passenger-car engines have oil pans that will hold about four quarts of oil. The oil-pan capacity is often dictated by the amount of ground clearance available below the engine. In some specialty engines, 4 quarts will not be enough. For example, a high-performance engine will be pumping oil so rapidly at high speed that the drain-back from the cylinder heads might not keep pace. A considerable portion of the oil reserve could therefore be concentrated in the upper part of the engine, and, under some circumstances, this could cause some bearings in the lower part to be oil starved. For this reason, high-performance engines may be equipped with larger-capacity oil pans or oil reservoirs.

2. *Oil churning.* Oil churning is another problem that may be encountered in high-performance engines. Of course, there is always some oil churning in the crankcase of the engine because of the rotation of the crankshaft and the motion of the connecting rods and pistons. In high-speed engines, however, a considerable amount of oil may be in motion in the crankcase at high engine speeds, and this can cause a significant loss of power. For example, when Coventry Climax engineers were developing their 1.5-liter V-8 racing engine, they had considerable trouble with oil churning. They lowered the oil sump 2 inches and found this gave them a sizeable power gain. The lowered sump greatly reduced the oil churning. Various baffles of different sizes and shapes were tried, also, but these gave little improvement. Finally, they tried a copper-gauze screen in the

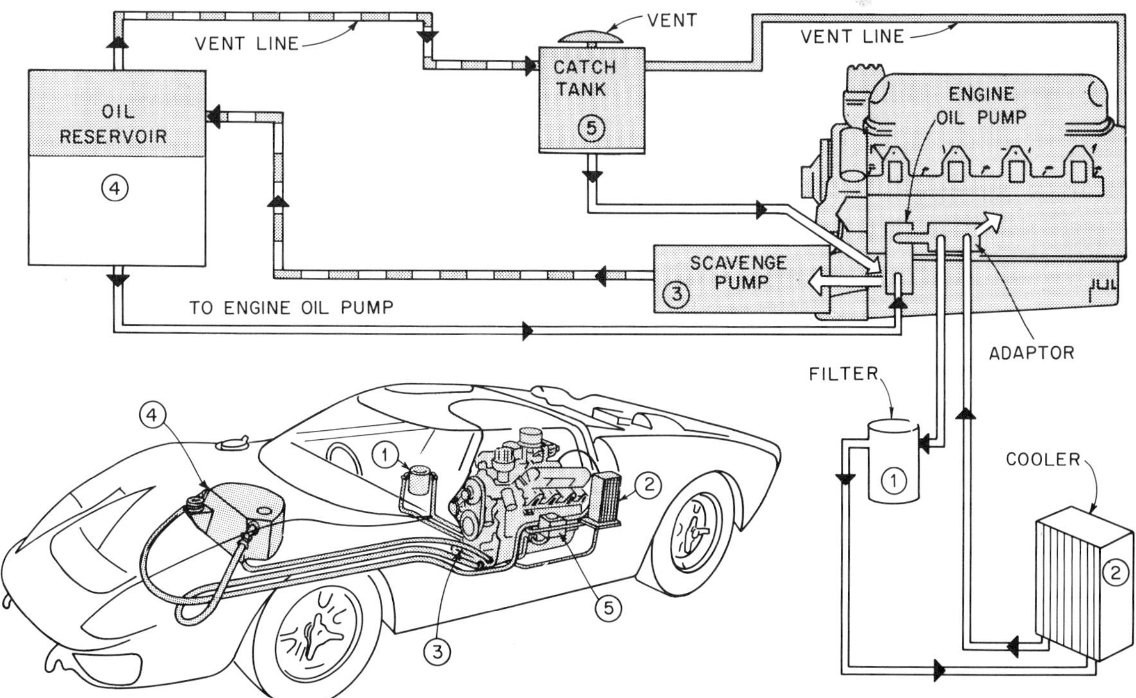

Fig. 19-28. Lubricating system for a high-performance engine—the Mark II-427 GT engine. (*Ford Motor Company*)

crankcase, shaped so it followed the path of the connecting rod big ends (Fig. 19-26). The screen acts as a one-way valve, in effect, allowing the oil to drain downward into the oil sump, but protecting the oil from the windage effects of the rotating components. With the oil screen in place, engineers then found they could raise the oil sump again to within 5/8 inch of the original position, thus regaining the ground clearance they needed, without significant loss of power.

3. *Oil pooling.* A different sort of problem was encountered by Chevrolet engineers during the early phases of their Turbo-Jet engine development program. They found that, at 5,000 rpm (revolutions per minute) and above, with maximum bearing clearances throughout the engine and only 3 quarts of oil in the engine, some bearings would be oil starved. This was found to be caused by the oil pooling ahead of the front slosh baffle which is used to keep the oil in the sump during panic stops (Fig. 19-27). Without this baffle, most of the oil would be thrown forward during panic stops, and there would not be enough oil left in the sump for the oil pump to work on. Thus, air would get into the oil lines and bearings throughout the engine would be temporarily oil starved. This could cause bearing failure. The oil baffle prevents this by holding most of the oil in the sump during panic stops, as shown to the lower left in Fig. 19-27. However, as noted above, this same baffle was preventing the oil from draining back into the sump rapidly enough at high speed. The engineers solved this problem by modifying the slosh baffle to include two troughs, one on each side. These troughs significantly improved drain-back into the sump and relieved the threat of oil starvation at high engine speeds.

4. *High-performance-engine lubricating systems.* Figure 19-28 illustrates the lubricating system used in the Ford Mark II-427 GT vehicle. This is a high-performance vehicle that has won impressive victories in important races. It was not possible, because of low ground clearances, to increase the size of the oil pan sufficiently to

handle the oil requirements. Therefore, a dry-sump system was substituted for the standard oil-pan system. A scavenge pump removes oil from the crankcase and delivers it to the oil reservoir. The oil reservoir has a vent line to a catch tank which deaerates (removes air from) the oil. The system also has a filter and an oil cooler, as shown.

5. *Cold-weather starts.* We have mentioned previously the problem of start-up wear (rapid wear that takes place in a cold engine after first starting, §271) and the accumulation of water sludge in the crankcase (§283). These conditions are difficult to control in start and stop driving, but they can be ameliorated to some extent by an engine design that has small water jackets for rapid engine warm-up. It takes so many Btu's (British thermal units) to warm the engine, and these Btu's accumulate only as the engine runs. In particularly adverse situations, as in frigid climates where the engine must be started at below-zero temperatures, some vehicle operators make provision for heating the engine. Sometimes this is done with a built-in heating element, located in the crankcase, that can be plugged in to a 110-volt circuit during the night. Other times it may be no more than an electric heater placed in front of the car radiator or under the engine. In either case, starting is made much easier because the engine oil and engine are already warm. In addition, because the engine is already warm, it reaches operating temperature much more quickly and start-up wear is thereby greatly reduced.

NOTE: Another factor here is that a warm battery can produce higher cranking current so the engine is cranked faster.

6. *Locating causes of excessive oil consumption.* A relatively new method of tracking down excessive oil consumption in new engines was announced recently. The test involves adding a minute quantity of radioactive bromine-82 to the engine oil, and then collecting samples of the exhaust gas from various cylinders (for example, from the two banks of a V-8 engine). The amount of radioactivity detected in the exhaust-gas samples is a measure of how much oil is being consumed. This is a useful test on the engine production line, and Buick (who first announced the test) is using it to check engines as they come off the end of the production line. The test is not designed to check all engines, but just samples—1 in every 200, for example. It is simply an additional quality check to assure that something hasn't gone wrong up the line somewhere.

SUMMARY

The primary purpose of the engine lubricating system is to provide a flow of lubricating oil to all engine parts so as to reduce possible wear and friction. However, the oil also removes heat from engine parts, absorbs shocks between bearings and other engine parts, forms a seal between piston rings and cylinder walls, and helps keep engines clean by carrying away dirt and other foreign matter.

Several additives are used in engine lubricating oil to give the oil certain desirable properties. These include pour-point depressants, detergent dispersants, extreme-pressure agents, viscosity-index improvers, and agents to inhibit oxidation, corrosion, rust, and foam.

Service ratings of oil are MS, MM, ML, and, for diesel-engine oils, DS and DG.

Engine oil must be tested in many ways to determine its ability to function satisfactorily under various engine conditions. These tests may be divided into two catagories: laboratory tests and road tests.

There are three types of lubricating systems for automotive engines: splash systems, pressure-feed systems, and combination splash and pressure-feed systems. The typical lubricating system contains an oil pump, oil passages, to all moving engine parts, a pressure relief valve, and an oil filter. Many cars have a pressure indicator which shows the pressure in the system and thus indicates its performance.

While the improved filters and lubricating oils of today have reduced the frequency of oil changes, it is still necessary to change the engine oil periodically.

Oil may be lost from the engine in three ways: burning in the combustion chamber, leakage in liquid form, and passing out of the crankcase in the form of vapor or mist.

Sludge formation in the crankcase can be very harmful to the engine. Sludge forms more readily if the car is used in short-trip, start and stop driving. Some work has been done on blow-by diversion, which would reduce sludge formation, particularly during cold-engine operation.

REFERENCES

1. Watson, R. D., From Crude Oil to Lube Oil—Refining Techniques, SAE (Society of Automotive Engineers), special publication SP-237, 1962.

2. Tyminski, R., What a Fleet Manager Needs to Know About Motor Oils and Lubricants, Standard Oil Company of Ohio (paper).

3. Kalil, P., From Crude Oil to Lube Oil—Development and Tests, SAE (Society of Automotive Engineers), special publication SP-237, 1962.

4. Colyer, C. C., L. J. Aliman, and R. M. Ladevich, Balanced Motor Oils for 1968 Engines, SAE (Society of Automotive Engineers) 670499, 1967 (paper).

5. Meckel, N. T., J. V. Moffitt, and R. D. Quillian, Jr., Cleaner Crankcase with Blowby Diversion, SAE (Society of Automotive Engineers) 801B, 1964 (paper).

QUESTIONS

1. Name and describe six functions of the oil in the engine.

2. Define viscosity, particularly as the term applies to engine lubricating oil.

3. What are the viscosity ratings of engine oil?

4. What is meant by viscosity index?

5. What is the purpose of pour-point depressants?

6. What is the purpose of oxidation inhibitors, and why are they important in engine oil?

7. Why are foaming inhibitors important in engine oil?

8. Explain the purpose and action of detergent dispersants in engine oil.

9. Describe the various laboratory tests given to oil.

10. Describe the road tests given to engine oil.

11. Describe various automotive lubricants. What are EP lubricants?

12. Describe a typical lubricating system for a modern engine, and explain the path of oil flow to the various engine parts.

13. What are two methods of lubricating the rocker arms and upper end of the push rods and valve stems?

14. Explain how the oil-pressure indicator works.

15. Explain why engine oil must be changed periodically.

16. Explain the three basic ways that oil is lost from the engine.

17. Describe water-sludge formation and its relationship to the type of engine operation.

18. Describe the purpose of blow-by diversion, and discuss some of the experimental methods which have been tried.

19. Discuss some of the considerations of lubricating-system design.

Ignition System

CHAPTER **20**

This chapter discusses the function, design, and operation of the various types of ignition systems that are currently in use in automotive engines, or that are proposed for the future.

§286. Function of ignition system The ignition system has the job of supplying high-voltage surges to the spark plugs in the engine cylinders.

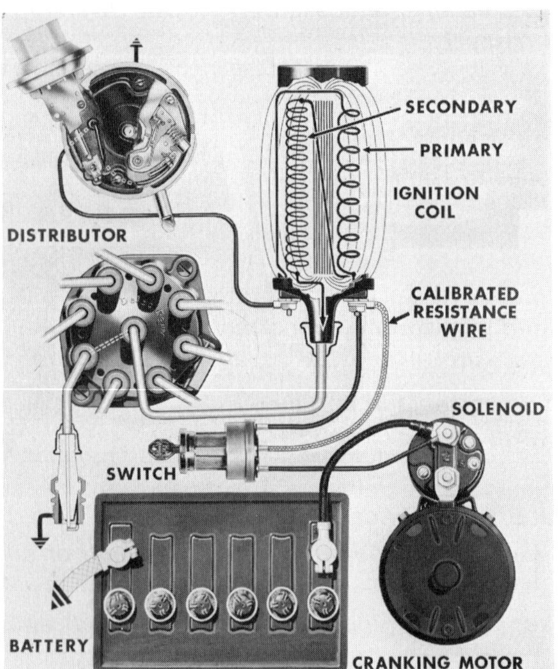

Fig. 20-1. Typical ignition system. It consists of the battery (source of power), ignition switch, ignition coil (shown schematically), distributor (shown in top view with its cap removed and placed below it), spark plugs (one shown in sectional view), and wiring. The coil is shown schematically, with magnetic lines of force indicated. (*Delco-Remy Division of General Motors Corporation*)

These high-voltage surges must be supplied at the exact instant that they are needed. That is, a surge must come along just as the piston nears TDC (top dead center) on the compression stroke. The surge then produces the spark that ignites the compressed air-fuel mixture.

The ignition system consists of the battery, switch, ignition distributor, ignition coil, wiring, and spark plugs (Fig. 20-1). The distributor is two separate devices in one—a fast-acting switch and a distributing mechanism. It is driven by gearing from the camshaft of the engine (Figs. 19-10 and 19-11). Briefly, this is how the distributor in a typical ignition system operates. The distributor

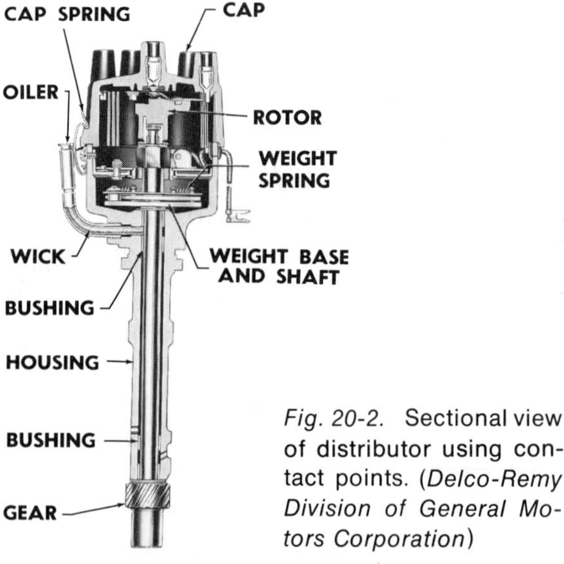

Fig. 20-2. Sectional view of distributor using contact points. (*Delco-Remy Division of General Motors Corporation*)

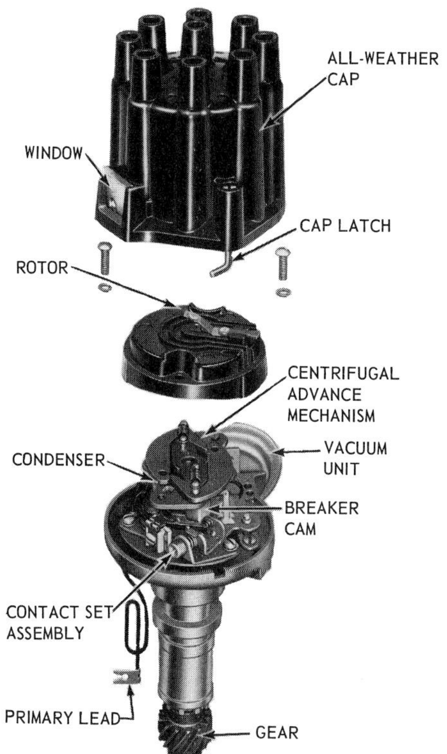

Fig. 20-3. Partial disassembled view of distributor using contact points. (*Delco-Remy Division of General Motors Corporation*)

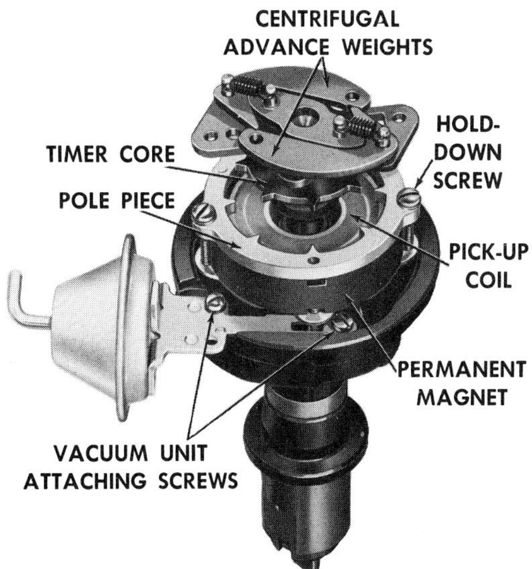

Fig. 20-4. Partial disassembled view of distributor with magnetic pick-up. (*Delco-Remy Division of General Motors Corporation*)

shaft rotates. A cam on the upper end of the shaft, as it rotates, causes contact points to close and open. When the points are closed, the ignition coil is connected to the battery. This loads the coil with electric (electromagnetic) energy. Then, when the points are opened (as the cam continues to rotate), this energy is unloaded from the coil in the form of a high-voltage surge. The surge is directed to the proper spark plug (in cylinder ready for firing) by the distributor cap and rotor (and ignition wiring), in a manner that is explained below.

Some ignition systems use transistors to reduce the electric-current load on the distributor contact points. Other ignition systems do not have contact points in the distributor, but instead use a combination of transistors and a magnetic pick-up in the distributor. These are discussed in fol-following articles.

§287. Ignition distributor As already noted, the ignition distributor does two jobs: it closes and opens the coil primary circuit, and it distributes the resulting high-voltage surges from the coil secondary to the engine spark plugs. Actually, there are two basic types of distributors: the type which uses contact points to close and open the coil primary circuit, and the type (without contact points) which uses a magnetic pick-up and a transistor-control unit to interrupt the current flow to the coil primary winding.

1. Distributor with contact points. The distributor using contact points (Figs. 20-2 and 20-3) consists of a housing, a drive shaft with breaker cam and advance mechanism, a breaker plate with contact points and condenser, a rotor, and a cap. The shaft is usually driven by the engine camshaft through spiral gears, and it rotates at one-half crankshaft speed. Usually, the distributor drive shaft is coupled with a shaft that drives the oil pump.

Rotation of the shaft and breaker cam causes the distributor contact points to open and close. The breaker cam usually has the same number of lobes as there are cylinders in the engine.* It rotates at half crankshaft speed, and the contact points close and open once for each cylinder with every breaker-cam rotation. Thus, for each cylinder one high-voltage surge is produced by the coil every two crankshaft revolutions. This ignites the air-fuel mixture compressed in each cylinder during every other crankshaft revolution.

The rotor rotates with the breaker cam on which it is mounted. As it does so, a metal spring and a segment on the rotor connect the center terminal of the cap with each outside terminal in turn, so that the high-voltage surges from the coil are directed, first to one spark plug, and then to another, and so on, according to the firing order.

2. Transistorized, no-contact ignition system.[1,2] With the cap on, the distributor for this system looks the same as the distributor using contact points. However, when the caps are removed, the difference between the two is apparent. Figure 20-4 shows the magnetic pick-up (or pulse) distributor with the cap and rotor removed. Figure 20-5 is a diagram of the ignition circuit. The transistorized pulse amplifier is connected between the ignition coil primary and the battery (through the ignition switch). It permits battery current to flow to the coil primary winding, and it interrupts this flow on signals from the distributor. This action is similar to what happens when the points close and open in the contact-point distributor.

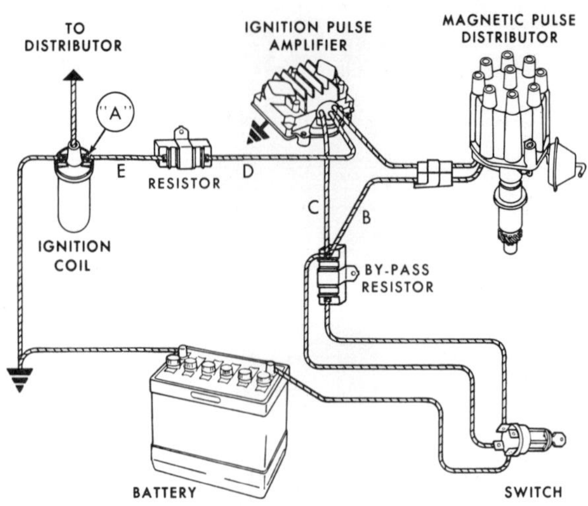

Fig. 20-5. Wiring diagram of ignition system using magnetic-pulse distributor and transistor-control unit. (*Delco-Remy Division of General Motors Corporation*)

The distributor is mounted and driven in the same manner as in other distributors. The magnetic pick-up (Fig. 20-4), which provides the signals to the amplifier, contains a permanent magnet on top of which is mounted a pole piece. The pole piece has a series of teeth pointing inward. There are the same number of teeth as there are cylinders in the engine. Inside the permanent magnet is a pick-up coil, containing many turns of wire. All these parts are assembled together over the main bearing of the distributor housing, and the assembly is attached to a vacuum unit which provides vacuum advance (§300).

The timer core, made of iron, is assembled on the distributor shaft through the centrifugal-advance mechanism and rotates with the shaft. It has the same number of teeth as there are cylinders in the engine. When the engine is operating and the distributor shaft is rotating, the timer-core teeth and the pole-piece teeth align eight times for every shaft rotation (for an eight-cylinder

* On some applications, the breaker cam has only one-half as many lobes as engine cylinders, but there are two sets of contact points that are arranged to close and open alternately. This produces the same effect as the breaker-cam and contact-point arrangement discussed above.

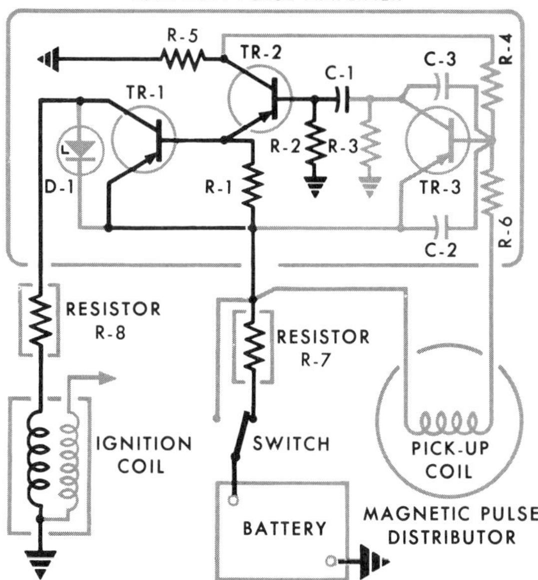

Fig. 20-6. Current flow (heavy lines) through ignition-pulse amplifier during time that ignition coil primary is being furnished with current from battery. (*Delco-Remy Division of General Motors Corporation*)

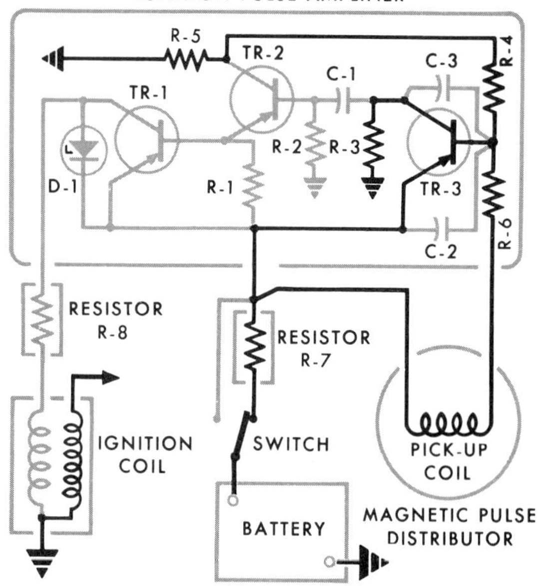

Fig. 20-7. Flow of current (heavy lines) through ignition-pulse amplifier when pick-up coil in distributor sends signal (pulse of current) to control unit. Transistors TR-2 and TR-3 have "turned off" to interrupt the flow of current to the ignition coil primary. The secondary, therefore, discharges high-voltage surge. (*Delco-Remy Division of General Motors Corporation*)

engine). This compares with the eight times that the points open (on an eight-cylinder engine) for every shaft revolution in the contact-point distributor. Each time the teeth align, a magnetic path is established through the pick-up coil; that is, magnetic lines of force from the permanent magnet cut through the turns of wire in the pick-up coil. Further shaft rotation moves the teeth apart so that the magnetic path is opened and the magnetic field quickly collapses. When this happens, a voltage is induced in the coil, and this sends a signal, or pulse of current, to the amplifier. This produces the same effect in the primary circuit as the opening of contact points.

Before the pick-up coil sends its signal to the amplifier, the conditions are as shown in Fig. 20-6 in the circuit. That is, current is flowing from the battery, through resistor R-7 and through the control unit (via R-1 and transistor TR-1) to the ignition oil primary winding.

But when the signal arrives in the amplifier from the pick-up coil, it causes transistor TR-3 to become conductive. The reason for this is that the pulse of current from the pick-up coil supplies the TR-3 transistor base with current carriers. When this happens, current flows as shown in Fig. 20-7. With TR-3 conductive, current carriers are drained away from the base of TR-2 so that TR-2 becomes a nonconductor. With no current flowing through TR-2 there is a reduced voltage drop across resistor R-1, and the base of TR-1 becomes approximately the same voltage as the lower TR-1 connection. Thus, there are no current carriers at the TR-1 base—the TR-1 transistor now becomes, in effect, a diode—and current stops flowing from the battery through TR-1 to the coil primary winding.

With the sudden stoppage of current to the ignition-coil primary winding, the magnetic field in the ignition coil collapses, inducing a high voltage in the ignition-coil secondary winding.

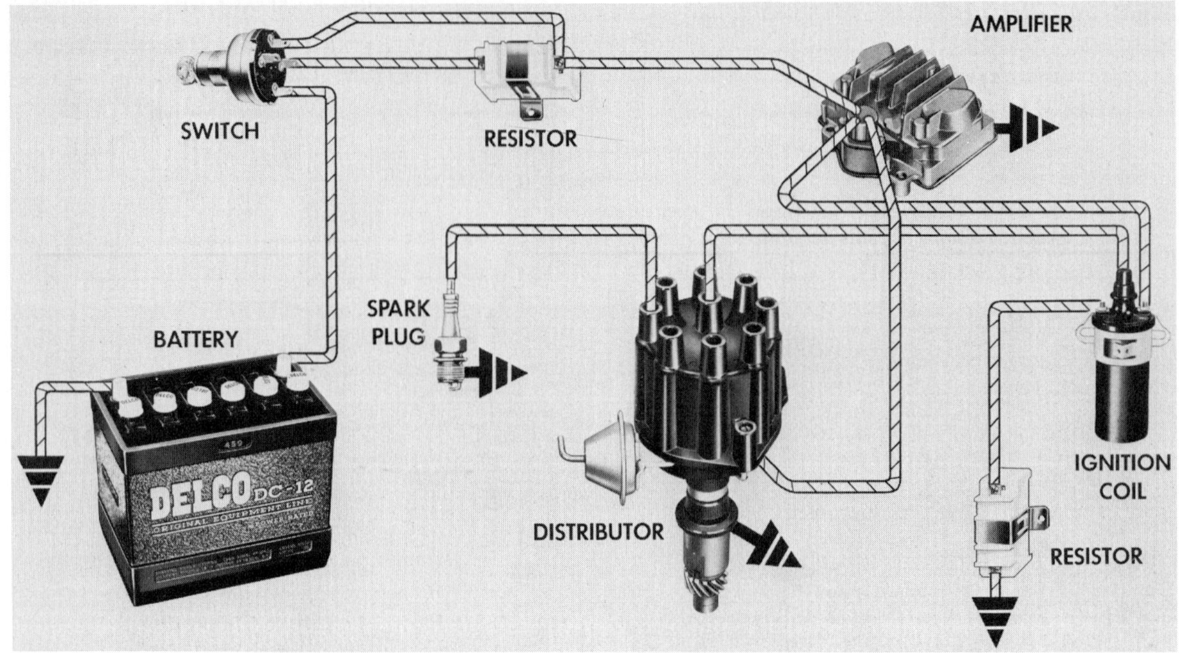

Fig. 20-8. Schematic view of an ignition system, using a distributor with contact points and a transistorized amplifier. (*Delco-Remy Division of General Motors Corporation*)

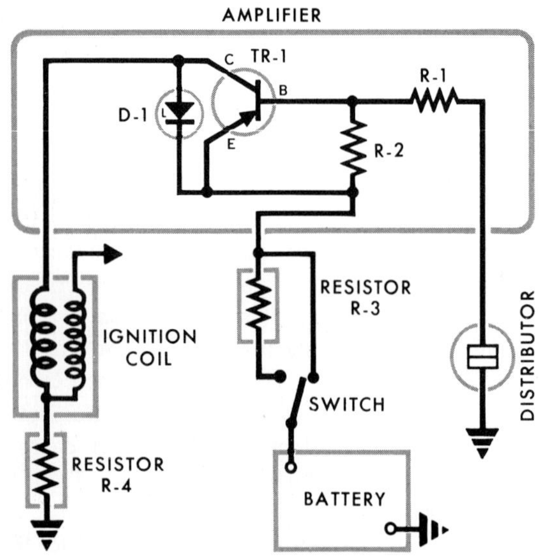

Fig. 20-9. Wiring circuit of the ignition coil and amplifier. (*Delco-Remy Division of General Motors Corporation*)

This high-voltage surge is delivered to the correct spark plug (the one ready to fire) by the distributor rotor and cap and the secondary wiring, exactly as for the distributor with contact points.

3. Distributor with contact points and transistorized amplifier. Figure 20-8 shows the wiring circuit of an ignition system using distributor contact points and a transistorized amplifier. The internal wiring circuit is shown schematically in Fig. 20-9.

When the ignition switch is turned on with the contact points closed, current enters the amplifier and flows through resistor R-2, transistor TR-1, resistor R-1, the distributor contact points, and the coil primary and resistor R-4 to ground. When the contact points are opened, this interrupts the flow of current through the emitter-base of the transistor (or E and B). This "shuts off" the emmiter-collector current (E and C). The flow of current through the coil primary winding therefore drops off sharply, and high voltage is induced in the coil secondary. The item marked "D-1" in Fig. 20-9 is a diode that protects the

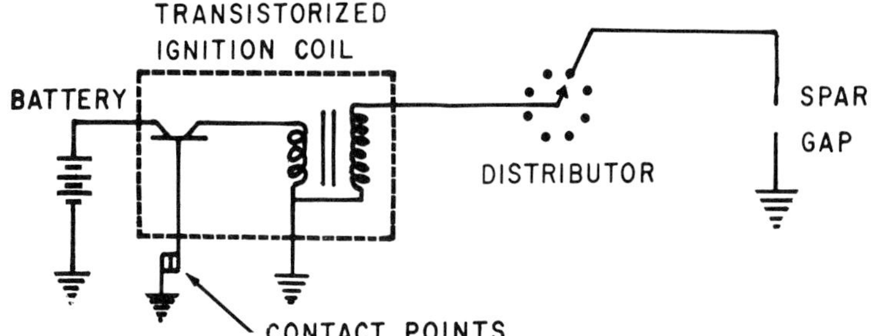

Fig. 20-10. Simplified schematic drawing of a transistorized ignition system.

transistor by limiting the size of transient voltages that might appear in the primary circuit.

The manufacturer claims two advantages for this system. Only a small current is carried through the distributor contact points so they last a long time. Secondly, a high current can be carried through the transistor and through the primary winding of the ignition coil. This means a higher secondary voltage and therefore better engine performance, especially at high speeds.

4. Distributor with contact points and transistorized coil. The wiring circuit of a distributor with contact points used with a transistorized ignition coil is shown in Fig. 20-10. The contact points are connected between the transistor base and the grounded side of the circuit. When the points are closed, the base is electrically connected to ground. Current carriers can now appear at the base, and current can flow through the coil primary winding. A magnetic field builds up. When the contacts are opened, current carriers no longer are available at the transistor base. Current stops flowing through the transistor, the magnetic field in the coil collapses, and a spark appears at a spark-plug gap. Note that only a small current flows through the contact points. The points therefore last a long time, since they are not required to break the coil primary circuit—the transistor does that.

§288. Construction of the ignition coil The ignition coil contains two windings (Fig. 20-11). It has a primary winding of a few hundred turns of relatively heavy wire and a secondary winding of many thousand turns of a very fine wire. Both are wound on the same core, the primary winding usually being wound on the outside of the secondary winding. The winding is sealed into a metal case to which a top made of insulating material is attached. Coil terminals are set into the top. The winding is immersed in insulating compound or oil.

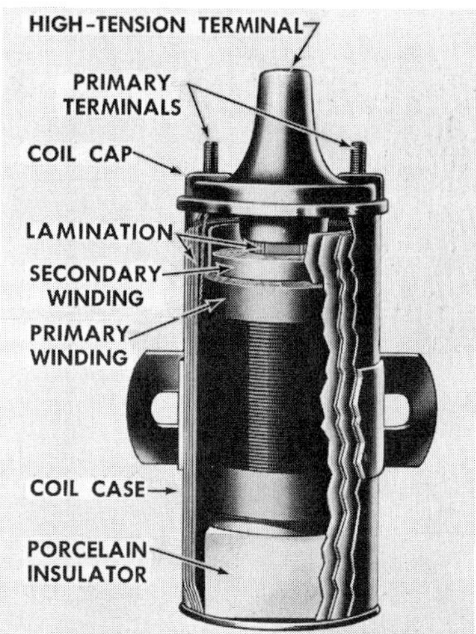

Fig. 20-11. Cutaway of an ignition coil. (*Delco-Remy Division of General Motors Corporation*)

§289. Mutual and self-induction in ignition coil The ignition coil is a type of transformer that uses mutual induction to produce high voltage in the coil secondary winding. The voltage produced is roughly in proportion to the ratio of the number of turns in the primary and secondary windings. The sequence of actions leading up to the production of the high voltage in the secondary winding is as follows: First, the contact points in the distributor close so that current begins to flow in the primary winding, and a magnetic field builds up around the winding. Self-induction prevents this current from peaking instantly (§290). When the contact points separate, the current stops flowing and the magnetic field collapses. This collapse induces a momentary voltage in the primary winding of more than 200 volts. At the same time, the magnetic-field collapse also produces

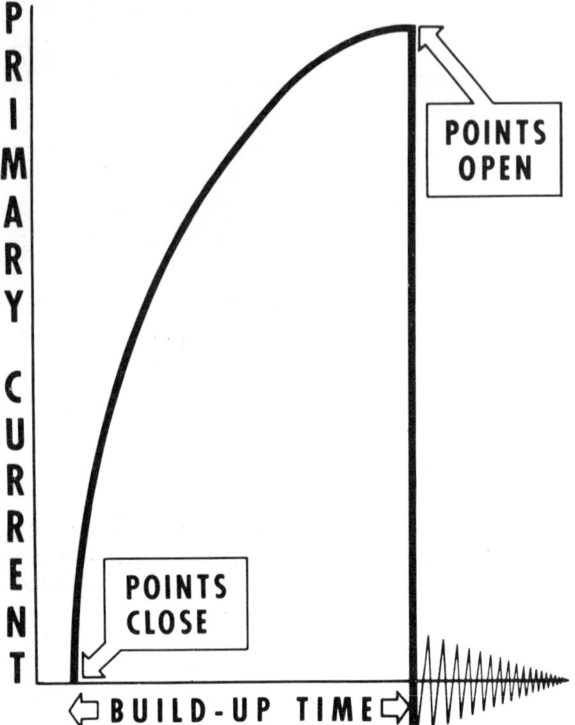

Fig. 20-12. Graph, showing coil build-up time. The distributor contact points are so arranged that as the current approaches its maximum, as determined by the primary resistance, the points open. At higher speeds, the points remain closed a shorter interval, so that build-up time is shortened.

in the secondary winding the high voltage needed to produce the spark at the spark-plug gap in the combustion chamber.

§290. Action in primary winding during build-up Self-induction (which produces a countervoltage) prevents the current from building up to a peak instantly when the primary winding is connected to the battery through the contact points. It takes a small fraction of a second—a few milliseconds—for the build-up to be completed (Fig. 20-12). Actually, during high-speed operation, the time interval between point closing and point opening is so short that the peak never occurs. But there is still sufficient build-up to produce adequate secondary voltage.

§291. Action in the secondary winding during build-up As the magnetic field builds up in the primary winding, it induces not only a countervoltage in the primary winding, but also a voltage in the secondary winding. This voltage, however, does not increase to a value sufficient to cause any action in the secondary side of the ignition system. In order for any activity to take place in the secondary winding, the voltage must increase to several thousand volts—enough to cause a spark to jump the spark-plug gap. During the build-up time, the secondary voltage does not reach a very high value. But when current stops flowing in the primary winding, a series of events begins that does produce a high voltage in the secondary winding.

§292. Self-induction in primary winding after current stops During the time that current flows from the battery through the primary winding, the coil is being "loaded" with energy in the form of magnetic lines of force. When the current stops flowing, the magnetic field starts to collapse. The collapsing magnetism induces current in the same direction as that in which it originally flowed from the battery. This is self-induction. Regardless of whether the magnetic field is building up or collapsing, it induces a voltage (or countervoltage) that opposes any change in the amount of current or magnetic strength. While the coil is being "loaded," the battery voltage must overcome this countervoltage in order to start the current flowing and bring it up to its maximum as determined by the resistance of the winding.

Also, when the battery is disconnected, the self-induction of the winding attempts to keep the current flowing. In the transistor-controlled system, the transistor quickly brings the current flow to a stop so that a rapid magnetic collapse and a high secondary voltage result. In the system using distributor contact points, a different situation exists. The increasing voltage (in the primary as well as the secondary winding) would quickly build up to a value sufficient to cause an arc to form across the contact points as they began to separate from each other, provided that some means of preventing this were not used. Contact points are mechanically operated; they cannot separate rapidly enough or far enough in the time allowable to prevent an arc. The instant the points separate (no more than $^1/_{1,000,000}$ inch) current stops flowing, and a partial collapse of the magnetism takes place. This induces enough voltage to push current across the gap between the points. Without some means of preventing this arc, most of the energy in the coil (stored in the form of magnetism) would be converted into current that would flow across the points. This would burn the points. Also, it would prevent the coil secondary winding from producing the high-voltage surge needed to fire the spark plug and ignite the mixture of vaporized gasoline and air in the cylinder.

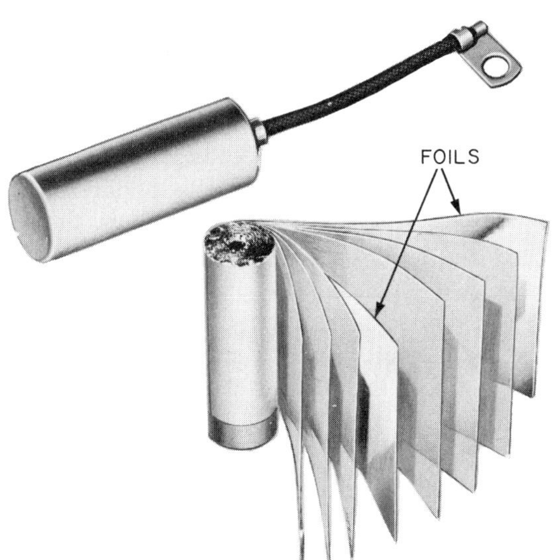

Fig. 20-13. Condenser assembled and with the winding partly unwound.

§293. Condenser action On ignition systems with distributor contact points, a condenser (also called a capacitor) is used to prevent this action. Thus, the ignition coil can release its energy through the secondary winding in the form of a high-voltage surge. The condenser is made up of two plates which are electrically insulated from each other (Fig. 20-13). Each plate is connected to a lead. The plates in an automotive-ignition condenser are two long, narrow strips of lead or aluminum foil, insulated from each other with special condenser paper and wrapped on an arbor to form a winding. One plate is connected to the condenser case, the other to the condenser lead. The winding is impregnated in oily or waxy substances to improve the insulating properties of the condenser paper.

The condenser is connected across the contact points. When the points begin to open, the condenser momentarily provides a place for the current (or electrons) to flow. Current flows into the condenser, charging it, instead of jumping across the gap between the separating contact points.

The instant the points separate, even as little as $^1/_{1,000,000}$ inch, current momentarily stops flowing in the primary winding. The magnetic field that is produced by the flow of current begins to collapse. A voltage is induced that attempts to keep the current moving. Without the condenser, the current would arc across the points. However, with the condenser this does not happen because the plates of the condenser provide "room" for the current (or electrons). The voltage, at first, does not have to be very high to push electrons into the condenser, and the condenser begins to become *charged.*

The induced voltage soon "fills up," or charges, the condenser; the current in the primary winding stops flowing. The magnetic field further collapses, inducing a higher voltage, which further charges the condenser. This creates still more opposition in the condenser to a flow of current, which forces additional magnetic-field collapse, still higher voltage, and so on. The voltage that may be reached in the primary winding may be as much as 250 volts. This must be thought of as a rapid and continuous process; the voltage constantly increases in an attempt to force current to flow. But as the voltage increases, the contact points continue to get farther and farther apart, so that the voltage does not at any time reach a value that would cause an arc across the points. What does happen is that the increasing voltage continues to charge the condenser further.

NOTE: During the first few millionths of a second after the points separate, arcing does take place across the points; however, this occurs *despite* condenser action, not because of it.

At the same time that all this is happening in the primary winding, events are reaching a climax in the secondary winding—events that will culminate in the production of a high-voltage surge of as much as 20,000 volts.

§294. Action in the secondary winding during magnetic collapse The secondary winding is connected to a spark-plug gap in a cylinder (Fig. 20-1). During the time that the primary winding is building up its magnetic field, the increasing magnetic field induces voltage in the secondary winding. We saw, however, that this voltage was not sufficient to cause any activity in the secondary winding (see §291). This is because the speed of the build-up is limited by the self-induction of the primary winding. If the build-up could be accomplished with extreme rapidity, the magnetic field would be moving rapidly enough across the secondary turns to induce a voltage sufficient to jump the spark-plug gap. It is not easy, however, to produce the high-voltage surge by this method. However, a high voltage can be induced if the primary-current flow can be stopped very quickly, since this causes a rapid collapse of the magnetic field.

The condenser action (in systems with contact points) or the transistor causes the flow of current in the primary winding to be very rapidly retarded. Consequently, the magnetic field produced by the current flow quickly collapses also. We saw that as much as 250 volts is induced in the primary as the magnetic field collapses, and the voltage continues to increase in an attempt to reach a value sufficient to set the current to flowing again in the primary.

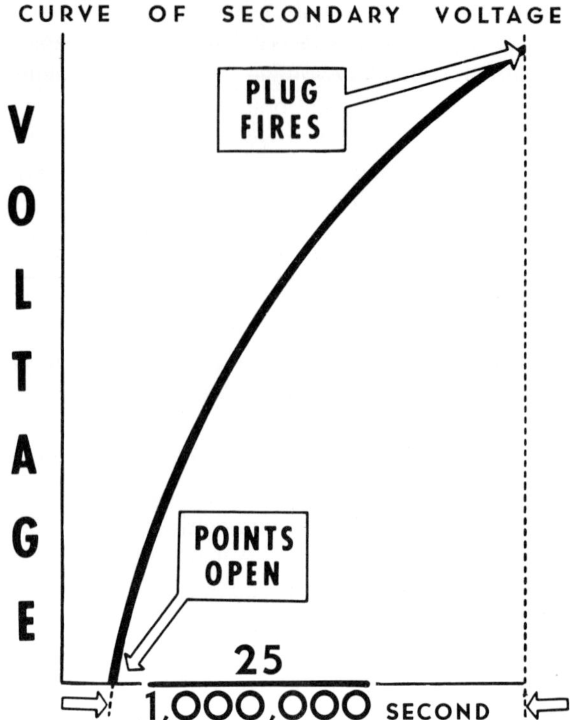

Fig. 20-14. Curve of secondary voltage, showing approximate interval of the time between opening of the points and the instant the spark occurs across the spark-plug gap.

The rapidly collapsing magnetic field also induces voltage in the secondary winding. Practically the same amount of voltage is induced in every turn of wire (primary or secondary) in the coil. There are about 100 times as many turns of wire in the secondary winding as in the primary winding, and consequently, the secondary voltage can go 100 times higher. The voltage of the secondary winding quickly increases to a value sufficient to jump the gap at the spark plug, somewhere between 4,000 and 20,000 volts (Fig. 20-14). Note that the firing voltage is attained in a few millionths of a second—a very short time indeed. The variation in voltage required is due to the width of the spark-plug gap, compression in the cylinder, temperature of spark-plug electrodes, and many other factors.

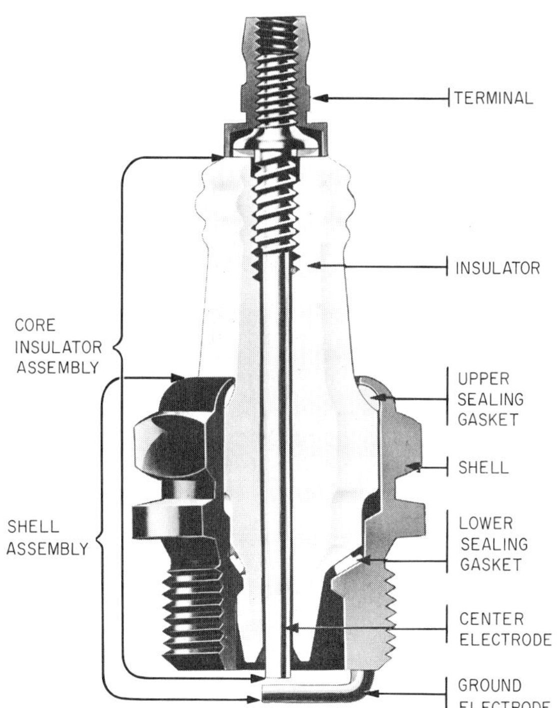

Fig. 20-15. Sectional view of a spark plug. (*AC Spark Plug Division*)

As soon as the plug fires, the energy in the ignition coil (stored momentarily in the form of magnetism) begins to be converted into a flow of current. This current flows through the secondary winding and across the spark-plug gap. Now, a reduction in voltage takes place for the following reason: The flow of current in the secondary winding produces a magnetic field. The magnetic field thus produced is in the same direction as that of the field already in existence (produced by the primary winding). The magnetic field, therefore, partially stops collapsing, and the induced voltage in the secondary drops to around 1,000 volts—all that is required to sustain the arc after it has formed.

§295. Spark plugs The spark plug (Fig 20-15) consists of a metal shell to which is fastened a porcelain insulator and an electrode extending through the center of the insulator. The metal shell has a short electrode attached to one side and bent in toward the center electrode. There are threads on the metal shell that allow it to be screwed into a tapped hole in the cylinder head. The two electrodes are of special heavy wire, and there is a gap of up to 0.040 inch between them. The electric spark jumps this gap to ignite the air-fuel mixture in the combustion chamber, passing from the center, or insulated, electrode to the grounded, or outer, electrode. The seals between the metal base, porcelain, and center electrode, as well as the porcelain itself, must be able to withstand the high pressure and temperature created in the combustion chamber during the power stroke.

Some spark plugs have been supplied with a built-in resistor, which forms part of the center electrode. The purpose of this resistor is to reduce radio and television interference from the ignition system. We have been talking of the high-voltage surge from the ignition coil secondary as though it were a single powerful surge that almost instantly caused the spark to jump across the spark-plug gap. Actually, the action is more complex than that. There may be a whole series of preliminary surges, and at the end of the sparking cycle, the spark may be quenched and may re-form several times. The effect of all this is that the ignition wiring acts like a radio-transmitting antenna; the surges of high voltage send out static that causes radio and television interference. However, the resistors in the spark plugs tend to concentrate the surges in each sparking cycle, reduce their number, and thus reduce the interference.

§296. Secondary wiring The secondary wiring consists of the high-tension cables connected between the distributor cap, the spark plugs, and the high-tension terminal of the ignition coil. These cables carry the high-voltage surges that produce the sparks at the plug gaps. Thus, they must be heavily insulated to contain the high voltage, and the insulation must be able to withstand the effects of high temperature and oil, as well as high voltage.

Before 1961, the cores of these cables were made of copper or aluminum wire. However, in 1961, all automotive manufacturers in the United States began to install cables which had carbon-impregnated linen cores. The carbon-impregnated linen forms a resistance path for the high-voltage surges, producing the same effect as the resistors in the spark plugs (§295). These cables thus do an effective job of eliminating radio and television interference from ignition systems.

In 1963, many cars began using cables with graphite-saturated fiberglass cores. These operate in the same manner as the carbon-impregnated, linen-core cables. However, it is claimed that they are less susceptible to breakage from pulling the cables off the spark plugs, and that they have less tendency to char from the high temperatures resulting from poor connections.

§297. Ignition-spark advance As engine speed and throttle opening vary, the instant that the spark appears in the cylinder (the "timing" of the spark) must also vary if maximum power is to be obtained. Each charge of air and vaporized gasoline taken into the cylinder must be ignited at the correct instant if it is to give up the maximum power available. When the engine is running at low speeds, the ignition system delivers the high-voltage surge with proper timing to produce the spark just before the piston reaches TDC (top dead center). At higher engine speeds, there is less time for the air-fuel mixture to burn because the piston is moving more rapidly.

To realize maximum power from the charge at higher speeds, it is necessary to ignite the mixture earlier in the cycle, or well before the piston reaches TDC. At high speeds, on some engines, the spark may occur as many as 45 degrees of crankshaft rotation before TDC. That is, the engine crankshaft may still have 45 degrees to rotate on the compression stroke, pushing the piston upward, at the time the spark occurs and the mixture begins to burn. The speed of the piston is so great, however, that it is over TDC and moving downward on the firing stroke before the burning of the charge and the pressure increase are well started. If the spark were not advanced at high speeds, the piston would be moving downward so rapidly as the charge began to burn that it would almost "keep step" with the pressure rise; thus there would be little increase in pressure, and most of the power would be lost.

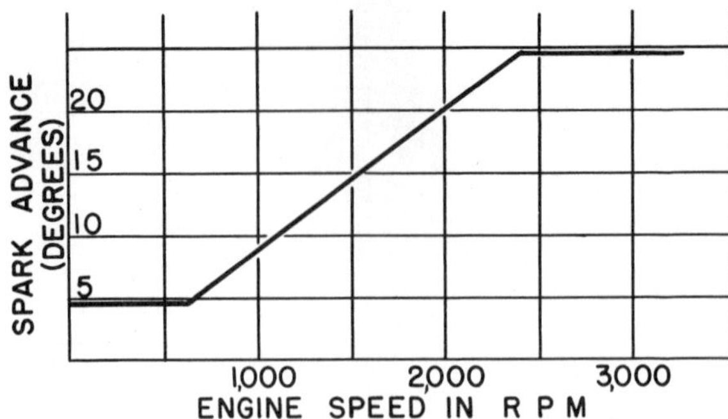

Fig. 20-16. Typical spark-advance curve. Not all advance curves are straight lines. Many of them bend or "dog-leg," to provide more rapid advance through some speed ranges than through others.

§298. Determination of spark-advance curve The graph in Fig. 20-16 illustrates a typical spark-advance curve. At idling speeds, the spark is set at 5 degrees before TDC. At higher speeds, the spark is advanced by a centrifugal device (see §299) to produce a spark advance based on engine speed. At 2,000 engine rpm (revolutions per minute), for example, the spark will occur at 20 degrees before TDC. The actual amount of spark advance for any engine speed is determined by operating the engine at that speed (with wide-open throttle) and gradually increasing the spark advance until maximum power is obtained. Since this amount of advance may cause some knocking, a slight retarding of the spark can then be made. The engine is tested at all speeds, the best spark advance (considering power and knocking) is found for each speed, and then the centrifugal-advance device is built to provide that advance.

§299. Centrifugal spark advance The correct instant for introducing the spark into the cylinder is determined by a number of variables, one of the most important of which is engine speed. As has been already shown (see §297), it is necessary to get the spark into the cylinder earlier in the compression stroke at high engine speeds so that the mixture can ignite and deliver its power to the piston. To obtain this advance of the spark based on engine speed, centrifugal-advance mechanisms

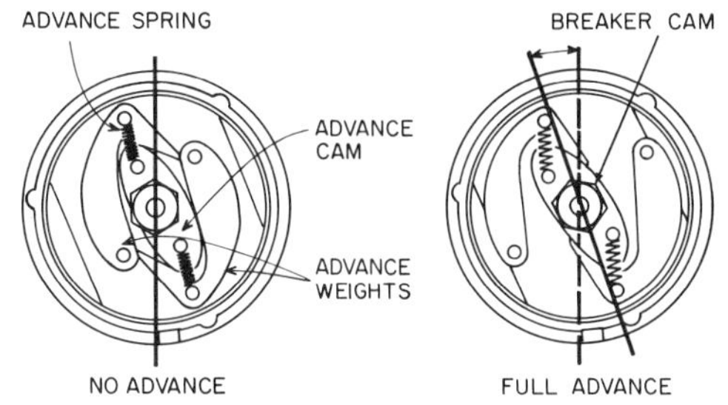

Fig. 20-17. Centrifugal-advance mechanism, showing no-advance and full-advance positions.

of various types are used. One type is shown in Fig. 20-17 (see also Fig. 8-12). It consists of two weights, which are pushed out by centrifugal force against spring tension as engine speed increases. This movement is transmitted through a toggle arrangement to the breaker cam (or the timer core on magnetic pick-up distributors). This causes the cam (or timer core) to move ahead or rotate with respect to the distributor drive shaft. On the contact-point distributor, this advance causes the cam to open and close the contact points earlier at high speeds. On the magnetic-pick-up distributor, the timer core is advanced so that the pick-up coil advances the timing of its signals to the transistor-control unit. With either system, the timing of the spark to the cylinder consequently varies from no advance at low speeds to full advance at high speeds, when the weights have reached the outer limits of their travel. The contours of the toggle arrangement (advance cam and weights) and the strength of the springs are designed to suit the special requirements of the engine and to produce the spark advance at each engine speed that will give maximum power and best performance (see §298).

§300. Intake-manifold vacuum advance There are other conditions besides the engine speed that must be considered in determining the proper spark advance of an engine. The centrifugal-advance curve is worked out with the engine operating at wide-open throttle. Under part throttle, the conditions in the cylinder during compression and combustion are such that more spark advance could be used.

When the throttle is only partly opened, the admission of air into the manifold is restricted, and a vacuum develops in the intake manifold. The speed of the engine and the amount of throttle opening determine the amount of vacuum. With vacuum in the intake manifold, less air and vaporized gasoline will be delivered to the cylinders. This means that the mixture that does get into the cylinder will be less highly compressed because there was less to start with.

With lower compression, the rate of flame propagation will be slower as the mixture is ignited and burns. Unless there is an additional spark advance, the full power of the charge will not be realized because the piston will be moving downward before the mixture is well ignited. In order to provide this additional advance, many applications have a vacuum-advance mechanism, which produces a spark advance based on intake-manifold vacuum

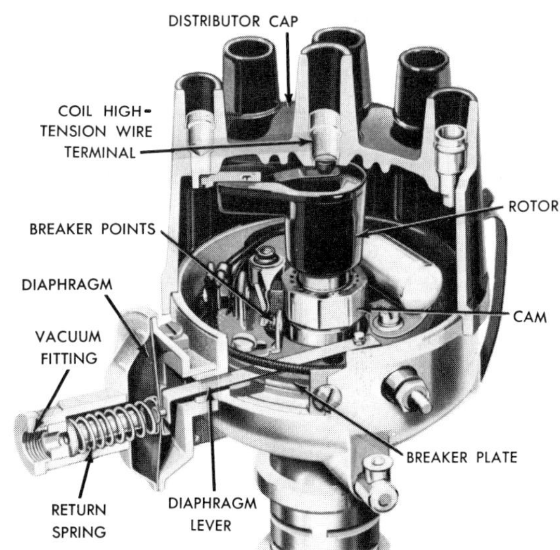

Fig. 20-18. Cutaway view of distributor, showing construction of vacuum-advance mechanism. (*Ford Motor Company*)

conditions. This spark advance is in addition to the centrifugal advance produced by the centrifugal-advance mechanism.

Figure 20-18 illustrates one type of vacuum-advance mechanism used on contact-point distributors. It contains a spring-loaded and airtight

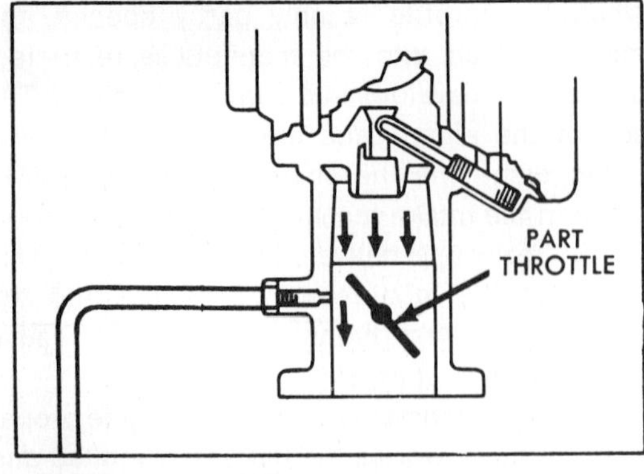

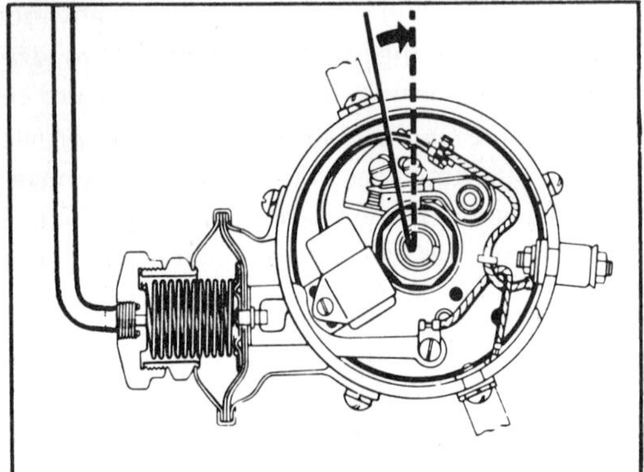

Fig. 20-19. Operation of vacuum-advance mechanism. When the throttle valve swings past the opening, a vacuum is admitted to the vacuum-advance mechanism on the distributor, and the breaker plate is rotated to advance the spark. (*Delco-Remy Division of General Motors Corporation*)

diaphragm connected by a linkage, or lever, to the breaker plate. The breaker plate is supported on a bearing so it can turn with respect to the distributor housing. It actually turns only a few degrees since the linkage to the spring-loaded diaphragm prevents any greater rotation than this.

The spring-loaded side of the diaphragm is connected through a vacuum line to an opening in the carburetor (Fig. 20-19). This opening is on the atmospheric side of the throttle valve when the throttle is in the idling position. There is no advance in this position.

As soon as the throttle is opened, however, it swings past the opening of the vacuum passage. The intake-manifold vacuum can then draw air from the vacuum line and the airtight chamber in the vacuum-advance mechanism. This causes the diaphragm to move against the spring. The linkage to the breaker plate then rotates the breaker plate. This movement carries the contact points around so that the cam, as it rotates, closes and opens the points earlier in the cycle. The spark consequently appears at the spark-plug gap earlier in the compression stroke. As the throttle is opened wider, there will be less vacuum in the intake manifold and less vacuum advance. At wide-open throttle, there will be no vacuum advance at all. The spark advance under this condition will be provided entirely by the centrifugal-advance mechanism.

On the magnetic-pick-up distributor, the vacuum-advance mechanism is attached to the magnetic-pick-up assembly (Fig. 20-4) so that this assembly is rotated to provide the vacuum advance.

§301. Combining centrifugal and vacuum advances At any particular speed, there will be a certain definite centrifugal advance due to engine

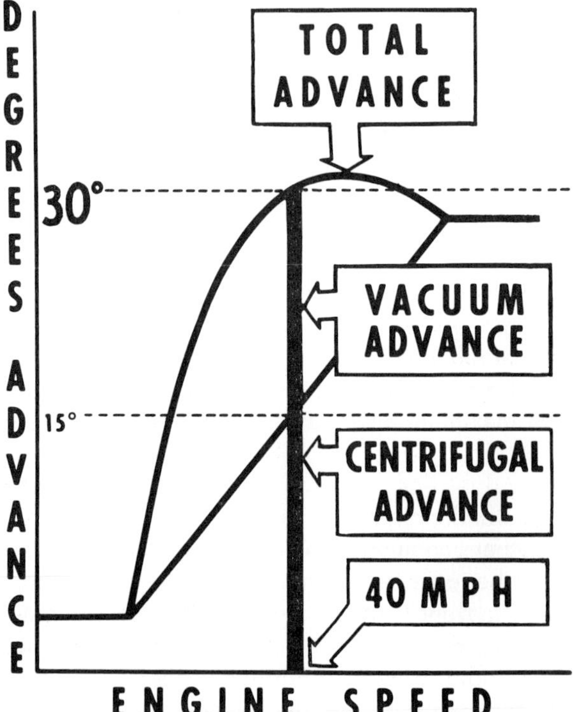

Fig. 20-20. Centrifugal- and vacuum-advance curves for one application.

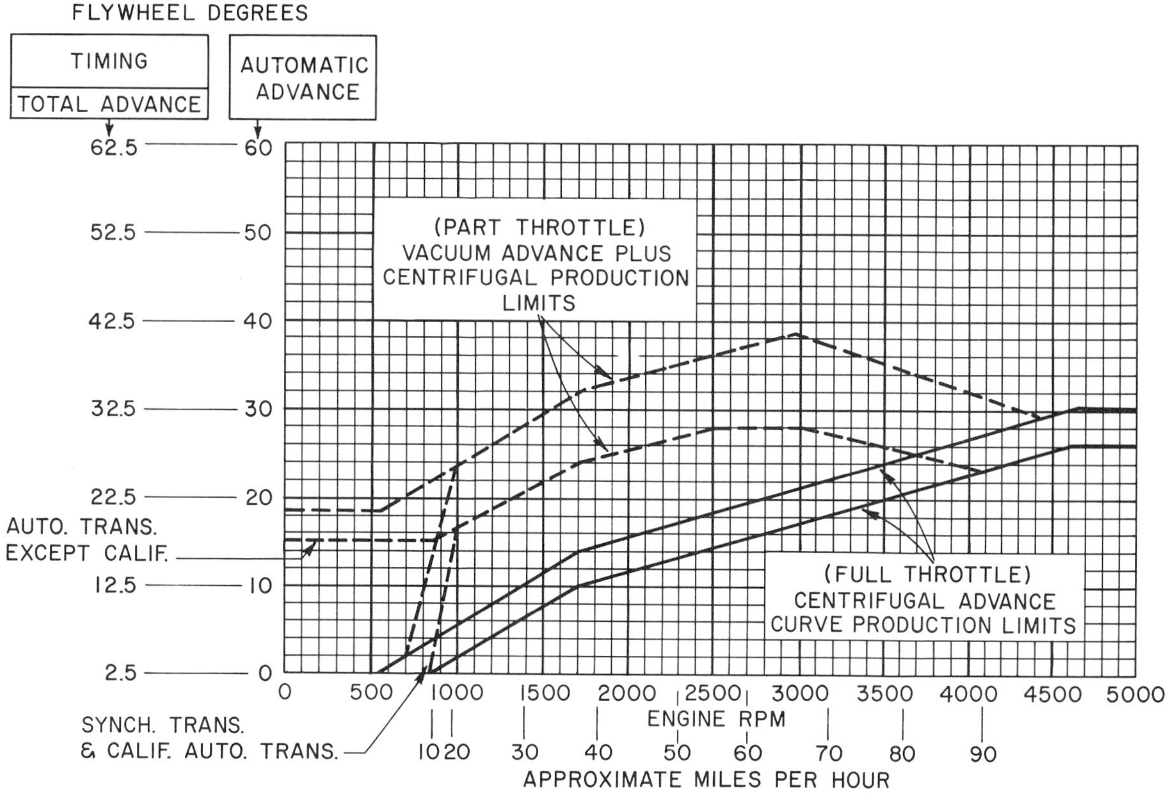

FLYWHEEL DEGREES

TIMING / TOTAL ADVANCE: 62.5, 52.5, 42.5, 32.5, 22.5, 12.5, 2.5

AUTOMATIC ADVANCE: 60, 50, 40, 30, 20, 10, 0

(PART THROTTLE) VACUUM ADVANCE PLUS CENTRIFUGAL PRODUCTION LIMITS

AUTO. TRANS. EXCEPT CALIF.

(FULL THROTTLE) CENTRIFUGAL ADVANCE CURVE PRODUCTION LIMITS

SYNCH. TRANS. & CALIF. AUTO. TRANS.

ENGINE RPM: 0, 500, 1000, 1500, 2000, 2500, 3000, 3500, 4000, 4500, 5000

APPROXIMATE MILES PER HOUR: 10, 20, 30, 40, 50, 60, 70, 80, 90

Fig. 20-21. Centrifugal- and vacuum-advance curves for a 340 cubic inch engine. (*Buick Motor Division of General Motors Corporation*)

speed, plus a possible additional spark advance resulting from vacuum conditions in the intake manifold. Figure 20-20 illustrates this. At 40 mph (miles per hour), the centrifugal-advance mechanism provides 15 degrees spark advance on this typical application. The vacuum-advance mechanism will supply up to 15 degrees additional advance under part-throttle conditions. However, if the engine is operated at wide-open throttle, this added vacuum advance will not be obtained. The advance, in the usual operating conditions, will vary somewhere between the straight line (centrifugal advance) and the curved line (centrifugal advance plus total *possible* vacuum advance) as the throttle is opened and closed, and as engine speeds change. Figure 20-21 shows the centrifugal- and vacuum-advance curves for a specific application.

The distributor illustrated in Fig. 20-22 does

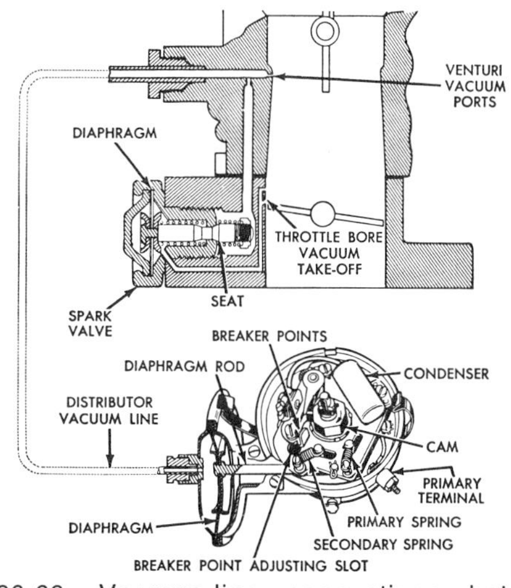

Fig. 20-22. Vacuum-line connections between carburetor and distributor, having full vacuum control. (*Ford Motor Company*)

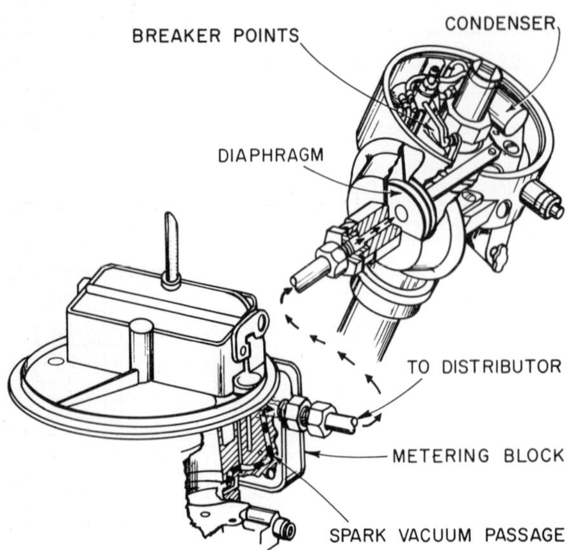

Fig. 20-23. Connection of vacuum line between carburetor and vacuum-advance mechanism on distributor. (*Ford Motor Company*)

not contain a centrifugal-advance mechanism, but utilizes vacuum from the carburetor venturi and intake manifold to produce the proper advance (Fig. 20-23). Full control by vacuum alone is possible because air speed through the carburetor air horn, and thus the vacuum in the venturi, are directly related to engine speed. Let us see how this system functions.

In the carburetor shown in Fig. 20-22, there are two vacuum openings in the air horn: one is at the venturi, and the other is just above the throttle when it is closed. The lower, or throttle, bore vacuum-take-off opening may have two ports on some models, as shown in Fig. 20-22. These openings are connected by vacuum passages to each other and to the distributor vacuum-advance mechanism by a vacuum line. Vacuum imposed on the diaphragm in the vacuum-advance mechanism causes the breaker-plate assembly to rotate. This is very similar to other vacuum-advance devices discussed above. Rotation of the breaker plate causes a spark advance.

As engine speed increases, the vacuum at the venturi in the carburetor increases because of increase of air speed through the venturi. This causes an increase spark advance that is related to engine speed. At the same time, under part-throttle operating conditions, there will be a vacuum in the intake manifold, and this acts at the throttle vacuum ports in the carburetor to pro-

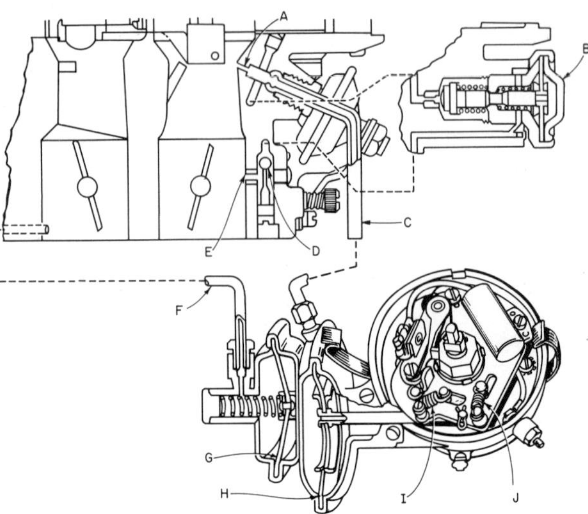

Fig. 20-24. Vacuum-line connections between four-barrel carburetor for V-8 engine and distributor with full vacuum control. *A,* primary venturi-vacuum passage; *B*, spark-control valve; *C*, distributor-vacuum line; *D*, vacuum-passage check ball; *E*, manifold-vacuum passage; *F*, manifold-vacuum line; *G*, secondary spark-control diaphragm; *H*, primary spark-control diaphragm; *I*, secondary breaker-plate spring; *J*, primary breaker-plate spring. (*Ford Motor Company*)

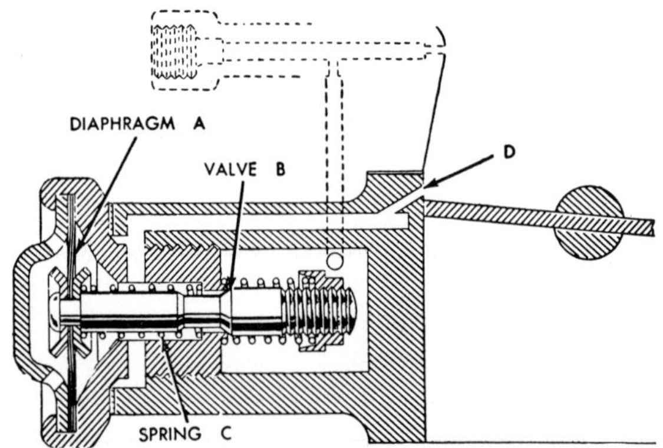

Fig. 20-25. Sectional view of spark-control valve. (*Ford Motor Company*)

duce a further vacuum advance. Thus, the interrelation of the vacuum conditions at the two points in the carburetor produces, in effect, a speed advance (as with a centrifugal-advance device) combined with a vacuum advance.

A variation of this design for V-8 engines with four-barrel carburetors uses a spark-control valve in the carburetor. The complete arrangement is shown in Fig. 20-24, and the valve details are shown in Fig. 20-25. The spark-control-valve device momentarily retards the spark during acceleration to prevent excessive ping. When the throttle is held steady in a partly opened position, manifold vacuum is sufficient to hold the spark-control valve open. The vacuum, acting through the vacuum opening D (Fig. 20-25), causes diaphragm A to be pulled in so that valve B is open. Now, intake-manifold vacuum can act through valve B and the additional vacuum passage (shown dotted in Fig. 20-25). This provides the part-throttle vacuum advance discussed previously. However, when the throttle is opened further for acceleration, manifold vacuum drops. Now, the vacuum against the diaphragm is reduced so much that the diaphragm spring can move the spark-control valve to the closed position. As the valve closes, there is a rapid spark retard; this reduces the chances of ping during acceleration. When the accelerator is again moved toward the closed position, or as engine speed builds up so that intake-manifold vacuum increases, then the spark-control valve will open again. This again produces the part-throttle vacuum advance.

On the model shown in Fig. 20-24, there are two spark-control diaphragms. The secondary spark-control diaphragm (G in Fig. 20-24) has the purpose of reducing or eliminating ping on sudden acceleration. When the throttle is opened suddenly, the intake-manifold vacuum falls sharply. This permits the spring in the secondary spark-control chamber to push the diaphragm inward. This pushes air into the primary spark-control chamber so that, for a moment, the primary spark-control diaphragm is pushed inward slightly. This action forces a momentary spark retard, while the distributor-vacuum line, carburetor-vacuum passages, and primary spark-control diaphragm become adjusted to the new pressure conditions which have developed. In this manner, the engine ping that could otherwise develop on quick acceleration is reduced or eliminated.

§302. Piezoelectric ignition This type of ignition system[3] does not use contact points, a battery, a condenser, or an ignition coil. Its operation depends on a peculiar property of some crystals. When these crystals are squeezed in a certain manner they produce a voltage on opposing faces. Such crystals are used in many microphones and phonograph pick-ups. In the phonograph pick-up, for example, the phonograph needle vibrates as it rides in the record groove. This vibration is applied to a crystal, and the crystal produces a varying voltage exactly matching the variations of pressure caused by the vibration. The voltage causes current to flow through an amplifier and speaker so that sound is produced.

This piezoelectric principle has recently been applied to some single-cylinder engines used on lawn mowers. There is a possibility that this principle will be developed for use in multiple-cylinder engines. The system for the single-cylinder engine is illustrated in Fig. 20-26. The cam is driven by the engine. It has a single lobe. At the proper time, the cam lobe comes up under the lever, causing the lever to apply pressure to the two piezoelectric crystals contained in an insulating tube. The outer ends of the crystals are grounded, and the inner ends are connected to the high-tension terminal. This terminal is connected to the spark plug. The

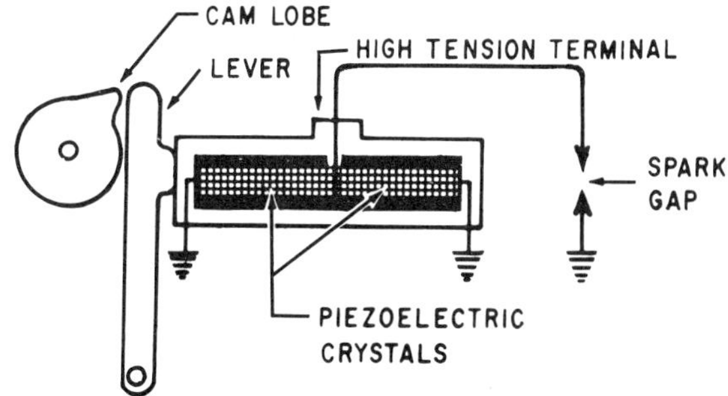

Fig. 20-26. Simplified schematic drawing of a piezoelectric ignition system for a single-cylinder engine.

pressure on the crystals causes them to produce a very high voltage (20,000 volts or more). This high voltage causes a spark at the spark-plug gap.

A piezoelectric crystal can continue to supply high-voltage surges in this manner almost indefinitely. A simple way of thinking about the process is to consider that a crystal is composed of atoms, formed into molecules. The atoms are partly made up of electrons and protons (see Chap. 5). These particles, which are negatively and positively charged, are in an orderly arrangement in the crystal. When pressure is applied, this orderly arrangement is disturbed, and the molecules and atoms are pushed out of position. In effect, all are turned in such a way that their negative sides point one way and their positive sides point the other. Then they act somewhat like battery cells connected in series. High voltages appear on the opposing faces of the crystal. If these opposing faces are connected by an electric circuit, current will flow through the circuit.

§303. Special ignition devices The following special features are used in different ignition systems.

1. *Primary resistor.* Many late-model, 12-volt ignition systems use a resistor or a resistance wire in the ignition-coil primary circuit (Fig. 20-1). This resistance is shorted-out by the ignition switch when it is turned to START. Full battery voltage is imposed on the ignition coil for good performance during cranking. After the engine is started and the ignition switch is turned to ON, the resistance is inserted in the ignition primary circuit, thus protecting the contact points from excessive current.

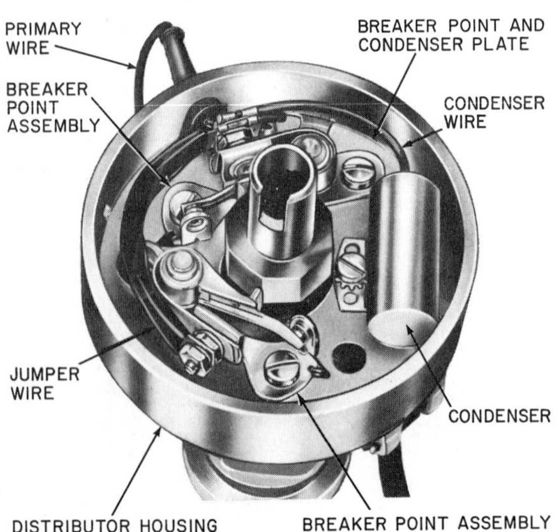

Fig. 20-27. Dual contact-point distributor, with cap removed so that breaker plate can be seen. (*Ford Motor Company*)

On some cars, the resistance consists of a separately mounted resistor unit. On most cars, the resistance consists of a length of resistance wire in the wiring harness.

2. *Double-contact-set distributor.* Some V-8 engines (Ford high-performance V-8s, for example) have used a distributor with two sets of contact points (Figs. 20-27 and 20-28). On this unit, both sets of contact points are in parallel. The primary winding of the ignition coil is connected to battery (through ground) when either set is closed. One set of points closes the circuit, and the other set opens it. By having a lag of several degrees (about 7 degrees) between the closing and opening of the two sets, a longer coil build-up time is achieved. That is, the coil is connected to the battery for a longer time, and it can therefore build up more magnetism (see §290 for information on build-up time). The coil can then deliver a stronger spark for better ignition at high engine speeds. In Fig. 20-28, you will note that one set of contact points always closes the circuit, and the other set always opens it.

3. *Distributor with built-in governor.* Some distributors have built-in governors for controlling engine speed. Figure 20-29 shows schematically one design. The distributor includes a centrifugal valve which is spring-loaded. At low speeds, slots and grooves in the valve shaft and in the distributor shaft line up so that air can flow freely through, as shown by the arrows. There is no appreciable vacuum developed in the carburetor-actuator diaphragm chamber. However, as the preset speed is approached, the centrifugal force on the valve causes it to move out against its restraining spring. Now, the flow of air is reduced, and the intake-manifold vacuum begins to act on the carburetor-actuator diaphragm. When this happens, the

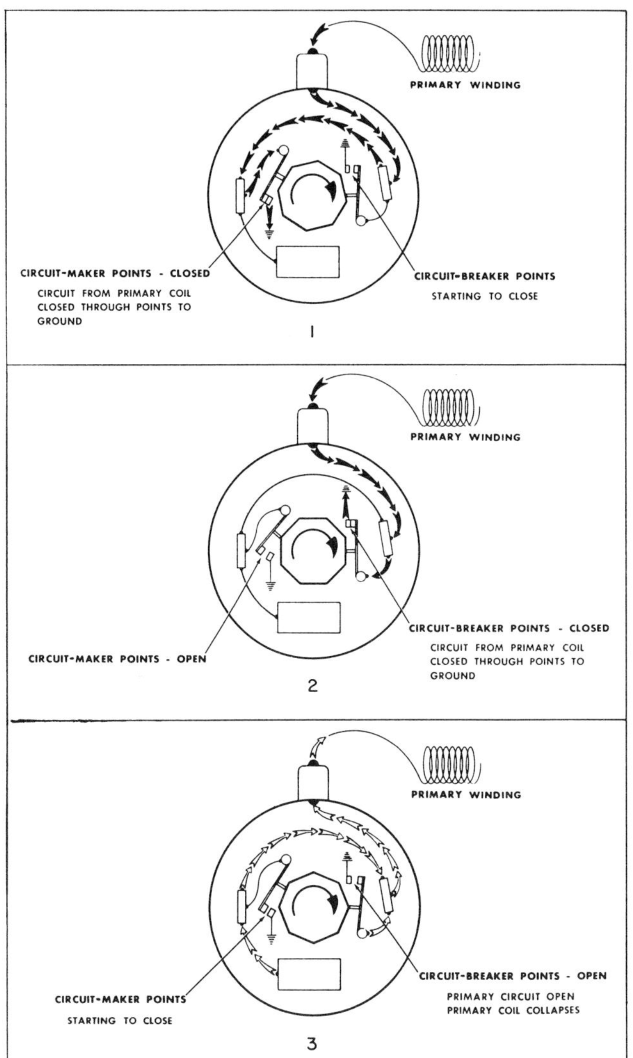

Fig. 20-28. Action of the two sets of contact points in a distributor: (1) circuit-maker points have closed, and the circuit-breaker points are about to close; (2) circuit-maker points have opened, and the circuit-breaker points, still closed, are about to open; (3) both sets are open, but the circuit-maker points are about to close. (*Chrysler Motors Corporation*)

butterfly valve in the carburetor is moved toward the closed position, reducing the flow of air-fuel mixture to the engine. The engine cannot develop greater power and thus cannot increase further in speed.

4. No-lubrication distributors. Some distributors have built-in oil reservoirs surrounding a porous bushing (Fig. 20-30). Oil seeps through the bushing to provide long-time lubrication. Recommendations call for refilling the reservoir with 20W oil every 10,000 miles.

Some distributors have a cam lubricator which

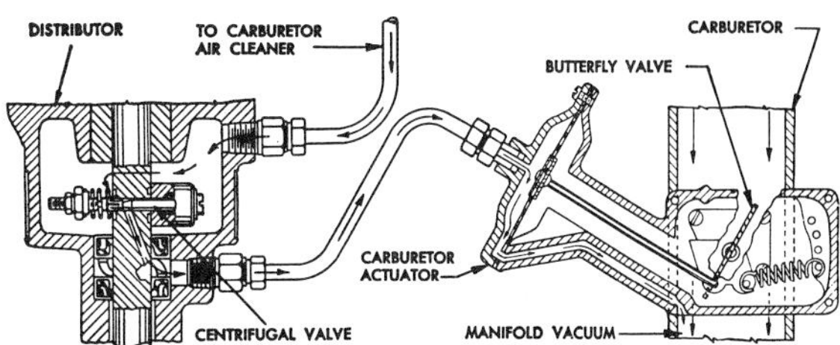

Fig. 20-29. Schematic drawing of a distributor that has a built-in engine governor and the carburetor with which it is used. Only the relevant parts of the units are shown. (*Delco-Remy Division of General Motors Corporation*)

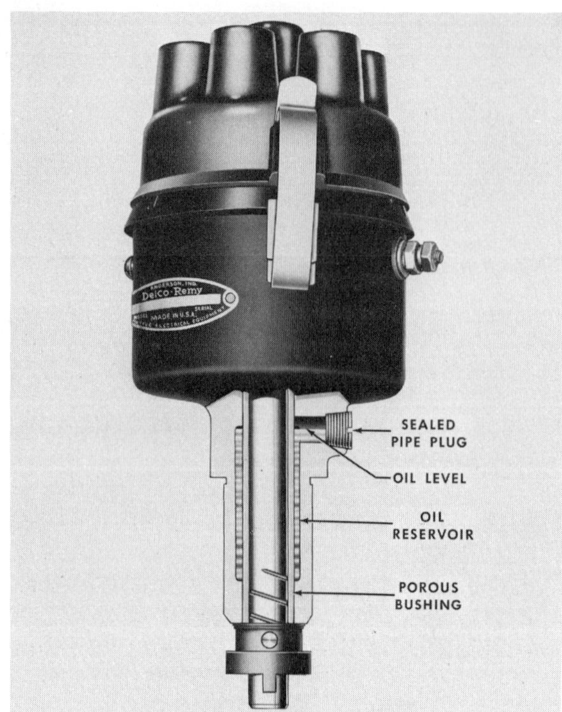

Fig. 20-30. Partial sectional view of a distributor, showing the oil reservoir. (*Delco-Remy Division of General Motors Corporation*)

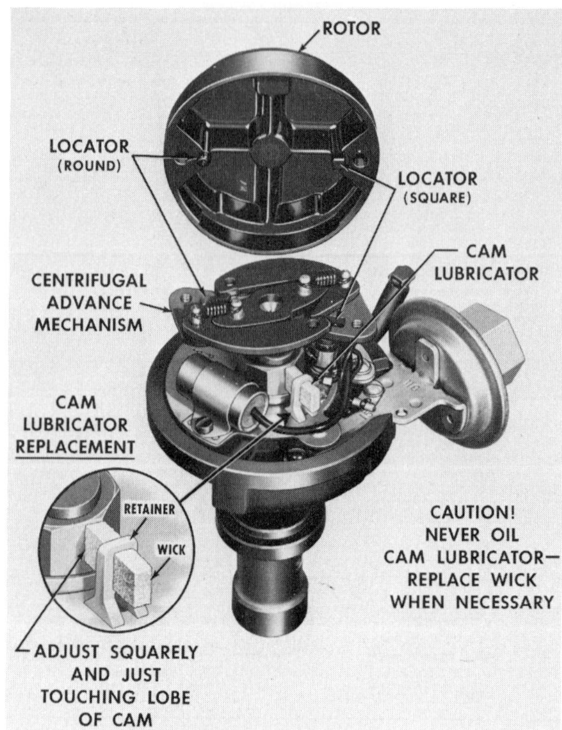

Fig. 20-31. External adjustment distributor with cap and rotor removed. Circle shows cam-lubricator wick. (*Delco-Remy Division of General Motors Corporation*)

keeps the breaker cam properly lubricated (Fig. 20-31). On these types, the wick should be replaced when it becomes worn or dry. It should not be oiled.

§304. Low-frequency vs. high-frequency ignition systems[4-6] The conventional ignition system, illustrated in Fig. 20-1 and described previously is termed a "low-frequency, high-impedance system." The impedance of the ignition-coil secondary, with its many thousands of turns, results in an alternating voltage of relatively low frequency (compared with other systems to be described below). This system functions well for most conditions; however, when the plugs foul, they may fail to fire properly. Plug fouling can be due to the engine design, type of operation, or use of the wrong fuels and lubricating oils for the type of operation. Any of these might cause an accumulation of carbon or other substance on the ceramic insulator of the spark plug. This foreign material

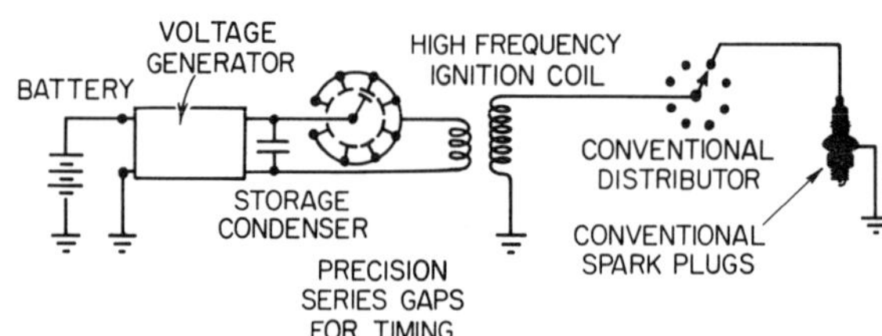

Fig. 20-32. High-frequency, high-voltage ignition system.

forms a relatively low-resistance path. Under certain circumstances, the voltage which the ignition coil builds up, and which could produce a spark, is drained off across the low-resistance path as fast as it builds up. As a result, no spark occurs. If the voltage could build up faster (higher frequency), then it could produce a spark instead of being drained away. The secondary voltage build-up time, however, is a function of the mag-

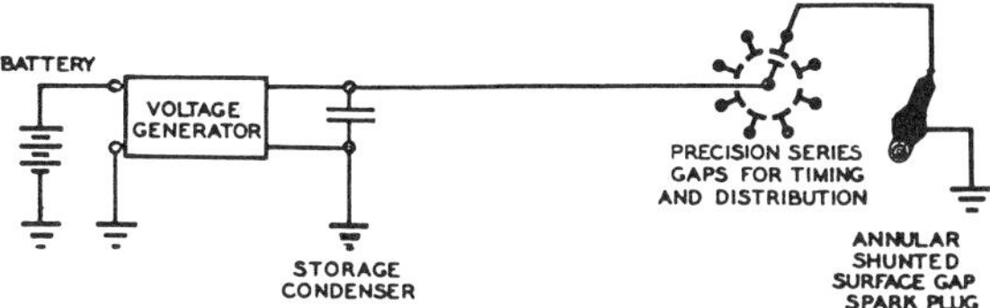

Fig. 20-33. Very-high-frequency ignition system.

netic-field collapse (§292 and 294). This collapse is retarded somewhat by the self-induction of the windings (that is, the windings have a high impedance). The result is that there is an upper limit to the frequency that this system can produce.

1. *High-frequency system.* Figure 20-32 shows a high-frequency, high-voltage system that will improve firing of fouled spark plugs. It consists of a voltage generator, storage condenser, rotating gap-type timer, high-frequency ignition coil, conventional distributor (cap and rotor of conventional ignition distributor), and wiring and spark plugs. In operation, the voltage generator stores a charge in the condenser. Then, the timer rotor moves opposite a metal segment in the timer ring. This minimizes the gap, and the condenser discharges across this gap. This discharge is at high frequency because there is comparatively little impedance in the circuit (only that of the primary winding of the ignition coil).

The high frequency applied to the primary winding produces a high-frequency high-voltage in the secondary winding, and this is distributed to the spark plugs by a conventional distribution system.

2. *Very-high-frequency system.* This system (Fig. 20-33) is a direct capacitor-discharge system with very little impedance. Practically all the energy is converted to very high frequencies of high amplitude. The system uses a special, surface-discharge spark plug (Fig. 20-34). In this spark plug, there is no plug gap. Instead, the active surfaces of the two electrodes are separated by an insulator in which partially conducting oxides are mixed. The spark propagates from one electrode to the other by skipping from one partially conducting particle to the next. It can be seen from this that surface contaminants, such as carbon, simply improve the fire-ability of these plugs. The frequency of the voltage applied is so great that it does not have a chance to drain away. Instead, it forms a series of arcs across the surface. This system has been used in some experimental installations, but there is little expectation of its widespread adoption as long as conventional systems continue to perform satisfactorily.

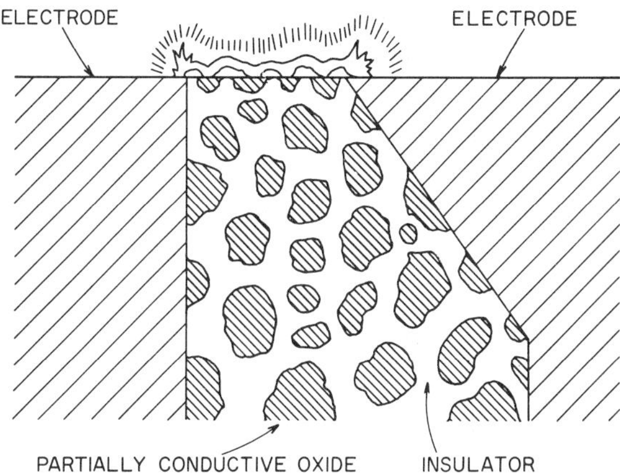

Fig. 20-34. Surface-gap firing.

SUMMARY

The standard ignition system used on modern automobiles is the low-frequency, high-impedance type. It consists of a source of power (alternator or battery), an ignition distributor, ignition coil, ignition switch, spark plugs, and wiring. In operation, the contact points in the ignition distributor close and open the primary circuit of the ignition coil, thus producing high-voltage surges in the ignition-coil secondary winding. These high-voltage surges are distributed to the spark plugs by the distributor rotor and cap and the secondary wiring. Advance mechanisms, centrifugal and vacuum, determine the timing of the spark for the best engine performance under different engine speeds and throttle openings.

Some high-performance engines use a transistorized ignition system, which reduces the current flow through the contact points while allowing a higher peaking voltage. Some systems use a breakerless ignition distributor, with a magnetic-pulse arrangement that triggers an amplifier to provide for starting and stopping the flow of current in the primary winding of the ignition coil.

Other ignition systems include piezoelectric and capacitor-discharge systems. The latter system uses a magnetic-pulse distributor to trigger a transistorized-capacitor system, which produces a quick primary current and thus a very-high-frequency secondary voltage.

REFERENCES

1. *Sharpe, J. W., Transistorized Ignition for High Speed Gasoline Engines, SAE (Society of Automotive Engineers) 650498, 1965 (paper).*

2. *Hogle, R. C., Mark II-GT Ignition and Electrical System, SAE (Society of Automotive Engineers) 670068, 1967 (paper).*

3. *Mosley, J. A., The Piezoelectric Ignition System, from SAE (Society of Automotive Engineers), special publication SP-237, 1962.*

4. *Dunne, C. J., Contemporary Ignition Systems, from SAE (Society of Automotive Engineers), special publication SP-237, 1962.*

5. *Hardin, J. T., Capacitor Discharge Ignition: The System Approach to Extended Performance and Life, SAE (Society of Automotive Engineers) S414, 1964 (paper).*

6. *Hetzler, L. R., and P. C. Kline, Engineering C-D Ignition for Modern Engines, SAE (Society of Automotive Engineers) 670116, 1967 (paper).*

QUESTIONS

1. *What is the function of the ignition system?*
2. *Describe the operation of the conventional ignition system using contact points.*
3. *Describe the operation of an ignition system using a magnetic pick-up.*
4. *Describe the operation of an ignition system with contact points and a transistorized amplifier.*
5. *Describe the construction and operation of an ignition system.*
6. *What is the purpose of the ignition condenser?*
7. *Describe the construction of a spark plug.*
8. *Describe the construction and purpose of the centrifugal-advance mechanism. Of the vacuum-advance mechanism.*
9. *Describe the operation of the piezoelectric ignition system.*
10. *Describe the operation of the capacitor-discharge ignition system.*

Bibliography

Chapter 1

Anderson, J., and E. Tatro, *Shop Theory*, 5th ed., McGraw-Hill Book Company, New York, 1968.

Burghardt, H. D., A. Axelrod, and J. Anderson, *Machine Tool Operation*, McGraw-Hill Book Company, New York, Part 1, 1959, and Part 2, 1960.

Burlingame, Roger, *Machines That Built America*, Harcourt, Brace & World, Inc., New York, 1953.

Diebold, J., *Beyond Automation*, McGraw-Hill Book Company, New York, 1964.

Feirer, J. L., and E. Tatro, *Machine Tool Metalworking*, McGraw-Hill Book Company, New York, 1961.

Grabbe, E. M., *Automation in Business and Industry*, John Wiley & Sons, Inc., New York, 1957.

Also, trade magazines such as *Automation, Automotive Industries, Factory*, and *Machine Design* carry articles on machine tooling, manufacturing methods, and automation.

Chapter 2

Cunningham, H. M., and W. F. Sherman, *Production of Motor Vehicles*, McGraw-Hill Book Company, New York, 1951.

Datsko, J., *Material Properties and Manufacturing Processes*, John Wiley & Sons, Inc., New York, 1966.

Nadler, G., "The Science of Design," SAE (Society of Automotive Engineers) 650390, 1965 (paper).

National Tool, Die, and Precision Machining Association, *Basic Die Making*, McGraw-Hill Book Company, New York, 1963.

Phelan, R. M., *Fundamentals of Machine Design*, McGraw-Hill Book Company, New York, 1962.

Society of Automotive Engineers, *SAE Handbook* (a yearly publication).

Chapter 3

Crouse, William H., *Automotive Engines*, 4th ed., McGraw-Hill Book Company, New York, 1970.

Crouse, William H., *Automotive Mechanics*, 6th ed., McGraw-Hill Book Company, New York, 1970.

Chapter 4

Crouse, William H., *Automotive Engines*, 4th ed., McGraw-Hill Book Company, New York, 1970.

Crouse, William H., *Automotive Mechanics*, 6th ed., McGraw-Hill Book Company, New York, 1970.

Chapter 5

Jones, J. B., and G. A. Hawkins, *Engineering Thermodynamics*, John Wiley & Sons, Inc., New York, 1960.

Lichty, Lester C., *Combustion Engine Processes*, McGraw-Hill Book Company, New York, 1967.

Taylor, C. F., and E. S. Taylor, *The Internal Combustion Engine*, International Textbook Company, Scranton, Pa., 1961.

Chapter 6

Crouse, William H., *Automotive Engines*, 4th ed., McGraw-Hill Book Company, New York, 1970.

Crouse, William H., *Automotive Mechanics*, 6th ed., McGraw-Hill Book Company, New York, 1970.

Chapter 7

Crouse, William H., *Automotive Engines*, 4th ed., McGraw-Hill Book Company, New York, 1970.

Crouse, William H., *Automotive Mechanics*, 6th ed., McGraw-Hill Book Company, New York, 1970.

Shop Manuals or Repair Manuals issued by automotive manufacturers.

Chapter 8

Crouse, William H., *Automotive Electrical Equipment*, 7th ed., McGraw-Hill Book Company, New York, 1970.

Crouse, William H., *Automotive Engines*, 4th ed., McGraw-Hill Book Company, New York, 1970.

Crouse, William H., *Automotive Fuel, Lubricating, and Cooling Systems*, 3d ed., McGraw-Hill Book Company, New York, 1967.

Crouse, William H., *Automotive Mechanics*, 6th ed., McGraw-Hill Book Company, New York, 1970.

Chapter 15

Crouse, W. H., *Automotive Engines*, 4th ed., McGraw-Hill Book Company, 1970.

Turkish, M. C., *Valve Gear Design*, Eaton Manufacturing Company, 1946.

Index

Air cleaner, 268–269
Alternator, 105
Aluminum-alloy pistons, 146–148
Antifreeze, 319–320
Antiknock values of fuels, 118, 125–126, 128
Assembling, automation of, 5
Atoms, 59–60
Automated cylinder-block processing, 4–5
Automatic screw machine, 2–4
Automatic-transfer machine, 255
Automatic turret lathe, 2–4
Automation, 2–6
  of assembling, 5
  designing for, 6
  factors to be considered, 5–6
Automobile designing, 10–25
Automotive engine (*see* Engine)
Automotive industry, opportunities in, 7–9
Autothermic pistons, 152, 160

Battery, 104–105
Bearings, 178–195
  crankshaft, 179
  design, 189–193
  failure analysis, 193–195
  load graphs, 188–189
  loading, 186–189
  lubrication, 181–184
  main, 179–180
Bearings, manufacture, 192
  materials, 185–186
  requirements, 184–185
  thrust, 181
  types, 184
Binder fluidic carburetor, 305–306
Block (*see* Cylinder block)
Blow-by, 164
Blow-by diversion, 343–344
Bore, 68
Boyle's law, 62
Brake horsepower, 71–72
Bucks, 18
Bushings, 179

Cam-ground piston, 151
Camaro, designing of, 18–19
Cams, 92–93, 231–234
  contour design, 232–234
  high performance, 239–241
  for hydraulic lifters, 238–239
Camshafts, 92–93
  overhead, 241–242
Carburetor, 101–103, 265–291
  air cleaner, 268–269
  choke, 271–273
  circuits, 268
  design, 287–291
  four-barrel, 283–287
  fundamentals, 267–268
  one-barrel, 279
Carburetor, quadrijet, 283–287
  requirements, 265–266
  two-barrel, 279–282
Centrifugal spark advance, 108, 358–359
Charles' law, 62
Chevrolet 427 piston, 159–161
Chevrolet Turbo-Jet engine cooling system, 321–322
Chevrolet Turbo-Jet engine intake manifold, 295–296
Chevrolet Turbo-Jet engine valves, 237–238
Choke, 271–273
Chrysler valve-port design, 218
Clay models, 16–18
Collision tests, 21–23
Combustion, 61
  chemistry of, 130
Combustion-chamber design, 132–142
Combustion-chamber requirements, 132–133
Compression ratio, 69–70
Compression rings, 91–92, 165–172
  (*See also* Piston rings)
Connecting rods, 28, 89–90, 178
Cooling system, 109–110, 309–323
  antifreeze solutions, 319–320
  Chevrolet Turbo-Jet engine, 321–322

Cooling system, design, 320–322
fan, 312–314
heat transfer in, 309–311
purpose, 309–311
radiator, 314–317
radiator pressure cap, 319
sealed, 317
temperature indicator, 320
thermostat, 317–319
water jackets, 311
water pumps, 311
Cope, 250
Cores, 250–255
Crankcase dilution, 117
Cranking motor, 105
Crankshaft, 86, 195–202
balance analysis, 197–199
crankpin throw, 200
design, 196–197
journal geometry, 201
journal size, 200–201
tests, 201–202
vibration dampers, 87–88, 202–203
Crush, bearing, 189–190
Cycle, constant-volume, 63–64
Cycles, idealized, 63–65
Cylinder block, 79–80, 247–263
aluminum, 259–263
casting, 252–253
cylinder liners, 259–263
design considerations, 247–250
finishing, 255–257
Ford 240 engine, 253–255
machining, 255–257
processing, automated, 4–5
thread repair in, 263
Cylinder heads, 80–82, 247–263
design considerations, 247–250, 257–259
Cylinder liners, 259–263
Cylinders, engine, 27

DAC, 15–16
Design, by computer, 15–16
Design, mechanical, 13–14
Design job, 23
Designing, for automation, 6
an automobile, 10–25
the Camaro, 18–19
for safety, 20–23
Die-sinking, 17–18
Diesel engine, 48–52
Distributor, 349–353
advance mechanisms, 358–363
centrifugal, 358–363
vacuum, 359–363
transistorized, 350–353
DOHC, 45, 241
Drag, 250
Dual carburetors, 279–282
Dual-exhaust system, 85
Dynamometer, 72

Efficiency, mechanical, 76, 114–115
thermal, 64, 113–114
volumetric, 65–66, 114, 136
Electric system, 104–109
Elements, 60
Engine, accessory systems, 100–110
assembly, 259
bearings, 88–89
combustion in, 61
construction, 79–99
cycles, 63–65
design, 111–115
diesel, 48–52
DOHC, 45
eight-cylinder, 42–43
F-head, 45
flat four, 39–40
four-cylinder, 36–40
free-piston, 52–53
fuel, 116–131
heat losses, 76–77
I-head, 44–45
L-head, 44
Engine, measurements, 68–77
operation of, 27–33
overhead camshaft, 45
principles of, 59–67
PV curve, 65
rotary, 57–58
six-cylinder, 40–41
SOHC, 45
Sterling, 55–57
three-cylinder, 35–36
two-cylinder, 35
two-stroke cycle, 46–48
types of, 34–58
V-4, 38–39
V-8, 42–43
valve arrangements in, 43–45
vibration mountings, 203–204
Wankel, 54–55
(*See also* specific entries such as Cylinders; Engine; Piston rings; Pistons; etc.)
Exhaust gases, 299–301
Exhaust manifold, 84–85, 296–297
Expansion control in piston, 150–153

F-head engine, 45
F-head valve train, 97
Fan, 312–314
Fhp, 73–74
Float circuit, 269
Flywheel, 86–87
Ford Mark II-427 GT intake manifold, 293–295
Ford's 240 engine cylinder block, 253–255
Foundry practice, 250–252
Free-piston engine, 52–53
Friction, 72–74
Friction horsepower, 73–74
Fuel-evaporation control, 301–302
Fuel gauge, 266–267
Fuel injection, 302–305

Fuel pump, 100–102
Fuel systems, 100–102, 265–307
  requirements, 265
  (*See also* specific entries such as Carburetor; Fuel pump; etc.)
Fuel tank, 100

Gas laws, 62
Gas turbine, 52
Gaskets, 83
Gasoline, volatility of, 116–118
Gasoline additives, 129–130
Gear lubricants, 331
Generator, 105
Grease, 331–334

Head (*see* Cylinder heads)
Head-land ring, 166–167
Heat, 62
Heat of compression, 118
Heat control in piston, 150
Heat flow, 62–63
Heat transfer in cooling system, 309–311
Hemispheric combustion chamber, 136–139
Horsepower, 70–72
Hydraulic valve lifter, 97–98
  cams for, 238–239

I-head versus L-head, 207–208
I-head engine, 44–45, 82
I-head valve train, 96–97
Idealized cycles, 63–65
Ignition-advance mechanisms, 107–109
Ignition coil, 353–357
Ignition distributor, 349–353
  advance mechanisms, 358–363
  centrifugal, 358–363
  transistorized, 350–353
  vacuum-advance mechanisms, 359–363
Ignition-spark advance, 358–363
Ignition system, 106–109, 348–368
  advance mechanisms, 358–363
    centrifugal, 358–363
  coil, 353–357
  distributor, 349–353
  function, 348–349
  high-frequency, 366–367
  low-frequency, 366–367
  piezoelectric, 363–364
  secondary wiring, 357–358
  spark plugs, 357
  transistorized, 350–353
  vacuum-advance mechanisms, 359–363
Ihp, 70–71
Indicated horsepower, 70–71
Induction system, 265
Intake manifold, 85–86, 291–296
  Chevrolet Turbo-Jet engine, 295–296
  Ford Mark II-427 GT, 293–295
  heat control, 273–274
  tuned, 292–293
Interchangeability, 1–2

Jernaes engine, 58

Kauertz engine, 57
Kinetic friction, 73
Knocking, 118–129
  causes of, 118–119
  control of, 123–129
    chemical, 125–128
  study of, 120–123

L-head versus I-head, 207–208
L-head engine, 44, 81–82
L-head valve train, 94–96
Lead time, 19–20
Loft lines, 16–18
Lubricants, 331–334
Lubricating system, 103–104, 324–347
  changing oil, 339–340
  design, 344–346
  oil consumption in, 340–341, 346
  oil filters, 338
  oil-pressure indicators, 338–339
  pump, 337
  purpose, 324–325
  relief valve, 337–338
  types of, 334–337
  water-sludge formation, 341–343

Mach number, 210
Machine tools, 2–6
Manifold (*see* Exhaust manifold; Intake manifold)
Manifold heat control, 273–274
Mark II-427 GT engine valve ports, 216–219
Mass distribution, 6–7
Mass production, 1–2
Mechanical design, 13–14
  versus styling, 19
Mechanical efficiency, 76, 114–115
Mercer engine, 57
Milling machines, computer-controlled, 20
Mockup, 17–18
Mold, 250–253
Molecules, 60–61

Octane rating, 123–129
Octane requirements, 129
OHC, 241–242
Oil, 325–330
  additives, 326–329
  changing, 339–340
  consumption, 340–341, 346
  pressure indicators, 338–339

Oil, properties, 326–329
  purpose, 324–325
  properties, 326–329
  purpose, 324–325
  service ratings, 329
  sources, 325–326
  tests of, 329–330
  viscosity, 326
  viscosity index, 326–327
  viscosity ratings, 326
Oil-control rings, 91–92, 172–176
  (*See also* Piston rings)
Oil filters, 338
Oil pan, 83–84
Oil pump, 337
ONR, 123–129
Overhead camshaft, 45, 241–242
Oversquare engine, 68

Patent infringement, 12–13
Patterns, 250–255
PCV system, 297–299
PCV valve, 299
Piezoelectric ignition, 363–364
Piston-pin attachment, 154
Piston-pin lubrication, 155
Piston-pin offset, 155–156
Piston rings, 27–28, 90–92,
    143–162, 164–177
  abrasive wear, 168
  compression, 165–172
  dimensions, 169
  failure analysis, 176
  head-land, 166–167
  joints, 165
  life of compression-type, 172
  materials, 167–169
  oil-control, 91–92, 172–176
  purpose, 164–165
  scuff wear, 168
  shapes, 166
  speed and oil control, 175–176
  tests of compression-type,
    171–172
  trends in compression-ring
    design, 169–171
  types of oil-control, 173–175
  wear, 167–169
Piston rings,
  wear, 167–169
Pistons, 90–92, 143–163
  aluminum, 146–148
  cam-ground, 151
  Chevrolet, 27, 159–161
  design, 143–146
  displacement, 68–69
  expansion control, 150–153
  failures analysis, 161–162
  forged, 148
  head design, 149–150
  heat control, 150
  materials, 146–148
  pin attachment, 154
  pin lubrication, 155
  pin offset, 155–156
  preignition failure, 162
  ring-groove fortification, 157
  ring-groove stresses, 156–157
  scuffing, 148–149, 161–162
  skirts, 153
  tests, 157–159
  weight, 153–154
Positive-crankcase ventilating
  system, 297–299
Preignition, 125
Prony brake, 71
Pumping loss, 115
Push-rod engine, 45
PV curve, 65

Quadrijet carburetors, 283–287
Quench. 134

Radiator, 314–317
Radiator pressure cap, 319
Ram-jet action, 66
Regulator, 105
Ring-groove fortification, 157
Ring-groove stresses, 156–157
Ring joints, 165
Rings, piston (*see* Piston rings)
Rocker arms, 229–231
Rods (*see* Connecting rods)
Rotary engine, 57–58
Rumble, 125

SAE, 24–25
  Handbook, 24
  horsepower, 74
Safety, designing for, 20–23
Screw machine, automatic, 2–4
Scuffing piston, 148–149
Secondary wiring, 357–358
SKETCHPAD, 15–16
Sleeve bearings, 179
Smog control, 297–302
Society of Automotive Engineers,
  24–25
Sodium valves, 215
SOHC, 45, 241
Spark advance, 107–109
Spark-plug placement, 140
Spark plugs, 357
Specific heat, 62–63
Spread, 189–190
Squish, 134
Static friction, 73
Sterling engine, 55–57
Stroke, 68
Styling versus mechanical
  design, 19
Stylists, 14–16
Supercharging, 296
Surface/valve ratio, 140–141
s/v ratio, 140–141

Tail-fin fad, 14
Tel, 128
Templates in design, 16–18
Tetraethyl lead, 128
Thermal efficiency, 64, 113–114
Thermostat, 317–319
Thermostatic fuel gauge, 267
Thread repair, 267
Torque, 74–76
Torsional-vibration damper,
  87–88

Transfer machine, automatic-, 255
Transistorized ignition system, 350–353
Tuned intake manifold, 292–293
Turbulence, 134–136
Turret lathe, automatic, 2–4
Two-stroke cycle engine, 46–48

Vacuum advance, 108–109, 359–363
Valves, 28–30, 93–94, 207–246
  arrangements, 43–45
  for Chevrolet Turbo-Jet engine, 237–238
  cooling, 139
  design, 209
  exhaust and gas flow, 210–211
  face angle, 211–212
  facings, 215–216
  failure analysis, 242–244
  guides, 219
  head proportions, 212–213
  head shape, 213–214
  intake and gas flow, 210
  intake-valve location, 218–219
  interference angle, 212
  lift, 209–210
  lifter, hydraulic, 97–98
Valves, lubrication, 225–227
  materials, 214–215
  port design, 216–219
  ports, 139
  requirements, 208–209
  rotation, 227–229
  seat inserts, 222–223
  siamesed, 220
  size, 211
  sodium, 215
  springs, 234–235
  stem seals, 226–227
  stem size, 213
  stems, 216
  temperatures, 223–225
  timing, 98
  tips, 216
  (*See also* Valve trains)
Valve seat, 94, 219–223
  cooling, 221–222
  design, 219–223
  durability, 222–223
  inserts, 222–223
  siamesed, 220
Valve trains, 207–224
  cams, 231–234
  design, 209
  dynamics, 235–237
  lubrication, 336–337
Valve trains, requirements, 208–209
  rocker arms, 229–231
  springs, 234–235
  (*See also* Valves)
Vapor recovery, 301–302
VI (viscosity index), 326–327
Vibration damper, 87–88, 202–203
Vibration mountings, 203–204
Virmel engine, 57
Viscosity, 326
Viscosity index, 326–327
Viscosity ratings, 326
Volatility of gasoline, 116–118
Volkswagen electronic fuel injection, 305
Volumetric efficiency, 65–66, 114, 136, 210–211

Wankel engine, 54–55
Water jackets, 139, 311
Water pumps, 311
Water-sludge formation, 341–343
Wedge combustion chamber, 136–139
Wind tunnel tests, 18–19